CLINICAL
PSYCHOLOGY

———

CLINICAL PSYCHOLOGY

ASSESSMENT, TREATMENT, AND RESEARCH

Editors

DAVID C. S. RICHARD, PhD
Rollins College, Department of Psychology,
Winter Park, Florida

STEVEN K. HUPRICH, PhD
Eastern Michigan University, Department of Psychology,
Ypsilanti, Michigan

ELSEVIER

AMSTERDAM • BOSTON • HEIDELBERG • LONDON
NEW YORK • OXFORD • PARIS • SAN DIEGO
SAN FRANCISCO • SINGAPORE • SYDNEY • TOKYO
Academic Press is an imprint of Elsevier

Elsevier Academic Press

30 Corporate Drive, Suite 400, Burlington, MA 01803, USA
525 B Street, Suite 1900, San Diego, California 92101-4495, USA
84 Theobald's Road, London WC1X 8RR, UK

This book is printed on acid-free paper. ⊚

Library of Congress Cataloging-in-Publication Data
Clinical psychology : assessment, treatment, and research / editors,
David C. S. Richard, Steven K. Huprich.
    p. ; cm.
  Includes bibliographical references and index.
  ISBN 978-0-12-374256-8 (hardcover : alk. paper)   1.   Clinical psychology.   I.
Richard, David C. S. II. Huprich, Steven Ken, 1966-
  [DNLM: 1.   Psychology, Clinical. 2.   Mental Disorders–diagnosis. 3.   Mental
Disorders–therapy. 4.   Psychotheraphy–methods. WM 105 C6415 2009]
  RC467.C58612 2009
  616.89–dc22

                                                                                      2008026459

British Library Cataloguing in Publication Data
A catalogue record for this book is available from the British Library

ISBN 13: 978-0-12-374256-8

For all information on all Elsevier Academic Press publications visit our Web site at
www.elsevierdirect.com

Printed in the United States of America
08 09 10 9 8 7 6 5 4 3 2 1

Contents

Contributors

Carmela Alcántara Department of Psychology, University of Michigan, Ann Arbor, MI 48109

Gordon J. G. Asmundson Center for Kinesiology Health and Sport, University of Regina, Regina, SK, S4S 0A2 Canada

Kira Hudson Banks Department of Psychology, Illinois Wesleyan University, Bloomington, IL 61702

Isabelle Beaulieu Center for Neuropsychology and Learning, Ann Arbor, MI 48109

Iruma Bello Department of Psychology, University of Hawai'i at Mānoa, Honolulu, HI 96822

Matteo Bertoni Pacific Graduate School of Psychology, Redwood City, CA 94063

Larry E. Beutler Redwood City, CA 94063

Kathi A. Borden Department of Clinical Psychology, Antioch University New England, Keene, NH 03431-3516

Robert F. Bornstein Derner Institute of Advanced Psychological Studies, Adelphi University, Garden City, NY

Nicole M. Cain Department of Psychology, Pennsylvania State University, University Park, PA 16802

Brett Deacon Department of Psychology, University of Wyoming, Laramie, WY 82071

Paul Emmelkamp Department of Clinical Psychology, University of Amsterdam, 1018 WB Amsterdam, The Netherlands

John P. Forsyth Department of Psychology, University of Albany, State University of New York, Albany, NY 55369

Arthur Freeman Freeman Institute for Cognitive Therapy, Fort Wayne, IN 46825

Elaine Gierlach Pacific Graduate School of Psychology, Redwood City, CA 94063

Erin T. Graham Department of Psychology, University of Michigan, Ann Arbor, MI 48109

Robert Gregory Department of Psychology, Wheaton College, Wheaton, IL 60187-5593

Heather D. Hadjistavropoulos Department of Psychology, University of Regina, Regina, SK, S4S 0A2 Canada

Thomas Hadjistavropoulos Department of Psychology, University of Regina, Regina, SK, Canada S4S 0A2

Stephen N. Haynes Department of Psychology, University of Hawai'i at Mānoa, Honolulu, HI 96822

Tiffany Haynes Department of Psychology, University of Michigan, Ann Arbor, MI 48109

Elaine M. Heiby Department of Psychology, University of Hawai'i at Mānoa, Honolulu, HI 96822-2216

John M. Houston Department of Psychology, Rollins College, Winter Park, FL 32789

Julia Humphrey Department of Psychology, Rollins College, Winter Park, FL 32789

Steven K. Huprich Department of Psychology, Eastern Michigan University, Ypsilanti, MI 48197

Joseph Keawe'aimoku Kaholokula Department of Native Hawaiian Health, John A. Burns School of Medicine, University of Hawai'i at Mānoa, Honolulu, HI 96813

Satoko Kimpara Pacific Graduate School of Psychology, Redwood City, CA 94063

Laura P. Kohn-Wood Department of Psychology, University of Michigan, Ann Arbor, MI 48109

Gerald P. Koocher Graduate School for Health Sciences, Simmons College, Boston, MA 02115

Erin Krauskopf Department of Psychology, Rollins College, Winter Park, FL 32789

Radhika Krishnamurthy School of Psychology, Florida Institute of Technology, Melbourne, FL 32901

Renée Lajiness-O'Neill Department of Psychology, Eastern Michigan University, Ypsilanti, MI 48197

Janet D. Latner Department of Psychology, University of Hawai'i at Mānoa, Honolulu, HI 96822-2216

Kenneth N. Levy Department of Psychology, Pennsylvania State University, University Park, PA 16802

E. John McIlvried School of Psychological Sciences, University of Indianapolis, Indianapolis, IN 46227

Joshua D. Miller Department of Psychology, University of Georgia, Athens, GA 30602

Andrea H. Nacapoy Department of Psychology, University of Hawai'i at Mānoa, Honolulu, HI 96822

William C. Oakley Midwestern University

Jenna Paunovich Wright Kitch, Drutchas, Wagner, Valitutti, & Sherbrook, Detroit, MI, 48226

Megan Phillips Antioch University New England, Keene, NH 03431-3516

Aaron L. Pincus Department of Psychology, Pennsylvania State University, University Park, PA 16802

Mark B. Powers Department of Clinical Psychology, University of Amsterdam, 1018 WB Amsterdam, The Netherlands

David C. S. Richard Department of Psychology, Rollins College, Winter Park, FL 32789

Sean C. Sheppard Department of Psychology, State University of New York, University of Albany, Albany, NY 12222

Robert Smither Department of Psychology, Rollins College, Winter Park, FL 32789

George C. Tremblay Antioch University New England, Keene, NH 03431-3516

Thomas A. Widiger Department of Psychology, University of Kentucky, Lexington, KY 40506-0044

Karryll Winborne Combined Program in Education and Psychology, University of Michigan, Ann Arbor, MI 48109

Preface

The profession of clinical psychology is a noble enterprise. Individuals choosing to enter the profession do so knowing that their training will take several years and that the financial rewards are modest at best. Despite these realities, applications to clinical training programs remain especially competitive — it is common for doctoral training programs to report acceptance rates in the single digits.

It is the nobility of the profession, however, that may be its main attractant. The desire to help others, and to do so in ways that engender long-lasting psychological development and change, transcends the profession and is rooted in the religious, cultural, and philosophical foundations of the modern world. The clinical psychologist's currency is not measured in dollars but in something more ethereal, optimistic, and enduring — human change. To know that one has helped another person through a process of change and to watch people grow and transform the way they view themselves and the world provide a tremendous sense of personal satisfaction. The fact that an entire profession is devoted specifically to helping others address psychological problems and suffering is, in many ways, validation of the need for clinical psychologists. In a society where it is not always clear that there are safety nets to catch those who have fallen, the clinical psychologist is the professional with the most training and greatest number of tools at his or her disposal. It is a responsibility not to be taken lightly.

Although all clinical psychologists share the common goal of engendering change to help others, the exact way in which this is done varies tremendously from one professional to the next. As a result, this book reflects the tremendous diversity of the field. Although the chapters are broadly organized into three major sections (i.e., assessment, treatment, and contemporary issues), what exactly a clinician does as part of assessment and treatment depends substantially on his or her theoretical orientation. This is a theme that will be explored throughout the book. Suffice it to say at this point that we consider theoretical diversity to be a strength of the field, not a weakness. Indeed, given the complexities of the human experience, we think it is untenable for any one theory to provide both a comprehensive and adequate account of psychological problems. Instead, the learned clinician will value diverse perspectives (if not always agree with them) for the illumination they provide in understanding the full range of issues associated with any clinical problem.

This book is unusual in that it was conceptualized from the beginning to be thoroughly eclectic. As you will see throughout the chapters, the ideas and points of view are often diverse, and the authors have taken liberty to write about and support their ideas while recognizing and respecting the diversity within professional clinical psychology. Thus, our goal from the beginning was to bring together diverse views within the profession with regard to assessment, treatment, and other germane issues. In doing this, we frequently found ourselves working not to impose our own theoretical predispositions on the work of our contributors. This was no easy task given that one of us is psychodynamic (SH) and the other cognitive-behavioral (DCR). Indeed, we occasionally found ourselves in theoretical and empirical debates using the commenting function in Microsoft Word as an impromptu forum for intellectual discourse, which our authors saw and were asked to grapple with. To our contributors, we offer a special thanks (and even congratulations) on surviving a feedback process that, at times, may have resembled the ramblings of dissociating editors rather than a theoretically coherent set of remarks.

Thus, the reader should look forward to a spirited text written in a mentoring style that is designed to expose the reader to the full range of contemporary thinking in our field. Each of the contributors took on his or her chapter knowing that the target audience was the first-year graduate student in clinical psychology or an advanced undergraduate. Thus, they focused their work in a way that is meant to be most useful to the clinician in training. We believe that this text serves as a solid foundation for your development as a clinician and that you will refer to it often in succeeding years. We hope it is a worthy introduction to your future profession, and we wish you nothing but the best in your journey.

David C. S. Richard, PhD
Rollins College
Winter Park, Florida

Steven K. Huprich, PhD
Eastern Michigan University
Ypsilanti, Michigan

CHAPTER

1

Professional Psychology Education and Training: Models, Sequence, and Current Issues

Kathi A. Borden
Antioch University New England

E. John McIlvried
University of Indianapolis

OUTLINE

In this chapter, we discuss education and training in clinical psychology. Because the doctoral degree has been considered the entry degree for **licensure** and practice for psychologists, we have focused on the doctoral level. First, we discuss the history of education and training in professional psychology. Included in this history are a sample of training conferences and a description of the models of education and training in clinical psychology that have developed over the years. The remainder of the chapter focuses on the sequence of education, training, and credentialing that leads to entry into the profession of psychology.

HISTORICAL OVERVIEW

"Psychology," in the general sense, has existed for all of recorded history. There have always been individuals who provided support and advice to others, and others who wondered about functions like memory, learning, and the meaning of dreams. When psychology first began to grow as a discipline in the nineteenth century, though, the formal discipline of psychology was founded. At that time, the only existing psychology programs focused on experimental psychology and on the observation and measurement of individual differences. In fact, a 1934 study by the American Psychological Association (**APA**) Committee on the PhD Degree in Psychology found that the only training commonality among the 22 institutions surveyed was that "training in experimental psychology is fundamental and required for all psychologists" (p. 71). Most programs required basic science courses for admission and agreed that "there must be close personal contacts with the candidate which will enable the department to evaluate his research ability and scientific imagination" (p. 71). The emphasis on science was clear, as was the lack of focus on practice. It may surprise students to know that venereal disease and war were largely responsible for increasing attention to education for practice and for moving psychology from an academic discipline to a profession.

Advanced, untreated syphilis can lead to the development of general paresis, a set of symptoms that resemble a severe psychological disorder. When antibiotics were discovered and found to be effective in the treatment of syphilis, the observation was made that this type of "insanity" could be cured. In addition, the "humane" or "moral" treatment of Pinel, Tuke, and Dix was observed to have a positive impact on those with mental illness. With the recognition that both medical and psychosocial interventions could help those with psychological problems, there was a change in prevailing views of mental health and illness. For the first time, mental illness was seen as treatable and even curable.

The two world wars brought with them an awareness that psychologists, with expertise in measurement and interest in the increasing number of approaches to the treatment of mental illness, might be helpful in evaluating military recruits and in treating traumatized soldiers, particularly after World War II. However, even after the war, there were no standards for how to teach psychologists to move from the laboratory into the clinic. Figure 1.1 summarizes the history of education and training in clinical psychology.

MODELS OF TRAINING

Boulder Scientist-Practitioner Model

With the growing participation of psychologists in applied activities following World War II, the need to examine the education and training of clinical psychologists became obvious. The Veterans Administration (**VA**) pledged support for the training of clinical psychologists but wanted the field of psychology to designate appropriate programs to receive funding. Thus began the concept of psychology program accreditation; however, clinical psychology did

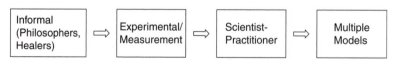

FIGURE 1.1   History of Education and Training in Clinical Psychology.

not have clear standards to apply in the program approval process. In an effort to define appropriate education and training in clinical psychology, the APA formed a Committee on Training in Clinical Psychology in 1947, chaired by David Shakow. The committee provided the first set of guidelines for training in clinical psychology (Committee on Training in Clinical Psychology of the American Psychological Association, 1947). The committee's recommendations discussed the "raw material" or characteristics of applicants likely to succeed in clinical psychology. In addition to intelligence and other traits, admissions criteria were to focus on finding applicants with "a reasonably well-adjusted and attractive personality" (p. 541). In addition, applicants were expected to have strong undergraduate science and humanities backgrounds. Program recommendations described by this committee became the basis for the **scientist-practitioner model** of training, developed at the Boulder conference in 1949 (Raimy, 1950). Specific recommendations were made for a four-year sequence including coursework, **practicum**, **internship**, and **dissertation**.

The pressured doctoral student of today will appreciate the committee's additional recommendation that "students must be given time to read and think" and develop strong critical thinking skills, asking questions and searching for scientific evidence to support their views. More recent restatements and clarifications of the model have been published (e.g., Belar, 2000; Belar & Perry, 1992). Approximately 52% of clinical psychology programs that indicated a training model in 2006 (the most recent year available) stated that they followed the scientist-practitioner model, and approximately 31% of clinical psychology degrees were awarded by these programs (APA, 2008). Many of these programs are members of the Council of University Directors of Clinical Psychology (**CUDCP**), a training council made up of member programs that meet to share ideas and improve and update scientist-practitioner training.

The Shakow report and Boulder model, supported by training grants from the (VA) and the United States Public Health Service (USPHS), focused clinical psychology on blending into the health-care system. The Boulder model's acceptance of the medical model and of training and practice in medical settings as primary has been criticized for ignoring education, business, and other settings where the need for psychological services was evident (Albee, 2000; Baker & Benjamin, 2000).

Vail Professional Model

The Boulder model of scientist-practitioner training was the only existing model for approximately 20 years. During the 1960s, legislation led to a plan for deinstitutionalization of the chronically mentally ill and to the development of community-based mental health centers (**CMHCs**) across the United States designed to offer a continuum of prevention and intervention services. The development of numerous CMHCs created jobs in administration, assessment, and intervention for psychologists. But many psychologists at that time who had been trained as scientist-practitioners had not received sufficient applied clinical training for these positions. Because the universities in which scientist-practitioner programs were housed generally rewarded faculty for research rather than clinical productivity, and because most early Boulder model program faculty had been trained as experimental psychologists, faculty and their programs focused more on training students for research than for practice. Thus, the balance proposed at the Boulder conference was not achieved. While many scientist-practitioner programs sought to train academic researchers, many graduates went into clinical practice, and the modal number of publications of those graduates was zero. Yet training for work in real-world clinical settings often was not sufficient in what had become research-focused programs. Some began to wonder if it was possible to train students equally well in both research and practice. The "Chicago conference" of 1965 was held to review alternative models of training for clinical psychologists, but the ultimate outcome was an endorsement of scientist-practitioner training (Hoch, Ross, & Winder, 1966).

Growing concern about the adequacy of clinical training for practitioners led to another well-known training conference, the Vail conference (Korman, 1973a), which yielded a description of an alternative model of training, the professional model. In the proceedings of the Vail conference, Pottharst (1973) pointed out that the Boulder model was developed in response to the need for programs to train psychology practitioners. However, locating practitioner training in psychology departments rather than in separate schools of psychology, accreditation criteria of the time, offering the PhD research degree rather than an alternative practice degree as is common in other professions, maintaining faculty who were researchers rather than practitioners, and related structural characteristics made it difficult to infuse sufficient practitioner training into clinical programs. The advanced level of clinical skills expected of doctoral-level practitioners was not achieved until after graduation or even licensure and was often learned on the job (Pottharst, 1973). Many felt that it was extremely difficult to train each student to be both a practitioner and a scientist with equal success (Albee, 1971; Peterson, 1991).

The Vail conference sought to remedy this situation by recommending more practice-based education and training activities. Students were still to be trained in the broad psychological foundations of practice and in research methods, and science was still to be integrated with practice, but these were done with the purpose of educating practitioners. The PsyD degree was recommended for those intending to practice and the PhD for those intending careers in research and teaching. University schools of psychology, medical schools, education departments, and free-standing schools of psychology as well as university departments of psychology were all described as appropriate settings for clinical psychology programs.

Because research has shown that much of the work done at the doctoral level can be done equally well by those with a master's degree, the delegates to the Vail conference recommended that doctoral-level psychologists engage in program development and evaluation, the development of new clinical procedures and models, the integration of practice with theory, supervision and training, and the management and administration of facilities and programs (Korman, 1973b). Delegates thus proposed the idea of training for **multiple roles**, a suggestion that has been realized in current accreditation criteria. Unfortunately, the master's vs. doctoral issue, including issues surrounding the continuity of education and the differentiation of practice domains, still has not been adequately addressed. However, the positive result of the Vail conference was attention to direct education for practice careers and a greater choice in training models, emphases, goals, degrees, and training settings available to students.

In 2006, approximately 22% of programs indicated that they followed the Vail **practitioner-scholar model** (the term that will be used for the remainder of this chapter for programs based on the Vail model), and approximately 42% of the degrees awarded in clinical psychology that year came from these programs (APA, 2008). Vail model programs usually maintain membership in their own training council, the National Council of Schools and Programs of Professional Psychology (**NCSPP**), which has further developed this training model (e.g., Peterson, Peterson, Abrams, & Stricker, 1997). Most NCSPP programs offer the doctor of psychology (PsyD) degree.

Some concerns have been expressed about the Vail model. Research training is often seen as one way to distinguish psychologists from other mental health practitioners, and some believe that practitioner programs do not emphasize science and research skills sufficiently. Others worry that locating programs outside of university psychology departments may mean insufficient resources for these programs, and that with larger class sizes than in most Boulder model programs the opportunity to learn through research mentorships might be lost. One strength of Vail model programs is the relevance of direct multiple roles training for the practice jobs most graduates are likely to hold.

Clinical Scientist Model

Since Vail, an additional model of training has entered the scene, the **clinical scientist model** of training (McFall, 1991, 2000; Hébert, 2002). This model (McFall, 1996) emphasizes first that "psychological services should not be administered to the public (except under strict experimental control) until they have satisfied" (p. 9) specific criteria for empirical validation. Second, "doctoral training programs in clinical psychology must ... produce the most competent clinical scientists possible" (p. 9). Programs using the clinical scientist model are typically members of the Academy of Psychological Clinical Science (**APCS**) and often maintain membership in CUDCP as well. In 2006, approximately 16.5% of programs indicated that they followed the clinical scientist model, and approximately 9.5% of clinical psychology doctorates were awarded by these programs (APA, 2008).

Critics of the clinical scientist model express two primary concerns (Peterson, 1996a, 1996b). First, McFall (1996) uses a very narrow definition of research support. Second, by limiting psychologists to "proven" methods, critics assert that we will be unable to discover new potentially effective methods or to address problems that do not yet have clearly demonstrated effective treatments. Even in medicine, when there is no cure for a particular type of cancer, medical professionals will focus on improving the comfort of the patient and treating secondary conditions resulting from the cancer. Many psychologists believe we should provide such assistance to people with psychological conditions for which there is no empirically supported treatment and do our best to see if there is some not-yet-proven technique that might be effective. In addition, some are concerned that the nonspecific factors effective in the treatment relationship are not given sufficient attention in these programs and that the "sanitary" environment of the laboratory rarely exists in the clinic. Nonetheless, the strength of this model is the attention it has focused on the need for testing new methods and demonstrating that what we do as professional psychologists works.

Education and Training Models: Putting It All Together

Despite the varied emphases of each model of treatment, there are many more similarities than differences among clinical psychology programs using different training models. Accreditation criteria have ensured that all programs provide broad and general training at the doctoral level; doctoral students are to be trained for general practice, and specialization is not expected until the postdoctoral level. All programs must provide grounding in the scientific foundations of psychology and the foundations of practice, provide adequate practicum experiences, and teach students to integrate science and practice. All must teach students about empirically supported interventions and evidence-based practice (APA, 2007b). Additional requirements for accreditation are presented in Highlight Box 1.1.

HIGHLIGHT BOX 1.1

DOMAINS FOR APA ACCREDITATION*

A. Eligibility
  a. Factors related to the institutional setting and structure
  b. Residency requirement
B. Program Philosophy, Objectives, and Curriculum Plan
  a. Stated philosophy, objectives, and curriculum plan
  b. Experiences to teach specific content areas
    i. Scientific foundation
    ii. Foundations of practice
    iii. Application
  c. Practicum
C. Program Resources
  a. Faculty
  b. Students
  c. Financial, clerical, technical, training materials, physical facilities, student support, practicum sites
D. Cultural and Individual Differences and Diversity
  a. Recruitment, support, and advancement of diverse students and faculty

  b. Education prepares students to work in a diverse world
E. Student-Faculty Relations
  a. Rights and ethics are respected, respect for diversity, written policies and procedures
  b. Faculty are accessible and serve as role models
  c. Complaints are handled appropriately
F. Program Self-Assessment and Quality Enhancement
  a. Program gathers short- and long-term data on student and program outcomes
  b. Changes are made to improve the program based on data collected
G. Public Disclosure
  a. All crucial information is readily available
H. Relationship with the Accrediting Body
  a. Abides by CoA guidelines and informs CoA of program changes
  b. Pays dues to CoA and makes required interim reports

---

*From American Psychological Association (2007b). Guidelines and principles for accreditation of programs in professional psychology. Washington, DC: Author.

The research-practice continuum is often used to distinguish different program models. One interesting observation is that *all* of the major training conferences and training councils in psychology have endorsed and even emphasized the need to integrate research and practice. All accredited programs must do this. Clinical science and scientist-practitioner programs are more likely to focus research training on traditional, experimental, generalizable studies and toward having graduates who produce and publish original research. Most practitioner-scholar programs focus on graduates conducting "disciplined inquiry" (Peterson, 1996b), functioning as "local clinical scientists" (Stricker & Trierweiler, 1995; Trierweiler & Stricker, 1998) or "scientific practitioners" (Peterson, 2000) who engage in science-based practice, critical thinking and logic, and local (i.e., not necessarily generalizable) quasi-experiments (including outcome and program evaluation) as they engage in clinical practice. In addition, some programs devote more resources to support faculty research and expect more publications in research journals, while others provide fewer resources for original faculty research and do not require the same number or types of publications. Despite these differences of emphasis, students in all models of clinical psychology programs should expect much of what they learn to be based on an integration of research and practice.

A recent survey of program directors found that there were no significant differences in professional psychology student exposure to measurement theory, research methods, or statistical analyses based on the program model and that the only difference based on degree was in the direction of more coverage of qualitative methods in PsyD than in PhD programs (Rossen & Oakland, 2008). It is clear that despite the program model or degree, students receive training in all of these areas. However, the Rossen and Oakland study did not examine whether differences in the programs' training goals influence the level of depth and detail in which these topics are taught. In addition, students being trained in CUDCP member programs indicated that about 37% of their time was spent in research training, 29% in clinical work, and 17% in their integration (Merlo, Collins, & Bernstein, 2008). It would be interesting to have comparative data for NCSPP and APCS programs as an indication of how different or similar we actually are on this dimension.

The issue of models and degrees may be quite confusing to outsiders. It has caused a fair amount of conflict within the field as well. Psychologists often lose their scientific, evidence-based focus and stubbornly hold the view that "if it is like me, it must be OK" and "if it's not like me, it must be deficient in some way" (Meehl, 1973). There is much overlap among the different models of training within clinical psychology, and more research-focused Vail model programs are hard to distinguish from

Clinical Scientist   Scientist-Practitioner   Practitioner-Scholar

← Greater Research Focus   Greater Practice Focus →

FIGURE 1.2 Theoretical Distribution of Research and Practice Emphasis of Programs Indicating Different Training Models.

more practice-focused Boulder model programs. If we placed all clinical psychology programs along a continuum based on research-practice emphasis, we would certainly have overlapping distributions among the models of training (see Figure 1.2). Clearly, psychology needs excellent researchers *and* excellent practitioners. The advantage of what may at first appear to be a chaotic state of affairs is that all aspects of psychology education and training are covered. The past animosity among proponents of each model damages psychology's public image and slows the progress we can make together when we join as a science and a profession to solve today's important problems. By allowing applicants to choose the training models, degrees, and programs that best fit their interests and career goals, we ensure the continuation and enhancement of research, practice, and their integration in professional psychology.

MOVEMENT TOWARD COMPETENCIES

Identification of Competencies

The development of a standardized core curriculum in psychology has been controversial for many years and has never fully succeeded

(Benjamin, 2001). One of the consequences of this failure is a weak understanding of what a psychologist is and does. Consistent with the lack of an agreed-upon core curriculum, the Guidelines and Principles for Accreditation (APA, 2007b) do not require a specific set of courses. Instead, to be accredited, programs must present their philosophy, model of training, goals, objectives, and curriculum plan to the Commission on Accreditation (**CoA**), engage in ongoing self-study and program evaluation to learn whether they are accomplishing what they set out to do, and demonstrate that they have improved their programs based on the evaluation data gathered. Allowing programs to vary has both pros and cons. On the one hand, diversity of educational programs, creativity, and the ability to change with new developments are encouraged. On the other hand, the lack of consistency across programs increases the confusion about what a psychologist is trained to do.

Defining the specific competencies that psychologists are trained in without prescribing specific courses or training experiences has been one way in which the field has addressed this problem. Competencies are comprised of the integration of knowledge, skills, and attitudes (**KSAs**) used in psychological practice (Bent, 1991). As pointed out by McIlvried and Bent (2003), **core competencies** are the most fundamental aspects of psychologist functioning, although they contribute to more advanced and specialized competencies learned later in one's development as a psychologist.

In 1986, NCSPP held a conference in Mission Bay, California, on standards of training. At that meeting, a paper by Bent and Cannon (1987) described the "key functional skills," or frequent professional activities of psychologists. From that list, the first set of core competencies in professional psychology was developed, including intervention, assessment, research and evaluation, relationship, management and supervision, and consultation and

teaching. Each competency was made up of essential KSAs. Current lists of psychologist competencies look very much like this original list. NCSPP added diversity as a separate competency outside of relationship in 2002 at a meeting where advocacy was also discussed as a potential competency.

Work on competencies continues. At the Competencies conference of 2002 (Kaslow et al., 2004), additional progress was made on the identification and conceptual organization of competencies. One helpful view of competencies was presented by Rodolfa et al. (2005) in the form of a competency cube (see Figure 1.3). The first dimension of the cube consists of foundational, or cross-cutting, competencies that are necessary to perform all psychologist functions. Examples include competency in ethics, diversity, relationship, oral and written communication, critical thinking, and information retrieval. The second dimension consists of functional competencies, including the tasks in which many professional psychologists engage. Examples include intervention, assessment, research and evaluation, management and administration, supervision and teaching, and consultation. The final dimension consists of a developmental timeline from graduate school through postdoctoral specialization and beyond. As psychologists move through their careers over time, they will notice the need to master different "blocks" in the competencies cube. In addition, graduate students may notice that their graduate program focuses more on some of these blocks than others, reflecting the diversity that exists in psychology education.

Teaching and Assessment of Competencies

If core competencies are defined as the minimum clusters of KSAs necessary for professional psychology practice, then it makes sense that doctoral, internship, and postdoctoral programs teach those competencies and assess them to make sure graduates are ready to enter

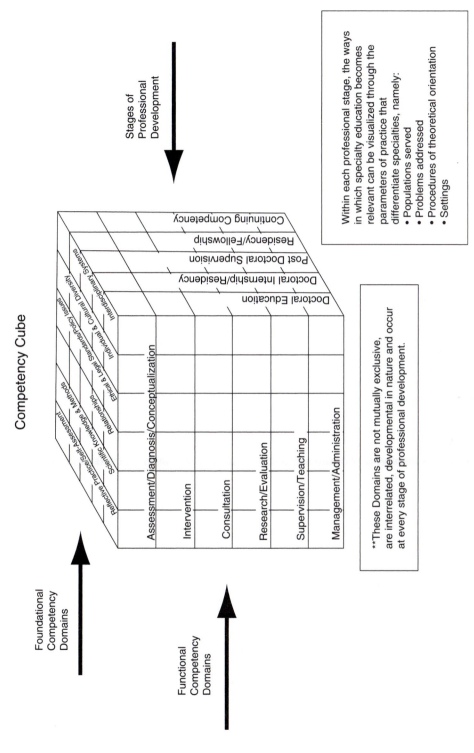

FIGURE 1.3 Cube model describing competency development in professional psychology. Copyright © 2005 by the American Psychological Association. Reproduced with permission.

the profession. As we described in an earlier chapter, different **pedagogies** may be appropriate to teach different material. For example, knowledge may best be taught didactically, skills through observation and practice, and attitudes through experiential activities, although there is considerable overlap and multiple methods might produce the most thorough learning (Borden & McIlvried, submitted for publication). Similarly, different types of material might be assessed in different ways.

Psychology faces numerous issues in the assessment of competencies and overall competence. For example, some competencies are easier to assess than others, and there is not a single agreed-upon "right" way to perform some essential clinical tasks. In general, the knowledge and skill components of competencies are easier to assess than attitudes. The need for graduates to conduct ongoing self-assessments to evaluate their competence and performance is another area that requires greater attention. There is a great deal more work to do in the area of assessment of competencies and of overall competence. A summary of current competency assessment issues can be found in Roberts, Borden, Christensen, and Lopez (2005).

To do adequate assessment, programs must have clear descriptions of each competency to be assessed and the level of performance expected at each stage of a student's career. Work toward defining these performance levels has only recently begun (APA, 2007a; NCSPP, 2007) and has yet to be fully integrated into psychology training programs.

Impact of Accreditation

Following the surge in demand for psychological services after World War II, APA began accrediting doctoral programs in professional psychology (Nelson, 2007). Prior to 1991, APA accreditation focused primarily on program "inputs" (e.g., courses offered) and resources (e.g., faculty and library) (APA, 1979). Concerns were raised that this approach had led to a "checklist mentality," missing the details and true quality of programs. Starting in 1991, the accreditation committee (now **Commission on Accreditation**) (CoA) of APA began to focus on "judging the degree to which a program has achieved the goals and objectives of its stated training model" (APA, 2007b, p. 2), thus switching to an "output-" or outcomes-based evaluation.

Several "professional principles and values" now appear in the accreditation guidelines. Programs must provide "broad and general" preparation for practice. As such, they must teach students about "broad theoretical and scientific foundations of the discipline and field of psychology in general" (APA, 2007b, p. 3), in addition to teaching the KSAs of the specific practice area (clinical, counseling, or school). In addition, all must teach students to integrate science and practice. All programs are evaluated in eight domains (see Highlight Box 1.1).

SEQUENCE OF TRAINING

Predoctoral Training

To assist the reader in understanding the literature on professional training, data will be included on various program characteristics. Much of the data comes from a recent (2005) self-study of the doctoral programs that comprise NCSPP (http://www.ncspp.info/). NCSPP represents most clinical psychology PsyD programs and some PhD programs across the country (over 67 APA-approved members). Since over half of the clinical doctorates in psychology awarded annually in the United States are PsyD degrees (APA, 2008), these data provide important information about the current status of professional training in our discipline. Data from APA also will be included to give broader information about both PhD and PsyD programs. Figure 1.4

QUESTIONS TO CONSIDER THROUGHOUT THE DOCTORAL TRAINING SEQUENCE

Decision to Enter Program
Is the program regionally accredited? Is the program APA/CPA accredited? Do the curriculum and length of program satisfy the requirements for licensure? Does the program satisfy the residency requirements for licensure? Does the program meet the joint designation criteria established by the NR and ASPPB?

Practicum
Will the number of practicum hours be competitive to obtain desired internship? Will the quality of the practicum experience enhance chances of obtaining internship?

Other Academic Requirements
Required to defend the dissertation proposal before being allowed to apply for internship? Required to defend the final dissertation before being allowed to apply for internship? Required to pass doctoral comps/quals before being allowed to apply for internship?

Internship
Is the internship APA/CPA accredited? Is the internship APPIC listed? CAPIC member? Will the number of internship hours, supervision, etc., satisfy licensure requirements? Does the internship meet NR guidelines?

GRADUATION

Postdoctoral Experience and Licensure
How many postdoctoral hours, direct contact hours, supervision hours needed for license? When permitted to take the EPPP? Jurisprudence or other exams required? How often must license be renewed? Continuing education requirements? Apply for NR and CPQ to enhance recognition and mobility? Apply for ABPP specialization?

FIGURE 1.4   Training Sequence in Clinical Psychology.

presents some of the important questions that students should consider as they progress through the doctoral training sequence.

Accreditation

A program's accreditation status influences whether or not it is recognized by licensing boards, professional organizations, and the public at large. In psychology, two kinds of accreditation are important: regional accreditation and accreditation by the professional body that represents our discipline.

The United States is divided into six areas for the purposes of regional accreditation (i.e., formal recognition) of institutions of higher learning (Council for Higher Education Accreditation, 2007), each with its own accrediting body. State licensing boards typically require regional accreditation to recognize one's degree as legitimate for licensing purposes. Regionally accredited institutions must demonstrate adequate resources, planning, institutional commitment, and the like before beginning a doctoral program and before admitting any students.

Accreditation by the professional body that represents the discipline (i.e., APA) is also important. Although not mandated by most licensing boards, APA accreditation is a mark of quality and streamlines the licensure process. APA first started accrediting clinical psychology doctoral programs in 1947 (Altmaier, 2003); accreditation of counseling and school psychology programs followed soon after. APA does not accredit master's programs.

General Program Structure and Coursework

Data from the APA suggest that the median amount of time to complete a doctoral program (including the one-year internship) is six years for PhD students and five years for PsyD students (Paszkiewicz et al., 2006). CoA requires at least three years of full-time study (or the equivalent), completion of an internship, and a minimum of two years spent at the degree-granting institution. At least one year must be spent in "full-time residence" or the equivalent (APA, 2007b).

Another area where students often have questions concerns the kinds of courses they will need to take. Generally, APA and various state laws do not mandate specific courses. Rather, they require that students demonstrate knowledge and competence in various important *areas*, including "(a) the breadth of scientific psychology, its history of thought and development, its research methods, and its applications" (e.g., biological, cognitive, affective, and social aspects of behavior; history and systems; measurement; research; statistics); "(b) the scientific, methodological, and theoretical foundations of practice" (e.g., development, psychopathology, ethics, etc.); "(c) diagnosing or defining problems through psychological assessment and measurement and formulating and implementing intervention strategies (including training in empirically supported procedures)" (e.g., assessment, intervention, consultation, supervision, etc.); "(d) cultural and individual diversity"; and "(e) attitudes essential for life-long learning, scholarly inquiry, and professional problem solving" (APA, 2007b, p. 7) (see Highlight Box 1.1). Programs have considerable latitude in how they meet these requirements.

As mentioned earlier, APA's position is that at the predoctoral level, training is **generalist** in nature. Thus, individuals wishing to specialize should receive further postdoctoral training in the specialty area. However, many doctoral programs offer concentration areas. While not constituting a formal specialization, this allows students to elect a sequence of courses in a particular area. This can be combined with a dissertation topic and practicum work in the same area in order to create a training focus within the broad and general preparation that the student is receiving. Approximately 78% of the doctoral programs represented in the NCSPP self-study (NCSPP, 2005) indicated that they offer concentration areas or tracks, the most common areas being child/adolescent (53.9%), health and neuropsychology (40.4%), family (36.6%), forensic (34.7%), and multicultural (19.2%).

In addition to completing coursework, students typically must demonstrate an ability to successfully engage in behaviors deemed as essential to the profession. For example, students must evidence professional and ethical behaviors, be able to engage in problem solving, demonstrate maturity and responsibility, and so on. Typically, programs evaluate students on these critical behaviors and provide feedback to students as well as assist with remediation if there are difficulties (Council of Chairs of Training Councils, 2004).

Master's-level preparation is often part of the training sequence. Students in stand-alone master's programs may complete a **terminal master's degree** (focus is on preparation for practice at the master's level) or participate in a nonterminal master's program that is intended to prepare students to apply for doctoral study. In addition to master's degrees in clinical psychology, a number of other types of master's-level programs are offered that prepare students for practice in the general arena of mental health (e.g., mental health counseling, marriage and family therapy, etc.). No specific curriculum is stipulated by APA for master's-level training, and master's-level clinicians cannot become licensed to practice as psychologists in most states. To address this gap, organizations such as the Council of Applied Masters Programs in Psychology (CAMPP, http://www.camppsite.org) have arisen that have formulated specific curriculum recommendations for master's-level training. Many states have some form of limited practice licensure for related mental and behavioral health areas (e.g., Marriage and Family Therapy, Mental Health Counseling) at the master's level. Typically, states have depended on other accrediting bodies such as the American Association of Marriage and Family Therapists

(AAMFT Commission on Accreditation for Marriage and Family Therapy Education, http://www.aamft.org/about/COAMFTE/index_nm.asp) and the Council for Accreditation of Counseling and Related Educational Programs (CACREP, http://www.cacrep.org/) for guidance in requirements to be eligible for master's-level licensure.

Many doctoral programs include either required or optional master's-level preparation as part of the doctoral degree; however, some programs do not offer this as an option. Requirements for these master's vary widely and may include any combination of coursework, clinical experience, examinations, theses, or clinical projects. Approximately 86% of the doctoral programs represented in the NCSPP self-study (NCSPP, 2005) indicated that students can earn a master's degree on the way to completing their doctorate, and about 84% of their students do complete the master's degree.

Practicum

While engaged in coursework, students are required to learn clinical skills through the supervised provision of clinical services (i.e., practicum). Practica have historically focused on assessment and therapy, although this has expanded as psychology has increased its focus on multiple roles in varied settings. Practicum placements now may focus on a combination of therapy, assessment, supervision of others, providing psychoeducation, consulting, participating in case conferences, and so on. In some programs, roles and functions may be separated; for example, assessment and therapy training may occur in two separate placements. The majority of doctoral programs in the NCSPP self-study (NCSPP, 2005) indicated that mixed practica (involving a combination of roles and activities) are most common. Clinical supervision of students typically occurs from someone at the practicum agency, and about 90% of the doctoral programs indicated that academic oversight of practicum students (typically, weekly contact) also is required. The median amount of weekly practicum supervision required is two hours, with at least one hour having to be individual face-to-face supervision from a doctoral-level licensed clinical psychologist.

Each program has its own policies about how many practicum hours students must minimally complete based on that program's goals, objectives, and educational approach. The median number of practicum hours that doctoral programs in the NCSPP self-study (NCSPP, 2005) required students to complete was 1,200 (i.e., minimum number of required hours). Of those, 500 hours on average were required to be direct contact with patients (as opposed to case conferences, report writing, supervision, etc.). However, the number of practicum hours that students typically complete has been steadily increasing over time. For example, in 1996 the average number of practicum hours that students reported as actually having been completed in their doctoral program was about 1,500 hours, whereas the average number of completed hours reported in 2006 was approximately 2,000 hours (Rodolfa, Owen, & Clark, 2007). This increase is largely due to the desire of students to be competitive for internship placements that they typically complete at the end of their program. Despite the students' belief that *more is better*, studies have failed to find a relationship between the number of practicum hours completed and internship status (Alden et al., 2000; Dixon & Thorn, 2000). Although some basic number of practicum hours is critical in securing an internship, it is likely that the *quality* of the practicum experience is more important than simply the quantity of hours after a certain point.

In most programs, students complete practicum placements at external agencies or sites outside of the program proper such as local community mental health centers, hospitals, social service agencies, clinics, and organized group private practices. About 46% of the doctoral programs represented in the NCSPP self-study (NCSPP, 2005) reported that they were affiliated with off-site agencies that trained only their students, and approximately 94% reported that they were affiliated with off-site agencies that trained students from their program as well as from other programs. About 48% of the doctoral programs reported that at least some of their practica paid a stipend to students, while 44% reported that no students received practicum stipends. Only about 4% reported that all practicum students received stipends.

Many programs also have an in-house clinic or psychological services center where students can obtain supervised experience. In some cases, these in-house experiences are mandated (or may occasionally be the only experiences available), while in other programs these may be optional or limited in scope (e.g., conducting an intake). The benefits of an in-house clinic are the focus on training, the faculty's increased knowledge of students' clinical work, and opportunities for enhanced integration of coursework, research, and clinical work. Approximately 67% of the doctoral programs represented in the NCSPP self-study (NCSPP, 2005) reported that they had an in-house clinic that trained at least some practicum students.

Almost all programs require practicum supervisors to submit ratings of the students' performance on different tasks or competency areas (e.g., ability to form a therapeutic alliance, awareness of one's own assumptions and biases, competence with various assessment techniques, openness to supervision, intervention planning and implementation). In addition, students may be required to attend a practicum seminar taught by a core faculty member where case presentations are required and students are evaluated on their KSAs. To address concerns about assessing the specific competencies expected of practicum students, some attempts have been made to establish more specific criteria for the KSAs expected prior to and following the practicum experience (see Hatcher & Lassiter, 2007; NCSPP, 2007).

Internship

To meet licensure and accreditation standards, all clinical, counseling, and school psychology programs require an **internship**. The predoctoral internship is a capstone clinical experience that occurs after all practica are completed but before the awarding of the student's degree. Clinical internships typically involve full-time placement at an agency or organization, although two-year part-time internships are more rarely available. A few programs have students complete a two-year half-time internship while they continue to take coursework (Mangione, VandeCreek, Emmons, McIlvried, Carpenter, & Nadkarni, 2006). In this latter case, questions have been raised about what differentiates an internship from completing an advanced practicum.

Internships are required to be *organized training programs* with a structured training focus. This differentiates internships from simply working for someone for a year. Similar to the system in place for medical residencies, most internships are independently operated by external agencies (although some academic programs operate affiliated or **captive internships** that primarily accept their own students).

Thus, recognition and accreditation of predoctoral internships occur separately from accreditation of the student's graduate program.

APA (and the Canadian Psychological Association, **CPA**, through a Memorandum of Understanding) accredits predoctoral internship programs and has the most elaborate and stringent set of standards of the various internship accrediting bodies. APA/CPA accreditation is therefore generally recognized as the highest form of accreditation and is rarely questioned by licensing boards or employers. As of 2007, APA voted to discontinue joint accreditation of doctoral and internship programs in Canada, and CPA will proceed with establishing their own independent criteria for the accreditation of these programs (Canadian Psychological Association, 2008). The Association of Psychology Postdoctoral and Internship Centers (**APPIC**, http://www.appic.org/) also is widely recognized as having created a set of criteria that meet the quality standards of most jurisdictions (see Highlight Box 1.2). APPIC does not *accredit* internships. However, internships can join APPIC if they meet APPIC's training standards. Other organizations such as the National Register (**NR**, http://www.nationalregister.org/) and Association of State

---

HIGHLIGHT BOX 1.2

WHAT DOES IT TAKE TO BE AN INTERNSHIP?

Graduate students hear a lot of stories about how important the internship is in their training. In addition, they hear about how hard it can be to find a good internship. So, what makes a good internship? Can students find any reputable site and simply arrange to get some experience there, or is there more to it than that? One widely accepted set of standards about what good quality internships must have was developed by APPIC (the Association of Psychology

Postdoctoral and Internship Centers). To be a member of APPIC,* internships must meet the following general criteria:

1. Internship organization — The internship must be an organized training program (not just supervised work or on-the-job training).
2. Internship oversight — The internship must have a licensed doctoral psychologist who is responsible for the

HIGHLIGHT BOX 1.2   (*continued*)

program and present at the facility at least 20 hours per week.

3. Internship staff — The internship program must have at least two licensed doctoral psychologists who are full-time staff members who are the primary supervisors of the interns. During the year, at least two different supervisors should oversee the work of the interns.

4. Internship supervision — Individual supervision of interns is provided by licensed doctoral psychologists (minimum of 1 hour of supervision for every 20 hours of intern services being provided). Supervisors should be staff members of the agency or affiliates that have clinical responsibility for the cases discussed.

5. Internship services — The program provides training in a variety of psychological assessment and intervention activities that are directly provided to clients.

6. Direct services — Interns must spend at least 25% of their time in direct contact with clients providing psychological services.

7. Didactic activities — The program must provide at least two hours per week of educational activities (e.g., seminars, case conferences, in-service training, grand rounds).

8. Timing of internship — The internship occurs after practica, externships, and clerkships have been completed but before the awarding of the doctoral degree.

9. Number of interns — There should be at least two predoctoral interns (minimum 20 hours per week) in training during any given internship year.

10. Title of interns — Individuals completing the program should have an official title such as intern, resident, or fellow that indicates their status as a trainee.

11. Public statements and materials — The program has written materials that describe the internship, list training goals and procedures, and outline specific expectations of interns' work.

12. Due process procedures — The program must have stated policies for handling concerns about interns' performance, interns' concerns about training, and appeals procedures.

13. Length of internship — The internship program must involve at least 1,500 hours and consist of no less than 9 months and no more than 24 months of training.

14. Certificate of completion — Interns should receive a certificate from the program verifying that they have completed a training program in psychology.

15. Formal written evaluations — Interns should receive evaluations at least twice a year.

16. Financial support — The program must have financial resources to achieve its training goals. Interns should receive a reasonable and fair stipend that is arranged in advance.

*See http://www.appic.org/about/2_3_1_about_policies_and_procedures_internship.html for more detailed information about the above requirements.

and Provincial Psychology Boards (**ASPPB**, http://www.asppb.org/) have developed their own criteria for internships to assist in the recognition of appropriately trained psychologists. Also, the Canadian Council of Professional Psychology Programs (**CCPPP**, http://www.ccppp.ca/) and the California Psychology Internship Council (**CAPIC**, http://www.capic.net/) have established internship training guidelines, most of which are similar to those developed by APA and APPIC.

Students are often concerned about how to sort through the various types of internships, apply, and be accepted to the internship of their choice. To facilitate this process, APPIC publishes a directory of member programs (currently around 600 internships) that provides detailed information about sites. CAPIC also publishes a database with information on member programs (currently around 165 internships). Many internships have application deadlines in November, and students should research programs well in advance.

For many students, the application and selection process can be overwhelming. To manage this, APPIC has established a uniform application and matching process in which most programs in the United States and many programs in Canada participate (Stedman, 2007). Students complete a standard application form (the "AAPI") and submit other required materials to sites in which they are interested. Typically, students apply to 12 to 13 programs (Rodolfa & Keilin, 2006). After four to six weeks, students are notified whether or not they will be invited for an interview at the various programs. Interviewing can be expensive and time consuming. Sometimes internships allow telephone interviews, but most students and sites prefer in-person interviews since this allows both parties to develop a better sense of the fit between the program and applicant. The American Psychological Association of Graduate Students (APAGS) has sponsored the development of a workbook to help students with this somewhat daunting application and matching process (Williams-Nickelson & Prinstein, 2007).

After interviewing is completed, both students and programs rank their preferences and submit them online for a computerized matching process overseen by APPIC. Because the computerized system does not result in a match for all students and internship sites, a **clearinghouse** has been established to help connect unmatched students with unfilled internship slots. Other clearinghouses also exist (e.g., CAPIC and the Association of Counseling Center Training Agencies, https://www.accta.net/default.asp).

Historically, more students have sought an internship each year than there are available slots in programs. Recent data suggest that about 75% of those participating in the APPIC match received an internship placement on the uniform notification day; this number increases to 88% of all participants obtaining an internship position after the clearinghouse process is completed (Keilin, Baker, McCutcheon, & Peranson, 2007). This imbalance is referred to as the supply-and-demand issue and has been increasing in severity over the past decade (Rodolfa, Bell, Bieschke, Davis, & Peterson, 2007). Common reasons given for failing to receive an internship placement include applying to too few sites or primarily applying to sites that are very competitive, applying within a limited geographic region, applying only for part-time internships, or applying only in popular metropolitan areas (Madson, Hasan, Williams-Nickelson, Kettmann, & Van Sickle, 2007). Some surveys (Neely & Borden, 1993) have shown that internship directors believe many applicants are qualified, and so they focus on a good match of interests, experience, and interpersonal style. Also, some internships consider factors that are beyond the applicant's control, such as having a balance of genders or diversity in the overall internship cohort.

Graduate programs may restrict the kinds of internships to which their students may apply.

This is especially pertinent since students who do not match for an internship may be tempted to arrange a placement with a site that is not accredited by or a member of APA/CPA, APPIC, or CAPIC. Approximately 25% of the doctoral programs represented in the NCSPP self-study (NCSPP, 2005) reported that they did not permit students to apply for non-APA/CPA, APPIC, or CAPIC internships. About 60% of the programs indicated that they do not allow students to arrange or develop their own internship at an agency. Despite the internship shortage, most graduates in clinical psychology are employed in a job that uses their doctoral education, and they are satisfied with that job (Wicherski & Kohout, 2007).

Other Program Elements

In addition to the aforementioned aspects of graduate training, another critical element is the **comprehensive examination** that is required by most programs. This exam is variously referred to as a comprehensive exam ("comps"), qualifying exam, or preliminary exam, but we will use the term *comps* to refer to all of these. Some programs ascribe different meanings to each of these terms, while other programs use these terms synonymously. Whatever name the program uses, these exams typically are given to ensure that students have mastered the core scientific knowledge and/or clinical knowledge and skills needed to go on internship.

Unfortunately, little normative information exists about comps, and there appears to be great variability among programs on the processes involved. Approximately 96% of the doctoral programs represented in the NCSPP self-study (NCSPP, 2005) reported that they require some kind of comps exam, most frequently after the third year of coursework and almost always (94%) prior to internship. Comps may be a single exam (36% of programs require one exam) or may be broken down into parts

(32% of programs require two exams), such as when students take one exam on the core scientific knowledge and another to demonstrate clinical knowledge and skill. Approximately 15% of the programs indicated that they require three or more exams (e.g., an exam at the end of each year in the program).

In the NCSPP self-study, the most common formats used for comps were written clinical work samples (77%), oral clinical work samples (60%), essay tests of theoretical knowledge (51%), oral exams of theoretical knowledge (49%), recordings of clinical sessions (47%), multiple-choice tests of theoretical knowledge (38%), theory papers (15%), and in-class or take-home assignments (13%). The majority of programs (57%) indicated that students are either dismissed or put on mandatory probation if they fail the comps exam twice, while about 4% of the programs indicated that students can only fail comps once and 13% of the programs indicated that there is no limit to the number of times students can attempt to take and pass comps.

A final scholarly capstone project such as a dissertation is required in most doctoral programs. Different titles are used for this by different programs depending on the model of training and focus of the program. Approximately 57% of the doctoral programs represented in the NCSPP self-study (NCSPP, 2005) reported that they require students to complete a dissertation, while about 31% said that their program requires a **clinical research project** and 16% of the programs indicated that they require some other type of project. In the NCSPP self-study, the most common types of projects that students conducted in different programs were analyses of archival data (82%), survey research (80%), systematic qualitative studies (78%), outcome studies (65%), theoretical analyses (61%), case studies (51%), group-based nomothetic investigations (47%), and program development studies (47%). More research-focused programs are more likely to limit dissertations to quantitative empirical studies.

Dissertations typically require that students form a committee of several members (with the adviser serving as the chairperson). Some programs require that at least one committee member be an "outside reader" or individual from another academic area. Most programs require that a student has passed a **proposal defense** before proceeding with the study, and depending on the type of project, approval of the school's institutional review board may be required to ensure the protection of study participants. Programs often require that students have at least passed their proposal defense before they apply for internship, and internships typically prefer to admit students who have made substantial dissertation progress. Some programs require that students complete the entire dissertation before internship.

The next section of this chapter discusses steps that typically occur following the awarding of the doctoral degree that are related to professional psychology practice. These include credentialing (i.e., licensing and certification), specialization, **mobility**, and lifelong learning and continuing education.

Postdoctoral Requirements

Licensure

The primary purpose of licensure is to create regulatory laws that will protect the public from incompetent or dishonest professionals. In addition, licensure often is used to establish legal recognition of a specific body of knowledge and its application and to limit the use of the title "psychologist" to those who possess that knowledge.

The first licensure law in psychology was passed in 1945 for school psychologists in Connecticut. Missouri became the last state to pass a psychology licensure law in 1977, and Prince Edward Island became the last province in Canada to pass legal regulation in 1990. Currently, all 50 states, the District of Columbia, 10 Canadian provinces, and several territories have instituted some form of legal regulation for psychologists (Reaves, 2006).

In most jurisdictions, licensure is generic, and anyone who engages in work of a *psychological nature* must be licensed. In many cases the license for clinical, counseling, industrial-organizational (I/O), and consulting psychologists is essentially the same (Blanton, 2006). For the purposes of this chapter, clinical psychologists who engage in the assessment, diagnosis, and treatment of mental and behavioral disorders must be licensed to practice. However, there are some exceptions depending on the particular jurisdiction (e.g., for state and federal employees, academic psychologists supervising practicum students).

Jurisdictions independently decide whether or not an applicant for licensure possesses adequate education, knowledge, and experience to be allowed to practice within that jurisdiction, and requirements do vary. In an attempt to develop more consistency in licensing, ASPPB, a coalition of licensure and certification boards, was formed in 1961. ASPPB has been responsible for creating the Examination for Professional Practice of Psychology (i.e., the licensure exam used throughout the United States and Canada), maintaining a credentials bank, facilitating communication and reciprocity, and engaging in various other activities aimed at improving mobility for psychologists (Van Horne, 2006). ASPPB provides information on licensure requirements in the various jurisdictions in *The Handbook of Licensing and Certification Requirements for Psychologists in the United States and Canada* (ASPPB, 2008), which is available online.

The first requirement for licensure is to demonstrate appropriate education. In the United States, one can demonstrate appropriate education by either having graduated from a doctoral program that is accredited by the APA/CPA or showing that the program is regionally accredited and meets all of the criteria specified in law. Many states have a *residency requirement* that is part of the licensure law, such that the individual's program must have involved some minimal amount of time where the student was physically present with the core faculty taking coursework.

The second element required for licensure is to demonstrate appropriate knowledge.

Knowledge is demonstrated by passing examinations required by the jurisdiction. There can be three kinds of exams that are required, depending on the particular jurisdiction.

First, individuals must pass the *Examination for Professional Practice of Psychology* (**EPPP**), a 200-item multiple-choice exam (Rehm & Lipkins, 2006), with passing points varying by jurisdiction but typically about 70%. Highlight Box 1.3 presents the areas assessed on the EPPP. The exam is taken on

---

HIGHLIGHT BOX 1.3

WHAT KIND OF TEST DO PSYCHOLOGISTS HAVE TO PASS IN ORDER TO BE LICENSED?

After spending considerable time and money getting a doctorate, individuals still must pass at least one exam in order to be licensed. The Examination for the Professional Practice of Psychology* (EPPP) is required for licensure in all states and provinces (except Quebec as noted in this chapter). So, what kinds of things are on this exam? What do individuals need to know in order to pass the EPPP? Following are examples of the content in areas covered by this exam.

Biological bases of behavior (11%): knowledge of biological and neural bases of behavior; psychopharmacology; behavioral genetics; interaction of biology and the environment; methods used to assess brain functioning.

Cognitive-affective bases of behavior (13%): knowledge of types of cognition; the neural bases of cognition and affect; learning theories and applications; theories and applications of emotion and motivation, memory, and executive function; influence of psychosocial factors.

Social and multicultural bases of behavior (12%): knowledge of social cognition and interpersonal processes; group dynamics; evolutionary

and ecological influences; theories of personality; diversity issues involving race, ethnicity, culture, gender, sexual orientation, age, and disability.

Growth and lifespan development (13%): knowledge of age-appropriate as well as atypical patterns of development across the life span; theories of development; normative and non-traditional families; risk and protective factors in development; life events and organism-environment interactions.

Assessment and diagnosis (14%): knowledge of psychometric theory; theories and models of assessment; assessment methods for individuals, couples, families, groups, and organizations; diagnostic systems and differential diagnosis.

Treatment, intervention, and prevention (15%): knowledge of theories of intervention; intervention approaches with individuals, couples, families, groups, organizations, and communities; consultation models and processes; career counseling; health promotion and prevention; working with health-care systems.

Research methods and statistics (7%): knowledge of research design and methods;

HIGHLIGHT BOX 1.3   (*continued*)

statistical methods and procedures; program evaluation; instrument selection and validation; critical evaluation of research findings.

Ethical, legal, and professional issues (15%): knowledge of ethical principles and codes of ethics; professional standards and guidelines for practice; legal mandates and restrictions; ethical decision-making processes; professional development; supervision.

*From the Association of State and Provincial Psychology Boards, 2007. See http://asppb.org/publications/pdf/IFC.pdf for more specific information.

---

computer and can be scheduled at test sites in most urban centers. The EPPP is required for licensure by 61 of the 62 jurisdictions that are members of ASPPB. Quebec only requires this exam for those seeking licensure from outside of the province (Melnyk & Vaughn, 2006).

Some jurisdictions have developed additional "complementary" examinations. These exams evaluate whether the individual demonstrates adequate abilities, judgment, and reasoning in the integration and application of psychological knowledge. Recent data from ASPPB indicate that out of 62 state and provincial licensing boards, 31 require an interview or oral examination, and 7 require both an oral examination and a written exam (Melnyk & Vaughn, 2006). Concerns have been voiced about the reliability and validity of these oral examinations.

Finally, most jurisdictions require that individuals pass a **jurisprudence exam** demonstrating knowledge of legal standards, ethics, and professional conduct in the jurisdiction where application for licensure is being made. Jurisprudence exams are often written and are less subject to criticisms of poor reliability and validity. Recent data from ASPPB indicate that 48 of the 62 state and provincial licensing boards require a jurisprudence exam for licensure (Melnyk & Vaughn, 2006). Licensing requirements change frequently, so individuals are cautioned to check with their local board of examiners for the most current requirements.

The third element required for licensure is appropriate experience, typically demonstrated by documenting minimum number of hours of supervised clinical practice. The exact number of required hours varies from state to state. Most states specify that a certain percentage of the required hours may be predoctoral, with the remaining hours needing to be obtained postdoctorally. With respect to internship, Bartle and Rodolfa (1999) reviewed licensure data from ASPPB and reported that 11 states required 2,000 hours of supervised clinical experience, 14 states required between 1,501 and 1,900 hours, and 14 states required 1,500 hours of supervised experience. To make matters more confusing, 11 states required one year of experience but did not specify the number of required hours. Further complication results because many internships (25%) require between 1,500 and 1,900 hours and thus do not fulfill the required predoctoral hours requirement in all jurisdictions.

With respect to postdoctoral hours, Kaslow and Echols (2006) reported that 39 states required one year (between 1,000 and 2,000 hours). Eight states and the District of Columbia mandated two years of supervised postdoctoral experience (between 1,500 and 4,000 hours), and two states did not have any supervised postdoctoral experience requirement for licensure. In addition, most states specified a minimum number of direct patient contact hours, varying between 450 and 1,000. Clearly, the disparities in required experience among jurisdictions create a serious challenge for our profession (Rodolfa & Keilin, 2006).

As previously noted, the number of hours of supervised predoctoral experience has been steadily increasing. Consequently, there has been considerable discussion about whether there is a need for postdoctoral hours for licensure. It has been argued that the postdoctoral experience requirement prolongs training, places an additional financial burden on individuals, creates difficulties in finding supervised postdoctoral positions, and is inconsistent with the licensing process in most other health professions (APA, 2001; Kaslow & Echols, 2006). As a result of these discussions, APA voted to revise its model licensure act in 2005 to recommend doing away with the postdoctoral hours requirement (APA, 2006). Each jurisdiction can decide whether or not to follow APA's recommendation (APA, 2001), and currently three states (Washington, Alabama, and Utah) do not require any postdoctoral hours, allowing students to complete all of their required hours during their doctoral programs.

Postdoctoral Recognition and Specialization

Most jurisdictions still require supervised postdoctoral experience for licensure. This postdoctoral experience may be informal, occurring in a regular work setting, or formal, with specialized or advanced training taking place within a structured program (Kaslow & Echols, 2006). Most formal postdocs are one or two years in length and involve some combination of direct service, training, didactic experiences, and possibly research.

After becoming licensed, psychologists can apply for specialty certification in a number of areas. The American Board of Professional Psychology (**ABPP**, http://www.abpp.org/) is probably the best known organization that provides specialty certification for psychologists. ABPP was established in 1947 with support from the APA. It offers psychologists specialty certification in one of 13 areas through its various boards (Packard & Simon, 2006). Certification is voluntary and requires that applicants meet a set of criteria and undergo an examination to receive their **diplomate**. Thirty jurisdictions offer expedited licensure review for those who have obtained ABPP certification (DeLeon & Hinnefeld, 2006).

In 1974 the National Register of Health Service Providers (NR) was established through a joint effort of APA and ABPP to go beyond generic licensure and credential individuals as *Health Service Providers in Psychology* (HSPs) (Wise, Hall, Ritchie, & Turner, 2006). Healthcare companies, insurance companies, governmental agencies, and the general public use the NR to identify individuals who meet basic quality standards.

Mobility

Individuals must be separately licensed in each jurisdiction where they will engage in independent practice. Because each state and province may have different laws, requirements, and tests, there is a significant possibility of confusion and difficulty when one wishes to move from one jurisdiction to another. This is typically referred to as an issue of **mobility**. Various attempts have been made to help psychologists deal with mobility issues.

The NR HSP credential (and the Canadian Register of Health Service Providers) can facilitate mobility in the over 40 jurisdictions that currently accept or are in the process of modifying their regulations to accept the NR HSP credential. These jurisdictions waive the requirements for documentation of a doctoral degree, internship year, and postdoctoral year for individuals credentialed by the NR. The majority of these jurisdictions also waive reporting of the EPPP score.

Students can also document each phase of their training with the NR by signing up for the National Psychologist Trainee Register (NPTR). Participation in the NPTR is free, and graduate students can submit documentation about each phase of training at the time it is completed and have it reviewed for compliance with national standards (Wise et al., 2006).

ASPPB provides several programs to assist professional psychologists with mobility. First, they have established a *credentials bank* that allows individuals to submit and archive critical documentation about their training, which provides protection for the psychologist if, for example, an internship program is discontinued or a supervisor cannot be located. Second, individuals can document their eligibility for licensure and earn the Certificate of Professional Qualification (**CPQ**) (DeMers & Jonason, 2006). Jurisdictions that accept the CPQ waive documentation of education, supervised experience, and EPPP scores for the purposes of licensure. Third, ASPPB has established an Agreement of Reciprocity. Jurisdictions that participate in this program have agreed to accept each other's licenses.

Lifelong Learning and Continuing Education

Psychologists are typically licensed for a specified period of time (e.g., two years) and then must renew their licenses. License renewal requires a fee and verification that they have not engaged in any unethical behavior, had their license revoked in any other jurisdiction, or had any legal actions taken against them.

Often, license renewal also involves psychologists verifying that they have maintained currency in the field through continuing education (CE) activities. Recent data indicate that CE requirements for licensure renewal now exist in 41 states and the District of Columbia (Sharkin & Plageman, 2003), although the number of required hours varies, often between 20 and 40 hours every two years. States may require CE in specific areas (e.g., ethics) and may limit the type of activities that may count toward CE requirements. Questions have been raised about the lack of evidence that CE activities actually improve or maintain professional services (VandeCreek, Knapp, & Brace, 1990), and alternative methods such as reexamination have been discussed.

SUMMARY

The world of professional psychology education and training has come a long way in the past 65 years, moving from the absence of standards and guidelines to our current situation with multiple training models and a specified training sequence to help students develop knowledge, skills, and professional attitudes in a set of specific competencies. There are numerous training councils and organizations dedicated to the development of psychologists. Despite our many differences, our core values (e.g., the need for research to inform practice and practice to inform research, respect for human dignity, an emphasis on human diversity in all of its forms, etc.) will continue to be reflected in our educational policies and practices. Nonetheless, it is likely that we will see continued change in the future, and education and training may be quite different by the time students reading this book begin to train the next generation of psychologists.

THOUGHT QUESTIONS

1.1. Psychology graduate programs attempt to select students based on academic, clinical, research, and personal/interpersonal experience and attributes. Programs continue to evaluate students on their personal and interpersonal qualities. What are some effective and fair ways in which programs might conduct this evaluation?

1.2. Many health professions have separate research and practice degrees. Psychology has traditionally awarded the PhD for both research and practice and now awards both the PhD and PsyD to future practitioners. What do you see as the advantages and disadvantages of this mixed-degree model?

1.3. We talk about training and evaluating students in a variety of areas of knowledge, skills, and attitudes. What attitudes do you believe are crucial for psychologists?

1.4. Should professional psychology have a standardized curriculum? What are the advantages and disadvantages of this standardization?

1.5. How might professional psychology address the supply-and-demand imbalance that currently exists in psychology internships? What are the implications of each solution?

1.6. Differences exist in the licensure requirements for various jurisdictions where psychologists may practice. How should our profession and our training programs address this situation so that psychologists are adequately prepared to practice wherever they choose to move? What are the obstacles to various possible solutions, and how can we address those obstacles?

1.7. Postdoctoral specialization is available in a number of areas of professional psychology. What are the advantages and disadvantages of seeking additional training in order to specialize? What are the opportunities and obstacles inherent in practicing as a specialist in our field?

Glossary

ABPP: American Board of Professional Psychology. The organization that awards the diplomate to psychologists with advanced or specialized knowledge and skill.

APA: American Psychological Association. The largest organization of psychologists in the world. APA represents the science, practice, education, and public interest applications of psychology.

APCS: Academy of Psychological Clinical Science. Training council for clinical scientist programs.

APPIC: Association of Psychology Postdoctoral and Internship Centers. Organization that serves those with interests in the predoctoral and postdoctoral training of professional psychologists. Runs the "internship match" program.

ASPPB: Association of State and Provincial Psychology Boards. Organization of certification and licensing boards in the United States and Canada.

CAPIC: California Association of Psychology Internship Centers. California-based organization that helps match students and internships Most CAPIC internships are half-time.

Captive internship: Internship administered by an academic program that may or may not be required of all students in that program and usually gives preference to students applying from the affiliated academic program.

CCPPP: Canadian Council of Professional Psychology Programs. Organization representing university-based academic and internship programs in clinical psychology, counseling psychology, and clinical neuropsychology in Canada.

Clearinghouse: Service through APPIC to facilitate additional internship placements by providing information on open internship positions following the official internship match.

Clinical Research Project: Final scholarly clinical capstone project required in some practitioner-scholar model doctoral programs in clinical psychology.

Clinical scientist model: Model based on the tenets that scientific clinical psychology is the only acceptable form of clinical psychology and that all students should be able to produce competent clinical scientists.

CMHC: Community Mental Health Center. Agency initially established to provide a range of prevention and intervention services to be delivered in local communities.

CoA: Commission on Accreditation. Group affiliated with APA that accredits doctoral, internship, and postdoctoral programs and develops accreditation policy in the United States.

Commission on Accreditation (CoA): Thirty-two member group that evaluates doctoral, internship, and postdoctoral programs in professional psychology for accreditation and sets accreditation policy in the United States.

Comprehensive examination: One or more achievement exams given to doctoral students to evaluate their knowledge of scientific foundations, theories, and/or clinical knowledge and skill. Passing this exam is often required prior to the internship or dissertation.

Core competencies: Constellations of fundamental knowledge, skills, and attitudes considered essential for all professional psychologists, and upon which all practice is based.

CPA: Canadian Psychological Association. Professional organization of psychologists in Canada striving to support research, education, and practice in psychology and to promote the health and welfare of the public.

CPQ: Certificate of Professional Qualification. Certificate awarded by ASPPB to psychologists with specific education and experience qualifications to facilitate mobility and streamline credentials reviews.

CUDCP: Council of University Directors of Clinical Psychology. Training council for scientist-practitioner programs.

Diplomate: American Board of Professional Psychology certification of advanced achievement in one of 13 specialty areas within professional psychology.

Dissertation: Final scholarly research capstone project required in many doctoral programs in clinical psychology across all program models.

EPPP ("E-triple P"): Examination for Professional Practice in Psychology. Multiple-choice examination of knowledge required for licensure by most states and provinces in the United States and Canada.

Generalist: Psychology training or practice that is broad-based and not specialized.

Internship: Capstone clinical experience that occurs after all practica are complete, but prior to the awarding of the doctoral degree. Students serve full-time or half-time conducting many of the same activities as clinical staff members and receive intensive training through supervision, seminars, and other learning experiences.

Jurisprudence examination: Test of knowledge of laws, ethics, and professional standards in the location where an applicant is seeking licensure.

KSAs: Knowledge, skills, and attitudes. The components of competencies taught and assessed in the professional development of clinical psychologists.

Licensure: State or provincial regulation of which individuals may call themselves psychologists and limits the use of various psychological techniques to licensed individuals.

Mobility: The ability of psychologists to move from one jurisdiction to another, or to practice in more than one jurisdiction.

Multiple roles: The many tasks that psychologists typically combine in their careers, for example, therapy, consultation, supervision, and administration.

NCSPP: National Council of Schools and Programs of Professional Psychology. Training council for practitioner scholar or professional model programs.

NR: National Register of Health Service Providers in Psychology. Group that certifies the background of psychologists wanting to serve as health service providers, a designation mostly used to qualify for third-party payment for services.

Pedagogy: Philosophy of teaching and education. Educational approach.

Practicum: Placement of students in a clinical setting where they engage in experiential learning by providing clinical services to clients or patients, typically under the supervision of a licensed psychologist.

Practitioner-scholar model (includes practitioner, professional, and scholar-practitioner models): Clinical psychology training model developed at the 1973 Vail conference that proposes an emphasis on direct training for clinical roles in psychology. All models integrate research with practice. Most professional model programs offer the PsyD degree.

Proposal defense: Meeting of a student and the dissertation committee to agree upon a dissertation project. Student usually presents a written proposal that is reviewed and approved by all committee members.

Scientist-practitioner model: Clinical psychology training model developed at the 1949 Boulder conference. Training should be as a scientist first, then a clinician. All models integrate research with practice. Most scientist-practitioner programs offer the PhD degree.

Terminal master's degree: Degree earned in a program designed to stop after the awarding of the master's degree. Program does not go beyond the master's level.

Training council: Group of representatives of training organizations (e.g., academic programs, internships) who meet to advance training and education.

VA: Veterans Administration. A department of the United States government dedicated to providing medical care and other services to veterans. Supported clinical psychology training in an effort to increase the availability of mental health care for veterans.

References

Albee, G. W. (1971). Role conflicts in psychology and their implications for a reevaluation of training models. *Canadian-Psychologist, 12*, 465–481.

Albee, G. W. (2000). The Boulder Model's fatal flaw. *American Psychologist, 55*, 247–248.

Alden, A., Van Tuyl, L., Chow, J., Davis, C., Del Rio, R., Peruzzi, N., et al. (2000, August). *1994–1999 Intern applicant practicum hours: an exploratory investigation.* Poster presented at the 108th Annual Convention of the American Psychological Association, Washington, DC.

Altmaier, E. M. (2003). The history of accreditation of doctoral programs in psychology. In E. Altmaier (Ed.), *Setting standards in graduate education: psychology's commitment to excellence in accreditation* (pp. 39–60). Washington, DC: American Psychological Association.

American Psychological Association (1979). *Criteria for accreditation of doctoral training programs and internships in professional psychology.* Washington, DC: Author.

American Psychological Association (2001). *Report of the Commission on Education and Training Leading to Licensure in Psychology*. Washington, DC: Author.

American Psychological Association (2006). *APA governance news*. Retrieved April 1, 2008 from http://www.apa.org/monitor/apr06/governance.html

American Psychological Association (2007a). *Assessment of competency benchmarks work group: a developmental model for the defining and measuring of competencies in professional psychology*. Retrieved April 1, 2008 from http://www.apa.org/ed/graduate/comp_benchmark.pdf.

American Psychological Association (2007b). *Guidelines and principles for accreditation of programs in professional psychology*. Washington, DC: Author.

American Psychological Association (2008). [Compilation of data from Graduate Study in Psychology, 2008 Edition]. Unpublished data.

American Psychological Association Committee on the Ph.D. Degree in Psychology (1934). Standards for the Ph.D. degree in psychology. *Psychological Bulletin, 31*, 67–72.

Association of State and Provincial Psychology Boards (2008). *Handbook of licensing and certification requirements for psychologists in the United States and Canada*. Retrieved April 1, 2008 from http://www.asppb.org/HandbookPublic/handbookreview.aspx

Baker, D. B. & Benjamin, L. T. (2000). The affirmation of the scientist-practitioner: a look back at Boulder. *American Psychologist, 55*, 241–246.

Bartle, D. D. & Rodolfa, E. R. (1999). Internship hours: proposing a national standard. *Professional Psychology: Research and Practice, 30*, 420–422.

Belar, C. D. (2000). Scientist-practitioner ≠ science + practice: Boulder is bolder. *American Psychologist, 55*, 249–250.

Belar, C. D. & Perry, N. W. (1992). The National Conference on Scientist-Practitioner Training for the Professional Practice of Psychology. *American Psychologist, 47*, 71–75.

Benjamin, L. T., Jr. (2001). American psychology's struggles with its curriculum: should a thousand flowers bloom? *American Psychologist, 56*, 735–742.

Bent, R. J. (1991). The professional core competency areas. In R. L. Peterson, J. D. McHolland, R. J. Bent, E. Davis-Russell, G. E. Edwall, K. Polite, D. L. Singer, & G. Stricker (Eds.), *The core curriculum in professional psychology*. Washington, DC: American Psychological Association.

Bent, R. J. & Cannon, W. G. (1987). Key functional skills of a professional psychologist. In E. F. Bourg, R. J. Bent, J. E. Callan, N. F. Jones, J. McHolland, & G. Stricker (Eds.), *Standards and evaluation in the education and training of professional psychologists: knowledge attitudes, and skills* (pp. 87–97). Norman, OK: Transcript Press.

Blanton, J. S. (2006). License issues for industrial/organizational psychologists and other non-health service providers. In T. J. Vaughn (Ed.), *Psychology licensure and certification: what students need to know* (pp. 145–154). Washington, DC: American Psychological Association.

Borden, K. A. & McIlvried, E. J. (2008). Applying the competency model to professional psychology education, training, and assessment: Mission Bay and beyond. In M. B. Kenkel & R. L. Peterson (Eds.), *Standards and processes for education in professional psychology*. Submitted for publication.

Canadian Psychological Association (2008). *Advocating for CPA accreditation in North America*. Retrieved April 1, 2008 from http://www.cpa.ca/accreditation/advocatingforcpaaccreditationinnorthamerica/

Committee on Training in Clinical Psychology of the American Psychological Association (1947). Recommended graduate training program in clinical psychology. *American Psychologist, 2*, 539–558.

Council for Higher Education Accreditation (2007). *Recognized accrediting organizations*. Retrieved April 1, 2008 from http://www.chea.org/pdf/CHEA_USDE_AllAccred.pdf

Council of Chairs of Training Councils (2004). *The comprehensive evaluation of student-trainee competence in professional psychology programs*. Retrieved April 1, 2008 from http://www.psychtrainingcouncils.org/pubs/NCSPP-%20CCTC%20model%20Student%20Competency.pdf

DeLeon, P. H. & Hinnefeld, B. J. (2006). Licensure mobility. In T. J. Vaughn (Ed.), *Psychology licensure and certification: what students need to know* (pp. 97–105). Washington, DC: American Psychological Association.

DeMers, S. T. & Jonason, K. R. (2006). The ASPPB Credentials Bank and the Certificate of Professional Qualification in Psychology: comprehensive solutions to mobility obstacles. In T. J. Vaughn (Ed.), *Psychology licensure and certification: what students need to know* (pp. 107–115). Washington, DC: American Psychological Association.

Dixon, K. E. & Thorn, B. E. (2000). Does the internship shortage portend market saturation? 1998 placement data across the four major national training councils. *Professional Psychology: Research and Practice, 31*, 276–280.

Hatcher, R. L. & Lassiter, K. D. (2007). Initial training in professional psychology: the Practicum Competencies Outline. *Training and Education in Professional Psychology, 1*, 49–63.

Hébert, R. (2002, January). We'd like to thank the Academy: APCS creates fusion of science and clinical training. *APS Observer, 15(1)*. Retrieved March 27, 2008 from http://www.psychologicalscience.org/observer/0102/apcs.html

Hoch, E. L., Ross, A. O., & Winder, C. L. (Eds.) (1966). *Professional preparation of clinical psychologists: Proceedings of the Conference on the Professional Preparation of Clinical Psychologists*. Washington, DC: American Psychological Association.

Kaslow, N. J., Borden, K. A., Collins, F. L., Jr., Forrest, L., Illfelder-Kaye, J., Nelson, P. D., et al. (2004). Competencies conference: future directions in education and credentialing in professional psychology. *Journal of Clinical Psychology, 60,* 699–712.

Kaslow, N. J. & Echols, M. M. (2006). Postdoctoral training and requirements for licensure and certification. In T. J. Vaughn (Ed.), *Psychology licensure and certification: what students need to know* (pp. 85–95). Washington, DC: American Psychological Association.

Keilin, W. G., Baker, J., McCutcheon, S., & Peranson, E. (2007). A growing bottleneck: the internship supply-demand imbalance in 2007 and its impact on psychology training. *Training and Education in Professsional Psychology, 1,* 229–237.

Korman, M. (Ed.) (1973a). *Levels and patterns of professional training in psychology: conference proceedings.* Washington, DC: American Psychological Association.

Korman, M. (1973b). Recommendations of the conference. In M. Korman (Ed.), *Levels and patterns of professional training in psychology: conference proceedings* (pp. 99–125). Washington, DC: American Psychological Association.

Madson, M. B., Hasan, N. T., Williams-Nickelson, C., Kettmann, J. J., & Van Sickle, K. S. (2007). The internship supply and demand issue: graduate student's perspective. *Training and Education in Professional Psychology, 1,* 249–257.

McFall, R. M. (1991). Manifesto for a science of clinical psychology. *The Clinical Psychologist, 44,* 75–88.

McFall, R. M. (1996). Making psychology incorruptible. *Applied & Preventive Psychology, 5,* 9–15.

McFall, R. M. (2000). Elaborate reflections on a simple manifesto. *Applied & Preventive Psychology, 9,* 5–21.

McIlvried, E. J. & Bent, R. J. (2003, January). *Core competencies: current and future perspectives.* Paper presented at the midwinter meeting of the National Council of Schools and Programs of Professional Psychology. Scottsdale, AZ.

Meehl, P. E. (1973). Why I do not attend case conferences. In P. E. Meehl (Ed.), *Psychodiagnosis: selected papers* (pp. 225–302). Minneapolis: University of Minnesota Press.

Melnyk, W. T. & Vaughn, K. S. (2006). Complementary examinations. In T. J. Vaughn (Ed.), *Psychology licensure and certification: what students need to know* (pp. 55–72). Washington, DC: American Psychological Association.

Merlo, L. J., Collins, A., & Bernstein, J. (2008). CUDCP-affiliated clinical psychology student views of their science training. *Training and Education in Professional Psychology, 2,* 59–65.

National Council of Schools and Programs of Professional Psychology (2005). 2005 NCSPP self study: final results. Retrieved April 1, 2008, from http://www.ncspp.info/2005%20NCSPP%20Self%20Study%20Final%20Report.pdf

National Council of Schools and Programs of Professional Psychology (2007). Competency developmental achievement levels (DALs) of the National Council of Schools and Programs of Professional Psychology (NCSPP). Retrieved April 1, 2008 from http://ncspp.info/DALof%20NCSPP%209-21-07.pdf.

Neely, F. & Borden, K. (1993, January). *Beyond the APPIC Directory: applicant characteristics preferred by directors of predoctoral internships.* Paper presented at the National Council of Schools of Professional Psychology Training in Professional Psychology Conference. La Jolla, CA.

Nelson, P. D. (2007). Striving for competence in the assessment of competence: psychology's professional education and credentialing journey of public accountability. *Training and Education in Professional Psychology, 1,* 3–12.

Packard, T. & Simon, N. P. (2006). Board certification by the American Board of Professional Psychology. In T. J. Vaughn (Ed.), *Psychology licensure and certification: what students need to know* (pp. 117–126). Washington, DC: American Psychological Association.

Paszkiewicz, W., Rabe, D. M., Adams, W., Gathercoal, K., Meyer, A., & McIlvried, E. J. (2006, January). *2005 NCSPP self study with complementary data from the 2006 Graduate Study in Psychology and 2004–2005 Faculty Salary Survey.* Presented at the meeting of the National Council of Schools and Programs of Professional Psychology. Las Vegas, NV.

Peterson, D. R. (1991). Connection and disconnection of research and practice in the education of professional psychologists. *American Psychologist, 46,* 422–429.

Peterson, D. R. (1996a). Making conversation possible. *Applied & Preventive Psychology, 5,* 17–18.

Peterson, D. R. (1996b). Making psychology indispensable. *Applied & Preventive Psychology, 5,* 1–8.

Peterson, D. R. (2000). Scientist-practitioner or scientific practitioner? *American Psychologist, 55,* 252–253.

Peterson, R. L., Peterson, D. R., Abrams, J. C., & Stricker, G. (1997). The National Council of Schools and Programs of Professional Psychology education model. *Professional Psychology: Research and Practice, 28,* 373–386.

Pottharst, K. E. (1973). A brief history of the professional model of training. In M. Korman (Ed.), *Levels and patterns of professional training in psychology: conference proceedings* (pp. 33–40). Washington, DC: American Psychological Association.

Raimy, V. C. (Ed.) (1950). *Training in clinical psychology.* Englewood Cliffs, NJ: Prentice Hall.

Reaves, R. P. (2006). The history of licensure of psychologists in the United States and Canada. In T. J. Vaughn (Ed.), *Psychology licensure and certification: what students need to know* (pp. 17–26). Washington, DC: American Psychological Association.

Rehm, L. P. & Lipkins, R. H. (2006). The examination for professional practice in psychology. In T. J. Vaughn (Ed.), *Psychology licensure and certification: what students need to know* (pp. 39–53). Washington, DC: American Psychological Association.

Roberts, M. C., Borden, K. A., Christiansen, M. D., & Lopez, S. J. (2005). Fostering a culture shift: assessment of competence in the education and careers of professional psychologists. *Professional Psychology: Research and Practice, 36,* 355–361.

Rodolfa, E. R., Bell, D. J., Bieschke, K. J., Davis, C., & Peterson, R. L. (2007). The internship match: understanding the problem—seeking solutions. *Training and Education in Professional Psychology, 1,* 225–228.

Rodolfa, E., Bent, R., Eisman, E., Nelson, P., Rehm, L., & Ritchie, P. (2005). A cube model for competency development: implications for psychology educators and regulators. *Professional Psychology: Research and Practice, 36,* 347–354.

Rodolfa, E. & Keilin, G. (2006). Internship training with licensure on the horizon. In T. J. Vaughn (Ed.), *Psychology licensure and certification: what students need to know* (pp. 73–83). Washington, DC: American Psychological Association.

Rodolfa, E. R., Owen, J. J., & Clark, S. (2007). Practicum training hours: fact and fantasy. *Training and Education in Professional Psychology, 1,* 64–73.

Rossen, E. & Oakland, T. (2008). Graduate preparation in research methods: the current status of APA-accredited professional programs in psychology. *Training and Education in Professional Psychology, 2,* 42–49.

Sharkin, B. S. & Plageman, P. M. (2003). What do psychologists think about mandatory continuing education? A survey of Pennsylvania practitioners. *Professional Psychology: Research and Practice, 34,* 318–323.

Stedman, J. M. (2007). What we know about predoctoral internship training: a 10-year update. *Training and Education in Professional Psychology, 1,* 74–88.

Stricker, G. & Trierweiler, S. J. (1995). The local clinical scientist: a bridge between science and practice. *American Psychologist, 50,* 995–1002.

Trierweiler, S. J. & Stricker, G. (1998). *The scientific practice of professional psychology.* New York: Plenum.

VandeCreek, L., Knapp, S., & Brace, K. (1990). Mandatory continuing education for licensed psychologists: its rationale and current implementation. *Professional Psychology: Research and Practice, 21,* 135–140.

Van Horne, B. A. (2006). Resources available from the Association of State and Provincial Psychology Boards. In T. J. Vaughn (Ed.), *Psychology licensure and certification: what students need to know* (pp. 27–38). Washington, DC: American Psychological Association.

Wicherski, M. & Kohout, J. (2007). *2005 Doctorate Employment Survey.* Retrieved April 8, 2008 from http://research.apa.org/des05.html#job

Williams-Nickelson, C. & Prinstein, M. J. (Eds.) (2007). *Internships in psychology: the APAGS workbook for writing successful applications and finding the right match.* Washington, DC: American Psychological Association.

Wise, E. H., Hall, J. E., Ritchie, P. L., & Turner, L. C. (2006). The National Register of Health Service Providers in Psychology and the Canadian Register of Health Service Providers in Psychology. In T. J. Vaughn (Ed.), *Psychology licensure and certification: what students need to know* (pp. 127–137). Washington, DC: American Psychological Association.

Ethics in Assessment, Treatment, and Research

Thomas Hadjistavropoulos
University of Regina

Gerald P. Koocher
Simmons College

OUTLINE

INTRODUCTORY STATEMENT

Unlike most professionals, practicing psychologists deal with the most personal, private, and sensitive matters that preoccupy individuals. The extremely sensitive knowledge they acquire from clients places them in a position of utmost responsibility and trust. In addition, a large portion of clients who seek consultation with psychologists do so during some of the most difficult and vulnerable times of their lives. This vulnerability creates an uneven power dynamic in the relationship between a client and a psychologist. Moreover, the clinician's "expert" status may foster a degree of dependence (Barnett, Lazarus, Vasquez,

Moorehead-Slaughter, & Johnson, 2007). For this reason, psychological practitioners, as a profession, have adopted very high standards of ethical conduct and ethics training. National, state, and provincial psychological associations and regulatory bodies have adopted and enforce codes of ethics. In addition, the accreditation standards adopted by the American Psychological Association (APA, Committee on Accreditation, 2008) and by the Canadian Psychological Association (CPA, 2002) for doctoral programs and internships in psychology explicitly specify requirements for training in ethics and professional standards.

Our high standards of ethical conduct not only serve to protect clients, research participants, and the general public but also safeguard the esteem and public image of our discipline. This chapter provides an overview of the ethics codes adopted by the APA and CPA and discusses some of the most central and common ethical themes that arise in the context of the practicing psychologist's work.

OUR CODES OF ETHICS

The American Psychological Association and the Canadian Psychological Association have each adopted codes of ethics (APA, 2002; CPA, 2000). Both codes focus on regulating only those activities that psychologists engage in by virtue of their professional roles. Private behavior does not fall under the purview of these codes (APA, 2002) unless it raises concerns about the competence or personal ability of the individual to carry out activities as a psychologist or undermines the public trust in the profession as a whole (CPA, 2000). For example, imagine a psychologist lies to a friend or intimate partner. Although such behavior may raise personal ethical issues, it does not fall under the purview of our professional codes because the psychologist engaged in the behavior as a private individual, not in a professional role. On the other hand, there are situations when a psychologist's behavior as a private citizen may undermine the public's trust in the profession in general (and, as such, may fall under the purview of our codes of ethics). Consider the hypothetical example of a group of psychologists in a small community who regularly attend the local bar, drink excessively, and subsequently find themselves arrested for public nudity. To the extent that members of the small community recognize the group as psychologists, the public's trust in the profession and its standards may be undermined.

We must remain mindful that our ethics codes and legal requirements do not always overlap congruently, and in situations of discrepancy between ethics and the law, psychologists must make known their commitment to **ethical principles** and attempt to resolve the conflict. If resolution of the conflict proves unfeasible, psychologists may adhere to the legal requirements and/or regulations in a manner consistent with upholding basic human rights (APA, 2002).

Codes of ethics usually consist of ethical principles and **ethical standards**. On one hand, we intend the principles to guide our behavior aspirationally, recognizing that such principles will prove difficult to enforce. On the other hand, we intend the specific standards listed in the ethics codes as enforceable rules (e.g., by disciplinary committees and state and provincial professional regulatory bodies).

The American Psychological Association established its first code of ethics in 1953, based on members' reports of problematic ethical incidents (Sinclair, Poizner, Gilmour-Barrett, & Randall, 1987). The most recent version of the code (APA, 2002), also based on a critical incident survey, consists of five ethical principles and many standards of practice:

1. Beneficence and nonmalificence (which refers to the obligation to maximize benefit and to minimize harm);

2. Fidelity and responsibility (which refers to the obligation to accept responsibility for one's professional behavior, setting and following high professional standards, forming relationships of trust, and consulting with colleagues);
3. Integrity (which refers to the general obligation to be truthful and honest);
4. Justice (which recognizes that fairness and justice entitle all people to have access to and benefit from competent and unbiased psychologists' contributions);
5. Respect for persons' rights and dignity (which stresses the importance of respect for the worth and dignity of all persons as well as the rights to self-determination, **confidentiality,** and **privacy**).

The various standards in the code are placed into 10 categories: (a) resolving of ethical issues (e.g., working with ethics committees and dealing with instances of conflict between ethical principles); (b) competence; (c) human relations; (d) privacy and confidentiality; (e) advertising and other public statements; (f) record keeping and fees; (g) education and training; (h) research and publication; (i) assessment; and (j) therapy.

Other national organizations of psychologists have organized their ethical standards and principles in different ways. For instance, the Canadian Code of Ethics for Psychologists (CPA, 2000) outlines four ethical principles:

1. Respect for the dignity of persons (emphasizes moral rights and autonomy)
2. Responsible caring (emphasizes caring and competence)
3. Integrity in relationships (emphasizes honesty, straightforwardness, and openness)
4. Responsibility to society (emphasizes respect for societal values as well as the importance of development of knowledge and activities that are beneficial for society)

Accompanying each principle of the Canadian code are detailed values statements and many ethical standards. The Canadian code takes a unique approach by articulating the four principles in order of importance. While all four principles are important, in instances where principles are in conflict, psychologists should place greater emphasis on principles standing earlier in the hierarchy (except in situations when a person's life seems in danger, in which case the principle of "responsible caring" takes precedence). Consider, for example, a client who decides to take an action that, in the psychologist's opinion, would not serve the client's best interests. In such a situation the principle of "respect for the dignity of persons," which stresses the importance of client autonomy, would conflict with the principle of "responsible caring," which emphasizes the importance of the psychologist making every effort to maximize benefit and minimize harm.

When a legal standard exists, as in the case of abuse or neglect of a child, the psychologist has clear legal guidance (e.g., the obligation to report to authorities that a child needs protection because of physical or sexual abuse). However, resolving ethical dilemmas (especially in instances where ethical principles conflict with one another) can prove challenging. In such cases, the Canadian Code of Ethics for Psychologists (CPA, 2002) offers a distinct advantage by outlining a series of dilemma-resolving steps one can follow (see Highlight Box 2.1).

The APA and CPA intend their codes not only to educate and guide psychologists' professional behavior, but also to act as factors for consideration by state and provincial regulatory bodies in evaluating complaints against psychologists. While our codes of ethics cover a wide variety of topics and situations, this chapter focuses on some of the most central ethical issues likely to arise in psychological practice and research.

HIGHLIGHT BOX 2.1

A PROCESS FOR RESOLVING ETHICAL DILEMMAS

The Canadian code of ethics for psychologists (CPA, 2000) outlines a series of decision-making steps that are designed to facilitate the resolution of ethical dilemmas. These steps are as follows:

"1 Identification of the individuals and groups potentially affected by the decision.

2. Identification of ethically relevant issues and practices, including the interests, rights and any relevant characteristics of the individuals and groups involved and of the system or circumstances in which the ethical problem arose.

3. Consideration of how personal biases, stresses, or self-interest might influence the development of or choice between courses of action.

4. Development of alternative courses of action.

5. Analysis of likely short-term, ongoing, and long-term risks and benefits of each course of action on the individual(s)/group(s) involved or likely to be affected (e.g., client,

client's family or employees, employing institution, students, research participants, colleagues, the discipline, society, self).

6. Choice of course of action after conscientious application of existing principles, values, and standards.

7. Action, with a commitment to assume responsibility for the consequences of the action.

8. Evaluation of the results of the course of action.

9. Assumption of responsibility for consequences of action, including correction of negative consequences, if any, or re-engaging in the decision-making process if the ethical issue is not resolved.

10. Appropriate action, as warranted and feasible, to prevent future occurrences of the dilemma (e.g., communication and problem solving with colleagues; changes in procedures and practices)."
CPA (2000), p. 3.

COMPETENCE

One of the most central ethical requirements for practicing psychologists involves the need to practice only within one's areas of competence. For example, work with children, forensic practice, family therapy, and neuropsychological assessment all require mastery of specialized content and supervised practice. Psychologists lacking specialized education and training should refrain from offering such services without appropriate supervision.

Permissible exceptions might occur in emergency situations or when alternate skilled providers are not available. However, such exceptions should end as the emergency resolves or alternate services become available. Psychologists also have an ethical obligation to maintain their competence and keep their skills current by engaging in continuing education or other such activities. One colleague estimated that what we learn while earning a doctoral degree in psychology becomes obsolete within 10 to 12 years (Dubin, 1972). In addition, we must strive for a continuing awareness of our own personal functioning and refrain from providing services when we become aware of a personal problem that may limit our ability to practice competently.

INFORMED CONSENT

Prior to entering any professional relationship as practitioners or researchers, psychologists have both ethical and legal obligations to initiate the process of consent. Some people like to use the term *informed consent*, although the term is redundant since consent implies having access to and comprehending all the information that might reasonably influence a person's decision. A valid consent requires three elements voluntariness, comprehensible information, and the competence to give consent (Freedman, 1975; Koocher & Keith-Spiegel, 2008).

Competence to give consent is defined on legal and/or psychological grounds. Specifically, in most circumstances, one must attain the age of majority as a precondition for legally valid consent. From a psychological standpoint, competence requires adequate cognitive ability and psychological maturity to comprehend, appreciate, and make choices based on the risks, benefits, voluntariness, and nature of participation requested.

Ethics codes and a variety of legal cases have established some of the minimal standards required in the consent process. Although providing written consent forms and inviting questions often prove helpful to clients, such practices have little value if the client cannot understand the content because of language differences or complexity. The consent process and any written materials should describe and clarify the limits to confidentiality (see next section); involvement of any third parties; the nature, purpose, and duration of the psychological assessment and/or intervention; as well as issues pertaining to billing. Consent pertaining

to clinical research should include additional elements such as an explanation of the purpose of the research, the voluntary nature of participation, right to withdraw, anticipated risks and benefits, as well as information on how to contact the person in charge of the research and the institutional (ethics) review board (termed an IRB in the United States and REB [Research Ethics Board] in Canada). If the individual cannot legally provide consent (e.g., due to age or diminished capacity), one must seek permission from the legal guardian and assent (i.e., agreement) from the potential participant. When considering whether to give permission, a legal guardian should place paramount importance on risks, benefits, and the preservation of dignity. Even when a psychological assessment/ intervention relates to a court order or other legal mandate, psychologists must still provide all pertinent information regarding the nature and purpose of the psychological service and the limits to confidentiality that apply (Knapp & VandeCreek, 2006; Koocher & Keith-Spiegel, 2008).

PRIVACY, CONFIDENTIALITY, AND PRIVILEGE

Client privacy and confidentiality lie at the heart of psychological practice. *Privacy* refers to individuals' right to choose for themselves the circumstances, timing, and the extent to which information about them and their behavior may be shared with or withheld from others (Siegel, 1979).

Confidentiality refers to the ethical responsibility of psychologists and other health-care professionals to protect clients and research participants from unauthorized disclosure of protected information (Corey, Corey, & Calaman, 1998). The professional must restrict disclosures to situations authorized by the client or otherwise mandated by law (Koocher & Keith-Spiegel, 2008).

Privilege, a legal right, prevents certain categories of information from disclosure in court proceedings (Koocher & Keith-Spiegel, 2008). In U.S. courts, information produced within the context of psychotherapeutic encounters is generally protected from compelled disclosure by state privilege or federal case law (*Jaffe v. Redmond*, 1996). In some jurisdictions, however, privilege may not extend to students and trainees, and it becomes incumbent on each practitioner to learn the specific laws of his or her practice jurisdiction (Koocher & Keith-Spiegel, 2008). Other limitations of privilege also vary across jurisdictions. In some jurisdictions, a judge may have discretion to override the privilege, and in other jurisdictions privilege extends only to civil proceedings (Koocher & Keith-Spiegel, 2008). Moreover, in many circumstances, the law mandates practitioners to report certain types of information to authorities. For example, in some jurisdictions the law addresses waiver of privilege in situations where clients are involved in criminal activity as either a perpetrator, victim, or third party. In most jurisdictions, the psychotherapist-client privilege belongs to the client and not the therapist (i.e., the client, not the therapist, has the right to waive the privilege). In Canada, communications between a psychologist and a client do not qualify as privileged, meaning that courts of law can readily subpoena psychological therapy and assessment records.

Because of such variability, it is imperative to inform clients before beginning assessment or psychotherapy of *all* the limitations to confidentiality that apply in the jurisdiction (e.g., the obligation to report to authorities that a child is in need of protection because of physical or sexual abuse). Similarly, when undertaking assessments done on behalf of a third party (e.g., an insurance company or potential employer), the client may choose to waive certain rights to confidentiality in advance of the assessment so that the information can be sent to the insurance company or employer. Psychologists should always document such waivers in writing.

Highlight Box 2.2 discusses the famous case of *Tarasoff v. Board of Regents of the University of California* and associated implications for confidentiality. In summary, the university and a psychologist employed at the student health center were successfully sued for not taking adequate steps to protect Ms. Tarasoff after Prosenjit Poddar, a psychotherapy client at the university counseling service, expressed specific and active intent to murder her. Ultimately, the California Supreme Court ruled that the psychologist owed a special duty of protection to Ms. Tarasoff and, in this case, should have informed Ms. Tarasoff of the danger as a possible way of fulfilling that duty to protect. However, a psychologist's duty to protect third parties could potentially extend to other types of situations. Consider, for example, cases involving possible HIV transmission (e.g., when an HIV seropositive client indicates having or planning unprotected sex; Huprich, Fuller, & Schneider, 2003). Such cases can differ from a *Tarasoff*-type situation in several respects (Hook & Cleveland, 1999; Palma & Iannelli, 2002; VandeCreek & Knapp, 2001; Wong-Wylie, 2003). First, consider the accuracy of the information (i.e., Do you know for certain the validity of the alleged HIV status?). Second, has the client identified a particular person as the object of sexual attention (i.e., Do you know who to possibly warn?). Third, does the stated plan to engage in behavior that may put unnamed others at risk rise to the level of dangerousness necessary to trigger an involuntary civil hospital commitment to protect people in the client's zone of dangerousness? Suppose that the client discloses having had unsafe sex in the past (as opposed to disclosing a plan or intention to have unprotected sex in the future), making the issue of forewarning moot, while leaving the former sex partner vulnerable and unknowing. In addition, unprotected sex involves risk, but not certainty of transmission of the virus (Wong-Wylie, 2003).

HIGHLIGHT BOX 2.2

TARASOFF v. REGENTS OF THE UNIVERSITY OF CALIFORNIA

The famous case of *Tarasoff v. Regents of the University of California* represents one of the most known ethical dilemmas faced by a psychologist (i.e., the need to break confidentiality in order to prevent serious harm). The case involved Prosenjit Poddar, who was a client of the student health facility at the University of California at Berkeley. Mr. Poddar pursued a romantic relationship with Tatiana Tarasoff. After she rejected him, he sought treatment at the student health facility where a psychiatrist referred him to a psychologist. During the sessions with the psychologist, Mr. Poddar disclosed that he intended to harm or kill Ms. Tarasoff. After consulting with two psychiatrists, the psychologist decided to pursue civil commitment as Mr. Poddar was diagnosed with paranoid schizophrenia. When the psychologist learned that Mr. Poddar had purchased a gun, he informed the campus police and asked them to detain Mr. Poddar for the purpose of emergency commitment. Mr. Poddar assured the police that he would stay away from Ms. Tarasoff and was released. No other attempts to commit him were made as the supervising psychiatrist decided that commitment was not necessary and requested that the letter sent to police and some therapy records be destroyed in order to protect confidentiality. Approximately two months later, Mr. Poddar stabbed Ms. Tarasoff to death after he had discontinued his sessions with the psychologist. Initially, the complaint was dismissed by the trial court and the court of appeal (Stone, 1976). Following two appeals to the California Supreme Court, the court vacated its original decision that made references to duty to warn for a more broadly formulated "duty to protect" (Stone, 1976). The psychologist and the counseling center were found liable (*Tarasoff v. the Regents of the University of California*, 1976) for not having taken enough steps to prevent harm. In the *Tarasoff* case the duty to protect could have been satisfied if the psychologist had warned Ms. Tarasoff, but the court outlined other ways in which the duty to protect could have been met.

According to VandeCreek and Knapp (2001), the legal requirements under the *Tarasoff* case seem consistent with conclusions that could be reached through ethical decision making. Generally, psychologists maximize client autonomy over the direction of major events of therapy. Under rare circumstances, however, such as when a client is at risk of causing imminent harm to others, psychologists have to consider whether taking action to prevent harm (e.g., breaking confidentiality) must override the need to protect client autonomy. The psychologist can minimize the infringement of autonomy and maximize the involvement of the client when designing interventions designed to reduce the probability of harm (VandeCreek & Knapp, 2001). Also, state and other laws or legal precedent may require certain actions (e.g., warning the intended victim).

The key to such dilemmas would involve direct discussion with the client regarding the client's behavior and risks to others. We know of no circumstances where anyone has successfully sued a mental health professional for failure to warn or protect against HIV infection by a client. Anyone contemplating such a suit would likely face a significant challenge: addressing their own failure to practice safe sex. Some jurisdictions also have statutes that preclude disclosure of a client's HIV status without permission. The greater challenge would involve practitioners working in residential facilities where disinhibited or mentally incompetent persons might face unknowing exposure to people with infectious diseases, including hepatitis and tuberculosis as well as HIV. It behooves clinicians to incorporate discussions of behavior toward others in any work with infectious clients. When in doubt, a consultation with expert colleagues constitutes the best practice.

An imminent risk of suicide presents another situation in which psychologists need to carefully consider the actions necessary to prevent harm. Understanding the signs of suicide risk and best practices for risk assessment constitutes an essential clinical competency. Informing clients in advance of such limits to confidentiality makes ethical dilemmas relating to risk to self and others much easier to resolve.

MULTIPLE RELATIONSHIPS

Multiple relationship dilemmas arise when a psychologist holds a professional role with a person while simultaneously fulfilling another role with the same person. We all hold many such multiple roles, especially in small communities, and these situations are not intrinsically unethical. Ethical dilemmas arise when the multiple roles might reasonably affect the psychologist's objectivity, competence, and effectiveness or when a risk of harm or exploitation exists. The APA and CPA codes stress that psychologists must refrain from entering into such relationships (i.e., those involving potential for harm and exploitation). The codes also indicate that if such relationships arise due to unforeseen circumstances, psychologists must take steps to resolve the problem while protecting the best interests of affected persons and with maximal

compliance to the codes of ethics. Certain types of dual relationships carry a great deal of risk of harm to the client and are specifically prohibited by our code of ethics (e.g., sexual relationships with current therapy clients are explicitly prohibited [APA standard 10.05 and CPA standard II.27], as are sexual relationships with close relatives of clients [APA standard 10.06] or providing therapy to one's former intimate partners [APA standard 10.07], while sexual relationships with former clients are also prohibited under most circumstances [APA standard 10.08 and CPA standard II.27]). The situation becomes more complicated in other contexts such as receiving invitations from clients to attend important social events (e.g., a wedding or a graduation) or receiving gifts from clients and bartering services.

The APA code of ethics specifically addresses bartering (standard 6.05) and permits it only when not clinically contraindicated and the exchange does not become exploitative. In such situations, potential for exploitation increases when a bartered service does not have a clear and definitive value (e.g., setting the value of the item or service becomes subjective or open to negotiation). In the United States, practitioners must also pay taxes on the imputed value of bartered goods or services received or face tax evasion charges. In Canada, barter transactions also fall within the purview of the income tax act.

In situations where clients offer gifts, potential for exploitation occurs, especially when gifts of particular value are involved. Small gifts (e.g., homemade cookies) are easier for psychologists to accept because of social protocol and because of the possibility that a client may take offense at any refusal. The latter possibility may prove especially salient among clients of specific cultural groups within which such gift giving is expected or has special meaning (Syme, 2006). On the other hand, accepting a gift can lead to powerful reinforcement of the gift-giving behavior, which could then recur (Gerig, 2004).

Psychologists must consider the circumstances of the gift in order to assess the risk of ethical compromise. Some have suggested that psychologists, in deciding whether or not to accept a gift, must consider the "therapeutic meaning" or a potential hidden motive associated with the gift (Gerig, 2004). Gerig suggests that if the gift holds high "therapeutic meaning," accepting it could entail a high level of risk for an ethical complaint (e.g., a client harboring erotic feelings toward a therapist brings a red rose to the therapist). One important clinical test involves asking oneself, "How will accepting or refusing this gift help the client?" Difficulty in answering that question may indicate respectful refusal as the best option. In many situations, it is important to discuss the gift giving with the client within the therapeutic context, especially in situations where the gift has therapeutic meaning or the therapist cannot accept the gift for ethical reasons (e.g., an expensive or intimate gift).

In some situations, multiple relationships can prove very difficult to avoid. Consider, for example, a small and isolated rural community where only one psychologist exists as the sole provider of mental health services. Clinicians in such circumstances may find themselves called upon to assist clients in crisis with whom they have preexisting relationships. In general, practitioners should consider several issues when deciding whether to pursue a professional relationship that may complicate relational roles. These might include consideration of the extent to which the relationship could potentially harm the client, the extent of any power imbalance, the duration of the relationship, the clarity of issues relating to termination of therapy or of another psychological service, any alternate options for the client, any likelihood that the secondary relationship could disrupt the professional relationship, and the extent to which the psychologist can maintain clinical objectivity

(Barnett et al., 2007; Gottlieb, 1993; Younggren & Gottlieb, 2004).

VULNERABLE POPULATIONS

Psychologists who work with vulnerable populations (e.g., children or adults with cognitive impairments) should exercise special caution. Often, vulnerable clients lack legal authorization to provide consent for treatment, assessment, and participation in research; however, we should seek their assent (i.e., agreement) to the extent possible. Although a small number of North American jurisdictions permit minors to consent to psychotherapy, most jurisdictions require parental or legal guardian consent before psychotherapy can begin (Koocher & Keith-Spiegel, 2008).

Just as the law in most jurisdictions requires the consent of parents or legal guardians prior to initiation of professional service delivery, these same persons typically control the privacy rights of their children. In essence, children have only those rights to privacy allowed by their parents. Although the law deems adults competent until proved otherwise, the reverse holds true for children. Such parental right of access could potentially compromise trust and limit the effectiveness of the intervention, particularly with adolescent clients.

We recommend having a discussion at the beginning of treatment, including the parents and child (or adolescent), to clarify the ground rules. Parents will typically agree to not seek certain types of information from the therapist. In the case of adolescent clients, the psychologist will almost certainly want to note that teenagers often talk about issues such as smoking, alcohol, sex, and other matters that they might prefer not to raise simultaneously (or ever) with their parents. By coming to a mutual understanding on such necessary secrets and points at which it may become necessary to breech confidentiality (e.g., threats of harm to self or others), the clinician can clarify acceptable limits with all parties at the outset of their work together. As part of the process, therapists will need to think through what sorts of issues may rise to the level of warranting parental disclosure.

Of course, none of this planning will cover every possible subsequent event. Even the most creative therapists will run into unanticipated behavioral adventures with their adolescent clients. Having pledged unconditional respect for their child's confidentiality at the outset of treatment, parents may change their minds and demand information from the therapist or access to their child's records with full legal authority.

RECORD KEEPING AND ACCESS TO RECORDS

Keeping careful records of psychological treatment and assessment services serves multiple purposes (Knapp & VandeCreek, 2006). Records help remind the psychologist what took place in previous sessions. They also serve to document services in order to justify, for third-party payers, the necessity of treatment. Client records can also prove useful to document important information to assist future treatment providers. Finally, in legal proceedings or disciplinary hearings, records also document the psychologist's account of the sessions.

State and provincial regulatory bodies may have requirements pertaining to the content of records. The APA (2007) has also published updated record-keeping guidelines. Generally, records include client demographic information, dates of services and consultations, session summaries, psychological test results, correspondence, diagnostic problem information, treatment plan, and any other information that may be required by a psychologist's jurisdiction (Koocher, 2005a).

State and provincial regulations differ with respect to how long after the termination psychologists must retain their records, but most specify *at least* five years for adult clients and at least a year beyond a child client's eighteenth birthday, whichever is of longer duration. Psychologists should confirm applicable standards in their practice jurisdictions.

The extent to which clients have the right to access their records varies from jurisdiction to jurisdiction. In the United States the Health Insurance Portability and Accountability Act (HIPAA) (see Highlight Boxes 2.3 and 2.4) allows clients (or the parents/guardians of minors) to have access to all records except psychotherapy notes. As used in the context of HIPAA, the term *psychotherapy notes* encompasses the therapist's notes taken for his or her own use in the treatment process, as opposed to the typical documentation described earlier that comprises a client's medical record. However, the laws of some states provide clients with more complete access. When state laws afford clients more protections than the federal HIPAA statute, the state law prevails.

Ethical issues could arise when clients request access to their records. For example, a record may contain information the client might experience as distressing (e.g., certain diagnostic labels). Psychologists would be wise to prepare all records cognizant of the possibility that clients may view them in the future and avoid statements or characterizations that might prove distressing or prone to misinterpretation by clients. When requesting records, clients will often be satisfied with a summary of their records prepared by the psychologist. If they still wish to exercise their right to view their full record, we recommend that the psychologist personally introduce and offer to interpret the information and answer questions.

Another issue related to assessment results involves test security. This refers to the fact that public disclosure of psychological test items might compromise the validity of the

---

HIGHLIGHT BOX 2.3

THE HEALTH INSURANCE PORTABILITY AND ACCOUNTABILITY ACT

The Health Insurance Portability and Accountability Act (HIPAA) is a 1996 United States act (also known as Public Law 104-191) that streamlined standards for transmitting electronic health claims. It also set standards for securing the storage of patient information and for protecting people's privacy (APA Practice Organization, 2002).

The HIPAA includes three key rules.

- The HIPAA *privacy rule* specifies to whom and under what circumstances confidential private information can be disclosed. The privacy rule was designed to serve as a minimum level of privacy protection (state laws requiring greater protection are not preempted by HIPAA) and has implications for dealing with requests to release psychological notes. For example, according to the privacy rule, general consent alone is not adequate when a third party requests treatment notes. Psychologists are required to obtain specific patient authorization for the use and release of such notes. They are also expected to ensure either that any party requesting therapy records has provided a valid authorization or that they themselves secure client authorization prior to releasing the material (APA Practice Organization, 2002). In many jurisdictions, HIPAA has served to ensure that clients have greater access to their health records (e.g., for inspection and amendment).

- The HIPAA *transaction rule* addresses technical aspects of electronic transfer of information as well as the formats that should be used when information is sent and received electronically.

- The HIPAA *security rule* (APA Practice Organization, not dated) is aimed to ensure the security of electronic confidential patient information. This includes consideration of a variety of potential hazards or threats such as computer viruses and inappropriate uses and disclosures of confidential information (such as accidentally transmitting electronic information to the wrong recipient). Among other requirements, there is an expectation that physical safeguards be placed (e.g., locating the computer in a locked office with access only by authorized employees). Additional expectations such as limiting access to patient information through procedures such as use of passwords are also articulated.

There is little question that the HIPAA standards have improved client protection in many jurisdictions. While serious penalties (including imprisonment and/or fines) could be imposed from failure to comply with the HIPAA rules, it is important to remain cognizant that the ethics codes adopted by APA and CPA, prior to HIPAA coming into effect, had already set the highest standards relating to the protection and autonomy of users of psychological services.

---

tests. For example, if intelligence test items (e.g., questions and answers) appeared in public media, coaching to yield high test scores might result in highly inaccurate findings. In addition, the standardization of widely used assessment tools can be an extensive and costly process, leading test publishers to claim "trade secret" or copyright protections. Psychologists have an obligation to safeguard the security of test items, as reflected in our codes of ethics.

HIGHLIGHT BOX 2.4

HIPAA VERSUS FERPA

Some people may tend to conflate aspects of the U.S. Family Educational Rights and Privacy Act (FERPA) with HIPAA. FERPA (officially codes as 20 U.S.C. § 1232g; 34 CFR Part 99) is a U.S. federal law detailing the privacy constraints on educational records.

- Like HIPAA, FERPA affords a right of inspection access to one's own educational records (or those of one's minor child). These rights transfer to the student when he or she reaches the age of 18 or attends a school beyond the high school level. In FERPA parlance, these are "eligible students."
- If the student/family believes that FERPA records contain an error, they may request correction and, if not satisfied, may seek a hearing and ultimately insert a page of their own comments as part of the record.
- Such records include privacy protection of student grades and evaluations. For example, FERPA prohibits teachers from piling up graded exams outside their office door for pick-up and potential viewing by others or posting of grades in any manner that might enable identification of the student.
- FERPA does not preclude release of information to school officials, schools to which a student transfers, financial aid authorities, accrediting organizations, or in response to health/safety emergencies or court orders.
- FERPA records do not acquire any legal privilege.

- In some instances, the files of educational institutions may include health information found in educational institution files (e.g., the immunization records of a child in kindergarten or psychological data attesting to special educational accommodations).
- The distinction between psychological test data (e.g., a person's responses to questions or puzzles) and test materials (e.g., manuals and objects in test kits) can become blurred. Consider the situation when a psychologist writes a client's responses on a copyright-protected test protocol form. HIPAA does allow for the protection of "trade secrets," and some test publishers may make such assertions regarding their testing forms. When in doubt, the psychologist can provide copies of the forms to another professional designated by the student/family or offer the data without the form.
- When in doubt about whether HIPAA applies to health or mental health data in the files of educational institutions, we recommend affording the higher level of protection to the student.
- Unlike HIPAA, however, FERPA is not enforceable as a civil action against individuals, only institutions. Under HIPAA, scalable penalties of $100 per incident up to $25,000 per year can be issued against individuals or institutions. Under FERPA, violations could possibly lead to institutional loss of federal funds, but severe penalties are rare.

In thinking about releasing test materials, one must distinguish between copyrighted test materials (e.g., manuals and test stimuli) and the responses clients give to the materials (i.e.,

test data). Although test materials and printed test forms may have copyright protection, writing test responses or observations about clients on the forms converts the material from test material into test data under the HIPAA standards (see Highlight Box 2.3). This does create an apparent conflict between copyright holders and the HIPAA privacy rule. HIPAA allows test publishers to claim "trade secret" exemptions from disclosure (see, for example, Harcourt Brace Assessment Inc., not dated).

Often, psychologists find themselves faced with requests to release psychological test data to persons who may lack the qualifications to interpret them. For example, such requests often come from lawyers. One course of action might involve contacting the lawyer and requesting the designation of a qualified psychologist to receive the material (following obtaining all necessary consents). However, some attorneys may not want to disclose the names of their potential experts before they have heard the opinions of those psychologists. In some cases involving litigation, the psychologist may have no option but to obey court-approved requests for release of raw data directly to attorneys (Knapp & VandeCreek, 2006; Koocher & Keith-Spiegel, 2008).

When the subpoenas to release test materials could compromise test security, the situation becomes even more complicated. The psychologist would need not only to address issues pertaining to client confidentiality but also to avoid dissemination of content that could threaten the test's validity. The psychologist may also have a contractual obligation pertaining to copyrighted materials (see Highlight Boxes 2.3 and 2.4).

The Committee on Legal Issues (COLI, 2006) of the APA has provided a detailed discussion of requests for the release of information (including but not limited to psychological test records) in a legal context. Subpoenas are legal documents commanding testimony, release of documents, or both. Although one should never ignore a subpoena, one need not always do exactly as the document instructs (Koocher, 2005b). For example, in the case of civil suits some subpoenas may be issued without judicial review. If the jurisdiction recognizes psychotherapist-client privilege, the psychologist may advise the client or client's attorney to assert the client's privilege (unless the client previously waived privilege or a legal exception applies).

The APA Committee on Legal Issues (COLI, 2006) has recommended several steps for psychologists confronted with subpoenas. First, one should determine whether the request to disclose sensitive content is legally valid. This step may require consultation with a lawyer (e.g., a subpoena issued in one jurisdiction may not be legally binding for a psychologist living and working in a different jurisdiction). The next recommended step involves informing the client (and possibly also consulting with the client's lawyer and/or the psychologist's own lawyer since the client's and the psychologist's interests may diverge during the legal proceedings). In some cases, the client may have no objections to the release of the information. The third step recommended by COLI is to negotiate with the requester and explore whether other ways exist to achieve the requester's objectives without divulging certain types of sensitive information. The psychologist (often through an attorney) can also seek guidance from the court if the requester insists that confidential information or psychological test data be released. The court can be advised of the ethical concerns (e.g., about the release of copyrighted psychological test materials) and suggest alternatives. Finally, one can file a motion to quash the subpoena (i.e., render it invalid or seek a protective order). A protective order may be tailored to meet legitimate interests (e.g., limiting the disclosure of test materials or other sensitive information). According to COLI, courts will more likely entertain requests to quash a subpoena that originate with the client's attorney. Once these options have been exhausted and a court order remains, a psychologist must comply or face a contempt of court ruling (COLI, 2006).

ADVERTISING

In a competitive marketplace, psychologists will be tempted to advertise their services. Many would also argue that advertising provides members of the public with important information about available services. Nonetheless, advertising could deceive or imply results that can never be guaranteed. The avoidance of false and deceptive statements in the advertising of psychological services is explicitly addressed in the APA and CPA codes. Moreover, under the CPA code, psychologists are expected to avoid statements that appeal to client fears and anxiety (if the services are not obtained), claims of one-of-a-kind abilities, or claims of comparative desirability of alternative treatments (Shead & Dobson, 2004). Generally, listing one's contact information along with the services offered and populations served will prove widely acceptable practice when done in a professional fashion.

CROSS-CULTURAL ISSUES

Diversity issues are discussed in more detail later in the book, but we address some key points related to ethics and standards here. Cross-cultural issues become of central importance in psychological assessment, therapy, and research, especially within the North American context where people from many diverse cultural backgrounds may walk into a psychologist's office. The APA ethical principle of Respect for People's Rights and Dignity emphasizes that psychologists respect cross-cultural differences. In addition, a number of specific standards stress the importance of considering cross-cultural issues in developing competence as well as in interpreting assessment results (APA standards 2.01a and 9.06). The importance of not discriminating against people based on diversity factors also appears

in the code (APA standards 3.01 and 3.03). The Canadian code of ethics also addresses culture very explicitly and consistently with the APA code.

We have long known that culture can affect the nature of responses to psychological test items; we should therefore apply culturally appropriate norms (e.g., Skinstad & Mortensen, 1992) where possible (or, at the very least, we should always consider the impact of culture on psychological test results [e.g., Lezak, 1995]). Multicultural competence also becomes very important in therapy where psychologists need the ability to understand and constructively relate to the uniqueness of each person in light of the diverse cultures that can influence each client's point of view (Stuart, 2004).

Hwang (2006) has pointed out that little research has been done on evaluating the efficacy of well-established psychological interventions with culturally diverse client groups. He cited evidence that ethnic minority clients are less likely to receive high-quality services and that they experience less positive treatment outcomes compared to other groups. Finally, we need to consider treatment adaptations in order to enhance the effectiveness of interventions in specific cross-cultural contexts (e.g., Lau, 2006).

In seeking to develop multicultural competence, clinicians should aim to acquire an understanding of the complexities of culture and to avoid stereotyping. Stuart (2004) has made several suggestions designed to assist clinicians in the development of multicultural competence. These included (but are not limited to) development of skills in discovering each client's unique cultural outlook as well as sensitivity to cultural differences without overemphasizing such differences. Moreover, Stuart stressed the importance of recognition and evaluation of possible personal biases, contextualization of assessment, recognition of the importance of clients' ethnic and worldviews in selecting therapists, and critical evaluation of methods used to collect culturally relevant information.

With respect to research, it is important to remember that psychological findings based on one cultural group may not generalize to people in a different culture. Moreover, consent methodologies will often require alteration to conform to the traditions of specific cultural groups. For example, in seeking research consent among many North American First Nations groups, consent by ceremony may be preferred over the more traditional contract-like consent forms (although each participant should receive a written record of the participation agreement). In all cases, participants must be able to choose to withdraw from research at any time.

PSYCHOLOGICAL TESTING

In both assessment and therapy, practitioners must achieve competence by virtue of specialized training and experience in the type of population with whom they work (e.g., adults, children, couples, or families). When using psychological tests, clinicians must have adequate familiarity with measurement theory and issues relating to test validity and reliability. They should remain aware of the limitations associated with the use of computerized interpretation systems for psychological tests. Specifically, such computer-generated interpretations cannot be accepted at literal face value, as they are often simulations of clinical decision making and may be of limited validity (Matarazzo, 1986). In all cases, practitioners should check computerized interpretations against other psychological tests, chart information, and interviews. Even developers of computerized reports advise against making any diagnostic or treatment decisions based solely on computerized interpretations (e.g., Archer & Psychological Assessment Resources [PAR] staff, 2003). They also stress that statements

generated in computerized interpretive reports should be integrated with other sources of information such as interviews, test findings, psychosocial history data, and the like (e.g., Archer & PAR staff, 2003). One must also make sure that the computerized interpretation system used includes evidence of reliability and validity for the particular evaluation context.

ASSESSMENTS REQUESTED BY A THIRD PARTY

One of the most complex ethical issues in assessments arranged by third parties relates to potential divided loyalties between the practitioner, the client, and the third party (e.g., the legal system or an insurance company) (Hadjistavropoulos, 1999). These issues are discussed in more detail later in the book but are briefly reviewed here. The adversarial nature of the legal and/or insurance system may imply that the client should be viewed with suspicion (e.g., when an insurance company seeks to assess malingering). At the same time, the client may approach the assessment situation with understandable defensiveness and fear that could affect his or her response style (e.g., a parental fitness evaluation).

According to Bellamy (1997), the role of the health professional generally involves being an advocate and helper for the client. However, the adversarial system of litigation may invite psychologists and especially those who engage in independent assessments for third-party payers to become suspicious of the client. This orientation can disrupt the trust that traditionally exists in the psychologist-client relationship and affect client disclosure. Furthermore, one can imagine that some third-party payers may send more referrals to psychologists who seem least sympathetic to client complaints (e.g., psychologists who, based on a third-party payer's past experience and opinion, are more likely to indicate that claimants' claims of disability are not valid and that the claimants should be expected to return to work as soon as possible). Some of these issues can be dealt with, at least to some extent, by clarifying and discussing business obligations, limits to confidentiality, and ethical obligations to the client and third parties while obtaining consent. The professional who emphasizes integrity and honesty during all interactions will most likely be received well by the majority of claimants and third-party payers.

Another ethical obligation of the psychologist is to provide feedback to the client following an assessment. This generally applies even where third-party assessments are concerned. In some circumstances, such as an independent disability or preemployment examination, the entity paying for the evaluation may preclude sharing of results by the examiner, asserting that the report will be their property and that it will only be released to them. Such conditions should be clarified with all parties during the consent process prior to the assessment. We recommend the use of an unambiguous consent process and form (in addition to affording clients an opportunity to have all their questions answered about the assessment).

ETHICS IN RESEARCH

The most significant impetus for research regulations throughout the world has its roots in the post–World War II Nuremberg trials of Nazi physicians who conducted experiments on nonconsenting concentration camp prisoners (Spitz, 2005; Tong, 2007). These experiments included injecting people with bacteria and various toxins or subjecting people to very low or high atmospheric pressures and temperatures in order to see how long they could survive. Prisoners refusing participation faced

immediate death (Tong, 2007). In response to such atrocities, the world scientific community worked together to draft a code of research ethics known as the Nuremberg Code, which stressed the importance of informed consent. A variety of ethical codes regulating research soon followed.

In both the United States and Canada, research conducted by psychologists who work at universities and major hospitals must undergo scrutiny by Institutional Review Boards (IRBs or REBs in Canada). IRBs perform oversight and regulate research. Before research projects that involve human participants can proceed, research protocols must be approved by the IRB or the REB based on ethical, scientific, and legal standards.[1]

Ethical standards concerning research appear in the codes of ethics of both APA and CPA. Fundamental to any research participation is the right of people to decide freely on whether or not they wish to enroll in the research, after a full disclosure of all known risks and benefits. Clients of psychologists may also feel obligated to participate in research if they fear that not doing so might compromise the quality of the services that they receive. It is important for psychologists at sites where both clinical and research activities take place to ensure that this does not occur (e.g., by having a mechanism whereby the treating psychologist does not know whether any given client has consented to participate in research projects).

Clinical psychologists often conduct research with vulnerable clients including (but not limited to) persons with limited capacity to provide consent for research participation because of cognitive impairments. In such cases, psychologists must seek informed permission from a proxy (e.g., a parent or legal guardian) as well as

---

[1]In the United States and Canada, research involving animals is regulated by Institutional Animal Care and Use Committees (as opposed to IRBs or REBs).

aim to seek assent[2] from the individual of limited capacity. Even when proxy consent is obtained, psychologists should not impose research participation on individuals of limited capacity who show behavioral and/or verbal indications of not wishing to participate and for whom there would be no major and direct benefits from such research participation.

Several psychological experiments are mentioned very frequently in discussions of research ethics in psychology. One of these experiments is the classic obedience experiment conducted by Stanley Milgram, in which an authority figure directed experimental participants to deliver what they thought was a potentially lethal level of electric shock to a confederate (Milgram, 1963). Although no electric shocks were ever administered and the confederate was never exposed to pain, the experiment raised questions about the ethics of scientific experimentation because of the extreme emotional stress suffered by some participants.

While it seems very unlikely that the Milgram experiment would gain approval by an IRB today, psychologists sometimes use deception (as Milgram did when misleading his participants). Other investigators may employ partial disclosure in their research, using the rationale that if participants are familiar with the goals of the study, they might respond in a way that could invalidate the data. The APA code of ethics specifies that deception can only be used if scientifically justified and no nondeceptive alternative procedures will suffice. It also specifies that deception that could reasonably be expected to cause harm or significant emotional distress should not be used. Moreover, participants should be debriefed (i.e., informed of the deception) as soon as possible and no later than the conclusion of their participation. At that time, one must also provide participants with the opportunity to withdraw their data. The CPA code has similar provisions.

The codes of ethics of APA and CPA also outline very high standards for the humane use of animals in research. Other research-related issues outlined in the codes include (but are not limited to) authorship credit (which should be granted for substantive intellectual contributions to the research and not merely for holding an institutional position such as department chair), the need to avoid coercive inducements for research participation, the importance of sharing one's research data (following publications) for the purposes of verification, and the accurate reporting of research results.

ETHICS COMMITTEE AND DISCIPLINARY HEARINGS

In the event that a psychologist engages in ethically problematic, unprofessional, and/or negligent behavior, clients can pursue several options. These range from civil suits and other avenues through the legal system to complaints to state and provincial professional regulatory bodies (e.g., the Illinois Board of Psychology Examiners or the College of Psychologists of British Columbia) or complaints to professional association ethics committees (i.e., if the psychologist belongs to the association). If a psychologist is deemed to have engaged in ethically inappropriate behavior following a disciplinary hearing, regulatory bodies will consider a variety of courses of action that range from education and/or warning letters, to directives for mandatory supervision, to permanent or temporary expulsion of the psychologist (e.g., removal of registration, certification, or license and/or monetary fines). The worst penalty a professional association can impose is expulsion. The seriousness of the ethical violation and/or risk of future violation will typically determine the severity of the sanction.

---

[2]The term *assent* simply implies agreement, but it is not, necessarily, legally valid. In contrast, we use the term *consent* to indicate agreement that is legally valid.

SUMMARY

Due to the nature of their work, psychologists may acquire extremely personal and sensitive information from their clients. This places them in a position of utmost trust. In addition, a large portion of clients see psychologists during some of the most difficult and vulnerable times of their lives. In order to maximize protection for their clients and to maintain the highest standards in our profession, psychologists adhere to codes of ethics such as those of the American Psychological Association and the Canadian Psychological Association. In this chapter we reviewed some of the key issues that are discussed in these codes, including competent practice, informed consent, confidentiality and its limits, protection of vulnerable clients, dual relationships, cross-cultural issues, advertising, and record keeping. We have also reviewed ways in which psychologists can address requests for access to records that can occur in dealings with the legal system. Finally, we have discussed some special issues pertaining to research ethics.

THOUGHT QUESTIONS

2.1. In the code of ethics that has been adopted by the Canadian Psychological Association (CPA), ethical principles are ranked in order of importance. This ranking is intended to facilitate decision making in situations when ethical principles conflict with one another (e.g., respecting client autonomy vs. ensuring that harm is avoided). The code of ethics that has been adopted by the American Psychological Association does not include such a ranking. An argument can be made both in favor of and against the ranking of ethical principles. In your opinion, what are some advantages and disadvantages of ranking ethical principles in a code of ethics?

2.2. Not all cultures place as high a value on autonomy as most North Americans. Can you think of a culture in which individual autonomy might stand lower in a decision-making hierarchy?

2.3. Consider the following fictitious vignette: A psychologist is supervising the clinical practicum of a graduate student who is treating a client showing symptoms of major depression, suicidal ideation, and fears of rejection by others. Over the course of the treatment, it becomes apparent to the supervisor that the student has developed significant mental health symptomatology that could compromise his ability to relate to the client and to act as an effective therapist. The psychologist believes that it would not be appropriate for the student to continue treating the client (as this could jeopardize the client) but is concerned about protecting both the student's privacy and the client (who may feel that she has been "rejected" by the student if the student were to stop treating her). The psychologist also recognizes that the client's treatment, given her suicidal ideation and severe depression, cannot be postponed. Take the perspective of the supervising psychologist and use the decision-making steps that have been adopted by the Canadian Psychological Association (see Highlight Box 2.1) in an effort to find the best possible resolution to this ethical dilemma. Consider issues such as privacy, confidentiality, dignity, and the need to maximize benefit and minimize harm.

Glossary

Confidentiality: Confidentiality refers to the ethical obligation not to disclose (without proper authorization) information obtained within the context of a professional relationship.

Ethical principle: The principles that guide our behavior aspirationally, recognizing that enforcement of such principles will prove difficult to enforce.

Ethical standard: The specific standards listed in the ethics codes as enforceable rules (e.g., by disciplinary committees and state and provincial professional regulatory bodies).

Privacy: A person's right to choose the extent to which his or her views, attitudes, and behaviors can be shared with others.

Privilege: A legal term that protects information obtained in the context of certain professional relationships from being disclosed in legal proceedings. The laws governing privilege vary from jurisdiction to jurisdiction.

References

American Psychological Association (1953). *Ethical standards of psychologists*. Washington, DC: Author.

American Psychological Association (2002). *Ethical principles of psychologists and code of conduct*. Washington, DC: Author.

American Psychological Association (2007). *Record keeping guidelines*. Washington, DC: American Psychological Association.

American Psychological Association Practice Organization (not dated). *The HIPPA security rule primer*. Washington, DC: Author.

American Psychological Association Practice Organization (2002). *Getting ready for HIPPA: a primer for psychologists*. Washington, DC: Author.

Archer, R. P. & Psychological Assessment Resources staff (2003). *MMPI-A interpretive system (version 3.10.021)*. Lutz, FL: Psychological Assessment Resources.

Barnett, J. E., Lazarus, A. A., Vasquez, M. J., Moorehead-Slaughter, O., & Johnson, W. B. (2007). Boundary issues and multiple relationships: fantasy and reality. *Professional Psychology: Research and Practice, 38*, 401–410.

Bellamy, R. (1997). Compensation neurosis. *Clinical Orthopedics and Related Research, 336*, 94–106.

Canadian Psychological Association (2000). *Canadian code of ethics for psychologists* (3rd ed.). Ottawa: Author.

Canadian Psychological Association (2002) *Accreditation standards and procedures for doctoral programmes and internships in professional psychology, Fourth Revision*. Ottawa: Author.

Committee on Accreditation (2008). *Guidelines and principles for accreditation of programs in clinical psychology*. Washington, DC: American Psychological Association.

Committee on Legal Issues (2006). Strategies for private practitioners coping with subpoenas or compelled testimony for client records or test data. *Professional Psychology: Research and Practice, 37*, 215–222.

Corey, G., Corey, M. S., & Callannan, P. (1998). *Issues and ethics in the helping professions* (5th ed.). Pacific Grove, CA: International Thomson Publishing Services.

Dubin, S. S. (1972). Obsolescence or lifelong education: a choice for the professional. *American Psychologist, 27*, 486–498.

Freedman, B. (1975). A moral theory of informed consent. *Hastings Center Report, 5*, 32–39.

Gerig, M. (2004). Receiving gifts from clients: ethical and therapeutic issues. *Journal of Mental Health Counseling, 26*, 199–210.

Gottlieb, M. C. (1993). Avoiding exploitative dual relationships: a decision making model. *Psychotherapy, 30*, 41–48.

Hadjistavropoulos, T. (1999). Chronic pain on trial: the influence of compensation and litigation on chronic pain syndromes. In A. R. Block, E. F. Kremer, & E. Fernandez (Eds.), *Handbook of pain syndromes: biopsychosocial perspectives* (pp. 59–76). Mahwah, NJ: Lawrence Erlbaum Associates.

Harcourt Brace Assessment, Inc. (not dated). HIPPA Position statement. San Antonio, Texas: Author. Retrieved February 11, 2008 from http:// harcourtassessment.com/ hai/images/pdf/legal/HIPAA_ Position.pdf

Hook, M. K. & Cleveland, J. L. (1999). To tell or not to tell: breaching confidentiality with clients with HIV and AIDS. *Ethics & Behavior, 9*, 365–381.

Huprich, S. K., Fuller, K., & Schneider, R. (2003). Divergent ethical perspectives on the Duty-to-Warn principle with HIV-positive patients. *Ethics and Behavior, 13*, 263–278.

Hwang, W. C. (2006). The psychotherapy adaptation and modification framework. *American Psychologist, 61*, 702–715.

Jaffe v. Redmond 116 S. Ct. 95-266, 64L.W. 4490 (June 13, 1996).

Knapp, S. L. & VandeCreek, L. D. (2006). *Practical ethics for psychologists*. Washington, DC: American Psychological Association.

Koocher, G. P. (2005a). Prototype Mental Health Records. In G. P. Koocher, J. C. Norcross, & S. S. Hill (Eds.), *PsyDR: Psychologists' Desk Reference* (2nd ed.). (pp. 649–651). New York: Oxford University Press.

Koocher, G. P. (2005b). Dealing with subpoenas. In G. P. Koocher, J. C. Norcross, & S. S. Hill (Eds.), *PsyDR:*

Psychologists' Desk Reference (2nd ed., pp. 570–571). New York: Oxford University Press.

Koocher, G. & Keith-Spiegel, P. (2008). *Ethics in psychology and the mental health professions: standards and cases* (3rd ed.). New York: Oxford University Press.

Lau, A. S. (2006). Making the case for selective and directed cultural adaptations of evidence-based treatments: examples from parent training. *Clinical Psychology: Science and Practice, 13,* 295–310.

Lezak, M. (1995). *Neuropsychological assessment* (3rd ed.). New York: Oxford University Press.

Matarazzo, J. D. (1986). Computerized clinical psychological test interpretations: unvalidated plus all mean and no sigma. *American Psychologist, 41,* 14–24.

Milgram, S. (1963). A behavioral study of obedience. *Journal of Abnormal and Social Psychology, 67,* 371–378.

Palma, T. V. & Iannelli, R. J. (2002). Therapeutic reactivity to confidentiality with HIV positive clients: bias or epidemiology? *Ethics & Behavior, 12,* 353–370.

Shead, N. W. & Dobson, K. S. (2004). Psychology for sale: the ethics of advertising professional services. *Canadian Psychology, 45,* 126–136.

Siegel, M. (1979). Privacy, ethics and confidentiality. *Professional Psychology, 10,* 249–258.

Sinclair, C., Poizner, S., Gilmour-Barrett, K., & Randall, D. (1987). The development of codes of ethics for psychologists. *Canadian Psychology, 28,* 1–8.

Skinstad, A. H. & Mortensen, J. K. (1992). Cross-cultural comparison of MMPI norms in alcoholics with and without a diagnosis of borderline personality disorder. *New Trends in Experimental & Clinical Psychiatry, 8,* 103–112.

Spitz, V. (2005). *Doctors from Hell: the horrific account of Nazi experiments on humans.* Boulder, CO: Sentient Publications.

Stone, A. A. (1976). The *Tarasoff* decisions: suing psychotherapists to safeguard safety. *Harvard Law Review, 90,* 358–378.

Stuart, R. B. (2004). Twelve practical suggestions for achieving multicultural competence. *Professional Psychology: Research and Practice, 35,* 3–9.

Syme, G. (2006). Fetters or freedom: dual relationships in counseling. *International Journal for the Advancement of Counselling, 28,* 57–69.

Tarasoff v. Regents of the University of California, 17 Cal. 3d 425, 131 Cal Rptr. 14, 551 P.2d 334 (1976).

Tong, R. (2007). *New perspectives in health care ethics.* Upper Saddle River, NJ: Pearson Education, Inc.

VandeCreek, L. D. & Knapp, S. L. (2001). *Tarasoff and beyond: legal and clinical considerations in the treatment of life-endangering patients* (3rd ed.). Sarasota, FL: Professional Resource Press.

Wong-Wylie, G. (2003). Preserving hope in the duty to protect: counselling clients with HIV or AIDS. *Canadian Journal of Counselling, 37,* 35–43.

Younggren, J. N. & Gottlieb, M. C. (2004). Managing risk when contemplating multiple relationships. *Professional Psychology: Research and Practice, 35,* 255–260.

CHAPTER

3

Assessment of Intelligence, Achievement, and Adaptive Behavior

Robert Gregory
Wheaton College

OUTLINE

INTRODUCTION: DEFINITIONS AND DISTINCTIONS

Since the early 1900s, the field of clinical psychology has developed a large number of methods for the assessment of human abilities. Indeed, these methods constitute the foundational achievements of the entire field (Meyer et al., 2001). Students of clinical psychology need to know the history of this broad enterprise, the key concepts and methods of the field, and critical issues and contemporary debates. That is the task of this chapter—a daunting task because of the sheer vastness of the topics. We begin with some important definitions and distinctions that are necessary to delineate the assignment at hand.

This chapter focuses exclusively on individual tests, as opposed to group tests. Thus, we begin by defining and distinguishing these two approaches to testing. **Group tests** are largely paper-and-pencil measures administered to a group of examinees and typically require little or no interaction between the examiner and the people being tested. The examiner often does nothing more than pass out forms, read instructions, and then monitor time limits. Typically, there are few ways by which to determine whether an individual student worked diligently on the test, stared out the window, or doodled aimlessly on the desk before answering questions with random check marks.

By their design and purpose, **individual tests** are intended for one-on-one interaction in which the examiner poses structured questions and tasks to the client. The goal is not only to obtain objective scores or other indices of performance but also to gain clinically relevant information such as the examinee's extent of effort, response to failure, degree of impulsiveness, and the like. This valuable information is useful in providing an overall assessment of the client, as opposed to merely collating a bunch of test scores.

This highlights another important distinction, namely, testing versus assessment. **Testing** is the narrow enterprise of learning how to administer and score tests correctly, which can be accomplished by most reasonably bright individuals who possess character habits of diligence and who take supervision well. **Assessment** involves synthesizing information from many sources, formulating an overall picture of the client, and making appropriate recommendations that take into account issues of psychometrics, client history, culture, and diversity. Meyer et al. (2001) provide a clear distinction between testing and assessment as follows:

In psychological testing, the nomothetic meaning associated with a scaled score of 10 on the Arithmetic subtest from the Wechsler Adult Intelligence Scale — Third Edition (Wechsler, 1997) is that a person possesses average skills in mental calculations. In an idiographic assessment, the same score may have very different meanings. After considering all relevant information, this score may mean a patient with a recent head injury has had a precipitous decline in auditory attention span and the capacity to mentally manipulate information. In a patient undergoing cognitive remediation for attentional problems secondary to a head injury, the same score may mean there has been a substantial recovery of cognitive functioning. In a third, otherwise very intelligent patient, a score of 10 may mean pronounced symptoms of anxiety and depression are impairing skills in active concentration.... The assessment task is to use test-derived sources of information in combination with historical data, presenting complaints, observations, interview results, and information from third parties to disentangle the competing possibilities. (Eyde et al., 1993; cited in Meyer et al. 2001)

Testing is to assessment as skill is to wisdom. The difference between testing and assessment is one reason why training to be a doctoral-level psychologist takes about five years instead of one semester plus a summer practicum.

A final introductory comment has to do with the importance of careful scoring in ability-based testing. The capacity to score tests correctly is essentially a character habit that requires unceasing vigilance and attention to details. Extended supervision in testing by skilled practitioners is vital for student trainees to develop these personal qualities.

Scoring errors are probably much more common than most clinicians want to admit and likely pose a substantial threat to the validity of testing. This observation is based not only on anecdotal evidence but also on a raft of research studies that demonstrate poor scoring proficiency among graduate students and experienced clinicians alike (e.g., Gregory, 1999; Hopwood & Richard, 2005; Loe, Kadlubek, &

Marks, 2007; Ryan, Prifitera, & Powers, 1983; Simons, Goddard, & Patton, 2002). For example, Ryan, Prifitera, and Powers (1983) found that scoring errors produced Full Scale **IQs** (derived from the same protocol) that deviated from the correct score by anywhere from 2 to 7 points in a sample of 19 practicing psychologists and 20 graduate students. The experienced psychologists made just as many errors as the graduate students. The author of this chapter has supervised ability-based testing for 35 years and observed colossal scoring errors made by graduate students and experienced clinicians alike. Sometimes these errors have shifted IQ scores by as much as 40 points off the true mark. A recent example involved a report written by a newly licensed psychologist in which the IQ scores somehow were inexplicably swapped with the percentile ranks for those scores. The case involved a high-functioning client whose IQ score was 140, which is at the 99th percentile of the general population. The narrative described the client as being in the "very superior" range of functioning, clearly possessing the intellectual skills needed for success in college, and possessing a Full Scale IQ of . . . 99. Errors like this (and other examples could be cited) arise mainly because of "zombie-like" carelessness, computational blunders, mechanically transcribing the wrong row of numbers, or a similar slapdash approach. Contrary to the popular outlook, this kind of scoring error has little to do with judgment differences in the scoring of indistinct answers. For example, on the various Wechsler intelligence scales, discussed later in this chapter, the examiner may need to determine whether an answer to a vocabulary question (e.g., "What does *radiant* mean") is worth 1 or 2 raw score points. Yet, this kind of judgment issue typically does not shift the overall IQ score by any significant margin, unless the examiner is scoring a protocol from an examinee at one of the extremes (high functioning

or low functioning) and consistently errs in a liberal or conservative direction.

HISTORICAL LANDMARKS IN ABILITY-RELATED ASSESSMENT

Why review history? Because, oddly, the history of testing is of more than historical interest! Here are some vital reasons to know a bit of history: it helps explain contemporary practices that might otherwise seem arbitrary or peculiar; the strengths and limitations of testing stand out better in historical context; and the history of testing includes a few lamentable episodes that serve as reminders to exercise caution in our applications and understandings of testing (Gregory, 2007). Later, we will provide a few instructive examples of this last point, but in the meantime consider the following cautionary tale from the related field of psychiatry. In 1949, the Nobel Prize for Medicine or Physiology was awarded to the Portuguese psychiatrist Egaz Moniz for his invention of the prefrontal lobotomy. Once heralded as a major breakthrough in the treatment of severe mental illness, this crude form of brain surgery is now completely discredited and stands as an historical warning that we should not be too eager to jump on the latest medical or psychological bandwagon. Additional warnings are recounted later in this chapter.

The origins of mental testing can be traced to Francis Galton, a British genius who devised a collection of largely sensory and motor measures that he displayed for the 1884 International Health Exhibit in London (Johnson, McClearn, Yuen, Nagoshi, Ahern, & Cole, 1985). His battery included physical characteristics such as head size, behavioral measures (such as grip strength), and sensory measures (such as auditory acuity and reaction time to visual and auditory stimuli). Remarkably, fair-goers actually paid him for the privilege of undergoing these tests. Even though his approach was highly influential for at least 20 years and was imported to the United States by James McKeen Cattell (1890), this sensory-based approach to testing, known as **brass instruments psychology**, eventually died out when it was found that such instruments did not predict real-world outcomes such as college grades (Wissler, 1901). The reference to "brass instruments" in naming this approach is just that — many of the testing tools were made of brass.

The advent of the modern ability test — that is, one with a focus on cognitive skills — can be traced to the scale introduced in 1905 in Paris by Alfred Binet and Theodore Simon (Binet & Simon, 1905). The first Binet-Simon scale consisted of 30 tasks ranging from very simple sensory tests (e.g., following a moving object with the eyes) to items of intermediate difficulty (e.g., repeating three spoken digits, telling how two common objects are alike) to highly complex perceptual and verbal tasks (e.g., identifying the resulting shape after folding and cutting a piece of paper, defining abstract words like *boredom*). By contemporary standards, it is remarkable that the 1905 scale did not offer a precise method for arriving at a total score. Instead, the examiner obtained a pattern of right and wrong answers. This information was nonetheless very helpful in identifying children who needed special placement, which was the entire purpose of the scale (Gregory, 2007). Of course, later versions of the scale provided scores and subscores in plenitude. In 1916, the Binet-Simon was given a sound empirical basis with good norms in the original American translation and revision known as

---

HIGHLIGHT BOX 3.1

THE BRASS INSTRUMENTS TRADITION IN MENTAL TESTING

What did the early brass instruments test batteries look like? With hindsight, the extent to which these batteries relied on the assessment of sensory and motor capacities is remarkable. Cattell (1890) presented his battery in a classic paper titled "Mental Tests and Measurements," as summarized by Gregory (2007):

1. Strength of hand squeeze as measured by dynamometer
2. Rate of hand movement through a distance of 50 centimeters
3. Two-point threshold for touch — minimum distance at which two points are still perceived as separate
4. Degree of pressure needed to cause pain — rubber tip pressed against the forehead
5. Weight differentiation — discern the relative weights of identical-looking boxes varying by 1 gram from 100 to 110 grams
6. Reaction time for sound — using a device similar to Galton's
7. Time for naming colors
8. Bisection of a 50-centimeter line
9. Judgment of 10 seconds of time
10. Number of letters repeated on one hearing

The inclusion of pain sensitivity (item 4) on a mental test is especially curious. Cattell assumed that pain sensitivity was inversely related to intelligence, that is, this item was scored in reverse. Thus, the more pressure required, the lower the examinee's score on this item.

the Stanford-Binet (Terman, 1916). The Binet-Simon tradition is still with us today in the latest American update, the Stanford-Binet: Fifth Edition (Roid, 2003).

But that is getting ahead of the story. Five years after Binet and Simon published their test in 1905, Henry H. Goddard translated it into English, with minor changes, so that it could be used with American children (Goddard, 1910) for the study of what was then known as "feeblemindedness" and what we would now describe as mental retardation or intellectual disability. Later, the commissioner of immigration invited Goddard to Ellis Island to study the intelligence of immigrant groups. The impetus for the study was a near-hysterical concern among some national leaders that too many immigrants of very low intelligence were arriving at our shores, a concern that Gould (1981) has satirically referred to as the "menace of feeblemindedness." In what was surely a colossal misuse of testing, Goddard tested hundreds of (most likely) frightened and disoriented immigrants who literally had just walked ashore, using translators with an instrument devised in French, translated into English, then translated into each immigrant's native language (Hungarian, Russian, Polish, Italian, and so forth). The results then were scored according to the original French norms, all as a basis for "proving" that certain unwanted groups posed a threat, through the hereditary transmission of low intelligence, to the entire nation. Goddard was a highly complex person who was following the social ideologies of his day, and there is much more to the story than we can portray here (see Gelb, 1986; Zenderland, 1998). The point of this brief excursion is to remind students of clinical psychology that what seems sensible in current historical context might be viewed years later as an abuse of testing.

Another early development in the history of testing that bears mention is the development of group tests for the examination of army recruits during World War I. Robert Yerkes, a Harvard psychology professor, spearheaded an effort to develop two screening tests: the Army Alpha, a verbally loaded test battery used with higher functioning recruits, and the Army Beta, a nonverbal group test designed for illiterate recruits and immigrants whose first language was not English (Yerkes, 1919). The relevance of the Alpha and Beta tests to contemporary assessment is that many of the specific formats were later borrowed by David Wechsler when he developed his individual intelligence tests. For example, contemporary Wechsler subtests such as Object Assembly, Arithmetic, Digit Symbol-Coding, and Picture Completion can be traced directly to the Alpha and Beta tests.

Other forms of contemporary testing also have roots in instruments developed in the early 1900s. From the very beginning of the profession of psychology, clinicians realized that measures of intelligence provided an incomplete picture of the functioning of persons with mental retardation. In addition to aspects of cognitive functioning, such as verbal and perceptual skills, what was needed was an assessment of practical matters such as self-sufficiency, personal responsibility, and community functioning. **Adaptive behavior**, discussed in more detail later, refers to the age-appropriate behaviors needed for a person to function independently in daily life, such as communication, social skills, and activities of daily living (e.g., eating, grooming, mobility).

The first standardized instrument for the assessment of adaptive behavior was the Vineland Social Maturity Scale (VSMS), developed by Edgar Doll (1936). At the time, Doll was the head of the Vineland Training School in New Jersey, a premier facility for the research and treatment of mental retardation. His conception of adaptive behavior was pivotal in the field and led him to develop the VSMS, which consisted of 117 discrete items arranged in a year-scale format. A knowledgeable informant indicated yes or no for each item. Arranged from youngest to oldest age-equivalent, examples of items on the scale included grasps objects within reach, removes coat or dress, bathes self unaided, goes to nearby places alone, and shares community responsibility. The Vineland is still a respected instrument in its modern and revised form, the Vineland Adaptive Behavior Scales-II (Sparrow, Cicchetti, & Balla, 2005).

CONTEMPORARY MEASURES OF INTELLIGENCE

The number of respectable individual tests of intelligence increases almost on a yearly basis, so it is difficult for a practitioner to know which test(s) to choose. In addition, the major contenders possess such a high degree of construct overlap that correlations among any two tests typically are very strong, often approaching $r = 0.80$ or so in heterogeneous samples of individuals. This would suggest that any well-normed test of intelligence will suffice if the only goal of the examiner is to produce a global score (Gregory, 2007). Yet, practitioners often want to understand the nuances of intellectual functioning such as might be found in subtest or area scores, which differ widely among mainstream intelligence tests. Seen in this light, each available instrument has its particular merits and also its specific shortcomings. Practitioners are advised to study the pros and cons of individual instruments and always to select a test in light of the assessment needs of the examinee. We can offer a few guidelines here, but this is more an illustration of how to think about tests than a definitive guide.

Stanford-Binet: Fifth Edition

We begin with the intelligence test that has the oldest lineage, the Stanford-Binet: Fifth Edition (SB5, Roid, 2003), parts of which can be traced back to the 1905 Binet-Simon scale. This

test recognizes five factors of intelligence, each measured in the two domains of nonverbal and verbal. This makes for 5×2, or 10, subtests. The five factors of intelligence are based on modern theories of cognition and include fluid reasoning, knowledge, quantitative reasoning, visual-spatial reasoning, and working memory. Each of these areas of intelligence is assessed by means of both a verbal and a nonverbal subtest. In all, then, the SB5 yields ten subtest scores (mean of 10 and standard deviation of 3), three IQ scores (Nonverbal, Verbal, and Full Scale), and the five factor scores noted above. The IQ and factor scores are normed to a mean of 100 and standard deviation of 15.

The test is suitable for persons from age 2 to age 85, which is one advantage over the Wechsler scales (discussed in this chapter), where the examiner would need to purchase and learn three separate instruments to achieve approximately the same age coverage. Perhaps a more important advantage of the SB5 is that the test includes extensive high-end items for assessing gifted persons (i.e., the test has a high ceiling) and a good number of low-end items for assessing persons with mental retardation (i.e., the test has a low floor). The concepts of **test ceiling** and **test floor** refer to the capacity of an instrument to make meaningful distinctions in ability at high and low levels of functioning, respectively. In fact, the range of IQ scores possible for the SB5 is 40 to 160, which is a wider range than is found on most individual tests of intelligence. Thus, one reason to prefer this instrument over others might be in the assessment of the extremes of intellectual functioning.

Kaufman Assessment Battery for Children: Second Edition

Another interesting test of cognitive ability, and one that provides alternative theoretical understandings of intelligence, is the Kaufman Assessment Battery for Children, Second

HIGHLIGHT BOX 3.2

HISTORY OF THE IQ CONCEPT

Almost immediately upon the advent of intelligence testing in the early 1900s, psychologists sought ways to summarize the overall score in a useful manner, which shortly led to the concept of Intelligence Quotient, or IQ. The definition and computation of IQ have shifted over the decades, so a brief review of its origin and history will prove helpful here, based on the summary provided by Gregory (2007). We begin by noting that the original Binet-Simon scale of 1905 provided only a patterning of right and wrong answers to 30 subtests, but it did not yield an overall score.

In 1911, the third revision of the Binet-Simon scale was published. This test consisted of exactly five items at each age level. This allowed examiners to derive a precise mental level for each child, which was the age equivalent of his or her mental functioning. Essentially, the examiner accomplished this by finding the **basal level** (the age at which all items were passed) and adding one-fifth of a year for each item passed at higher age levels up to the **ceiling level** (the age at which all items were failed). Soon, the mental level was known as the mental age (MA), and examiners were comparing this with the chronological age (CA). For example, a 9-year-old who was functioning at the mental age of a 6-year-old was known to be retarded by three years.

Stern (1912) was quick to point out that being retarded by three years meant something quite different for a 6-year-old (functioning at a 3-year-old level) than it did for a 13-year-old (functioning at a 10-year-old level). He recommended computing an Intelligence Quotient by dividing the mental age by the chronological age. In publishing the Stanford-Binet, Terman (1916) recommended multiplying this quotient by 100 to get rid of annoying fractions, thus yielding the formula of $IQ = 100 \times MA/CA$. He was also the first to use the IQ abbreviation.

The formula noted above works reasonably well for children into their teenage years but then falls apart for examinees in their adult years. For example, a normal 50-year-old adult functioning at the mental age of an average 25-year-old would be cognitively quite competent, but the formula still confers an IQ of only 50 ($100 \times 25/50$), which would (inaccurately) indicate a moderate level of mental retardation. For this and other reasons, psychologists soon abandoned the use of MA and CA in the calculation of IQ and began to use a standardized score approach instead. In this method, scores are calibrated on the assumption that the average IQ at every age is 100, with a standard deviation of about 15. In this approach, the calculation of the IQ is in reference to other individuals of the same age rather than directly utilizing mental age or chronological age in a formula.

Edition, or KABC-II (Kaufman & Kaufman, 2004). This test is suitable for children ages 3 to 18 and consists of 20 brief subtests that yield five subtest scores and an overall global score. Not all subtests are used with every age group, so it is possible to complete the full battery in 35 to 70 minutes.

The KABC-II can be scored and interpreted within two different theoretical frameworks. One use of the test provides for a neuropsychological understanding within the model proposed by the legendary Russian neuropsychologist Alexander Luria (Luria, 1973). Within this approach, selected subtests are administered to provide scale scores in four neuropsychologically relevant areas: Simultaneous Processing, Sequential Processing, Planning Ability, and Learning Ability. A global Mental Processing Index also is derived. Examiners who think and work within a neuropsychological framework find this use of the KABC-II to be highly companionable.

The second theoretical framework available with the same test is based on the Cattell-Horn-Carroll (CHC) theory of intelligence. The CHC theory is a modern and influential approach derived from the reanalysis of over 400 data sets spanning nearly a century of research on cognitive functioning (Carroll, 1993; McGrew, 1997). The CHC project used factor analysis to identify a number of broad abilities, including the five scales that can be obtained from selected subtests of the instrument: Visual Processing, Short-Term Memory, Fluid Reasoning, Long-Term Storage and Retrieval, and Crystallized Ability. **Factor analysis** is a statistical technique that permits researchers to identify the latent structure of a measurement instrument. (For example, factor analysis can help researchers identify those scales within a test that appear to measure similar constructs — for example, nonverbal reasoning skills — based on the degree to which scores on the scales correlate with scores on other scales.) Examiners who prefer a contemporary factor-analytically based understanding of intelligence are at ease with this use of the KABC-II.

In addition to allowing for two different theoretical understandings of cognitive functioning, the KABC-II possesses other desirable features. For example, the subtests are different, intriguing, and, in some cases, unique. The game-like qualities of many items fascinate and entrance children, helping to hold their interest. For instance, one subtest involves riddles, while another requires the child to identify from memory one face among a group of people.

Another desirable feature of the KABC-II is the psychometric excellence of the test. The instrument was carefully normed on over 3,000 representative children. The composite scales show reliabilities ranging from 0.88 to 0.93, whereas the global scales reveal split-half reliabilities of 0.95 to 0.97. One psychometric quality bears special mention — namely, group differences among ethnic and cultural groups are smaller than those found on other mainstream instruments. For example, when scores are corrected for the educational level of the mother, the average scores on the sequential scale were:

African American	100
American Indian	97
Asian American	103
Hispanic	95
White	101

In general, group differences on all the scales of the test were found to be reduced in comparison to other prominent tests of general intelligence such as the Wechsler scales (Kaufman & Lichtenberger, 2002). Furthermore, because the subtests of the KABC-II rely less on verbal skills than most other mainstream tests, one important application of the test is with children who possess limited English language proficiency or whose first language is not English.

Wechsler Intelligence Scales

In any discussion of intelligence tests, we would be remiss not to mention the extraordinary contributions of David Wechsler (1896–1981), who originated a family of instruments that now dominates the field in the assessment of intelligence. The genius of Wechsler is that he fashioned his first instrument from the sometimes failed and discarded remnants of other tests (especially the Army Alpha and Beta tests) using a simple methodology that he carried forward from one instrument to the next.

With each of the Wechsler intelligence tests, the practitioner administers 12 subtests to every examinee (although some variation in the number of subtests is possible), starting each subtest at an easy level and continuing until a number of consecutive items have been failed. Scoring is simple and straightforward in comparison to some other instruments. Wechsler also used very similar subtests across his several instruments, so that transfer of training was easy for examiners. His instruments have been successively revised by colleagues at the Psychological Corporation and now consist of the WPPSI-III (Wechsler Preschool and Primary Scale of Intelligence, Third Edition), used with children ages 2½ to 7 years and 3 months; the WISC-IV (Wechsler Intelligence Scale for Children, Fourth Edition), used with children ages 6 through 16; and the WAIS-III (Wechsler Adult Intelligence Scale, Third Edition), normed for persons 16 through 89 years of age. The subtests and index scores of the most recent test, the WISC-IV, are shown in Table 3.1. Although no hard data can be cited, anecdotal evidence suggests that the Wechsler tests are used in the majority of assessments in school and neuropsychological settings. Certainly, it is true that doctoral programs and internship sites expect training and expertise in the Wechsler scales.

The Wechsler tests can be praised for their ease of administration and their psychometric excellence in norming, reliability, and validity studies, but they have one minor shortcoming: the ceiling does not go very high, and the floor does not go as low as might be needed for some applications. In other words, the WAIS-III does not contain enough difficult items to discriminate at the high end of intelligence (ceiling effect) and does not contain enough easy items to discriminate at the low end of functioning (floor effect).

We are not recommending the practice, and we intend no disrespect to persons with serious disabilities, but it will be instructive in

TABLE 3.1 Index Scores and Subtests of the WISC-IV

Index	Subtests
Verbal Comprehension	Similarities
	Vocabulary
	Comprehension
Perceptual Reasoning	Block Design
	Picture Concepts
	Matrix Reasoning
Working Memory	Digit Span
	Letter-Number Sequencing
Processing Speed Index	Coding
	Symbol Search
Supplemental Subtests	Picture Completion
	Cancellation
	Information
	Arithmetic
	Word Reasoning

Note: A Full Scale IQ score also is derived from the first ten subtests.

understanding the idea of floor effect to consider what would happen if the WAIS-III were administered to a bedridden adult who was in a deep, unresponsive coma. Following the rules, the examiner would pose a question or a task, wait for a response within time limits (if applicable), and then assign a raw score of zero to the failed items. After a certain number of failed items, the examiner would proceed to the next subtest. Raw scores would be added together to obtain subtest scores of zero, which are further compiled and compared to table values and so forth. In the end, consulting the appropriate table in the test manual, our patient in a coma would "earn" a Full Scale IQ of 45. This is the same score that might be earned by an individual with moderate mental retardation who was able to answer some of the easiest items on each scale. In sum, the WAIS-III does a poor job of discriminating levels of performance in the low ranges of intellectual functioning. The test has a mirrored problem of ceiling effect at the high end — persons who just barely answer all the questions correctly and earn an IQ of 155 (the highest score possible) are not discriminated by their results from individuals who yet might know ten times more and solve even harder problems and whose true IQ is literally off the charts.

TEST BIAS AND TEST FAIRNESS

Individual ability tests — especially those known as intelligence tests — have been widely criticized by the lay public and even some professionals as being *biased* against minorities, the poor, and others with inadequate access to education. Perhaps the primary foundation for this criticism is the fact that, on average, certain minority groups score significantly lower than persons of European American descent. Indeed, this is a correct observation — group differences have been widely documented over a span of many decades. For example, the most widely studied difference is between African American and white populations, where a divergence of 15 points in average IQ scores is characteristic (Jensen, 1998).

The very existence of this kind of group discrepancy in test results is taken by many as ipso facto proof that ability tests are biased against many ethnic and racial minorities. But is this a fair conclusion? We will propose an argument here that while traditional intelligence tests certainly merit close scrutiny in regard to their societal consequences, these instruments nonetheless do not possess test bias, at least not in the manner that psychometric specialists understand test bias. While the sources of group differences in IQ test scores are not entirely understood, the more likely explanations include social and environmental features such as poverty and its cofactors (Brooks-Gunn, Klebanov, & Duncan, 1996; Wilson, 1994).

Test bias has a very specific and objective definition, and group differences do not necessarily figure into the designation. In particular, **test bias** refers to *differential validity:*

> Bias is present when a test score has meanings or implications for a relevant, definable subgroup of test takers that are different from the meanings or implications for the remainder of the test takers. Thus, bias is differential validity of a given interpretation of a test score for any definable, relevant subgroup of test takers. (Cole & Moss, 1998)

Entire books and many lengthy chapters have been written on the nature, definition, and detection of test bias. We can provide only the most cursory coverage here. We begin by describing one specific approach to the examination of test bias.

One way to get at the issue of test bias is to consider the relative difficulty levels of specific items within a subtest of an instrument under question. For example, consider the Information subtest found on the Wechsler tests. This subtest consists of a series of information-related questions of graded difficulty, including very easy items similar to "What is the day that comes after Monday?" or intermediate items like "On what continent is Egypt?" or harder items such as "Who wrote *Canterbury Tales*?" In an unbiased test, the rank order of item difficulties (as indexed by the percentage of same-aged individuals who pass each item) will be identical or nearly identical that is, the easiest item for one subgroup will also prove to be the easiest item for other identifiable subgroups, and likewise for intermediate and very difficult items. Note that we are speaking of the *relative* difficulty level of items — we are not looking for equivalent passing rates for the individual test items in the relevant subgroups.

When prominent individual intelligence tests are scrutinized to determine if the rank order of item difficulties is the same across relevant subgroups, the nearly universal result is that the rank order is virtually identical for all relevant subgroups (Gregory, 2007). When test bias is evaluated through a variety of empirical procedures such as:

- factor analysis (to determine if the factorial structure of individual tests is similar across groups),
- regression equations (to determine if relevant subgroups fall along the same regression line for predicting a criterion from test scores),
- intragroup comparisons of items nominated by experts for "bias" (to determine if "biased" items really are relatively more difficult for relevant subgroups),

the overwhelming conclusion is that prominent intelligence tests do not show any reliable evidence of test bias (e.g., Reynolds, 1994).

Does this mean that mainstream tests receive a free "pass" and can be used for important decisions? The answer to this question is complicated and hinges on an understanding of test fairness. **Test fairness** refers to the extent to which the social consequences of test usage are thought to be fair to minorities and other subgroups when tests are used for selection decisions (Gregory, 2007).

Consider the use of mainstream individual intelligence tests such as the WISC-IV or the SB5 in the evaluation of children for possible placement in special education classes. This practice, common in the 1970s and 1980s, continues in one form or another to the present day in many (but not all) school systems. The quandary posed by this tradition is that minority children are two to three times more likely to be assigned to these special classes than white children (Agbenyega & Jiggetts, 1999). If special education were superior to regular education (e.g., the best teachers, the most resources, the smallest classes, the highest overall morale), there would be no debate about the use of individual intelligence tests for selection purposes — or possibly the debate would

be about the diametrically opposite issue of selecting students with *high* scores for this privilege. But as Scarr (1987) noted decades ago, special education often is inherently inferior education that perpetuates educational disadvantage.

No wonder, then, that many advocates have come forth to question the use of mainstream intelligence tests for placement purposes. Legal challenges date back to at least 1967 with *Hobson v. Hansen*, a case that challenged the use of ability tests to "track" students on the grounds that such tests discriminate against minority students. More noteworthy, in 1979 with *Larry P. v. Riles*, the California court system ruled that traditional IQ tests are culturally biased against African American children and barred their use for placement purposes with minority children. Although the courts used the term *bias*, it is clear from the context that the real complaint was about the *fairness* of the tests, that is, their continued use was perceived to maintain a heritage of mistreatment of African American students. Of course, this topic remains controversial within the field of psychology, and not all psychologists agree with the interpretations offered here. For contrary positions, see Herrnstein and Murray (1994) and Rushton and Jensen (2005).

THE CHALLENGE OF THE FLYNN EFFECT

The **Flynn effect** refers to the fact that throughout the twentieth century, each successive generation has apparently shown small gains in overall IQ that cumulatively amount to massive population gains of as much 18 points in Full Scale IQ in as little as 55 years (Flynn, 2007a). These gains are deduced from the process of revising and renorming major instruments such as the Wechsler Intelligence Scale for Children, now in its fourth edition

(WISC-IV, Wechsler, 2003). A span of about 12 years separated the standardization and release of the WISC-IV from its predecessor, the WISC-III. In studying the psychometric qualities of the new version, both the WISC-IV and the WISC-III were administered to a representative sample of 244 children, in counterbalanced order. The average Full Scale IQs for this sample were 104.5 on the WISC-IV and 107.0 on the WISC-III. In other words, this sample of children, representative of the current general population, performed 2.5 points higher on the older test, indicating that they were that much smarter than children tested earlier, with an apparent population gain of 2.5 IQ points in the 12 years separating the standardization of these two instruments. In like manner, performance of prior representative samples can be looked up in the relevant technical manuals, comparing the WISC-III with its predecessor, the WISC-R, and the WISC-R with the original WISC, and so forth, in a calibration of overall scores reaching backward to the Wechsler-Bellevue-I and beyond (Flynn, 2007b). In the case of the WISC-IV, the cumulative increase over prior generations is a staggering 18 points. Similar increases have been reported for other instruments such as the Raven's Progressive Matrices and in other nations such as Denmark, although just to complicate matters further, some have argued that trends have now stabilized or possibly have even turned downward (Teasdale & Owen, 2005).

Explaining the Flynn effect has proven challenging, and various factors such as improved nutrition and health care, combined with improvements in education, have been cited (e.g., Neisser, 1998). Yet, it strains credulity to believe that the intelligence of a population, in any real and meaningful sense, could be catapulted upwards so far in such a short period of time. At one point in his career, Flynn concluded flatly that we should question what so-called intelligence tests measure:

> Psychologists should stop saying that IQ tests measure intelligence. They should say that IQ tests measure abstract problem-solving ability (APSA), a term that accurately conveys our ignorance. We know people solve problems on IQ tests; we suspect these problems are so detached, or so abstracted from reality, that the ability to solve them can diverge over time from the real-world problem-solving ability called intelligence; thus far we know little else. (Flynn, 1987)

In more recent writings, Flynn has offered a much more complex and nuanced understanding of the phenomenon that bears his name (Flynn, 2007b). Regardless of how the historical changes in test scores ultimately are explained, the very existence of such sharp alterations in normative scores is a reminder that our understanding of intelligence is yet tentative, still a work in progress. And from a practical standpoint, another lesson is available here: norms for major tests do shift over time, sometimes substantially. It remains imperative for test developers to provide new standardization data, ideally every ten years or so.

ADAPTIVE BEHAVIOR MEASURES AND MENTAL RETARDATION

The most important application for measures of adaptive behavior is in the assessment of persons with known or suspected **mental retardation**. These instruments are useful for many other forms of assessment (e.g., children with autism, persons with moderate or severe head injury, individuals struggling with serious mental illness), but their most common use by far is in the assessment of mental retardation. Before introducing useful measures, a brief summary of definitions and issues in this area of assessment will be helpful. An authoritative source on the topic is the American Association on Intellectual and Developmental Disability (AAIDD, 2002), which offers this definition:

Mental retardation is a disability characterized by significant limitations both in intellectual functioning and in adaptive behavior as expressed in conceptual, social, and practical adaptive skills. This disability originates before age 18.

In practical terms, this definition translates to an IQ below 70 on a mainstream test such as a Wechsler scale or the Stanford-Binet: Fifth Edition *and* deficits in adaptive behavior that are two or more standard deviations below the mean for conceptual, social, or practical skills. If a person first manifests these criteria after age 18 (for example, from a serious head injury in adulthood), he or she faces major adaptive challenges, but the diagnostic label of mental retardation simply does not fit well. The practical reason for restricting the diagnosis of mental retardation to those cases in which the limitations arise in childhood (as opposed to being acquired in adulthood) is that the typical lifelong trajectory, the approaches to rehabilitation, and the types of supports needed differ substantially in these two broad scenarios.

What does the AAIDD mean by conceptual, social, and practical skills? These are discussed in detail in their reference book (AAIDD, 2002), but we can give a quick summary here. Conceptual skills refer to language usage, reading and writing, money concepts, and self-directions. Social skills involve a sense of responsibility, interpersonal skills, self-esteem, following rules and laws, and avoiding victimization. Practical skills involve activities of daily living (eating, dressing, and hygiene), instrumental activities of daily living (preparing meals, taking medication, managing money), occupational skills, and maintaining a safe environment.

How can a psychologist possibly evaluate the functioning of a client in so many diverse areas of adaptive behavior? Fortunately, a number of excellent instruments are available for this purpose, including the AAMR Adaptive Behavior Scales: Second Edition (ABS-2, Nihira, Leland, & Lambert, 1993), the Vineland Adaptive Behavior Scales: Second Edition (Vineland-II, Sparrow, Cicchetti, & Balla, 2005), the Scales of Independent Behavior-Revised (SIB-R, Bruininks, Woodcock, Weatherman, & Hill, 1996), and the Inventory for Client and Agency Planning (ICAP, Hill, 2005). Regarding these tests, the reader can find detailed information on publishers, authors, year of release, ordering information, and so forth by using any major Internet search engine. We will focus here on just one representative instrument, the Vineland-II (Sparrow, Cicchetti, & Balla, 2005).

With the Vineland-II, a teacher, parent, or other reliable informant provides information to the examiner about the functioning of the client. A number of forms are available (Survey Interview, Parent/Caregiver Rating Form, Expanded Interview, Teacher Rating Form), but all of them involve the same methodology of rating discrete items of adaptive behavior on this 3-point scale:

2: Usually or habitually performed without help or reminders
1: Performed sometimes or partially without help or reminders
0: Never performed without help or reminders

In addition, ratings of "no opportunity" and "don't know" also are allowed. Raw scores on individual items are then collated within subdomains, which in turn yields domain scores and an overall score for adaptive functioning. The domain and subdomain scales are listed in Table 3.2. In addition, a separate and optional index of maladaptive behavior can be obtained. This index includes scores on Internalizing, Externalizing, and Other forms of maladaptive behavior.

The Adaptive Behavior Composite (i.e., the overall score) and the Domain scales are normed to a mean of 100 and standard deviation of 15 for the general population. The Subdomain scales are reported as V-scale scores, with a mean of 15 and standard deviation of 3.

TABLE 3.2 Domain and Subdomain Scales of the Vineland-II

Domain Scales	Subdomain Scales
Communication	Receptive
	Expressive
	Written
Daily Living Skills	Personal
	Domestic
	Community
Socialization	Interpersonal Relationships
	Play and Leisure Time
	Coping Skills
Motor Skills	Fine
	Gross

The norm group consisted of a nationally representative sample of 3,687 individuals tested in 2003 and 2004.

One reason for the careful and objective evaluation of adaptive behavior is that the behaviors included within this broad domain are prone to ongoing change, especially when persons with intellectual disabilities receive needed intervention and support (Verdugo, 2003). Modern conceptions of mental retardation focus not only on the capacities and limitations of the person undergoing an assessment but also on the supports and opportunities that society will need to provide for optimal client functioning. This is a not-so-subtle philosophical shift that offers a far more optimistic tone than merely assigning persons with intellectual disabilities to the outdated categories of mild, moderate, severe, or profound mental retardation.

ACHIEVEMENT MEASURES AND LEARNING DISABILITIES

The purpose of an **achievement test** is to appraise what an individual has learned in regard to traditional areas of school curriculum such as reading, spelling, mathematics, and written expression. There are literally dozens of well-designed *group* tests of achievement, and anyone schooled in the United States has encountered these instruments at least yearly, if not more often. Our focus here is on *individual* tests of achievement, those administered one to one for purposes such as the assessment of learning problems. For this application, the number of suitable tests is much smaller. The most respected instruments include the Kaufman Test of Educational Achievement-II (KTEA-II), the Wechsler Individual Achievement Test-II (WIAT-II), the Diagnostic Achievement Battery-3 (DAB-3), and the Woodcock-Johnson-III Tests of Achievement (WJ-III). Again, we note that abundant information about these instruments can be found by using any major Internet search engine. Here we provide modest detail on one typical and representative instrument, the KTEA-II.

The KTEA-II is normed on a nationally representative sample of persons ranging from 4½ through 25 years of age. The core of the test consists of eight subtests that provide composite scores in four areas: Reading, Math, Written Language, and Oral Language. These composite scores, highly useful in the assessment of learning problems, are reported as standard scores with mean of 100 and standard deviation of 15 in the general population. In addition, a variety of supplemental subtests can be used to assess functioning in a number of reading-related areas such as phonological awareness, word recognition, and naming fluency. The test also provides an overall achievement score for the entire battery, normed to a mean of 100 and standard deviation of 15. The subtests and composites of the KTEA-II are listed in Table 3.3.

The overall composite score rarely is used. In the assessment of learning problems, the area composite scores in reading, mathematics, written language, and oral expression are

TABLE 3.3   Composite Areas and Subtests of the
KTEA-II

Composite	Subtests
Reading	Reading Comprehension
	Letter & Word Recognition
Math	Math Computation
	Math Concepts & Applications
Written Language	Written Expression
	Spelling
Oral Language	Oral Expression
	Listening Comprehension

Note: The KTEA-II Comprehensive Form includes
diagnostically valuable reading-related subtests and also
provides for an overall Comprehensive Achievement
Composite.

typically more useful than the overall composite because of their practical application in the assessment of **learning disabilities** (LDs). Although a variety of definitions for LD can be found, most of them refer to learning problems that are:

> (a) *not* due to inadequate opportunity to learn, general intelligence, or to significant physical or emotional disorders, but to *basic* disorders in specific psychological processes, (b) these specific psychological processing deficits are a reflection of neurological, constitutional, and/or biological factors, and (c) there is a psychological processing deficit that depresses only a limited aspect of academic or contextually appropriate behaviour. (Swanson, 2003)

Consistent with this definition, many authorities argue that LD can be identified, in part, as a discrepancy of at least one standard deviation (i.e., 15 points) between general ability as measured by overall IQ and specific achievement as measured by composite achievement score for reading, math, written language, or oral expression (Gregory, 2007). Thus, the existence of achievement tests like the KTEA-II,

with composite scores normed to the same metric as IQ scores (i.e., mean of 100 and standard deviation of 15), provides an objective statistical approach to the assessment and identification of LD — namely, look for a significant discrepancy between overall IQ and specific achievement in reading, math, written language, or oral expression.

Yet, others argue that discrepancy formulas contain methodological flaws and do not account for statistical anomalies (e.g., regression to the mean) or subtle differences among instruments that can result in different classification decisions depending on which specific tests are used. For example, suppose a child meets the necessary discrepancy of 15 points or more between Full Scale IQ of 107 on the WISC-IV and Reading Composite of 91 on the KTEA-II and is otherwise qualified for the diagnosis, for example, has received adequate opportunity to learn, and so forth. Would this child also meet the criteria for LD classification if administered the SB5 and WIAT-II instead? Maybe yes, maybe no. As noted above, normative standards and the test scores based on them shift with time and show differences among mainstream instruments. Due to such factors, the WISC-IV and the SB5 do not provide exactly identical results for overall scores, and neither do the KTEA-II and the WIAT-II for the individual composite scores that would be pivotal in determining LD according to the discrepancy approach.

A study by Schultz (1997) bears on this point. In this study, 62 fifth graders considered at-risk for LD were evaluated first with the WISC-R and then later with the WISC-III. The achievement levels of the children were evaluated with the Woodcock-Johnson–Revised Tests of Achievement. Then the usual 15-point discrepancy — between Full Scale IQ and achievement scores in specific areas like reading and math — was consulted to determine eligibility for an LD diagnosis. When the WISC-R was used as the measure of general ability, 86% of the children qualified, whereas when the WISC-III was applied to the formula, only 48% of the children met the criteria.

Because of problems like this, some experts in LD (e.g., Shaw, Cullen, McGuire, & Brinckerhoff, 1995) propose a different approach, one less statistically laden, in which an *intraindividual* discrepancy in academic functioning (listening, speaking, reading, writing, reasoning, and math) is the hallmark of this group of disorders. Gregory (2007) describes this more flexible approach as follows:

> In this approach, the first task is to identify one or more intraindividual weaknesses in the core areas. These are always relative to strengths in several other core areas. In other words, persons who are slow learners in all areas do not meet the criteria of LD. The second step is to trace the learning difficulties to central nervous system dysfunction, which may manifest as problems with information processing. For example, a young adult with a severe weakness in listening (as judged by her inability to learn from the traditional lecture approach to teaching) might exhibit a deficit on a test of verbal memory — confirming that an information-processing problem was at the heart of her disability. The purpose of the third step (examining psychosocial skills, physical and sensory abilities) is to specify additional problems that may need to be addressed for program-planning purposes. Finally, in the fourth step the examiner rules out non-LD explanations for the learning difficulties (since these explanations would mandate a different strategy for remediation).

This approach is not as straightforward as the statistical analysis of discrepancy scores. Thus, it does permit for greater latitude of clinical judgment on the part of the examiner, which could open the door for incorrect classifications. Yet, when enacted by a careful and well-trained clinician, the advantage is that children truly in need of intervention will not be exempted from services because of the rigidity of a discrepancy formula that often just doesn't work.

SUMMARY

Since the early 1900s, clinical psychologists have developed hundreds of ability-based tests useful for working with clients in a variety of settings. In general, these instruments are among the paramount accomplishments of the entire field. At the same time, it is essential to learn from the history of psychological testing, which does reveal a few regrettable episodes in which tests were used for questionable purposes, including the restriction of immigration in the 1920s based on the low test scores of certain immigrant groups.

Contemporary measures of intelligence are especially helpful in identifying the extremes of functioning — individuals with intellectual giftedness, and those with intellectual disabilities. Intelligence tests are part of the equation in the assessment of mental retardation, but measures of adaptive behavior also are essential. Alongside measures of academic achievement, intelligence measures also provide an excellent starting point in the assessment of learning disabilities, which often involve a discrepancy between general intelligence and specific achievement.

Ability-based tests are not without controversy. A longstanding concern has to do with possible test bias, which is defined as differential validity — the same test result means something different for a member of one subgroup (e.g., a racial minority) than for a member of another subgroup (e.g., the Caucasian majority). For the most part, major ability tests such as intelligence tests do not show test bias in this strict psychometric sense of differential validity. On the other hand, ability-based tests do raise questions as to test fairness, which is defined as the extent to which the social consequences of test usage are considered fair to relevant subgroups.

THOUGHT QUESTIONS

3.1. What might be some of the advantages and disadvantages of individual one-on-one testing versus administering tests in a group setting?

3.2. In general, doctoral-level psychologists are intelligent and careful individuals who care deeply about their profession. In light of this, why do scoring errors still occur, at least among some psychologists?

3.3. What might be some reasons for learning about the history of psychological testing?

3.4. Why do you suppose that the earliest mental tests mainly relied on the assessment of sensory and motor functions in the evaluation of intelligence?

3.5. What are some advantages and disadvantages of mainstream tests of intelligence such as the Stanford-Binet: Fifth Edition and the various Wechsler scales?

3.6. What are some advantages of the Kaufman Assessment Battery, Second Edition, over other tests of intellectual functioning?

3.7. Define test bias and distinguish it from test fairness. How do group differences figure into our understanding of whether or not a test is biased?

3.8. What is the Flynn effect? What are some possible implications of this effect?

3.9. What is the definition of mental retardation? Why is a low IQ not a sufficient basis for making a designation of mental retardation?

3.10. What is a learning disability? What are some prominent approaches to defining a learning disability?

Glossary

Achievement test: A test that assesses the degree of learning or accomplishment in an academically related subject matter.

Adaptive behavior: Practical skills of everyday life such as communication, self-care, meal preparation, money management, and ability to find one's way in the community.

Assessment: The broad enterprise of evaluating the level or magnitude of individual attributes and interpreting them in the context of an examinee's life.

Basal level: In an age-graded test, the level at which an examinee passes all items.

Brass instruments psychology: The late 1800s historical era in psychology in which brass instruments were used to evaluate sensory and motor skills in the belief that these were the underpinnings of intelligence.

Ceiling level: In an age-graded test, the level at which an examinee fails all items.

Factor analysis: A family of statistical procedures used to summarize relationships among variables so as to identify a small number of underlying factors.

Flynn effect: The observation that test norms have shifted over the decades with the apparent implication that the IQ of the general population has risen significantly in the last century.

Group tests: Mainly paper-and-pencil tests suitable for testing large groups of individuals at the same time.

Individual tests: Instruments designed for the purpose of one-on-one testing, which provides for clinical observations as well as the derivation of scores.

IQ: Intelligence Quotient. A standardized score that represents a person's relative rank on a measure on an intelligence test. Although computed differently in the early days of psychology, IQ scores today are entirely norm-referenced. Most IQ tests have a mean of 100 and a standard deviation of either 15 or 16 points, depending on the test.

Learning disabilities: A group of disabilities in which individuals manifest academic achievement that is lower than expected in one or more areas (e.g., reading, math, oral expression) given their level of intelligence.

Mental retardation: Limitations in both intellectual functioning and adaptive behavior as expressed in conceptual, social, and practical adaptive skills, with onset before age 18.

Test bias: Differential validity for an identifiable subgroup; that is, the same test result means something different for a person for one subgroup than for persons from other subgroups.

Test ceiling: The highest level of ability or functioning for which an instrument is able to make meaningful distinctions.

Test fairness: The extent to which the social consequences of test usage are considered fair for identifiable subgroups.

Test floor: The lowest level of ability or functioning for which an instrument is able to make meaningful distinctions.

Testing: The narrow enterprise of administering, scoring, and reporting test results.

References

Agbenyega, S. & Jiggetts, J. (1999). Minority children and their over-representation in special education. *Education, 119*, 619–633.

American Association on Intellectual and Developmental Disabilities (2002). *Mental retardation: definition, classification, and systems of supports* (10th ed.). Washington, DC: Author.

Binet, A. & Simon, T. (1905). Methodes nouvelles pour le diagnostic du niveau intellectual des anormaux. *Annee Psychologique, 11*, 191–244.

Brooks-Gunn, J., Klebanov, P., & Duncan, G. (1996). Ethnic differences in children's intelligence test scores: role of economic deprivation, home environment, and maternal characteristics. *Child Development, 67*, 396–408.

Bruininks, R., Woodcock, R., Weatherman, R., & Hill, B. (1996). *Scales of Independent Behavior-Revised, Interviewer's Manual.* Allen, TX: DLM Teaching Resources.

Carroll, J. B. (1993). *Human cognitive abilities.* New York: Cambridge University Press.

Cattell, J. McK (1890). Mental tests and measurements. *Mind, 15*, 373–380.

Cole, N. & Moss, P. (1998). Bias in test use. In R. L. Linn (Ed.), *Educational measurement* (3rd ed.). Westport, CT: Oryx Press.

Doll, E. A. (1936). Preliminary standardization of the Vineland Social Maturity Scale. *American Journal of Orthopsychiatry, 6*, 283–293.

Eyde, L., Robertson, G., Krug, S., Moreland, K., Robertson, A., Shewan, C., Harrison, P., Hammer, A., & Primoff, E. (1993). *Responsible test use: case studies for assessing human behavior.* Washington, DC: American Psychological Association.

Flynn, J. R. (1987). Massive IQ gains in 14 nations: what IQ tests really measure. *Psychological Bulletin, 101*, 171–191.

Flynn, J. R. (2007a). Solving the IQ puzzle. *Scientific American Mind*, October/November, 24–31.

Flynn, J. R. (2007b). *What is intelligence?* New York: Cambridge University Press.

Gelb, S. (1986). Henry H. Goddard and the immigrants, 1910–1917: the studies and their social context. *Journal of the History of the Behavioral Sciences, 22*, 324–332.

Goddard, H. H. (1910). A measuring scale for intelligence. *The Training School, 6*, 146–155.

Gould, S. J. (1981). *The mismeasure of man.* New York: W.W. Norton.

Gregory, R. J. (1999). *Adult intellectual assessment: the WAIS-III and other tests in clinical practice.* Boston: Allyn & Bacon.

Gregory, R. J. (2007). *Psychological testing: history, principles, and applications* (5th ed.). Boston: Allyn & Bacon.

Herrnstein, R. J. & Murray, C. (1994). *The bell curve: intelligence and class structure in American life.* New York: Free Press.

Hill, B. (2005). ICAP User's Group Home Page. Retrieved from www.cpinternet.com/bhill/icap September 13, 2005.

Hopwood, C. & Richard, D. (2005). Effect of varying WAIS-III scoring requirements and Full Scale IQ on scoring accuracy. *Assessment, 12*, 445–454.

Jensen, A. R. (1998). *The g factor: the science of mental ability.* Westport, CT: Praeger.

Johnson, R., McClearn, G., Yuen, S., Nagoshi, C., Ahern, F., & Cole, R. (1985). Galton's data a century later. *American Psychologist, 40*, 875–892.

Kaufman, A. S. & Kaufman, N. L. (2004). *Kaufman Assessment Battery for Children* (2nd ed.). Circle Pines, MN: American Guidance System Publishing.

Kaufman, A. S. & Lichtenberger, E. O. (2002). *Assessing adolescent and adult intelligence* (2nd ed.). Boston: Allyn & Bacon.

Loe, S., Kadlubek, R., & Marks, W. (2007). Administration and scoring errors on the WISC-IV among graduate student examiners. *Journal of Psychoeducational Assessment, 25,* 237–247.

Luria, A. R. (1973). *The working brain.* New York: Basic Books.

McGrew, K. (1997). Analysis of the major intelligence batteries according to a proposed comprehensive Gf-Gc framework. In D. P. Flanagan, J. L. Genshaft, & P. L. Harrison (Eds.), *Contemporary intellectual assessment: theories, tests and issues* (pp. 151–179). New York: Guilford Press.

Meyer, G., Finn, S., Eyde, L., Kay, G., Moreland, K., Dies, R., Eisman, E., Kubiszyn, T., & Reed, G. (2001). Psychological testing and psychological assessment: a review of evidence and issues. *American Psychologist, 56,* 128–165.

Neisser, U. (Ed.). (1998). *The rising curve: long-term gains in IQ and related measures.* Washington, DC: American Psychological Association.

Nihira, K., Leland, H., & Lambert, N. (1993). *Adaptive Behavior Scale-Residential and Community* (2nd ed.). Washington, DC: American Association on Mental Retardation.

Reynolds, C. (1994). Bias in testing. In R. J. Sternberg (Ed.), *Encyclopedia of human intelligence.* New York: Macmillan.

Roid, G. (2003). *Stanford-Binet Intelligence Scales* (5th ed.). Itasca, IL: Riverside Publishing.

Rushton, J. & Jensen, A. (2005). Thirty years of research on race differences in cognitive ability. *Psychology, Public Policy, and Law, 11,* 235–294.

Ryan, J., Prifitera, A., & Powers, L. (1983). Scoring reliability on the WAIS-R. *Journal of Consulting and Clinical Psychology, 51,* 149–150.

Scarr, S. (1987). Forward. In R. Elliott (Ed.), *Litigating intelligence: IQ tests, special education, and social science in the courtroom.* Dover, MA: Auburn House.

Schultz, M. (1997). WISC-III and WJ-R tests of achievement: concurrent validity and learning disability identification. *Journal of Special Education, 31,* 377–386.

Shaw, S., Cullen, J., McGuire, J., & Brinckerhoff, L. (1995). Operationalizing a definition of learning disabilities. *Journal of Learning Disabilities, 28,* 586–597.

Simons, R., Goddard, R., & Patton, W. (2002). Hand scoring errors in psychological testing. *Assessment, 9,* 292–300.

Sparrow, S. S., Cicchetti, D. V., & Balla, D. A. (2005). *Vineland Adaptive Behavior Scales:* (2nd ed.). (Vineland II), Survey Interview Form/Caregiver Rating Form, Livonia, MN: Pearson Assessments.

Swanson, H. L. (2003). Learning disabilities. In R. Fernandez-Ballesteros (Ed.), *Encyclopedia of psychological assessment* (pp. 553–558). London: SAGE.

Teasdale, T. & Owen, D. (2005). Long-term rise and recent decline in intelligence test performance: the Flynn Effect in reverse. *Personality and Individual Differences, 39,* 837–842.

Terman, L. M. (1916). *The measurement of intelligence.* Boston: Houghton Mifflin.

Verdugo, M. (2003). Mental retardation. In R. Fernandez-Ballesteros (Ed.), *Encyclopedia of psychological assessment* (pp. 579–584). London: SAGE.

Wechsler, D. (1997). *WAIS-III: Wechsler Adult Intelligence Scale* — (3rd ed.). San Antonio, TX: Psychological Corporation.

Wechsler, D. (2003). *WISC-IV: Wechsler Intelligence Scale for Children* — (4th ed.). San Antonio, TX: Psychological Corporation.

Wilson, M. N. (1994). African Americans. In R. J. Sternberg (Ed.), *Encyclopedia of human ntelligence,* New York: Macmillan.

Wissler, C. (1901). The correlation of mental and physical tests. *The Psychological Review,* Monograph Supplement 3(6).

Yerkes, R. (1919). Report of the Psychology Committee of the National Research Council. *Psychological Review, 26,* 83–149.

Zenderland, L. (1998). *Measuring minds: Henry Herbert Goddard and the origins of American intelligence testing.* New York: Cambridge University Press.

Psychological Diagnosis

Thomas A. Widiger
University of Kentucky

Joshua D. Miller
University of Georgia

OUTLINE

PSYCHOLOGICAL DIAGNOSIS

The **diagnosis** of psychopathology has had a historically (Rosenhan, 1973; Szasz, 1961), and currently (Caplan & Cosgrove, 2004; Kirk, 2005; Kutchins & Kirk, 1997), rocky reputation. Clinicians can be reluctant to attach "labels" to the persons they are trying to help. They want to recognize that each person is a unique individual who cannot be adequately described by just one word, particularly if that word is stigmatizing, if not denigrating. Some psychologists may also be reluctant to use diagnoses because the predominant labeling system used today, the American Psychiatric Association's (2000) *Diagnostic and Statistical Manual of Mental Disorders* (DSM-IV-TR), might not be optimally compatible with their own theoretical perspective (Beach, Wamboldt, Kaslow, Heyman, & Reiss, 2006; Charney et al., 2002; Folette & Houts, 1996; PDM Task Force, 2006), or perhaps even because this manual was constructed by a rival profession they consider to be tainted, if not corrupt (Caplan, 1995; Kutchins & Kirk, 1997; Schacht, 1985).

71

Some form of labeling and diagnosis is largely unavoidable, however. Even clinicians who claim to reject diagnostic labels must use words to communicate with their colleagues and with their clients, to describe verbally what they consider to be the problem(s) affecting their clients. In addition, it is imperative that clinicians and researchers be able to communicate effectively with one another, and to do so one must use a common language. The primary purpose of an official diagnostic **nomenclature** is to provide a common language that minimizes the use of idiosyncratic concepts (Kendell, 1975; Sartorius et al., 1993). The impetus for the development of an official diagnostic nomenclature was the crippling confusion generated by its absence (Widiger, 2008). As Kendell (1975) observed, "For a long time confusion reigned. Every self-respecting alienist, the nineteenth-century term for a psychiatrist, and certainly every professor, had his own classification" (p. 87).

> The production of a new system for classifying psychopathology became a right of passage in the nineteenth century for the young, aspiring professor. To produce a well-ordered classification almost seems to have become the unspoken ambition of every psychiatrist of industry and promise, as it is the ambition of a good tenor to strike a high C. This classificatory ambition was so conspicuous that the composer Berlioz was prompted to remark that after their studies have been completed a rhetorician writes a tragedy and a psychiatrist a classification. (Zilboorg, 1941, p. 450)

Effective communication was essentially impossible with each clinician and each researcher being allowed to develop his or her own diagnoses, or even if they used the same diagnostic labels, they applied them idiosyncratically. A uniform diagnostic system is a necessity for progress in scientific research and clinical treatment. However, an official diagnostic nomenclature, as the authoritative language of communication, can be exceedingly powerful, impacting significantly many important

social, forensic, clinical, and other professional decisions (Schwartz & Wiggins, 2002). Persons think in terms of their language, and the predominant language of psychopathology is the American Psychiatric Association's (2000) DSM-IV-TR. As such, this nomenclature has a substantial impact on how clinicians, researchers, social agencies, and the general public conceptualize psychopathology.

Work is now beginning on the development of the fifth edition of this authoritative nomenclature (see Highlight Box 4.1). The first meeting of its Task Force was held in November of 2006, with an anticipated publication date of 2012. Six issues worth highlighting with respect to this effort are (1) the process through which the diagnostic system is constructed, (2) the definition of mental disorder, (3) the threshold for a diagnosis, (4) categorical versus dimensional classification, (5) value judgments, and (6) psychological tests. Each of these issues will be discussed in turn.

CONSTRUCTION OF THE DIAGNOSTIC SYSTEM

One of the more common criticisms of the American Psychiatric Association's diagnostic manual is that its compilation is simply the result of arbitrary committee decisions rather than scientific evidence (Caplan, 1991, 1995; PDM Task Force, 2006; Westen & Shedler, 1999). It is certainly true that the authors of the diagnostic manual have at times approved the inclusion of diagnoses that have since been rejected due to insufficient empirical support, such as self-defeating personality, **paraphiliac** rapism, idiosyncratic alcohol intoxication, and sadistic personality (Pincus, Frances, Davis, First, & Widiger, 1992). More importantly, however, it would be virtually impossible to construct a diagnostic manual without having committees, unless one takes the position that the authority for the decisions should be given to just one person. In addition, decisions are not, and cannot, be made by a scientific study. Studies are considered and interpreted, and persons will disagree as to the precise implications of any particular study. No study will ever be sufficiently conclusive or so well designed that the decision for how the diagnostic manual should be impacted by the study will be unambiguous or undebatable.

The construction of the most recent edition of the diagnostic manual, DSM-IV-TR (American Psychiatric Association, 2000), was not extensive in its effort to be guided by scientific research, as this edition was confined simply to a revision of the narrative text (no new diagnoses were added, none was deleted, and no **criterion sets** were revised in any way). However, the development of DSM-IV (American

Psychiatric Association, 1994) proceeded through an explicit and systematic process for obtaining all relevant published and unpublished empirical data, for conducting field trials, and for documenting the scientific evidence for all of the central decisions (Widiger et al., 1991). The authors of DSM-V can do even better (Widiger & Clark, 2000). Briefly discussed will be membership selection, criteria for revision, pilot testing, and critical review.

Membership Selection

Perhaps the most important decision to be made in developing the diagnostic manual is who will serve on the task force and work groups, as these persons will have the primary

---

HIGHLIGHT BOX 4.1

DSM HISTORY

The first edition of the DSM was published in 1952. It came into existence largely because of World War II, which brought together mental health professionals from around the world. The need for a common language of communication became very apparent as clinicians with literally different languages tried to communicate with one another. Even for clinicians with the same language, communication was difficult. For example, in the U.S. armed forces, there were independent diagnostic systems within the army, navy, and Veterans Administration.

Perhaps the most innovative shift in the classification of mental disorders arrived with DSM-III, chaired by Robert Spitzer and published in 1980. Its major innovation was the inclusion of specific and explicit diagnostic criteria, which improved substantially the potential ability of clinicians, and certainly the ability of researchers, to obtain

reliable diagnoses. Additional innovations included the provision of a multiaxial system (information regarding level of functioning, psychosocial stressors, and medical disorders, along with the mental disorder diagnosis) and the substantial broadening of information within the text of the diagnostic manual (e.g., family history, course, and associated features).

The major innovation of DSM-IV, chaired by Allen Frances and published in 1994, was the publication of the scientific basis for all of the decisions made by the committee members, including literature reviews, data analyses, and field trials. This information was provided in an accompanying four volume *DSM-IV Sourcebook*.

It is not yet clear what the major innovation of DSM-V will be. Speculation is that it will be the inclusion of explicit shifts to more dimensional classifications of mental disorders.

authority and power in constructing the manual. Yet, this is the one aspect of the development process that is least open to public scrutiny or review. Sadler (2005) suggested that much of the controversy and disgruntlement with each edition of the American Psychiatric Association's diagnostic manual has been due to the absence of adequate opportunity for persons with divergent viewpoints to participate in the decision-making process. He, therefore, proposed that the final decisions be based on a democratic vote of clinicians. Spitzer, Williams, and Skodol (1980), however, have argued that opinion surveys should not be conducted because "no one wanted to repeat the scene of the general membership voting on a presumably 'scientific' issue, as was done in 1973 on the issue of the elimination of homosexuality from the DSM-II classification" (p. 152). Voting on whether or not paraphiliac rapism, homosexuality, or premenstrual dysphoric disorder should be included within the diagnostic manual would make the decision more open, but also perhaps more political and less scientific (see Highlight Box 4.2).

Decisions should, however, be informed by a fair hearing of the diversity of perspectives, and these viewpoints and perspectives should be systematically, comprehensively, and enthusiastically solicited. Nevertheless, the most scientifically valid decision may at times be "politically incorrect." The authors of the diagnostic manual should then have the authority to make innovative decisions that are scientifically justified even when they are contrary to general clinical consensus (Widiger & Clark, 2000). DSM-III (American Psychiatric Association, 1980) was innovative in large part because its chair, Dr. Robert Spitzer, was willing to go against the stream (e.g., the inclusion of specific and explicit diagnostic criterion sets, rejected at that time by the World Health Organization for the international classification of psychopathology).

A number of persons originally selected to be involved in the development of DSM-V were ultimately excluded because of the amount of

financial support they were receiving from the pharmaceutical industry. Degree of financial connection to the pharmaceutical industry, though, is a rather fallible indicator of problematic bias. Ideally, perhaps, the membership should consist of "consensus scholars," or persons who will consider the existing evidence with no a priori expectations and biases (Frances, Widiger, & Pincus, 1989). It can be difficult, however, to find persons who do not already have strong opinions regarding what decisions should be made. It is possible that the persons who have the most experience, or have conducted the most informative research, may have the strongest opinions (Widiger & Trull, 1993). Many of the persons selected for membership on the DSM-IV Task Force or Work Group were chosen precisely to represent a particular perspective.

Sadler (2005) suggested further that if the final decisions cannot be decided by a vote, then at least the persons who make the ultimate decisions should themselves be elected through a democratic process. A variation on this proposal would be to have the committee memberships determined by a panel of researchers (or clinicians) whose deliberations are open to some form of public review or critique. In any case, it is unlikely that the American Psychiatric Association will surrender the power it has over the selection of committee membership, nor perhaps is it even likely that the process of selection will itself be open to critical review.

Criteria for Revision

If it is helpful to have specific and explicit criteria for making a diagnosis (Spitzer et al., 1980), then perhaps it would be useful to have specific and explicit criteria for the persons literally making (i.e., constructing) the diagnoses. Blashfield, Sprock, and Fuller (1990) proposed specific and explicit criteria for committee decisions, analogous to the reliance on specific and explicit diagnostic criteria that constrain the decision-making power of practicing clinicians. Clinicians, left to their own criteria for clinical diagnosis, naturally and inevitably provide diagnoses that are idiosyncratic and thereby unreliable. The same could perhaps be said for members of DSM-V work groups as they deliberate on revisions to the diagnostic criterion sets and the addition or deletion of diagnostic categories.

It would be difficult to reach a consensus on the precise number of studies and quality of methodology required to alter, add, or delete a diagnosis. Nevertheless, the process of working toward the development of a uniform set of explicit algorithms for making decisions about revisions, additions, or deletions might facilitate more consistent and objective decision making as well as develop a fuller understanding and appreciation of the many variables and concerns that can impact these decisions.

Pilot Testing

It is well beyond the expertise of the authors of a diagnostic manual to fully anticipate the effects of their decisions (Blashfield, Blum, & Pfohl, 1992). The field testing conducted for DSM-IV was funded by the National Institute of Mental Health (NIMH), and these studies were much more substantial than had been conducted for prior editions of the manual (Widiger & Clark, 2000). Nonetheless, the pilot research still fell far short of being comprehensive. Only a very small subset of the diagnostic criterion sets were field tested (Widiger et al., 1998). This is disappointing, to say the least, given the great significance of this official nomenclature for many important social, forensic, and clinical decisions. The budget for a sufficient number of field trials to cover all of the proposed revisions would be substantial and well beyond reasonable support by NIMH, but the costs may be well within the range of the profits that have been generated by the sales of DSM-IV and DSM-IV-TR.

Critical Review

The DSM-IV Task Force addressed, in part, skepticism regarding the ability of persons to reach fair, balanced, or optimal interpretations of inconclusive or inadequate research by obtaining critiques of the literature reviews and proposals (Frances et al., 1989). Critical review is fundamental to the scientific process, and it was integral to the construction of DSM-IV (Widiger & Trull, 1993). Nevertheless, the critical reviews obtained during the course of developing DSM-IV were not themselves published. All that was published were the final literature reviews, data reanalyses, and field trials (Widiger et al., 1998). The critical review process would be improved by obtaining written critiques of the literature reviews and pilot studies, with the full understanding that these critiques would themselves be published within the official archival document alongside the final reports (Widiger & Clark, 2000).

DEFINITION OF MENTAL DISORDER

DSM-IV-TR includes a rather lengthy and cumbersome operational definition of mental disorder, developed originally by Spitzer and Endicott (1978) to have a set of specific and explicit criteria for what constitutes a mental disorder, analogous to the criterion sets used to identify the presence of specific disorders (Spitzer et al., 1980). Wakefield (1992, 2007) has since provided quite thorough and compelling critiques of the Spitzer and Endicott definition of mental disorder and as an alternative has offered his own "harmful dysfunction" conceptualization. Dysfunction is a failure of an internal mechanism to perform a naturally selected function as developed through evolution, and harm is a value judgment that the design failure is harmful to the individual. Wakefield's harmful dysfunction definition has drawn considerable attention, including even an endorsement by Spitzer (1999), the chair of DSM-III and DSM-III-R, and a consideration for inclusion in DSM-V (Rounsaville et al., 2002). Attractive features of his definition include its conceptual elegance, its evolutionary perspective, and its recognition of the need to include a value judgment along with objective scientific criteria (Rounsaville et al., 2002; Spitzer, 1999).

Wakefield's definition, however, has also received quite a number of compelling critiques (e.g., Bergner 1997; Fulford & Thornton, 2007; Henriques, 2002; Houts, 2001; Jablensky, 2007; Kirmayer & Young 1999; Lilienfield & Marino 1999; McNally, 2001; Widiger & Sankis, 2000). One fundamental limitation is its conjoining with evolutionary theory, thereby limiting its relevance and usefulness to psychodynamic, social-interpersonal, cognitive-behavioral, and even neurochemical models of **etiology** and pathology that concern more proximate dysfunctions (Bergner, 1997; McNally, 2001). In addition, it would be difficult, if not impossible,

---

HIGHLIGHT BOX 4.2

HOMOSEXUALITY

Homosexuality was one of the more controversial diagnoses in the history of the APA diagnostic manual. In DSM-II, any instance of homosexuality was considered a mental disorder. In DSM-III, only those instances in which homosexuality was "ego-dystonic" (i.e., the person is distressed over his or her sexual orientation) was classified as a mental disorder. This revision was fairly successful in subduing the controversy, but it was little more than a political revision. It still allowed clinicians to diagnose homosexuality in persons who were troubled by their sexual orientation (i.e., persons seeking treatment), while not allowing clinicians to diagnose it in persons who objected to the existence of the diagnosis (i.e., were not distressed by their sexual orientation). It wasn't until DSM-IV that homosexuality was not considered to be a mental disorder even if the person found his or her sexual orientation to be distressing.

Homosexuality is usually accompanied by impairments, the most significant one being distress. However, this distress can usually be attributed to the prejudice, discrimination, and even abuse homosexuals receive from other members of the society. The distress often disappears when homosexuals live in a community or society that is accepting and accommodating.

Homosexuals do have one inherent impairment: they are impaired in their ability to consummate a sexual relationship with a member of the opposite sex. However, this impairment is no worse than that of an obligate heterosexual being unable to consummate a sexual relationship with a member of the same sex. In a society that fully accepted both orientations, either impairment would be comparable in level of severity.

Homosexuals do have one unique impairment. They are unable to procreate their own biological child. This is not necessarily a trivial impairment, as many heterosexual couples will testify. However, it is not at all clear that this specific limitation warrants a classification as a mental disorder. In any case, classifying homosexuality as a mental disorder will certainly increase the stress experienced by homosexuals, as it would fuel further discrimination and prejudice.

for clinicians (or for the authors of a diagnostic manual) to determine with any confidence the precise "intentions" of the ongoing process of evolution (Jablensky, 2007; Kirmayer & Young, 1999). More specifically, it is questionable how one could effectively or convincingly use evolutionary theory to determine which conditions should and should not be included within the diagnostic manual. Any such discussion would be so conjectural and speculative that its reliability and validity would be sorely inadequate (McNally, 2001).

Ironically, Wakefield's model might even be inconsistent with some sociobiological models of psychopathology. For example, psychopathology might not always be the result of a failure of a mechanism to perform as intended through evolution. Psychopathology can instead be the result of cultural evolution outstripping the pace of biological evolution, rendering some designed functions that were originally adaptive within earlier time periods maladaptive in the current environment (Lilienfeld & Marino, 1999; Widiger & Sankis, 2000). For example, "the existence in humans of a preparedness mechanism for developing a fear of snakes may be a relic not well designed to deal with urban living, which currently contains hostile forces far more dangerous to human survival (e.g., cars, electrical outlets) but for which humans lack evolved mechanisms of fear preparedness" (Buss, Haselton, Shackelford, Bleske, & Wakefield, 1998, p. 538). Yet, Wakefield (2007) would exclude from the diagnostic manual "danger signals that were adaptive in the past, when failure in such situations could lead to ... a consequent threat to survival" (p. 154) precisely because such phobic reactions represent an internal mechanism performing one of its naturally selected functions.

In addition, missing entirely from Wakefield's (1992, 1997) conceptualization is any reference to dyscontrol. Mental disorders are perhaps better understood as dyscontrolled impairments in psychological functioning (Bergner, 1997; Kirmayer & Young 1999; Klein, 1999; Widiger & Trull,

1991). As Klein (1999) suggested, "Involuntary impairment remains the key inference" (p. 424). Dyscontrol is one of the fundamental features of mental disorder emphasized in Bergner's (1997, 2004) "significant restriction" and Widiger and Sankis's (2000) "dyscontrolled maladaptivity" definitions of mental disorder. To these authors, the concept of a mental disorder implies the presence of impairments to feelings, thoughts, or behaviors over which a normal (healthy) person is considered to have adequate control. They place more emphasis on the absence of adequate control than on the presence of pathology. To the extent that a person willfully, intentionally, freely, or voluntarily engages in harmful sexual acts, drug usage, gambling, or child abuse, the person would not be considered to have a mental disorder. It is when the person effectively loses control of these behaviors and experiences clinically significant impairment that a diagnosis of mental disorder becomes warranted. Persons seek professional intervention in large part to obtain the insights, techniques, skills, or other tools (e.g., medications) that increase their ability to better control their mood, thoughts, or behavior.

Including the concept of dyscontrol within a definition of mental disorder provides a fundamental distinction between mental and physical disorder, as dyscontrol is not a meaningful consideration for, or a fundamental component of, physical disorder. This stands in stark contrast to the definition of Wakefield (2007), who argues that the concept of a mental disorder should "fall under the broader medical concept of disorder" (p. 150). A criticism of dyscontrol as a fundamental component of mental disorder is that it may imply the existence of free will, a concept that is, at best, difficult to scientifically or empirically verify (Bargh & Ferguson, 2000; Howard & Conway, 1986). However, the presence versus absence of free will may have no bearing on the extent to which a person effectively controls his or her behavior, as machines (and organisms) that lack free will also vary in the extent of their behavioral flexibility and their ability to respond effectively to external threats. A person with a mental disorder could be analogous to a computer lacking the necessary software to execute effective programs or combat particular viruses. **Pharmacotherapy** alters the neural connections of the central nervous system (the hardware), whereas psychotherapy alters the cognitions (the software) in a manner that increases a person's behavioral repertoire. A computer provided with new software has not been provided with free will, but it has been provided with more options to act and respond more effectively.

DIAGNOSTIC THRESHOLD

One of the fundamental purposes of a diagnostic manual is to demarcate the boundary between normal and abnormal psychological functioning. Nearly everyone at some point has feelings of anxiety or sadness; many persons smoke cigarettes; many drink alcohol; and many engage in sexual fantasies and behaviors that might be considered to be deviant, or at least idiosyncratic. At what point would these feelings, behaviors, or predilections become a mental disorder? The answer to this question is obviously important, for it has substantial social, clinical, forensic, and public health implications.

In order to be diagnosed with pedophilia, DSM-III-R (American Psychiatric Association, 1987) required only that an adult have recurrent intense urges and fantasies involving sexual activity with a prepubescent child over a period of at least six months and have acted on them (or be distressed by them). The authors of DSM-IV were concerned that these criteria were not providing adequate guidance for determining when deviant sexual behavior reflects a personal preference rather than a mental disorder as every adult who engaged

in a sexual activity with a child for longer than six months would meet these diagnostic criteria (Frances et al., 1995). Deviant or repugnant behavior alone has not traditionally been considered sufficient for a diagnosis (Houts, 2001). Presumably, some persons can engage in deviant, aberrant, and even heinous activities without being compelled to do so by the presence of psychopathology. The authors of DSM-IV, therefore, added the requirement that "the behavior, sexual urges, or fantasies cause clinically significant distress or impairment in social, occupational, or other important areas of functioning" (American Psychiatric Association, 1994, p. 523).

Spitzer and Wakefield (1999), however, argued that the presence versus absence of impairment would not actually distinguish between a normal and abnormal sexual interest in children and may in fact contribute to a normalization of pedophilic and other paraphilic behavior by allowing the diagnoses not to be applied if the persons who engaged in these acts were not themselves distressed by their behavior or did not otherwise experience impairment. In response, Frances et al. (1995) had argued that pedophilic sexual "behaviors are inherently problematic because they involve a nonconsenting person (exhibitionism, voyeurism, frotteurism) or a child (pedophilia) and may lead to arrest and incarceration" (p. 319). Therefore, any person who engaged in an illegal sexual act (for longer than six months) would be experiencing a clinically significant social impairment. However, using the illegality of an act as a basis for identifying the presence of a disorder is problematic. First, it undermines the original rationale for the inclusion of the impairment criterion (i.e., to distinguish immoral or illegal acts from abnormal or disordered acts). Second, it is inconsistent with the stated definition of a mental disorder that indicates that neither deviance nor conflicts with the law are sufficient to warrant a diagnosis (American Psychiatric Association, 1994, 2000).

Wakefield (1997, 2007) has provided further examples that are less socially controversial than pedophilia that may also illustrate a failure to make a meaningful distinction between maladaptive problems in living and true psychopathology due to a sole reliance on indicators of distress or impairment. For example, the DSM-IV-TR criterion set for major depressive disorder currently excludes most instances of depressive reactions to the loss of a loved one (i.e., uncomplicated bereavement). Depression after the loss of a loved one can be considered a mental disorder if "the symptoms persist for longer than two months" (American Psychiatric Association, 2000, p. 356). Allowing two months to grieve before one is diagnosed with a mental disorder might be as arbitrary and meaningless as allowing a person to engage in a sexually deviant act only for six months before the behavior is diagnosed as a paraphilia. In addition, many other losses may lead to depressed mood (e.g., loss of job or physical health), yet these are not treated in the same manner as the loss of a loved one (Wakefield, Schimtz, First, & Horwitz, 2007).

Regier and Narrow (2002) have raised similar concerns regarding the diagnosis of common anxiety and mood disorders. They suggested that the prevalence rates for many of the anxiety, mood, and other mental disorders obtained by the NIMH Epidemiologic Catchment Area program (ECA) and the National Comorbidity Survey (NCS) were excessive. "Based on the high prevalence rates identified in both the ECA and NCS, it is reasonable to hypothesize that some syndromes in the community represent transient homeostatic responses to internal or external stimuli that do not represent true psychopathologic disorders" (Regier et al., 1998, p. 114).

Wakefield and First (2002) have therefore argued that the distinction between disordered and nondisordered behavior requires an assessment for the presence of an underlying internal pathology (e.g., irrational cognitive schema or neurochemical dysregulation), and not simply the presence or degree of impairment (Spitzer & Wakefield, 1999). The inclusion of pathology within diagnostic criterion sets (e.g., irrational cognitive schemas, unconscious defense mechanisms, or neurochemical dysregulations) would be consistent with the definition of mental disorder provided in DSM-IV-TR, which states that the syndrome "must currently be considered a manifestation of a behavioral, psychological, or biological dysfunction in the individual" (American Psychiatric Association, 2000, p. xxxi).

In addition, there is a more general interest in separating the diagnosis of mental disorder from the presence of impairment (Lehman et al., 2002) because (in theory) some disorders could in fact be present in the absence of impairment, analogous to certain medical conditions (e.g., high blood pressure). For instance, even though a person is currently suffering no impairment from a particular phobia of heights, snakes, or water largely because the respective stimuli are not within the person's environment, it might still be useful for such a person to become aware of his or her propensity to be irrationally avoidant prior to an unanticipated exposure. Such a person might be diagnosed with the disorder on the basis of the apparent pathology (e.g., through psychological testing), even though he or she is currently suffering no impairment.

A limitation of diagnosing a disorder on the basis of pathology rather than impairment, however, is that there is currently little agreement over the specific pathology that underlies any particular disorder. There is insufficient empirical support to give preference to one particular cognitive, interpersonal, neurochemical, psychodynamic, or other theoretical model of pathology. The precise nature of this pathology could perhaps be left undefined or characterized simply as an "internal dysfunction" (Wakefield, Pottick, & Kirk, 2002), but an assessment of an unspecified pathology is unlikely to be reliable. Clinicians will have very different perspectives and will make radically different judgments as to the nature and presence of a patient's internal dysfunction.

In addition, the concern of Regier and Narrow (2002) and Wakefield (1997, 2007) that the nomenclature is subsuming normal problems in living may also be misguided. Persons critical of the nomenclature have decried the substantial expansion of the diagnostic manual over the past 50 years (e.g., Caplan, 1995; Haby & Lafner, this volume; Horwitz, 2002; Houts, 2000, 2002; Kutchins & Kirk, 1997). However, perhaps it would have been more surprising to find that scientific research and increased knowledge have failed to lead to the recognition of more instances of psychopathology (Wakefield, 1998). In fact, the current manual might still be inadequate in its coverage. Quite often the most common diagnosis in general clinical practice is not otherwise specified (NOS, Clark, Watson, & Reynolds, 1995). The NOS diagnosis is provided when a clinician has determined that psychopathology is present but the symptomatology fails to meet criteria for any one of the existing disorders. That clinicians are providing the diagnosis of NOS for anxiety, mood, personality, and other disorders is a testament to inadequate coverage. Perhaps the problem is not that depression in response to a loss of a job or physical disorder should not be a disorder, analogous to bereavement (Wakefield, 2007); perhaps the problem is that bereavement should be a mental disorder when the depression is both impairing and dyscontrolled (Bonanno et al., 2007; Forstmeier & Maercker, 2007; Widiger & Sankis, 2000).

Optimal psychological functioning, as in the case of optimal physical functioning, might represent an ideal that is achieved by only a very small minority of the population. The current assumption that only a small minority of the population currently has, or will ever have, a mental disorder (Regier & Narrow, 2002) is questionable. Very few persons fail to have at least some physical disorders, and all persons suffer from quite a few physical disorders during the course of their life. It is unclear why it should be different for mental disorders, as if most persons have been fortunate to have obtained no problematic genetic dispositions or vulnerabilities and have never experienced significant stress, pressure, or conflict that strained or injured their psychological functioning. The rejection of a high prevalence rate of psychopathology may reflect the best of intentions, such as concerns regarding the stigmatization of mental disorder diagnoses (Kutchins & Kirk, 1997) or the potential impact on funding for treatment (Regier et al., 1998), but these social and political concerns could also hinder a more dispassionate and accurate recognition of the true rate of a broad range of psychopathology within the population (Widiger & Sankis, 2000).

CATEGORICAL VERSUS DIMENSIONAL MODELS OF CLASSIFICATION

As stated in DSM-IV, "DSM-IV is a categorical classification that divides mental disorders into types based on criterion sets with defining features" (American Psychiatric Association, 2000, p. xxxi). The intention of the diagnostic manual is to help the clinician determine which particular disorder is present, the diagnosis of which would purportedly indicate the presence of a specific pathology that would explain the occurrence of the symptoms and suggest a specific treatment that would ameliorate the patient's suffering (Frances et al., 1995; Kendell, 1975). However, as expressed by the chair (Dr. Kupfer) and vice chair (Dr. Regier) of DSM-V, the classification system has not been particularly successful in meeting this goal.

In the more than 30 years since the introduction of the **Feighner criteria** by Robins and Guze, which eventually led to DSM-III, the goal of validating these syndromes and discovering common etiologies has remained elusive. Despite many proposed candidates, not one laboratory marker has been found to be specific in identifying any of the DSM-defined syndromes. Epidemiologic and clinical studies have shown extremely high rates of comorbidities among the disorders, undermining the hypothesis that the syndromes represent distinct etiologies. Furthermore, epidemiologic studies have shown a high degree of short-term diagnostic instability for many disorders. With regard to treatment, lack of treatment specificity is the rule rather than the exception. (Kupfer, First, & Regier, 2002, p. xvii)

The existing diagnostic nomenclature does not appear to be identifying qualitatively distinct conditions (Krueger, Markon, Patrick, & Iacono, 2005; Watson & Clark, 2006; Widiger & Samuel, 2005). "In the past 20 years ... the disease entity assumption has been increasingly questioned as evidence has accumulated that prototypical mental disorders such as major depressive disorder, anxiety disorders, schizophrenia, and bipolar disorder seem to merge imperceptibly both into one another and into normality ... with no demonstrable natural boundaries or zones of rarity in between" (Rounsaville et al., 2002, p. 12). The modern effort to demarcate a **taxonomy** of distinct clinical conditions is traced to Kraepelin (1917), but Kraepelin had himself acknowledged that "wherever we try to mark out the frontier between mental health and disease, we find a neutral territory, in which the imperceptible change from the realm of normal life to that of obvious derangement takes place" (p. 295).

Most mental disorders appear to be the result of a complex interaction of an array of interacting biological vulnerabilities and dispositions and environmental, psychosocial events (Rutter, 2003). The symptoms and pathologies of mental disorders appear to be highly responsive to a wide variety of neurochemical, interpersonal, cognitive, and behavioral experiences; unconscious dynamics; and other mediating and moderating variables that help to develop, shape, and form a particular individual's psychopathology profile. This complex

etiological history and individual psychopathology profile are unlikely to be well described by a single diagnostic category that attempts to make distinctions at nonexistent discrete joints along the continuous distributions (Widiger & Samuel, 2005).

A model for the future might be provided by one of the more well-established diagnoses, mental retardation. A dimensional classification of mental disorders is viewed by some as a radical departure, but DSM-IV-TR already includes this compelling precedent. The point of demarcation for the diagnosis of mental retardation is an arbitrary quantitative distinction along the normally distributed levels of hierarchically and multifactorially defined intelligence. The current point of demarcation is an intelligence quotient of 70, along with a clinically significant level of impairment. This point of demarcation is arbitrary in the sense that it does not carve nature at a discrete joint, but it was not randomly or mindlessly chosen (Haslam, 2002). It is a well-reasoned and defensible selection that was informed by the impairments in functioning commonly associated with an IQ of 70 or below (Zachar, 2000).

Many researchers are now turning their attention to the identification of underlying spectra of dysfunction that cut across the existing diagnostic categories (Krueger et al., 2005; Watson & Clark, 2006; Widiger & Samuel, 2005). The first of a series of DSM-V research planning conferences was in fact devoted to identifying the research that would lead the field to a dimensional classification of personality disorder (Widiger, Simonsen, Krueger, Livesley, & Verheul, 2005). Krueger et al. (2005) and Watson and Clark (2006) suggest a revision of the classification of mood, anxiety, substance use, and personality disorders into two broad dimensions of internalizations and externalizations that parallel closely the internalization and externalization distinction proposed for the same reasons many years ago for disorders of childhood by Achenbach (1966, 2002). Widiger and Trull

(2007) have suggested a dimensional classification of the personality disorders that integrates the psychiatric classification of personality disorders with the five-factor model of general personality structure developed within psychology. A four-step procedure for the diagnosis of personality disorders from the perspective of the five-factor model has been developed by Widiger, Costa, and McCrae (2002).

VALUE JUDGMENTS

The DSM-V Researching Planning Nomenclature Work Group asserted that "the most contentious issue is whether disease, illness, and disorder are scientific biomedical terms or are sociopolitical terms that necessarily involve a value judgment" (Rounsaville et al., 2002, p. 3). Wakefield's (1992) definition of mental disorder has been considered innovative in part because it accepts that a definition of mental disorder includes a value judgment (Spitzer, 1999). To some, however, this is simply an admission that the concept of mental disorder is fundamentally flawed as an arbitrary moral judgment relative to local social-cultural values (Maddux, Gosselin, & Winstead, 2008; Sadler, 2005). This is perhaps a misunderstanding of the value component, fed in part by Wakefield (2007) himself suggesting at times that "a condition is a mental disorder only if it is harmful according to social values" (p. 150).

Different societies and cultures (and, of course, the persons within a particular society or culture) will disagree as to what constitutes optimal or pathological biological and psychological functioning (Lopez & Guarnaccia, 2008). An important and difficult issue is how best to understand these differences of opinion (Alarcon et al., 2002; Kirmayer, 2006). Do differences of opinion that are secondary or related to social-cultural values reflect perspectives that have equal validity, or do they reflect differences of opinion that should and can be resolved through scientific research? Maddux et al. (2008) argue that the construct of mental disorder is itself a culture-bound belief that reflects the local biases of Western society and that the science of psychopathology is valid only in the sense that it is an accepted belief system of a particular culture. Speaking from a strict **social constructivist** perspective, "the solution ... is to accept the fact that the problem has no solution — at least not a solution that can be arrived at by scientific means" (Maddux et al., 2008, p. 11).

The value judgment that is inherent to the general concept of mental disorder is not specific to any particular local culture but is instead consistent with the universal value judgment that is inherent to the concept of physical disorder (Widiger, 2002). It is necessary for the survival of the human species to value physical health. In a world in which there were no impairments or threats to physical functioning, the construct of a physical disorder would have no meaning except as an interesting thought experiment. Meaningful and valid scientific research on the etiology, pathology, and treatment of physical disorders occurs because in the world as it currently exists there are real impairments and threats to physical functioning. It is provocative and intriguing to conceive of a world in which physical health and survival would or should not be valued or preferred over illness, suffering, and death, but this form of existence is unlikely to emerge anytime in the near future. Placing a value on adequate or optimal physical functioning is a natural result of evolution within a world in which there are threats to functioning and survival.

Similarly, in the world as it currently exists, there are real impairments and threats to adequate psychological functioning. It is provocative and intriguing to conceive of a society (or world) in which psychological health would or should not be valued or preferred, but this form of existence is also unlikely to emerge anytime in the near future. Placing a value on adequate, necessary, or optimal psychological functioning might be inherent to and a natural result of existing in our world. Any particular definition of what would constitute adequate, necessary, or optimal psychological functioning will be biased to some extent by local cultural values, but this is perhaps best understood as only a local failure to adequately determine what is optimal psychological functioning.

The society that is able to determine most accurately what specifically constitutes healthy biological and psychological functioning will be the society that is most likely to survive, grow, and develop. It is in this precise determination of what constitutes healthy biological and psychological functioning that problematic social and cultural biases can emerge (Lopez & Guarnaccia, 2008), but this effort is not simply the imposition of local social-cultural values. It is an effort that should in fact move past local culture values for the sake of the further growth and development of the species as a whole. Determining what constitutes optimal or healthy psychological functioning is exceedingly difficult in part because this judgment can be distorted by social-cultural biases and personal value judgments, and because this determination must often consider the social and cultural context in which the person is functioning, which at times may itself be unhealthy (Lopez & Guarnaccia, 2008). Optimal psychological health may at times be inconsistent with local social-cultural values. In this regard, what is considered to be disordered is not simply an imposition of or an appeal to local social values, as Wakefield (2007) has suggested. It may in fact be precisely inconsistent with the predominant values of the culture or society. In sum, there may indeed be a factual answer to the question of what constitutes optimal biological and psychological functioning (i.e., an answer that does not simply reflect personal, social, or cultural biases), but the effort to

answer the question is readily susceptible to distortions, errors, and biases secondary to personal, social, and cultural values.

PSYCHOLOGICAL TESTS

"Diagnoses in the rest of medicine are often heavily influenced by laboratory tests" (Frances et al., 1995, p. 22). Laboratory tests within medical practice go beyond the assessment of symptoms. They provide a more direct and objective assessment of an underlying physical pathology. A hope is that laboratory tests could do the same for psychiatry as they have done for other domains of medicine (Rounsaville et al., 2002; Steffens & Krishnan, 2003). "The increasing use of laboratory tests in psychiatric research raises the question of whether and when these tests should be included within the diagnostic criteria sets" (Frances et al., 1995, p. 22).

Substantial attention is being given to structural and functional brain imaging, with the expectation that these instruments could be used eventually to diagnose a psychiatric neurophysiological pathology (Epstein, Isenberg, Stern, & Silbersweig, 2002). However, clearly limiting the potential of these and other neurophysiological measures for incorporation within diagnostic criterion sets is the virtual absence of research indicating their ability to provide independent blind diagnoses. Despite the enthusiasm for their potential diagnostic value, there are currently no studies that have assessed the sensitivity and specificity of neuroimaging techniques for the diagnosis or differential diagnosis of specific mental disorders (Steffens & Krishnan, 2003).

Most sleep disorder specialists use the International Classification of Sleep Disorders (ICSD) developed by the American Sleep Disorders Association (1990). The ICSD requires the use of polysomnographic information for a number of sleep disorders (e.g., time of onset of rapid-eye movement sleep). The 12 DSM-IV-TR sleep disorder diagnoses are coordinated with the

---

HIGHLIGHT BOX 4.3

ASSESSMENT TOOLS

A number of assessment tools are germane to psychological evaluation and diagnosis. Some would suggest that semistructured interviews are at the top of the "assessment hierarchy" in terms of (1) comprehensiveness and breadth, (2) convergence with the DSM-IV, and (3) methodological rigor. These instruments, which exist for both Axis I and II disorders, provide set questions (e.g., "Have you ever intentionally hurt yourself") for the interviewer to use while allowing some flexibility in that the interviewer can ask nonspecified follow-up questions. Due to the explicit congruence between these many measures (e.g., Structured Clinical Interview for DSM Disorders) and the DSM-IV, resultant data can be transformed quite easily into clinical diagnoses. In addition, administration of these broad measures provides coverage of the entirety of the DSM-IV diagnoses, which is often important in both clinical and research work, in that they do not allow initial impressions or symptom reports to guide or bias assessment (i.e., failing to assess for disorders that are not immediately apparent).

More narrowly constructed interviews also exist; these interviews often attempt to gather a greater level of detail about one specific disorder (e.g., Borderline Personality Disorder). As an alternative to interview methodologies, a number of self-report instruments exist and provide information of varying width (e.g., one disorder; 10 disorders; multiple domains of psychopathology), depth, and convergence with the DSM-IV. For instance, the Beck Depression Inventory-II uses 21 questions to cover the array of symptoms often associated with depression (e.g., sadness; frequency of crying). Although this information can be used to inform diagnostic decisions and measure change in depression across time, the scoring is not explicitly tied to the DSM-IV criteria for a Major Depressive Episode. Similarly, the Minnesota Multiphasic Personality Inventory-2 provides information on a variety of psychopathology dimensions, such as depression and paranoia, which are found across clinical diagnoses. While data on these scales are clinically relevant, they are not as explicitly tied to any single DSM-IV diagnosis.

Some view the MMPI-2 approach as a strength in that it recognizes the problematic construct overlap within the current diagnostic system and does not try to re-create it and its substantial comorbidity. Ultimately, decisions regarding the utilization of various assessment tools must take into account extant data pertaining to the reliability and validity of the available assessment instruments (including their relevance to a specific population), as well as constraints imposed by the setting (e.g., assessment time; training) and situation.

ICSD but differ significantly in failing to include polysomnographic diagnostic criteria. Detailed references are made to polysomnographic findings within the text of DSM-IV (and DSM-IV-TR), and its authors acknowledged that "for sleep disorders other than insomnia, such as narcolepsy and sleep apnea, the utility of sleep laboratory testing is widely accepted" (Buysse, Reynolds, & Kupfer, 1998, pp. 1104–1105). Nevertheless, polysomnography findings were not required in DSM-IV because of the extensive cost of the technology and their lack of availability within many clinical settings (Buysse et al., 1998; Frances et al., 1995).

DSM-IV-TR already establishes a precedent for the requirement of test findings obtained by a laboratory specialist. Laboratory tests are fundamental components of the diagnostic criteria for learning disorders and mental retardation. For example, "the essential feature of Mental Retardation is significantly subaverage general intellectual functioning ... [and] general intellectual functioning is defined by the intelligence quotient (IQ or IQ-equivalent) obtained by assessment with one or more of the standardized, individually administered intelligence tests (e.g., Wechsler Intelligence Scales for Children, 3rd Edition; Stanford-Binet, 4th Edition; Kaufman Assessment Battery for Children)" (American Psychiatric Association, 2000, p. 41). Psychological tests administered by a trained specialist using standardized equipment are essentially equivalent to the provision of laboratory testing. A diagnosis of mental retardation by a practicing clinician without the input of individually administered IQ tests would be highly problematic and controversial.

The precedent established by mental retardation and learning disorders should perhaps be extended to other disorders (Widiger & Clark, 2000). "Although diagnostic criteria are the framework for any clinical or epidemiological assessment, no assessment of clinical status is independent of the reliability and validity of the methods used to determine the presence of a diagnosis" (Regier et al., 1998, p. 114). The DSM-III (American Psychiatric Association, 1980) innovation of providing relatively specific and explicit diagnostic criteria is not realized if clinicians do not in fact adhere to the criterion sets and assess them in a comprehensive, systematic, and consistent fashion (Rogers, 2003). Researchers would be hard-pressed to get their findings published if they failed to document that their diagnoses were based on a systematic, replicable, and objective method, yet no such requirements are provided for clinical diagnoses, with the exception of mental retardation and learning disorders. Clinicians generally prefer to rely on their own experience,

expertise, and subjective impressions obtained through **unstructured interviews** (Westen, 1997), but it is precisely this reliance upon subjective and idiosyncratic clinical interviewing that often undermines the reliability and ultimately the validity of clinical diagnoses (Garb, 2005; Rogers, 2003).

One of the new additions to the text of DSM-IV was a section devoted to laboratory and physical exam findings (American Psychiatric Association, 1994). This material was intended to provide the initial step toward the eventual inclusion of laboratory tests within diagnostic criterion sets (Frances et al., 1995). However, a noteworthy exclusion from this text is any reference to psychological tests (Rounsaville et al., 2002; Widiger & Clark, 2000). It is ironic that psychological tests are already included within the criterion sets for mental retardation and learning disorders, yet virtually no reference is made to any psychological test within the sections devoted to laboratory test findings for all other mental disorders (see Highlight Box 4.3).

The discussion of laboratory instruments is confined in DSM-IV-TR to measures of neurophysiology (e.g., functional brain imaging and the dexamethasone suppression test). Unfortunately, semistructured interviews and self-report inventories that assess the cognitive, behavioral, affective, dynamic, or other components of psychological functioning that explicitly comprise the diagnostic criterion sets for these disorders are not included. This is surprising as there is a substantial body of research that provides specificity and sensitivity rates for these psychological tests that are not obtained by the neurophysiological instruments. The semistructured interviews and self-report inventories should at least be acknowledged along with the neurophysiological measures. Perhaps no mention is made of their existence because the inclusion of additional psychological tests within diagnostic criterion sets might have professional implications for the necessary qualifications to render a clinical diagnosis (as in the case of sleep disorders). For example, it is unclear whether many psychiatrists and even some psychologists are sufficiently trained in the administration and interpretation of the most informative and valid psychological tests. However, the American Psychiatric Association has already developed an authoritative guideline for what they consider to be the best "psychiatric" instruments (many of which were developed by psychologists) to use for the assessment of each disorder included within DSM-IV-TR (Rush, First, & Blacker, 2008).

SUMMARY

Nobody is fully satisfied with DSM-IV-TR, and it is not difficult to find harsh critics. Zilboorg's (1941) suggestion that budding nineteenth-century theorists and researchers cut their first teeth by providing a new classification of mental disorders still applies, although perhaps the rite of passage today is to provide a critique of the latest edition of the American Psychiatric Association's diagnostic manual.

Clinicians, theorists, and researchers will at times feel frustrated at being required to use DSM-IV-TR. It can be difficult to obtain a grant, publish a study, or receive insurance reimbursement without reference to a DSM-IV-TR diagnosis. The benefits of an official diagnostic nomenclature do, however, appear to outweigh the costs. Despite its significant flaws, DSM-IV-TR does at least provide a useful point of comparison that ultimately facilitates the development of new ways of conceptualizing and diagnosing psychopathology. Viable alternatives to particular sections of DSM-IV-TR are being developed, some of which will eventually be incorporated within future revisions of the diagnostic manual.

THOUGHT QUESTIONS

4.1. How should the DSM-V be constructed?
4.2. Is homosexuality a mental disorder?
4.3. A 43-year-old man was arrested for having sex with a 6-year-old girl, as was a 17-year-old boy for drinking an entire six-pack of beer. Do they have mental disorders?
4.4. Do we even need a diagnostic manual?
4.5. What would be your definition of a mental disorder?
4.6. Is the diagnosis of a mental disorder an arbitrary value judgment?

Glossary

Criterion sets: A list of symptoms and rules for their application that are specified for the diagnosis of each disorder included in the *Diagnostic and Statistical Manual for Mental Disorders.*

Diagnosis: The establishment, through the use of various assessment procedures, of whether an individual meets the criteria for a psychological disorder. The diagnostic criteria used for this process are most commonly found in the most up-to-date versions of the *Diagnostic and Statistical Manual for Mental Disorders* or the International Classification of Diseases.

Etiology: The cause(s) of a disorder.

Feighner criteria: Published in 1972, Feighner and colleagues at the Department of Psychiatry at Washington University put forth specific diagnostic criteria (i.e., symptoms, decision rules regarding timing of symptoms, number of symptoms present) for 15 psychological disorders. This occurred at a time when the

Diagnostic and Statistical Manual for Mental Disorders provided only general descriptions of the various psychological disorders. This idea, which the *Diagnostic and Statistical Manual for Mental Disorders* later adopted, had a substantial impact on increasing the reliability of psychological diagnoses.

Nomenclature: The names for the constructs (e.g., panic attack) and disorders (e.g., panic disorder) found in the official classification systems for psychological disorders such as the *Diagnostic and Statistical Manual for Mental Disorders* and the International Classification of Diseases.

Paraphiliac: Refers to behavior (e.g., rape) engaged in as part of a paraphilia, which is a class of disorders that the *Diagnostic and Statistical Manual for Mental Disorders-IV* defines as "recurrent, intense, sexually arousing fantasies, sexual urges, or behaviors generally involving 1) nonhuman objects, 2) the suffering or humiliation of oneself or one's partner, or 3) children or other nonconsenting persons that occur over a period of at least 6 months" (APA, 2000, p. 566). Examples of paraphilias include voyeurism, exhibitionism, frotteurism, and pedophilia.

Pharmacotherapy: Use of drugs to treat illnesses or disorders (e.g., depression).

Social constructivist perspective: A theory that suggests that all knowledge or information is specific to an individual culture or place and that reality is subjective. As this applies to psychological disorders, it suggests that behavior, emotions, and/or cognitions considered pathological in one society may be considered more normative in another.

Taxonomy: A classification system. For psychological disorders, the recognized classification system is typically derived from either the *Diagnostic and Statistical Manual for Mental Disorders* or the International Classification of Diseases. When classifying medical or psychological diseases or disorders, the term *taxonomy* is often replaced with "nosology."

Unstructured interviews: Diagnostic interviews without an explicit set of ordered questions to guide the interviewer. Some perceived benefits of this include greater flexibility and spontaneity for the interviewer, although this may come at the cost of decreased reliability.

References

Achenbach, T. M. (1966). The classification of children's psychiatric symptoms: a factor-analytic study. *Psychological Monographs, 80* (No. 615).

Achenbach, T. M. (2002). Empirically based assessment and taxonomy across the life span. In J. E. Hulzer & J. J. Hudziak (Eds.), *Defining psychopathology in the 21st century: DSM-V and beyond* (pp. 155–168). Washington, DC: American Psychiatric Publishing.

Alarcon, R. D., Bell, C. C., Kirmayer, L., Lin, K-H., Ustun, B., & Wisner, K. (2002). Beyond the fun-house mirrors: research agenda on culture and psychiatric diagnosis. In D. J. Kupfer, M. B. First, & D. A. Regier (Eds.), *A research agenda for DSM-V* (pp. 219–281). Washington, DC: American Psychiatric Publishing.

American Psychiatric Association (1980). *Diagnostic and statistical manual of mental disorders* (3rd ed.). Washington, DC: Author.

American Psychiatric Association (1987). *Diagnostic and statistical manual of mental disorders* (3rd ed., rev. ed.). Washington, DC: Author.

American Psychiatric Association (1994). *Diagnostic and statistical manual of mental disorders* (4th ed.). Washington, DC: Author.

American Psychiatric Association (2000). *Diagnostic and statistical manual of mental disorders, Text Revision* (4th ed., rev. ed.). Washington, DC: Author.

American Sleep Disorders Association (1990). *International classification of sleep disorders: diagnostic and coding manual*. Rochester, MN: Author.

Bargh, J. A. & Ferguson, M. J. (2000). Beyond behaviorism: on the automaticity of higher mental processes. *Psychological Bulletin, 126,* 925–945.

Beach, S. R. H., Wamboldt, M. Z., Kaslow, N. J., Heyman, R. E., & Reiss, D. (2006). Relational processes and mental health: a bench-to-bedside dialogue to guide DSM-V. In S. R. H. Beach, M. Z. Kaslow, R. E. Hyman, M. B. First, L. G. Underwood, & D. Reiss (Eds.), *Relational processes and DSM-V: neuroscience, assessment, prevention, and intervention* (pp. 1–18). Washington, DC: American Psychiatric Publishing.

Bergner, R. M. (1997). What is psychopathology? And so what? *Clinical Psychology: Science and Practice, 4,* 235–248.

Bergner, R. M. (2004). An integrative framework for psychopathology and psychotherapy. *New Ideas in Psychology, 22,* 127–141.

Blashfield, R. K., Blum, N., & Pfohl, B. (1992). The effects of changing Axis II diagnostic criteria. *Comprehensive Psychiatry, 33,* 245–252.

Blashfield, R. K., Sprock, J., & Fuller, A. (1990). Suggested guidelines for including/excluding categories in the DSM-IV. *Comprehensive Psychiatry, 31,* 15–19.

Bonanno, G. A., Neria, Y., Mancini, A., Coifman, K. G., Litz, B., & Insel, B. (2007). Is there more to complicated grief than depression and posttraumatic stress disorder? A test of incremental validity. *Journal of Abnormal Psychology, 116,* 342–351.

Buss, D. M., Haselton, M. G., Shackelford, T. K., Bleske, A. L., & Wakefield, J. C. (1998). Adaptations, exaptations, and spandrels. *American Psychologist, 53,* 533–548.

Buysse, D. J., Reynolds, C. F., & Kupfer, D. J. (1998). DSM-IV sleep disorders: final overview. In T. A. Widiger, A. J. Frances, H. A. Pincus, R. Ross, M. B. First, W. Davis, & M. Kline (Eds.), *DSM-IV sourcebook* (vol. a, pp. 1103–1122). Washington, DC: American Psychiatric Association.

Caplan, P. J. (1991). How do they decide who is normal? The bizarre, but true, tale of the DSM process. *Canadian Psychology, 32,* 162–170.

Caplan, P. J. (1995). *They say you're crazy. How the world's most powerful psychiatrists decide who's normal.* Reading, MA: Addison-Wesley.

Caplan, P. J. & Cosgrove, L. (Eds.) (2004). *Bias in psychiatric diagnosis.* New York: Basic Books.

Charney, D. S., Barlow, D. H., Botteron, K., Cohen, J. D., Goldman, D., Gur, R. E., Lin, K-M., Lopez, J. F., Meador-Woodruff, J. H., Moldin, S. O., Nestler, E. J., Watson, S. J., & Zaleman, S. J. (2002). Neuroscience research agenda to guide development of a pathophysiologically based classification system. In D. J. Kupfer, M. B. First, & D. A. Regier (Eds.), *A research agenda for DSM-V* (pp. 31–84). Washington, DC: American Psychiatric Association.

Clark, L. A., Watson, D., & Reynolds, S. (1995). Diagnosis and classification of psychopathology: challenges to the current system and future directions. *Annual Review of Psychology, 46,* 121–153.

Epstein, J., Isenberg, N., Stern, E., & Silbersweig, D. (2002). Toward a neuroanatomical understanding of psychiatric illness: the role of functional imaging. In J. E. Helzer & J. J. Hudziak (Eds.), *Defining psychopathology in the 21st century* (pp. 57–69). Washington, DC: American Psychiatric Press.

Folette, W. C. & Houts, A. C. (1996). Models of scientific progress and the role of theory in taxonomy development: a case study of the DSM. *Journal of Consulting and Clinical Psychology, 64,* 1120–1132.

Forstmeier, S. & Maercker, A. (2007). Comparison of two diagnostic systems for complicated grief. *Journal of Affective Disorders, 99,* 203–211.

Frances, A. J., First, M. B., & Pincus, H. A. (1995). *DSM-IV guidebook.* Washington, DC: American Psychiatric Press.

Frances, A. J., Widiger, T. A., & Pincus, H. A. (1989). The development of DSM-IV. *Archives of General Psychiatry, 46,* 373–375.

Fulford, K. W. M. & Thornton, T. (2007). Fanatical about "harmful dysfunction." *World Psychiatry, 6,* 161–162.

Garb, H. (2005). Clinical judgment and decision making. *Annual Review of Clinical Psychology, 1,* 67–89.

Haslam, N. (2002). Kinds of kinds: a conceptual taxonomy of psychiatric categories. *Philosophy, Psychiatry, & Psychology, 9,* 203–217.

Henriques, G. R. (2002). The harmful dysfunction analysis and the differentiation between mental disorder and disease. *The Scientific Review of Mental Health Practice, 1,* 157–173.

Horwitz, A. (2002). *Creating mental illness.* Chicago: University of Chicago Press.

Houts, A. C. (2000). Fifty years of psychiatric nomenclature: reflections on the 1943 war department technical bulletin, medical 203. *Journal of Clinical Psychology, 56,* 935–967.

Houts, A. C. (2001). Harmful dysfunction and the search for value neutrality in the definition of mental disorder: response to Wakfield, part 3. *Behaviour Research and Therapy, 39,* 1099–1132.

Houts, A. C. (2002). Discovery, invention, and the expansion of the modern diagnostic and statistical manuals of mental disorders. In M. L. Malik & L. E. Beutler (Eds.), *Rethinking the DSM: a psychological perspective* (pp. 17–65). Washington, DC: American Psychological Association.

Howard, G. S. & Conway, C. G. (1986). Can there be an empirical science of volitional action? *American Psychologist, 41,* 1241–1251.

Jablensky, A. (2007). Does psychiatry need an overarching concept of "mental disorders"? *World Psychiatry, 6,* 157–158.

Kendell, R. E. (1975). *The role of diagnosis in psychiatry.* London, England: Blackwell Scientific Publications.

Kirk, S. A. (Ed.) (2005). *Mental disorders in the social environment: critical perspectives.* New York: Columbia University Press.

Kirmayer, L. J. (2006). Beyond the new cross-cultural psychiatry: cultural biology, discursive psychology and the ironies of globalization. *Transcultural Psychiatry, 43,* 126–144.

Kirmayer, L. J. & Young, A. (1999). Culture and context in the evolutionary concept of mental disorder. *Journal of Abnormal Psychology, 108,* 446–452.

Klein, D. F. (1999). Harmful dysfunction, disorder, disease, illness, and evolution. *Journal of Abnormal Psychology, 108,* 421–429.

Kraepelin, E. (1917). *Lectures on clinical psychiatry* (3rd ed.). New York: William Wood.

Krueger, R. F., Markon, K. E., Patrick, C. J., & Iacono, W. G. (2005). Externalizing psychopathology in adulthood: a dimensional-spectrum conceptualization and its implications for DSM-V. *Journal of Abnormal Psychology, 114,* 537–550.

Kupfer, D. J., First, M. B., & Regier, D. A. (Eds.) (2002). *A research agenda for DSM-V*. Washington, DC: American Psychiatric Association.

Kutchins, H. & Kirk, S. A. (1997). *Making us crazy. DSM: the psychiatric bible and the creation of mental disorders*. New York: The Free Press.

Lehman, A. F., Alexopoulos, G. S., Goldman, H. H., Jeste, D. V., Offord, D., & Ustun, T. B. (2002). Mental disorder and disability: time to reevaluate the relationship? In D. J. Kupfer, M. B. First, & D. A. Regier (Eds.), *A research agenda for DSM-V* (pp. 201–218). Washington, DC: American Psychiatric Press.

Lilienfeld, S. O. & Marino, L. (1999). Essentialism revisited: evolutionary theory and the concept of mental disorder. *Journal of Abnormal Psychology, 108,* 400–411.

Lopez, S. R. & Guarnaccia, P. J. (2008). Cultural dimensions of psychopathology: the social world's impact on mental illness. In J. E. Maddux & B. A. Winstead (Eds.), *Psychopathology: foundations for a contemporary understanding*. 2nd ed. (pp. 19–38). Mahwah, NJ: Lawrence Erlbaum.

Maddux, J. E., Gosselin, J. T., & Winstead, B. A. (2008). Conceptions of psychopathology: a social constructionist perspective. In J. E. Maddux & B. A. Winstead (Eds.), *Psychopathology: foundations for a contemporary understanding*. 2nd ed. (pp. 3–18). Mahwah, NJ: Lawrence Erlbaum Associates.

McNally, R. J. (2001). On Wakefield's harmful dysfunction analysis of mental disorder. *Behaviour Research and Therapy, 39,* 309–314.

PDM Task Force (2006). *Psychodynamic diagnostic manual*. Silver Spring, MD: Alliance of Psychoanalytic Organizations.

Pincus, H. A., Frances, A., Davis, W., First, M., & Widiger, T. (1992). DSM-IV and new diagnostic categories: holding the line on proliferation. *American Journal of Psychiatry, 149,* 112–117.

Regier, D. A., Kaelber, C. T., Rae, D. S., Farmer, M. E., Knauper, B., Kessler, R. C., & Norquist, G. S. (1998). Limitations of diagnostic criteria and assessment instruments for mental disorders: implications for research and policy. *Archives of General Psychiatry, 55,* 109–115.

Regier, D. A. & Narrow, W. E. (2002). Defining clinically significant psychopathology with epidemiologic data. In J. E. Hulzer & J. J. Hudziak (Eds.), *Defining psychopathology in the 21st century: DSM-V and beyond* (pp. 19–30). Washington, DC: American Psychiatric Publishing.

Rogers, R. (2003). Standardizing DSM-IV diagnoses: the clinical applications of structured interviews. *Journal of Personality Assessment, 81,* 220–225.

Rosenhan, D. L. (1973). On being sane in insane places. *Science, 179,* 250–258.

Rounsaville, B. J., Alarcon, R. D., Andrews, G., Jackson, J. S., Kendell, R. E., Kendler, K. S., & Kirmayer, L. J. (2002). Toward DSM-V: basic nomenclature issues. In D. J. Kupfer, M. B. First, & D. A. Regier (Eds.), *A research agenda for DSM-V* (pp. 1–29). Washington, DC: American Psychiatric Press.

Rush, A. J., First, M. B., & Blacker, D. (Eds.) (2008). *Handbook of psychiatric measures* (2nd ed.). Washington, DC: American Psychiatric Publishing.

Rutter, M. (2003, October). *Pathways of genetic influences on psychopathology*. Zubin Award Address at the 18th Annual Meeting of the Society for Research in Psychopathology. Toronto, Ontario.

Sadler, J. Z. (2005). *Values and psychiatric diagnosis*. New York: Oxford University Press.

Sartorius, N., Kaelber, C. T., Cooper, J. E., Roper, M., Rae, D. S., Gulbinat, W., Ustun, T. B., & Regier, D. A. (1993). Progress toward achieving a common language in psychiatry. *Archives of General Psychiatry, 50,* 115–124.

Schacht, T. E. (1985). DSM-III and the politics of truth. *American Psychologist, 40,* 513–521.

Schwartz, M. A. & Wiggins, O. P. (2002). The hegemony of the DSMs. In J. Sadler (Ed.), *Descriptions and prescriptions: values, mental disorders, and the DSM* (pp. 199–209). Baltimore, MD: Johns Hopkins University Press.

Spitzer, R. L. (1999). Harmful dysfunction and the DSM definition of mental disorder. *Journal of Abnormal Psychology, 108,* 430–432.

Spitzer, R. L. & Endicott, J. (1978). Medical and mental disorder: proposed definition and criteria. In R. L. Spitzer & D. F. Klein (Eds.), *Critical issues in psychiatric diagnosis* (pp. 15–39). New York: Raven Press.

Spitzer, R. L. & Wakefield, J. C. (1999). DSM-IV diagnostic criterion for clinical significance: does it help solve the false positives problem? *American Journal of Psychiatry, 156,* 1856–1864.

Spitzer, R. L., Williams, J. B. W., & Skodol, A. E. (1980). DSM-III: The major achievements and an overview. *American Journal of Psychiatry, 137,* 151–164.

Steffens, D. C. & Krishnan, K. R. R. (2003). Laboratory testing and neuroimaging: implications for psychiatric diagnosis and practice. In K. A. Phillips, M. B. First, & H. A. Pincus (Eds.), *Advancing DSM: dilemmas in psychiatric diagnosis* (pp. 85–104). Washington, DC: American Psychiatric Association.

Szasz, T. S. (1961). *The myth of mental illness*. New York: Hoeber-Harper.

Wakefield, J. C. (1992). The concept of mental disorder: on the boundary between biological facts and social values. *American Psychologist, 47*, 373–388.

Wakefield, J. C. (1997). Diagnosing DSM-IV—Part I: DSM-IV and the concept of disorder. *Behavioral Research and Therapy, 35*, 633–649.

Wakefield, J. C. (1998). The DSM's theory-neutral nosology is scientifically progressive: response to Follette and Houts (1996). *Journal of Consulting and Clinical Psychology, 66*, 846–852.

Wakefield, J. C. (2007). The concept of mental disorder: diagnostic implications of the harmful dysfunction analysis. *World Psychiatry, 6*, 149–156.

Wakefield, J. C. & First, M. B. (2002). Clarifying the distinction between disorder and nondisorder: confronting the overdiagnosis (false positives) problem in DSM-V. In K. A. Phillips, M. B. First, & H. A. Pincus (Eds.), *Advancing DSM: dilemmas in psychiatric diagnosis* (pp. 23–55). Washington, DC: American Psychiatric Association.

Wakefield, J. C., Pottick, K. J., & Kirk, S. A. (2002). Should the DSM-IV diagnostic criteria for conduct disorder consider social context? *American Journal of Psychiatry, 159*, 380–386.

Wakefield, J. C., Schmitz, M. F., First, M. B., & Horwitz, A. V. (2007). Extending the bereavement exclusion for major depression to other losses — evidence from the National Comorbidity Survey. *Archives of General Psychiatry, 64*, 433–440.

Watson, D. & Clark, L. A. (2006). Clinical diagnosis at the crossroads. *Clinical Psychology: Science and Practice, 13*, 210–215.

Westen, D. (1997). Divergences between clinical and research methods for assessing personality disorders: implications for research and the evolution of Axis II. *American Journal of Psychiatry, 154*, 895–903.

Westen, D. & Shedler, J. (1999). Revising and assessing Axis II, Part I: developing a clinically and empirically valid assessment method. *American Journal of Psychiatry, 156*, 258–272.

Widiger, T. A. (2002). Values, politics, and science in the construction of the DSM. In J. Sadler (Ed.), *Descriptions and prescriptions: values, mental disorders, and the DSM* (pp. 25–41). Baltimore, MD: Johns Hopkins University Press.

Widiger, T. A. (2008). Classification and diagnosis: historical development and contemporary issues. In J. Maddux & B. Winstead (Eds.), *Psychopathology: foundations for a contemporary understanding*. 2nd ed. (pp. 83–101). Mahwah, NJ: Lawrence Erlbaum Associates.

Widiger, T. A. & Clark, L. A. (2000). Toward DSM-V and the classification of psychopathology. *Psychological Bulletin, 126*, 946–963.

Widiger, T. A., Costa, P. T., & McCrae, R. R. (2002). A proposal for Axis II: diagnosing personality disorders using the five factor model. In P. T. Costa & T. A. Widiger (Eds.), *Personality disorders and the five factor model of personality* (2nd ed., pp. 431–456). Washington, DC: American Psychological Association.

Widiger, T., Frances, A., Pincus, H., Davis, W., & First, M. (1991). Toward an empirical classification for DSM-IV. *Journal of Abnormal Psychology, 100*, 280–288.

Widiger, T. A., Frances, A. J., Pincus, H. A., Ross, R., First, M. B., Davis, W. W., & Kline, M. (Eds.) (1998). *DSM-IV sourcebook* (vol. 4). Washington, DC: American Psychiatric Association.

Widiger, T. A. & Samuel, D. B. (2005). Diagnostic categories or dimensions: a question for DSM-V. *Journal of Abnormal Psychology, 114*, 494–504.

Widiger, T. A. & Sankis, L. M. (2000). Adult psychopathology: issues and controversies. *Annual Review of Psychology, 51*, 377–404.

Widiger, T. A., Simonsen, E., Krueger, R., Livesley, J., & Verheul, R. (2005). Personality disorder research agenda for the DSM-V. *Journal of Personality Disorders, 19*, 317–340.

Widiger, T. A. & Trull, T. J. (1991). Diagnosis and clinical assessment. *Annual Review of Psychology, 42*, 109–133.

Widiger, T. A. & Trull, T. J. (1993). The scholarly development of DSM-IV. In J. A. Costa e Silva & C. C. Nadelson (Eds.), *International review of psychiatry* (vol. 1, pp. 59–78). Washington, DC: American Psychiatric Press.

Widiger, T. A. & Trull, T. J. (2007). Plate tectonics in the classification of personality disorder: shifting to a dimensional model. *American Psychologist, 62*, 71–83.

Zachar, P. (2000). Psychiatric disorders are not natural kinds. *Philosophy, Psychiatry, Psychology, 7*, 167–182.

Zilboorg, G. (1941). *A history of medical psychology*. New York: W.W. Norton.

Assessment of Personality

Robert F. Bornstein
Adelphi University

OUTLINE

PERSONALITY ASSESSMENT

Most people associate clinical psychology primarily with psychotherapy, but personality assessment's clinical history is at least as long as that of psychological treatment. Although the first use of the term *mental test* in the psychological literature referred only to intellectual assessment (Cattell, 1890), it did not take long for interest in personality testing to follow. Two years after Cattell's seminal (1890) paper, Kraepelin (1892) described the use of a formal free association test for use with psychiatric patients; several years after that he outlined a series of personality tests designed to quantify basic aspects of character and temperament (Kraepelin, 1895). Most psychologists trace modern personality assessment to the development of Woodworth's Personal Data Sheet during World War I (see Franz, 1919) and to the publication of *Psychodiagnostik*, Hermann Rorschach's (1921) monograph describing procedures for interpreting patients' responses to his now-famous inkblots.

Personality assessment continues to play an important role in contemporary clinical psychology. As Groth-Marnat (1999) pointed out, there are at least 35 different categories of mental health professionals who perform psychological treatment for mental disorders, but only psychologists are trained and qualified to conduct personality assessments. Understanding the basic principles of personality assessment is critical to becoming a competent clinician, and two distinctions are central to this understanding.

The first distinction is between **diagnosis** and **psychological assessment**. Although these terms are sometimes used interchangeably, even in the professional literature, they are actually quite different. Diagnosis involves identifying and documenting a patient's symptoms, with the goal of classifying that patient into one or more categories whose labels represent shorthand descriptors of psychological syndromes (e.g., social phobia, bulimia nervosa, avoidant personality disorder). Assessment, in contrast, involves administering one or more personality tests (and sometimes intellectual and neuropsychological tests as well) to disentangle the complex array of dispositional and situational factors that interact to determine a patient's subjective experiences, core beliefs, coping strategies, and behavior patterns. Put another way, diagnosis is key to understanding a patient's *pathology*; assessment is key to understanding the *person* with this pathology (Bornstein, 2005, 2007).

As is true for diagnosis and assessment, psychologists often use the terms **psychological testing** and **psychological assessment** interchangeably, but they, too, mean very different things. Handler and Meyer (1998, pp. 4–5)

provided an excellent summary of the conceptual and practical differences between psychological testing and psychological assessment. They wrote:

> Testing is a relatively straightforward process wherein a particular test is administered to obtain a particular score or two. Subsequently, a descriptive meaning can be applied to the score based on normative, nomothetic findings.... Psychological assessment, however, is a quite different enterprise. The focus here is not on obtaining a single score, or even a series of test scores. Rather, the focus is on taking a variety of test-derived pieces of information, obtained from multiple methods of assessment, and placing these data in the context of historical information, referral information, and behavioral observations in order to generate a cohesive and comprehensive understanding of the person being evaluated.

Handler and Meyer's (1998) insightful analysis has been echoed and elaborated by numerous clinicians and clinical researchers (e.g., Bornstein, 2007; Groth-Marnat, 1999; Meyer et al., 2001; Widiger & Samuel, 2005). Cates (1999, p. 637) put it well when he noted that in the realm of psychological assessment, "art rests on science." Psychological testing requires precision, objectivity, and the kind of scientific detachment that facilitates accurate data-gathering. Psychological assessment involves integration, synthesis, and clarification of ambiguous — even conflicting — evidence obtained during the testing process. These are skills that cannot be taught directly but must be built up over time, through experience.

This chapter discusses the role of personality assessment in clinical psychology, beginning with a simple but important question: Why assess personality? What unique information does personality assessment provide the clinician? Following this discussion, the major personality assessment methods are described, and techniques for maximizing the validity and utility of assessment data are discussed. Strategies for integrating personality test findings from various sources are then considered, followed by a brief discussion of current controversies in personality assessment.

WHY ASSESS PERSONALITY?

The skeptical clinician (or patient) might wonder how personality assessment data help the clinician do his or her job better — how these data can increase the accuracy of clinical judgment or enhance the effectiveness of psychological treatment. Personality assessment helps the clinician in at least three ways.

Refining Diagnosis

Although personality assessment data by themselves should never be used to render diagnoses, knowing something about a patient's underlying personality structure can help the clinician differentiate between two syndromes with similar or overlapping surface characteristics (see Bornstein, 2001; Huprich & Ganellen, 2006; Weiner, 2000). Assessment data can also inform the clinician regarding the relationships among comorbid symptom patterns and provide evidence regarding which syndrome is "primary" (i.e., onset first) and which syndrome may be — in whole or in part — a consequence of (or "secondary to") the initial diagnosis.

Consider, for example, a patient who reports a history of intermittent depressive episodes and presents during the initial interview with an exaggerated sense of self-importance, inflated self-esteem, and grandiosity. If assessment reveals an underlying narcissistic personality structure, the clinician should consider the possibility that the patient's depressive episodes may be secondary to his or her narcissism, with periods of depression following instances wherein the patient sustained narcissistic injuries or insults (e.g., negative feedback regarding job performance). If assessment reveals low levels of narcissism, the possibility of an underlying narcissistic character cannot be ruled out conclusively, but in this case the clinician should consider more strongly the possibility that the

patient's grandiosity may reflect a bipolar or cyclothymic (rather than narcissistic) process.

Contextualizing Diagnosis

Beyond aiding in differential diagnosis, assessment can help contextualize diagnoses by providing information regarding personality traits that (1) play a role in symptom onset and (2) modify symptom course. For example, two depressed patients may present with similar (even identical) DSM symptoms, but if assessment reveals that one patient is highly dependent whereas the other is more self-critical, the clinician has obtained important information regarding the etiology and dynamics of these patients' ostensibly similar depressions. Studies show that in dependent patients the onset of depression often follows interpersonal conflict or loss (e.g., the breakup of a romantic relationship); in self-critical patients, depression often onsets following work/achievement-related stressors (e.g., failure to get a hoped-for promotion). With respect to syndrome course, research indicates that depressed patients are more likely to make suicide attempts (and suicidal gestures) when they have a self-critical personality style than when their personality style is characterized by excessive dependency (see Bornstein, 2005; Duberstein, Seidlitz, & Conwell, 1996).

Structuring Treatment

A third advantage of combining diagnostic data with assessment data is that assessment data can help structure treatment in ways that diagnostic data cannot. Unless one assumes that psychological treatment should target symptom reduction exclusively with no attention to associated thought processes and personality dynamics, then assessment information is vital in treatment planning. Among the kinds of assessment data useful in this regard are those bearing on the patient's self-concept, underlying and expressed motives, impulse control, defense and coping style, perceptual style, and cognitive complexity.

Consider, for example, two patients with borderline personality disorder (a disorder characterized by relationship instability, emotional lability, and a pattern of self-defeating, self-destructive behavior) who are both undergoing psychotherapy. Though their symptoms are similar, assessment reveals that the first patient is capable of using relatively mature defenses (e.g., intellectualization, rationalization) and has reasonably good impulse control, whereas the second patient relies exclusively on less mature defenses (e.g., projection, denial) and has greater difficulty controlling impulses. Based on these assessment results, the clinician may decide to adopt a relatively unstructured, uncovering treatment strategy in therapy with the first patient, probing and challenging on occasion to help the patient gain insight into the origins and dynamics of her difficulties. The second patient likely requires a more structured and supportive therapeutic approach, with insight taking a back seat to strengthening of defenses and bolstering of coping skills.

MAJOR PERSONALITY ASSESSMENT METHODS

Personality assessment plays a major role in contemporary clinical psychology, but some psychologists contend that assessing behavior directly may be more useful than assessing personality traits that are presumed to underlie patients' behavior patterns and predispositions. **Behavioral assessment** — measurement of an individual's behavior through direct observation or other means (e.g., analysis of the patient's records of daily behaviors kept in diary format) — has the advantage of yielding a quantitative index of behavior frequencies, along with contextual information (e.g., behavioral antecedents and consequences) that can help the psychologist understand the environmental factors that

sustain the behavior in various situations and settings (see Richard & Bobicz, 2003; Richard & Gloster, 2006). Some psychologists advocate use of behavioral assessment in lieu of formal personality assessment; others argue that behavioral and personality assessment data can be usefully combined, yielding a richer picture of patient functioning than would be afforded by either method alone.

Although literally hundreds of different personality tests are used in clinical settings today, the vast majority of these measures fall into one of two categories: **self-report tests** and **free-response tests**. Many self-report tests emerged from what has come to be known as the *psychometric tradition* in personality assessment — a perspective that emphasizes careful construction and empirical validation of personality test items to assess a broad array of traits and behavior patterns. Most free-response tests, in contrast, emerged from a *psychodynamic tradition* wherein responses to ambiguous stimuli (like inkblots) are thought to reveal underlying features of personality that the person cannot (or will not) verbalize directly. In the following sections, the key characteristics of self-report and free-response tests are discussed, and the most commonly used tests in each category are briefly described.

Self-report Tests

Self-report tests (formerly known as *objective tests*) typically take the form of questionnaires wherein patients are asked to (1) acknowledge whether a series of trait-descriptive statements is true of them, or (2) rate the degree to which each of these statements describes them accurately. As McClelland, Koestner, and Weinberger (1989) pointed out, such measures assess "self-attributed" traits, motives, emotions, and need states — characteristics that a patient recognizes in him- or herself and acknowledges as being representative of his or her day-to-day functioning and experience.

The psychological processes involved in responding to self-report test items are, for the most part, consistent across patients and form a predictable sequence. Upon first encountering a self-report personality test item, patients turn their attention inward to determine whether that test statement captures some aspect of their feelings, thoughts, motives, or behaviors. They then engage in a retrospective autobiographical memory search to try to recall instances wherein the feelings, thoughts, motives, or behaviors described in that item were experienced or exhibited. If such instances come to mind easily, the patient is likely to acknowledge that item as being true; if not, the patient is likely to deny that item.

It is important to note in this context that although responses to self-report tests typically begin with introspection and retrospection, another very different process — deliberate self-presentation — often follows. Consider how a patient might respond to the statement "I have difficulty controlling my anger." Even if a patient can recall numerous instances of angry outbursts, that patient could still choose to respond *No* to that item to present him- or herself in a positive light. Conversely, a patient might choose to respond *Yes* to that item even in the absence of anger-related memories if the goal is to appear unhealthy rather than healthy. Thus, self-report personality test scores reflect two related (and sometimes competing) dynamics: (1) the degree to which a patient recognizes a personality trait in him- or herself and (2) the degree to which that patient is willing to acknowledge this trait when asked.

In the sections that follow, the most widely used self-report personality tests in clinical settings are briefly described, along with key references for further information regarding each measure.

Minnesota Multiphasic Personality Inventory–2 (MMPI-2) The original version of the MMPI was published in 1940 and was intended to be a cost-efficient questionnaire for deriving psychiatric diagnoses without having to conduct one-on-one interviews with patients (Hathaway & McKinley, 1940, 1952). Although flaws in initial test development and validation procedures (e.g., overlapping item content in different MMPI subscales, use of psychiatric patients' family members as a nonclinical comparison group) limited the usefulness of the MMPI as a diagnostic tool, it became a widely used measure of personality style in clinical settings. A revised version of the original MMPI — the MMPI-2 — was published in 1989 and includes updated item content and refined scoring and interpretation procedures.

Like its predecessor, the MMPI-2 includes 566 true-false items that comprise ten *clinical scales* assessing various dimensions of personality and psychopathology (e.g., hypochondriasis, masculinity-femininity, paranoia, psychasthenia [obsessiveness]). The MMPI-2 also includes an array of *validity scales* that assess each patient's response style, that is, his or her approach to the test (e.g., being defensive, faking bad, faking good). Rather than using individual clinical scale scores to draw inferences regarding a respondent's personality, MMPI-2 interpretation involves summarizing these scores (along with those of the validity scales) on a summary sheet and interpreting the patient's overall profile — the interrelationships and patterns of elevations among different clinical and validity scales. Additional information regarding MMPI-2 administration, scoring, and interpretation can be found in Butcher (1990) and Graham (2000).

Millon Clinical Multiaxial Inventory–III (MCMI-III) Originally published in 1977 to assess DSM-III (APA, 1980) personality disorder symptoms, the MCMI is now in its third edition (Millon, Millon, & Davis, 1994) and includes 175 true-false items that tap (1) traits and behaviors associated with each

DSM-IV (APA, 1994) personality disorder and (2) symptoms of various clinical syndromes (e.g., psychotic thinking, alcohol abuse). In addition, the MCMI-III includes several validity scales (called *modifying indices*) that provide interpretive context for clinical scale scores. Like MMPI-2 scores, MCMI-III scores are summarized in the form of a visual profile to facilitate pattern analysis and interpretation. Although the MCMI-III is of limited use as a diagnostic tool because many of its subscales yield a high proportion of false positive diagnoses, it continues to be widely used as an index of personality disorder–related traits and predispositions. Further information regarding use of the MCMI-III in clinical settings is provided by Millon et al. (1994) and Strack and Millon (2007).

Personality Assessment Inventory (PAI) Morey's (1991) PAI was designed in part to be a psychometrically improved variant of the MMPI. To accomplish this goal, its developers employed more stringent item development procedures than were used in the development of the MMPI, along with a 4-point response scale that allowed for greater variation (and enhanced precision) in patients' self-reports regarding the degree to which a given PAI statement characterizes their day-to-day functioning and behavior. The PAI's 344 items assess various dimensions of psychopathology and interpersonal functioning (e.g., anxiety, paranoia, warmth) that can be combined using pattern analysis to draw conclusions regarding patients' personality, social adjustment, and treatment-related behavior. Among the potential advantages of the PAI as an index of personality traits are its well-validated validity scales and its interpretive focus on clinical and risk-management issues (Kurtz & Blais, 2007). Detailed discussions of PAI administration, scoring, and interpretation are provided by Morey (1991, 2003).

NEO Personality Inventory–Revised (NEOPI-R) The NEOPI-R is a 240-item questionnaire designed to tap five major dimensions (or *factors*) of personality that have frequently emerged in studies of people's descriptions of themselves and others: neuroticism, extraversion, openness, agreeableness, and conscientiousness. Patients respond to each NEOPI-R item on a 5-point disagree-agree scale; the measure is also available in an "other report" format (Form O) wherein individuals who know the patient well complete the scale to describe the patient's characteristic patterns of behavior. Although much research involving the NEOPI-R has focused on the five major factors, in recent years clinicians and researchers have devoted increasing attention to interpreting the array of more specific behavior patterns (typically called *facets*) that comprise each factor. The cross-cultural generalizability of NEOPI-R has also been a topic of considerable interest and is regarded as a particular strength of the instrument. Information regarding use of the NEOPI-R in personality assessment is provided by Costa and McCrae (1992), Costa and Widiger (1994), and Widiger and Lowe (2007).

California Psychological Inventory (CPI) Originally developed by Gough (1957, 1987) to assess normal (nonpathological) features of personality, the current version of the CPI is a shortened version of the original instrument and includes 434 of the original 480 true-false items. The CPI yields scores for 20 separate dimensions of personality (e.g., dominance, empathy, tolerance, flexibility), along with scores for three personality *vectors* — externality/internality, norm doubting/norm favoring, and ego integration — that are conceptualized as underlying temperament-like variables that help shape and direct the behavioral tendencies reflected in the personality scales themselves. Like many of the self-report tests already discussed, the CPI includes a set of validity scales that helps place each patient's personality profile in context, providing information regarding each patient's approach to the test (e.g., faking bad, faking good). A detailed discussion of CPI administration, interpretation, and scoring is provided by Gough and Bradley (1996) and Megargee (2002).

Free-response Tests

Psychological measures that require patients to interpret ambiguous stimuli have long been labeled *projective tests*, but because the degree to which projection shapes responses to these stimuli is unclear, more recently these instruments have been described as free-response tests (see Bornstein, 2007; Meyer et al., 2001). As McClelland et al. (1989) noted, free-response tests assess "implicit" aspects of personality, that is, traits, motives, and need states that shape behavior automatically and reflexively, often without any awareness on the patient's part that his or her responses are affected by these factors. In this context McClelland et al. (1989, pp. 698–699) suggested that free-response tests:

> provide a more direct readout of motivational and emotional experiences than do self-reports that are filtered through analytic thought and various concepts of self and others, [because] implicit motives are more often built on early, prelinguistic affective experiences, whereas self-attributed motives are more often built on explicit teaching by parents and others as to what values or goals it is important for a child to pursue.

Whatever the specific nature of the ambiguous stimuli may be (e.g., inkblots, drawings), the fundamental challenge confronting the patient engaged in a free-response test is to attribute meaning to stimuli that can be interpreted in multiple ways. Free-response tests often have complex scoring criteria and require extensive training and experience to administer and interpret properly. Although free-response tests in

general — and the Rorschach Inkblot Method (RIM) in particular — have been criticized vociferously in recent years (e.g., Hunsley & Bailey, 1999; Wood, Lilienfeld, Nezworski, & Garb, 2001), evidence confirms that when scoring criteria are constructed carefully and validated properly, free-response tests can yield valid and reliable information regarding a patient's cognitive style, coping resources, and underlying personality structure (see Bornstein & Masling, 2005; Huprich, 2006; Viglione 1999; Weiner, 2000).

In the sections that follow, the most widely used free-response personality tests in clinical psychology today are briefly described, along with key references for further information regarding each measure.

Rorschach Inkblot Method (RIM) Originally developed by Hermann Rorschach nearly 90 years ago, the RIM stimulus materials consist of ten bilaterally symmetrical inkblots: five black and white; two black, red, and white; and three multicolored. Test administration consists of two phases. In the *free association* phase, the examiner presents the cards to the patient one at a time, in order, with minimal instructions (the typical introductory statement upon presenting the first card to the patient is, "What might this be?") and with little guidance from the examiner as to appropriate types or numbers of responses. The examiner records verbatim each description offered by the patient, so that in the *inquiry* phase the examiner can read back the patient's descriptions one at a time, asking the patient to explain where in the inkblot he or she saw each image and what aspects of the inkblot caused him or her to see it that way. The examiner also records the patient's explanations word-for-word to facilitate scoring (Exner & Weiner, 1986).

A vast array of structural and content variables can be scored from an RIM protocol. Structural variables typically reflect the more cognitive/perceptual components of RIM responses (e.g., whether the entire inkblot or only part of the inkblot was used, whether there is a good or poor fit between the image and the parts of the inkblot where it was perceived), whereas content variables reflect the thematic imagery of RIM responses (e.g., whether the response included people, whether the response included violent activity). These structural and content variables are then combined into various ratios and percentages that yield information regarding a broad array of clinically relevant issues (e.g., impulse control, suicidality, experienced stress). Although the most common method for scoring and interpreting RIM data is Exner's (1993) *Comprehensive System*, a number of other RIM scoring systems are also available (Bornstein & Masling, 2005). Additional information regarding RIM scoring and interpretation is provided by Exner and Erdberg (2005) and Huprich (2006).

Thematic Apperception Test (TAT) The TAT was originally developed by Henry Murray (1943) and consists of 31 cards, 30 of which depict various scenes and 1 of which is blank. Cards are grouped into those appropriate for girls and women (GF cards), boys and men (BM cards), and those appropriate for both genders. The typical TAT protocol in most clinical settings includes 20 or fewer cards selected based on the patient's gender and age and on the nature of the referral question. (Unlike the RIM, different TAT cards are intended to tap different themes, issues, and interpersonal conflicts.) In introducing the TAT, the examiner usually describes it as a test of "imagination," and the patient is encouraged to tell detailed stories which include (1) what has led up to the scene depicted on the card; (2) what is happening at that moment; (3) what the characters are thinking and feeling; and (4) what the final outcome will be. Traditional TAT scoring involves assessing the primary *needs* (i.e., motives and goals) and *press* (i.e., factors that promote or inhibit the attainment of these goals) of the main character (sometimes called the "hero"). However, in recent years several alternative TAT scoring systems have been developed, the most influential of which are Westen, Lohr, Silk, Gold, and Kerber's (1989) Social Cognition and Object Relations Scale (SCORS) and Cramer's (1991) Defense Mechanism Manual (DMM). Information regarding TAT scoring and interpretation is provided by Aronow, Weiss, and Reznikoff (2001) and Teglasi (2001).

Sentence Completion Tests Several sentence completion tests are used in clinical settings, including Rotter's Incomplete Sentences Blank (ISB, Rotter, Lah, & Rafferty, 1992), Loevinger's Sentence Completion Test (SCT, Loevinger, 1985), and Lanyon's Incomplete Sentences Test (IST, Lanyon & Lanyon, 1980). These tests share a common format: the patient is presented with a form listing a series of incomplete sentences and is asked to complete each however he or she chooses. Typical incomplete sentences include "I like...", "I want to know...", "Back home...", and "I regret...". Unlike the RIM and TAT, there are no well-validated scoring systems for quantifying and integrating the results of a sentence completion test. Instead, the examiner interprets the patient's responses informally, in the context of results obtained from other personality tests, with sentence completion responses used to confirm and amplify the conclusions obtained via these other, more extensively validated measures. Additional information regarding the use of sentence completion tests in clinical settings is provided by Hy and Loevinger (1996) and Lanyon and Goodstein (1997).

Projective Drawings The first modern use of projective drawings was by Goodenough (1926),

HIGHLIGHT BOX 5.1

DESIGNING AN ASSESSMENT BATTERY

Once upon a time most assessment batteries looked pretty much the same: the clinician would administer a self-report personality test (usually the MMPI), a free-response test (almost always the RIM, sometimes accompanied by the TAT), an intelligence test, and a brief neurological screen. Things have changed in the age of managed care, and now the clinician must justify the inclusion of each assessment instrument, explaining how each measure helps answer the question(s) being addressed in the assessment and how each measure adds incremental validity to the battery, providing unique information not provided by any other measure (see Acklin, 2002; Weiner & Greene, 2008).

Although experienced clinicians sometimes bemoan the demise of the standard assessment battery, use of more personalized batteries is in many ways a good thing. It forces the assessor to think more carefully about the purpose of each test he or she administers, compels the assessor to select tests that have adequate construct validity data and norms, and helps make designing an assessment battery a more mindful, goal-driven process. Two principles should be used to select tests for inclusion in an assessment battery:

1. The referral question

On occasion a psychiatrist, family physician, school counselor, or other referral source will simply ask a psychologist to conduct an assessment, with no specific question to be addressed. Often the referrer frames this request as an attempt to "find out if there are any psychological issues I should be aware of." Such a question is not really answerable (it is simply too vague), so when this occurs, the psychologist must contact the referring colleague and try to determine what specific issues are to be addressed in the assessment. After all, it is no more reasonable to send a patient for an open-ended "psychological assessment" than it would be to send a patient to a physician and ask that physician to conduct some unspecified "medical tests."

The request for a specific referral question is likely to bring one of three responses. First, the referring colleague may indicate that he or she had no particular question in mind but that, hopefully, psychological testing will help him or her better understand the patient. This situation represents an opportunity for the psychologist to educate the referrer as to the nature and goals of psychological assessment.

Second, the referring colleague may describe an inappropriate question — one that cannot be addressed via psychological assessment (e.g., he or she may want to know whether the patient will adhere to a medication regimen or whether the patient's marriage is likely to succeed). Again, this represents an opportunity to help the referring colleague understand what psychological testing can and cannot do.

The third possibility is that the referrer will, upon being asked, describe a question or issue that can reasonably be addressed via psychological assessment. If, for example, a psychiatrist would like psychological testing to delineate the underlying personality style of a substance-abusing or bulimic patient or help determine whether a depressed patient is likely to engage in self-destructive (e.g., suicidal) behavior, these questions can be addressed via a combination of self-report and free-response test data.

HIGHLIGHT BOX 5.1   (*continued*)

2. The types of information provided by each test
    Although each test must contribute unique information, it is also useful to include in the battery tests that assess similar constructs in different ways. As noted earlier, there is much to be learned about a patient by scrutinizing the degree to which scores on different measures of similar constructs converge or diverge. Thus, even though many assessment batteries still include both self-report and free-response personality tests, the way in which these test results are interpreted has changed over the years, with clinicians exploring more systematically the meaning of test score divergences (e.g., discontinuities between self-report and free-response indicators of impulse control, defense effectiveness, and other clinical indicators).

    In exploring test score convergences and divergences, two general classes of personality tests may be used. First, it is often useful to include two comprehensive "omnibus" tests, each of which addresses a broad range of personality variables, but in different ways (e.g., the PAI and RIM). This enables the clinician to determine the degree to which a given patient shows general consistency between expressed (self-reported) and underlying (free-response-based) traits. Second, it may be useful to include more narrow instruments that assess one variable (or a small number of variables) specifically related to the referral question (e.g., the Beck Depression Inventory [Beck & Steer, 1983], the Rosenberg [1965] Self-Esteem Scale, Spielberger's [1989] State-Trait Anxiety Inventory). This enables the clinician to determine the degree to which these particular traits and experiences show consistency across assessment modality (e.g., whether self-reported anxiety or self-esteem scores are consistent with RIM-derived indices of these variables).

---

who evaluated children's intelligence by assessing the level of detail and conceptual sophistication in their drawings of a man. Several decades later, psychoanalytic clinicians adapted Goodenough's technique and used it to assess latent (i.e., unconscious) aspects of children's psychological functioning, including their wishes, fears, conflicts, and mental representations of self and significant others. Several projective drawing methods remain in use today, although these are generally only included in test batteries for children through their early teens. Current projective drawing methods include Machover's (1949) Draw a Person (DAP) technique, Buck's (1948) House-Tree-Person (HTP) technique, and Burn's (1982) Kinetic Family Drawing (KFD). Extending Goodenough's original method, the DAP asks the patient to draw a person of the same gender (with no stick figures allowed). The HTP asks the patient to draw a scene including a house, a tree, and a person (the relations among which are then interpreted using a psychodynamic framework), while the KFD asks the patient to draw the members of his or her family doing something together (with the drawing then used as a stimulus to encourage the patient to describe different family members, their roles, and characteristic interaction patterns). Evidence for the construct validity and clinical utility of projective drawings is mixed; information regarding the uses and limitations of these methods is provided by Leibowitz (1999) and Sopchak, Sopchak, and Kohlbrenner (1993).

MAXIMIZING THE VALIDITY AND UTILITY OF ASSESSMENT

Any useful personality test must provide documented evidence of *construct validity*—evidence that the test actually measures the trait(s) it purports to assess. Because personality traits are theoretical constructs that cannot be observed directly, documenting the construct validity of a personality test can be challenging. Among the other types of validity evidence that should be described in the manual accompanying every personality test are **convergent validity** (test scores should be positively associated with theoretically related variables) and **discriminant validity** (test scores should be unrelated to variables that are theoretically distinct from the construct being assessed), **concurrent validity** (test scores should be able to predict current behavior if the test is designed to assess some aspect of functioning in the here-and-now), and **predictive validity** (test scores should be able to predict future behavior if the test is designed to assess some aspect of future functioning, such as risk for future depression).

In addition to providing evidence of various aspects of validity, any useful personality test should also provide evidence of **retest reliability** (most personality test scores should be stable over periods of several months or longer) and **inter-rater reliability** (for tests wherein patients' responses are open-ended and must be evaluated or rated by the clinician, there should be evidence that two scorers unaware

of each other's evaluations come to similar conclusions). Detailed discussions of validity and reliability in personality tests are provided by Butcher (2002), Lanyon and Goodstein (1997), McIntire and Miller (2007), and Weiner and Greene (2008).

In addition to good validity and reliability evidence, the utility of a personality test depends on the adequacy of the available **norms** for that test — the average scores and typical score distributions obtained by patients with known characteristics. For example, even if a test of obsessiveness yields scores that can potentially range from 0 to 50, it does not follow that a patient who obtains a score of 40 is necessarily highly obsessive. To interpret this patient's test score, one must know the norms for that test so that the patient's score can be compared to that of other patients. Moreover, the greater the specificity of the available norms, the more confidence the clinician can have in interpreting a patient's test score. Thus, tests that provide norms for psychiatric inpatients within relatively narrow age ranges and socioeconomic statuses (and separately by gender and ethnic background) are easier to interpret than tests that simply provide average scores for "psychiatric inpatients."

For personality measures that include multiple subscales, norm-based test score interpretation can be aided by use of *scaled scores* (sometimes called *standardized scores*). When scaled scores are used, the mean score on each subscale is set at a fixed number, regardless of the number of items in that subscale, or patients' average raw score on that scale. For example, because different MMPI-2 scales have different numbers of items and yield very different means, raw scores on the MMPI-2 are converted to scaled scores prior to interpretation (for the MMPI-2, *T scores*, which have a mean of 50 and a standard deviation of 10, are used). Thus, by definition each MMPI-2 subscale has the same standard score mean, making it easier to compare a patient's performance across subscales.

In evaluating the construct validity of a personality test, two caveats should be kept in mind. First, no test is perfect, and no test is likely to produce flawless construct validity data in every domain or provide norms that approximate every type of patient one might ever encounter. Thus, the clinician should realistically seek tests that show good construct validity, not perfect construct validity.

Second, even if a test does show excellent construct validity evidence in validation studies, it is still up to the clinician to administer, score, and interpret the test in ways that maximize its utility within the particular setting in which it is being used. In other words, it is possible that a test can be valid in the laboratory, or in the setting in which it was initially developed, but still not yield useful data in a particular setting for a particular patient. Three strategies will help the clinician maximize the validity and utility of any assessment tool.

Using Standardized Procedures

Ironically, using standardized procedures tends to be a greater challenge for experienced testers than novice ones. When a clinician is first learning to administer and score personality tests, there is a natural tendency to "go by the book," adhering closely to guidelines described in the test manual. With experience, however, confidence grows, and the clinician is more likely to depart from the guidelines and "freelance," making subtle changes in test administration that can have a powerful impact on test results. The best defense against this tendency is to recall Handler and Meyer's (1998) advice and remember that personality testing is intended to be a standardized, almost mechanical procedure. The clinician's intuition, expertise, and personal insight should come

into play when test scores are interpreted and integrated, not while test data are being collected.

Minimizing Self-presentation Effects

Many patients strive to respond to personality test items as accurately as possible, but some deliberately try to present themselves in an overly positive way (sometimes called "faking good") or in a negative way ("faking bad"). There are many reasons patients fake good, including trying to impress the tester, avoid treatment (or gain discharge from the hospital), or obtain a job (if personality assessment is part of a prescreening process). Similarly, patients fake bad for many reasons, and these may include attempting to obtain treatment (or remain in the hospital) or avoid responsibility for past actions (if testing is taking place in a forensic setting).

Some personality tests such as the MMPI-2 have built-in scales to assess faking good and faking bad (as well as other self-presentation strategies patients may use), but it is still up to the clinician to minimize self-presentation effects throughout the testing procedure. Useful strategies in this regard include taking time to develop a rapport with the patient before testing begins, explaining the goals of testing in a way the patient can understand, letting the patient know who will (and will not) have access to test results, and engaging the patient in the testing procedure in such a way that patient and tester are data-gathering allies rather than adversaries (Finn, 2005; Handler & Hilsenroth, 1998). In this latter realm, it is particularly helpful to inform the patient before testing begins that the two of you will meet once the test results have been scored and interpreted to discuss the findings. Curiosity alone is enough to motivate many patients to cooperate during testing in the hope they will learn something interesting about themselves afterward.

Managing Tester Expectancy Effects

Clinicians, like patients, sometimes have difficulty entering into the testing situation without biases, expectations, and hidden agendas. Numerous studies have shown that clinicians bring to their work all sorts of preconceptions regarding particular patients — stereotypes, really — based on various patient characteristics. Age, gender, ethnic background, socioeconomic status, and sexual orientation are among the patient characteristics that have been shown to influence clinicians' expectations, creating unintended "expectancy effects" that subtly bias the way personality test data are obtained, recorded, and interpreted.

Expectancy effects can be minimized simply by being aware that they exist and reminding oneself periodically not to let preexisting beliefs affect how one perceives a given patient's behavior. However, studies also show that stereotypes about people — once internalized — can never really be fully overcome and can affect our behavior in ways we cannot see, much less fully control (see Nosek, Greenwald, & Banaji, 2005). Hence, we can see the importance of rule-guided, by-the-book test administration and scoring. Only when the clinician approaches testing as an objective standardized procedure can subtle expectancy effects truly be managed (though never eliminated altogether).

INTEGRATING PERSONALITY TEST DATA

Personality test data are like medical test results. Viewed in isolation, any piece of personality test data yields limited information, but when these data are combined with other sources of information, patterns begin to emerge. So it is with medical test data: the results of a blood test or an electrocardiogram by themselves are usually somewhat ambiguous, but when these different sources of data are contextually integrated, the picture becomes clearer.

Integrating personality test data involves two related tasks. First, the clinician must combine results from different personality tests (self-report, free response, etc.) to derive a more complete picture of the patient's personality dynamics. Second, the clinician must combine personality test data with other sources of information (e.g., diagnostic information, life history data) to place these data in context.

Combining Data from Different Personality Tests

Most clinicians — especially beginning clinicians — intuitively value converging results from different personality tests, in part because converging results are reassuring and increase their confidence in test-derived clinical predictions. Moreover, until relatively recently most writing on test score integration focused primarily on test score convergences (e.g., Campbell & Fiske, 1959; Scott & Johnson, 1972). Only within the past 15 years or so have psychologists written extensively on interpreting test score divergences as well as convergences (e.g., Archer & Krishnamurthy, 1993a, 1993b; Bornstein, 2002; Meyer, 1996, 1997), with most of these writings focusing on divergences between self-report and free-response test scores. As Meyer (2000) and Meyer et al. (2001) noted, when different personality assessment tools use different formats and engage different psychological processes in the testee, divergences in scores on these tests can be particularly informative, with each test adding **incremental validity** (i.e., unique information not provided by any other measure) to the assessment battery.

Consider, for example, a series of studies wherein Bornstein and his colleagues found that discontinuities between self-report and free-response dependency test scores provided important information regarding personality dynamics that neither test alone could provide (Bornstein, 1998; Bornstein, Bowers, & Bonner, 1996a, 1996b; Bornstein, Rossner, Hill, & Stepanian, 1994). These studies were all based on an oft-observed pattern: although many patients obtain consistently high (or consistently low) scores on self-report and free-response dependency tests, some patients score high on one type of test but low on the other (see Bornstein, 2002, 2005). Those who obtain high free-response but low self-report dependency scores have a personality style characterized by *unacknowledged dependency*; those who obtain the reverse pattern — low free-response but high self-report dependency scores — have a *dependent-self presentation*, exaggerating dependent feelings and urges as a means of obtaining rewards in social and work relationships. Moreover, college students who score high on self-report and free-response dependency tests tend to have high levels of dependent personality disorder symptoms, whereas students who obtain high free-response but low self-report dependency scores tend to have histrionic rather than dependent features (Bornstein, 1998). Similar conclusions have emerged in studies contrasting self-report and free-response measures of other personality traits, including need for power (Koestner, Weinberger, & McClelland, 1991), achievement (Spangler, 1992), and intimacy (Craig, Koestner, & Zuroff, 1994).

Combining Personality Test Data with Other Sources of Information

Three other sources of information are potentially useful in this context: diagnostic data, the results produced by other psychological tests, and life history data, (e.g., intelligence tests, neuropsychological measures). By combining personality test data with diagnostic information, the clinician can obtain a more complete picture of the psychological processes that underlie a patient's difficulties and areas of strength that can be drawn upon during therapy. As noted earlier, even within a diagnostic category there is considerable variability in patients' intra- and interpersonal functioning, and personality test data can help identify salient underlying personality dynamics that have implications for treatment, risk management, and other clinical issues.

The same is true of combining personality test data with information derived from intellectual and neurological testing. For example, intellectual testing may reveal that one patient suffering from post-traumatic stress disorder (PTSD) is well above average in both verbal and quantitative intelligence, whereas another patient with similar PTSD symptoms is below average in intelligence; studies show that high IQ is linked with faster and more complete recovery from various forms of PTSD (see Blanchard & Hickling, 2004; Taylor, 2006). Along somewhat different lines, neuropsychological assessment may indicate difficulties in the processing and integration of visual information (e.g., due to abnormalities in the functioning of the occipital cortex), which would suggest that a schizotypal patient's aberrant perceptions are due in part to neurological rather than psychological factors.

Finally, integrating personality test data with life history information can not only help clarify individual test results but also provide a context for interpreting test score discontinuities. For example, knowing that a particular patient was raised in a chaotic, dysfunctional household wherein one or both parents were often absent or psychologically unavailable can help the clinician better understand test results that indicate this patient has a pronounced need for control over the environment. Knowing that another patient was raised in a home where both parents were highly religious and adhered rigidly to fundamentalist tenets regarding acceptable moral behavior can help explain why that patient might produce a relatively benign MMPI-2 record with a defensive validity scale profile, along with an RIM protocol characterized by evidence of powerful underlying affect and barely contained impulses.

HIGHLIGHT BOX 5.2

THERAPEUTIC ASSESSMENT

Traditionally, psychological assessment has been viewed as a method for systematically gathering information regarding a patient's psychological functioning prior to the start of therapy to help refine diagnoses and formulate a treatment plan. Therapeutic assessment (TA), developed by Finn and his colleagues in the early 1990s (e.g., Finn & Tonsager, 1992), alters the focus of assessment by recognizing that beyond supplying critical information, assessment can have therapeutic value in and of itself. TA conceptualizes assessment as a collaborative process rather than one driven exclusively by the clinician. As Tharinger, Finn, Wilkinson, and Schaber (2007, p. 297) noted, TA differs from traditional psychological testing "in its explicit goal of leaving clients positively changed at the end of an assessment. This goal is achieved through an ongoing focused dialogue between clients and assessors, which can lead to the 'coauthoring' of a 'new story' about the clients, their strengths, their significant relationships, and their problems in living."

TA has been applied to patients with a broad array of diagnoses and presenting problems (e.g., patients with attention deficit disorder, children with behavior problems, eating-disordered patients, survivors of child sexual abuse) and has been used effectively in inpatient, outpatient, and educational settings. Three features of TA stand out.

Collaborative Interpretation

In contrast to traditional assessment, in TA the interpretation of test results is a collaborative endeavor involving input from both patient and clinician. When conclusions from a given test (or set of tests) are reasonably clear and unambiguous, the clinician typically offers the patient an interpretation of these test results and asks the patient for his or her impressions. When conclusions from a given test are less clear, the clinician may offer two or more tentative interpretations and work with the patient to determine which interpretation seems most accurate and useful.

Assessment as a Means of "Getting Unstuck"

Although psychological assessment usually takes place prior to the start of psychotherapy, periodic assessments may sometimes occur at various points during treatment to gauge progress, quantify changes in salient domains of personality and psychopathology, and refine the treatment plan. As Finn (2003) noted, an additional advantage of TA in this context is that it represents an opportunity for patient and therapist to step back, gain perspective, and "get unstuck" during those moments when therapy appears to have reached a temporary impasse.

HIGHLIGHT BOX 5.2   (*continued*)

Engagement through Feedback

By shifting the interpretation of test results from a clinician-driven process to a collaborative process, patients are empowered and assume greater "ownership" of assessment results. Collaborative interpretation not only enables patients to gain insight regarding their strengths, and the challenges they face, but because these insights are formulated by clinician and patient working together, patients become more fully engaged in the treatment process.

CURRENT CONTROVERSIES IN PERSONALITY ASSESSMENT

As is true of any widely studied, rapidly evolving topic with important social implications, contemporary personality assessment is characterized by a number of ongoing controversies and areas of dispute. Three stand out.

Validity of Free-response Test Data

Although free-response tests in general — and the RIM in particular — have been criticized vociferously in recent years (e.g., Wood et al., 2001), the situation is more complex than many of these critiques suggest. It is true that there have been numerous instances wherein free-response test results have been used to make clinical predictions that were not grounded in the results of controlled empirical studies. Even today, clinicians who depart from standardized test administration, scoring, and interpretation procedures may sometimes draw incorrect and unwarranted conclusions from free-response test data. However, evidence confirms that when free-response test data are collected using appropriate methods, scored using established guidelines and norms, and interpreted according to the results of sound construct validity studies, these data can increase the accuracy of clinical prediction in numerous ways. Among the dimensions usefully assessed using free-response test results are those related to thought disorder, impulse control, stress tolerance, perceptual style, defense style, implicit motives, object representations, and psychotherapy potential (Bornstein & Masling, 2005; Cramer, 2006; Exner & Erdberg, 2005; Huprich, 2006; Silverstein, 2007).

Thus, the best way to think about the validity of free-response test data is to move beyond a global "Is this test valid?" debate and frame the issue in a more precise and nuanced way: For what types of questions can this test provide useful information, and what scoring and interpretation procedures are available to address these questions? By doing this, psychologists can move beyond entrenched positions and evaluate the validity of free-response test data in a more useful and constructive manner.

Cost-effectiveness of Personality Assessment

During the past several decades, it has become increasingly difficult for clinicians to be reimbursed for psychological assessments under the auspices of managed care; when reimbursements are forthcoming, they are often so modest that psychological testing is virtually a pro bono activity (the exception to this trend being neuropsychological testing, which continues to be reimbursed at reasonably high rates). Moreover, while use of certain psychological tests (e.g., the Beck Depression Inventory; Beck & Steer, 1983) may be acceptable and uncontroversial, use of other tests that yield demonstrably useful data (e.g., the RIM or TAT) is rarely deemed acceptable by managed care organizations.

This situation has resulted in part from a paucity of evidence documenting the cost-effectiveness of personality assessment — the decrease in treatment costs (both short and long term) that can result from the use of personality test data in refining diagnosis, enhancing clinical prediction, and structuring treatment. Initial findings from studies in this area suggest that despite the initial increase in patient care costs that results from a thorough testing at the outset of treatment, personality assessment data can decrease care costs in the long run by making psychological intervention more efficient and effective (Porcelli & McGrath, 2007; Quirk, Erdberg, Crosier, & Steinfeld, 2007). Continued research is needed to document more precisely the ways in which personality assessment results can enhance the effectiveness of psychological treatment in cost-effective ways.

Assessing the Mind and Assessing the Brain

Modern neuroimaging techniques have provided unique insights into the neurological underpinnings of various psychological processes, and as a result many researchers and clinicians believe that the evolution of personality assessment during the twenty-first century will be characterized by an inexorable shift from psychological to neurological measurement techniques. In some ways, this view reflects a long-standing reductionist perspective that continues to be influential in various areas of psychology, which holds that progress in psychological science is reflected in the degree to which we are able to explain mental processes and mental disorders in biological rather than psychological terms.

While there is much to be gained from enhancing our understanding of the neurological underpinnings of psychopathology, it is important to keep in mind that neuroimaging and personality assessment are not interchangeable but employ different methods to achieve different goals. Moreover, these two techniques ask very different questions to begin with. Neuroimaging techniques are designed to measure structural changes in the brain and subtle functional changes in neural activity that result from (or precede) these structural changes. Personality assessment, by contrast, assesses cognition, affectivity, and other underlying psychological processes using a broad array of instruments, some of which emphasize self-report (either verbal or questionnaire based) and some of which are derived from free-response test data wherein patients' behavior is sampled in a standardized testing situation. Thus, whereas neuroimaging techniques are designed to provide unique insights into the functioning of the *brain*, personality assessment is intended to provide unique insights into the functioning of the *mind*. These two assessment tools yield complementary types of information that, taken together, can provide unique information regarding myriad aspects of human mental life.

ADVANCED TRAINING OPTIONS

The single best source for information regarding advanced training opportunities in personality assessment is the Society for Personality Assessment (SPA) Web site (www.personality.org). SPA provides links to a variety of training programs and workshops, as well as a periodically updated list of assessment courses and field placements offered by various graduate programs and internship sites. In addition, the SPA annual meeting, which takes place each spring, includes numerous symposia and presentations on personality assessment by leading clinicians and researchers, along with accredited

Continuing Education (CE) courses in this area. Other good sources of information on advanced training options include the Rorschach Workshops Web site (www.rorschachworkshps.com) and the MMPI-2/MMPI-A Workshops Web site (www.upress.umn.edu/tests/workshops).

The American Psychological Association Web site (www.apa.org) includes a page listing accredited pre- and postdoctoral internship programs. Although this online listing does not include information regarding assessment opportunities within each program, perusal of individual internship Web sites is a useful way to determine which programs offer advanced training in personality assessment.

SUMMARY

In clinical settings, personality assessment can be used to refine diagnoses, place these diagnoses in the broader context of a patient's overall psychological functioning, and help structure treatment. A wide variety of personality tests are in use today, including self-report personality scales (e.g., the Minnesota Multiphasic Personality Inventory–2, the Personality Assessment Inventory), which are designed to assess self-attributed traits (i.e., traits patients see in themselves and acknowledge when asked), and free-response tests (e.g., the Rorschach Inkblot Method, the Thematic Apperception Test), which assess implicit (i.e., underlying, often unconscious) traits, motives, and need states.

It is important to use personality tests that have good construct validity, but even then the clinician must maximize the validity and utility of assessment by employing standardized test administration and scoring procedures, minimizing patients' self-presentation effects, and managing examiner expectancy effects that can bias and distort test results. A number of controversies characterize contemporary personality assessment and include questions regarding the validity of free-response test data, the cost-effectiveness of personality assessment, and the value of neuroimaging techniques in relation to traditional psychological tests. These controversies notwithstanding, evidence confirms that careful integration of the results obtained with different personality tests, and integration of personality test results with other sources of information (e.g., life history data), can yield unique and valuable information that aids in diagnosis, treatment planning, clinical decision making, and risk management.

THOUGHT QUESTIONS

5.1. You just finished assessing a patient who is potentially suicidal. Which would worry you more: (1) finding that the patient scored high on an RIM index of underlying stress and also reported high levels of experienced stress on a questionnaire measure or (2) finding that the patient scores high on an RIM index of underlying stress but reports *low* levels of experienced stress on a questionnaire?

5.2. If you intended to administer a test battery consisting of a self-report test, a free-response test, an intelligence test, and a brief neurological screen, in what order would you administer these tests? Why?

5.3. Suppose a managed care organization agrees to pay for a thorough personality assessment of one of your patients. You administer the tests, the patient provides the responses, and the company pays for the testing. Who actually "owns" these test results?

Glossary

Behavioral assessment: Measurement of an individual's behavior through direct observation or other means (e.g., analysis of patients' records of their daily behaviors kept in diary format).

Concurrent validity: The degree to which scores on a personality test predict current behavior if the test is designed to assess some aspect of functioning in the here-and-now (as would be required of a measure of current ongoing depression).

Construct validity: The degree to which any test that is designed to assess an unobservable theoretical construct (like personality) actually measures the variables(s) it purports to assess.

Convergent validity: The degree to which test scores are positively associated with theoretically related variables (e.g., the degree to which narcissism scores are associated with high scores on a measure of self-esteem).

Diagnosis: The process of identifying and documenting a patient's symptoms to classify that patient into one or more diagnostic categories whose labels represent shorthand descriptors of psychological syndromes (e.g., social phobia, bulimia nervosa, avoidant personality disorder).

Discriminant validity: The degree to which test scores are unrelated to variables that are theoretically distinct from the construct being assessed (e.g., the degree to which narcissism scores are unrelated to intelligence).

Free-response test: Type of psychological test that requires patients to interpret ambiguous stimuli like inkblots (formerly labeled *projective tests*); free-response tests assess "implicit" aspects of personality, that is, traits, motives, and need states that shape behavior automatically, often without any awareness on the patient's part that his or her responses are affected by these factors.

Incremental validity: The degree to which a test adds predictive value to an existing test battery, allowing the clinician to make more precise and accurate predictions.

Inter-rater reliability: The degree to which two independent raters unaware of each other's judgments come to similar conclusions regarding the scoring of open-ended test responses (e.g., patients' descriptions of inkblots).

Norms: Average scores and typical score distributions obtained by patients with known characteristics.

Predictive validity: The degree to which scores on a personality test predict future behavior if the test is designed to assess some aspect of future functioning (as would be required of a measure designed to assess risk for future depression).

Psychological assessment: Integration of data from one or more personality tests (and sometimes intellectual and neuropsychological tests as well) to understand the dispositional and situational factors that interact to determine a patient's subjective experiences, core beliefs, coping strategies, and behavior patterns (see also *Psychological testing*).

Psychological testing: The process of administering and scoring one or more psychological tests (see also *Psychological assessment*).

Retest reliability: The degree to which personality tests yield similar results when administered to a patient on two occasions (most personality test scores should be stable over periods of several months or longer).

Self-report test: Formerly known as *objective tests*, self-report tests typically take the form of questionnaires wherein patients are asked to acknowledge whether a series of trait-descriptive statements is true of them or rate the degree to which each of these statements describes them accurately; self-report tests assess "self-attributed" traits, motives, and need states — characteristics that a patient recognizes in him- or herself and acknowledges when asked.

References

Acklin, M. (2002). How to select personality tests for a test battery. In J. N. Butcher (Ed.), *Clinical personality assessment* (2nd ed., pp. 13–23). New York: Oxford University Press.

American Psychiatric Association (1980). *Diagnostic and statistical manual of mental disorders* (3rd ed.). Washington, DC: Author.

American Psychiatric Association (1994). *Diagnostic and statistical manual of mental disorders* (4th ed.). Washington, DC: Author.

Archer, R. P. & Krishnamurthy, R. (1993a). Combining the Rorschach and MMPI in the assessment of adolescents. *Journal of Personality Assessment, 60*, 132–140.

Archer, R. P. & Krishnamurthy, R. (1993b). A review of MMPI and Rorschach interrelationships in adult samples. *Journal of Personality Assessment, 61*, 277–293.

Aronow, E., Weiss, K., & Reznikoff, M. (2001). *A practical guide to the Thematic Apperception Test: The TAT in clinical practice*. New York: Brunner-Routledge.

Beck, A. T. & Steer, R. A. (1983). *Beck Depression Inventory manual*. San Antonio, TX: Psychological Corporation.

Blanchard, E. B. & Hickling, E. J. (2004). The Albany Treatment Study: a randomized, controlled comparison on cognitive-behavior therapy and SUPPORT in the treatment of chronic PTSD secondary to MVAs. In E. J. Hickling & E. B. Blanchard (Eds.), *After the crash: psychological assessment and treatment of survivors of motor vehicle accidents* (pp. 315–347). Washington, DC: American Psychological Association.

Bornstein, R. F. (1998). Implicit and self-attributed dependency needs in dependent and histrionic personality disorders. *Journal of Personality Assessment, 71*, 1–14.

Bornstein, R. F. (2001). Clinical utility of the Rorschach Inkblot Method: reframing the debate. *Journal of Personality Assessment, 77*, 39–47.

Bornstein, R. F. (2002). A process dissociation approach to objective-projective test score interrelationships. *Journal of Personality Assessment, 78*, 47–68.

Bornstein, R. F. (2005). *The dependent patient: a practitioner's guide*. Washington, DC: American Psychological Association.

Bornstein, R. F. (2007). Might the Rorschach be a projective test after all? Social projection of an undesired trait alters Rorschach Oral Dependency scores. *Journal of Personality Assessment, 88*, 354–367.

Bornstein, R. F., Bowers, K. S., & Bonner, S. (1996a). Effects of induced mood states on objective and projective dependency scores. *Journal of Personality Assessment, 67*, 324–340.

Bornstein, R. F., Bowers, K. S., & Bonner, S. (1996b). Relationships of objective and projective dependency scores to sex role orientation in college students. *Journal of Personality Assessment, 66*, 555–568.

Bornstein, R. F. & Masling, J. M. (Eds.) (2005). *Scoring the Rorschach: seven validated systems*. Mahwah, NJ: Lawrence Erlbaum Associates.

Bornstein, R. F., Rossner, S. C., Hill, E. L., & Stepanian, M. L. (1994). Face validity and fakeability of objective and projective measures of dependency. *Journal of Personality Assessment, 63*, 363–386.

Buck, J. N. (1948). The HTP test. *Journal of Clinical Psychology, 4*, 151–159.

Burns, R. C. (1982). *Self-growth in families: Kinetic family drawing (KFD) research and applications*. New York: Brunner/Mazel.

Butcher, J. N. (1990). *MMPI-2 in psychological treatment*. New York: Oxford University Press.

Butcher, J. N. (Ed.) (2002). *Clinical personality assessment* (2nd ed.). New York: Oxford University Press.

Campbell, D. T. & Fiske, D. (1959). Convergent and discriminant validation by the multitrait-multimethod matrix. *Psychological Bulletin, 56*, 81–105.

Cates, J. A. (1999). The art of assessment in psychology: ethics, expertise, and validity. *Journal of Clinical Psychology, 55*, 631–641.

Cattell, J. M. (1890). Mental tests and measurements. *Mind, 15*, 373–381.

Costa, P. T. & McCrae, R. R. (1992). *Revised NEO Personality Inventory (NEOPI-R) and NEO Five-Factor Inventory (NEO-FFI) professional manual*. Sarasota, FL: Professional Resources Press.

Costa, P. T. & Widiger, T. A. (Eds.) (1994). *Personality disorders and the five-factor model of personality*. Washington, DC: American Psychological Association.

Craig, J. A., Koestner, R., & Zuroff, D. C. (1994). Implicit and self-attributed intimacy motivation. *Journal of Social and Personal Relationships, 11*, 491–507.

Cramer, P. (1991). *The development of defense mechanisms: theory, research, and assessment*. New York: Springer-Verlag.

Cramer, P. (2006). *Protecting the self: defense mechanisms in action*. New York: Guilford Press.

Duberstein, P. R., Seidlitz, L., & Conwell, Y. (1996). Reconsidering the role of hostility in completed suicide: a life-span perspective. In J. M. Masling & R. F. Bornstein (Eds.), *Psychoanalytic perspectives on developmental psychology* (pp. 257–323). Washington, DC: American Psychological Association.

Exner, J. E. (1993). *The Rorschach: a comprehensive system*, vol. 1. (Basic foundations). New York: Wiley.

Exner, J. E. & Erdberg, P. (2005). *The Rorschach: Advanced interpretation*. New York: Wiley.

Exner, J. E. & Weiner, I. B. (1986). *The Rorschach: a comprehensive system*, vol. 3 (*Assessment of children and adolescents*). New York: Wiley.

Finn, S. E. (2003). Therapeutic assessment of a man with "ADD." *Journal of Personality Assessment, 80*, 115–129.

Finn, S. E. (2005). How psychological assessment taught me compassion and firmness. *Journal of Personality Assessment, 84,* 29–32.

Finn, S. E. & Tonsager, S. E. (1992). The therapeutic effects of providing MMPI-2 feedback to college students awaiting psychotherapy. *Psychological Assessment, 4,* 278–284.

Franz, S. I. (1919). *Handbook of mental examination methods* (2nd ed.). New York: Macmillan.

Goodenough, F. L. (1926). *Measurement of intelligence by drawings.* Yonkers-on-Hudson, N.Y.: World Book.

Gough, H. G. (1957). *California Psychological Inventory manual.* Palo Alto, CA: Consulting Psychologists Press.

Gough, H. G. (1987). *California Psychological Inventory: administrator's guide.* Palo Alto, CA: Consulting Psychologists Press.

Gough, H. G. & Bradley, P. (1996). *California Psychological Inventory manual* (3rd ed.). Palo Alto, CA: Consulting Psychologists Press.

Graham, J. R. (2000). *MMPI-2: assessing personality and psychopathology.* New York: Oxford University Press.

Groth-Marnat, G. (1999). Current status and future directions of psychological assessment. *Journal of Clinical Psychology, 55,* 781–785.

Handler, L. & Hilsenroth, M. J. (Eds.) (1998). *Teaching and learning personality assessment.* Mahwah, NJ: Lawrence Erlbaum Associates.

Handler, L. & Meyer, G. J. (1998). The importance of teaching and learning personality assessment. In L. Handler & M. J. Hilsenroth (Eds.), *Teaching and learning personality assessment* (pp. 3–30). Mahwah, NJ: Lawrence Erlbaum Associates.

Hathaway, S. R. & McKinley, J. C. (1940). A Multiphasic Personality Schedule, I: construction of the schedule. *Journal of Psychology, 10,* 249–254.

Hathaway, S. R. & McKinley, J. C. (1952). *Minnesota Multiphasic Personality Inventory manual.* New York: Psychological Corporation.

Hunsley, J. & Bailey, J. M. (1999). The clinical utility of the Rorschach: unfulfilled promises and an uncertain future. *Psychological Assessment, 11,* 266–277.

Huprich, S. K. (Ed.) (2006). *Rorschach assessment of the personality disorders.* Mahwah, NJ: Lawrence Erlbaum Associates.

Huprich, S. K. & Ganellen, R. J. (2006). The advantages of assessing personality disorders with the Rorschach. In S. K. Huprich (Ed.), *Rorschach assessment of the personality disorders* (pp. 27–53). Mahwah, NJ: Lawrence Erlbaum Associates.

Hy, L. X. & Loevinger, J. (1996). *Measuring ego development.* Hillsdale, NJ: Lawrence Erlbaum Associates.

Koestner, R., Weinberger, J., & McClelland, D. C. (1991). Task-intrinsic and social-extrinsic sources of arousal for motives assessed in fantasy and self-report. *Journal of Personality, 59,* 57–82.

Kraepelin, E. (1892). *Uber die beeinflussung einfacher psychischer vorgagne durch einige arzneimittel.* Jena: Fischer.

Kraepelin, E. (1895). Der psychologische Versuch in der Psychiatrie. *Psychologische Arbeiten, 1,* 1–91.

Kurtz, J. E. & Blais, M. A. (2007). Introduction to the Special Series on the Personality Assessment Inventory. *Journal of Personality Assessment, 88,* 1–4.

Lanyon, R. I. & Goodstein, L. D. (1997). *Personality assessment* (3rd ed.). New York: Wiley.

Lanyon, B. P. & Lanyon, R. I. (1980). *Incomplete Sentences Task manual.* Chicago: Stoelting.

Leibowitz, M. (1999). *Interpreting projective drawings: a self-psychological approach.* Philadelphia, PA: Brunner/Mazel.

Loevinger, J. (1985). Revision of the Sentence Completion Test for ego development. *Journal of Personality and Social Psychology, 48,* 420–427.

Machover, K. (1949). *Personality projection in the drawing of the human figure.* Springfield, IL: Charles C. Thomas.

McClelland, D. C., Koestner, R., & Weinberger, J. (1989). How do self-attributed and implicit motives differ? *Psychological Review, 96,* 690–702.

McIntire, S. A. & Miller, L. A. (2007). *Foundations of psychological testing* (2nd ed.). Thousand Oaks, CA: Sage.

Megargee, E. I. (2002). *California Psychological Inventory handbook* (2nd ed.). San Francisco: Jossey-Bass.

Meyer, G. J. (1996). The Rorschach and MMPI: toward a more scientific understanding of cross-method assessment. *Journal of Personality Assessment, 67,* 558–578.

Meyer, G. J. (1997). On the integration of personality assessment methods: the Rorschach and MMPI. *Journal of Personality Assessment, 68,* 297–330.

Meyer, G. J. (2000). Incremental validity of the Rorschach Prognostic Rating Scale over MMPI Ego Strength Scale and IQ. *Journal of Personality Assessment, 74,* 356–370.

Meyer, G. J., et al. (2001). Psychological testing and psychological assessment: a review of evidence and issues. *American Psychologist, 56,* 128–165.

Millon, T., Millon, C., & Davis, R. (1994). *Millon Clinical Multiaxial Inventory-III manual.* Minneapolis, MN: National Computer Systems.

Morey, L. C. (1991). *Personality Assessment Inventory professional manual.* Odessa, FL: Psychological Assessment Resources.

Morey, L. C. (2003). *Essentials of PAI assessment.* New York: Wiley.

Murray, H. A. (1943). *Thematic Apperception Test manual.* Cambridge, MA: Harvard University Press.

Nosek, B. A., Greenwald, A. G., & Banaji, M. R. (2005). Understanding and using the Implicit Association Test: method variables and construct validity. *Personality and Social Psychology Bulletin, 31,* 166–180.

Porcelli, P. & McGrath, R. E. (2007). Introduction to the special issue on personality assessment in medical settings. *Journal of Personality Assessment, 89*, 211–215.

Quirk, M. P., Erdberg, P., Crosier, M., & Steinfeld, B. (2007). Personality assessment in today's health care environment: therapeutic alliance and patient satisfaction. *Journal of Personality Assessment, 89*, 95–104.

Richard, D. C. S. & Bobicz, K. (2003). Computers and behavioral assessment: six years later. *The Behavior Therapist, 26*, 219–223.

Richard, D. C. S. & Gloster, A. (2006). Technology integration and behavioral assessment. In M. Hersen (Ed.), *Clinician's handbook of adult behavioral assessment* (pp. 461–495). San Diego, CA: Elsevier Academic Press.

Rorschach, H. (1921). *Psychodiagnostik*. Berne: Huber.

Rosenberg, M. (1965). *Society and the adolescent self-image*. Princeton, NJ: Princeton University Press.

Rotter, J. B., Lah, M. I., & Rafferty, J. E. (1992). *Rotter Incomplete Sentences Blank manual*. San Antonio, TX: Psychological Corporation.

Scott, W. A. & Johnson, R. C. (1972). Comparative validities of direct and indirect personality tests. *Journal of Consulting and Clinical Psychology, 38*, 301–318.

Silverstein, M. L. (2007). *Disorders of the self: a personality guided approach*. Washington, DC: American Psychological Association.

Sopchak, A. L., Sopchak, A. M., & Kohlbrenner, R. J. (1993). *Interpersonal relatedness from projective drawings: applicability in diagnostic and therapeutic practice*. Springfield, IL: Charles C. Thomas.

Spangler, W. D. (1992). Validity of questionnaire and TAT measures of need for achievement: two meta-analyses. *Psychological Bulletin, 112*, 140–154.

Speilberger, C. D. (1989). *State-Trait Anxiety Inventory: a comprehensive bibliography*. Palo Alto, CA: Consulting Psychologists Press.

Strack, S. & Millon, T. (2007). Contributions to the dimensional assessment of personality disorders using Millon's model and the Millon Clinical Multiaxial Inventory (MCMI-III). *Journal of Personality Disorders, 89*, 56–69.

Taylor, S. (2006). Clinician's guide to PTSD: a cognitive-behavioral approach. New York: Guilford Press.

Teglasi, H. (2001). Essentials of TAT and other storytelling techniques. New York: Wiley.

Tharinger, D. J., Finn, S. E., Wilkinson, A. D., & Schaber, P. M. (2007). Therapeutic assessment with a child as a family intervention: a clinical and research case study. *Psychology in the Schools, 44*, 293–309.

Viglione, D. J. (1999). A review of recent research addressing the utility of the Rorschach. *Psychological Assessment, 11*, 251–265.

Weiner, I. B. (2000). Using the Rorschach properly in practice and research. *Journal of Clinical Psychology, 56*, 435–438.

Weiner, I. B. & Greene, R. L. (2008). *Handbook of personality assessment*. New York: Wiley.

Westen, D., Lohr, N., Silk, K. R., Gold, L., & Kerber, K. (1989). *Measuring social cognition and object relations using the TAT: a scoring manual*. Unpublished manuscript. Ann Arbor: University of Michigan.

Widiger, T. A. & Lowe, J. R. (2007). Five-factor model assessment of personality disorder. *Journal of Personality Assessment, 89*, 16–29.

Widiger, T. A. & Samuel, D. B. (2005). Evidence-based assessment of personality disorders. *Psychological Assessment, 17*, 278–287.

Wood, J. M., Lilienfeld, S. O., Nezworski, T. M., & Garb, H. N. (2001). Coming to grips with negative evidence for the Comprehensive System for the Rorschach: a comment on Gacano, Loving and Bodholdt, Ganellen, and Bornstein. *Journal of Personality Assessment, 77*, 48–70.

6

Behavioral Assessment and Functional Analysis

Joseph Keawe'aimoku Kaholokula
University of Hawai'i, Mānoa

Iruma Bello
University of Hawai'i, Mānoa

Andrea H. Nacapoy
University of Hawai'i, Mānoa

Stephen N. Haynes
University of Hawai'i, Mānoa

OUTLINE

INTRODUCTION

Behavioral assessment is an evolving science-based, psychological assessment paradigm with an interrelated set of concepts, methods, and strategies that *describe* and *explain* human behavior (Haynes & Kaholokula, 2008). It is an evolving psychological assessment paradigm because its methods and strategies are informed by up-to-date empirical research and enhanced by incorporating new technology. It is a science-based approach to psychological assessment because it involves the use of observation, measurement, and experimentation in describing and explaining human behavior.

In assessing human behavior, we are interested in describing the *attributes* (e.g., what it looks like) and *dimensions* (e.g., frequency, intensity, duration, and onset latency) of a behavior and in explaining what variables account for its *variance* (e.g., change over time and across contexts), how and why it occurs (e.g., its causes), and what affects its dimensions. Thus, a major tenet of behavioral assessment is that our investigation of human behavior be empirically based, testable, and refutable with data collected from measurements that are *valid* (i.e., how well they measure what they purport to measure) and *precise* (i.e., how accurately and sensitively they measure a specific behavior, variable, or event).

The *measurement* of human behavior, its causes, and their changes over time and across contexts are an important aspects of behavioral assessment. Measurement occurs whenever we assign a numerical value or other symbols to a dimension (e.g., rate, intensity, and duration) or attribute (e.g., specific behaviors, environmental events, and phenomena) of a variable so that it best reflects the dimension or attribute being measured. Whether for research or for applied clinical applications, our judgments about a person's behavior problem and its causes, the most appropriate treatment strategy,

or the effectiveness of a treatment must be based on the best available science-based measures. Thus, advocates of behavioral assessment encourage the use of (1) valid and precise measures of target behaviors, events, and phenomena and (2) empirically based (i.e., informed by prior research) assessment methods and strategies.

Behavioral assessment has several interrelated foci. First, the focus is on the specification of a person's behavior problem and the goals of assessment. Second, the focus is on the identification of the *functional relations* (i.e., how variables are related and covary over time and across contexts) between a person's behavior problem and its causes.[1] At the same time, the focus is on the measurement of *lower-order* and *less inferential* variables (e.g., the frequency, rate, and duration of specific behaviors under specific conditions) versus higher-order and highly inferential variables (e.g., general personality traits or coping styles). The focus is also on *important* (e.g., improves quality of life) and *modifiable* (i.e., amenable to change) causes of a person's behavior problem. Finally, behavioral assessment focuses on contemporaneous environmental causes (e.g., events that co-occur in time) as well as cognitive (e.g., dysfunctional thoughts) and physiological (e.g., rapid heart rate) causes of a person's behavior problem.

Behavioral assessment is an *idiographic* approach to psychological assessment. It allows the assessor to examine the unique causes of a person's behavior problem, how they can differ in unique ways over time and across contexts, and how causal agents and functional relations can differ across people with similar behavior problems. It also allows the assessor to match the assessment methods and strategies to the

---

[1]Functional relations will be discussed in more detail later in this chapter. Briefly, two variables or events have a functional relationship when they covary. Covariance or correlation does not imply a causal relationship but rather the conditional probability of one event given the co-occurrence of another event (Haynes & O'Brien, 2000).

assessment goals of the person being assessed. Thus, behavioral assessment is a conceptually based and methodologically diverse psychological assessment paradigm that involves frequent measures of behaviors and their causes with data integrated from *multiple methods of data collection* (e.g., direct observation and functional interviews) and from *multiple sources of data* (e.g., spouses, parents, teachers).

Because of the idiographic emphasis in behavioral assessment, the assessor is guided toward an orientation to psychological assessment that is highly sensitive to the individual being assessed and individual differences that could influence the assessment process and outcome. The assessor obtains informed consent to respect the rights and autonomy of a person, ensures a good client-assessor relationship throughout the assessment process, and works collaboratively in setting assessment goals with the person or persons being assessed. The assessor is also sensitive to individual differences — a person's age, sex, ethnicity, socioeconomic status, sexual orientation, religious affiliation, and physical and cognitive limitation — that might affect the validity of the data collected and the judgments made (e.g., treatment decisions and outcome evaluations) from those data. Thus, the behavioral assessment paradigm encourages sensitivity to the autonomy and uniqueness of an individual and the client-assessor relationship.

Because behavioral assessment is idiographic, conceptually based, and methodologically diverse, it is well suited for a wide range of clinical and research applications in describing and explaining human behavior. Some examples of its application can be found in clinical case formulation (Haynes, Nelson, Thatcher, & Kaholokula, 2002), experimental psychopathology (Lenzenweger & Hooley, 2002), treatment outcome research (Haynes, Kaholokula, & Yoshioka, 2007), personnel and workplace assessment (Murphy, 2004), school-based (Shapiro & Kratochwill, 2000) and institutional-based (Serper, Goldberg, & Salzinger, 2004) interventions, managed care (Strosahl & Robinson, 2004), and program evaluation (Wholey, Hatry, & Newcomer, 2004). It has been used across different settings, such as in inpatient (e.g., general and psychiatric hospitals) and outpatient (e.g., community health centers) settings; in schools, workplaces, and homes; and among different populations, such as children, adults, couples, families, and DSM-IV diagnoses.

One of the many clinical and research applications for which behavioral assessment is well suited is in *functional analysis* because of its focus on describing and explaining the relationship (i.e., functional relations) between behavior and its causes. As a behavioral clinical case formulation,[2] functional analysis is the identification of important and modifiable functional relations of a person's behavior problem. Its primary application is to organize and inform clinical judgments, such as selecting the best treatment foci and evaluating treatment effects. Within the fields of behavior analysis, "functional analysis" often refers to the systematic manipulation of an independent variable (e.g., the effect of attention from peers or the presence of different teachers on aggressive behaviors in the classroom) and the observation of its effects on behavior in well-controlled single-subject experimental research (e.g., ABAB replication designs where A = baseline condition and B = intervention condition).

In this chapter, we provide an overview of the behavioral assessment paradigm and illustrate just one of its many clinical and research applications — the functional analysis. First, we highlight the most commonly used assessment methods and strategies and the basic principles of behavioral assessment. Second, we review the characteristics of functional

---

[2]There are many other behavioral clinical case formulation models with behavioral assessment applications, such as those proposed by Nezu and colleagues (1997), Persons and Tompkins (1997), and Koerner and Linehan (1997).

analysis and illustrate the application of behavioral assessment for functional analysis in both behavioral clinical case formulation and single-subject experimental research. Finally, we conclude with recommendations for conducting a behavioral assessment and functional analysis. Recognizing that a comprehensive discussion of behavioral assessment and functional analysis is not possible in a single chapter, we refer you to more extensive discussions from other authors, notably Haynes and O'Brien (2000), Haynes and Heiby (2004), Hersen (2006a, 2006b), and Shapiro and Kratochwill (2000).

METHODS AND STRATEGIES OF BEHAVIORAL ASSESSMENT

How we collect data during the assessment process, as well as the methods and strategies we use, affects the kinds of data we collect and their validity.[3] Consequently, the data we collect during the assessment process, whether in the applied or research settings, affect the validity of our judgments about a person's behavior problems and treatment goals. Thus, the behavioral assessment paradigm employs assessment methods and strategies that can capture the dynamic and conditional nature of a person's behavior problem, that is, how behavior and its causes can change across time (e.g., daily or weekly changes), settings (e.g., home vs. work), and contexts (e.g., different states of the person). This emphasis on sensitivity to change is designed to improve the validity of our judgments in clinical research and clinical case formulation, thereby facilitating treatment decisions, predicting the risk of harm or post-treatment relapse, and estimating treatment outcomes.

---

[3]Definitions for the assessment methods, strategies, and psychometric terms used in this chapter can be found at http://www2.hawaii.edu/~sneil/ba/.

In this section, we review the utility, assets, and limitations of several behavioral assessment methods and strategies. We illustrate how data collection is often idiographic and specific to the goals of assessment by providing a brief clinical or research scenario at the beginning of each method being reviewed. A summary of the methods we review is provided in Table 6.1. Throughout this section we emphasize the collection of data using multiple methods of data collection (e.g., functional interviews and analogue observations) from multiple sources (e.g., spouse, coworkers, and teachers) to improve the validity of the judgments we make based on such data. We refer you to Haynes and Heiby (2004) and Hersen (2006a and 2006b) for more extensive discussions of the methods and strategies used in behavioral assessment.

Functional Behavioral Interviews, Questionnaires, and Checklists

Scenario: A clinical psychologist at a psychiatric inpatient hospital is asked to develop a treatment plan for a patient who frequently screams at unit staff, disrupts group therapy sessions, hits other patients, and often refuses to eat his food.

In the above scenario, the psychologist is not interested in a diagnosis but rather in the functional relations of the patient's multiple behavior problems (e.g., what happens before, during, and after a disruptive behavior is exhibited) across settings (e.g., inside vs. outside of the unit) and contexts (e.g., in the presence of different staff). The identification of the functional relations of the patient's behavior problems facilitates the formulation of a treatment plan that will have the greatest *magnitude of effect* in modifying the problem behaviors across different settings and contexts. "Magnitude of effect" is the change in behaviors or events that leads to the greatest improvements in quality of life, achievement of treatment goals, or greatest reduction in the rate, duration, and intensity of behavior problems.

TABLE 6.1 Summary of behavioral assessment methods and their major assets and limitations

Methods	Descriptions	Assets	Limitations
Functional Behavioral Interviews, Checklists, Questionnaires	• Self-report methods for assessing behavior problems and their causes and correlates	• Allows for the identification of dimensions and response modes of overt and covert behaviors • Allows for the assessment of functional relations • Highly flexible and cost- and time-efficient • Easy to administer and requires minimum training • Brief checklists and questionnaires can be used in time-series assessment strategies	• Subject to recall biases and difficulties • Subject to interviewer (e.g., skill level) and rater biases • Depends on the respondent's level of cooperation and willingness to be assessed • For questionnaires, the predictive validity of measures can vary across instruments
Naturalistic Observations	• Direct observation of behavior problems and their causes in their natural environments	• Allows for precision in assessing behavior-environment interactions • Amenable to time-series assessment strategies • Can be done with outside observers or by participant observers • High ecological validity	• Sources of error include the reactive effects of being observed and observer biases • Dependent on the reliability of coding system employed and the training of the coder
Analogue Behavioral Observations	• Direct observation of behavior-environment and behavior-behavior interactions in a contrived setting	• Allows for observation of less observable and low-frequency behaviors • Amenable to time-series assessment strategies • More cost-effective than naturalistic observations • Allows for the design, manipulation, and control of specific situations and conditions	• Subject to assessment reactivity such as changes in behavior due to the presence of the observer • Lower ecological validity than naturalistic observations

Continued

TABLE 6.1   (*Continued*)

Methods	Descriptions	Assets	Limitations
Self-monitoring	• Person records the instances of thoughts, emotions, behaviors, and environmental events over a specified period of time	• Less affected by recall biases • Allows for the collection of real-time data in the real-world setting • Amenable to time-series assessment strategies • Use of electronic devices can increase the validity of data and ease of data collection • More cost-effective than direct observation methods	• Electronic devices can be expensive and difficult to use • Utility is limited by the person's cognitive ability and level of motivation to understand and comply with the self-monitoring strategy
Clinic-based Psychophysiological Assessment	• Physiological monitoring devices used to gather data about physiological, cognitive, and emotional reaction to stimuli presented in the clinic environment	• Allows for measurement of multiple dimensions of behavior • Higher precision and reliability in measurement • Amenable to time-series and sequential analysis assessment strategies and within-subject interrupted time-series designs	• Use of equipment may be limited to laboratory settings • Equipment and training required can be expensive and highly technical, and equipment can be difficult to use • Can have less ecological validity
Ambulatory Biosensors	• Person wears a device that records physiological responses (e.g., heart rate, blood pressure) to environmental events, thoughts, or affective states during specific time periods	• Measurements can be taken in clinic and real-world settings and in conjunction with other assessment methods, such as self-monitoring • Allows for the measurement of multiple dimensions of behavior • Amenable to time-series assessment strategies • High ecological validity	• Devices are expensive and their use may not be feasible in large-scale studies • May be costly and time-consuming to retrieve and manage the data collected • Data gathered can be voluminous and challenging to interpret

Functional behavioral interviews, questionnaires, and checklists are useful self-report methods for the idiographic assessment of a person's behavior problem. They are "functional" behavioral self-report methods because they are designed to describe and explain human behavior, that is, they help to identify the important dimensions (i.e., rate, intensity, duration, onset latency), *response modes* (i.e., affective, cognitive, physiological, and motor), and functional relations of a person's behavior problem across settings and contexts (Barbour & Davison, 2004; Fernandez-Ballesteros, 2004). Thus, not all assessment interviews, questionnaires, and checklists allow for the specification of behavior problems and identification of their functional relations across settings and contexts.

Functional behavioral interviews, questionnaires, and checklists are particularly useful for examining low-frequency behaviors (e.g., physical aggression), less observable behaviors (e.g., attitudes and beliefs), and socially sensitive behaviors (e.g., sexual behaviors). In our scenario, these self-report methods can be used to identify whether the patient screams at all staff members or only some of those on the unit; whether the patient only hits specific people, what provokes the hits, and the consequences of hitting; and whether certain conditions affect the patient's eating. They are also time-efficient and cost-effective for gathering data from *multiple informants*. For example, a functional behavioral questionnaire about the patient's disruptive behaviors could be administered to several staff members in the psychiatric unit.

As illustrated, functional behavioral interviews, questionnaires, and checklists can be tailored to an individual's specific behavior problem and assessment goals and thus are useful across various populations and in clinical and research applications. They can also be relatively easy to administer, with appropriate training, and are cost-effective and time-efficient compared to some other assessment methods. However, they also have their limitations, such as being subject to self-reporting biases and cognitive limitations of the respondents. Interviews can also be subject to interviewer biases, such as when an interviewer's preconceived notions about a person's behavior problem inadvertently influence the information obtained.

In our scenario, the patient's willingness to cooperate with the assessment and his psychological state (e.g., medicated or actively delusional state) during the assessment process could affect the validity of data collected using self-report methods. An interviewer's past experience with the patient could lead to questions that seek to confirm rather than disconfirm a hypothesis about the cause of the patient's psychotic episodes. There are assessment strategies to reduce self-reporting biases. For example, the *time-line follow-back* procedure, which is a structured interview technique using calendars and memory anchor points to reconstruct a daily behavior (e.g., alcohol consumption) during a specific time period, can be used (Sobell & Sobell, 1992).

Gender, ethnic, and socioeconomic differences, to name a few, between an assessor and person being assessed can also affect the information obtained from self-report methods. For example, a male patient may be hesitant in discussing sexual impulses with a female assessor, or a female client who was sexually assaulted by a male in the past may be reluctant to discuss her sexual functioning with a male assessor. A recent immigrant to the United States who is having difficulties with his employer may be hesitant to share his thoughts of being discriminated against with an assessor whose ethnicity and socioeconomic background are similar to those of his employer. We refer you to Tanaka-Matsumi (2004) for a more detailed discussion on individual differences affecting behavioral assessment.

Naturalistic Observation

Scenario: A fifth grade teacher reports to the school psychologist that one of her students has difficulty sitting still in class, gets up from his seat and goes to other students' desks without permission; continuously interrupts her when she is teaching a lesson; and appears to have difficulty completing assignments.

In the above scenario, the focus of behavioral assessment is on identifying the functional relations relevant to the child's multiple behavior problems in the classroom setting. Thus, the assessment goal is to identify *behavior-environment interactions* to select the treatment strategies that will best address the student's disruptive classroom behaviors. Some questions regarding behavior-environment interactions an assessor might think about are "In what situations is the student most likely to interrupt the class?" and "Are there teacher or classmate responses that might be maintaining the child's behaviors?"

Naturalistic observations are powerful assessment methods to address questions involving behavior-environment interactions. They have good *ecological validity*, which concerns how well the data obtained from a particular assessment method are representative of the data that would have been obtained from the same targets in the natural environment of interest. They can be performed by an outside observer or a participant observer, like a teacher's aide, who is already part of the natural environment. Direct observations in the natural environment can be useful in measuring highly specific events associated with the dimensions and *functions* (i.e., response contingencies, such as attention or avoidance of an aversive task, that can serve to maintain a behavior) of a behavior problem and their conditional probabilities (i.e., the likelihood of occurring) over time (Hartmann, Barrios, & Wood, 2004). In our scenario, the teacher's aide could observe and record how often the student interrupts the teacher during a class period as well as what happens just before (i.e., antecedent events) and after (i.e., consequences) the interruption.

With naturalistic observations, various sampling strategies can be used alone or in combination. These may include subject-sampling, which focuses on observing only a subset of the target group (e.g., entire class vs. teacher-child interaction); behavior-sampling, which focuses on observing a subset of behaviors (e.g., verbal vs. nonverbal disruptions); and time-sampling, which consists of observations during predetermined times. In our scenario, the teacher's aide may observe the number of times the student (subject-sampling) verbally interrupts (behavior-sampling) the teacher during a 30-minute math lesson (time-sampling) in the actual classroom setting.

When performing naturalistic observations, the occurrences of problem behaviors and environmental events can be manually recorded and coded in real time, or they can be recorded using instrumentation (e.g., video or tape recorder) and later coded for problem behaviors (Dishion & Granic, 2004). Observers can also use laptop or PDA computers to record event occurrences in real time as well as develop a systematic coding system or adopt previously developed coding systems that include operational definitions of the behaviors and environmental events of interest (Kerig & Lindahl, 2001). In our scenario, the student and class could be video recorded for later coding rather than having the teacher's aide record her observations during class periods.

Naturalistic observations allow for increased precision and specificity in the measurement of behavior-environment interactions unique to an individual. It is a flexible and simple assessment method (e.g., it can be done by anyone who is trained in the coding system), and it can be used across behaviors, populations, and settings (e.g., school, home, social situations). Behavioral observation is also amenable to time-series assessment strategies, a powerful strategy for identifying functional relationships between behavior problems and potential controlling factors (Kahng & Iwata, 1998).

The utility of behavioral observation can be limited by the degree to which behaviors are displayed at the time of observation and thus less useful for low-frequency and socially sensitive behaviors. Reactive effects may also occur, which decrease the ecological validity of the data in that a person's behavior or environment can be influenced by the presence of an observer or recording device. The reliability of the coding system and the skills of the observer can also affect the validity of the data collected.

Analogue Behavioral Observation

Scenario: A counseling psychologist is treating a couple for marital discord. The treatment has focused on improving the couple's communication style (e.g., negative attributions, lack of "listening" skills, distracting comments), and the psychologist wants to assess the effects of her treatment after six therapy sessions.

In the above scenario, the psychologist is interested in determining the effects of her treatment on the couple's problem behavior. Thus, she wants to observe the couple's communication style while discussing a problematic situation to evaluate whether or not improvements are evident or the treatment needs to be modified.

Analogue behavioral observations are a powerful, cost-effective (vs. naturalistic observations) assessment method, especially for low-frequency behaviors. During an analogue behavioral observation, the assessor can design and manipulate a particular situation in a contrived setting (e.g., clinic or lab) that approximates the real-world setting to directly observe specific behaviors and their functional relations (Heyman & Slep, 2004; also see Special Section on behavioral analogue observation in *Psychological Assessment*, 23, no. 1, March 2001). In our scenario, the therapist might ask the couple to discuss several problem areas in their relationship, such as financial problems and disagreements about parenting,

for 10 minutes in her office, which will allow her to directly observe their interaction. During this time, she can easily track the number of times the problem behaviors are displayed by the wife (e.g., shouting and invalidating statements) and husband (e.g., use of derogatory words), as well as the emotional tone of the discussion and paralinguistic events (e.g., shrugs, frowns, and smiles).

Analogue behavioral observations can be used for testing a hypothesis as well as for evaluating treatment effects. In our scenario, the psychologist may arrange analogue behavioral observations to test the hypothesis that the husband's lack of reflective or "active listening" comments is leading to the wife's feelings of rejection by the husband. Thus, analogue behavioral observations can be tailored to an individual or a group of persons (e.g., a couple, teacher-child interaction), to the assessment goals (e.g., case formulation, examining treatment effects), and to the specific behaviors of interest (e.g., verbal communication, parent-child interaction). They allow for the identification of environmental triggers (e.g., wife's tangential comments) of a specific behavior or emotion (e.g., husband's derogatory remarks or feeling unsupported) and the observation of social interactions in highly controlled situations. However, because of the contrived nature of the assessment process, some data (e.g., the rates of particular behaviors) gathered during analogue behavioral observations can have reduced ecological validity. We refer you to Haynes (2001) for a more extensive discussion on the psychometric characteristics of analogue behavioral observations and to the Special Section in *Psychological Assessment* (2001) for additional discussions of the applicability, utility, and limitations of analogue behavioral observations.

Self-Monitoring

Scenario: A primary care psychologist is beginning to treat a patient who reports that he always feels sad and never has enough energy to get things accomplished. Retrospectively, the patient rates his mood as a 10 (on a scale of 1 to 10, 10 being the most sad) for all day, every day of the week.

In the above scenario, the psychologist knows that there is variability in mood, even in individuals with major depression, and that many settings and events can affect the patient's depressed mood. Thus, the assessment goal with this patient is to identify causal variables (e.g., thoughts, criticism from a coworker) that could explain changes in the dimensions (e.g., duration and intensity) and response modes (e.g., affective and motor) of the patient's depressed mood over time.

Self-monitoring (i.e., self-assessment) can be a useful assessment method to capture the functional relations of a person's behavior problem (e.g., behavior-environment interactions) in real time and in real-world settings, making it amenable to time-series assessment strategies. We refer you to the Special Section on Self-Monitoring in *Psychological Assessment*, 11, no. 4, December 1999, and to Sigmon and LaMattina (2006) for more detailed discussions on self-monitoring methods.

In our scenario, the therapist might ask the patient to record his thoughts, co-occurring events, and mood every hour throughout the day, for several days, using an electronic diary to identify the factors that affect his mood. Thus, self-monitoring can be used in many different real-world contexts to evaluate a wide range of behaviors and their functional relations either randomly or at specified times of the day. The same data-sampling strategies we reviewed for naturalistic observations apply to self-monitoring.

Self-monitoring can be done using paper and pencil or electronic equipment (e.g., PDA (Personal Digital Assistants) or electronic diaries; see Hufford, Stone, Shiffman, Schwartz, & Broderick, 2002). It can be an efficient method for measuring the effects of environmental events and for gathering data on low-frequency and less observable behaviors. It helps to

reduce the effects of recall biases associated with retrospective self-report methods. However, the validity of self-monitoring data is limited by the person's ability and level of motivation to understand and comply with the self-monitoring strategy and instructions. Electronic devices can help to ensure the real-time recording of data by prompting a person to record (e.g., alarm on a PDA), and data can be transmitted electronically (e.g., Bluetooth technology) with minimum effort on the part of the person self-monitoring (Smyth & Stone, 2003). The primary drawback is that these devices can be expensive and require some training in their use.

Psychophysiological Assessment and Ambulatory Biosensors

Scenario: A research psychologist is examining psychophysiological, emotional, and cognitive responses to naturally occurring environmental stimuli of war veterans with and without post-traumatic stress disorder (PTSD). The participants are asked to record their mood, any intrusive thoughts, and stressful environmental situations while wearing an ambulatory device that records heart rate, blood pressure, and muscle tension every half-hour of the waking hours for a week.

In this scenario, the researcher is interested in identifying the psychophysiological responses, thoughts, and emotions associated with stressful and nonstressful situations that most strongly differentiate between war veterans with and without PTSD.

Psychophysiological assessment, either in the clinic or via the use of ambulatory biosensors in the natural environment, is a powerful method of assessing physiological responses (e.g., heart rate, increase in cortisol levels) to changes in environmental conditions. A wide range of physiological and motor behaviors can be assessed with psychophysiological measurements, such as cardiovascular reactivity, cortisol and blood glucose levels, respiration, skin conductance, muscle tension, and physical activity.

Psychophysiological measures are often used in conjunction with other assessment methods, such as self-monitoring, to gather data about a person's physiological responses to stimuli that one may not be able to readily report or observe (Haynes & Yoshioka, 2007). Often, physiological and motor behaviors are the primary interest in behavioral assessment, such as research on treatment outcome with essential hypertension, diabetes, or chronic pain (Stetter & Kupper, 2002). In other applications, psychophysiological measures are considered markers of higher-level constructs, such as anxiety or sleep quality. In the context of functional analysis, we are often interested in covariation among psychophysiological responses and cognitive processes (e.g., irrational thoughts) and environmental events, such as when we are interested in identifying behaviors and environmental stressors most strongly associated with blood glucose levels for a patient with subclinical diabetes.

Because clinic-based psychophysiological measures can have low ecological validity, assessors might use ambulatory biosensors, which allow for the collection of motor and physiological responses in real-world settings with minimum disruption. In our scenario, multiple assessment methods — self-monitoring and ambulatory biosensors — are used to gather cognitive (e.g., "I cannot trust these people"), emotional (e.g., anger), motor (e.g., increased muscle tension), and physiological responses (e.g., blood pressure) to specific environmental events over time.

Compared to self-report methods of assessing physiological and motor responses, psychophysiological methods can yield more reliable and precise measurements. They can also provide extensive data across time, which makes them ideal for time-sampling and time-series analytic strategies (Griffin & Gottman, 1990). However, the instrumentation can be expensive, technologically challenging (e.g., requires special training), and cumbersome (e.g., wearing a blood pressure cuff during a physical activity) to use. We refer you to Cacioppo, Tassinary, and Berntson (2007) for a more detailed discussion about psychophysiological assessment methods.

USE OF MULTIPLE METHODS, MULTIPLE INFORMANTS, AND VALID MEASURES

We provided clinical and research scenarios to illustrate a few applications of behavioral assessment methods. However, behavioral assessment methods are not restricted to these applications. For example, a naturalistic observation with a participant observer could have been used to collect data on the functional relations of the psychiatric patient's disruptive behaviors on the unit instead of, or in addition to, using self-report methods. In addition to self-monitoring, a functional behavioral interview could have also been used to identify the functional relations of the patient's depressed mood. The behavioral assessment paradigm emphasizes the use of multiple methods of data collection (e.g., direct observation and self-monitoring) and multiple sources of data (e.g., spouse, coworkers, teachers, and health professionals).

The rationale for using multiple methods and multiple informants is that each method has its own strengths and limitations, as we highlighted throughout this section and summarized in Table 6.1. Each assessment method provides unique information when assessing similar behavior problems and their causes as well as having unique sources of error (Meyer et al., 2001). For instance, self-report measures can be good at capturing a person's attitudes and beliefs about environmental events that lead to panic attacks, but they are subject to recall and other biases that threaten the validity of the data. Having a person self-monitor her panic episodes might allow for the identification of specific environmental triggers, but the validity of the data can be influenced by the person's adherence to self-monitoring instructions (e.g., recording events as they occur). Furthermore, people can differ in their perspectives and biases concerning their own and others' behavior problems and causes, and people can differ in the settings (e.g., school for a teacher, home for a parent) in which their perceptions are based. Thus, the use of multiple methods and multiple informants in the assessment process can increase the internal and ecological validity of our judgments about a person's behavior problems by reducing the sources of error unique to each method and increasing the contexts from which data are derived.

Underscoring the use of multiple methods and multiple informants is the use of valid measures. The degree to which our judgments about a person's behavior problems are valid is affected by the degree to which the measures we use are valid. The validity of a measure is determined by the degree to which it accurately reflects the construct or variable of interest. However, the validity of a measure, such as a score from a questionnaire or data from a biosensor, is *conditional*, that is, a measure's validity is limited to its intended use (e.g., clinical vs. research), population (e.g., age, ethnic, and socioeconomic groups), setting (e.g., schools vs. work), and conditions (e.g., timed vs. untimed performance) for which its validity was established. As we illustrate more fully in the next section, our measures should be valid, precise, and sensitive to change in order to improve the validity of our judgments about a person's behavior problem.

PRINCIPLES OF BEHAVIORAL ASSESSMENT

The methods and strategies of behavioral assessment are guided by several principles relevant to the nature of behavior problems, their

causes, and their measurement. In this section, we discuss the basic principles of the behavioral assessment paradigm. We discuss how people often have multiple and functionally related behavior problems that can differ in their dimensions (e.g., rate, intensity, and duration) and response modes (e.g., affective, motor, physiological, and cognitive) and that can change over time and across settings. We also discuss how similar behavior problems across persons can have different causal relationships that can also change over time and across settings.

Persons Have Multiple and Functionally Related Behavior Problems

Persons who seek, or are in need of, psychological services often have multiple or *comorbid* behavior problems. For example, as many as 99% of children with schizophrenia or schizoaffective disorder have at least one comorbid behavior disorder, such as depression (30%), oppositional defiant disorder (43%), and attention-deficit hyperactivity disorder (84%; Ross, Heinlein, & Tregellas, 2006). In persons who abuse inhaled substances (e.g., amyl nitrate and nitrous oxide), there is a high comorbidity of mood (48%), anxiety (36%), and personality disorders (45%; Wu & Howard, 2007). Comorbid behavior problems can also be found in persons without a formal psychiatric diagnosis, such as when job stressors lead to sleep problems (Knudsen, Ducharme, & Roman, 2007) or when marital conflicts lead to depressive symptoms (Balog et al., 2003). We refer you to Haynes and Kaholokula (2008), Krueger and Markon, (2006), and Lilienfeld, Waldman, and Israel (1994) for further discussions of comorbidity.

Behavior problems can covary because one behavior problem causes other behavior problems, as illustrated by Functional Relation A in Figure 6.1, such as when a person's marital discord causes both sexual dysfunctions

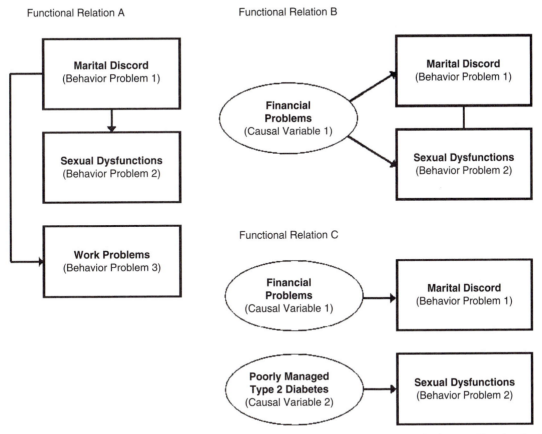

Functional Relation A

Functional Relation B

Functional Relation C

FIGURE 6.1   The three diagrams illustrate how a person's multiple behavior problems can be functionally related using an example of a person who is seeking treatment for marital discord.

(e.g., low sexual urge and arousal) and work problems (e.g., frequent sick days). Functional Relation B depicts how behavior problems can covary because they share the same causal variable, such as when a person's marital discord and sexual problems are caused by financial problems. As depicted in Functional Relation C, behavior problems can covary because of different but covarying causal variables, such as when a person's marital discord is due to financial problems while sexual dysfunctions are due to a poor self-management of type 2 diabetes. Note that, as depicted in Functional Relation C, the independent causal variables must be

operating at the same time for comorbidity to be occurring.

Knowing, or not knowing, that a person has multiple and possibly interrelated behavior problems affects how we conduct an assessment and the judgments we make, such as treatment foci, based on the data obtained. Take, for example, the treatment foci that would have the greatest magnitude of effect for each of the three functional relations depicted in Figure 6.1. In Functional Relation A of Figure 6.1, the treatment target that would have the greatest magnitude of effect on all three behavior problems is the person's marital discord because any improvement in this behavior problem would most likely lead to corresponding improvements in sexual functioning and work performance. In this case, a treatment that targeted his sexual dysfunctions would not be as effective and would have a smaller magnitude of effect on all three behavior problems because the important causal variable was not being targeted. Contrast this with Functional Relation C, where multiple treatment targets are needed to have the greatest magnitude of effect on his multiple behavior problems. In this case, a treatment strategy that targeted both his financial problems and the self-management of his diabetes would most likely have the greater magnitude of effect on his comorbid behavior problems. We discuss additional variables affecting treatment outcome later in this section and later in this chapter.

Figure 6.1 also indicates how our estimation of the *direction* of functional relations between behavior problems can influence the foci of treatment. Imagine, for example, how our treatment target would change if in Functional Relation A the person's work problems were causing his marital problems and sexual dysfunctions rather than how the relations between these behavior problems are currently depicted. In this case, a treatment strategy that focused on the person's work-related problems would have the greatest magnitude of effect. Thus, the degree to which we can describe and explain the functional relations among a person's comorbid behavior problems affects the degree to which we can make appropriate treatment recommendations, predict the risk of harm or post-treatment relapse, and estimate treatment outcomes.

To capture a person's comorbid and functionally interrelated behavior problems, the best assessment methods and strategies are those that allow us to explain as well as describe the problem behaviors. Therefore, an important emphasis in behavioral assessment is on identifying the functional relations between a client's behavior problems. Functional behavioral interviews, direct observations, and self-monitoring of behavior problems are useful in identifying co-occurring behaviors and in explaining their functional relations. Functional interviews can help to identify the presence of multiple behavior problems and their functional relations with such questions as "Have you noticed other areas of difficulties associated with your avoidance of large social groups?" or "What happens after you have too much to drink?" Observing antecedent events (e.g., husband's negative attributions toward wife) of a behavior problem (e.g., wife's depressed mood) and its consequences (e.g., social withdrawal) as they occur in their natural setting or during an analogue situation can help identify comorbid behavior problems and their functional relations.

Behavior Problems, Their Causes, and Functional Relations Are Idiographic and Dynamic in Nature

The attributes of a behavior problem can differ across persons in their most important dimensions (i.e., rate, duration, intensity, and onset latency), response modes (i.e., motor, cognitive, physiological, and affective), and *time-course* (i.e., changes in dimensions and response modes over time). For example, two people experiencing a major depressive episode may both have insomnia, loss of appetite, and difficulty concentrating, but one of them may have a more disruptive sleep pattern and more eating problems, while the other may have more frequent and greater difficulties in concentration. They could also differ on the primary response mode of their depressive episode where one person experiences guilty and bothersome self-deprecating thoughts (cognitive response mode), while the other experiences psychomotor agitation and bouts of extreme irritability (physiological and motor response mode).

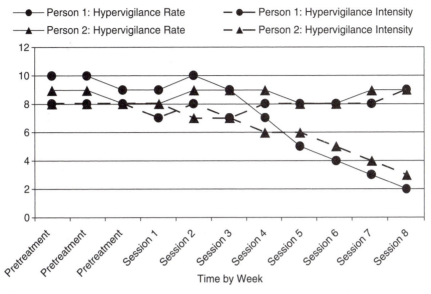

FIGURE 6.2 This figure depicts the time-series data of the rate and intensity of hypervigilance in two different persons with PTSD over the course of three assessment occasions and eight therapy sessions.

We depict the time course of hypervigilance on two dimensions (rate and intensity) across two persons being treated for PTSD in Figure 6.2 in order to illustrate how the dimensions of a behavior problem can differ in its time course across persons. Although the rate and intensity of both persons' hypervigilance in crowded settings are about the same initially, they change dramatically over the course of treatment but in different ways. For person 1, there is a large decrease in the rate of his hypervigilance with little change in intensity, whereas the inverse has occurred for person 2. We depict the time course of hypervigilance over three assessment occasions and eight treatment sessions, but differential responses to causal variables could also lead to similar changes in the two dimensions over time in the absence of a formal intervention. The change in person 1's rate of hypervigilance could be due to the presence of a new friend, while change in person 2's hypervigilance

intensity could be due to a recent move to a new neighborhood. These differences in causal factors and differential changes in the dimensions of a behavior problem also point to the conditional nature of behavior problems and their causal variables.

Individual differences in the dimensions, response modes, and time course of behavior problems have several implications for the clinical applications of behavioral assessment. First, the assessment should focus on identifying the important dimensions and response modes of a person's behavior problem and their changes over time within a person or across persons. Assessment is also often more clinically useful when focused on the precise (i.e., accurate, specific, and sensitive) measurement of lower-order variables (e.g., specific behaviors and thoughts) rather than higher-order variables that are aggregates of multiple facets of a construct (e.g., summary measures of "depression" and "social phobia").

Measures of aggregated variables can be helpful in understanding a person's behavior problems, but they do not allow for the identification of important dimensions and response modes of a person's behavior problems. Often, the variables that affect one dimension of a behavior problem, such as frequency, can be different from the variables that affect other dimensions, such as the duration or intensity of a behavior problem. In addition, the dimensions (e.g., decreasing the frequency of tension headaches) and response modes (e.g., decreasing a person's cognitive distortions or increasing his or her verbal social skills) are the targets of focused behavioral and cognitive interventions.

Not only are people's behavior problems idiographic and dynamic, but so are their causal variables and relations. For example, people's overt behaviors (e.g., physical aggression, alcohol consumption, time devoted to a task), emotions (e.g., negative and positive affect), and thoughts (e.g., attitudes, worries) can change in important ways across time. Many of these changes are often in response to changes in environmental events (e.g., a new job or a recent divorce), response contingencies (e.g., attention from peers for oppositional behavior), triggering stimuli (e.g., physical abuse), and contexts (e.g., home vs. work environment), which can also change in important ways across time. Of most interest in behavioral assessment are changes in the dimensions of a behavior problem and changes in the variables that affect those dimensions, such as changes in the rate and intensity of a person's delusional thoughts in response to changes in situational demands or changes in a person's sleep onset latency in response to changes in work hours.

Haynes and Kaholokula (2008) outlined several ways in which behavior problems can change over time in response to changes in causal variables and their functional relations. First, the repeated or prolonged exposure to a causal variable can result in the extinction, sensitization, or habituation of a behavior problem, such as when a fear of flying subsides after repeated exposure to flying in a computer-based flight simulator. Second, new causal variables may emerge while old causal variables cease to operate on a behavior problem, such as when a person's poor eating was maintained by work stress but is now maintained by a fear of gaining weight. Often the changes in the operating causal variables are due to changes in contextual or situational factors, such as when a child's disruptive classroom behaviors decrease due to a change in schools. Finally, the role of a *mediator* (i.e., a variable that accounts for, or explains, the relationship between two other variables) and *moderator* (i.e., a variable that affects the strength of the relationship or directionality of two other variables) can change over time, such as when a person's depressed mood is improved by the acquisition of new friends or manifested because of a change in thyroid-stimulating hormone levels.

The idiographic and dynamic nature of a person's behavior problems, their causal variables, and their functional relations has several implications for behavioral assessment. One implication is that a variable's state (a snapshot measure of the variable at one point in time) as well as its phase (the value of a variable in the context of prior time periods) should be measured in both clinical and research applications to capture change over time and across persons and conditions. We refer you to Haynes, Blaine, and Meyer (1995) for a discussion of *state-phase functions*. Another implication is that a person's behavior problems and causal variables should be measured repeatedly over time via a time-series assessment strategy, which involves repeated and ongoing measurements during assessment and treatment. As we illustrated earlier, assessment methods such as self-monitoring, behavioral observations and questionnaires, and psychophysiological measurements are conducive to time-series assessment strategies.

We have illustrated, thus far, that a person's behavior problem, its causes, and functional relations can change over time, and they can change in different ways across people with similar behavior problems. In a clinical setting, the implication for behavioral assessment is that it is desirable to keep measuring a person's behavior problem, its causal variables, and their functional relations over time and across contexts to improve the validity of our clinical judgments. In research, where we are often concerned with the assessment of multiple people, the systematic examination of changes in a behavior problem, its causes, and their functional relations across time can reveal important individual (e.g., age, sex, ethnic) and contextual (e.g., settings) differences in the effects of an intervention and the time course of treatment effects. Whether in the applied clinical or research setting, static or snapshot (e.g., single moment in time) measurements of a person's behavior problem, its causes, and their functional relations cannot capture their idiographic, dynamic, and contextual nature.

Behavior Problems Are Conditional

As we mentioned earlier, a person's behavior problems are often conditional: they can differ in their likelihood or other dimensions across situations and contexts. For example, a young child with autism may be more likely to injure herself in response to changes in academic demands but less likely to do so during play or while left alone by her teacher (O'Reilly, Sigafoos, Lancioni, Edrisinha, & Andrews, 2005). A woman recovering from alcohol abuse may be more likely to have a relapse in response to marital conflict than to other types of interpersonal conflicts (Walitzer & Dearing, 2006). A person may experience marital problems due to the use of an antidepressive medication that causes a decrease in sexual urge (Williams et al., 2006).

The conditional nature of a behavior problem can also differ across persons with similar behavior problems. For example, one person could be more likely to have an alcohol relapse in response to negative affect or interpersonal problems, while another person is more likely to have an alcohol relapse in response to social pressures to drink (Walitzer & Dearing, 2006). One person with a diagnosis of panic disorder with agoraphobia may experience panic attacks while riding in an elevator but not in an airplane, while the opposite might be true for another person with the same diagnosis.

As the previous examples illustrate, the conditions that affect a person's behavior problems can include social situations (e.g., the presence of unfamiliar people vs. familiar people), physical settings (e.g., classroom vs. home), psychological or physiological states (e.g., medication, intoxication, fatigue), and recent events (e.g., interpersonal conflict, loss of a loved one or a job). The examples also illustrate how the effects of such conditions can differ across persons with similar behavior problems. Moreover, they illustrate how contextual factors and settings often serve as causal variables for behavior problems and how they can affect the dimensions and attributes of a behavior problem. Often the meaning attributed (e.g., "No one likes me") to an environmental event (e.g., large social gathering) can affect the dimensions and attributes of a behavior problem (e.g., increased social withdrawal or worsening depressive episodes). Note that treatment foci would differ across persons as a function of differences in the settings associated with the occurrence of their behavior problem.

The best assessment strategies to capture the conditional nature of behavior problems require the examination of *differential conditional probabilities* — differences in the rate, duration, intensity, and latency to onset of behavior problems across contexts. The use of assessment methods such as functional interviews, direct observations, self-monitoring, and ambulatory biosensors is helpful in examining the conditional nature of behavior problems. For example, ambulatory biosensors can be used to measure changes in heart rate and galvanic skin response to different types of environmental events (e.g., driving in traffic, sitting in a crowded room) in a person with panic attacks. A person with social anxiety disorder can self-monitor the rate, duration, and intensity of his or her apprehensive expectations (e.g., people will laugh at me) and co-occurring environmental events (e.g., number of people present) across different settings (e.g., work and shopping).

The Causes of Behavior Problems Are Often Linked to Contemporaneous Environmental Events or Conditions

A large proportion of the variance in behavior problems across time and conditions for a person and between persons can often be explained by contemporaneous behavior-environment interactions. As indicated by many studies, contemporaneous environmental events or conditions can often explain why a behavior problem can differ in its rate, duration, and intensity across persons, time, and settings. Consider, for example, how a child only engages in self-injury when trying to avoid a demanding task or how a person might only experience a panic attack when in unfamiliar places.

The postulate that contemporaneous behavior-environment interactions often can account for a significant proportion of variance in a person's behavior problems has several implications for behavioral assessment. The primary focus of assessment is often on contemporaneous (e.g., what happens in the environment before, during, and after a behavior problem)

versus historical, or distal, causal variables. While historical (or distal) causal variables are important in understanding why some but not other persons develop a behavior problem, contemporaneous causal variables are often the best explanation of behavior variance across time, are more amenable to change, and, therefore, are more useful in therapy.

In clinical settings, we are often presented with clients who have been experiencing a behavior problem for an extended period of time. People seldom seek treatment following the initial onset or in the early phases of a problem. They are more likely to seek treatment after long periods of relationship difficulties, depression, headaches, anxiety, or inability to manage their children. Thus, our focus is often on identifying variables that are maintaining those problems rather than variables associated with their onset. We might ask "Why is it that our client is still depressed two years after a difficult divorce?" or "What is happening at home that might be maintaining a child's oppositional and aggressive behavior?"

Although the focus is on contemporaneous behavior-environment interactions, behavioral assessment is also concerned with contemporaneous cognitive (e.g., outcome expectations, self-evaluative thoughts) and emotional and physiological responses that serve to maintain a behavior problem. Thus, it is important to examine the differential operations of environmental and response contingencies and cognitive, affective, and physiological factors when differential conditional probabilities for a behavior problem (e.g., the likelihood of occurrence differs across settings) are evident. Behavioral observations, self-monitoring, and ambulatory biosensors are powerful assessment methods for identifying the relative importance of contemporaneous behavior-environment interactions and co-occurring cognitive, affective, and physiological variables that may affect a person's behavior problem.

FUNCTIONAL ANALYSIS: A CLINICAL AND RESEARCH APPLICATION OF BEHAVIORAL ASSESSMENT

As we mentioned earlier and illustrated throughout this chapter, behavioral assessment is well suited for a wide range of clinical and research applications because of its idiographic focus, conceptual basis, and methodological diversity. Functional analysis is just one application of behavioral assessment. Various definitions of the term *functional analysis* have been used across disciplines and by scholars in behavior therapy. We define functional analysis as the idiographic identification (when discussing behavioral clinical case formulation) or the systematic manipulation (when discussing experimental research) of important and modifiable functional relations of specific behavior problems in specific settings and conditions.

In this section, we briefly outline the characteristics of functional analysis. We then review functional analysis for behavioral clinical case formulation with an example of a client seeking outpatient treatment and illustrate the application of behavioral assessment in this context. Finally, we review a study by Christensen, Young, and Marchant (2007) to illustrate the use of behavioral assessment and functional analysis in the context of single-subject experimental research. In both contexts, we illustrate the components of functional analysis. We refer you to Haynes et al. (2002) for a more detailed discussion of the application of behavioral assessment to functional analysis as a behavioral clinical case formulation model and to Kazdin (2002) for single-subject experimental research designs.

Characteristics of Functional Analysis

We briefly outline the key characteristics of functional analysis to illustrate how it is consistent with the behavioral assessment paradigm and how it is useful in the idiographic identification of important and modifiable functional relations of a person's specific behavior problems.

The key characteristics of functional analysis are as follows:

- A functional analysis emphasizes the identification of *important* (e.g., greatest magnitude of effect), *controllable* (e.g., amenable to modification in treatment) causal variables that are functionally related to a person's behavior problem.
- A functional analysis is based on our *best estimates* or working hypotheses of a person's behavior problem, its causes, and their functional relations. Thus, it is a set of tentative and modifiable clinical judgments, based on the acquisition of new data and integration with prior research.
- A functional analysis is *nonexclusionary* to the possibility of other existing and valid functional relations. For example, a strong functional relationship between negative thoughts about weight gain and smoking relapse does not exclude the possibility of a strong functional relationship between increased life stressors and smoking relapse.
- A functional analysis is *dynamic, in that it can change over time.* Thus, it is modifiable based on clinical judgments derived from additional data about changes in a person's behavior problem, its causal variables, and their functional relations over time.
- A functional analysis is *conditional* because its validity is limited to specific domains (e.g., setting, person's psychological state or developmental stage). For example, a functional analysis of the likelihood of a person having a smoking relapse during a social gathering

will be different from a functional analysis of her likelihood of having a smoking relapse at home or work.

- The *level of specificity* can differ for a functional analysis. The degree to which higher- (e.g., depression) and lower-order (e.g., hypersomnia or loss of appetite) variables are used in a functional analysis varies depending on its specific purpose.

- A functional analysis is compatible with a *goal-oriented constructional approach* to assessment where the goal is to increase desirable behaviors while reducing undesirable behaviors. Thus, a constructional approach to assessment seeks to identify a person's strengths, available resources, and positive intervention goals (Haynes & O'Brien, 2000). Goal-oriented constructional intervention strategies also depend on assessment-based estimates of shared variance[4] and magnitude of effect.

- A functional analysis is the integration of nomothetically based empirical research findings with qualitative and quantitative assessment data for a single client. The validity of a functional analysis for a person can be increased if assessors are knowledgeable about the current empirical research relevant to a specific behavior problem and its most common functionally related variables. This information can guide initial assessments with a person and help to generate reasonable hypotheses about possible causes of a person's behavior problem.

- A functional analysis should include extended *social systems*, especially when they have treatment implications for a person's behavior problem. For example,

chains of causal variables may be related to the behaviors of parents, teachers, supervisors, staff members who are also affected by the behavior of other people, life stressors, and policies at the workplace.

- Functional analysis has other characteristics not outlined here, such as the consideration of noncontiguous variables (e.g., causal variables not temporally related) of a behavior problem and the functional response classes of a behavior. We refer you to Haynes and O'Brien (2000) for more elaboration on the characteristics of functional analysis.

Functional Analysis for Clinical Case Formulation

We illustrate functional analysis as a behavioral clinical case formulation strategy and the application of behavioral assessment in this context with an example of a client seeking services at an outpatient community health center. The client was Mr. Kanoa, a 45-year-old married male of mixed Asian American and Pacific Islander ethnic ancestries, who presented with marital problems. In describing Mr. Kanoa's functional analysis, we use the Functional Analytic Clinical Case Model (FACCM), which is a vector diagram that illustrates and quantifies important elements of a functional analysis (Haynes & O'Brien, 2000). The FACCM is used to assist us with organizing pre-intervention data and hypotheses, making appropriate assessment decisions, and selecting intervention targets. The FACCM depicting Mr. Kanoa's functional analysis after three assessment occasions is presented in Figure 6.3, and the legend for the FACCM is presented in Figure 6.4.

Mr. Kanoa's assessment process began by obtaining his informed consent for the goals and methods of the behavioral assessment. The first focus of the assessor was the specification of his behavior problems (e.g., their

---

[4]Shared variance is the amount of the same thing being measured by, or reflected in, two or more variables. For example, both marital discord and work problems can account for the frequency of a person's binge drinking.

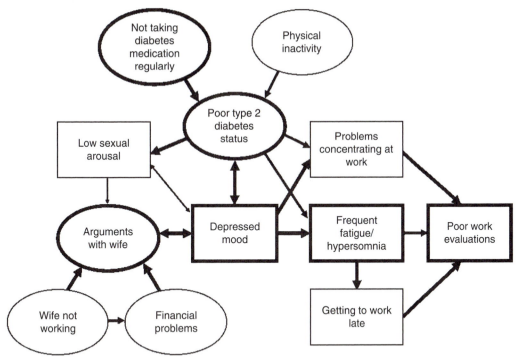

FIGURE 6.3   The Functional Analytic Clinical Case Model (FACCM) illustrates Mr. Kanoa's behavioral clinical case formulation (functional analysis) with data derived from multiple assessment methods (e.g., interviews and questionnaires) and from multiple informants (e.g., wife and primary care physician).

dimensions and response modes) and intervention goals. This was done in collaboration with Mr. Kanoa to help guide subsequent assessment methods and foci. The initial semistructured behavioral interview with Mr. Kanoa identified him as having clinical depression (i.e., intense, persistent feelings of sadness) four times a week on average over the past six months, being frequently (three times in the past workweek) late to work, having difficulty concentrating at work, and having problems being sexually intimate with his wife (e.g., difficulty obtaining and maintaining erections). Mr. Kanoa stated that his marital problems stem from his problems with sexual intimacy, and thus his main intervention goal was to be more sexually intimate with his wife. Mr. Kanoa gave permission to interview Mrs. Kanoa.

Over three assessment occasions, multiple assessment methods were used to collect data from multiple informants. Semistructured interviews were conducted with Mr. and Mrs. Kanoa, separately, to specify Mr. Kanoa's behavior problems, their causes, and factors that might be affecting them at home and at work. Mrs. Kanoa was also interviewed about her marital concerns and other concerns she had for her husband. They also completed questionnaires and checklists to assess their marital problems (e.g., Marital Satisfaction Inventory, Revised, Snyder, 1997; Spouse Observation Checklist, Birchler, Weiss, & Vincent, 1975), and Mr. Kanoa completed questionnaires to specify the dimensions and response modes of his depressive symptoms (e.g., Beck Depression Inventory-II, Beck, Steer, & Brown, 1996).

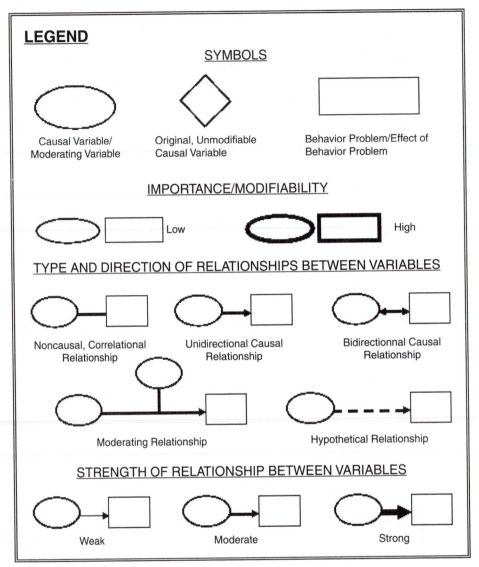

FIGURE 6.4   FACCM legend explaining the symbols used to depict the types of variables, the type and direction of relationships, and the strength and importance/modifiability of variables and their relationships.

Mr. Kanoa also monitored, with a PDA, his depressed mood, along with concurrent thoughts about his marital relationship, several times a day over the course of five working days to gather real-time data on his depressed mood in the home and work environment. Early on in the assessment process, Mrs. Kanoa reported that her husband was recently diagnosed with type 2 diabetes. In a brief telephone interview with Mr. Kanoa's primary care physician, she stated that his diabetes was not well controlled and that he may have had diabetes for a number of years before being diagnosed. To assess Mr. Kanoa's diabetes self-care, he completed the Summary of Diabetes Self-care Activities measure, a brief self-report questionnaire (Toobert, Hampson, & Glasgow, 2000).

After a review of the scientific literature on the relationships between depression and diabetes, the assessor found that comorbid depression occurred in about one-third of persons with type 2 diabetes (Anderson et al., 2001) and that many of the symptoms of depression overlap with the symptoms of diabetes (e.g., fatigue, concentration difficulties, and sexual problems in males).

The assessor's clinical judgments about Mr. Kanoa, based on multimethod and multisource clinical assessment data and relevant empirical literature, were organized using the FACCM. We refer you to the FACCM legend in Figure 6.4 for an explanation of the symbols used to depict the type of variables, the type and direction of relationships, and their magnitude of effects (e.g., their strengths) and importance/modifiability in Mr. Kanoa's FACCM.[5] His FACCM illustrates the identified causal variables and functional relations hypothesized to affect his behavior problems and how his behavior problems are functionally related. It also illustrates the magnitude of effect estimated for each causal variable and its relation to a behavior problem. What is not illustrated in Figure 6.3 is how Mr. Kanoa's FACCM changed (e.g., modification of causal variables and relations) over the three assessment occasions as more data were collected. Thus, his FACCM depicted in Figure 6.3 is tentative and can change as his behavioral problems, their causes, and their modifiability change over time, as new assessment data are collected and as treatment progresses.

The magnitude of effect for each variable and the direction and strength of the relationship between variables were estimated from the assessment data. For example, the degree to which Mr. Kanoa's marital problems were affecting his depression was assessed by examining the relationship between his depressed mood and positive and negative thoughts about his marriage from his self-monitoring data. Inquiries designed to estimate conditional probabilities (e.g., the likelihood that depressed mood would be elevated, given a particular event or context) were made to Mr. Kanoa, such as "Tell me about your thoughts, feelings, and behavior after you have attempted to be intimate with your wife." Mr. Kanoa was also asked to separately rate the degree to which his marital and work problems, his depression, and his diabetes were adversely affecting his quality of life by rating their impact on a scale of 1 to 10, with 1 having the weakest and 10 having the strongest impact. Thus, data from his self-monitoring, functional interviews, and impact ratings were helpful in determining the direction of the causal relationships and their magnitude of effect.

Mr. Kanoa's current FACCM suggests that a treatment targeting his marital distress and his diabetes self-care would have the greatest magnitude of effect on his depressed mood and low sexual arousal, and his diabetes (e.g., chronic hyperglycemia) and depression symptoms affecting his work performance (e.g., concentration difficulties and fatigue). Furthermore, his depressed mood and the poor management of his diabetes were both hypothesized to account for variance (i.e., shared variance) in his poor concentration, fatigue, and low sexual arousal. Mr. Kanoa's strengths and personal resources identified in his functional analysis included his love for the outdoors (important for increasing his physical activity) and his wife (important for improving their relationship) and his strong spiritual beliefs (important as sources of support and guidance).

A treatment plan was collaboratively worked out with Mr. Kanoa that involved marital therapy with he and his wife focusing on increasing their sexual intimacy and communication skills and helping him better manage his diabetes

---

[5]The authors would like to acknowledge Marcin Bury for creating and allowing us to use the FACCM legend (Figure 6.4) in this chapter.

(e.g., increasing his physical activity). His personal strengths and resources were integrated into the treatment plan, such as using his love for the outdoors as a means of having quality time with his wife and increasing his physical activity.

Throughout the course of Mr. Kanoa's treatment, frequent and ongoing assessments of his behavioral problems, their causes, and their functional relations were done. Frequent measurements (e.g., weekly) of his depressed mood and marital relationship were done via self-report measures, such as functional questionnaires and brief interviews. His diabetes self-management was assessed daily via the use of a PDA to self-monitor his symptoms of diabetes and to record his blood glucose (before and after meals) and each occurrence, duration, and intensity of physical activity. The ongoing assessment of Mr. Kanoa's treatment helped to continuously evaluate its effects and inform treatment modifications, if any were needed.

Although we stress the importance of the functional analysis in selecting the most effective treatment foci, we also want to emphasize that additional factors affect ultimate treatment strategies and outcome. In conducting hundreds of functional analyses, it is our experience that rarely is an ultimate treatment focus based entirely on the functional analysis. A few of the other factors that affect treatment foci include the theoretical orientation and expertise of the therapist, the cost of the treatment and economic resources of the client, the resources and policies of the service providers, staffing and supervision patterns of hospitals and schools, support and barriers from the client's family and friends, time constraints of the client and therapist, and the client's previous therapy experiences.

A major thesis of this chapter is that, in many cases, the effectiveness of a treatment is associated with the degree to which it focuses on important and modifiable causal variables. However, many of the factors mentioned in the previous paragraph also affect treatment outcome, along with others such as the therapist's fidelity to empirically supported treatment strategies, the client's adherence to treatment recommendations, the client's expectations regarding the costs and benefits of behavior change, the nature of the client-therapist relationship, new moderating and mediating events that occur during treatment, and the negative and positive side-effects of the treatment.

Functional Analysis in Experimental Research

To illustrate functional analysis and the application of behavioral assessment in the context of single-subject experimental research, we review a study by Christensen and her colleagues (2007). They systematically examined an assessment-based intervention to increase the prosocial classroom behaviors of Jose, a socially withdrawn third grade Hispanic child with a learning disability. Several behavioral assessment methods and strategies were used to identify Jose's specific classroom behavior problems and behavior-environment interactions and to examine the effectiveness of an intervention designed specifically for him.

Christensen and her colleagues used multiple methods and multiple informants in their initial behavioral assessment of Jose to identify targets and strategies for intervention. For example, a functional behavioral interview was done with Jose's teacher to identify the specific behaviors of concern and the settings most academically and socially problematic for him, as well as the settings in which he was most successful (e.g., exhibited prosocial classroom behaviors). Direct classroom observations were made of Jose's interactions with his classmates for several hours during his general education class by the school's behavior specialist. The behavior specialist collected data on the frequency and quality of his social interactions (e.g., initiating conversations and being assertive) with other children. Using a goal-oriented constructional approach to assessment, they also identified a *response class* of positive alternative behaviors, such as attending to and complying with the teacher's instructions, initiating social interactions with peers, and being assertive with peers (e.g., standing up for himself).

From the initial behavioral assessment process, Christensen et al. determined that the intervention goals were to increase Jose's prosocial classroom behaviors with the idea that, by doing so, his academic performance would also improve. They also determined that the focus of the intervention would be to increase seven specific prosocial classroom behaviors (e.g., attending to teacher and getting her attention appropriately) using a combination of intervention strategies (i.e., skill development, self-management with reinforcers, and peer mediation). The intervention foci and strategies they employed were informed by prior empirical research and the idiographic assessment data they collected. To systematically test the effects of the intervention, they employed an ABAB single-subject withdrawal design (see Franklin, Allison, & Gorman, 1996; Kazdin, 2002). We illustrate an ABAB single-subject withdrawal design in Figure 6.5 using a hypothetical case of a child who received a similar

intervention to increase her prosocial classroom behaviors.

In Christensen et al.'s study, the first baseline period (first phase A) in the ABAB design consisted of direct classroom behavioral observations to collect data on Jose's prosocial classroom behaviors prior to implementing the intervention. The observations were done using a 10-second whole-interval recording strategy. Observations were made for 10 consecutive school days for 25 to 40 minutes per day. The first intervention period (first phase B) was the implementation of the intervention for 7 consecutive school days while continuing to observe and record Jose's prosocial classroom behaviors. The intervention was then withdrawn for 4 consecutive school days while continuing to observe and record Jose's prosocial classroom behaviors (return to baseline; second phase A). Finally, the intervention was reintroduced (second phase B) with systematic changes in the reinforcement schedule (i.e., thinning) while observations continued over 20 more consecutive school days. The researchers also observed and recorded the same prosocial classroom behaviors of the other 18 students in Jose's third grade class in order to have comparison group data. Interobserver agreement estimates for all observational data were calculated to ensure a high degree of consistency across observers,

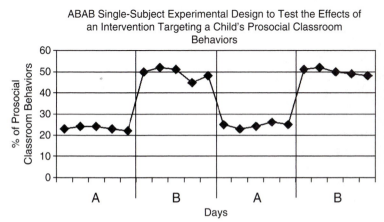

FIGURE 6.5 This figure depicts an ABAB single-subject withdrawal design to examine the effects of an intervention to increase prosocial classroom behaviors in a child. The first A phase is the initial baseline phase, the first B phase is the introduction of the intervention, the second A phase is the withdrawal of the intervention, and the final B phase is the reintroduction of the intervention. During each phase, the number of prosocial classroom behaviors exhibited by the child was observed over a five-day period.

which were in 90% agreement for Jose's prosocial classroom behaviors and 82% agreement for those of the comparison group.

Similar to the trends depicted in Figure 6.5, Christensen et al. found that Jose exhibited prosocial behavior an average of 48% of the time across the observation sessions in the initial baseline phase (first phase A) but that it increased to an average of 94% when the intervention was first introduced (first phase B). When the intervention was withdrawn (second phase A), the child's average prosocial classroom behaviors dropped down to 67%. It then increased to as high as 97% after reintroducing the intervention (final phase B). During the baseline phases, Jose's prosocial classroom behaviors were well below the mean (77%) of those exhibited by his peers but considerably higher than peers during the intervention phases.

Beyond illustrating experimental functional analysis as a single-subject experimental research strategy to identify causal factors for a behavior problem and the use of behavioral assessment, the study by Christensen and her colleagues also illustrates the importance of assessment data in designing an effective intervention. Their study also illustrates some of the key components of experimental functional analysis, such as the systematic manipulation of an independent variable (e.g., an intervention) while simultaneously examining changes in a dependent variable (e.g., child's prosocial classroom behaviors) over time.

RECOMMENDATIONS FOR ASSESSMENT

We conclude this chapter with assessment recommendations pertinent across a wide range of clinical and research applications. As we did throughout this chapter, we emphasize that our assessments should (1) identify important functional relations among behavior problems and causal variables, (2) capture the idiographic, dynamic, and conditional nature of a person's behavioral problems, their causes, and their functional relations, (3) be sensitive to individual differences and the client-assessor relationship, and (4) enhance the validity of our judgments about a person's behavior problem, the important targets of treatment, the best treatment strategies, and the effects and outcomes of our treatments. Thus, our recommendations are outlined as follows:

1. *Survey for multiple behavior problems.* Evaluate whether a person, couple, family, or group of individuals have other behavior problems beyond the presenting problem(s) or problems of interest.
2. *Estimate how multiple behavior problems are functionally related.* Look at how one behavior problem affects the other. Do they covary because they affect each other or share a common causal variable, or do they both have different causal variables?
3. *Identify the most important dimensions (i.e., rate, duration, intensity, and onset latency) and response modes (i.e., motor, physiological, affective, and cognitive) of a behavior problem.* This is important because most treatments are designed to affect specific dimensions and response modes of a behavior problem.
4. *Identify the important and modifiable functional relations of a behavior problem.* Identify the factors that affect a client's behavior problem and the ones that are most amenable to change during treatment.
5. *Use time-series assessment strategies to investigate how behavior problems change over time and across settings and contexts.* Keep measuring important behaviors across time and in pertinent situations and contexts during the assessment process and treatment.
6. *Employ multiple methods of data collection from multiple sources.* Augment self-report

methods with other methods of assessment (e.g., self-monitoring and analogue behavioral observation). In addition to the person being assessed, collect data from other relevant people, such as spouses, teachers, coworkers, and other health professionals.

7. *Use valid and precise measures that are sensitive to change.* Select measures that are the most valid and sensitive for the client and the goals of the assessment.

8. *Be sensitive to individual differences.* Match the assessment methods, strategies, and measures and the assessment goals to the individual. Be aware of how a person's ethnicity, gender, age, religious affiliation, physical and cognitive limitations, and sexual orientation can affect the assessment process, treatment goals, causal factors, and you as the assessor.

9. *Maintain a positive relationship with the person being assessed.* Take a collaborative, constructional, and supportive approach to assessment — focus also on a person's strengths.

10. *Maintain informed consent throughout the assessment process.* A person being assessed, whether a client or research participant, should know the methods (including the use of informants), purposes, and goals of assessment.

11. *Take a hypothesis testing approach.* Keep in mind that our assessments result in tentative clinical judgments that are likely to change with new information or because of natural changes in a person over time. Thus, be open to data that refute your hypothesis, and be willing to change your clinical judgments with new information.

12. *Go beyond diagnosis — specify the behavior problems and their causes.* A diagnosis is sometimes useful for describing a constellation of behavior problems, but it is often imprecise and insensitive to individual differences between persons with the same diagnosis, and it does not explain why a specific behavior problem occurs or why it changes over time and across contexts.

Glossary

Behavioral Assessment: A science-based psychological assessment with an interrelated set of concepts, methods, and strategies that describe and explain human behavior. Advocates of behavioral assessment encourage the use of valid and precise (i.e., accurate) assessment measures of lower-order behaviors, events, and phenomena using empirically-based assessment methods and strategies.

Functional Analysis: The idiographic identification (when discussing behavioral clinical case formulation) or the systematic manipulation (when discussing experimental research) of hypothesized important and modifiable functional relations of specific behavior problems in specific settings and conditions.

References

Anderson, R. J., Freedland, K. E., Clouse, R. E., & Lustman, P. J. (2001). The prevalence of comorbid depression in adults with diabetes. *Diabetes Care, 24,* 1069–1078.

Balog, P., Imre, J., Leineweber, C., Blom, M., Wamala, S. P., & Orth-Gomér, K. (2003). Depressive symptoms in relation to marital and work stress in women with and without coronary heart disease. The Stockholm Female Coronary Risk Study. *Journal of Psychosomatic Research, 54,* 113–119.

Barbour, K. A. & Davison, G. C. (2004). Clinical interviewing. In S. N. Haynes, E. H. Heiby, & M. Hersen (Eds.), *Comprehensive handbook of psychological assessment*, Volume 3, *Behavioral assessment* (pp. 181–193). Hoboken, NJ: Wiley.

Beck, A. T., Steer, R. A., & Brown, G. K. (1996). *Manual for the Beck Depression Inventory* (2nd ed.). San Antonio: The Psychological Corporation.

Birchler, G. R., Weiss, R. L., & Vincent, J. P. (1975). A multimethod analysis of social reinforcement exchange between maritally distressed and nondistressed spouse and stranger dyads. *Journal of Personality and Social Psychology, 31,* 349–360.

Cacioppo, J. T., Tassinary, L., & Berntson, G. G. (2007). *Handbook of psychophysiology* (3rd ed.). New York: Cambridge University Press.

Christensen, L., Young, K. R., & Marchant, M. (2007). Behavioral intervention planning: increasing appropriate behavior of a socially withdrawn student. *Education and Treatment of Children, 30,* 81–103.

Dishion, T. J. & Granic, I. (2004). Naturalistic observation of relationship process. In S. N. Haynes, E. H. Heiby, & M. Hersen (Eds.), *Comprehensive handbook of psychological assessment,* vol. 3, *Behavioral assessment* (pp. 143–161). Hoboken, NJ: Wiley.

Fernandez-Ballesteros, R. (2004). Self-report questionnaires. In S. N. Haynes, E. H. Heiby, & M. Hersen (Eds.), *Comprehensive handbook of psychological assessment,* vol. 3, *Behavioral assessment* (pp. 194–221). Hoboken, NJ: Wiley.

Franklin, R. D., Allison, D. B., & Gorman, B. S. (1996). (Eds.), *Design and analysis of single case research.* Mahwah, NJ: Lawrence Erlbaum Associates.

Griffin, W. & Gottman, J. (1990). Depression and aggression in family interaction. In G. R. Patterson (Ed.), *Depression and aggression in family interaction: advances in family research* (pp. 131–168). Hillsdale, NJ: Lawrence Erlbaum Associates.

Hartmann, D. P., Barrios, B. A., & Wood, D. D. (2004). Principles of behavioral observation. In S. N. Haynes, E. H. Heiby, & M. Hersen (Eds.), *Comprehensive handbook of psychological assessment,* vol. 3, *Behavioral assessment* (pp. 108–127). Hoboken, NJ: Wiley.

Haynes, S. N. (2001). Clinical applications of analogue observation: dimensions of psychometric evaluation. *Psychological Assessment, 13,* 73–85.

Haynes, S. N., Blaine, D., & Meyer, K. (1995). Dynamical models for psychological assessment: phase-space functions. *Psychological Assessment, 7,* 17–24.

Haynes, S. N. & Heiby, E. (Eds.) (2004). *Behavioral assessment.* (vol. 3 as part of 5-volume Wiley *Comprehensive handbook on psychological assessment*). (Michel Hersen, Series Editor). Hoboken, NJ: Wiley.

Haynes, S. N. & Kaholokula, J. K. (2008). Behavioral assessment. In M. Hersen, & A. M. Gross (Eds.), *Handbook of clinical psychology.* New York: Wiley.

Haynes, S. N., Kaholokula, J. K., & Yoshioka, D. T. (2007). Principles and methods of behavioral assessment in treatment research. In A. M. Nezu & C. Nezu (Eds.), *Evidenced-based outcome research: A practical guide to conducting randomized controlled trials for psychosocial interventions.* New York: Oxford University Press.

Haynes, S. M., Nelson, K. G., Thatcher, I., & Kaholokula, J. K. (2002). Outpatient behavioral assessment and treatment target selection. In M. Hersen & L. K. Porzelius (Eds.), *Diagnosis, conceptualization, and treatment planning for adults: A step-by-step guide.* Mahwah, NJ: Lawrence Erlbaum Associates.

Haynes, S. N. & O'Brien, W. O. (2000). *Principles and practices of behavioral assessment.* New York: Plenum/Kluwer Press.

Haynes, S. N. & Yoshioka, D. T. (2007). Clinical assessment applications of ambulatory biosensors. *Psychological Assessment, 19,* 44–57.

Hersen, M. (Ed.) (2006a). *Clinician's handbook of child behavioral assessment.* San Diego, CA: Elsevier Academic Press.

Hersen, M. (Ed.) (2006b). *Clinician's handbook of adult behavioral assessment.* San Diego, CA: Elsevier Academic Press.

Heyman, R. E. & Slep, A. M. S. (2004). Analogue behavioral observation. In S. N. Haynes, E. H. Heiby, & M. Hersen (Eds.), *Comprehensive handbook of Psychological Assessment,* vol. 3, *Behavioral assessment* (pp. 162–180). Hoboken, NJ: Wiley.

Hufford, M. R., Stone, A. A., Shiffman, S., Schwartz, J. E., & Broderick, J. E. (2002). Paper vs. electronic diaries. *Applied Clinical Trials, 11,* 38–43.

Kahng, S. W. & Iwata, B. A. (1998). Computerized systems for collecting real-time observational data. *Journal of Applied Behavior Analysis, 31,* 253–261.

Kazdin, A. E. (2002). *Research designs in clinical psychology* (4th ed.). Boston: Allyn & Bacon.

Kerig, P. K. & Lindahl, K. M. (Eds.) (2001). *Family observational coding systems — resources for systemic research.* Mahwah, NJ: Lawrence Erlbaum Associates.

Knudsen, H., Ducharme, L. J., & Roman, P. M. (2007). Job stress and poor sleep quality: data from an American sample of full-time workers. *Social Science and Medicine, 64,* 1997–2007.

Koerner, K. & Linehan, M. M. (1997). Case formulation in dialectical behavior therapy. In T. D. Eells (Ed.), *Handbook of psychotherapy case formulation* (pp. 340–367). New York: Guilford Press.

Krueger, R. F. & Markon, K. E. (2006). Reinterpreting comorbidity: a model based approach to understanding and classifying psychopathology. *Annual Review of Clinical Psychology, 2,* 111–133.

Lenzenweger, M. & Hooley, J. (2002). *Principles of experimental psychopathology: essays in honor of Brendan A. Maher.* Washington, DC: American Psychological Association.

Lilienfeld, S. O., Waldman, I. D., & Israel, A. C. (1994). A critical examination of the use of the term and concept of comorbidity *in psychopathology research. Clinical Psychology Science and Practice, 1,* 71–103.

Meyer, G. J., Finn, S. E., Eyde, L. D., Kay, G. G., Moreland, K. V., Dies, R. R., Eisman, E. J., Kubiszyn, T. W., & Reed, G. M. (2001). Psychological testing and psychological assessment: a review of evidence and issues. *American Psychologist, 56,* 128–165.

Murphy, K. (2004). Assessment in work settings. In S. N. Haynes, E. H. Heiby, & M. Hersen (Eds.), *Comprehensive handbook of psychological assessment,* vol. 3, *Behavioral assessment* (pp. 346–364). Hoboken, NJ: Wiley.

Nezu, A. M., Nezu, C. M., Friedman, S. H., & Haynes, S. N. (1997). *Case formulation in behavior therapy: a problem-solving perspective* (pp. 9–34). Champaign, IL: Research Press Co.

O'Reilly, M., Sigafoos, J., Lancioni, G., Edrisnha, C., & Andrews, A. (2005). An examination of the effects of a classroom activity schedule on levels of self-injury and engagement for a child with severe autism. *Journal of Autism and Developmental Disorders, 35,* 305–311.

Persons, J. B. & Tompkins, M. A. (1997). Cognitive-behavioral case formulation. In T. D. Eells (Ed.), *Handbook of psychotherapy case formulation* (pp. 314–339). New York: Guilford Press.

Ross, R. G., Heinlein, S., & Tregellas, H. (2006). High rates of comorbidity are found in childhood-onset-schizophrenia. *Schizophrenia Research, 88,* 90–95.

Serper, M. R., Goldberg, B. R., & Salzinger, K. (2004). Behavioral assessment of psychiatric patients in restrictive settings. In S. N. Haynes, E. H. Heiby, & M. Hersen (Eds.), *Comprehensive handbook of psychological assessment,* vol. 3, *Behavioral assessment* (pp. 320–345). Hoboken, NJ: Wiley.

Shapiro, E. S. & Kratochwill, T. R. (2000). *Behavioral assessment in schools, theory research and clinical foundations.* (2nd ed.). New York: Guilford Press.

Sigmon, S. T. & LaMattina, S. M. (2006). Self assessment. In M. Hersen (Ed.), *Clinician's handbook of adult behavioral assessment* (pp. 145–164). San Diego, CA: Elsevier Academic Press.

Smyth, J. M. & Stone, A. A. (2003). Ecological momentary assessment research in behavioral medicine. *Journal of Happiness Studies, 4,* 35–52.

Snyder, D. K. (1997). *Marital Satisfaction Inventory, Revised.* Los Angeles, CA: Western Psychological Services.

Sobell, L. C. & Sobell, M. B. (1992). Timeline follow-back: A technique for assessing self-reported alcohol consumption. In R. Z. Litten & J. P. Allen, *Measuring alcohol consumption: psychosocial and biochemical methods* (pp. 41–72). Totowa, NJ: Humana Press.

Stetter, F. & Kupper, S. (2002). Autogenic training: a meta-analysis of clinical outcome studies. *Applied Psychophysiology & Biofeedback, 27,* 45–98.

Strosahl, K. D. & Robinson, P. J. (2004). Behavioral assessment in the era of managed care: understanding the present, preparing for the future. In S. N. Haynes, E. H. Heiby, & M. Hersen (Eds.), *Comprehensive handbook of psychological assessment,* vol. 3, *Behavioral assessment* (pp. 427–452). Hoboken, NJ: Wiley.

Tanaka-Matsumi, J. (2004). Individual differences and behavioral assessment. In S. N. Haynes, E. H. Heiby, & M. Hersen (Eds.), *Comprehensive handbook of psychological assessment,* vol. 3, *Behavioral assessment* (pp. 128–139). Hoboken, NJ: Wiley.

Toobert, D. J., Hampson, S. E., & Glasgow, R. E. (2000). The Summary of Diabetes Self-care Activities measure. *Diabetes Care, 23,* 943–950.

Walitzer, K. S. & Dearing, R. L. (2006). Gender differences in alcohol and substance use relapse. *Clinical Psychology Review, 26,* 128–148.

Wholey, J. S., Hatry, H. P., & Newcomer, K. E. (Eds.) (2004). *Handbook of Practical Program Evaluation.* San Francisco: Jossey-Bass.

Williams, V. S., Baldwin, D. S., Hogue, S. L., Fehnel, S. E., Hollis, K. A., & Edin, H. M. (2006). Estimating the prevalence and impact of antidepressant-induced sexual dysfunction in 2 European countries: a cross-sectional patient survey. *Journal of Clinical Psychiatry, 67,* 204–210.

Wu, L.-T. & Howard, M. O. (2007). Psychiatric disorders in inhalant users: results from the National Epidemiologic Survey on Alcohol and Related Conditions. *Drug and Alcohol Dependence, 88,* 146–155.

Clinical and Forensic Neuropsychology Assessment

Renée Lajiness-O'Neill
Eastern Michigan University
and Henry Ford Hospital

Isabelle Beaulieu
Center for Neuropsychology,
Learning, and Development of
Oakland County

Jenna Paunovich Wright
Kitch, Drutchas, Wagner,
Valitutti, & Sherbrook

OUTLINE

INTRODUCTION

Clinical neuropsychology "is a specialty that applies the principles of assessment and intervention based on the scientific study of human behavior as it relates to normal and abnormal functioning of the central nervous system. The specialty is dedicated to enhancing the understanding of brain-behavior relationships and the application of such knowledge to human problems" (American Psychological Association [APA], 1996, 2003, p. 149). Neuropsychologists are concerned with expanding our understanding of both brain structure and function and its relationship to human emotion, cognition, and behavior. As such, it is a discipline rooted in both psychology and the neurosciences. The levels of neuropsychological inquiry and domains of interest are vast (Figure 7.1) (Bigler, 2003). Neuropsychologists work with children and adults with developmental and acquired disorders for which alterations in cognitive, behavioral, and emotional functioning are evident.

Neuropsychologists obtain doctoral training that provides the generic psychology and clinical core. This is followed by an APA or

CPA-approved internship training program and a postdoctoral residency with specialty education in clinical neuropsychology (APA, 1998). Neuropsychologists are typically employed in hospitals and medical centers with academic affiliations, psychiatric settings, and private practice. While many neuropsychologists choose to specialize in either pediatric or adult neuropsychology, a substantial number evaluate and treat individuals across the developmental spectrum.

Given that a strong foundation in the neurosciences, including an understanding of cortical organization and function, is critical for an appreciation of the elaborate interplay between emotions, cognitions, and behavior, the chapter will begin with a brief review of the organization of the central nervous system. This will be followed by a review of higher-order functions of attention, memory and learning, spatial processing, language, executive functioning, emotion, and social cognition as well as a discussion of syndromes that occur when disruptions occur in these domains. A general overview of neuropsychological assessment will be

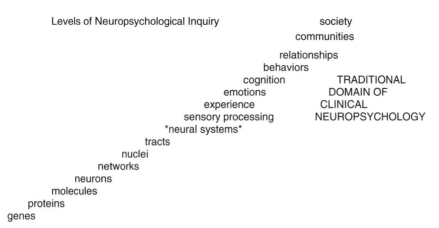

FIGURE 7.1   The different levels of neuropsychological inquiry from genes to complex social relationships that form societies. Traditional psychology has been primarily concerned with issues above the point of asterisks. (Acknowledgment: This chart from Bigler (2003) is a modification of a graph from O'Connor & Tasman, 1990.)

addressed. A review of how the recent science of neuropsychology has informed us about brain-behavior relationships in a number of clinical populations, both pediatric and adult, will follow. The chapter will address the current literature in frequently encountered disorders and is not intended to offer an exhaustive description of the populations seen by clinical neuropsychologists. For example, infectious, neoplastic, and vascular disorders will not be covered. Finally, the chapter will conclude with a review of forensic neuropsychology, a rapidly growing area of specialization within neuropsychology, particularly for private practitioners.

STRUCTURE AND FUNCTION OF THE CENTRAL NERVOUS SYSTEM

Cortical Organization

The human nervous system consists of the *central nervous system (CNS)* and the *peripheral nervous system (PNS)*. The CNS consists of the brain and spinal cord, while the PNS contains the autonomic and peripheral sensory and motor systems. Starting with lower brain structures and moving upward, the CNS can be further subdivided into the spinal cord, *brain stem* (midbrain, pons, and medulla), cerebellum, diencephalon, and telencephalon. The *diencephalon* includes the thalamus and hypothalamus, while the structures of the *telencephalon* include the cortex, limbic system, and basal ganglia.

Before proceeding further, a description of the six anatomical planes will be helpful as many of the structures of the brain are referenced by their relationship to one another or an imaginary central point within the brain. The planes include superior (top), lateral (side), medial or mesial (middle), ventral (bottom), anterior (front), and posterior or dorsal (back). Rostral

and caudal are also used to refer to structures close to the nose (anterior) or tail (tip of spinal cord).

Afferent or sensory information courses through the ventral horn of the spinal cord and through the brain stem to the cortex, while efferent or motor output passes from the cortex through the brain stem (e.g., corticospinal or pyramidal tract) and dorsal horn of the spinal cord. The brain stem, which consists of the midbrain, pons, and medulla, is critical for basic regulatory functions such as eating and drinking, body temperature, and sleep and waking. The nuclei of most of the 12 cranial nerves (CN) (except CN I and II) that assist in the regulation of these functions are found in the brain stem. The *reticular formation*, which is critical for attention and arousal, extends rostrally (i.e., toward the nose) from the medulla through the pons and midbrain. The reticular formation is involved when individuals experience coma. The midbrain (also called the mesencephalon) is divided into the tectum and tegmentum (dorsal and ventral sections) and is involved in sight/hearing and movement, respectively.

The *cerebellum*, which protrudes above the core of the brain stem, plays a critical role in the coordination and learning of skilled movements and balance. More recently, it has been found to play a role in cognition (Ben-Yehudah, Guediche, & Fiez, 2007). Damage to the cerebellum can result in *ataxia* (an awkward posture and gait), **intention tremor** (evident during movement), or **nystagmus** (a repetitive tremor-like jerking of the eyes).

The diencephalon consists of the thalamus and hypothalamus. The *thalamus* is composed of a number of nuclei and plays a critical role in relaying sensory information to the cortex. There are three nuclei that relay information directly from sensory systems to specific sensory cortex: the lateral geniculate body (LGB) receives visual projections that

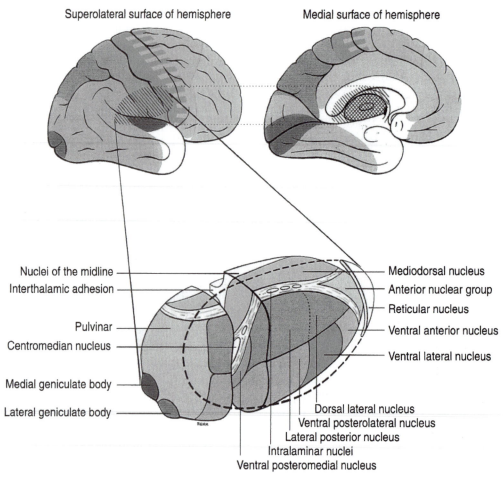

Superolateral surface of hemisphere   Medial surface of hemisphere

Nuclei of the midline
Interthalamic adhesion

Pulvinar
Centromedian nucleus

Medial geniculate body

Lateral geniculate body

Mediodorsal nucleus
Anterior nuclear group
Reticular nucleus
Ventral anterior nucleus
Ventral lateral nucleus

Dorsal lateral nucleus
Ventral posterolateral nucleus
Lateral posterior nucleus
Intralaminar nuclei
Ventral posteromedial nucleus

FIGURE 7.2   The relationship between the thalamic nuclei and the areas of the brain to which they project. (Source: Baars, B. J. (2007). The brain. In B. J. & N. M. Gage (Eds.), *Cognition, brain, and conciousness: introduction to cognitive neuroscience*. New York: Academic Press, p. 143.)

are projected to the visual cortex; the medial geniculate body (MGB) receives auditory projections that are projected to the auditory cortex; and the ventral-posterior lateral nucleus (VPL) receives touch, pressure, pain, and temperature projections from the body and projects these to the somatosensory cortex. Figure 7.2 illustrates the relationship between the thalamic nuclei and the areas of the brain to which they project. The *hypothalamus* is also a gray matter structure composed of many small nuclei. It assists with feeding,

sleeping, sexual and emotional behavior, temperature regulation, autonomic function, and movement.

The structures of the telencephalon include the cortex, limbic lobe (system), and basal ganglia. The cortex consists of two symmetrical hemispheres (right and left), separated by the longitudinal or interhemispheric fissure. A *fissure* is a cleft that extends deeply into the brain and is larger than a sulcus. The hemispheres are connected via the *corpus callosum*. Each hemisphere is further divided into four

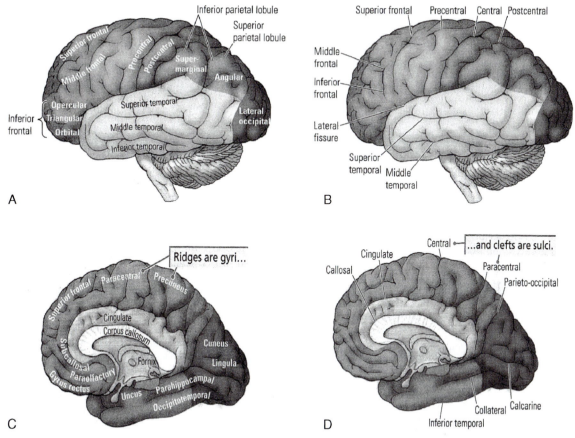

FIGURE 7.3 A review of major fissures, sulci, and gyri of the brain. (A) and (B) are lateral and medial views of gyri; (C) and (D) are lateral and medial views of sulci. (Source: Kolb & Wishaw, 2003.)

major lobes: frontal, parietal, temporal, and occipital. The frontal and parietal lobes are separated by the *central sulcus*, and the temporal lobes are separated from the frontal and parietal lobes by the *sylvian (lateral) fissure* (Figure 7.3).

The *limbic lobe* consists of the cingulate gyrus, hippocampal formation, amygdala, anterior thalamus, fornix, and the mammillary bodies (Figure 7.4). More recent conceptualizations also include the prefrontal cortex and hypothalamus. The limbic system is a complex system that is involved in emotion and memory, and it may play a role in spatial behavior (Kolb & Whishaw, 2003).

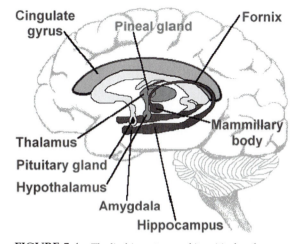

FIGURE 7.4 The limbic system and its critical pathways.

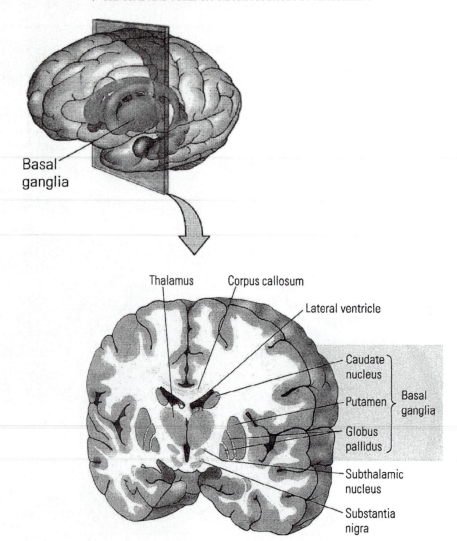

FIGURE 7.5   Coronal section of the cerebral hemispheres reveals the basal ganglia relative to surrounding structures. (Source: Kolb & Wishaw, 2003.)

The *basal ganglia* include a group of nuclei that lie in the anterior and inferior neocortex. The nuclei include the caudate, putamen, globus pallidus, and amygdala (also part of the limbic system) (Figure 7.5). The structures are also part of the striatum and are an integral part of the frontostriatal system. The caudate receives input from all regions of the neocortex and sends projections through the putamen and globus pallidus to the thalamus and to the motor regions of the cortex. Disruptions in the basal ganglia result in deficits in the quality of motor performance.

Cortical Function

The regions of the neocortex have specialized functions that reveal complex neural systems.

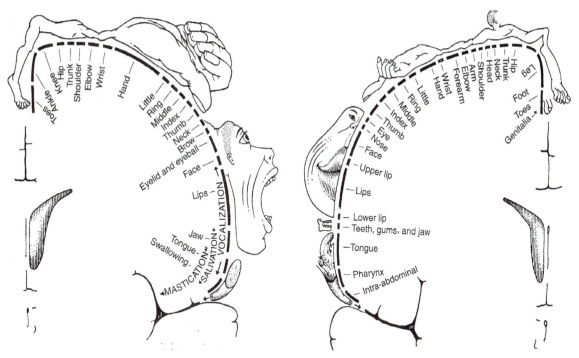

FIGURE 7.6 Motor and somatosensory information, respectively, and their homotopic representation depicted in the homunculi. (Source: Baars, B. J. (2007). The brain. In B. J. & N. M. Gage (Eds.), *Cognition, brain, and conciousness: introduction to cognitive neuroscience*. New York: Academic Press, p. 137.)

Primary projection areas either project to spinal motor systems or receive information from sensory systems. The *precentral and postcentral gyri* represent two of the primary projection areas for motor and somatosensory information, respectively, and their homotopic representation is frequently depicted in the homunculi (Figure 7.6). Primary auditory and visual projection areas are in the temporal and occipital cortices. Lesions in the primary motor areas result in **hemiplegia** (paralysis) or **hemiparesis** (weakness) to the **contralateral** (opposite) rather than **ipsilateral** (same) side of the body. Depending on the site of the disruption, lesions in primary sensory areas can result in deficits in touch, proprioception-stereognosis, pain-temperature, or cortical blindness. The primary sensory areas send projections to adjacent areas, while primary motor areas receive fibers adjacent to them, the so-called **secondary areas**. While the primary areas have direct connections with sensory receptors and motor neurons, the secondary areas play a role in interpreting perceptions and organizing movements. The areas of cortex between the secondary areas are the *tertiary (association)* areas that connect and coordinate secondary areas. The association areas mediate complex functions such as attention, memory, language, and executive abilities. Lesions or disruptions in secondary or association cortices can result in complex disorders such as **agnosia** (individuals are able to see or hear adequately but are unable to recognize objects), **aphasia** (loss or impairment in language), or **apraxia** (loss of the ability to carry out purposeful skilled actions), even though sensory and motor systems are intact. Given that each lobe contains

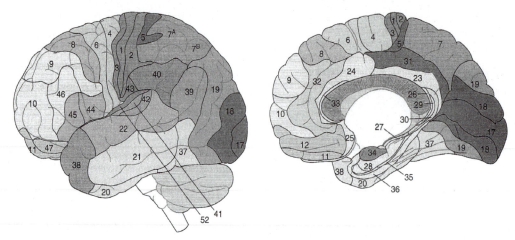

FIGURE 7.7   Brodmann's (BA) map, which is based on the cytoarchitectonic (cellular) structure of the brain. (Source: Baars, B. J. (2007). The brain. In B. J. & N. M. Gage (Eds.), *Cognition, brain, and conciousness: introduction to cognitive neuroscience*. New York: Academic Press, p. 124.)

one primary projection area, each has been associated with a general function: frontal — motor; parietal — somatosensory; temporal — auditory; occipital — visual. The projection maps also roughly correspond to a widely used map of the cortex, ***Brodmann's (BA) map***, which is based on the cytoarchitectonic (cellular) structure of the brain (Figure 7.7). Contemporary views of functional organization have further segregated the brain into dorsal ("where") and ventral ("what") streams responsible for processing both visual and auditory information (Scott, 2005, Ungerleider, Courtney, & Haxby, 1998).

While outside the scope of this chapter, the integrity of the arterial (e.g., anterior, posterior, and middle cerebral arteries) and neurotransmitter systems (e.g., catecholamines, indolamines, and amino acids) is essential to the functioning of these structures and systems.

Attention and Consciousness

Attention allows the CNS to select and focus on stimuli in our environment and integrate that information with our past and current thoughts and beliefs so that we take appropriate action. The neural mechanisms that underlie attention are vast and include a complex network of structures primarily in the frontal and parietal lobes (Baars, 2007). Attention is concerned with "selecting" one event rather than another, and these events should be distinguished from "conscious" events, which are those that individuals can report accurately (Baars, 2007), that is, information may be attended to but is not always consciously perceived. In fact, recent investigations have shown that while frontoparietal regions appear to underlie conscious perception, unconscious stimuli typically activate focal visual areas (Rees & Lavie, 2001). Nonetheless, attentional selection typically results in conscious perception.

Inattention is a phenomenon that we all experience, and the vulnerability of our attention is evident in tasks of inattentional blindness and change blindness. *Inattentional blindness* occurs when individuals fail to notice an event that occurs during a competing task, while *change blindness* occurs when they fail to notice change in the presence, identity, or location of objects in a scene. The frailty of the attentional system is further evident in attentional disorders such as ***sensory neglect or inattention*** due to disruption in the attentional network from traumatic brain injury or cerebral vascular accident (stroke), most often noted with involvement in the right cerebral hemisphere. Individuals with sensory neglect do not attend to (hence, perceive) images in the contralateral visual field (external space) or may completely neglect an entire half of their body (motor neglect), despite intact basic sensory processing.

Perception

There is substantial overlap in both structure and function of attentional and spatial processing. As noted, an individual may experience a sensory or hemispatial neglect, and this most often involves the right posterior parietal cortex. This disorder is typically perceived as a disorder of *spatial attention* or spatial representation. Sometimes the lesion will be more extensive, involving the occipitotemporoparietal junction, and individuals will experience difficulty with both object recognition and spatial location. If the visual pathway projections from the optic nerve to the striate (visual) cortex are disrupted, an individual will experience an actual visual field loss rather than merely inattention, such as in a *hemianopia* in which an individual is unable to see the contralateral half of space. In contrast, if the lesion is more anterior and involves both frontal and parietal regions, an individual may experience a *constructional apraxia*, that is, problems with construction such as drawing and building. In this case, there are deficits in visuoperception, visually guided action, and executive function. Substantial research has demonstrated differences in quality of performance in right versus left hemispheric impairment, which is often revealed through a *"process"-oriented approach* to testing (Kaplan, 1990). In general, left-sided impairment causes sparse production given that the left hemisphere is important for detail, whereas individuals with right-sided lesions display abundant detail, but their constructions are spatially disorganized. Patients may also suffer from a variety of agnosias. For example, a patient with a visual or object **agnosia** is unable to recognize objects by sight even though they can by

sound or touch, whereas **prosopagnosia** occurs when an individual is unable to recognize familiar faces.

Memory and Learning

Memory consists of a number of interrelated cognitive processes, and there are multiple memory systems that require the integrity of many brain regions. Baddeley and Hitch (1974) proposed a theory of *working memory* as an alternative way of characterizing short-term memory that focuses on the maintenance of information through rehearsal. Working memory consists of a visuospatial sketchpad and phonological loop, which are the slave systems for maintaining information in working memory. The third component, the central executive, controls how the slave systems are used. The dorsolateral prefrontal cortex (DL-PFC) and supramarginal gyrus have been implicated in both verbal and spatial working memory, while the frontal eye fields have been reported to assist the visuospatial sketchpad and the inferior frontal gyrus is involved in verbal rehearsal (phonological loop). Working memory is critical for all aspects of cognition including language and executive functions. Once information has been successfully encoded and consolidated, which relies heavily on limbic structures, memories are eventually stored in the neocortex and await retrieval.

Schacter and Tulvig (1994) proposed a classification system for the various aspects of memory (Figure 7.8) that includes both **declarative** and *nondeclarative* types of memory. Declarative memories include both *semantic* (knowledge/facts) and *episodic* (events) memory and rely heavily on mesial temporal brain regions. Declarative memory is impaired in *amnesia* and is often an early area of damage in Alzheimer's disease given the pathophysiological mechanisms of these disorders. Nondeclarative or implicit memories are learned in the absence of explicit awareness. For example, we rely on **procedural memory** when we ride a bicycle, which refers to

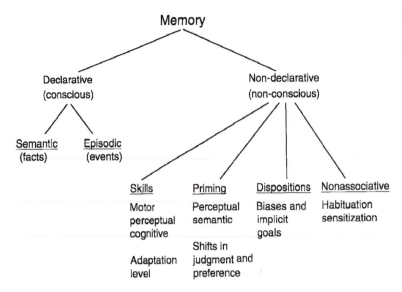

FIGURE 7.8 A classification system for the various aspects of memory proposed by Schacter and Tulvig (1994).

sensorimotor habits or automatic skills that one is generally able to retrieve without conscious awareness. Implicit and procedural memory are spared in amnesia, given that subcortical regions likely underlie these forms of memory.

Language

Language is the fundamental means by which humans express their thoughts and feelings. Speech is the motor production of words, while language allows one to communicate with and understand the ideas of others, although these aspects of communication are intricately interwoven. The left hemisphere is dominant for language in most individuals. The best-known neuropsychological model of language is that of Geschwind's model (1979), for which *Broca's* and *Wernicke's* areas establish a clear demarcation between *expressive* and *receptive* language. However, advances in neuroimaging reveal considerable overlap in regions that underlie speech production, semantics (the meaning of words and phrases), and the understanding of sentences and text (Vigneau et al., 2006).

The posterior superior temporal gyrus has traditionally been identified as critical for language comprehension (Wernicke's), which is connected via the *arcuate fasciculus* with the left inferior frontal gyrus (L-IFG) (Broca's), noted to be the primary region involved in speech planning and language production. More recent comprehensive and distributed models reveal a complex system of language implicating BA 42 and BA 44 for phonological segmentation and sequencing, the superior temporal gyrus for identification of work form and category, and the middle temporal gyrus and left frontal lobe for the integration of semantic and morpho-syntactic information (Friederici, 2002). Following stroke or head injury, an individual may lose the ability to understand language or communicate effectively. The clinical syndromes of language impairment or **aphasia** involve some aspect of reduced language output as well as impaired comprehension, repetition, and naming (Table 7.1). Disruptions in the quality of speech production may also occur and include poor articulation (**dysarthria**), poor melodic line (**dysprosody**), or low volume (*hypophonia*).

TABLE 7.1 The clinical syndromes of aphasia

	Fluent	Repetition	Comprehension	Naming	Right-side Hemiplegia	Sensory Deficits
Broca	no	poor	good	poor	yes	few
Wernicke	yes	poor	poor	poor	no	some
Conduction	yes	poor	good	poor	no	some
Global	no	poor	poor	poor	yes	yes
Transcortical motor	no	good	good	poor	some	no
Transcortical sensory	yes	good	poor	poor	some	yes
Transcortical mixed	no	good	poor	poor	some	yes
Anomia	yes	good	good	poor	no	no

Executive Processes and Control

Executive functions are linked to the frontal lobes, and in particular the prefrontal cortex (PFC). The PFC consists of the vast majority of the frontal cortex anterior to the motor and premotor regions. The PFC can be grossly subdivided into lateral (side), medial (midline), ventral (bottom), and anterior regions. The lateral regions can be further subdivided into the commonly known regions of the dorsolateral PFC (DL-PFC) and ventrolateral PFC (VL-PFC) (Figure 7.9). Finally, the orbitofrontal (OF-PFC) and ventromedial PFC reside on the inferior surface of the PFC. The OF-PFC is important for understanding future reward and changes in reward contingencies as well as selecting goals. Damage to the OF-PFC may result in problems with **behavioral inhibition** (Davidson & Irwin, 1999).

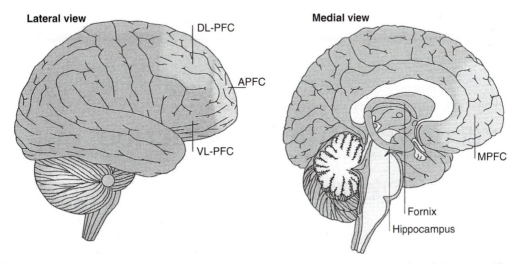

FIGURE 7.9 Regions of the Prefrontal Cortex (PFC). The PFC is divided into lateral and medial portions. The lateral PFC is further divided into dorsolateral (DL-PFC) and ventrolateral regions (VL-PFC). APFC is the anterior portion of the PFC. (Adopted from Goldberg & Bougakov in Baars & Gage, 2007.)

Traditionally, the PFC has been purported to coordinate goals and actions, and broadly speaking, the PFC assists with two general classes of cognitive operations: (1) an individual's ability to plan and guide behavior and (2) an individual's ability to inhibit one's plan and alter behavior (Goldberg & Bougakov, 2007). The latter suggests that an important aspect of executive functioning is an individual's ability to shift mental or cognitive set — **cognitive flexibility**. However, executive functions consist of a vast array of higher-order cognitive processes including, but not limited to, initiating, planning, establishing goals, organizing, problem solving, decision making, reasoning, monitoring, adapting, sustaining attention, storing and updating working memory, and unifying the sound, syntax, and meaning of language. The PFC is also involved in both feeling emotions and regulating emotional impulses. More recent research has revealed the role of the PFC in anticipating future events based on past experiences, the ability to deal with cognitive novelty, and veridical versus adaptive decision making (Goldberg & Bougakov, 2007).

Impairment to the frontal lobes and PFC results in marked changes in behavior and personality, with two of the classic syndromes being the dorsolateral (pseudodepressed personality) and orbitofrontal (pseudopsychopathic) syndromes. Individuals with *dorsolateral syndrome* display decreased initiation and spontaneity, **perseverative** (once a behavior is started, they can't terminate) and field-dependent behavior, apathy, and little overt emotion. In **orbitofrontal syndrome**, individuals are emotionally and behaviorally disinhibited. They display inappropriate social behavior, including sexual disinhibition, lack of concern for others, and an inappropriate jocular attitude.

Emotion and Social Cognition

By the time you have reached this section in the chapter, either you are feeling elated with all of the neuropsychology jargon you have just learned or you are frustrated because it feels like a foreign language (and if you wanted to learn a foreign language, you wouldn't have gone into psychology). Nonetheless, you are feeling or having an emotional experience. We not only experience and express emotion, but work by Paul Ekman (2003) has demonstrated that there are six universal facial expressions of basic emotions recognized by humans of all cultures: anger, fear, disgust, surprise, happiness, and sadness.

The first major theory of the emotional brain was proposed by Papez in 1937 and included the previously discussed limbic system. However, more contemporary theories of emotion suggest that emotion and cognition are intimately interconnected and likely require coordinated neural systems. The *limbic lobe* has rich connections with the ventromedial prefrontal cortex (VM-PFC), referred to as the feeling part of the thinking brain, as well as the insular cortex. A vital structure of the emotional brain is that of the *amygdala*, which underlies fear responses and is critical for social cognition. Along with the amygdala, the *ventral striatum* and *orbitofrontal cortices* mediate the association of perceptual representations with emotional response, cognitive processing, and a motivational component. The left prefrontal, right parietal, and cingulate regions have been suggested to help one develop an internal model of the social environment, develop representations of others and others with self, as well as reasoning about one's behavior in a social group (Adolphs, 2003). Emotion is tightly linked to social functioning, and there is substantial overlap in the brain regions that underlie these processes.

The temporal lobe has been found to be critical in processing facial information with the *fusiform gyrus* involved in the structural, static properties of faces, while the superior temporal gyrus (STG) has been found to be important for responding to the changeable elements of faces such as eye movements and expressions. These movement cues might generate attributions of animacy, intentionality, and agency.

The concept of intentionality is a critical construct in a major theory of social cognition known as *theory of mind (ToM)*. ToM refers to a complex metacognitive ability to think about what others might be thinking and representing what might be going on in another's mind. We also understand other people's behavior, in part, by simulation — putting ourselves in their shoes. The *Mirror Neuron System (MNS)* has been purported to allow us to imitate another's action through observation and includes a network that consists of the *superior temporal sulcus (STS)*, inferior parietal lobule, and inferior and ventral prefrontal regions. Iacoboni (2005a, 2005b) suggests that the MNS may be a plausible neurophysiological mechanism for complex social behaviors from imitation to empathy and encoding of others' intentions.

Social cognition is becoming one of the fastest-growing areas of neuroscience and neuropsychology, given the pivotal role that social impairment plays in all aspects of psychopathology and brain-related impairment. However, clinical neuropsychology's current assessment methods are woefully inadequate in examining this aspect of functioning, and much of what we know is based on research and particularly with functional neuroimaging.

NEUROPSYCHOLOGICAL ASSESSMENT

Neuropsychologists use traditional psychometric measures such as tests of attention and memory to examine an individual's cognitive strengths and weaknesses, aid in diagnostic decision making, and render treatment recommendations as warranted. Recent advances in neuroimaging (e.g., fMRI, PET, MEG) over the past several decades have equipped neuropsychologists with more sophisticated methods to inform the science. While imaging technology is not yet used for clinical diagnostic decision making, the field is making rapid advances through imaging research identifying important phenotypic and endophenotypic variables of developmental, psychiatric, and degenerative disorders.

As with other areas of clinical psychology, the assessment begins with an examination of the *clinical presentation* or *presenting problem*, obtained from multiple informants such as the referral source, patient, spouse, parent or legal guardian, and in some cases a child, depending on his or her age. The *mental status examination* often provides the clinician with initial information about gross level of functioning and typically includes an assessment of (1) general appearance and behavior, (2) orientation, (3) thought content and process, (4) insight and judgment, (5) affect and mood, (6) conversational speech and language, and (7) attention and memory. Consistency and contradictions in the nature and severity of presenting problems described by various informants must be considered. Adult referrals are often interested in examining a specific complaint such as memory, as seen in dementia, while referrals for children are often prompted by learning or behavioral difficulties. The second component consists of a comprehensive review of the relevant *history*. This involves obtaining information about the individual's developmental history, medical and psychiatric history including relevant family history, academic and employment history, and long-standing functioning in social, emotional, and adaptive domains. After sufficient appraisal of the presenting problems and the relevant historical data, the neuropsychologist develops hypotheses about the possible etiology, pattern of strengths and weaknesses, and severity of neuropsychological deficits that are reasonable to expect.

The final element is the *neuropsychological examination* itself. This involves the utilization of a variety of technical procedures. Selection of procedures depends, in part, on the nature of the referral question. It also depends on the individual's age and on his or her physical and mental capacities. The specific tests used in a neuropsychological examination will vary according to the neuropsychologist's own preferences. Despite these variations, the comprehensive neuropsychological examination will attempt to measure, at least in a molar fashion, all domains of neuropsychological functions believed to be of importance for supporting the individual's abilities to successfully interact in his or her environment. Making decisions as to which tests are most appropriate under what circumstances requires substantial sophistication and training. Such training includes an understanding of the psychometric characteristics of the procedures themselves and of their validity and reliability in the context in which they are being considered. A number of excellent books and reviews of psychological and neuropsychological tests used in the context of neuropsychology are available (e.g., Baron, 2004; Lezak, 1995; Spreen and Strauss, 1998).

Neuropsychologists have traditionally used a "fixed battery" approach to assessment, and two of the most widely used batteries historically have been the Halstead-Reitan Neuropsychological Test Battery (HRNTB, Reitan & Davison, 1974) and the Luria-Nebraska Neuropsychological Battery (LNNB, Golden, Purisch, & Hammeke, 1979). Recently, a computerized version of a fixed battery, CANTAB, the has been developed by a team at Cambridge University (Robbins et al., 1998) that offers convenience with highly structured administration. However, currently less than 15% of neuropsychologists employ a fixed battery approach (Sweet, Nelson, & Moberg, 2006). In fact, there is often an advantage of approaching assessment from a flexible battery method, given that developmental and neuroscience research continually reveals additional cognitive processes that may be important predictors of outcome or critical components of a diagnostic phenotype — hence, the need to frequently update our tools and batteries. The flexible battery allows the neuropsychologist to "accurately describe a patient's behavior and cognitive status and utilize standardized measures that depict a level of function that permits diagnosis and monitoring of a patient's neurobehavioral status" (Randolph, in Bigler, 2007, p. 48). The development of pediatric measures has appropriately evolved from being atheoretical in its approach to being significantly more grounded in developmental and neuroscience theory (Korkman, 1999). Early batteries such as the Halstead-Reitan Test Battery for Children (Reitan & Wolfson, 1985) and the Luria-Nebraska Test Battery for Children (Golden, 1987) further advised a fixed battery approach, that is, all subtests of a well-defined battery were administered in a generally fixed manner. As pediatric neuropsychology began to embrace a more diverse referral base that included preschool-aged children and those with complex neurodevelopmental and medical conditions, more flexibility has been necessary to garner the appropriate data.

Neuropsychological domains are not entirely or even mostly independent constructs. However, they do have some level of functional independence from each other, and neuropsychological tests are commonly labeled based on the primary domain that the test putatively measures (e.g., memory, speech and language, executive). Although clinicians can vary substantially in the specific tests included in their neuropsychological test batteries, there is substantial agreement about which neuropsychological constructs or domains of functioning should be measured in order to obtain a comprehensive assessment. Domains to be considered include intellectual, academic achievement, speech and language, visuospatial and perceptual-motor, memory and learning, and attention and executive functioning. In addition, assessment of basic sensory and motor functions is typically included because of their established importance for diagnosing and lateralizing brain dysfunction as well as their importance for understanding the potential contribution of impaired performance on "cognitive tasks" that have a sensorimotor component. A broad-based comprehensive examination is necessary in order to provide the clinician with multiple data points from which to make inferences. The data will provide the clinician with a profile or pattern of strengths and weaknesses from which to generate diagnoses as well as compensatory, remedial, therapeutic, and rehabilitation recommendations. Behavioral, social, and emotional adjustments are also evaluated in the comprehensive neuropsychological examination.

Developmental Issues

The nature and extent of the neuropsychological examination are, in part, determined by the developmental level of the individual. Many pediatric neuropsychologists develop expertise that extends to patients as young as 2 years of age, while those clinicians interested in dementia should be familiar with a host of issues in gerontology. Over the past decade or so, a number of measures have been developed to assess neurocognitive and developmental levels of functioning in young children such as the Differential Ability Scales-2 (DAS-2, Elliott, 2006), NEPSY-II Developmental Neuropsychological Assessment Battery (NEPSY II, Korkman, Kirk, & Kemp, 2005), and Mullen Scales of Early Learning (Mullen, 1995). Likewise, measures have been developed to specifically screen for issues in geriatrics such as the Dementia Rating Scale-2 (DRS-2, Mattis, 2002).

Domains of Neuropsychological Functioning

General Intelligence

Measures of intelligence, most commonly represented by IQ tests, provide an assessment of cognitive abilities and intellectual potential that can be used to compare a person's relative standing with that of his or her age peers and corresponding demographic factors. These measures are essential to examine giftedness as well as mental retardation for which a concurrent measure of adaptive functioning (e.g., Vineland Adaptive Behavior Scales) is required. Several tests have been designed to assess intellectual potential such as the well-known Wechsler series for toddlers (WPPSI-III), children and adolescents (WISC-IV), and adults (WAIS-III).

Developmental Assessments

As noted, a number of measures have been constructed based on developmental models and use developmentally appropriate tasks to assess a child's developmental level of functioning to guide early intervention efforts, such as the Bayley Scales of Infant Development-Third Edition BSID-III (Bayley, 2006) and the Mullen Scales of Early Learning (Mullen, 1995). Other measures focus on basic concept acquisition and emergence of preliteracy skills in order to determine a child's readiness for school or to identify those who are at risk of developing learning disabilities without appropriate and more intensive instructions.

Academic Abilities

Many individuals with a reading disorder or **dyslexia** have difficulty with one or more aspects of the reading process that cannot be accounted for by intellectual limitations, functional impairments, or inadequate schooling. Some individuals have difficulty decoding words, others have problems acquiring a sight vocabulary or accessing words rapidly, still others have difficulty comprehending (Catts et al., 2002). Specific tests can be used to examine cognitive processes found to be critical predictors of reading success, such as phonological awareness, through nonword decoding or rapid automatized naming. Several aspects of writing should be examined when a disorder of written expression or **dysgraphia** is suspected (Sandler et al., 1992), such as legibility, fluency, spelling, punctuation, and written grammar. The ability to express ideas through a written modality should also be assessed to evaluate organization, cohesion, and sense of audience, as well as other skills discussed above. A specific learning disability that affects primarily the acquisition of arithmetic skills (Shalev & Gross-Tsur, 2001) is referred to as a mathematics disorder or **dyscalculia**. Dyscalculia is diagnosed when individuals exhibit significant difficulty with computations and/or difficulty with problem-solving abilities; however, individuals with visual-spatial difficulties can display problems understanding quantitative and measurement concepts or aligning numbers properly to perform calculations.

Sensorimotor Functions

Evaluation of sensorimotor skills can provide clinicians with information regarding acquisition of motor skills and quality of performance, lateralization of functions and evidence of lateralized dysfunction, and sensory processing. The motor evaluation typically includes examining handedness, bilateral fine motor speed and dexterity, motor accuracy and coordination, and strength. The motor evaluation provides the clinician with a gross assessment of the integrity of the frontostriatal and cerebellar systems. The clinical neuropsychologist should be alert to evidence of *hemiplegia* or **hemiparesis**. The finger oscillation test or grooved pegboard is often used to examine fine motor speed. The clinician should be alert to disruptions in the quality of performance such as *tremor* or *athetoid* and *dystonic* movements that may suggest cerebellar or subcortical involvement, respectively. Individuals may struggle with

movement representation, motor planning, and performance of sequential movements to accomplish an action even when sensory and motor systems are intact, referred to as an **apraxia** (Luria, 1974). In children, motor deficits of a developmental nature may manifest as a *developmental coordination disorder* and interfere with the performance of activities of daily living.

A comprehensive examination of sensory processes and the integrity of the primary sensory cortices will include an assessment of auditory, visual, and somesthetic functions. The integrity of the cranial nerves can be conducted by an examination of basic skills such as oculomotor and oral-motor functions. Tests of finger recognition, sensory neglect (double simultaneous stimulation), graphesthesia (the ability to discriminate between numbers and letters written on the palm or finger of the hand), and stereognosis (the ability to distinguish form with the tactile sense) are conducted.

Visuospatial/Visuoconstructional/ Visuoperceptual Skills

Both developmental and acquired disorders can result in deficits in visuospatial abilities. Children may avoid or be reluctant to engage in drawing or handwriting. Following injury, children or adults may have difficulty with copying or constructing two- or three-dimensional shapes or designs. Impairment or disruptions in the integrity of the right parietal, frontoparietal, and occipitoparietal regions often interfere with these abilities. Many tests exist that measure different aspects of visual-spatial abilities ranging from basic perceptual processes to basic drawing abilities, visuospatial orientation, figure-ground discrimination, visuospatial reasoning, and so on.

Speech and Language

Speech refers to the mechanics of oral communication, while language refers to the ability to communicate information. Difficulties in communication, in either receptive and/or expressive language functions, may be developmental (e.g., *developmental language disorder*) or acquired (e.g., aphasia). Clinicians may use a wide variety of measures to assess these skills, from an individual's ability to name objects and pictures to more complex skills such as providing word definition and formulating and expressing ideas and thoughts orally. Pragmatic communication involving the ability to use language as well as nonverbal communication for various social functions may also be examined.

Attention, Concentration, Speed of Information Processing

Examining attention and concentration includes assessing focused, selective, divided, and sustained attentional skills. Speed of information processing is often disrupted in brain injury and degenerative disorders. Tests are conducted that examine one's ability to stay focused despite the presence of distractors, attend to more than one task at a time or "multitask," perform two types of tasks simultaneously, mentally shift one's attention from one task to another, and maintain vigilance and performance over time.

Memory and Learning

Problems with memory are one of the most frequent reasons for a referral for a neuropsychological evaluation in older adults. However, true amnestic disorders in children are rare and often the result of a cerebral insult such as epilepsy or head injury (Vargha-Khadem et al., 2003; Williams and Sharp, 1999). Memory tasks have been developed for children as young as 3 and typically involve tasks that assess verbal and nonverbal memory processes, or both simultaneously. Verbal memory can be examined by asking an individual to repeat stories, sentences, and lists of words. Nonverbal memory tasks may involve remembering faces, locations, and designs or pictures, for example. The individual's performance across separate memory tests will provide the clinician with a reliable pattern of strengths and weaknesses (e.g., visual vs. verbal learning), assist in diagnostic decision making, and guide with intervention strategies.

Executive Functions

As previously noted, executive functions refer to a wide variety of complex cognitive processes including, though not limited to, working memory, mental flexibility, inhibition, initiation, planning, organization, and problem solving. Attention-deficit hyperactivity disorder (ADHD) is the prototypical disorder of executive functioning for which frontostriatal disruptions are implicated. Historically, tests such as the Category Test, Tower of Hanoi, and Wisconsin Card Sorting Test have been used to examine executive skills such as concept formation, strategy, and problem solving. More contemporary measures such as the Cognitive Bias Task (Goldberg et al., 1994) have been developed as cognitive neuroscience has expanded our conceptualization of executive functions. In fact, only recently has a battery of tests been developed to assess a broad array of executive functions across the life span, specifically the Delis-Kaplan Executive Function System (DKEFS, Delis, Kaplan, & Kramer, 2001).

Personality and Psychosocial Functioning

The evaluation of psychological, social, and behavioral factors is an important part of the neuropsychological evaluation. Standardized and objective personality and behavioral questionnaires are typically employed for both children and adults. The assessment of these issues is addressed elsewhere in this book and will not be comprehensively covered here. Frequently, measures of effort will be necessary for adults who are involved in litigation, and these are addressed in the forensic section.

A representative sample of neuropsychological measures used to examine the relative domains of functioning is presented in Table 7.2.

TABLE 7.2   A representative sample of neuropsychological measures used to examine the relative domains of functioning

Cognitive Domains	Representative Tests/Measures
Intelligence	Wechsler Scales (WPPSI, WAIS, WISC)
	Stanford-Binet Intelligence Scale
Development	Bayley Scales of Infant Development
	Differential Ability Scale
	Mullen Scales of Early Learning
Achievement	Wechsler Individual Achievement Test
	Woodcock-Johnson Test of Achievement
	Comprehensive Test of Phonological Processing
Attention and Concentration	Test of Variables of Attention
	Continuous Performance Test
Visuospatial/Perceptual-Motor	Developmental Test of Visual-Motor Integration
	Rey-Osterreith Complex Figure Test
Speech and Language	Clinical Evaluation of Language Fundamentals
	Peabody Picture Vocabulary Test
	Boston Naming Test
	Phonemic and Semantic Fluency
Learning and Memory	California Verbal Learning Test
	Test of Memory and Learning
	Wide Range Assessment of Memory and Learning
	Wechsler Memory Scale
Executive Function	Wisconsin Card Sorting Test
	Category Test
	Cognitive Bias Task
	Delis-Kaplan Executive Function System
Personality and Psychosocial	Minnesota Multiphasic Personality Inventory
	Personality Assessment Inventory
	Conners' Rating and Adult ADHD Scales
	Behavioral Assessment Schedule for Children
Effort and Malingering	Test of Memory Malingering
	Word Memory Test

Note: To simplify the table, relative editions or versions were not noted.

Interpretations and Recommendations

If the test data are judged to be a valid and reliable measure of the individual's abilities, then multiple methods of inference are used to interpret the neuropsychological data. Historically, the major methods of inference have been level of performance, pattern of performance, pathognomonic signs, right-left patterns, and test-retest performance patterns. As brain-behavior relationships have become more fully illuminated, other axes and networks of dysfunction can now be examined in hypothesis development such as cortical-subcortical, anterior-posterior, orbitomedial and dorsolateral, and dorsal-ventral stream patterns of performance. As the field of neuropsychology has evolved and as the complexity of neural organization has been revealed (Booth et al., 2004; Sporns et al., 2004), the goal is no longer to uncover merely an "organic" etiology or "lesion localization" but instead to examine the patterns of performance to aid in diagnostic decision making and to illuminate strengths and weaknesses so that appropriate interventions can be recommended.

PEDIATRIC NEUROPSYCHOLOGY

Pediatric neuropsychology has seen significant advances over the past several decades, surfacing as an area of unrivaled growth in psychology. Pediatric neuropsychologists typically evaluate populations for which developmental, learning, and behavioral difficulties are evident such as in learning disability, ADHD, autistic spectrum disorders (ASD), genetic and metabolic syndromes, epilepsy, head injury, and neoplastic disorders (Lajiness-O'Neill et al., 2006; Yeates, Ris, & Taylor, 1999). A sizable empirical knowledge base has developed demonstrating that medical disorders secondarily affecting the CNS (e.g., craniofacial) or primarily affecting nonbrain organ systems can,

under certain conditions, have neuropsychological sequelae as well, such as cardiac, renal, pulmonary, and immune disorders (Fennell, 1999; Pulsifer & Aylward, 1999). Children with teratogen exposure often present to the pediatric neuropsychologist due to significant behavioral and learning difficulties. For example, children who have chronic and significant lead exposure will experience a predictable pattern of difficulties that includes substantial dysregulation and features of ADHD, aggression, and learning disorders (Ris, 2003; Trask & Kosofsky, 2000).

Recently, the first comprehensive compendium strictly devoted to the measures and methods used in the neuropsychological assessment of children including the compilation of normative data was published (Baron, 2004). A number of disorders could easily be addressed as topics in both childhood and adulthood such as epilepsy and head injury. In order to minimize redundancy, epilepsy will be addressed in the pediatric section, while head injury will be discussed with disorders that frequently occur in adulthood.

Learning Disability and ADHD

Outpatient pediatric neuropsychological practices include referrals of a large number of children whose difficulties are recognized primarily within the classroom setting. Diagnosis and treatment planning can be substantially aided by comprehensive neuropsychological assessment. As research has informed clinical practice, the focus has shifted from using purely discrepancy based models in identifying learning disability to the identification of process variables known to be disrupted in learning disability such as phonological processing and speeded naming (Rudel & Denckla, 1974; Denckla & Rudel, 1976). Three brain regions have been found to underlie these reading and reading-related processes: (1) a region in the inferior frontal cortex critical for word analysis (decoding), (2) a region in the temporoparietal cortex for phonological processing or assembled phonology, and (3) a region in the inferior occipitotemporal region for skilled, fluent (automatic word recognition) reading (Shaywitz & Shaywitz, 2005). As such, measures such as the Comprehensive Test of Phonological Processing (CTOPP, Wagner, Torgesen, & Rashotte, 1999) have been developed to assess these process variables. A complex issue that frequently surfaces in the academic setting is that of the distinction between ADHD and a learning disability, such as dyslexia and/or dysgraphia. Nonetheless, it is important to recognize that many individuals with ADHD also have comorbid learning disorders, with rates as high as 10% to 25% reported (DSM-IV, American Psychiatric Association, 1994). While reading disability is a language disorder, primary receptive and expressive language disorders can significantly interfere with the acquisition of reading as well. Likewise, sensorimotor deficits may negatively impact graphomotor and written language abilities. Neuropsychological evaluation may also help the treatment provider and family members understand why a child is having difficulty socially. Clinicians and researchers have begun to identify additional forms of learning disorders, such as nonverbal learning disability (NLD) (Rourke, 1995), which may serve as a marker for other developmental (e.g., Asperger syndrome) and psychiatric conditions for which social problems are a key feature. Children with NLD display a predictable pattern of cognitive strengths and weaknesses that are purported to underlie their social deficits. Children with NLD exhibit deficits in sensorimotor, visuospatial, perceptual-motor functioning, nonverbal memory, and novel problem solving with a concomitant weakness in mathematics. The constellation of deficits is purported to contribute to the child's inability to accurately interpret the subtle nuances in social exchanges, which interferes with appropriate reciprocity in relationships and subsequently cascades into significant interpersonal deficits. Emotional and interpersonal adjustment difficulties are commonly seen in combination with cognitive deficits. The neuropsychological assessment can help to distinguish a primary anxiety or mood disorder from an attentional or learning disorder.

Autism Spectrum Disorders and Developmental Delay

Although prediction from infants' and young children's test performance to later ability level is possible at the extremes of the ability distribution, there has been generally poor success with predicting later skill levels from test scores obtained in infancy among those infants who were not unusually delayed or gifted (Aylward et al., 1987; Bornstein & Sigman, 1987; Gibbs, 1990). Nonetheless, distinguishing a global developmental delay (GDD) from a specific delay in development (e.g., mixed receptive and expressive language disorder) can be an important question answered by neuropsychological testing, which will subsequently guide immediate therapeutic efforts. The distinction between GDD and mental retardation is often a perplexing one for clinicians examining children of toddler age and frequently surfaces as a comorbid issue in children within the autistic spectrum. Typically, the diagnosis of GDD is reserved for younger children (i.e., typically less than 5) who exhibit age-specific deficits in learning and adaptation (i.e., two standard deviations or more below the mean on an age-appropriate norm-referenced test) and for which the etiology is heterogeneous (Shevell et al., 2003). In general, a diagnosis of mental retardation should rarely be made prior to age 5 when the assessment of intellectual abilities is much less valid and reliable and the degree of improvement following intervention is yet to be determined.

An equally difficult distinction to make is between children with pervasive developmental disorder, not otherwise specified and those with significant developmental language disorders. Neuropsychological testing can often illuminate many of the distinguishing features with standardized tools such as the Autism Diagnostic Interview–Revised (ADI-R, Lord, Rutter, & LeCouteur, 1994) or the Autism Diagnostic Observation Schedule (ADOS: WPS Edition, Lord et al., 1999) in conjunction with traditional neuropsychological measures, which also have the potential of identifying important phenotypic variables. For example, Lajiness-O'Neill and Menard (2007) recently identified a possible autistic spectrum subtype expressed through family psychopathology coupled with autistic probands' cognitive functioning (i.e., an endophenotypic profile). Specifically, significantly higher visuospatial functioning was noted in ASD probands for which there were higher rates of mood disorder on the maternal side, suggesting a possible marker for an ASD subtype. In general, the cognitive abnormalities in ASD follow a triad of weak CC (e.g., placing a premium on the extraction of detail at the expense of gestalt) (Happe, Briskman, & Frith, 2001), poor ToM (i.e., the inability to think and reason about mental states) (Baron-Cohen & Hammer, 1997), and impaired executive functions (EF).

Epilepsy

Childhood epilepsy is one of the most prevalent forms of chronic illness in childhood, and given that it disrupts typical maturation of the brain, it is believed to produce nonspecific consequences such as mental and behavioral impairment (Lassonde, Sauerwein, Jambaque, Smith, & Helmstaedter, 2000). The neuropsychological sequelae of childhood epilepsy are based on the site of the epileptic focus. Children with frontal lobe epilepsy typically display a profile of deficits consistent with what is often noted in adults with frontal lobe injury. More specifically, children will exhibit impairments in sustained attention, behavioral inhibition, planning, problem solving, mental flexibility, visuospatial organization, motor coordination, and complex motor movements (e.g., apraxia). Behavioral ratings further suggest more problems with attention, atypical behaviors (e.g., Thought Disorders Scale of CBCL), and social functioning (Lassonde et al., 2000).

Temporal lobe epilepsy (TLE) in childhood, with a typical spike focus in the anterior temporal lobes, is more variable and less common than in adults (Bourgeois, 1998). The neuropsychological profile typically includes deficits that follow the pattern of lateralization of brain functioning, including impairments in verbal learning and memory associated with left-hemispheric pathology and nonverbal impairment noted with right-hemispheric pathology. TLE has also been associated with poor reading development, again with a greater degree of difficulty noted in those with left- compared to right-hemispheric involvement. Finally, childhood TLE has been shown to be associated with substantially higher rates of psychopathology than in the general population, including aggressiveness and atypical behaviors. However, it is important to note that recent studies have shown that the predisposition to develop more severe forms of psychopathology in TLE such as psychotic disorder may be more strongly related to those who have intellectual disability (Buelow et al., 2003; Matsuura et al., 2005).

Genetic Disorders

The role of pediatric neuropsychology in the assessment of children with suspected or known genetic disorders that present with comorbid psychiatric illness is also becoming increasingly prevalent. Genomic disorders such as velocardiofacial syndrome (VCFS) (22q11.2 deletion syndrome), William syndrome, Prader-Willi syndrome, and Angelman syndrome present with characteristic physical, cognitive, and behavioral features (Lajiness-O'Neill et al., 2006; Nichols et al., 2004). For example, the rate of schizophrenia, bipolar disorder, and possibly obsessive compulsive disorder has been reported to be as high as 30% in individuals with 22q11 deletion syndrome, significantly higher than the general population (Eliez et al., 2001). As discussed by Finegan (1998), behavioral phenotypes will play a critical role in (1) understanding syndrome delineation, (2) illuminating intrasyndrome variability, (3) spawning theory development, and (4) understanding brain-behavior relationships and the genetic bases of behavior.

ADULT NEUROPSYCHOLOGY

Dementia

In geriatric medicine, clinical neuropsychology has made invaluable contributions to clarification of the distinctions among the types of dementia, identification of cognitive and behavioral markers and sensitive cognitive measures for screening, and investigation of the relationship of cognitive deficits to functional decline in the dementias such as Alzheimer's disease (AD), vascular dementia (VaD), diffuse Lewy body disease (DLB), and frontotemporal dementia (FTD) (Savla & Palmer, 2005). AD is the most common cause of dementia. Approximately 1% of the population over age 60–64 years have AD; however, the prevalence nearly doubles every 5 years after age 60, making the prevalence among those 85 years and older at approximately 30% to 45% (Fratiglioni, De Ronchi, & Agüero-Torres, 1999).

Dementia research has frequently been concerned with whether there are observable cognitive distinctions between those dementias with known cortical (e.g., AD) and subcortical (e.g., Parkinson's disease [PD]) neuropathology. Cortical dementias are associated with disruptions in higher-order cognitive processes such as memory, language, and semantic knowledge (Libon, Price, Davis Garrett, & Giovannetti, 2004). The cognitive profile often noted in subcortical dementias is consistent with frontostriatal pathology and involves deficits in speed of performance during visuospatial tasks and impaired retrieval during memory tasks (Lineweaver et al., 2005). In contrast, patients with AD often demonstrate impaired accuracy, but not speed, on visuospatial tasks and severe remote memory loss that follows a temporal gradient such that there is more impaired memory for recent events (Sadek et al., 2004), suggestive of impairments in memory consolidation consistent with cortical temporal hippocampal disruption. With respect to early cognitive markers for AD, the literature consistently reports deficits in verbal episodic memory (e.g., recalling what one had for breakfast) (Guarch, Marcos, Salamero, & Blesa, 2004).

In general, patients with dementias with a vascular etiology have been reported to exhibit a "spotty" profile of cortical cognitive deficits consistent with multiple infarcts. Individuals with subcortical VaD, however, demonstrate impairments on tests of executive functioning consistent with other subcortical dementias such as Parkinson's and Huntington's dementia. Executive control deficits observed in subcortical VaD are rather pervasive, while the executive control deficits observed in AD are typically context specific and related to lexical/semantic (i.e., language) functions (Libon et al., 2004).

The Mini-mental Status Examination (MMSE, Folstein, Folstein, & McHugh, 1975) is one of the most widely used cognitive measures in the screening of dementia. More recently, the sensitivity and specificity of alternative measures including the Seven Minute Screen (7MS) (Meulen et al., 2004) and Montreal Cognitive Assessment (MoCA) (Nasreddine et al., 2005) have been investigated and found to be effective when screening for non–Alzheimer's disease cognitive disorders.

Traumatic Brain Injury

Clinical neuropsychologists serve as quintessential diagnostic and treatment team members as well as investigators into the neurobiological and pathophysiological mechanisms that underlie the cognitive, neurobehavioral, and emotional impairment observed following traumatic brain injury (TBI) (Bigler, 2003; Goldstein & Levin, 2001), which is the most common cause of brain injury in children and young adults. TBI includes both closed head injury (CHI), which constitutes the majority of injuries, as well as penetrating head injury (PHI). Recently, the pathophysiological mechanisms and cognitive deficits secondary to blast injuries have been an area of investigation given the number of casualties from overseas wars (Cemak, Wang, Jiang, Bian, & Savic, 2001). TBIs in children are most likely to occur from falls, whereas in adults TBIs most commonly occur in the context of motor vehicle accidents (Annegers, Grabow, Kurland, & Laws, 1980). In adults, neurological injury affects the cognitive-behavioral substrate (the brain) after the individual has acquired and mastered skills. In children, however, brain damage often has a cascading effect on later developing cognitive and neurobehavioral functions, with a particular impact on prefrontal and executive functions (Eslinger & Biddle, 2000).

Severity of injury is a critical predictor of outcome and has been defined based on Glasgow Coma Scale (GCS), loss of consciousness (LOC), and/or post-traumatic amnesia (PTA). Coup-contracoup and acceleration and deceleration effects, which result in axonal injury and shearing, are two of the primary mechanisms of injury following TBI. Research has demonstrated that even in mild traumatic brain injury (MTBI) without demonstrable changes on neuroimaging such as CT or MRI, individuals can experience substantial changes in cognitive and behavioral functioning. MTBI (see Highlight Box 7.1) is pathologically similar to more severe TBI, but to a lesser degree. As stated by Bigler (2003), "an injury can occur when the tensile effects on axons or parenchyma deformations do not surpass the level where structural damage occurs, but biochemical perturbations are induced" (p. 604). More recent research has recently focused on additional factors affecting outcome such as severity, size and location of lesion, age at injury, presence of family support (Bigler, 2003; Ewing-Cobbs et al., 2003; Goldstein & Levin, 2001; Wade et al., 2003). Likewise, clinical neuropsychologists have relied on measures such as the Disability Rating Scale (DRS,

---

HIGHLIGHT BOX 7.1

CASE STUDY OF MILD TRAUMATIC BRAIN INJURY (MTBI)

This 15-year-old, left-handed female was referred for an evaluation due to problems with attention, memory, and learning, as well as reported changes in behavioral regulation (e.g., disinhibition and high-risk behaviors) following a series of three minor head injuries that occurred during an 18-month period. All three produced brief loss of consciousness (LOC), confusion, dizziness, fatigue, and headaches lasting two to three weeks. The last injury occurred following a fall from a trampoline in which she hit her head on a fence. Developmental and medical history was unremarkable, and she was an A-B student. Her parents both received their doctoral degrees.

The girl's cognitive and neurobehavioral profile was consistent with mild traumatic brain injury. Likewise, her general pattern of performance was below what would be expected given demographic variables. Her profile suggested mild lateralized right-hemispheric inefficiencies noted with respect to motor and perceptual-motor skills, as well as some indication of subtle frontal inefficiencies. This was most evident in problems with attention, mental flexibility, perseveration, speed of information processing, and behavioral inhibition. Note mild distortion in recall of Rey Complex Figure (Figure 7.10). The following represents Standard (SS) Scores, Scaled Scores (ss), and T-scores obtained on selected tests SS Mean (M) = 100, Standard Deviation (SD) = 15; ss M = 10, SD = 3; T M = 50; SD = 10):

HIGHLIGHT BOX 7.1   (*continued*)

Domain of Functioning	Standard Scores	Qualitative Description
Intellectual		
Verbal Comprehension	118	High Average
Perceptual Reasoning	89	Low Average
Working Memory	107	Average
Processing Speed	89	Low Average
Full Scale IQ	101	Average
Academic (SS)		
Word Reading	111	High Average
Spelling	109	Average
Arithmetic	100	Average
Motor Examination		
Finger Tapping Test	Dominant = 36.7	Left motor slowing
	Nondominant = 42.2	
Perceptual-Motor		
VMI (SS)	79	Borderline
Rey-Complex Figure Test (Copy)	11–16th percentile	Low Average
Speech and Language		
D-KEFS Phonemic Fluency (ss)	9	Average
D-KEFS Semantic Fluency (ss)	15	Superior
Boston Naming	55	Within Normal Limits
Learning and Memory (WRAML2) (ss)		
Story Memory	13	High Average
Verbal Learning	10	Average
Design Memory	6	Low Average to Borderline
Picture Memory	9	Average
Rey Complex Figure Immediate	8th percentile	Borderline
Attention and Executive		
CPT Omissions (T-score)	T = 46	Average
CPT Commissions (T-score)	T = 41	Low Average
CPT Reaction Time (T-score)	T = 42	Low Average
D-KEFS Trails Making — L-N Switching	9	Average
Verbal Fluency — Switching	13	High Average
Design Fluency — Switching	8	Average
WCST — Conceptual	102	Average
WCST — Perseveration	88	Low Average

Note: VMI, Developmental Test of Visual Motor Integration; D-KEFS, Delis-Kaplan Executive Function System; WRAML-2, Wide Range Assessment of Memory and Learning-2nd Edition; CPT, Continuous Performance Test; WCST- Wisconsin Card Sorting Test.

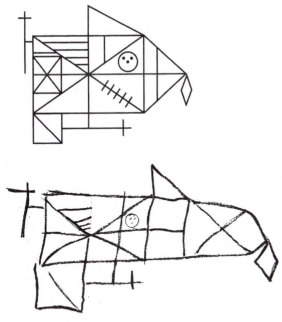

FIGURE 7.10   Rey Complex Figure.

Rappaport, Hall, Hopkins, Belleza, & Cope, 1982) and Glasgow Outcome Scale (GOS, Hall, Cope, & Rappaport, 1985) to assist with determining level of recovery and degree of disability.

Psychiatric Disorders

The presence of wide-ranging neuropsychological deficits in the major forms of mental illness such as depression, the anxiety disorders, and schizophrenia has been well established (Chamberlain, Fineberg, Blackwell, Robbins, & Sahakian, 2006; Murphy & Sahakian, 2001). Neuropsychological research has focused on establishing relationships between areas of cognitive impairment and brain regions that subserve these cognitive domains. Recent investigations have begun to focus on the identification of specific cognitive and behavioral profiles of psychiatric illness in the search for endophenotypic markers (Chamberlain,

Fineberg, Blackwell, Robbins, & Sahakian, 2005; Gottesman & Gould, 2003).

Verbal and visual memory (Burt, Zembar, & Niederehe, 1995) and executive abilities such as problem solving and planning (Elliott, Sahakian, Michael, Paykel, & Dolan, 1998; Franke et al., 1993) are often disrupted in depression, with results consistent with frontotemporal dysfunction in the pathogenesis of depression. More recent research in depression is attempting to elucidate the subtle differences between types or phases of depression. For example, Murphy and colleagues (2001) examined the interaction between cognitive and affective processing in patients with mania or depression using a novel "affective go/no-go" task. Subjects were required to respond to target words of either positive or negative affective tone by pressing a keyboard and inhibiting this response to words of the competing affective category. Patients with mania displayed a bias toward positive stimuli and demonstrated problems with behavioral inhibition and focused attention. In contrast, subjects with depression demonstrated a bias toward negative stimuli only. Similarly, the medial PFC and OF-PFC have been found to differentially activate during periods of depression and mania (Drevets et al., 1997), consistent with these findings.

Neuropsychological investigations of obsessive compulsive disorder (OCD), as an illustration of our understanding of a subtype of anxiety disorders, frequently suggests unique structural and functional abnormalities in the orbitofrontal cortex, anterior cingulate, and basal ganglia (particularly caudate) (Brambilla, Barale, Caverzasi, & Soares, 2002). However, these regions are crucial components of the "lateral orbitofrontal loop," a circuit that has also been implicated in the etiology of depression and mania (Chamberlain et al., 2005). Patients with OCD frequently display deficits in spatial recognition memory and spatial working memory (SWM) (Nielen & Den Boer, 2003; Purcell, Maruff, Kyrios, & Pantelis, 1998). Impairments in executive abilities such as set shifting (i.e., mental flexibility or shifting conceptual set), response inhibition, and attentional processing are also reported in OCD. Response inhibition failures have been demonstrated on "go/no-go" tasks, which require the inhibition of a prepotent motor response (Aycicegi, Dinn, Harris, & Erkmen, 2003; Muller et al., 2003). As such, inhibitory impairment in OCD on these tasks has been suggested to be consistent with lateral orbitofrontal loop dysfunction (Chamberlain et al., 2005). Some investigators have suggested that inhibitory failures may actually mediate set-shifting errors in OCD, as set-shifting requires not only the ability to shift attentional set and adopt a new rule but also an ability to inhibit a response to the previous rule (Evans, Lewis, & Iobst, 2004).

FORENSIC NEUROPSYCHOLOGY

Forensic neuropsychology, a practice subspecialty within the field, applies neuropsychological principles and practice to civil and criminal legal proceedings (Heilbronner, 2004; Hom, 2003). Forensic neuropsychology is a hybrid that combines neuropsychological science and practice with forensic science and practice (Heilbronner, 2004). Neuropsychological assessments can be used on behalf of a *plaintiff*, the person or parties who are bringing a lawsuit or claim against an entity or an individual, or on behalf of the *defendant*, the person or parties defending a claim or lawsuit against an individual or an entity. Legal referrals account for nearly one-third of private practice referrals, and only neurology and psychiatry are currently more important referral sources for neuropsychologists than attorneys (Hom, 2003). Thus, it is important for those interested in the practice of neuropsychology to understand all of the context and situations that lead up to a forensic assessment by a neuropsychologist and the significant implications and factors involved in a forensic assessment.

Clinical neuropsychologists are frequently called upon to conduct independent medical examinations (IMEs), render expert opinions, and provide the "trier of fact" (e.g., judges and juries) with information about cognitive, behavioral, emotional, and motivational functioning of individuals in both civil and criminal proceedings (Denney & Wynkoop, 2000; Heilbronner, 2004; Hom, 2003). In civil litigation, neuropsychologists may assist in cases involving educational due process within public schools, child custody, medical malpractice, personal injury, workers' compensation, disability determination, and competency (Heilbronner, 2004; Sweet, 1999). Criminal proceedings may involve expert testimony on competency to stand trial, sanity, diminished capacity or responsibility, or dangerousness (Denney & Wynkoop, 2000). The readership is referred to reviews in special issues of journals (Heilbronner, 1992; Larabee, 2000a) and books for a more thorough discussion on the practice of forensic neuropsychology (Larabee, 2000b, 2005; Sweet, 1999).

Training in Forensic Neuropsychology

There is currently no consensus on what constitutes competency or practice guidelines in this subspecialty, and individuals must decide if they have the prerequisite training, education, skills, and experience to serve in this role (Heilbronner, 2004). There are no formal training programs or licensure requirements for forensic neuropsychology (Hom, 2003). Predoctoral interns and postdoctoral fellows typically obtain experience through didactics or supervision by those who engage in forensic practice. Although no additional formal training or board certification requirements exist to practice forensic neuropsychology, board certification in clinical neuropsychology is perceived as the "clearest evidence" of the type of expertise expected to practice forensic neuropsychology (Heilbronner, 2004; Larabee, 2000b).

Case Precedent and Admissibility of Evidence

Forensic neuropsychologists may be called upon to render an opinion about the nature and extent of brain impairment and to ascertain whether it is due to a neurological or psychological etiology or is instead factitious. However, there is no current consensus about the clinical neuropsychologist's ability to opine on the **causal determination** of the brain impairment (Hom, 2003). Nonetheless, the ability of a clinical neuropsychologist to provide expert testimony regarding brain impairment was successfully argued in the precedent-setting case *Indianapolis Union Railway v. Walker* (1974).

Neuropsychologists employ the scientific method to obtain data and render results about impairment. However, this does not guarantee those data as admissible in court. From 1923 until 1993, the standard for admissibility of scientific testimony was set forth in the case of *Frye v. United States* (1923), which states that "while courts will go a long way in admitting expert testimony deduced from well-recognized scientific principles or discovery, the thing from which the deduction is made must be sufficiently established to have gained general acceptance in the particular field in which it belongs." A new evidentiary standard of admissibility of scientific testimony was set by the U.S. Supreme Court in 1993 in the case of *Daubert v. Merrell Dow Pharmaceuticals*. At that time, Federal Rule of Evidence 702 was established as the standard of admissibility of expert testimony, which states: "If scientific, technical, or other specialized knowledge will assist the trier of fact to understand the evidence or to determine a fact in issue, a witness qualified as an expert by knowledge, skills, experience, training, or education may testify thereto in the form of an opinion or otherwise." Currently, 33 states are using some version of the *Daubert* standard, while 17 continue to use the *Frye* standard (Reed, 1999).

Ethics, Specialty and Practice Guidelines

Those who engage in forensic neuropsychology are confronted with a host of ethical issues that are not often encountered in other areas of practice. Forensic neuropsychology by its very nature is often adversarial and antagonistic, and clinicians are frequently asked to render opinions regarding the training of and evaluations by other clinicians of the opposing side. Clinicians must be careful not to engage in what has been described as "opportunistic practice ethics" (Adams, 1997, p. 295), such as being overly critical of assessments by other colleagues and rendering opinions that are biased in favor of those whom one represents (plaintiff or defense). Individuals who practice forensic neuropsychology are required to follow the laws relevant to the practice of psychology in the state in which they practice, and while they are not necessarily required to follow APA Ethical Principles and Code of Conduct if they are not members of APA, nearly all states incorporate APA principles in their practice standards.

Guidelines have been set forth by the American Law Society's Specialty Guidelines for Forensic Psychologists (SGFP, Committee on Ethical Guidelines for Forensic Psychologists, 1991) and the American Academy of Forensic Psychology for neuropsychologists interested in forensic practice. In addition, in 1990 APA established two sets of aspirational guidelines related to the practice of forensic psychology: Guidelines for Child Custody Evaluations in Divorce Proceedings (APA, 1994) and Guidelines for Psychological Evaluations in Child Protection Matters (APA, 1998). These guidelines do not establish a standard of care in forensic neuropsychology, but they do address issues related to evaluator competence, informed consent, and confidentiality that may serve as a guide for those interested in forensic practice.

A goal of the forensic evaluator is to remain objective and obtain the "truth" about one's functioning. The nature of the relationship between the clinical neuropsychologist and the individual being assessed is qualitatively different from that in clinical practice. In essence, the goal of the forensic assessment is to evaluate the individual with respect to the claims being made rather than to exclusively inform subsequent treatment decisions (Denney & Wynkoop, 2000). The clinician should clarify the relationship and the role of the neuropsychologist during the initial evaluation, including informing the client that test and assessment results will not be confidential. A number of publications address specific issues often encountered during forensic evaluations, including the nature of informed consent (Johnson-Greene, Hardy-Morraix, Adams, Hardy, & Bergloff, 1997), the use of psychometricians (Division 40 Task Force, 1989; National Academy of Neuropsychology, 2000a), test security issues surrounding the release of raw data (American Psychological Association, 1996; National Academy of Neuropsychology, 2000b), and the role of third-party observers (National Academy of Neuropsychology, 2000c).

Whether the neuropsychologist is conducting a clinical assessment to guide treatment efforts or a forensic examination to address claims brought forth by a plaintiff, the goal continues to be to "accurately describe a patient's behavior and cognitive status and to utilize standardized measures that depict a level of function that permits diagnosis and monitoring of a patient's neurobehavioral status" (Bigler, 2007, p. 48). This further implies using the most appropriate tests and scientifically informed approaches to aid in decision making, including age, education, and demographically adjusted norms as available. As noted, an apparent asset of the flexible battery is that it allows for the use of more contemporary measures that are informed by rapidly changing information from neurodiagnostic (e.g., brain imaging), clinical, and cognitive neuroscience research (Bigler, 2007).

Pediatric Issues

Pediatric forensic neuropsychology historically has been primarily involved in civil litigation in traumatic injuries similar to that in adult cases. However, neuropsychologists may be called upon to render opinions in legal cases involving medical malpractice claims, usually against a physician, a clinician, or an institution, or all of the above.

In pediatric suits, it is important to recognize that children are often very young and in a phase of rapid growth and development, and issues related to CNS development are critical in decision making. For example, the traditional method for examining brain-behavior relationships has been the lesion method (Lezak, 1995), which has been used as a framework with adults to map brain function. This method assumes a direct correspondence between the cognitive process compromised and the location of the lesion, and this correspondence is altered in injuries in childhood. For example, injury in posterior temporal regions typically results in impaired language comprehension in adults, while children with similar injuries display deficits in language production (Bates et al., 1999). Moreover, as previously noted, studies in children have demonstrated substantial plasticity and resiliency in cognitive and behavioral development (Stiles et al., 2003), though residual deficits are evident.

Prospective studies of language development after early focal brain injury in children reveal more pronounced global linguistic impairments followed by considerable improvement in language extending to the school-aged period (Eisele, Lust, & Aram, 1998). In studies of visuospatial processing in children with early focal injuries, deficits in spatial processing are similar, though milder, than those noted in adults with similar injuries (Akshoomoff, Feroleto, Doyle, & Stiles, 2002). In contrast, a pattern of *emerging* deficits has been reported in studies of general cognitive ability (Levin, 1993) and in executive functioning for those who have sustained frontal lobe injury (Eslinger, Warner, Grattan, & Easton, 1991) that also suggests limitations on the capacity of the developing cognitive system to compensate for impairment. Results of these studies indicate that one should err in the direction of caution when issuing opinions on causation and prognosis in children with early injuries. There is a complex interaction between early injury and normal mechanisms of development that results in atypical structural and functional development and hemispheric specialization for which traditional adult lesion methods are less informative (Moses & Stiles, 2002).

Adult Issues

Neuropsychologists who practice forensic neuropsychology with adult populations should have expertise in the relevant area for which they are being consulted, that is, a clinician with expertise in dementia and competency would not likely be prepared to conduct an evaluation on dangerousness in a criminal proceeding (Denney & Wynkoop, 2000). There are significant theoretical and practical differences both between and within civil and criminal assessments (Heilbronner, 2004). Civil cases are those for which a neuropsychologist is recruited to render an opinion regarding level of functioning, strengths and weaknesses, etiology, and possible prognosis in cases such as competency, traumatic injury, and medical malpractice. Criminal cases might include those for which the neuropsychologist is called upon to render an opinion about competency to stand trial or insanity.

Forensic Process and Procedures

A neuropsychologist may be consulted at any of a number of stages in the legal suit. A *notice of intent* is usually required by most states to be filed first on behalf of the plaintiff, which provides notice of an intention to file a suit to the defendant. This is followed by the *complaint*, or the formal document of a lawsuit. In the complaint, facts from medical records or events are reiterated and listed, as well as the allegations of the plaintiff. These allegations often include theories of negligence, wherein the plaintiff states that the defendants or care providers were negligent in actions or inactions toward the plaintiff or patient. The complaint must also allege whose actions or inactions of negligence allegedly caused the plaintiff's problems or injuries. Finally, the complaint must allege what has been encountered in terms of damages. This most often involves claims of cognitive impairment or deficits as well as physical and motor impairment or deficits. Once the case has been filed via the complaint, there is a process called *discovery*, during which time the plaintiff can "discover" information relating to the claim through his or her attorneys. During this process of discovery, the clinical neuropsychologist may be consulted by the plaintiff or defense side to serve as *expert witness*. As an "expert," the neuropsychologist may be requested to review claims, records, and the facts at issue or perform an IME. Neuropsychologists may also be required to render opinions about the aforementioned in a formal process called a *deposition*.

A typical clinical neuropsychological evaluation includes a comprehensive interview with the client and relevant informants, a review of pertinent records, and a comprehensive neuropsychological examination. The forensic neuropsychological evaluation requires a much more extensive review of multiple sources of information to supplement the examination, including school and employment records, past medical records, and interviews with those familiar with the client. Significant emphasis is placed on objective test results and observation rather than subjective complaints and self-report measures. The IME report can become extremely significant in a legal case. It is important to realize that when a report is generated from a neuropsychologist in a forensic setting, every word in the report is perceived as the neuropsychologist's *opinions*. The neuropsychologist is held accountable for those opinions. It is customary that whatever side requests the neuropsychology exam and report, that side must proffer a copy of the report to the other side. Thus, a neuropsychologist must be cognizant that the other side (plaintiff or defense) will be privy to the report. During the deposition, a neuropsychologist is also often asked to state the basis of his or her opinions and knowledge. A neuropsychologist will be asked what journals, journal articles, textbooks, text excerpts, or other publications are felt to be authoritative or reliable in the field. In a forensic case, reliable or *authoritative* means that that expert deems that publication or writing to be 100% accurate in every context without exception. Thus, it is prudent for neuropsychologists to carefully consider and review any literature or data source to which they have referred in support of their opinions for scientifically accurate and thorough testing and methodology, reporting, and context.

Depending on the state and venue, if the neuropsychologist has performed one exam of the individual, the examination and report are usually sufficient until the time of trial. However, some venues can have cases that last more than five years from the inception of the case until trial. In those instances, it may be advantageous for the neuropsychologist to either request or be requested to perform another medical exam of the individual more contemporaneous to the time of trial so that the findings are most accurate as they relate to the individual's cognitive and neurobehavioral functioning. The neuropsychological examination and report

assist in the determination of *damages* in a legal case — that is, the amount of money at which the case is valued. For example, if a child is examined by a neuropsychologist and found to be significantly cognitively impaired as well as motorically impaired, these findings can essentially translate into lost earning capacity in the future, loss of activities of daily living and need for household services, need for attendant care or supervisory care, and need for therapies in the future. In cases involving children, the plaintiff will often use an economist and/or long-term care expert to project expenses over the life expectancy of the child. As such, these "damages" can add up to multimillion-dollar totals.

Effort and Malingering

As noted, in forensic neuropsychology the neuropsychologist should make every attempt to ensure that the data are valid and reliable and that exaggeration and inconsistencies are minimized and discovered. In civil and criminal litigation, secondary gain (e.g., financial or avoiding of incarceration) brings issues of potential malingering to the forefront, and competent evaluations must include measures of malingering and dissimulation. Base rates of malingering brain injury in civil litigation have been reported to range between 2% and 64% (Gouvier, Hayes, & Smirolodo, 1998; Heaton, Smith, Lehman, & Vogt, 1978). Assessing effort during forensic neuropsychological examinations is necessary to support the validity of the data. Instruments such as the Test of Memory Malingering (TOMM) and the Word Memory Test (WMT) are commonly used symptom validity tests with adequate psychometric properties that are frequently employed to examine effort (Bauer, O'Bryant, Lynch, McCaffrey, & Fisher, 2007). Currently, there are extremely limited data on the frequency of malingering or dissimulation in pediatric cases (Constantinou & McCaffrey, 2003; Donders, 2005), and no studies have been conducted to examine effort in pediatric forensic cases. However, the TOMM has been shown to be a valid measure that can be used with pediatric populations in clinical neuropsychological evaluations (Constantinou & McCaffrey, 2003; Donders, 2005). While there is likely to be much less concern about effort from young children for secondary gain, effort and malingering may be important issues for which the neuropsychologist should be attuned when obtaining data from adolescents, who can be coached, or from parents or legal guardians, who may have motives (e.g., financial) for embellishing results on behavioral indices. More recent indices such as the Behavioral Assessment Schedule for Children (BASC) allow for a direct examination of the validity of the measure.

SUMMARY

In summary, clinical neuropsychology is a subspecialty of psychology that utilizes assessment methods to identify an individual's cognitive and neurobehavioral strengths and weaknesses to guide clinicians in diagnostic decision making and treatment planning. Clinical neuropsychologists utilize a vast array of tools including observation, psychometric measures, and neuroimaging technologies to assist them in the development of hypotheses regarding brain-behavior relationships. While the focus of this chapter is on neuropsychological assessment, several important factors were considered in the development of the chapter that likely alter its emphasis from other assessment chapters.

First, we chose to begin this chapter with a thorough discussion on the biological substrates of cognition and behavior. Learning the neuropsychological approach to assessment and the assessment tools without a cogent theoretical understanding of the brain structures and systems for which these tools were developed is akin to being a brain surgeon who knows how to use a scalpel but has no knowledge of the structure and function of the organ of interest, the brain.

Second, we chose to avoid an elaborate discussion on measures used by neuropsychologists as there are currently several extensive compendiums of assessment measures that were previously discussed and to which the readership is referred.

Finally, it is important to recognize that the currently perceived critical cognitive constructs and tools to measure these abilities are constantly undergoing revision as cognitive neuroscience moves at warp speed to inform us of necessary modifications in our theoretical conceptualization of brain-behavior relationships. The current method of assessment that relies exclusively on the use of paper-and-pencil and computerized assessment tools is likely to become obsolete in the next several decades. Instead, and consistent with the current trend, future neuropsychologists will likely add complex neuroimaging tools to their armamentarium, such as functional MRI (fMRI), magnetoencephalography (MEG), and positron emission tomography (PET). When coupled with technologies that may have greater ecological validity (e.g., virtual reality), these methods will provide a more direct and objective measure of the integrity of the brain; they will likely assist the neuropsychologist in the examination of brain-behavior relationships and guide diagnostic decision making through the twenty-first century.

Glossary

Agnosia: The loss or impairment of the ability to recognize an object by sight, hearing, or touch, although there is no impairment in the basic sensory processes of vision, hearing, or touch.

Amnesia: A loss or impairment of memory due to damage to the temporal lobes.

Aphasia: The loss or impairment of language that is due to injury or illness to the left (language dominant) hemisphere.

Apraxia: The loss or impairment of the ability to carry out purposeful, skilled actions, even though sensory and motor systems are intact.

Ataxia: An awkward posture or gait due to damage to the cerebellum.

Cognitive flexibility: An aspect of executive functioning that allows one to shift mental or conceptual set.

Contralateral: On the opposite side of the body.

Declarative memory: Includes both semantic (knowledge/facts) and episodic (events) memory and relies heavily on mesial temporal regions.

Dorsolateral syndrome: A syndrome secondary to injury to the dorsolateral prefrontal cortex (DL-PFC) that results in decreased initiation, perseveration, field dependency, apathy, and decreased overt emotion.

Dysarthria: A disruption in speech production that results in poor articulation.

Dyscalculia: Mathematics disorder.

Dysgraphia: Disorder of written expression — a written language disorder.

Dyslexia: Reading disorder — a language disorder of reading and reading-related processes such as phonological awareness and speeded naming.

Dysprosody: Poor melodic line in speech.

Hemiparesis: Weakness on one-half of the body and is contralateral to the side of the lesion or injury.

Hemiplegia: Paralysis on one-half of the body and is contralateral to the side of the lesion or injury.

Intention tremor: A tremor evident during movement often indicative of cerebellar damage.

Ipsilateral: On the same side of the body.

Nystagmus: A repetitive tremor-like jerking of the eyes due to damage to the central nervous system.

Orbitofrontal syndrome: A syndrome secondary to injury to the orbitofrontal prefrontal

cortex (OF-PFC) that results in emotional and behavioral disinhibition, lack of concern, and jocularity.

Perseveration: Once a behavior or thought is started, an individual has difficulty terminating the behavior or thought.

Procedural memory: Sensorimotor habits or automatic skills that one is able to retrieve without conscious awareness and that rely heavily on subcortical regions.

Prosopagnosia: The loss or impairment of the ability to recognize familiar faces.

References

Adams, K. M. (1997). Comments and ethical considerations in forensic neuropsychological consultation. *The Clinical Neuropsychologist, 11,* 294–295.

Adolphs, R. (2003). Cognitive neuroscience of human social behavior. *Nature Reviews, 4,* 165–178.

Akshoomoff, N. A., Feroleto, C. C., Doyle, R. E., & Stiles, J. (2002). The impact of early unilateral brain injury on perceptual organization and visual memory. *Neuropsychologia, 40,* 539–561.

American Psychiatric Association (1994). *Diagnostic and statistical manual of mental disorders* (4th ed.). Washington, DC: Author.

American Psychological Association (1996). Committee on Psychological Tests and Assessments: Statement on the Disclosure of Test Data. *American Psychologist, 31,* 644–648.

American Psychological Association (1996, re-approved 2003). *Description of the specialty of clinical neuropsychology approved by APA Council of Representatives.* Retrieved January 31, 2008 from http://www.div40.org/def.html

American Psychological Association (1998). Policy Statement, Houston Conference on Specialty Education and Training in Clinical Neuropsychology. Retrieved January 31, 2008 from http://www.div40.org/pub/Houston_conference.pdf

Annegers, J. F., Grabow, J. D., Kurland, L. T., & Laws, E. R., Jr. (1980). The incidence causes, and secular trends of head trauma in Olmstead County, Minnesota, 1935–1974. *Neurology, 30,* 912–919.

Aycicegi, A., Dinn, W. M., Harris, C. L., & Erkman, H. (2003). Neuropsychological function in obsessive-compulsive disorder: effects of comorbid conditions on task performance. *European Psychiatry, 18,* 241–248.

Aylward, G. P., Gustafson, N., Verhulst, S. J., et al. (1987). Consistency in the diagnosis of cognitive, motor, and neurologic function over the first three years. *Journal of Psychology*, 12, 77–98.

Baars, B. J. (2007). Attention and consciousness. In B. J. Baars & N. M. Gage (Eds.), *Cognition, brain, and consciousness: introduction to cognitive neuroscience*. New York: Academic Press.

Baddeley, A. D. & Hitch, G. J. (1974). Working memory. In G. A. Bower (Ed.), *Recent advances in learning and motivation*. Vol. 8 (pp. 47–90). New York: Academic Press.

Baron, I. S. (2004). *Neuropsychological evaluation of the child*. New York: Oxford University Press.

Baron-Cohen, S. & Hammer, J. (1997). Parents of children with Asperger syndrome: what is the cognitive phenotype? *Journal of Cognitive Neuroscience*, 9, 548–555.

Bates, E. (1999). Language and the infant brain. *Journal of Communication Disorders*, 32, 692–697.

Bauer, L., O'Bryant, S. E., Lynch, J. K., McCaffrey, R. J., & Fisher, J. M. (2007). Examining the test of Memory Malingering Trial 1 and Word Memory Test Immediate Recognition as screening tools for insufficient effort. *Assessment*, 12, 215–222.

Bayley, N (2006). *Bayley Scales of Infant Development* (3rd ed.). New York: Harcourt.

Ben-Yehudah, G., Guediche, S., & Fiez, J. A. (2007). Cerebellar contributions to verbal working memory: beyond cognitive theory. *Cerebellum*, 6, 193–201.

Bigler, E. D. (2003). Neurobiology and neuropathology underlie the neuropsychological deficits associated with traumatic brain injury. *Archives of Clinical Neuropsychology*, 18, 595–621.

Bigler, E. D. (2007). A motion to exclude and the 'fixed' versus 'flexible' battery in 'forensic' neuropsychology: challenges to the practice of clinical neuropsychology. *Archives of Clinical Neuropsychology*, 22, 45–51.

Booth, J. R., Burman, D. D., Meyer, J. R., et al. (2004). Brain-behavior correlation in children depends on the neurocognitive network. *Human Brain Mapping*, 23, 99–108.

Bornstein, M. H. & Sigman, M. D. (1987). Continuity in mental development from infancy. *Child Development*, 57, 251–274.

Bourgeois, B. F. (1998). Temporal lobe epilepsy in infants and children. *Brain Development*, 20, 135–141.

Brambilla, P., Barale, F., Caverzasi, E., & Soares, J. C. (2002). Anatomical MRI findings in mood and anxiety disorders. *Epidemiological Psychiatric Society*, 11, 88–99.

Buelow, J. M., Austin, J. K., Perkins, S. M., Shen, J., Dunn, D. W., & Fastenau, P. S. (2003). Behavior and mental health problems in children with epilepsy and low IQ. *Developmental Medicine and Child Neurology*, 45, 683–692.

Burt, D. B., Zembar, M. J., & Niederehe, G. (1995). Depression and memory impairment: a meta-analysis of the association, its pattern, and specificity. *Psycholological Bulletin*, 117, 285–305.

Catts, H. W., Gillispie, M., Leonard, L. B., et al. (2002). The role of speed of processing, rapid naming, and phonological awareness in reading achievement. *Journal of Learning Disabilities*, 35, 509–524.

Cernak, I., Wang., Z., Jiang, J., Bian, X., & Savic, J. (2001). Cognitive deficits following blast injury-induced neruotrauma: possible involvement of nitric oxide. *Brain Injury*, 15, 593–612.

Chamberlain, S. R., Fineberg, N. A., Blackwell, A. D., Robbins, T. W., & Sahakian, B. J. (2005). The neuropsychology of obsessive compulsive disorder: the importance of failures in cognitive and behavioral inhibition as candidate endophenotypic markers. *Neuroscience Biobehavioral Review*, 29, 399–418.

Chamberlain, S. R., Fineberg, N. A., Blackwell, A. D., Robbins, T. W., & Sahakian, B. J. (2006). Motor inhibition and cognitive flexibility in obsessive-compulsive disorder and trichotillomania. *American Journal of Psychiatry*, 163, 1282–1284.

Committee on Ethical Guidelines for Forensic Psychologists (1991). Specialty guidelines for forensic psychologists. *Law and Human Behavior*, 15, 655–665.

Constantinou, M. & McCaffrey, R. J. (2003). Using the TOMM for evaluating children's effort to perform optimally on neuropsychological measures. *Child Neuropsychology*, 9, 81–90.

Daubert v Merrell Dow Pharmaceuticals. 509 US 579 (1993).

Davidson, R. J. & Irwin, W. (1999). The functional neuroanatomy of emotion and affective style. *Trends in Cognitive Science*, 3, 11–21.

Delis, D. C., Kaplan, E., & Kramer, J. H. (2001). *Delis-Kaplan Executive Function System*. San Antonio, TX: Psychological Corporation.

Denckla, M. B. & Rudel, R. G. (1976). Rapid "automatized" naming (R.A.N.): dyslexia differentiated from other learning disabilities. *Neuropsychologia*, 14, 471–479.

Denney, R. L. & Wynkoop, T. F. (2000). Clinical neuropsychology in the criminal forensic setting. *The Journal of Head Trauma Rehabilitation*, 15, 804–828.

Division 40 Task Force (1989). Report of the Division 40 Task Force on Education, Accreditation, and Credentialing. Guidelines regarding the use of nondoctoral personnel in clinical neuropsychological assessment. *The Clinical Neuropsychologist*, 3, 23–24.

Donders, J. (2005). Performance on the test of memory malingering in a mixed pediatric sample. *Child Neuropsychology*, 11, 221–227.

Drevets, W. C., Price, J. L., Simpson, J. R., Jr., Todd, R. D., Reich, T., Vannier, M., & Raichle, M. E. (1997). Subgenual prefrontal cortex abnormalities in mood disorders. *Nature*, 386, 824–827.

Eisele, J. A., Lust, B., & Aram, D. M. (1998). Presupposition and implication of truth: linguistic deficits following early brain lesions. *Brain and Language*, 15, 376–394.

Ekman, P. (2003). Emotions inside out: 130 years after Darwin's 'the expressions of the emotions in man and animal.' *Annuals of the New York Academy of Science, 1000,* 1–6.

Eliez, S., Antonarakis, S. E., Morris, M. A., Dahoun, S. P., & Reiss, A. L. (2001). Parental origin of the deletion 22q11.2 and brain development in velocardiofacial syndrome: a preliminary study. *Archives of General Psychiatry, 58,* 64–68.

Elliot, C. D. (1990). *Differential Ability Scales* (2nd ed.) (DAS II). San Antonio, TX: Psych Corp. Harcourt Assessments.

Elliott, R., Sahakian, B. J., Michael, A., Paykel, E. S., & Dolan, R. J. (1998). Abnormal neural response to feedback on planning and guessing tasks in patients with unipolar depression. *Psycholological Medicine, 28,* 559–571.

Eslinger, P. J. & Biddle, K. R. (2000). Adolescent neuropsychological development after early right prefrontal cortex damage. *Developmental Neuropsychology, 18,* 297–329.

Eslinger, P. J., Warner, G. C., Grattan, L. M., & Easton, J. D. (1991). Frontal lobe utilization behavior associated with paramedian thalamic infarction. *Neurology, 41,* 450–452.

Evans, D., W., Lewis, M. D., & Iobst, E. (2004). The role of the orbitofrontal cortex in normally developing compulsive-like behaviors and obsessive-compulsive disorder. *Brain and Cognition, 55,* 220–234.

Ewing-Cobbs, L., Barnes, M. A., & Fletcher, J. M. (2003). Early brain injury in children: development and reorganization of cognitive function. *Developmental Neuropsychology, 24,* 669–704.

Fennell, E. B. (1999). End-stage renal disease. In K. O. Yeates, D. H. Ris, & M. D. Taylor (Eds.), *Pediatric neuropsychology: research, theory and practice.* New York: Guilford Press.

Finegan, J. A. (1998). Study of behavioral phenotypes: goals and methodological considerations. *American Journal of Medical Genetics, 28,* 148–155.

Folstein, M., Folstein, S. E., & McHugh, P. R. (1975). "Mini-Mental State," a practical method for grading cognitive state of patients for the clinician. *Journal of Psychiatric Research, 12*(3), 189–198.

Franke, P., Maier, W., Hardt, J., Frieboes, R., Lichtermann, D., & Hain, C. (1993). Assessment of frontal lobe functioning in schizophrenia and unipolar major depression. *Psychopathology, 26,* 76–84.

Fratiglioni, L., De Ronchi, D., & Agüero-Torres, H. (1999). Worldwide prevalence and incidence of dementia. *Drugs and Aging, 15,* 365–375.

Friederici, A. D. (2002). Towards a neural basis of auditory sentence processing. *Trends in Cognitive Science, 6,* 78–84.

Friederici, A. D. (2002). Towards a neural basis of auditory sentence processing. *Trends in Cognitive Science, 6,* 78–84.

Frye v. United States. 293 F. 1013 (D. C., Cir 1923).

Geschwind, N. (1979). Specialization of the human brain. *Scientific American, 241,* 180–199.

Gibbs, E. D. (1990). Assessment of infant mental ability: conventional tests and issues of prediction. In E. D. Gibbs & D. M. Teti (Eds.), *Interdisciplinary assessment of infants: a guide for early intervention professionals.* Baltimore: Paul H. Brooks Publisher.

Goldberg, E. & Bougakov, D. (2007). Goals, executive control and action. In B. J. Baars & N. M. Gage (Eds.), *Cognition, brain, and consciousness: introduction to cognitive neuroscience.* New York: Academic Press.

Goldberg, E., Harner, R., Lovell, M., Podell, K., & Riggio, S. (1994). Cognitive bias, functional cortical geometry, and the frontal lobes: laterality, sex, and handedness. *Journal of Cognitive Neuroscience, 6,* 276–293.

Golden, C. J. (1987). *Luria-Nebraska Neuropsychological Battery: Children's Revision.* Los Angeles, CA: Western Psychological Services.

Golden, C. J., Purisch, A. D., & Hammeke, T. A. (1979). *The Luria-Nebraska Neuropsychological Battery: a manual for clinical and experimental uses.* Lincoln: University of Nebraska Press.

Goldstein, F. C. & Levin, H. S. (2001). Cognitive outcome after mild and moderate traumatic brain injury in older adults. *Journal of Clinical and Experimental Neuropsychology, 23,* 739–753.

Gottesman, I. I. & Gould, T. D. (2003). The endophenotype concept in psychiatry: etymology and strategic intentions. *American Journal of Psychiatry, 160,* 636–645.

Gouvier, W. D., Hayes, J. S., & Smirolodo, B. B. (1998). The significance of base rates, test sensitivity, test specificity, and subjects' knowledge of symptoms in assessing TBI sequelae and malingering. In C. R. Reynolds (Ed.), *Detection of malingering during head injury litigation* (pp. 55–79). New York: Plenum Publishing.

Guarch, J., Marcos, T., Salamero, M., & Blesa, R. (2004). Neuropsychological markers of dementia in patients with memory complaints. *International Journal of Geriatric Psychiatry, 19,* 352–358.

Hall, K., Cope, D. N., & Rappaport, M. (1985). Glasgow Outcome Scale and Disability Rating Scale: comparative usefulness in following recovery in traumatic head injury. *Archives of Physical Medicine and Rehabilitation, 66,* 35–37.

Happe, F., Briskman, J., & Frith, U. (2001). Exploring the cognitive phenotype of autism: weak "Central Coherence" in parents and siblings of children with autism: I. Experimental Tests. *Journal of Child Psychology and Psychiatry, 42,* 299–307.

Heaton, R. K., Smith, H. H., Jr., Lehman, R. A., & Vogt, A. T. (1978). Prospects for faking believable deficits on neuropsychological testing. *Journal of Consulting and Clinical Psychology, 46,* 892–900.

Heilbronner, R. L. (1992). Special section on forensic neuropsychology. *Forensic Reports, 5,* 219–220.

Heilbronner, R. L. (2004). A status report on the practice of forensic neuropsychology. *The Clinical Neuropsychologist, 18*, 312–326.

Hom, J. (2003). Forensic neuropsychology: are we there yet? *Archives of Clinical Neuropsychology, 18*, 827–845.

Iacoboni, M. (2005). Neural mechanisms of imitation. *Current Opinions in Neurobiology, 15*, 632–637.

Iacoboni, M., Molnar-Szakacs, I., Gallese, V., et al. (2005). Grasping the intentions of others with one's own mirror neuron system. *PLoS Biol, 3*, 529–535.

Indianapolis Union Railway v. Walker (1974). Court of Appeals of Indiana, First District, 578–590.

Johnson-Greene, D., Hardy-Morraix, C., Adams, K. M., Hardy, C., & Bergloff, P. (1997). Informed consent and neuropsychological assessment: ethical considerations and proposed guidelines. *The Clinical Neuropsychologist, 11*, 454–460.

Kaplan, E. (1990). The process approach to neuropsychological assessment of psychiatric patients. *Journal of Neuropsychiatry abd Clinical Neurosciences, 2*, 72–87.

Kolb, B. & Whishaw, I. Q. (2003). *Fundamentals of human neuropsychology* (5th ed.). New York: Worth Publishers.

Korkman, M. (1999). Applying Luria's diagnostic principles in the neuropsychological assessment of children. *Neuropsychology Review, 9*, 89–105.

Korkman, M., Kirk, U., & Kemp, S. (2005). *NEPSY-II: Administrative Manual.* San Antonio, TX: Psych Corp. Harcourt Assessments.

Lajiness-O'Neill, R. R., Beaulieu, I., Asamoah, A., Titus, J. B., Bawle, E. V., Ahmad, S., Kirk, J. W., & Pollack, R. (2006). The neuropsychological phenotype of velocardiofacial syndrome (VCFS): relationship to psychopathology. *Archives of Clinical Neuropsychology, 21*, 175–184.

Lajiness-O'Neill, R. & Menard, P. (2007). An autistic spectrum subtype revealed through familial psychopathology coupled with cognition in ASD. *Journal of Autism and Developmental Disorders.* Nov 22 [Epub ahead of print].

Larabee, G. T. (2000a). Forensic neuropsychology: *Special issue of the Journal of Head Trauma Rehabilitation, 15.*

Larabee, G. T. (2000b). Forensic neuropsychological assessment. In R. Vanderploeg (Ed.), *Clinician's guide to neuropsychological assessment* (2nd ed.). Mahwah, NJ: Lawrence Erlbaum Associates.

Larabee, G. T. (2005). *Forensic neuropsychology: a scientific approach.* New York: Oxford University Press.

Lassonde, M., Sauerwein, H. C., Jambaque, I., Smith, M. L., & Helmstaedter, C. (2000). Neuropsychology of childhood epilepsy: pre- and postsurgical assessment. *Epileptic Disorders, 2*, 3–14.

Levin, H. S., Culhane, K. A., Mendeksohn, D., Lilly, M. A., Bruce, D., Fletcher, J. M., Chapman, S. B., Harward, H., & Eisenberg, H. M. (1993). Cognition in relation to magnetic resonance imaging in head-injured children and adolescents. *Archives of Neurology, 50*, 897–905.

Lezak, M. D. (1995). *Neuropsychological assessment* (3rd ed.). New York: Oxford University Press.

Libon, D. J., Price, C. C., Davis Garrett, K., & Giovannetti, T. (2004). From Binswanger's disease to leukoaraiosis: what we have learned about subcortical vascular dementia. *Clinical Neuropsychology, 18*, 83–100.

Lineweaver, T. T., Salmon, D. P., Bondi, M. W., & Corey-Bloom, J. (2005). Differential effects of Alzheimer's disease and Huntington's disease on the performance of mental rotation. *Journal of International Neuropsychological Society, 11*, 30–39.

Lord, C., Rutter, M., DiLavore, P. C., & Risi, S. (1999). *Autism Diagnostic Observation Schedule.* Los Angeles, CA: Western Psychological Services.

Lord, C., Rutter, M., & LeCouteur, A. (1994). Autism Diagnostic Interview-Revised: a revised version of a diagnostic interview for caregivers of individuals with possible pervasive developmental disorders. *Journal of Autism and Developmental Disorders, 24*, 659–685.

Luria, A. R. (1974). *The working brain: an introduction to neuropsychology* (B. Haigh, Trans.). London: Penguin.

Matsuura, M., Adachi, N., Muramatsu, R., Kato, M., Onuma, T., Okubo, Y., Oana, Y., & Hara, T. (2005). Intellectual disability and psychotic disorders of adult epilepsy. *Epilepsia, 46*, 11–14.

Mattis, S. (2002). *Dementia Rating Scale-2 (DRS-2).* Odessa, FL: Psychological Assessment Resources.

Meulen, E. F., Schmand, B., van Campen, J. P., de Koning, S. J., Ponds, R. W., Scheltens, P., & Verhey, F. R. (2004). The Seven Minute Screen: a neurocognitive screening test highly sensitive to various types of dementia. *Journal of Neurology, Neurosurgery, & Psychiatry, 75*, 700–705.

Moses, P. & Stiles, J. (2002). The lesion method: contrasting views from adult and child studies. *Developmental Psychobiology, 40*, 266–277.

Mullen, E. M. (1995). *Mullen Scales of Early Learning.* Circle Pines, MN: American Guidance Service.

Muller, S. V., Johannes, S., Wieringa, B., Weber, A., Muller-Vahl, K., Matzke, M., Kolbe, H., Dengler, R., & Munte, T. E. (2003). Disturbed monitoring and response inhibition in patients with Gilles de la Tourette syndrome and co-morbid obsessive compulsive disorder. *Behavioral Neurology, 14*, 29–37.

Murphy, F. C. & Sahakian, B. J. (2001). Neuropsychology of bipolar disorder. *British Journal of Psychiatry, 178*, S120–S127.

Nasreddine, Z. S., Phillips, N. A., Bedirian, V., Charbonneau, S., Whitehead, V., Collin, I., Cummings, J. L., & Chertkow, H. (2005). The Montreal Cognitive Assessment, MoCA: a brief screening tool for mild cognitive impairment. *Journal of the American Geriatric Society, 53*, 695–699.

National Academy of Neuropsychology (2000a). The use of neuropsychology test technicians in clinical practice: official statement of the National Academy of Neuropsychology. *Archives of Clinical Neuropsychology*, 15, 381.

National Academy of Neuropsychology (2000b). Test security: official statement of the National Academy of Neuropsychology. *Archives of Clinical Neuropsychology*, 15, 383–386.

National Academy of Neuropsychology (2000c). Presence of third party observers during neuropsychological testing: official statement of the National Academy of Neuropsychology. *Archives of Clinical Neuropsychology*, 15, 379–380.

Nichols, S., Jones, W., Roman, M. J., et al. (2004). Mechanisms of verbal memory impairment in four neurodevelopmental disorders. *Brain and Language*, 88, 180–189.

Nielen, M. M. & Den Boer, J. A. (2003). Neuropsychological performance of OCD patients before and after treatment with fluoxetine: evidence for persistent cognitive deficits. *Psychological Medicine*, 33, 917–925.

O'Connor, S. & Tasman, A. (1990). The application of electrophysiology to research in alcoholism. *Journal of Neuropsychiatry and Clinical Neurosciences*, 2, 149–158.

Pulsifer, M. B. & Aylward, E. H. (1999). Human Immunodeficiency Virus. In K. O. Yeates, D. H. Ris, & M. D. Taylor (Eds.), *Pediatric neuropsychology: research, theory and practice*. New York: Guilford Press.

Purcell, R., Maruff, P., Kyrios, M., & Pantelis, C. (1998). Neuropsychological deficits in obsessive compulsive disorder: a comparison with unipolar depression, panic disorder, and normal controls. *Archives of General Psychiatry*, 55, 415–423.

Rappaport, M., Hall, K. M., Hopkins, K., Belleza, T., & Cope, D. N. (1982). Disability Rating Scale for severe head trauma: coma to community. *Archives of Physical Medicine and Rehabilitation*, 63, 118–123.

Reed, J. (1999). Current status of the admissibility of expert testimony after Daubert and Joiner. *Journal of Forensic Neuropsychology*, 1, 49–69.

Rees, G. & Lavie, N. (2001). What can functional imaging reveal about the role of attention in visual awareness? *Neuropsychologia*, 39, 1343–1353.

Reitan, R. M. & Davison, L. A. (1974). *Clinical neuropsychology: current status and applications*. Washington D.C: Winston.

Reitan, R. M. & Wolfson, D. (1985). *The Halstead-Reitan Neuropsychological Test Battery*. Tucson, AZ: Neuropsychology Press.

Ris, M. D. (2003). Causal inference in lead research: introduction to the special section on the neurobehavioral effects of environmental lead. *Child Neuropsychology*, 9, 1–9.

Robbins, T. W., James, M., Owen, A. M., Sahakian, B. J., Lawrence, A. D., McInnes, L., & Rabbitt, P. M. A. (1998). A study of performance on tests from the CANTAB battery sensitive to frontal lobe dysfunction in a large sample of normal volunteers: implications for theories of executive functioning and cognitive ageing. *Journal of the International Neuropsychological Society*, 4, 474–490.

Rourke, B. P. (1995). *Syndrome of nonverbal learning disabilities: neurodevelopmental manifestations*. New York: Guilford Press.

Rudel, R. & Denckla, M. B. (1974). Relationship of forward and backward digit repetition to neurological impairment in children with learning disabilities. *Neuropsychologia*, 12, 109–118.

Sadek, J. R., Johnson, S. A., White, D. A., Salmon, D. P., Taylor, K. I., Delapena, J. H., Paulsen, J. S., Heaton, R. K., & Grant, I. (2004). Retrograde amnesia in dementia: comparison of HIV-associated dementia, Alzheimer's disease, and Huntington's disease. *Neuropsychology*, 18, 692–699.

Sandler, A. D., Watson, T. E., Footo, M., et al. (1992). Neurodevelopmental study of writing disorders in middle childhood. *Journal of Developmental and Behavioral Pediatrics*, 13, 17–23.

Savla, G. N. & Palmer, B. W. (2005). Neuropsychology in Alzheimer's disease and other dementia research. *Current Opinions in Psychiatry*, 18, 621–627.

Schacter, D. L. & Tulvig, E. (1994). *Memory systems*. Cambridge, MA: MIT Press.

Scott, S. K. (2005). Auditory processing — speech, space, and auditory objects. *Current Opinions in Neurobiology*, 15(2), 197–201.

Shalev, R. S. & Gross-Tsur, V. (2001). Developmental dyscalculia. *Pediatric Neurology*, 24, 337–342.

Shaywitz, S. E. & Shaywitz, B. A. (2005). Dyslexia: specific reading disability. *Biological Psychiatry*, 57, 1301–1309.

Shevell, M., Ashwal, S., Donley, D., et al. (2003). Practice parameter: evaluation of the child with global developmental delay. *Neurology*, 60, 367–380.

Sporns, O., Chialvo, D. R., Kaiser, M., & Hilgetag, C. C. (2004). Organization, development and function of complex brain networks. *Trends in Cognitive Neuroscience*, 8, 418–425.

Spreen, O. & Strauss, E. (1998). *A compendium of neuropsychological tests: administration, norms, and commentary* (2nd ed.). New York: Oxford University Press.

Stiles, J., Moses, P., Roe, K., et al. (2003). Alternative brain organization after prenatal cerebral injury: convergent fMRI and cognitive data. *Journal of International Neuropsychology Society*, 9, 604–622.

Sweet, J. J. (1999). *Forensic neuropsychology: fundamentals and practice*. Lisse: Swets & Zeitlinger.

Sweet, J. J., Nelson, N. W., & Moberg, P. J. (2006). The TCN/AACN 2005 "salary survey": professional practices, beliefs, and incomes of U.S. neuropsychologists. *Clinical Neuropsychologist*, 20, 325–364.

Trask, C. L. & Kosofsky, B. E. (2000). Developmental considerations of neurotoxic exposures. *Neurology Clinics*, 18, 541–562.

Ungerleider, L., Courtney, S. M., & Haxby, J. V. (1998). A neural system for human visual working memory. *Proceedings from the National Academy of Science, USA*, 95, 883–890.

Vargha-Khadem, F., Salmond, C. H., Watkins, K. E., et al. (2003). Developmental amnesia: effect of age at injury. *Proceedings from the National Academy of Science, USA*, 100, 1055–1060.

Vigneau, M, Beaucousin, V., Herve, P. Y., et al. (2006). Meta-analyzing left hemisphere language areas: phonology, semantics, and sentence processing. *Neuroimage*, 30(4), 1414–1432.

Wade, S. L., Taylor, H. G., Drotar, D., et al. (2003). Parent-adolescent interactions after traumatic brain injury: the relationship to family adaptation and adolescent adjustment. *Journal of Head Trauma Rehabilitation*, 18, 64–76.

Wagner, R., Torgesen, J. K., & Rashotte, C. (1999). *Comprehensive Test of Phonological Processing*. Austin, TX: Pro-Ed.

Williams, J. & Sharp, G. B. (1999). Epilepsy. In K. O. Yeates, M. D. Ris, & H. G. Taylor (Eds.), *Pediatric neuropsychology: research, theory and practice*. New York: Guilford Press.

Yeates, K. O., Ris, M. D., & Taylor, H. G. (1999). *Pediatric neuropsychology: research, theory and practice*. New York: Guilford Press.

Psychodynamic and Psychoanalytic Psychotherapy

Kenneth N. Levy
Pennsylvania State University

Writing about psychodynamic psychotherapy is difficult because it is not a unified approach. In fact, it is often said that psychoanalysis, though frequently used singularly, is in actuality a plural noun representing an array of theoretical ideas and technical applications. Nevertheless, we can say that psychodynamic psychotherapies are approaches to helping people that derive from the ideas of Sigmund Freud and his collaborators and followers. Contemporary psychoanalytic and psychodynamic psychotherapies are influenced by at least four broad frameworks or schools: (1) *ego psychology*, derived from the classic psychoanalytic theory of Freud and elaborated by Hartman, Rapaport, and Bellak among others; (2) *object relations theory*, derived from the work of Melanie Klein and members of the "British School," including Fairbairn, Guntrip, Winnicott, and Balint and best represented by the work of Kernberg; (3) *self psychology*, developed by Heinz Kohut and elaborated by subsequent contributors such as Ornstein and Adler; and (4) *attachment theory*, developed by John Bowlby and Mary Ainsworth and elaborated by a number of clinical and developmental researchers including Peter Fonagy and Mary Target. Volumes have been written on each of these schools of thought, and within each of these psychoanalytic approaches there are multiple perspectives.

WHAT IS PSYCHODYNAMIC AND PSYCHOANALYTIC PSYCHOTHERAPY?

The terms *psychodynamic* and *psychoanalytic* are often used interchangeably. However, within the psychodynamic and psychoanalytic communities, *psychoanalysis* is the term used when referring to a psychological treatment where the therapist, called a psychoanalyst or analyst, adheres to standard techniques focused on *interpretation* leading to insight in the context of the transference. In psychoanalysis the patient usually attends treatment three to five times weekly for 45- to 50-minute sessions. Treatment usually involves the patient lying on a couch and the analyst sitting behind the patient while the patient free associates — that is, says whatever comes to mind. Psychodynamic psychotherapy is characterized by the same basic techniques as

psychoanalysis but tends to be briefer and less intensive than psychoanalysis. Although any given session of psychodynamic psychotherapy may be indistinguishable from a psychoanalytic session, in psychodynamic psychotherapy the therapist is more likely to be actively engaged with the patient, to resonate emotionally with the patient's affect states, and rely more on the interpersonal relationship between client and therapist than in psychoanalysis.

Basic Tenets and Concepts

A number of basic tenets and concepts are central to psychodynamic psychotherapy. These include the idea that some mental processes, such as motives, desires, and memories, are not available to awareness or conscious introspection. This idea is often referred to as **unconscious** *mental functioning* or *unconscious processing*. While attention to *unconscious* mental life remains central to psychoanalytic or psychodynamic psychotherapy, this is not to say that all important processes are out of our awareness or *unconscious*. Of course, much of our experience is available and accessible for introspection, reflection, and conscious decision making. Moreover, as Wachtel (2005) has noted, consciousness is better conceptualized as a matter of degree of accessibility and articulation than as a discrete division between conscious and *unconscious*.

Another tenet of the psychodynamic approach is the defense or **defense mechanism** — while some mental processes are out of our awareness, this is a process in which people are also motivated to push threatening thoughts or feelings from awareness. This concept of defense is generally well supported in the empirical literature examining narratives of adults (Main, 2000), psychophysiological data (Adams, Wright, & Lohr, 1996; Shedler, Mayman, & Manis, 1993), and neuroscience data (Anderson, Ochsner, Kuhl et al., 2004; Westen, Blagov, Harenski, Kilts, & Hamann, 2006) and is generally well accepted (Meehl, 1997). There is much evidence from experimental, social, and neuroscience research suggesting the importance of *unconscious* mental processes; however, the data are still unclear as to whether or not this noncouscious processing is motivated.

A third tenet central to psychodynamic theory is that of a *developmental perspective* in which childhood relationships with caregivers are seen as playing a role in shaping current relationships. This is not to imply a linear relationship or critical period between early experience and later development. Psychodynamic theory, consistent with a developmental psychopathology perspective, is probabilistic rather than deterministic regarding this relationship. In addition, this does not mean that the psychodynamic perspective fails to recognize the importance of biological contributions to development — quite the contrary. From the very beginning of his theorizing, Freud discussed how these childhood experiences, in concert with genetic (what Freud called constitutional) factors, influence people's internal experience of themselves and their overt behavior.

Finally, a psychodynamic perspective emphasizes the importance of *individual or personal meaning* of events. Psychodynamic clinicians are interested in the patient's phenomenological experience — how the patient experiences himself, important others, the world in general. In this way, psychodynamic clinicians are focused on what those from the cognitive-behavioral therapy tradition call schemas or schemata. The difference, however, is that in a psychodynamic model, these schemas are seen as having explicit, conscious, and implicit *unconscious* aspects, and the implicit parts can be simply out of awareness or kept out of awareness for defensive purposes. The psychoanalytic model posits that individuals may use one set of representations to defend against other intolerable representations. There is also greater attention to the emotional aspects of these schemas or representations and to the structural aspects of representation, that is, the degree of differentiation and hierarchical integration of representations (see Blatt, Auerbach, & Levy,

1997). Evidence from developmental, clinical, and neuroscience provides validation for these basic premises (see Westen, 1999, for a review).

Several other concepts are central to the psychodynamic approach in addition to the ideas of *unconscious* processes, *defense mechanisms*, a developmental perspective, and subjectivity. These include **transference, countertransference,** and **resistance**. With the exception of transference (see Berk & Andersen, 2000; Brumbaugh & Fraley, 2005), these issues have less empirical support at this time. However, interestingly, countertransference has recently become of interest to those from the behavioral (Kohlenberg & Tsai, 1994; Koerner, Kohlenberg, & Parker, 1996) and cognitive-behavioral paradigms (Linehan, 1993). Although other concepts have been stressed within psychoanalysis at various times, such as the Oedipus complex or psychosexual stages, it should be noted that these concepts are not as central or crucial to the psychoanalytic and psychodynamic models as the other tenets we have identified.

DEVELOPMENT OF PSYCHODYNAMIC PSYCHOTHERAPY

Freud developed psychoanalysis over the course of many years and was influenced by a number of colleagues and experiences. Between 1895 and 1938 Freud was a prodigious writer. His compiled works amount to 23 volumes and cover thousands of pages of writing. During the time he was developing psychoanalysis, his ideas changed, sometimes drastically, and he abandoned ideas when they did not coincide with new data. Many people are confused about his ideas because of the amount of writing he did and the fact that his ideas developed and changed over time, which has resulted in conflicting ideas. For these reasons it can be difficult to understand psychoanalytic psychotherapy without some basic understanding of the context of how Freud's ideas developed.

Although Freud is often portrayed as unscientific, he was a first-rate scientist and an active contributor in his day. While in medical school at the University of Vienna (1873–1881), Freud studied with the great physiologist Ernst Wilhelm von Brücke, the noted mechanist who in 1874 published *Lectures on Physiology* in which he discussed the principles of psychodynamics. Based on thermodynamics, Brücke suggested that all living organisms are energy systems, governed by the principle of energy conservation. Freud was supervised by Brücke during his first year in medical school and later worked in his lab as an assistant. Many years later he would borrow the idea of a "dynamic" from physiology to help conceptualize how the human mind worked.

In medical school, Freud enjoyed his scientific work and never intended to practice medicine. In his research he described nerve cells of small fish, protomyazin, and sexual organs of eels, supplying a missing link in the development of nerve cells from their forms in primitive species to their form in more evolved species. In 1877, Freud began working in Brücke's laboratory, where he investigated brain anatomy and histology. Examining questions related to Darwin's evolutionary theory, he also determined that the spinal neurons in humans and frogs were the same type; this work proved important at the time in providing evidence for evolutionary theory. Although Freud was a scientist, he was more typically an observer than an experimenter. This is an important distinction because observation is the method he brought to the study of behavior. Thus, he attempted to map out the mind just as he did nerve pathways in fish, eels, and frogs.

Freud would gladly have remained Brücke's assistant working on evolutionary anatomy of the nervous system where the quality of his research was strong. However, in 1881 he met Martha Barneys, the sister of a classmate.

A year later at age 26, they became secretly engaged. Freud desperately wanted to marry Martha, but both were from poor families, and he would need money to support himself, Martha, and the children they wanted to have. Brücke advised Freud that despite his good work, his prospects for promotion were poor and that private practice as a physician was his most viable option. The prospects of Freud's advancement in the professoriate were slim due in large part to the particularities of the European academic system. Unfortunately for Freud, there were two other assistants in the lab who had seniority and would most likely receive promotion before Freud. Furthermore, he was Jewish. Regardless of promotion, science and university academics did not portend of a particularly lucrative career. Thus, at Brücke's advice, Freud reluctantly went into the private practice of medicine as a neurologist.

Freud initially took a position at Vienna General Hospital in order to gain experience treating patients prior to commencing private practice. After some time in surgery and dermatology, he began in the psychiatry department headed by Theodor Meynert. In his heart, however, Freud saw himself as a scientist, as evidenced by the fact that he authored scientific monographs on topics ranging from cocaine (Freud, 1884) to aphasia (Freud, 1891) and several books on paralysis in children, of which he was considered an authority, having developed expertise during his time at Vienna General Hospital.

In private practice, most of his patients were young middle-class women who suffered from a host of "neurological" symptoms — paralysis, partial blindness, hallucinations, loss of motor control — that appeared to have no real neurological cause. The prevailing view in Vienna, where Freud, was practicing, was that these clients were malingering or faking it. Freud, however, realized that his patients were not simply "faking it." Because he thought that many of his patients were talented and very bright, he not only believed his patients but took their problems seriously. For most of the 1880s and well into the 1890s, he used the treatments popular at the time, including combinations of massage, rest therapy, hot baths, and weak electric currents. But he could tell that these treatments did not work very well on what we would today call psychosomatic disorders, and so he became interested in finding better procedures.[1]

In an effort to learn more about how to treat these patients, Freud applied for and won a grant to travel to Paris to study under famed neurologist Jean-Martin Charcot for six months at the Salpêtrière mental hospital in Paris. Charcot was a well-respected psychiatrist, the director of the Salpêtrière, who had turned his interest toward the problem of hysteria. Charcot had found that many patients experienced paralyses, pains, coughs, and a variety of other symptoms with no demonstrable physical etiology. Prior to Charcot's work, women were thought to have a wandering uterus (hence the Greek name "hysteria") for which pregnancy was often the prescribed treatment. In contrast, Charcot believed that after a physical trauma, a "hypnoid state" developed that made people who were predisposed to hysteria susceptible to the induction of hysterical symptoms. Thus, in contrast to the Viennese view that those suffering from hysteria were malingering, Charcot hypothesized that hysteria developed from mental degeneration or mental weakness.

Freud attended Charcot's lectures and demonstrations on hysteria. He managed to gain Charcot's attention by offering to translate

some of his writings into German. In consultation, Charcot suggested to Freud that he write a paper analyzing the differences between hysterical and organic paralysis. This was a definitive work in the area. What he found was something called glove and sock paralysis, in which the physical symptoms corresponded to how the hysterical individual thought the symptom should be expressed (e.g., paralysis of the arm from the top of the shoulder to the tips of the fingers rather than paralysis that followed the actual nerve pathways) that is, hysterical symptoms were delimited according to popular beliefs, which led to a presentation that was not consistent with actual nerve tracts. This was for Freud a major breakthrough and led to what might be considered his first great discovery on the way to developing psychoanalysis — that ideas can create and shape physical symptoms. He shared this idea with Charcot, who promptly rejected it, preferring his own idea that hysteria was a disorder of function rather than structure.

Upon returning to Vienna, Freud employed hypnosis on his patients but found it inadequate because not everyone is hypnotizable. Only about 20% to 30% of people make really good hypnotic subjects. Therefore, in 1889 Freud returned to France to work with Hippolite Bernhiem at the Nancy School in Nancy, France, to try to perfect his hypnotic technique. Bernhiem was a well-known physician who became interested in hypnosis through the work of a country doctor named Auguste Liebeault. As opposed to Charcot, Bernhiem believed that hypnosis was a normal phenomenon. While working with Bernhiem, Freud learned four principles that influenced his thinking:

1. Posthypnotic suggestions — Normal patients were highly suggestible with regard to both onset and diminishment of physical symptoms. Further, the symptoms were indistinguishable from those of hysterics.

---

[1]Freud remained a scientist at heart; he wanted to figure out what caused these problems — a perspective he learned while working with Brücke. In contrast to typical physiologists of the time, Brücke was concerned with the function of particular cells and organs, not just with their structure. Brücke's work thus focused on the attempt to discover basic physical laws that governed the processes that took place in living systems.

2. A hypnotized person can be virtually compelled, through posthypnotic suggestion, to perform a series of actions for reasons outside of his or her awareness. Importantly, when questioned, the individual would provide *a seemingly rational but demonstrably irrelevant explanation.* This rational but irrelevant explanation was important in Freud's development of different levels of psychic functioning, later to become conscious and *unconscious.*

3. Posthypnotic amnesia is not absolute. Ideas that were not conscious had the power to affect behavior and could be recovered to consciousness.[2]

4. Hypnotic lucidity. The mind has a storehouse of information that is not available to consciousness but is accessible under hypnosis.

Freud was also strongly influenced by the case he heard about in 1882 from Dr. Josef Breuer, an older mentor and medical colleague in Vienna. Breuer was treating a patient by the name of Bertha Pappenhiem, who is popularly known as Anna O. According to Breuer, Anna was an intelligent woman of 21 with a strict upbringing, leaving her sexually immature. In July of 1880 her father became seriously ill. She nursed him day and night until she collapsed in December. Her symptoms included a severe nervous cough, a squint, visual disturbances, paralysis of the right arm and neck, and a strange speech problem whereby she often replied to the German language questions in English. She was also agitated by hallucinations. She seemed to improve until her father's death. Then the hallucinations became more violent during the daytime, and at night she fell into a quiet trance and mumbled words to herself. Breuer repeated

her words back to her as a way to encourage her to elaborate on her hallucinations, and when she came out of the trance, she reported having felt better. If she did not talk about her experience, she would continue with the symptom. Anna herself called this the "talking cure" or used the metaphor of chimney sweeping to represent the experience. However, she kept developing new symptoms: hydrophobia and a trance-like state. Breuer noticed that each symptom disappeared when it was traced back to its first occasion and that the symptoms were removed by recalling forgotten unpleasant events. Furthermore, the symptom emerged with greatest force while it was being talked away

Thus, from Breuer's work with Anna O., Freud concluded that suppressed memory of a traumatic event gave rise to a symptom. Whereas Charcot thought that a physical trauma (e.g., train accident) combined with a mental defect (e.g., susceptibility to hypnoid states) caused hysterical symptoms, Freud believed that the cause was a psychic trauma and when the patient experienced the full force of the emotion, then the symptom disappeared. This process of the symptom remitting as the patient experiences the full force of emotional expression is referred to as a *catharsis.*

Thus, in his own work with patients, his studies with Charcot and Bernheim, and his consultations with Breuer, Freud learned that:

1. Preconceived but incorrect ideas could influence symptom expression (with Charcot).

2. Physical symptoms can be suggested, and those symptoms are indistinguishable from symptoms of hysterics (with Charcot and Bernheim).

3. Posthypnotic suggestion compelled the person to perform actions for reasons he or she was unaware of, but they will give seemingly rational but demonstrably irrelevant explanations (with Bernheim).

---

[2]I use only the word *conscious* because Freud himself had not yet postulated the idea of an *unconscious.*

4. Posthypnotic amnesia is not absolute — memory of events that are not conscious can be recalled to consciousness (with Bernheim).
5. Symptoms may be caused by *unconscious* "memories" of traumatic events (from Breuer's work with Anna O.).
6. Catharsis as shown by Breuer with Anna O. (the uncovering of *unconscious* events accompanied by the commensurate emotion) can eliminate corresponding symptoms.
7. The mind is a storehouse of information that is not available to consciousness but is accessible under hypnosis.

With this knowledge in hand, Freud had the elements of a theory. In Freud's view, a person who has experienced a *traumatic* event and is unable to experience or express fully the *appropriate emotion* often experiences *conflict* over the feelings and the person's own moral standards. The painful memory is pushed out of one's conscious awareness and is lost to memory (e.g., later conceptualized as repressed and having become *unconscious*), but the memory is not completely lost, and it continues to have effects. It obtrudes into consciousness disguised as a symptom. When catharsis occurs, indirect expression is no longer necessary. This account is known as Freud's trauma theory.[3] Breuer and Freud published a short preliminary communication, "Ueber den psychischen Mechanismus hysterische Phänomene" (On the Psychical Mechanism of Hysterical Phenomena, 1893, trans. 1909) in the *Neurologische Centralblatt*, which they more fully developed in *Studien über Hysterie* (1895). Although neither was well received by the medical community, these publications marked the beginning of psychoanalysis.

Freud learned a great deal from hypnosis, but for a number of reasons, he slowly abandoned it. First, as mentioned earlier, not everyone is hypnotizable. Second, he found that hypnotism provided only partial and/or temporary symptom relief (which we also know today). Third, he believed that hypnotism also increased the erotic element of treatment by intensifying the transference, something that happened both to Mesmer and to Breuer with Anna O. and was now happening with Freud's patients. Finally, he thought that it was wrong to suggest away a symptom when the patient's suffering was *real* (as others who were using hypnosis were doing). But how is repression to be lifted if one does not use hypnosis? Influenced by Brücke, who was a determinist, and based on his own findings while working with Charcot, Freud felt that hysterical symptoms had meaning and that nothing happened by chance. This idea that everything that happens in the mind is predetermined is referred to as *psychic determinism*. **Psychic determinism** postulates that nothing in the psyche happens by chance; all mental and physical behavior is determined by prior causes. Random thoughts, the inability to recall a familiar word or idea, saying or writing of wrong words, self-inflicted injuries, bungled actions, dreams, neurotic symptoms — all have underlying reasons, which may be *unconscious*. Thus, the forgetting of an appointment or a college exam happens for definite reasons. The explanation of these "parapraxes" may be fairly simple, such as anger toward the person to be met or spite regarding the exam. However, the causes of psychic phenomena are usually numerous and multidetermined. In a bold move, Freud reasoned that if nothing in the mind happens by chance, then all one needs to do is let the patient say whatever comes to mind and sooner or later the patient will give a clue to what the trouble is. This technique is referred to as *free association*. Free association held the promise of revealing associational networks and mental transformations of ideas and feelings in which patients revealed interpersonal cognitive-affective-

[3] Also known as the seduction theory.

behavioral patterns that the analyst could observe directly.

During free association, many of Freud's patients referred to dreams, and he realized that often dreams give clues to *unconscious* conflicts. For this reason, Freud referred to dreams as the "royal road to the *Unconscious*." Freud also discovered what most of us take for granted today: that dreams were symbolic and specific to the dreamer. Using free association, Freud found that patients reported sexual assaults in childhood in the first 18 cases of hysteria he treated. Although some of the experiences were single or isolated instances perpetrated by pedophiles, most of the experiences were carried out by adults who were looking after the child. In 1897, after 15 years of work and only 2 or so years after he had gone out on a limb — publicly proclaiming that childhood sexual abuse is the direct cause of hysteria — Freud repudiated this theory, citing a number of reasons including the difficulty of teasing out actual memories from fantasies. (Some of Freud's patients later recanted their original stories of childhood seduction, and other patients' stories were found to be untrue or were implausible.) He also began to worry that his line of questioning and the forceful manner he applied during free association might have pressured patients to report such events. Importantly, Freud acknowledged his own neurotic symptoms and discovered during self-analysis (begun after his father's death) that as a child he had sexual fantasies about his mother, although he was never abused. Most importantly, however, was Freud's realization that the trauma or seduction theory was limited in its explanatory power because the relationship between sexual abuse and hysteria was not perfectly predictive, that is, he knew that not all victims of sexual abuse developed hysteria and that not all sufferers of hysteria had been sexually abused. Thus, many were not actual events but were fantasies. This presented a real crisis in Freud's theory, for he had spent years

analyzing cases within the trauma paradigm. Because he had been working toward a rather tightly integrated theory that would yield a rational basis for treating neurosis, the discovery of this anomaly appeared to destroy what he had laboriously achieved over a period of 15 years.

Freud soon came to the conclusion, however, that the theory of an actual seduction was a dispensable element. Charcot thought that the cause of neurosis was a physical trauma, and Freud initially thought that it was a psychic trauma caused by sexual abuse. Now he was carrying the theory one step further in proposing that sometimes the psychic trauma was simply a fantasy that was completely or partly imaginary. This is not to say that Freud did not realize that sexual abuse occurred or that it had profound effects on those who experienced it. He never totally repudiated his original seduction theory, maintaining to the end of his life that actual incest did occur and that these instances contributed to the development of psychopathology. In fact, he had estimated the prevalence of sexual abuse at about 30%, an estimate we now know is accurate. However, in suggesting that children have sexual fantasies (known as infantile sexuality), he still needed an explanation for its occurrence. Here Freud proposed the concept of drives, which he thought tended to be aggressive and sexual in nature. (Later, John Bowlby and other object relations theorists would stress the importance of the drive for relatedness.) The idea of aggressive and sexual drives did not necessarily come out of the blue. Freud had approached this idea early in his theorizing when listening to patients who described conflicts around aggressive and sexual wishes, desires, and internalized inhibitions. If Freud was alive today, no doubt he would not be surprised that we have censors for our TV and movies that focus almost exclusively on sexual and aggressive themes.

The drive theory became closely tied to what is referred to as the Freudian conflict model of

compromise formation. This model posits that many of the conflicts that cause symptoms of mental and physical illness have a particular form: on one side there are intense wishes or desires, often of a selfish, sexual, or aggressive nature, and opposing these motives or drives are strong and disturbing feelings of guilt and fear. Negative emotion causes a person to repress, deny, or redirect troublesome needs and wishes, which then are expressed only indirectly — in symptoms, dreams, jokes, and slips of the tongue or "accidental" behavior (so-called Freudian slips). These drives or desires, and the prohibitions against their manifested behaviors, give rise to inner conflicts and then neurosis. Thus, what had started as a purely clinical theory of hysteria grew into a deep theory of personality and development.

Freud is often portrayed as unscientific because many of the methods he used would be considered inadequate today. Critics often cite his famous postcard in 1934 to Saul Rosenzweig, in which he replies to Rosenzweig's studies of repression by indicating that he "cannot put much value on these confirmations because the wealth of reliable observations on which these assertions rest make them independent of experimental verification." However, he also said that "science is no illusion but it would be an illusion that we could get anywhere what it cannot give us" (Freud, 1927/1953, p. 102). What this chapter hopes to show is that Freud was a serious scientist of his time and that he approached complex clinical problems scientifically. He was a consumer of most cutting-edge scientific knowledge of his time, integrating the theorizing and experimental work of Brücke, Darwin, Charcot, and Bernheim into his thinking. He also carried out his own scientific research, which was integrated into his theory. In this manner, Freud was one of the first translational scientists, who translated basic research into ideas useful for applied work.

COMPONENTS OF PSYCHOANALYTIC AND PSYCHODYNAMIC PSYCHOTHERAPY

The aim of psychodynamic psychotherapy is to make what is *unconscious* conscious in an effort to better understand a person's motivations and thus respond to them in reality more honestly. Three essential features of the psychoanalytic method are *interpretation*, including *clarification* and *confrontation*, and technical neutrality, and analysis of the transference.

Clarification, Confrontation, and Interpretation

The three main techniques used in psychodynamic psychotherapy are clarification, confrontation, and interpretation. **Clarifications** simply are requests for more information or further elaborations in order to better understand the patient's subjective experience. Beginning therapists, and those with only a cursory understanding of psychodynamic psychotherapy, often neglect this technique and move prematurely to *interpretation*. Even if a therapist could determine the appropriate interpretation without clarifying, it would be difficult for the patient to integrate it without first properly clarifying. Clarifying and confronting a patient's experience are preparatory steps for interpretation. The therapist should clarify thoroughly until both the therapist and the patient have a clear understanding of any areas of vagueness. It is important to recognize vague communications, which is not easily done because therapists prematurely foreclose clarification by inserting their own preconceptions when patients are vague or unclear. For example, if a patient says he feels depressed, the therapist should clarify what the patient means by the term. A standard technique is to start with short open-ended questions and become more specific as needed. For example, a therapist might simply respond by saying "Can you say more about that?" A recommended device for determining if *clarification* is required is to ask oneself whether a patient's presentation could be veridically described to a supervisor or consulting colleague. Frequently, a patient will become puzzled by contradictions in his or her thinking or experience during the clarification process.

Confrontations sound harsher than they are because they actually involve tactfully pointing out discrepancies or incongruities in the patient's narrative or the patient's verbal and nonverbal behavior (affect or actual behavior). It is difficult to successfully confront a patient without thoroughly clarifying because the patient may not be aware of what the therapist is observing. (Conversely, without clarifying, the therapist may incorrectly confront the patient regarding material that would otherwise be clear.) The therapist uses the clarified material or information that is contradictory for further exploration and understanding. This is done in an effort to better understand conflicting mental states or representations of experience that implicitly address the patient's defensive operations.

Interpretations focus on the *unconscious* meaning of what has been clarified and confronted. *Interpretations* can be made regarding experience in the therapy or about the relationship between the patient and the therapist (interpretations of the "here and now") or about relationships outside the therapy, with either important others or other people in the patient's life. Interpretations about relationships outside of therapy are referred to as **extratransferential interpretations**. Interpretations made about early experiences with caregivers are called **genetic interpretations**. In any regard, it is important that interpretations be timely, clear, and tactful and made in a collaborative manner only after clarifying the patient's experience and pointing out gaps

and inconsistencies. The interpretation is not offered until the patient is just about ready to discover it by him- or herself. Interpretation is offered as a hypothesis in the context of a collaborative endeavor and not as a pronouncement from an all-knowing authority as is frequently portrayed in movies, the media, and poorly trained individuals.

Technical Neutrality

The psychodynamic psychotherapist uses the techniques of clarification, confrontation, and interpretation in the context of technical neutrality. **Technical neutrality**, or therapeutic neutrality, is an often misinterpreted construct whereby the psychodynamic therapist mistakenly believes that he or she needs to adopt a stone face or blank screen, say very little, refuse to self-disclose, or provide no advice, support, or reassurance. The therapist is seen as nonactive, passive, maybe even bland, monotonous, or indifferent and at worst cold and lacking in concern. This is not what technical neutrality is supposed to be. Technical neutrality is a therapeutic strategy in which the therapist avoids communicating any judgment about the patient's conflicts while they are being discussed (i.e., remains equidistant from all sides of the patient's conflicts). Typically, therapists refrain from providing advice, praise, or reproof of the patient, and they restrain their own needs for a particular type of relationship (to be liked, valued, idealized, or the center of attention). Technical neutrality fosters warmth and genuine human *concern*. A nonjudgmental, noncritical stance provides the patient with a sense of safety that allows the exploration of previously avoided memories, thoughts, and feelings. Adopting this position encourages the patient to become more fully aware of his or her mental life and can be validating to the patient. Connecting with the entirety of the patient's internal experience is experienced as empathic. This strategy also helps the therapist avoid enactments and collusions with the patient. Finally, it is important to note that technical neutrality is modified to the extent required to maintain the structure of the treatment.

Transference

A cornerstone of psychodynamic theory and practice is the psychological phenomenon of transference. **Transference** is a universal phenomenon in which aspects of important and formative relationships (such as with parents and siblings) are *unconsciously* ascribed to unrelated current relationships. This fundamental *unconscious* process also occurs in relationships between therapists and patients. In clinical practice, recognition of underlying fantasies that surround the therapeutic relationship can prove helpful to patients, regardless of the type of treatment or the therapeutic orientation of the therapist. From a psychodynamic perspective, the transference situation has far-reaching effects and necessarily influences therapeutic outcome regardless of the therapeutic modality employed.

Countertransference has also been a central concept in psychodynamic psychotherapies. Initially, Freud defined *countertransference* as the analyst's transference to the patient, which referred to the emergence of the analyst's own unresolved or unanalyzed *unconscious* conflicts protruding into the patient's therapy. Initially, Freud saw this as a nuisance that interfered with the therapist's ability to treat the patient and recommended that he or she overcome his or her countertransference. Thus, the origin of countertransference was viewed as neurotic conflicts in the analyst or therapist. This conceptualization is often referred to as the classical approach. However, since Freud's initial conceptualization, the concept has undergone considerable elaboration. Winnicott (1965), in working with personality disordered patients, saw some countertransference reactions as a natural reaction to the patient's outrageous behavior, implying that anyone would react similarly to such provocative behavior. This position is often referred to as the totalistic standpoint in that it holds that countertransference broadly includes the therapist's conscious and total emotional reaction to the patient, which is seen as appropriate to the patient's behavior. As Winncott implied and Kernberg (1965) elaborated, countertransference is not seen as *unconscious* reaction toward the patient deriving from the therapist's *unconscious* needs and neurotic conflict but as a valuable diagnostic and therapeutic tool that provides the therapist with an emotional window or channel into the patient's internal and interpersonal world. Of course, the narrow (classical) and broad (totalistic) conceptions of countertransference are not mutually exclusive. The task of the therapist is to monitor his or her reaction to a patient to discern between an internal conflict within the therapist and a reaction that would be evoked in most anyone. Gabbard (1995) points out that this is now the prevailing view across most theoretical schools. Therapists must be able to analyze and understand the source of their countertransference, which may be difficult and require reflection. Racker (1957) distinguished between *concordant countertransference* and *complementary countertransference*. In concordant countertransference, the therapist identifies with the patient's current self-representation, which provides the therapist with a sense of the patient's current internal state. In complementary countertransference, the therapist identifies with the patient's projected or split-off mental states, which provides the therapist with a sense of what the patient may be defending against or may be concerned about.

Core Aspects of Psychodynamic Psychotherapy

A number of studies are particularly informative regarding the core aspects of psychodynamic psychotherapy. The late Enrico Jones and his colleagues, particularly Stuart Ablon, investigated the psychotherapy process (Ablon

& Jones, 1999; Jones & Pulos, 1993). In an initial study, Jones and Pulos (1993) used archival records to compare the therapy process in 30 brief psychodynamic and 32 cognitive-behavioral therapies. Verbatim transcripts of 186 treatment sessions were rated with the Psychotherapy Process Q-set (Jones, 1985), which was designed to provide a standard language for the description of psychotherapy process. Factor analysis of the ratings of the Q-set items found four factors: psychodynamic technique, cognitive-behavioral technique, negative emotions, and *resistance*. Cognitive-behavioral therapy promoted control of negative emotions through the use of intellect and rationality combined with vigorous encouragement. Psychodynamic therapy emphasized (1) evocation of emotions; (2) bringing of troublesome feelings into awareness; (3) integration of current difficulties with previous life experience; and 4) use of the therapist-patient relationship to foster change. Blagys and Hilsenroth (2000) used the PsycLit database to perform a computer search to identify empirical studies that compared the process and technique of manualized psychodynamic psychotherapy with that of manualized cognitive-behavioral therapy. Their systematic literature review indicated that psychodynamic psychotherapy had seven distinctive features: (1) focus on affect and expression of emotion; (2) exploration of attempts to avoid aspects of experience; (3) identification of recurring themes and patterns; (4) discussion of past experience; (5) focus on interpersonal relations; (6) focus on the therapeutic relationship; and (7) exploration of wishes, dreams, and fantasies.

VARIANTS OF CLASSICAL OR FREUDIAN PSYCHOANALYSIS

Kleinian Psychoanalysis. Kleinian psychoanalysis is a highly expressive object relations–based treatment that emphasizes how external reality is perceived and shaped by the inner world of the patient. There is a strong focus on the primacy of the analysis of the transference, even early in treatment. Kleinian analysts are more likely than other analysts to explore early childhood causes of neurosis. They are also known for the use of "deep" *interpretations* — that is, particularly bold, penetrating statements about *unconscious* motivations (historically, with less attention to preparing the patient for such *interpretations*). There is also a greater emphasis on the analysis of primitive object relations, defenses, and aggressive drives than on libidinal needs. Contemporary Kleinian techniques focus more on the analysis of *unconscious* meaning in the "here and now" and take a more graduated and cautious approach to genetic reconstructions (that is, explaining how past events influence present ones).

Expressive Techniques. Expressive techniques are those that encourage exploration of the patient's internal world, particularly *unconscious* wishes, fears, and desires, along with the defensive processes that keep such thoughts and feelings out of awareness. As noted earlier, these techniques include *clarification, confrontation,* and *interpretation*. Expressive therapies stress technical neutrality and minimize supportive interventions in order to enhance transference.

Supportive Psychotherapy (SPT). There are a number of different supportive psychotherapies (Appelbaum, 2005; Novalis, Rojcewicz, & Peele, 1993; Pinsker, 1997; Rockland, 1989; Winston et al., 1994), many of which have derived from psychodynamic psychotherapy. The primary goal of SPT is to bring about change through developing a healthy collaborative relationship with the therapist and to replace self-destructive enactments with verbal expressions of conflicts. This transformation is thought to occur through the patient's identification with the reflective capacities of the therapist rather than through *interpretation*. SPT therapists focus on fostering the patient's positive experience of the therapist and the working alliance by creating an atmosphere of safety and security and facilitating a collaborative relationship between the patient and therapist.

In contrast to psychoanalysis or more expressive psychotherapies, in SPT the therapists provide advice, encouragement, and/or self-disclosure. The SPT therapist may provide cognitive and emotional support by reinforcing adaptive compromises between impulses and defenses as well as supporting mastery of impulse and affect by expressing inspiration, hope, persuasion, advice, encouragement, suggestion, reassurance, praise, or concern. In addition, the SPT therapist may provide direct environmental intervention with relatives or other mental health providers or services that help to stabilize the patient's life when necessary. Typically, SPT therapists are attuned to dominant affect (the most central affect being expressed) and type of transference without interpreting it and will accept and utilize the positive transference.[4] In contrast, certain object relations–based therapies (e.g., Kernberg) suggest interpreting the positive transference. In SPT, more attention is given to clarification and confrontation and less to interpretation per se. Although the therapist identifies and attends to the transference by tracking it or following it, transference is not often interpreted. Finally, technical neutrality is systematically abandoned, and the therapist advocates whatever position enhances the patient's adaptive functioning and potential. Thus, for an emotionally constricted patient, the therapist might encourage the expression of an inhibited impulse, whereas for an impulsive patient, the therapist might systematically support patient awareness of harmful consequences, encourage sublimation, or help develop in the patient other socially acceptable modes of impulse expression (e.g., exercise, sports).

Supportive-expressive (SE) Techniques. A number of writers have noted that a basic distinction or dimension in psychoanalytic psychotherapy is between expressive treatments and supportive treatments. Some theoreticians and clinicians have attempted to integrate these approaches (Gabbard, 1995; Luborsky & Crits-Christoph, 1989). Supportive-expressive (SE) psychotherapy derives from contemporary ego psychology *interpretation* of classical psychoanalytic principles. The techniques have been modified to make the treatment applicable to a broader range of patients. SE psychotherapies explicitly incorporate supportive techniques to promote the working alliance with those of the more classical expressive techniques designed to promote exploration of the patient's mind in order to encourage self-understanding. The premise is that providing support allows for greater tolerance of exploration in the patient. The relative emphasis on expressive or supportive techniques is based on therapist evaluation of the patient's suitability for expressive interventions. Therapists use largely expressive techniques with patients who are relatively healthy, motivated, psychologically minded, and not in crisis. For these patients, therapy resembles a more traditional psychoanalytic treatment. For patients with poor anxiety tolerance, greater emphasis is placed on supportive techniques designed to enhance the alliance and promote adaptive functioning.

Relational Psychoanalysis. Developed by Stephen Mitchell and colleagues (1988, 2000; Mitchell & Black, 1996), relational psychoanalysis draws on a diverse set of writings within psychoanalysis and combines interpersonal psychoanalysis with object relations theory. Those practicing from a relational perspective emphasize how the individual's personality is shaped by both real and imagined relationships with others and how these relationship patterns are reenacted in the

---

[4]Positive transference is the good feelings the patient has toward the therapist. From some perspectives, such as Kernberg's, positive transference early in treatment is conceptualized as idealization and interpreted. In supportive psychotherapy, positive transference is used to strengthen the therapeutic alliance, especially the working alliance.

interactions between analyst and patient. Generally speaking, relational analysts focus on the interaction between therapist and patient and each party's subjective experience of the interaction. Thus, countertransference is used to enter the dynamics of the patient's subjective experience. These theorists challenge the idea that the analyst can be a neutral outsider commenting objectively on the internal dynamics of the patient and regard objectivity as impossible. They see the transference-countertransference dynamic as constructed jointly by the two parties. In contrast to standard psychodynamic technique, the relational analyst relies on self-disclosure to the client of feelings evoked in the therapist. This is done in the interest of understanding what is being re-created in the clinical setting.

RESEARCH ON PSYCHODYNAMIC PSYCHOTHERAPY

One major misconception about psychodynamic psychotherapy is that it lacks an empirical base. This misconception has become more problematic with the development of evidence-based medicine and empirically supported treatments. Many therapists assume either that psychodynamic treatments have not been tested or that they have been found to be less effective. Although it is true that psychoanalytic and psychodynamic psychotherapies possess a smaller research base than cognitive-behavioral therapy, the truly informed clinician should be cognizant of the extant research. What follows is a review of the empirical status of psychodynamic psychotherapy for various psychological disorders.

Depression

Although the database is not nearly as large for psychodynamic treatments of depression as it is for cognitive behavioral therapy (CBT), there are enough data to suggest that psychodynamic psychotherapy (PP) is as effective as CBT and that further research is warranted on psychodynamic approaches. This conclusion is based on three sets of findings reviewed next: (1) meta-analytic studies; (2) randomized controlled trial (RCT); and (3) process-outcome studies.

Meta-analytic Studies. There are five meta-analytic studies that examine the efficacy of psychodynamic psychotherapy as compared with CBT (Churchill, Hunot, Corney, Knapp, McGuire, Tylee et al., 2001; Crits-Christoph, 1992; Gloaguen, Cottraux, Cucheret, & Blackburn, 1998; Leichsenring, 2001; Svartberg & Stiles, 1991). Two of them show no differences between psychodynamic psychotherapy and CBT (Crits-Christoph, 1992; Leichenring, 2001), while the other three have found various levels of superiority for CBT over psychodynamic (Churchill et al., 2001; Gloaguen et al., 1998; Svartberg & Stiles, 1991). In the Churchill et al. review, they found superiority for CBT in terms of percent recovered from depression; however, there were no significant differences between groups post-treatment in symptoms, symptom reduction, or dropout. Furthermore, there were no differences between groups at 3 months and 1 year follow-up. In addition, the differences in recovery from depression between the groups disappeared when examining only the severely depressed patients. Finally, the authors note that in half the treatments they examined, the psychodynamic treatments were not bona fide therapies (see Wampold, 1997) as they were employed as a control condition that confounds the findings in favor of CBT. In the Gloaguen and colleagues' meta-analysis, Wampold and colleagues (Wampold et al., 2002) showed that the superiority of CBT over other therapies could no longer be demonstrated once non–bona fide therapies were removed from the comparisons. The most recent meta-analytic review comparing short-term psychodynamic psychotherapy for major depression to behavioral and CBT treatments found no significant differences between therapy modalities in terms of depressive symptoms, general psychiatric symptoms, or social functioning (Leichenring, 2001). All three treatments appeared equally effective. Effect sizes for psychodynamic psychotherapy were quite large (between 0.90 and 2.80), with the average depressed patient treated in psychodynamic psychotherapy better off than 82% to 100% of depressed patients before therapy. As a point of comparison, the effect sizes for antidepressant medications range between 0.24 for citalopram (Celexa) and 0.31 for escitalopram (Lexapro) (Turner et al., 2008). Effect sizes decrease when antidepressants are compared to active placebos (e.g., noninert placebo that mimics the side effects of an antidepressant drug but do not have antidepressant components).

Randomized Controlled Trials (RCT). Initially, brief dynamic therapy was used as a comparison from which to assess the validity of other treatments (Hersen et al., 1984). In these studies, psychodynamic psychotherapy was not a bona fide treatment as little attention was paid to the model of treatment, the appropriateness of the therapists, or the fidelity of the treatment. More recent studies have paid more attention to these issues and tend to show that psychodynamic treatment is as effective as other modalities (Barkham et al., 1999; Cooper et al., 2003; Gallagher-Thompson & Steffen, 1994; Shapiro et al., 1994, 1995). For example, in a randomized controlled trial (RCT), Gallagher-Thompson and Steffen (1994) found that 20 sessions of brief psychodynamic psychotherapy were as effective as 20 sessions of CBT in reducing depression in caregivers of elderly family members. Shapiro et al. (1994, 1995) randomized patients to 8 or 16 weeks of psychodynamic-interpersonal psychotherapy (IPT) or CBT. They found that both treatments were equally effective for the 8-week and 16-week conditions and that there were no group differences at 1-year follow-up. In both therapy conditions, severe depressions responded better to 16 weeks of intervention. Thus, similar effect sizes were found when psychodynamic psychotherapy was compared with

CBT, and these effects were comparable to those reported in other studies of CBT and IPT.

Process-outcome Studies. A number of process studies also suggest the value of a psychodynamic approach for depression. Jones and Pulus (1993), described earlier, found that although patients in both CBT and psychodynamic psychotherapy treatment improved, improvement in both therapies was dependent on the use of psychodynamic techniques. Indirect evidence for the importance of psychodynamic process also comes from the findings of Castonguay, Goldfried, Wiser, Raue, and Hayes (1996). In examining mechanisms of change in CBT for depression, they found that focusing on distorted cognitions was inversely related to successful treatment outcome. However, a focus on feelings about the self, while elaborating and integrating emotional experience to develop an in-depth self-understanding, predicted positive treatment outcome. These findings suggest that cognitive-behavioral therapists use psychodynamic strategies, at least occasionally, and that it was these techniques that were associated with positive treatment outcome for patients of both psychodynamic and cognitive-behavioral therapists.

Anxiety Disorders

Seven RCTs of psychodynamic psychotherapy have been published with regard to the anxiety disorders (Alstrom, 1984a, 1984b; Bögels, 2003; Brom, 1989; Durham et al., 1994; Milrod et al., 2007a; Wiborg & Dahl, 1996). Overall, the evidence suggests that psychodynamic therapy may be beneficial for anxiety disorders. Three RCTs found that psychodynamic treatment was superior to a waitlist control or minimal care group, and one RCT found that psychodynamic treatment combined with pharmacotherapy was more effective in preventing relapse for panic disorder than pharmacotherapy alone. Two RCTs compared psychodynamic psychotherapy with CBT (Bögels et al., 2003; Durham et al., 1994); one found no difference between the treatments (Bögels et al., 2003), and the other found that analytic therapy provided significant improvement but to a lesser degree than CBT (Durham et al., 1994). However, in the Durham et al. study, in contrast to the CBT treatment, the dynamic treatment was not manualized, there was no specific training of therapists, and there was no adherence checks or treatment fidelity monitoring for the dynamic therapists.

The most recent and exciting trial comes from Milrod and colleagues (2007). They manualized a psychodynamic treatment based on theory and case reports that focused on symptom reduction through exploring *unconscious* determinants, such as unacknowledged anger and conflicts regarding autonomy and dependence. Panic focused psychodynamic psychotherapy (PFPP) is aimed at helping patients understand the underlying emotional meaning of their panic. Once that is achieved, patients can acknowledge previously unacceptable feelings and ideas that have led to panic in the past. This contrasts with CBT, which relies on exposure to panic triggers (e.g., bodily sensations such as breathlessness, tightness in the chest, heart palpitations) and a highly structured set of exercises aimed at easing attacks. Milrod and colleagues compared PFPP to applied relaxation therapy (ART), a standard and structured relaxation-focused approach that has often been used in trials aimed at assessing the effectiveness of other treatment approaches in a 12-week randomized, controlled clinical trial. The 26 patients in the PFPP group had a greater reduction in their symptoms compared to the 23 patients in the ART group. In fact, by the trial's end, 73% of patients treated with the psychoanalytic approach met criteria for "response," using standard definitions of "response" criteria in the field, compared to just 39% of those in the ART cohort. In a second report examining personality disorders as a moderator of treatment response, Milrod and colleagues (Milrod et al., 2007b) found that those panic patients with comorbid

personality disorders did particularly well in the PFPP group. These findings are especially important given that a host of reviews suggest that anxiety patients with comorbid personality disorders do not do well in standard CBT (Brooks, Baltazar, & Munjack, 1989; Massion, Dyck, Shea, Phillops, Warshaw, & Keller, 2002; Noyes, Reich, Christiansen et al., 1990; Pollack, Otto, & Rosenbaum, 1992; Reich, 1991; Yonkers, Dyck, Warshaw, & Keller, 2000; see review by Mennin & Heimberg, 2000) and point to an important evidence-based conclusion: If a patient presents for treatment with symptoms of panic disorder and a comorbid personality disorder, PFPP should be the initial treatment of choice.[5]

Borderline Personality Disorders

There are three psychodynamic treatments for borderline personality that have empirical support: Russell Meares's interpersonal-self psychological approach, Bateman and Fonagy's mentalization based therapy, and Kernberg's transference focused psychotherapy. The last two have been shown to be efficacious in RCTs.

Interpersonal Self-psychological Approach. Russell Meares developed an interpersonal self-psychological approach (IP) for the treatment of borderline personality disorder (BPD) guided by the conversational model of Hobson (1985), the main aim of which is to foster the emergence of reflective consciousness that William James called *self consciousness* (James, 1890). A basic tenet of this approach is that self-consciousness is achieved through a particular form of conversation and reflects a deeper sense of relatedness. The nearest North American equivalent to this approach comes from Kohut (1971) and his followers (Ornstein, 1998).

A pre-post study that evaluated the effects of this approach for patients with BPD found that

---

[5]This conclusion is preliminary given the fact that PFPP is considered a probably supported treatment at this time.

patients at the end of treatment showed an increase in time employed and decreases in number of medical visits, number of self-harm episodes, and number and length of hospitalizations (Stevenson & Meares, 1992). Although the inferences that can be drawn from this study are limited by the lack of a control group, these findings supported the development and study of psychodynamic treatments for BPD. In a later quasi-experimental study (Meares, Stevenson, & Comerford, 1999), researchers compared BPD patients treated twice weekly for one year with those in a treatment-as-usual waitlist control group (all waitlisted patients received their usual treatments, which consisted of supportive psychotherapy, crisis intervention only, cognitive therapy, and pharmacotherapy). In all, 30% of IP-treated patients no longer met criteria for a DSM-III (American Psychiatric Association, 1980) BPD diagnosis at the end of the treatment year, whereas all of the treatment as usual (TAU) patients still met criteria for the diagnosis. These results demonstrated that psychotherapy based on psychodynamic principles is generally beneficial to patients with BPD in a naturalistic setting, having strong ecological validity. A five-year follow-up found that improvements were maintained (Stevenson, Meares, & D'Angelo, 2005). A recently completed second quasi-experimental study (Korner, Gerull, Meares, & Stevenson, 2006) replicated these findings.

Mentalization-based Therapy. Bateman and Fonagy (2006) developed mentalization-based therapy (MBT) based on the developmental theory of mentalization, which integrates philosophy (theory of mind), ego psychology, Kleinian theory, and attachment theory. Fonagy and Bateman (2006) posit that the mechanism of change in all effective treatments for BPD involves the capacity for mentalization — the capacity to think about mental states in oneself and in others in terms of wishes, desires, and intentions. Mentalizing involves both (1) implicit or *unconscious* mental processes that are activated along with

the attachment system in affectively charged interpersonal situations and (2) coherent integrated representations of mental states of self and others. The concept of mentalization has been operationalized in the Reflective Function (RF) scale (Fonagy et al., 1997).

In an RCT (Bateman & Fonagy, 1998), the effectiveness of 18 months of a psychoanalytically oriented day hospitalization program was compared with routine general psychiatric care for patients with BPD. Patients randomly assigned to the psychoanalytic day hospital program, now called mentalization-based therapy (Bateman & Fonagy, 2004), showed statistically significant improvement in depressive symptoms and better social and interpersonal functioning, as well as significant decreases in suicidal and parasuicidal behavior and number of inpatient days. Patients were reassessed every 3 months for up to 18 months post-discharge (Bateman & Fonagy, 2001). Short-term follow-up results indicated that patients who completed the MBT not only maintained their substantial gains but also showed continued steady and significant improvement on most measures, suggesting that BPD patients can continue to demonstrate gains in functioning long after treatment has ended. At 18-month post-discharge follow-up, 59.1% of patients treated with MBT were below the BPD diagnostic threshold, compared to only 12.5% of those treated in routine general psychiatric care. In a second follow-up, 8 years post-randomization and 5 years post–end of treatment, even more impressive findings were obtained: those treated with MBT showed not only statistical superiority in reduced suicidality, service utilization, medication use, and increases in global and vocational functioning but a remarkable level of clinical change (only 13% met criteria for BPD compared to 87% of those in the TAU group).

Findings that establish the long-term significance of MBT are particularly important given the entrenched and chronic nature of BPD.

Follow-up studies of CBT treatments for BPD have typically examined relatively short time frames (between 6 and 18 months), leaving the long-term efficacy of these treatments unclear. In addition, the outcomes for these studies have generally been mixed. For example, whereas the overall results of Linehan's outpatient psychotherapy study support the value of dialectic behavior therapy (DBT), results from her naturalistic follow-up of patients in DBT were uneven (Linehan et al., 1994). At the six-month follow-up, there were no differences between DBT and the TAU group in the number of days hospitalized, and at the end of a one-year follow-up there was no difference between groups in number of days hospitalized or in self-destructive acts. In addition, a six-month follow-up from the Verheul et al. (Verheul et al., 2001) study found no differences between DBT and the TAU control on impulsive behavior, parasuicidality, alcohol use, and both soft and hard drug use (van den Bosch et al., 2005). Finally, in Linehan et al.'s (2006) recent RCT comparing DBT with community treatment by experts (CTBE), the authors found that at one-year follow-up, there were no differences between the DBT and CTBE groups in terms of parasuicidality or crisis services utilization. In addition, although patients in DBT were half as likely to make a suicide attempt as patients in the CTBE group if the treatment year and follow-up period are combined, this difference disappeared when examining only the follow-up period (Lynch, 2004). Taken together, these findings suggest variable maintenance of treatment effects and ongoing impairment in functioning in patients who may have initially experienced symptom relief.

Transference Focused Psychotherapy. The major goals of transference focused psychotherapy (TFP) are to reduce suicidality and self-injurious behaviors and to facilitate better behavioral control, increased affect regulation, more gratifying relationships, and the ability to pursue life goals (Clarkin, Yeomans, & Kernberg, 2006; Kernberg, Yeomans, Clarkin, & Levy, in press). This is believed to be accomplished through the development of integrated representations of self and others, the modification of primitive defensive operations, and the resolution of identity diffusion that perpetuate the fragmentation of the patient's internal representational world. In this treatment, analysis of the transference is the primary vehicle for the transformation of undifferentiated and unintegrated (e.g., split and polarized) to advanced (e.g., complex, differentiated, and integrated) and benign mental representations of self and others.

Using the triad of *clarifications, confrontations,* and *interpretations,* the TFP therapist provides the patient with the opportunity to integrate cognitions and affects that were previously split and disorganized. In addition, the engaged, interactive, and emotionally intense stance of the therapist is typically experienced by patients as emotionally holding (containing) because the therapist conveys that he or she can tolerate the patient's negative affective states. The therapist's expectation of the patient's ability to have a thoughtful and disciplined approach to emotional states (i.e., that the patient is a fledgling version of a capable, responsible, and reflective adult) is thought to be experienced as cognitively holding. The therapist's timely, clear, and tactful interpretations of the dominant affect-laden themes and patient enactments in the here and now of the transference frequently shed light on the reasons that representations remain split off and thus facilitate integrating polarized representations of self and others.

There is now accumulating evidence for the effectiveness and efficacy of TFP. The initial study (Clarkin et al., 2001) examined the effectiveness of TFP in a pre-post study. Participants were women between the ages of 18 and 50 recruited from various treatment settings within the New York metropolitan area who met criteria for BPD through structured interviews. Overall, the major finding in this pre-post study was that patients with BPD who were treated with TFP showed marked reductions in the severity of parasuicidal behaviors; fewer emergency room visits, hospitalizations, and days hospitalized; and reliable increases in global functioning. The effect sizes were large and no less than those demonstrated by other BPD treatments (Bateman & Fonagy, 1999; Linehan et al., 1991). The one-year dropout rate was 19.1% and no patient committed suicide. These results compared well with other treatments for BPD: Linehan et al. (1991) had a 16.7% dropout rate and one suicide (4%); Stevenson and Meares's study (1992) had a 16% dropout rate and no suicides; and Bateman and Fonagy's study (1999) had a 21% dropout rate and no suicides. None of the treatment completers deteriorated or were adversely affected by the treatment. Therefore, it appears that TFP is well tolerated. Furthermore, 53% of participants no longer met criteria for BPD after one year of twice-weekly outpatient treatment (Clarkin & Levy, 2003). This rate compared quite well with that found by others (Bateman & Fonagy, 2001; Stevenson & Meares, 1992).

A second quasi-experimental study (Levy et al., 2007) provided further support for the effectiveness of TFP in treating BPD. In this study, 26 women diagnosed with BPD and treated with TFP were compared to 17 patients in a TAU group. There were no significant pretreatment differences between the treatment group and the comparison group in terms of demographic or diagnostic variables, severity of BPD symptomatology, baseline emergency room visits, hospitalizations, days hospitalized, or global functioning scores. The one-year attrition rate was 19%. Patients treated with TFP, compared to those treated with TAU, showed significant decreases in suicide attempts, hospitalizations, and number of days hospitalized, as well as reliable increases in global functioning. All of the within-subject and between-subject effect sizes for the TFP-treated participants indicated favorable change. The within-subject effect sizes ranged from 0.73 to 3.06 for the TFP-treated participants, with an average effect size of 1.19 (which is well above what is considered "large"; see Cohen, 1988).

In a recent controlled trial (Clarkin et al., 2007; Levy et al., 2006), 90 clinically referred patients

between the ages of 18 and 50 with BPD were evaluated using structured clinical interviews and randomized to one of the three treatments: TFP, DBT, and a credible psychodynamic SPT (Appelbaum, 2005). Results of individual growth-curve analysis indicated that both TFP- and DBT-treated groups, but not the SPT group, showed significant decrease in suicidality. Both *transference*-focused psychotherapy and supportive treatment were associated with improvement in anger and with improvement in facets of impulsivity. Only the TFP-treated group demonstrated significant improvements in irritability, verbal assault, and direct assault.

In an earlier report on this sample, Levy and colleagues (Levy et al., 2006) examined changes in attachment organization and reflective function as putative mechanisms of change. Attachment organization was assessed using the Adult Attachment Interview (AAI, George, Kaplan, & Main, 1985) and the RF coding scale (Fonagy et al., 1998). After 12 months of treatment they found a significant increase in the number of patients classified as secure with respect to attachment state of mind for TFP, but not the other two treatments. Significant changes in narrative coherence and RF were found as a function of treatment, with TFP showing increases in both constructs during the course of treatment. Findings suggest that 1 year of intensive TFP can increase patients' narrative coherence and reflective function. These findings are important because they show that TFP not only is an efficacious treatment for BPD but works in a theoretically predicted way and thus has implications for conceptualizing the mechanism by which patients with BPD may change. In addition, patients in TFP did better on these putative mechanisms (e.g., reflective function) than those in DBT and SPT. Our findings are especially important given the literature showing that many treatments do not show specific effects on specific theory-driven mechanisms (Ablon & Jones, 1998; Ablon, Levy, & Katzenstein, 2002; Castonguay, Goldfried,

Wiser, & Raue, 1996; DeRubeis & Feeley, 1990; DeRubeis et al., 1990; Ilardi & Craighead, 1994; Jones & Pulos, 1993; Shaw et al., 1999; Trepka, Rees, Shapiro, Hardy, & Barkham, 2004).

TFP was also examined as a control condition in a study in Amsterdam by Arntz and colleagues (Giesen-Bloo et al., 2006). They compared TFP with Young's schema focused therapy (Young, 1990; SFT), an integrative approach based on cognitive-behavioral or skills-based techniques along with object relations and gestalt approaches. Their study is unique in examining two active treatments over three years. Patients benefited from both treatments. At first glance, SFPT appeared more efficacious. However, a number of serious limitations argue against this conclusion.

First, despite randomization, the TFP condition included twice as many recently suicidal patients (76% vs. 38%); there was also a trend ($p = .09$) for the TFP condition to include more patients with recent self-injury behavior. (It has been shown that suicidality influences treatment outcome [Oldham, 2006]).

Second, the differences between the two groups were only apparent in the intent-to-treat (ITT) analyses but not in the completer analyses (Arntz, 2004; Kellogg & Young, 2006). A major factor in this difference appears to have been that patients in the TFP condition were significantly more likely to prematurely drop out of their treatment. Whereas intent-to-treat analyses speak to the external validity (e.g., generalizability), completer analyses speak to the issue of sufficient dose and thus the internal validity or integrity of the study. Differences in outcome between completer analyses and ITT suggest loss of validity due to nonrandom dropout. This can negate the control provided by randomization (Howard et al., 1986). Completer analyses did not show any statistically significant advantage for SFPT (Arntz, 2004; Kellogg & Young, 2006).

Third, the findings suggest inadequate implementation of TFP as indicated by lack of adherence by the TFP therapists. The authors report the median adherence level for TFP was 65.6. Given that a score of 60 is considered adherent, about 50% of TFP therapists were nonadherent. In contrast, the SFT group had a median score of 85.6 (again with 60 as adherent), suggesting that 50% of the SFT were not just adherent but exceptionally so. Not only were adherence ratings relatively poor for TFP, but they also appear to be significantly lower than for SFT. Suffice it to say, the report compares an exceptionally well-delivered treatment with an inadequately delivered one. There should be no surprise that the exceptionally delivered treatment outperformed the poorly delivered treatment, but it is not a fair test, and this fact alone may explain the differential outcome between the two treatments.

Fourth, treatment integrity includes having experienced treatment cell leaders, choosing experienced and adherent therapists with a proven track record, providing expert supervision, providing ongoing monitoring of adherence, and having plans for dealing with nonadherence (Clarkin et al., 2004). Each of these issues was problematic in the current study. Supervision was carried out in the form of peer supervision, known as intervision (Yeomans, 2006). Intervision may work well when carried out by exceptionally adherent therapists as was the case for the SFPT. However, such a model would not work well with nonadherent therapists and would be more akin to the blind leading the blind. The authors indicate that treatment integrity was monitored by means of supervision, but who was doing that monitoring? Yeomans (2006) reports the clinical observation that half the therapists were nonadherent, which is consistent with the author's own independently rated adherence scores. Most disturbing, however, is Yeomans' report (2006) that he informed the study's principal investigator of the nonadherence problem on numerous occasions, including by email and fax, and that no action was taken to deal with this problem.

Finally, therapists and assessors were not blind to ongoing outcome. Partial results were presented prior to study completion (Arntz, 2004; Giesen-Bloo et al., 2001, 2002; Young et al., 2003), creating another possible confound, which could have caused therapist demoralization in the TFP therapists or enhanced motivation in SFPT therapists (Chalmers et al., 1981). Given these concerns, it would be premature and irresponsible to conclude that TFP is not as efficacious as SFPT.

Accumulating evidence indicates that TFP may be an effective treatment for BPD. As more data from the RCT are assessed, we will have a better understanding of how the treatment performs under more stringent experimental conditions. Because the RCT better controls for unmeasured variables through randomization, offers controls for attention and support, and compares TFP to an already established, well-delivered alterative treatment, its outcome will be a strong indicator of the treatment's efficacy and effectiveness. In addition to assessment of outcome, the RCT has also generated process-outcome studies designed to assess the hypothesized mechanisms of action in TFP that result in the changes seen in these patients (Clarkin & Levy, 2006; Levy et al., 2006).

Mixed and Other Personality Disorders

Three studies have examined psychodynamic psychotherapy for personality disorders (Abbas, Sheldon, Gyra, & Kalpin, 2006; Winston, Pollach, McCullough, Flegenheimer, Kestenbaum, & Trujullo, 1991; Winston, Laiken, Pollack, Samstag, McCullough, & Muran, 1994). Winston and colleagues compared a short-term psychodynamic psychotherapy based on the work of Malan (1976) and Davanloo (1992) and a short-term psychodynamic psychotherapy called brief adaptive

psychotherapy (BAP) with a waitlist control in a group of patients predominantly diagnosed with cluster C personality disorders. Both treatments address defensive behavior and elicit affect in interpersonal contexts, although the BAP treatment is less *confrontational*. The authors found that both treatment groups showed significant change on the global severity index (GSI) of the sympton checklist (SCL)-90 (approximately 1 SD) and some changes on the social adjustment scale. An 18-months post-treatment follow-up indicated the maintenance of treatment gains (Winston et al., 1994). Abbas et al. (2006) examined STPP for outpatients with a range of personality disorders. The authors found significant improvement in interpersonal problems, significantly more hours worked, and better employment outcomes relative to controls. One study using an RCT examined outpatients with cluster C personality disorders (avoidant, dependent, obsessive-compulsive; Svartberg, Stiles, & Seltzer, 2004). The authors examined a 40-week STPP compared with CT and found no statistically significant difference between the short-term psychotherapy group and CT groups on any measure for any time period. At two-year follow-up, 54% of the short-term dynamic psychotherapy patients and 42% of the CT patients had recovered symptomatically.

META-ANALYSIS OF PSYCHODYNAMIC PSYCHOTHERAPY FOR PERSONALITY DISORDERS

There have been two meta-analyses of psychotherapy for personality disorders (Leichsenring & Leibing, 2003; Perry et al., 1999). Perry and colleagues (1999) identified 15 studies, including 6 RCTs, and found pre-post effect sizes ranging from 1.1 to 1.3, which decreased to 0.7 when an active control treatment was used. In a second meta-analysis, Leichsenring and Leibing (2003) examined the efficacy of both psychodynamic psychotherapy (14 studies) and CBT (11 studies) in the treatment of patients with personality disorders. Eleven of the studies were RCTs. They reported pretreatment to post-treatment effect sizes using the longest-term follow-up data reported in the studies. For psychodynamic psychotherapy (mean length of treatment was 37 weeks), the mean follow-up period was 1.5 years after treatment end, and the pretreatment to posttreatment effect size was 1.46. The findings again indicate that psychodynamic treatment benefits endure over time. For CBT (mean length of treatment was 16 weeks), the mean follow-up period was 13 weeks, and the pretreatment to post-treatment effect size was 1.0. The authors concluded that both psychodynamic therapy and CBT demonstrated effectiveness for patients with personality disorders. However, evidence for long-term effectiveness is stronger for psychodynamic psychotherapy. There was a nonsignificant correlation between treatment length and outcome. Thus, based on limited data, psychodynamic and CBT treatments appear to be equally effective for personality disorders, longer-term treatments might yield better outcomes, and psychodynamic treatments may have longer-lasting effects.

Eating Disorders

Eight RCTs have examined a psychodynamic treatment (Bachar et al., 1999; Crisp et al., 1991; Dare et al., 2001; Fairburn et al., 1986; Garner et al., 1993; Gowers et al., 1994; Hall & Crisp, 1987; Russell et al., 1987). The general finding is that for anorexia nervosa, psychodynamic treatment is as effective as other treatments, including behavioral and strategic family therapy (Crisp et al., 1991; Dare et al., 2001; Gowers et al., 1994; Hall & Crisp, 1987; Russell et al., 1987). Gowers et al. found significant

improvements in weight and body mass index as compared to a TAU control condition. Dare and colleagues found that both psychodynamic psychotherapy and family therapy were significantly superior to routine treatment in terms of weight gain. With regard to bulimia nervosa, Fairburn et al. (1986) and Garner et al. (1993) found that psychodynamic and CBT treatments resulted in comparable improvements in bulimic episodes and self-induced vomiting, although CBT was superior on other measures of psychopathology. At follow-up both were equally effective and superior to behavior therapy (Fairburn et al., 1995). Thus, although the initial findings favored CBT, the longer-term outcome was comparable and differentiated from behavior therapy, suggesting that both CBT and psychodynamic treatment are preferred choices over behavior therapy, although CBT may work more quickly. More long-term follow-up is needed to determine the long-term significance of these findings.

Marital Therapy

In a controlled outcome study, Snyder et al. (1991) followed up 59 couples four years after receiving either behavioral or insight-oriented martial therapy. There were no group differences between the two treatment conditions at either termination or six-month follow-up. However, at four-year follow-up, couples who received the insight-oriented therapy were more likely to be happily married (79% vs. 50%), whereas the couples who received the behavioral therapy were more likely to be divorced (38% vs. 3%).

Summary of Empirical Findings with Psychodynamic Psychotherapy

In summary, contrary to uniform stereotypes, psychodynamic psychotherapy appears to be as effective as other treatments; effect sizes from meta-analyses suggest that it is more effective than psychotherapy in general, as effective as CBT, and more effective than antidepressants. However, there is no evidence from RCTs for psychoanalysis or for longer-term therapies for depression or anxiety disorders. The data from studies of depression strongly suggest the need for more intensive treatment because the long-term efficacy of CBT, IPT, medication, and psychodynamic psychotherapy treatments appears poor. Despite the consistency of the findings, no specific psychodynamic psychotherapy meets the criteria as an empirically supported treatment (Chambless & Hollon, 1998) because no two studies by independent research groups are of the same form of psychodynamic psychotherapy. Nevertheless, a number of psychodynamic psychotherapies do meet criteria for probably being empirically supported (Bateman & Fonagy, 1999, 2001, 2008; Clarkin et al., 2007; Gallagher-Thompson & Steffen, 1994; Levy et al., 2006; Milrod et al., 2007a, b; Snyder et al., 1989, 1991; Woody et al., 1985). Some particularly striking findings that deserve additional study concern (1) the outcome in marital therapy in terms of happiness and divorce rates, which strongly suggests an advantage for insight-oriented psychotherapy; (2) the long-term outcomes of mentalization-based therapy; and (3) the efficacy and effectiveness of TFP given the changes in hypothesized mechanisms of action.

COMMON MISCONCEPTIONS REGARDING PSYCHODYNAMIC AND PSYCHOANALYTIC PSYCHOTHERAPY

There are a number of common misconceptions regarding psychodynamic psychotherapy that the reader can now defend.

1. *Myth:* Psychodynamic constructs and therapy cannot be studied empirically.

Reality: Although it can be difficult to operationalize many psychoanalytic constructs, with effort and attention to avoiding post hoc explanations, it can be accomplished.

2. *Myth:* There is no empirical research on psychoanalysis. *Reality:* There is a much larger body of research on psychoanalytic ideas than is generally known or acknowledged. As evidence, there are now many studies of psychoanalytic constructs, particularly of *unconscious* and defensive processes that have found support for basic psychoanalytic ideas. Interested readers are directed to a review paper by Westen (1999) in *Psychological Bulletin* and to the 10 volumes of a series titled Empirical Studies of Psychoanalytic Theories edited or co-edited by Joseph Masling. Masling (cited in Hoffman, 2002, p. 507) contends that "in fact, psychoanalytic theories have proven to be so robustly heuristic they have probably inspired more research in personality than any other set of ideas."

3. *Myth:* Psychodynamic psychotherapy is not or cannot be codified or manualized. *Reality:* There are a number of excellent examples of psychoanalytic or psychodynamic psychotherapy manuals. More recently, there has been increased emphasis on clear explanation of techniques, including the development of treatment manuals. This trend began with the detailed description of psychodynamic treatments for patients with interpersonal difficulties by Luborsky (1984) and Strupp (1984) and recently has been expanded with descriptions of psychodynamic treatments for those with severe personality disorders (Bateman & Fonagy, 2003; Clarkin, Yeomans, & Kernberg, 2006), panic disorder

(Milrod et al., 2007), and depression (Busch, Rudden, & Shaprio, 2004). These manuals tend to be less prescriptive and more principle based. For a review of pertinent issues in developing a psychodynamic manual, see Caligor (2005).

4. *Myth:* Psychodynamic therapists are largely silent, cold, and stone-faced. *Reality:* The psychoanalytic psychotherapist pays special attention to fostering the therapeutic alliance, being real, and showing warmth and concern for his or her clients. One recognizes that one's office location, office furniture and decorations, dress, jewelry, and so on all provide the patient with information about the therapist, as do his or her style and demeanor. Neutrality is not about creating an impossible situation or taking an expert authoritarian posture. Neutrality is a stance taken toward dealing with conflict within the patient to encourage exploration.

5. *Myth:* Psychoanalytic approaches focus exclusively or almost exclusively on *unconscious* processes. *Reality:* As indicated earlier in the chapter, *unconscious* motivations are clearly an important aspect of psychoanalytic work, but not to the extent of denying or failing to attend to conscious experience. Psychodynamic psychotherapists are keenly interested in phenomenology and intersubjectivity.

6. *Myth:* The main focus of therapy is the patient's sexuality, early childhood relationships, or traumatic experiences. *Reality:* Process research indicates that although psychodynamic psychotherapists may connect current relationship patterns with earlier patterns, the treatments tend to focus on current difficulties and interaction patterns and are more likely to connect these issues to the here and now of the therapy session than to reconstruct the past.

7. *Myth:* Psychodynamic psychotherapy is interminable. *Reality:* Although a traditional analysis will require the commitment of a number of sessions a week for many years, there are a host of short-term treatments for depression, anxiety, and eating disorders. Psychodynamic treatments tend to be longer for personality disorders, as are cognitive-behavioral treatments for these types of problems.

8. *Myth:* Psychodynamic psychotherapy lacks an evidence base, and what exists indicates that it is largely ineffectual. Thus, it is probably unethical to utilize it as a treatment. *Reality:* There is excellent evidence for psychodynamic psychotherapies for many disorders, including depression, panic, PTSD, eating disorders, BPD, cluster C personality disorders, and marital therapy. The effect sizes are generally as large for CBT. When there are differences favoring CBT, they usually disappear by follow-up and appear to be the result of allegiance effects (Luborsky et al., 1999; Robinson et al., 1990). There is also some evidence that effect sizes increase for psychodynamic treatments over time, suggesting that their effects may show themselves more slowly but also result in increased effectiveness over other treatments (e.g., Bateman & Fonagy, 2008). This process whereby patients continued to improve after psychodynamic therapy ends has been referred to as a "sleeper effect."

HIGHLIGHT BOX 8.1

ADVANCED TRAINING OPTIONS

There are fewer and fewer options available to individuals interested in psychodynamic training. Even at the undergraduate level, those interested in psychoanalytic ideas often cannot find them taught within psychology departments and instead take classes in the humanities where psychodynamic thought is better accepted (Cohen, 2007). At the graduate level, the vast majority of clinical training programs are cognitive-behavioral in their training orientation (Levy, 2008; Sayette, Mayne, & Norcross, 2006). A number of programs within the New York City area have a critical mass of psychoanalytic faculty (e.g., CUNY, Adelphi, Long Island University, New School University). However, only a handful of major research universities have psychodynamic faculty (e.g., Penn State, Emory, Tennessee). Most training programs have only one or maybe two dynamically trained faculty members. These numbers are down significantly from the situation in the 1950s through the 1980s when core faculty at major programs such as Michigan, Yale, NYU, Columbia, and Boston University were predominately psychodynamic in their orientation. Even PsyD programs are becoming less psychodynamic (Levy, 2008; Sayett, Mayne, & Norcross, 2007).

One possible reason for this change is the victorious antitrust lawsuit against the AMA in the 1980s, which resulted in psychologists having access to psychoanalytic institutes for advance training (*Welch v. the American Psychoanalytic Association*). This event, combined with the need for practitioners that arose in the 1970s and 1980s, the increasing emphasis in academia on obtaining grants, and the perception in academia that psychodynamic theory has been discredited or lacks empirical support resulted in a flood of dynamically oriented students giving up research-oriented careers and entering private practice. Nevertheless, there is an issue about how to get advanced training in psychodynamic psychotherapy at the doctoral level. The American Psychological Association Division 39 (Psychoanalysis) has an outreach link on its Web site that lists doctoral programs, internships, and postdoctoral sites that have psychodynamic representation. In addition, the American Psychoanalytic Association (APsA) lists psychoanalytic training institutes on its Web site. The APsA Web site lists only those programs that they have accredited. Many good training programs are not approved by the APsA but are approved by the International Psychoanalytic Association (IPA). Cities such as New York, Boston, Chicago, and Los Angeles often have multiple training institutes. Training is available in smaller cities such as Philadelphia, Pittsburgh, Cleveland, Durham, Atlanta, Houston, and Albany, among others.

For an accessible jargon-free introduction to the principles underlying psychodynamic psychotherapy, the reader is directed to a triad of books by Nancy McWilliams: *Psychoanalytic Diagnosis, Psychoanalytic Case Formulations*, and *Psychodynamic Psychotherapy: A Practitioner's Guide* (McWilliams, 1999). These books offer guidance for both beginning psychotherapists and more experienced psychotherapists who are interested in a psychodynamic approach. In addition, Glenn Gabbard has a number of books, including *Psychodynamic Psychiatry in Clinical Practice* and *Long-term Psychodynamic*

HIGHLIGHT BOX 8.1   (*continued*)

Psychotherapy: A Basic Text, which are useful for both psychology doctoral students and psychiatry residents. Interested readers should also consult Huprich's (2008) *Psychodynamic Therapy: Conceptual and Empirical Foundations*. These works provide an excellent introduction to contemporary psychodynamic psychotherapy. For those working with more severely disturbed patients, there are a number of books by Kernberg and colleagues, including *Handbook of Dynamic Psychotherapy for Higher Level Personality Pathology* (Caligor et al., 2007), *Psychotherapy for Borderline Personality: Focusing on Object Relations* (Clarkin et al., 2007), and *A Primer of Transference-focused Psychotherapy for the Borderline Patient* (Yeomans et al., 2003). Fonagy and his group also have a number of books on mentalization-based therapy, including *Psychotherapy for Borderline Personality Disorder, Mentalization-Based Treatment for Borderline Personality Disorder, The Handbook of Mentalization-based Treatment*, and *Affect Regulation, Mentalization, and the Development of the Self*, which the reader would probably find useful.

THOUGHT QUESTIONS

8.1. You're sitting with a new patient whom you have only seen a few times. Although his affect and demeanor are friendly, he comments about your office being small: "This is the nicest broom closet I've ever seen." Later he makes a disparaging comment about one of the paintings on your wall. In another session, he comments about not having bottled water available for patients. As the therapy progresses, you make what you feel are appropriate interventions. However, you begin to feel inadequate as a therapist, unhelpful, and demoralized about the prospects of the patient improving. Upon reflection, you realize that you generally don't feel incompetent or inadequate as a therapist. You recall that your supervisors have consistently given you high ratings across a number of domains, and despite occasional self-doubts about your clinical work, your patients have generally improved. You recognize that you are experiencing *countertransference*, but what type of *countertransference* is it, narrow (classical) or broad (totalistic)? Is it complementary or concordant?

8.2. You have just been assigned a patient with panic disorder and a comorbid personality disorder. The clinic director is strongly supportive of providing evidence-based medicine and empirically supported therapies. Although you have been interested in working psychodynamically with a patient, she strongly advises you to proceed to choose a CBT supervisor for this patient. How might you respond to your supervisor's advice?

8.3. A college-age student is admitted as your patient after a suicide attempt to an inpatient psychiatry unit where you are working as an extern. The patient is young, smart, articulate, but very distressed. She explains that she tried to kill herself because she was the victim of sexual abuse by her older brother. The abuse started when she was very young and continued for many years into her teens and included intercourse. She explains that prior to this admission she had not told anyone of the abuse, not even her parents. You find the patient to be very compelling, and the case evokes a lot of feelings in you. You find yourself enraged at the brother for perpetrating such a terrible act on your patient, and you find yourself also angry at the parents for letting such a thing happen and continue for so long. During your sessions, she is very open with her anger and disgust toward her older brother and her parents. At times, you find yourself so angered by what happened that you share with her your anger about the events and toward the brother. You work with the patient to help her tell her parents about what happened and to confront the older brother. The night before a family meeting with her parents, she attempts to kill herself by ingesting medications that she had been cheeking all week (i.e., hiding her medication in the side of her mouth). She was discovered accidentally during nightly rounds because she fell forward to the floor as opposed to back on her bed. Upon hearing the news, you feel angry toward the older brother, feeling that she tried to kill herself again because of what he had done. When you speak to her in the hospital, she is very tearful, and you try to allay her guilt by acknowledging how badly she feels about the abuse. However,

she surprises you when she tells you that the abuse is not why she tried to kill herself. She then shares with you that she wanted to die because you had been so angry at the older brother for abusing her. She then confides in you that just as she had been sexually abused by her older brother, she had engaged her younger brother in sexual behavior for which she felt guilty, especially when you became angry at the older brother. How might a concept like technical neutrality have aided you in working with this patient? How would you continue in therapy while remaining technically neutral?

8.4. You are seeing a parasuicidal patient who has been in therapy for a number of months. The patient calls one night in a suicidal crisis. You contract with him to go to his local emergency room. In your first meeting with the patient after his discharge from the hospital, he begins recounting in detail how foolish the staff at the hospital was because they allowed him to cut himself while under supervision (he had snuck in a razor blade in a book and cut himself under his long-sleeve shirt). As the patient recounts this story, his affect is extremely positive and gleeful. You comment that perhaps he thought that you were incompetent or foolish, too, in that he may feel you didn't take his suicidality seriously enough and that you suggested that he go to the hospital emergency room, an emergency room staffed by "incompetent" orderlies. He responds with a big satisfied smile. At this point, you ask the patient if he realized he was smiling, to which he responds yes. You point out that although he was talking about suicide, possibly dying and being cared for by "fools" and "incompetents," he was smiling and you wondered what he might be taking pleasure in. He did not seem to know, and you point out that maybe he was taking some pleasure in the fact that he perceived you and the hospital staff as inept. It is at this point that the patient realizes that he has been taking pleasure in the hospital staff's ineptness. Your question as to whether the patient was aware of the smile could be conceptualized as what psychodynamic technique? Your comments about the patient's affect and its discordance from the content of what he was discussing could be conceptualized as what psychodynamic technique? What might be your next technical move? Think about what you might say.

Glossary

Clarification: A request for more information or further elaboration in order to better understand the patient's subjective experience.

Compromise formation: In the Freudian conflict model, a compromise formation posits that many of the conflicts that cause symptoms of mental and physical illness have a particular form: on one side there are intense wishes or desires, often of a selfish, sexual, or aggressive nature, and opposing these motives or drives are strong and disturbing feelings of guilt and fear. This kind of negative emotion causes a person to defend (e.g., repress or deny) or redirect the troublesome needs and wishes, which then can be expressed only indirectly -- in symptoms, dreams, jokes, and slips of the tongue or "accidental" behavior (so-called Freudian slips).

Confrontation: Tactfully pointing out discrepancies or incongruities in the patient's narrative or the patient's verbal and nonverbal behavior.

Countertransference: Originally viewed as the therapist's reaction to the patient, revealing unresolved conflicts in the therapist, but now seen more as a valuable diagnostic and therapeutic tool that provides the therapist with an emotional window or channel into the patient's internal and interpersonal world.

Defense mechanisms: Means by which people push threatening thoughts or feelings from awareness.

Extratransferential interpretations: Interpretations about relationships outside of therapy.

Genetic interpretations: Interpretations made about early experiences with caregivers.

Interpretation: Focus on the unconscious meaning of what has been clarified and confronted regarding experience in therapy, the relationship between the patient and therapist, or relationships outside of therapy.

Psychic determinism: The idea that nothing in the mind happens by chance, that all mental and physical behavior is determined by prior psychological causes.

Resistance: A reluctance to engage in treatment. Resistance can be an unconscious process designed to maintain current maladaptive ways of functioning because they are comfortable or because change is potentially scary.

Technical neutrality: A therapeutic strategy in which the therapist avoids communicating any judgment about the patient's conflicts while they are being discussed.

Transference: Believed to be a universal phenomenon in which aspects of important and formative relationships (such as with parents and siblings) are unconsciously ascribed to unrelated current relationships.

Transference interpretation: The process of interpreting a patient's exhibition of transference.

Unconscious: Some mental processes, such as motives, desires, and memories, that are not available to awareness or conscious introspection.

References

Abbass, A. A., Hancock, J. T., Henderson, J., & Kisley, S. (2006). Short-term psychodynamic psychotherapies for common mental disorders. *The Cochrane Database of Systematic Reviews*, 4: CD004687.

Ablon, J. S. & Jones, E. E. (1998). How expert clinicians' prototypes of an ideal treatment correlate with outcome in psychodynamic and cognitive/behavioral therapy. *Psychotherapy Research*, 8, 71–83.

Ablon, J. S. & Jones, E. E. (1999). Psychotherapy process in the National Institute of Mental Health treatment of depression collaborative research program. *Journal of Consulting and Clinical Psychology*, 67, 64–75.

Ablon, J. S., Levy, R. A., & Katzenstein, T. (2002). Beyond brand names of psychotherapy: identifying empirically supported change processes. *Psychotherapy: Theory, Research, Practice, and Traning*, 23, 15.

Adams, H. E., Wright, L. W., & Lohr, B. A. (1996). Is homophobia associated with homosexual arousal? *Journal of Abnormal Psychology*, 105, 440–445.

Alstrom, J. E., Norlund, C. L., Persson, G., Harding, M., & Ljungqvist, C. (1984a). Effects of four treatment methods on agoraphobic women not suitable for insight-oriented psychotherapy. *Acta Psychiatrica Scandinavica*, 70, 1–17.

Alstrom, J. E., Norlund, C. L., Persson, G., Harding, M., & Ljungqvist, C. (1984b). Effects of four treatment methods on social phobic patients not suitable for insight-oriented psychotherapy. *Acta Psychiatrica Scandinavica*, 70, 97–110.

American Psychiatric Association (1980). *Diagnostic and statistical manual of mental disorders* (3rd ed.) Washington, DC: Author.

Anderson, M., Ochsner, K., Kuhl, B., Robertson, E., Gabrieli, S., Glover, G., & Gabrieli, J. (2004). Neural systems underlying the suppression of unwanted memories. *Science*, 303, 232–235.

Appelbaum, A. H. (2005). Supportive psychotherapy. In J. M. Oldham, A. E. Skodol, & D. S. Bender (Eds.), *Textbook of Personality Disorders* (pp. 335–346). Washington, DC: American Psychiatric Publishing.

Arntz, A. (2004). Borderline personality disorder. In T. A. Beck, A. Freedman, & D. D. Davis (Eds.), *Cognitive Therapy of Personality Disorders* (2nd ed.), pp. 187–215. New York: Guildford Press.

Bachar, E., Latzer, Y., Kreitler, S., & Berry, E. M. (1999). Empirical comparison of two psychological therapies: self psychology and cognitive orientation in the treatment of anorexia and bulimia. *Journal of Psychotherapy Practice Research*, 8, 115–128.

Barkham, M., Shapiro, D. A., Hardy, G. E., & Rees, A. (1999). Psychotherapy in two plus-one sessions: outcomes of a randomized controlled trial of cognitive behavioral and psychodynamic-interpersonal therapy for subsyndromal depression. *Journal of Consulting and Clinical Psychology*, 67, 201–211.

Bateman, A. W. & Fonagy, P. (1999). The effectiveness of partial hospitalization in the treatment of borderline personality disorder: a randomized controlled trial. *American Journal of Psychiatry*, 156, 1563–1569.

Bateman, A. W. & Fonagy, P. (2001). Treatment of borderline personality disorder with psychoanalytically oriented partial hospitalization: an 18-month follow-up. *American Journal of Psychiatry*, 158, 36–42.

Bateman, A. W. & Fonagy, P. (2003). The development of an attachment-based treatment program for borderline personality disorder. *Bulletin of the Menninger Clinic*, 67, 187–211.

Bateman, A. W. & Fonagy, P. (2004). Mentalization-based treatment of BPD. *Journal of Personality Disorders*, 18, 36–51.

Bateman, A. W. & Fonagy, P. (2006). *Mentalization based treatment for borderline personality disorder: a practical guide*. Oxford, UK: Oxford University Press.

Bateman, A. & Fonagy, P. (2008). Comorbid antisocial and borderline personality disorders: Mentalization-based treatment. *Journal of Clinical Psychology*, 64, 181–194.

Berk, M. S. & Andersen, S. M. (2000). The impact of past relationships on interpersonal behavior: behavioral confirmation in the social-cognitive process of transference. *Journal of Personality and Social Psychology*, 79, 546–562.

Blagys, M. D. & Hilsenroth, M. J. (2000). Distinctive feature of short-term psychodynamic-interpersonal psychotherapy: a review of the comparative psychotherapy process literature. *Clinical Psychology: Science and Practice*, 7, 167–188.

Blatt, S. J., Auerbach, J. S., & Levy, K. N. (1997). Mental representations in personality development, psychopathology, and the therapeutic process. *Review of General Psychology*, 1, 351–374.

Bögels, S., Wijts, P., & Sallaerts, S. (2003). Analytic psychotherapy versus cognitive behavioral therapy for social phobia. Paper presented at European Congress for Cognitive and Behavioural Therapies. Prague: Czech Republic.

Breuer, J. & Freud, S. (1895/1970). *Studien zur Hysterie.* (Neuausgabe Ed.). (Sigmund Freud Standard Edition, Vol. 2). Frankfurt/M.: Fischer Taschenbuch Verlag.

Breuer, J. & Freud, S. (1956). On the physical mechanism of hysterical phenomena. *International Journal of Psycho-Analysis, 37,* 8–13.

Brom, D., Kleber, R. J., & Defares, P. B. (1989). Brief psychotherapy for posttraumatic stress disorder. *Journal of Consulting and Clinical Psychology, 57,* 607–612.

Brooks, R. B., Baltazar, P. L., & Munjack, D. J. (1989). Co-occurrence of personality disorders with panic disorder, social phobia, and generalized anxiety disorder: a review of the literature. *Journal of Anxiety Disorders, 3,* 259–285.

Brumbaugh, C. C. & Fraley, R. C. (2005). Transference and attachment: how do attachment patterns get carried forward from one relationship to the next? *Personality and Social Psychology Bulletin, 32,* 552–560.

Busch, F. N., Rudden, M., & Shapiro, T. (2004). *Psychodynamic treatment of depression.* Washington, DC: American Psychiatric Publishing.

Caligor, E. (2005). Treatment manuals and psychotherapy research. *Clinical Neuroscience Research, Special Issue,* 387–398.

Caligor, E., Kernberg, O. F., & Clarkin, J. F. (2007). *Handbook of dynamic psychotherapy for higher level personality pathology.* Washington, DC: American Psychiatric Publishing.

Castonguay, L. G., Goldfried, M. R., Wiser, S. L., Raue, P. J., & Hayes, A. M. (1996). Predicting the effect of cognitive therapy for depression: a study of unique and common factors. *Journal of Consulting and Clinical Psychology, 64,* 497–504.

Chalmers, T., Smith, H., Blackburn, B., Silverman, B., Schroeder, B., Reitman, D., & Ambroz, A. (1981). A method for assessing the quality of a randomized controlled trial. *Controlled Clinical Trials, 2,* 31–49.

Chambless, D. L. & Hollon, S. D. (1998). Defining empirically supported therapies. *Journal of Consulting and Clinical Counseling, 66,* 7–18.

Churchill, R., Hunot, V., Corney, R., Knapp, M., McGuire, H., Tylee, A., & Wessely, S. (2001). A systematic review of controlled trials of the effectiveness and cost-effectiveness of brief psychological treatments for depression. *Health Technology Assessment, 5,* 1–187.

Clarkin, J. F., Foelsch, P. A., Levy, K. N., Hull, J. W., Delaney, J. C., & Kernberg, O. F. (2001). The development of a psychodynamic treatment for patients with borderline personality disorder: a preliminary study of behavioral change. *Journal of Personality Disorders, 15,* 487–495.

Clarkin, J. F. & Levy, K. N. (2003). A psychodynamic treatment for severe personality disorders. *Psychoanalytic Inquiry, 23,* 248–267.

Clarkin, J. F. & Levy, K. N. (2006). Psychotherapy for patients with borderline personality disorder: focusing on the mechanisms of change. *Journal of Clinical Psychology, 62,* 405–410.

Clarkin, J. F., Levy, K. N., Lenzenweger, M. F., & Kernberg, O. F. (2004). The Personality Disorders Institute/Borderline Personality Disorder Research Foundation randomised controlled trial for borderline personality disorder: rationale, methods, and patient characteristics. *Journal of Personality Disorders, 18,* 52–72.

Clarkin, J. F., Levy, K. N., Lenzenweger, M. F., & Kernberg, O. F. (2007). Evaluating three treatments for borderline personality disorder: a multiwave study. *American Journal of Psychiatry, 164,* 922–928.

Clarkin, J. F., Yeomans, F. E., & Kernberg, O. F. (2006). *Psychotherapy for borderline personality: focusing on object relations.* Washington, DC: American Psychiatric Publishing.

Cohen, J. (1988). *Statistical power analysis for the behavioral sciences* (2nd ed.). Hillsdale, NJ: Lawrence Erlbaum Associates.

Cohen, P. (2007). Freud is widely taught at universities, except in the psychology department. *New York Times,* November 25, 2007.

Cooper, P. J., Murray, L., Wilson, A., & Romaniuk, H. (2003). Controlled trial of the short- and long-term effect of psychological treatment of post-partum depression, I. impact on maternal mood. *British Journal of Psychiatry, 182,* 412–419.

Crisp, A. H., Norton, K., Gowers, S., & Halek, C. (1991). A controlled study of the effect of therapies aimed at adolescent and family psychopathology in anorexia nervosa. *British Journal of Psychiatry, 159,* 325–333.

Crits-Christoph, P. (1992). The efficacy of brief dynamic psychotherapy: a meta-analysis. *American Journal of Psychiatry, 149,* 151–158.

Dare, C., Eisler, I., Russell, G., Treasure, J., & Dodge, L. (2001). Psychological therapies for adults with anorexia nervosa: randomised controlled trial of out-patient treatments. *British Journal of Psychiatry, 178,* 216–221.

Davanloo, H. (1992). *Short-term dynamic psychotherapy.* Jason Aronson: New York, New York.

DeRubeis, R. J., Evans, M. D., Hollon, S. D., Garvey, M. J., Grove, W. M., & Tuason, V. B. (1990). How does cognitive behavioral therapy work? Cognitive change and symptom change in cognitive therapy and pharmacotherapy for depression. *Journal of Consulting and Clinical Psychology, 58,* 862–869.

DeRubeis, R. J. & Feeley, M. (1990). Determinants of change in cognitive behavioral therapy for depression. *Cognitive Therapy and Research, 14,* 469–482.

Durham, R. C., Murphy, T., Allan, T., Richard, K., Treliving, L. R., & Fenton, G. W. (1994). Cognitive therapy, analytic psychotherapy and anxiety management training for generalised anxiety disorder. *British Journal of Psychiatry*, *165*, 315–323.

Fairburn, C. G., Kirk, J., O'Connor, M., & Cooper, P. J. (1986). A comparison of two psychological treatments for bulimia nervosa. *Behaviour Research Therapy*, *24*, 629–643.

Fairburn, C. G., Norman, P. A., Welch, S. L., & O'Connor, M. E. (1995). A prospective study of outcome in bulimia nervosa and the long-term effects of three psychological treatments. *Archives of General Psychiatry*, *52*, 304–312.

Fonagy, P. & Bateman, A. W. (2006). Mechanisms of change in mentalization-based treatment of BPO. *Journal of Clinical Psychology*, *62*, 411–430.

Fonagy, P., Target, M., Steele, M., & Steele, H. (1998). Reflective-Functioning Manual: Version 5.0. For Application to the Adult Attachment Interviews. Unpublished manuscript, University College London.

Freud, S. (1927). *The future of an illusion*. Standard edition, Vol. 21, p. 34–63. Garden City, NY: Doubleday & Company.

Gabbard, G. O. (1995). Countertransference: the emerging common ground. *International Journal of Psycho-Analysis*, *76*, 475–485.

Gallagher-Thompson, D. & Steffen, A. M. (1994). Comparative effects of cognitive behavioral and brief psychodynamic psychotherapies for depressed family caregivers. *Journal of Consulting and Clinical Psychology*, *62*, 543–549.

Garner, D. M., Rockert, W., Davis, R., Garner, M. V., Olmstead, M. P., & Eagle, M. (1993). Comparison of cognitive-behavioral and supportive-expressive therapy for bulimia nervosa. *American Journal of Psychiatry*, *150*, 37–46.

George, C., Kaplan, N., & Main, M. (1985). The attachment interview for adults. Unpublished manuscript, University of California, Berkeley.

Giesen-Bloo, J. H., Arntz, A., van Dijck, R., Spinhoven, P. H., & van Tilburg, W. (2001). Outpatient treatment of borderline personality disorder: analytical psychotherapy versus cognitive behavior therapy. Paper presented at the World Congress of Behavioral and Cognitive Therapies, July 17–21, 2001, Vancouver.

Giesen-Bloo, J. H., Arntz, A., Van Dyck, R., Spinhoven, P., & Van Tilburg, W. (2002, September). Outpatient treatment of borderline personality disorder: analytical psychotherapy versus cognitive behavioral therapy. Paper presented at the Transference Focused Psychotherapy for Borderline Personality Symposium, New York, NY.

Giesen-Bloo, J., van Dyck, R., Spinhoven, P., van Tilburg, W., Dirksen, C., van Asselt, T., et al. (2006). Outpatient psychotherapy for borderline personality disorder: randomized trial of schema-focused therapy vs. transference-focused psychotherapy: correction. *Archives of General Psychiatry*, *63*, 1008.

Gloaguen, V., Cottraux, J., Cucherat, M., & Blackburn, I. (1998). A meta-analysis of the effects of cognitive therapy in depressed patients. *Journal of Affective Disorders*, *49*, 59–72.

Gowers, S., Norton, K., Halek, C., & Crisp, A. H. (1994). Outcome of outpatient psychotherapy in a random allocation treatment study of anorexia nervosa. *International Journal of Eating Disorders*, *15*, 165–177.

Hall, A. & Crisp, A. H. (1987). Brief psychotherapy in the treatment of anorexia nervosa: outcome at one year. *British Journal of Psychiatry*, *151*, 185–191.

Hersen, M., Bellack, A. S., Himmelhoch, J. M., & Thase, M. E. (1984). Effects of social skill training, amitriptyline, and psychotherapy in unipolar depressed women. *Behavior Therapy*, *15*, 21–40.

Hobson, R. F. (1985). *Forms of feeling: the heart of psychotherapy*. London: Tavistock.

Hoffman, L. (2002). Review of psychotherapy for personality disorders. *American Journal of Psychiatry*, *159*, 504–507.

Howard, K. I., Kopta, S. M., Kraase, M. S., & Orlinsky, D. E. (1986). The dose-effect relationship in psychotherapy. *American Psychologist*, *41*, 159–164.

Huprich, S. K. (2008 in press). *Psychodynamic therapy: conceptual and empirical foundations*. New York: Taylor & Francis.

Ilardi, S. S. & Craighead, W. E. (1994). The role of nonspecific factors in cognitive-behavior therapy for depression. *Clinical Psychology: Science and Practice*, *1*, 138–156.

James, W. (1890). *The principles of psychology*. New York: Holt.

Jones, E. E. (1985). Manual for the Psychotherapy Process Q-set. Unpublished manuscript, University of California, Berkeley.

Jones, E. E. & Pulos, S. M. (1993). Comparing the process in psychodynamic and cognitive-behavioral therapies. *Journal of Consulting and Clinical Psychology*, *61*, 306–316.

Kellog, S. H. & Young, J. E. (2006). Schema therapy for borderline personality disorder. *Journal of Clinical Psychology*, *62*, 445–458.

Kernberg, O. F. (1965). Countertransference. *Journal of the American Psychoanalytic Association*, *13*, 38–56.

Kernberg, O.F., Yeomans, F.E., Clarkin, J. F., & Levy, K. N. Transference focused psychotherapy: overview and update. *International Journal of Psychoanalysis* (in press).

Kohlenberg, R. J. & Tsai, M. T. (1994). Functional analytic psychotherapy: a radical behavioral approach to treatment and integration. *Journal of Psychotherapy Integration*, *4*, 175–201.

Kohut, H. (1971). *The analysis of the self*. New York: International Universities Press.

Koerner, K., Kohlenberg, R. J., & Parker, C. R. (1996). Diagnosis of personality disorder: a radical behavioral alternative. *Journal of Consulting and Clinical Psychology*, 64, 1169.

Korner, A., Gerull, F., Meares, R., & Stevenson, J. (2006). Borderline personality disorder treated with the conversational model: a replication study. *Comprehensive Psychiatry*, 47, 406–411.

Leichsenring, F. (2001). Comparative effects of short-term psychodynamic psychotherapy and cognitive-behavioral therapy in depression: a meta-analytic approach. *Clinical Psychology Review*, 21, 401–419.

Leichsenring, F. & Leibing, E. (2003). The effectiveness of psychodynamic therapy and cognitive behaviour therapy in the treatment of personality disorders: a meta-analysis. *American Journal of Psychiatry*, 160, 1223–1232.

Levy, K. N. (2008). The decline of psychodynamic psychology in academia. Unpublished manuscript.

Levy, K. N., Meehan, K. B., Kelly, K. M., Reynoso, J. S., Clarkin, J. F., & Kernberg, O. F. (2006). Change in attachment patterns and reflective function in a randomized controlled trial of transference-focused psychotherapy for borderline personality disorder. *Journal of Consulting and Clinical Psychology*, 74, 1027–1040.

Levy, K. N., Yeomans, F. E., & Diamond, D. (2007). Psychodynamic treatments of self-injury. *Journal of Clinical Psychology*, 36, 1105–1120.

Linehan, M. M. (1993). *Cognitive behavioral treatment of borderline personality disorder*. New York: Guilford Press.

Linehan, M. M., Armstrong, H. E., Suarez, A., & Allmon, D. (1991). Cognitive-behavioral treatment of chronically parasuicidal borderline patients. *Archives of General Psychiatry*, 48, 1060–1064.

Linehan, M. M., Comtois, K. A., Murray, A. M., Brown, M. Z., Gallop, R. J., Heard, H. L., et al. (2006). Two-year randomized controlled trial and follow-up of dialectical behavior therapy vs. treatment by experts for suicidal behaviors and borderline personality disorder. *Archives of General Psychiatry*, 63, 757–766.

Linehan, M. M., Tutek, D. A., Heard, H. L., & Armstrong, H. E. (1994). Interpersonal outcome of cognitive behavioral treatment for chronically suicidal borderline patients. *American Journal of Psychiatry*, 151, 1771–1776.

Luborsky, L. (1984). *Principles of psychoanalytic psychotherapy: a manual for supportive-expressive treatment*. New York: Basic Books.

Luborsky, L. & Crits-Christoph, P. (1989). A relationship pattern measure: the core conflictual relationship theme. *Psychiatry: Journal for the Study of Interpersonal Processes*, 52, 250–259.

Luborsky, L., Diguer, L., Seligman, D. A., Rosenthal, R., Krause, E. D., Johnson, S., et al. (1999). The researcher's own therapy allegiances: a "wild card" in comparisons

of treatment efficacy. *Clinical Psychology: Science and Practice*, 6, 95–106.

Lynch, T. R. (2004, July). *Dialectical behavior therapy: recent research and developments*, Conference presentation: NIMH's international think tank for the more effective treatment of borderline personality disorder. Bethesda, MD.

Main, M. (2000). The organized categories of infant, child, and adult attachment: flexible vs. inflexible attention under attachment-related stress. *Journal of the American Psychoanalytic Association*, 48, 1055–1096.

Malan, D. H. (1976). *The frontier of brief psychotherapy*. New York: Plenum.

Massion, A. O., Dyck, I. R., Shea, M. T., Phillips, K. A., Warshaw, M. G., & Keller, M. B. (2002). Personality disorders and time to remission in generalized anxiety disorder, social phobia, and panic disorder. *Archives of General Psychiatry*, 59, 434–440.

McWilliams, N. (1999). *Psychoanalytic case formulation*. New York, NY: Guilford Press.

Meares, R., Stevenson, J., & Comerford, A. (1999). Psychotherapy with borderline patients: I. a comparison between treated and untreated cohorts. *Australian and New Zealand Journal of Psychiatry*, 33, 467–472.

Meehl, P. E. (1997). Credentialed persons, credentialed knowledge. *Clinical Psychology: Science and Practice*, 4, 91–98.

Mennin, D. S. & Heimberg, R. G. (2000). The impact of mood and personality disorder comorbidity in the cognitive-behavioral treatment of panic disorder. *Clinical Psychology Review*, 20, 339–357.

Milrod, B., Leon, A. C., Busch, F., Rudden, M., Schwalberg, M., Clarkin, J., et al. (2007a). A randomized controlled clinical trial of psychoanalytic psychotherapy for panic disorder. *American Journal of Psychiatry*, 164(2), 265–272.

Milrod, B., Leon, A. C., Busch, F., Rudden, M., Schwalberg, M., Clarkin, J., Aronson, A., Singer, M., Turchin, W., Klass, E. T., Graf, E., Teres, J. J., & Shear, M. K. (2007b). Erratum: A randomized controlled clinical trial of psychoanalytic psychotherapy for panic disorder. *American Journal of Psychiatry*, 164(3), 259.

Mitchell, S. A. (1988). *Relational Concepts in psychoanalysis*. Cambridge, MA: Harvard University Press.

Mitchell, S. A. (2000). *Relationality: from attachment to intersubjectivity*. Mahwah, NJ: Analytic Press.

Mitchell, S. A. & Black, M. J. (1996). *Freud and beyond: a history of modern psychoanalytic thought*. New York, NY: Basic Books.

Novalis, P. N., Rojcewicz, Jr., S. J., & Peele, R. (1993). *Clinical manual of supportive psychotherapy*. Washington, DC: American Psychiatric Association.

Noyes, R., Reich, J., Christiansen, J., Suelzer, M, et al. (1990). Outcome of panic disorder: relationship to diagnostic subtypes and comorbidity. *Archives of General Psychiatry*, 47, 809–818.

Oldham, J. M. (2006). Borderline personality and suicidality. *American Journal of Psychiatry*, 163, 20–26.

Ornstein, M. (1998). Trend report: survey research. *Current Sociology*, 46, 1–137.

Perry, J. C., Banon, E., & Ianni, F. (1999). Effectiveness of psychotherapy for personality disorders. *American Journal of Psychiatry*, 156, 1312–1321.

Pinsker, H. (1997). *A primer of supportive psychotherapy*. Mahwah, NJ: Analytic Press.

Pollack, M. H., Otto, M. W., & Neimeyer, R. A. (Eds) (1992). *Challenges in psychiatric treatment: pharmacologic and psychosocial perspectives*. New York, NY: Guilford Press.

Racker, H. (1957). The meanings and uses of countertransference. *Psychoanalytic Quarterly*, 26, 303–357.

Reich, J. H. (1991). Avoidant and dependent personality traits in relatives of patients with panic disorder, patients with dependent personality disorder, and normal controls. *Psychiatry Research*, 39, 89–98.

Robinson, L. A., Berman, J. S., & Neimeyer, R. A. (1990). Psychotherapy for the treatment of depression: a comprehensive review of controlled outcome research. *Psychological Bulletin*, 108, 30–49.

Rockland, L. H. (1989). *Supportive therapy: a psychodynamic approach*. New York: Basic Books.

Russell, G. F. M., Szmukler, G. I., Dare, C., & Eisler, I. (1987). An evaluation of family therapy in anorexia nervosa and bulimia nervosa. *Archives of General Psychiatry*, 44, 1047–1056.

Sayette, M. A., Mayne, T. J., & Norcross, J. C. (2006). *Insider's guide to graduate programs in clinical and counseling psychology*. New York, NY: Guilford Press.

Shapiro, D. A., Barkham, M., Rees, A., Hardy, G. E., Reynolds, S., & Startup, M. (1994). Effects of treatment duration and severity of depression on the effectiveness of cognitive-behavioral and psychodynamic-interpersonal psychotherapy. *Journal of Consulting and Clinical Psychology*, 62, 522–534.

Shapiro, D. A., Rees, A., Barkham, M., & Hardy, G. E. (1995). Effects of treatment duration and severity of depression on the maintenance of gains after cognitive-behavioral and psychodynamic-interpersonal psychotherapy. *Journal of Consulting and Clinical Psychology*, 63, 378–387.

Shaw, B. F., Elkin, I., Yamaguchi, J., Olmsted, M., Vallis, T. M., Dobson, K. S., et al. (1999). Therapist competence ratings in relation to clinical outcome in cognitive therapy of depression. *Journal of Consulting and Clinical Psychology*, 67, 837–846.

Shedler, J., Mayman, M., & Manis, M. (1993). The illusion of mental health. *American Psychologist*, 48, 1117–1131.

Snyder, D. K. & Willis, R. M. (1989). Behavioral versus insight-oriented marital therapy: effects on individual and interspousal functioning. *Journal of Consulting and Clinical Psychology*, 57, 39–46.

Snyder, D., Willis, R., & Grady-Fletcher, A. (1991). Long-term effectiveness of behavioral versus insight-oriented marital therapy. *Journal of Consulting and Clinical Psychology*, 59, 138–141.

Stevenson, J. & Meares, R. (1992). An outcome study of psychotherapy for patients with borderline personality disorder. *American Journal of Psychiatry*, 149, 358–362.

Stevenson, J., Meares, R., & D'Angelo, R. (2005). Five-year outcome of outpatient psychotherapy with borderline patients. *Psychological Medicine*, 35, 79–87.

Strupp, H. H. (1984). Psychotherapy research: reflections on my career and the state of the art. *Journal of Social and Clinical Psychology*, 2, 3–24.

Svartberg, M. & Stiles, T. C. (1991). Comparative effects of short-term psychodynamic psychotherapy: a meta-analysis. *Journal of Consulting and Clinical Psychology*, 59, 704–714.

Svartberg, M., Stiles, T., & Seltzer, M. H. (2004). Randomized, controlled trial of the effectiveness of short-term dynamic psychotherapy and cognitive therapy for cluster C personality disorders. *American Journal of Psychiatry*, 161, 810–817.

Trepka, C., Rees, A., Shapiro, D., Hardy, G., & Barkham, M. (2004). Therapist competence and outcome of cognitive therapy for depression. *Cognitive Therapy and Research*, 28, 143–157.

Turner, E. H., Matthews, A. M., Linardatos, E., Tell, R. A., Rosenthal, R. (2008). Selective publication of antidepressant trials and its influence on apparent efficacy. *New England Journal of Medicine*, 358, 252–260.

van den Bosch, L. M. C., Koeter, M. W. J., Stijnen, T., Verheul, R., & van den Brink, W. (2005). Sustained efficacy of dialectical behavior therapy for borderline personality disorder. *Behavior Research Therapy*, 43, 1231–1241.

Verheul, R. (2001). Comorbidity of personality disorders in individuals with substance use disorders. *European Psychiatry*, 16(5):274–282.

Verheul, R., van den Bosch, L. M. C., Koeter, M. W. J., de Ridder, M. A. J., Stijnen, T., & van den Brink, W. (2003). Dialectical behaviour therapy for women with borderline personality disorder. *British Journal of Psychiatry*, 182, 135–140.

Wachtel, P. L. (2005). Anxiety, consciousness, and self-acceptance: placing the idea of making the unconscious conscious in an integrative framework. *Journal of Psychotherapy Integration*, 15, 243–253.

Wampold, B. E. (1997). Methodological problems in identifying efficacious psychotherapies. *Psychotherapy Research*, 7, 21–43.

Wampold, B. E., Minami, T., Baskin, T. W., & Tierney, S. C. (2002). A meta-(re) analysis of the effects of cognitive therapy versus "other therapies" for depression. *Journal of Affective Disorders*, 68, 159–165.

Welch v. American Psychoanalytic Association, No. 85 Civ. 1651 (JFK), 1986 U. S. Dist. Lexis 27182 (S. D. N. Y., April 14, 1986).

Westen, D. (1999). The scientific status of unconscious processes: is Freud really dead? Journal of the American Psychoanalytic Association, 47, 1061–1106.

Westen, D., Blagov, P. S., Harenski, K., Kilts, C., & Hamann, S. (2006). Neural bases of motivated reasoning: an fMRI study of emotional constraints on partisan political judgment in the 2004 U.S. presidential election. Journal of Cognitive Neuroscience, 18, 1947–1958.

Wiborg, I. M. & Dahl, A. A. (1996). Does brief dynamic psychotherapy reduce the relapse rate of panic disorder? Archives of General Psychiatry, 53, 689–694.

Winnicott, D. W. (1965). The maturational processes and the facilitating environment: studies in the theory of emotional development. London: Hogarth Press.

Winston, A., Laikin, M., Pollack, J., Samstag, L. W., McCullough, L., & Muran, J. C. (1994). Short-term psychotherapy of personality disorders. American Journal of Psychiatry, 151, 190–194.

Winston, A., Pollach, J., McCullough, L, Flegenheimer, W., Kestenbaum, R., & Trujillo, M. (1991). Brief psychotherapy of personality disorders. Journal of Nervous and Mental Disease, 179, 188–193.

Woody, G. E., McLellan, A. T., Luborsky, L., & O'Brien, C. P. (1985). Sociopathy and psychotherapy outcome. Archives of General Psychiatry, 42, 1081–1086.

Yeomans, F. E. (2006). Questions concerning the randomized trial of schema-focused therapy vs. transference-focused psychotherapy. Archives of General Psychiatry, 64(5), 609–310.

Yeomans, F. E., Clarkin, J. F., & Kernberg, O. F. (2003). A primer of transference-focused psychotherapy for the borderline patient. Northvale, NJ: Jason Aronson.

Yonkers, K. A., Dyck, I. R., Warshaw, M., & Keller, M. B. (2000). Factors predicting the clinical course of generalised anxiety disorder. British Journal of Psychiatry, 176, 544–549.

Young, J. E. (1990). Cognitive therapy for personality disorders: a schema-focused approach. Sarasota, FL: Professional Resource Press.

Young, J. E., Klosko, J. S., & Weishaar, M. E. (2003). Schema therapy: a practitioner's guide. New York: Guilford Press.

Interpersonal Psychotherapy

Aaron L. Pincus
Pennsylvania State University

Nicole M. Cain
Pennsylvania State University

OUTLINE

INTRODUCTION TO INTERPERSONAL PSYCHOTHERAPY

Psychotherapies and interpersonal relationships are inextricably bound together at many levels. There is a therapeutic relationship between therapist and patient (or patients — in group treatments). Beyond the therapeutic relationship, many patients seek help because they experience interpersonal problems that lead to difficulties forming relationships or repeatedly experiencing painful, conflictual, exploitative, enmeshed, or other maladaptive relationship patterns. Even when a patient seeks therapy for a specific anxiety, mood, eating, or substance use disorder, treatment will likely include examination of some of the various family, marital, social, and occupational relationships in the patient's life. And finally, most approaches to psychotherapy also propose that there are interpersonal relationships that exist inside both therapist and patient. The psychological concept of mental representation (Blatt, Auerbach, & Levy, 1997) represents a pantheoretical construct of intrapsychic mental models of interpersonal relationships. Whether referred to as interpersonal schemas (cognitive therapies), internal object relations (psychodynamic psychotherapies), or internal working models (attachment-based therapies), these internalized relationships impact motivation, regulation, social perception, and interpersonal behavior in myriad ways.

Given the ubiquitous nature of interpersonal relationships in psychotherapy, it might seem strange to propose that a particular approach be called *interpersonal psychotherapy*. In one sense we agree with this sentiment, as we see interpersonal functioning as a nexus for understanding personality, personality disorder, psychopathology, and psychotherapy (Pincus, 2005a, 2005b; Pincus & Ansell, 2003; Pincus & Gurtman, 2006; Pincus, Lukowitsky & Wright, in press). Thus, examination of interpersonal issues and potential interventions for interpersonal problems should exist across the spectrum of clinical theories and are, in fact, key elements of most effective psychotherapies (Castonguay & Beutler, 2006; Norcross, 2002). The fact that interpersonal concepts permeate psychotherapeutic practice means it would be simplistic to assert that the uniquely defining characteristic of interpersonal psychotherapy is a focus on interpersonal functioning.

What uniquely defines the interpersonal approach to psychotherapy we outline in this chapter is *how* the clinician focuses on interpersonal functioning. A comprehensive nomological net, hereafter referred to as the **interpersonal tradition** in clinical psychology, is used by the therapist for case conceptualization, intervention, and understanding the therapeutic process. The interpersonal tradition is a synthesis of theory and empirical research that has evolved through three generations of clinicians and investigators, reflecting nearly 60 years of effort integrating clinical science and practice. Beginning with American psychiatrist Harry Stack Sullivan's paradigm-shifting and highly generative **interpersonal theory of psychiatry** (Sullivan, 1953a, 1953b, 1954, 1956, 1962, 1964), the history of the interpersonal tradition reflects remarkably broad influences. Sullivanian thinking was operationalized in groundbreaking empirical work by Timothy Leary and associates (LaForge, 2004; Leary, 1957) and extended by a diverse set of clinical scientists such as Donald J. Kiesler, an original member of Carl Rogers's psychotherapy research team (e.g., Kiesler, 1966, 1982); Lorna Smith Benjamin, a student of primatologist Harry Harlow (e.g., Benjamin, 1973, 1996); and many others.

The resulting therapeutic paradigm synthesizes (a) rich clinical theory, (b) empirically validated models for systematic description of interpersonal functioning, (c) dynamic principles of reciprocal interpersonal impact and influence, and (d) a transactional framework for understanding interpersonal relationships. The interpersonal approach to psychotherapy applies the lens of the interpersonal tradition to understand the etiology and maintenance of patients' symptoms and difficulties and employs a variety of intervention techniques to promote new interpersonal awareness and learning, resulting in improved relational capacity and a reduction in symptoms.

Origins of the Interpersonal Tradition

Harry Stack Sullivan and the Interpersonal Theory of Psychiatry: Theoretical Principles

> I had come to feel over the years that there was an acute need for a discipline that was determined to study not the individual organism or the social heritage, but the interpersonal situations through which persons manifest mental health or mental disorder. (Sullivan, 1953b, p. 18)

> Personality is the relatively enduring pattern of recurrent interpersonal situations which characterize a human life. (Sullivan, 1953b, pp. 110–111)

In the first half of the twentieth century, psychotherapeutic practice was dominated by psychoanalytic assumptions based strongly in Freud's topographic model of the mind and drive theory. The therapeutic relationship was structured to minimize therapists' impact on patients (i.e., establish therapeutic neutrality) in order to encourage free association and the development of transference, promoting analysis of unconscious motives, impulses, conflicts, and memories that were acting outside the patient's awareness due to psychological defenses. Therapists' countertransference reactions to the patient were considered impediments to neutrality and analyzed outside the therapeutic relationship. Sullivan was opposed to Freud's drive concepts as the source of personality structuralization and saw the individual as developing relationally in communal existence with others. To Sullivan, the important contents of the mind were not repressed unconscious material but rather the learned patterning of behavior associated with the vicissitudes of anxiety, security, and esteem in relation to others. Emerging from continuous social learning processes, individuals develop patterns of behavior, or **dynamisms,** which support a consistent but malleable self-concept and concepts of important others. The emphasis on relational experience led Sullivan to assert that **interpersonal situations** are fundamental experiences for personality development and psychotherapeutic practice.

Sullivan's emphasis on the interpersonal situation as the focus for understanding both personality and psychopathology set a new course for psychology and psychiatry. Interpersonal theory thus begins with the assumption that the most important expressions of personality and psychopathology occur in phenomena involving more than one person. Sullivan (1953a, 1953b) suggested that individuals express integrating tendencies that bring them together in the mutual pursuit of satisfactions (generally, a large class of biologically grounded needs), security (i.e., anxiety-free functioning), and self-esteem. These integrating tendencies develop into increasingly complex dynamisms of interpersonal experience. From infancy throughout the life span, these dynamisms are encoded in memory via age-appropriate social learning. According to Sullivan, interpersonal learning of self-concept and social behavior is based on an anxiety gradient associated with interpersonal situations. All interpersonal situations range from rewarding (highly secure, esteem-promoting) through various degrees of anxiety and end in a class of situations associated with such severe anxiety that they are dissociated from experience. The interpersonal situation underlies genesis, development, maintenance, and mutability of personality and psychopathology through the continuous patterning and repatterning of interpersonal experience in an effort to increase security and self-esteem while avoiding anxiety. Over time, this gives rise to mental representations of self and other (Sullivan's **personifications**) as well as to enduring patterns of adaptive or disturbed interpersonal relating, referred to as the **self-system**.

Individual variation in learning occurs due to the interaction between the developing person's level of cognitive maturation and the characteristics of the interpersonal situations encountered. Interpersonal experience is understood differently depending on the developing person's grasp of cause-and-effect logic and the use of consensual symbols such as language. This affects how one makes sense of the qualities of significant others (including their "reflected appraisals," which communicate approval or disapproval of the developing person), as well as the ultimate outcomes of interpersonal situations characterizing a human life. Pincus and Ansell (2003) summarized Sullivan's concept of the interpersonal situation as "the experience of a pattern of relating self with other associated with varying levels of anxiety (or security) in which learning takes place that influences the development of self-concept and social behavior" (p. 210). In one way or another, all perspectives on personality, psychopathology, and psychotherapy within the interpersonal tradition address elements of the interpersonal situation. These elements include individual differences, reciprocal interpersonal patterns of behavior, internal psychological processes, and the transactional framework for understanding interpersonal relations that we review in this chapter.

A second major assumption of interpersonal theory is that the term *interpersonal* is meant to convey a sense of primacy, directing psychotherapy to a set of fundamental phenomena important for personality development and structuralization, psychopathology, and adjustment. The term is not meant as a geographical indicator of locale; it does not imply a dichotomy between what is inside the person and what is outside the person, nor does it limit the scope of interpersonal psychotherapy to observable behavioral interactions between two proximal people (Benjamin, 2005; Kiesler, Schmidt, & Wagner, 1997; Pincus, 2005a). Mitchell (1988) pointed out that Sullivan was quite amenable to incorporating internal psychological structures and processes into interpersonal theory as he viewed the most important contents of the mind to be the consequence of lived interpersonal experience. For example, Sullivan (1964) asserted that "everything that can be found in the human mind has been put there by interpersonal relations, excepting only the capabilities to receive *and elaborate* the relevant experiences" (p. 302; see also Stern, 1985, 1988). Sullivan clearly viewed the interpersonal situation as equally likely to be found within the mind of the person as it is

to be found in the observable interactions between two people. For example, Sullivan (1964) defined psychiatry as "the study of phenomena that occur in configurations of two or more people, all but one of whom may be more or less completely illusory" (p. 33). These illusory aspects of the interpersonal situation involve personifications. Sullivan (1953b) was forceful in asserting that personifications are elaborated organizations of past interpersonal experience, stating "I would like to make it forever clear that the relation of the personifications to that which is personified is always complex and sometimes multiple; and that personifications are not adequate descriptions of that which is personified" (p. 167).

Thus, interpersonal situations occur between proximal interactants *and* within the minds of those interactants via the capacity for mental representation. Interpersonal theory does suggest that the most important clinical phenomena are relational in nature, but it does not suggest that such phenomena are limited to contemporaneous observable behavior. They also occur in covert interpretations of ongoing interpersonal experiences, memories of past interpersonal experiences, and fantasies of future interpersonal experiences. Regardless of the level of accuracy or distortion in these perceptions, memories, and fantasies, both internal and proximal interpersonal situations continuously influence an individual's learned relational strategies and self-concept. Psychopathology is therefore inherently expressed via *disturbed interpersonal relations* (Sullivan, 1953b).

Harry Stack Sullivan and the Interpersonal Theory of Psychiatry: Therapeutic Innovations

Sullivan's initial psychotherapeutic efforts focused on treating psychotic and obsessional patients, and his work ultimately bifurcated

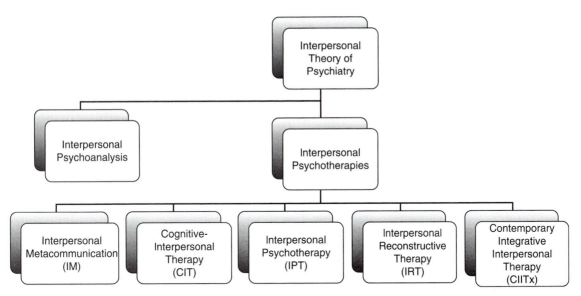

FIGURE 9.1   Therapeutic approaches based on Sullivan's interpersonal theory of psychiatry.

into two main influential lines of practice (see Figure 9.1). Sullivan joined the American psychoanalytic movement in the 1920s during a time of growth and transition from its Freudian roots (Thompson, 1952). His work has consistently been identified as psychoanalytic (e.g., Greenberg & Mitchell, 1983) and is the foundation for the treatment paradigm referred to as **interpersonal psychoanalysis** (Levenson, 2006; Lionells, Fiscalini, Mann, & Stern, 1995). This is a vibrant psychoanalytic movement, and we encourage interested students to explore the area in depth. However, the remainder of this chapter will focus on Sullivan's influences on contemporary *interpersonal psychotherapies*. These interrelated approaches to treatment integrate Sullivanian conceptual foundations with an empirically derived taxonomy of interpersonal motives, dispositions, and behaviors (Leary, 1957; Wiggins, 1982 — reviewed in the next section) to create the contemporary lens through which interpersonal psychotherapists view clinical phenomena.

The psychotherapeutic innovations that catalyzed contemporary approaches included Sullivan's new perspective on the therapeutic relationship and his emphasis on social learning processes (Chapman, 1978). Unlike the neutral psychotherapist who is the recipient of the patient's unconscious projections and transference, Sullivan saw the therapeutic relationship as an interpersonal situation. Thus the therapist is considered a **participant observer** engaged in a real relationship with the patient. From this perspective, case conceptualization and the main mechanisms of therapeutic change are derived from the therapeutic relationship itself. Because the therapist is an active participant in an ongoing relationship, reactions to the patient reflect the prominent interpersonal impacts of the patient's behavior on others rather than problematic countertransference and are viewed as fundamental **interpersonal communications** that inform clinical understanding and intervention decisions.

But the therapist is more than a participant; he or she is also an observer. Sullivan was clear that a particular stance be taken when observing the therapeutic relationship. Specifically, therapists should be acutely attuned to (a) the interpersonal communication occurring via behavior, voice tone, gesture, and symptoms and (b) indications of interpersonal anxiety or anxiety avoidance via the interpersonal communications of the patient's presentation. Such observation allows the therapist to identify those dynamisms associated with security and self-esteem and those associated with anxiety and its avoidance. For example, some patients are secure when taking a passive, cooperative relational stance but can be quite anxious with self-assertion or disagreement. For others, the opposite is true. Depressive symptoms may convey the submissive interpersonal message "help me; I can't do it by myself." Suicidality may convey the hostile interpersonal message "you're to blame for my misery" in one context, and the affiliative interpersonal message "I desperately need someone to take care of me" in another context. While waiting for a consultation on an inpatient unit, a schizophrenic patient haltingly approached the first author and said glumly, "I'm being punished for breathing fire." One common reaction to such a statement in an inpatient context is to see it as a psychotic symptom and disregard it since human beings do not breathe fire. However, when the interpersonal communication was considered, the patient appeared to be relaying a sense of frustration and hurt. When I replied, "That must feel unfair," the patient relaxed and was able to explain that he was reprimanded for smoking in his room rather than in a designated area.

The interpersonal communications of the patient's presentation will also demonstrate **security operations**, which serve to minimize anxiety via activation or inhibition of certain behaviors, and may operate outside the patient's awareness. Concretely, when without awareness, a patient changes the subject abruptly, fails to comprehend the therapist, refuses to respond, exhibits nonverbal and affective shifts, or reports new symptoms, the therapist should consider "what is the interpersonal meaning of such phenomena?" Sullivan suggested that when such behaviors interfere with the integration of the therapeutic relationship, the patient is employing learned strategies that minimize interpersonal anxiety and increase security. Thus participant observation allows the therapist to conceptualize the patient's problems directly via relational experience. Since the same learned relational patterns are assumed to be common across the interpersonal situations that characterize the patient's life, these data can then be used to plan treatment that encourages new interpersonal learning within the therapeutic relationship.

Finally, the interpersonal communication of the patient may also include clues of **parataxic distortion** in the therapist-patient relationship. This occurs when, outside of awareness, the patient organizes his or her experience of the therapist and therapeutic relationship in inaccurate ways that conform to certain prominent dynamisms and personifications. It is important to distinguish parataxic distortions from Freud's notion of transference. Distorted perceptions of others based on previous relationships were first recognized by Freud and called transference. Transference implies the unconscious reliving or repetition of aspects of past relationships based on libidinal development. In contrast, parataxic distortions are the immediate, often maladaptive, application of learned relational patterns in the covert interpretation of the present relationship. Parataxic distortions are not the reliving of traumatic aspects of past relationships but simply the unique organizing tendencies and relational patterns the patient has learned across the interpersonal situations that characterize his or her life.

The fundamental therapeutic implication of this distinction is that such maladaptive relational patterns may be addressed in the therapeutic relationship directly without requiring the working through of unresolved past conflicts with parental figures (although this is not precluded in Sullivan's approach).

Sullivan's innovations changed the nature of how therapists view interpersonal functioning by emphasizing the real relationship between therapist and patient, the interpersonal communications associated with the patient's behavior and symptoms, the patient's learned patterns of relational behavior associated with maintaining security and self-esteem and avoiding anxiety, the potential for disturbed interpersonal relations to arise from parataxic distortion, and the self-perpetuating nature of disturbed interpersonal patterns. These innovations implied a wide variety of intervention opportunities, including social learning via the immediate therapeutic relationship (relational emphasis), skills acquisition and practice in relationships outside of therapy (behavioral emphasis), mutual examination of the social-cognitive and affective processes of interpersonal perception (cognitive emphasis), and the exploration of relational antecedents of current interpersonal functioning (interpretive emphasis). Sullivan's attitude was clearly pragmatic and flexible, but he also recognized that therapy was not easy for patients, stating, "We can take your experience into the shop and fix it. It has to be fixed in you, by you, and there will be quite a bit of anxiety connected with the process. If something makes that worth undergoing, okay. If it doesn't, it won't happen" (White, 1952, p. 126).

The University of California, Berkeley/ Kaiser Foundation Group

The first articulation of the **interpersonal circle** (IPC, also referred to as the **interpersonal circumplex**) was developed from an extensive investigation of group psychotherapy conducted by graduate students, clinicians, and faculty associated with the University of California and the Kaiser Foundation Health Plan in Oakland, California. Guided by the theoretical influences of Sullivan and Kurt Lewin, the clinical goal was to understand the relations between group interaction and personality structure, and the research approach was an attempt to systematize and operationally define many of Sullivan's concepts, particularly those related to the interpersonal communications in patient behavior and symptomology. The results of this work are documented in a series of articles that appeared in the early 1950s (Coffey, Freedman, Leary, & Ossorio, 1950; Freedman, Leary, Ossorio, & Coffey, 1951; LaForge, Leary, Naboisek, Coffey, & Freedman, 1954; LaForge & Suczek, 1955; Leary & Coffey, 1955) and comprehensively summarized and expanded by Leary (1957). The history of the IPC is well documented (e.g., LaForge, 2004; LaForge, Freedman, & Wiggins, 1985; Wiggins, 1996), and we will only briefly cover it in this chapter. What is most important to note is that since its initial derivation, the IPC has had a reciprocal relationship with interpersonal theory itself, with developments in each impacting the other (Pincus, 1994). That is why we refer to the interpersonal tradition as a nomological net that combines rich clinical theory with an empirically based model of interpersonal description (Pincus, 2005b).

Leary and his associates observed interactions among group psychotherapy patients and asked, "What is the subject of the activity, e.g., the individual whose behavior is being rated, doing to the object or objects of the activity?" (Freedman et al., 1951, p. 149). In this regard, topical content was not of specific interest. Instead, observations reflected the interpersonal communications between group members. This context-free cataloguing of patients' interpersonal behavior eventually led to an empirically derived circular structure

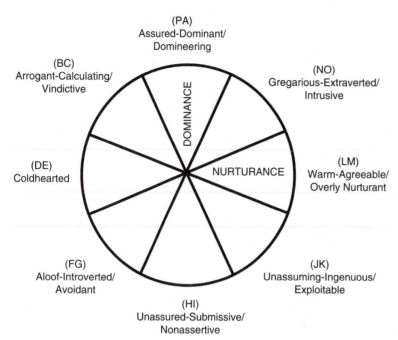

FIGURE 9.2 The Interpersonal Circle (Traits/Problems).

based on the two underlying dimensions of dominance-submission on the vertical axis and nurturance-coldness on the horizontal axis. While the model has been empirically refined and extended over the years, its fundamental characteristics have been repeatedly validated. A contemporary version is presented in Figure 9.2.

Emergence of Interpersonal Psychotherapies

During the 1960s and 1970s, continued development of theory and research on interpersonal functioning and IPC assessment attracted a diverse array of investigators and practitioners, culminating in the seminal publication of Anchin and Kiesler's (1982) *Handbook of Interpersonal Psychotherapy*. The two striking aspects of this book were the integrative nature of the emerging interpersonal paradigm and the initial formulations of what would become the contemporary interpersonal tradition. When reviewing the contributions to the volume, one finds a remarkable pluralistic range of psychodynamic, cognitive, behavioral, systems, gestalt, and experiential perspectives, all centered on the interpersonal nature of personality, psychopathology, and psychotherapy. In his thoughtful closing synthesis, Anchin (1982) made several conclusions and identified points of convergence to further guide and stimulate the integration of clinical science and practice through the formal features of the emerging interpersonal tradition. It was noted that "Clearly, there is no single interpersonal psychotherapy. Rather, interpersonal therapy embraces a variety of distinguishable treatment approaches emanating from the shared view that present-day interpersonal processes are centrally involved in the patient's distress" (p. 313). However, despite roots spanning nearly 30 years through the early

1980s, the emerging contemporary interpersonal tradition was still nascent, and "the theory, practice, and scientific study of individual psychotherapy and behavior change have yet fully and systematically to incorporate the knowledge and measurement methodologies associated with this rich and productive interpersonal tradition" (Anchin, 1982, p. 324). Fortunately, many of the important theoretical developments and empirical inquiries that were recommended at that time (e.g., Anchin, 1982; McLemore & Benjamin, 1979; Wiggins, 1982) have come to fruition in the following 25 years, leading to the contemporary interpersonal tradition in clinical psychology (e.g., Benjamin, 1996, 2003; Horowitz, 2004; Kiesler, 1996; Pincus, 2005a; Pincus et al., in press).

Anchin (1982) identified four convergent themes that can help define the nomological net of the interpersonal tradition (see Table 9.1). First, all interpersonal psychotherapies develop and expand Sullivanian theory. Prominent progress includes (a) advances in understanding and assessing the interpersonal communications of patient presentation and therapeutic interaction (e.g., Kiesler, 1979, 1982, 1988); (b) updating Sullivan's concepts like parataxic distortion,

personification, dynamism, and security operations in terms of contemporary cognitive psychology and social learning theory such as prototypes, schemas, expectancies, and information processing (e.g., Benjamin, 1996; Carson, 1982; Golding, 1978; Horowitz, 1979; Safran, 1990a, 1990b); (c) integrating Sullivan's maturational concepts with modern developmental and motivational theories (e.g., Benjamin, 1993; Horowitz, 2004); and (d) linking Sullivan's concepts of internal interpersonal processes with current concepts of mental representation (e.g., Benjamin, 2003; Pincus, 2005a).

Second, all interpersonal psychotherapies adopt an ecological/reciprocal emphasis. Specifically, the interpersonal psychotherapist "acknowledges the ongoing, reciprocal interaction between overt and covert processes vis-à-vis social-environmental stimuli in inducing, eliciting, and maintaining abnormality" (Anchin, 1982, p. 313). Disturbed interpersonal relations involve ongoing reciprocal transactions and social reinforcement via "an unbroken causal loop between social perception, behavioral enactment, and environmental reaction" (Carson, 1982, p. 66). This is the basis for the contemporary transactional framework of

TABLE 9.1 Defining Features of Interpersonal Psychotherapies

- Development and Expansion of Sullivanian Theory
  - o Integrations with cognitive psychology, social learning theory, communications theory, attachment theory, object relations theory, evolutionary theory.
- Ecological/Reciprocal Deterministic Emphasis
  - o Both psychopathology and therapeutic change involve reciprocal social reinforcements via interpersonal transactions between persons that influence behavior, cognition, affect, and symptomology (i.e., interpersonal situations).
- Circumplex Models of Interpersonal Dispositions and Behavior
  - o Provide a systematic language to describe interpersonal communication patterns and interpersonal transactions associated with clinical problems and psychotherapeutic interventions.
- Procedural Variability; Diverse Levels, and Targets of Intervention
  - o Flexible use of relational, cognitive, behavioral, and interpretive techniques as indicated by diagnostic factors, stages of therapeutic work, and the therapeutic alliance.

the interpersonal tradition reflected in concepts such as self-fulfilling prophecy (Carson, 1982), maladaptive transaction cycle (Kiesler, 1991), impact messages (Kiesler, Schmidt, & Wagner, 1997), interpersonal complementarity (Kiesler, 1983), and interpersonal predictive principles and copy processes (Benjamin, 2003).

Third, to a greater or lesser extent, interpersonal psychotherapies incorporate IPC models of individual differences in interpersonal dispositions and behavior "to provide a systematic language for the description of interpersonal transactions and to demonstrate that this language permits specification of a set of variables that are common to the enterprises of assessment, diagnosis, and treatment" (Wiggins, 1982, p. 183). Importantly, major classes of psychopathology have been systematically related to the IPC (e.g., Horowitz & Vitkus, 1986; Pincus & Wiggins, 1990), and beyond psychiatric diagnoses, a large number of patients seek treatment for interpersonal problems themselves (Horowitz, Rosenberg, Baer, Ureño, & Villaseñor, 1988). These explicit interpersonal difficulties can also be modeled by the IPC (Alden, Wiggins, & Pincus, 1990; see Box 9.1). Importantly, the systematic language and framework provided by IPC models also provide guidelines for intervention within the therapeutic relationship (e.g., Benjamin, 1996; Kiesler, 1988; Tracey, 1993).

Finally, interpersonal psychotherapies vary in how they are conducted, consistent with Sullivan's broad conception of interpersonal situations and contemporary theoretical integrations and extensions already noted. Interpersonal psychotherapy intervention strategies are pluralistic, employing relational, cognitive, behavioral, and interpretive techniques. These include the use of the therapeutic relationship as the here-and-now experiential mechanism for new social learning and change, collaborative examination of cognitive-affective interpersonal schemas as they impact the patient's relationships in and out of therapy, enhancing problem-solving strategies for typical interpersonal difficulties, and examination of the developmental origins of dysfunctional interpersonal patterns. Importantly, variable use of intervention techniques is also guided by considerations such as "the precise nature of the patient's maladaptive style, the stage of therapy, the quality of the therapist-patient relationship at any point in treatment, the interpersonal issues thus far examined, and the therapist's own personality characteristics" (Anchin, 1982, p. 322; see also Tracey, 1993; Tracey & Hays, 1989).

KEY CONCEPTS AND IDEAS

Interpersonal Description

There are two major, empirically validated, structural models of interpersonal description predominantly used in the interpersonal tradition.

The Interpersonal Circle

The IPC model (Figure 9.2) is a geometric representation of individual differences in interpersonal dispositions and behaviors (Locke, 2006). The former include interpersonal traits (Wiggins, 1979, 1995), interpersonal problems (Alden et al., 1990), and interpersonal values and motives (Locke, 2000). The latter include verbal and nonverbal interpersonal behaviors (Gifford, 1991; Kiesler, 1985; Kiesler, Goldston, & Schmidt, 1991; Moskowitz, 1994), covert interpersonal impacts (Schmidt, Wagner, & Kiesler, 1999), and social support behaviors (Trobst, 2000). Thus all qualities of individual differences within these domains can be described as blends of the circle's two underlying dimensions located along the 360° perimeter. Interpersonal qualities close to one another on the perimeter are conceptually and statistically similar, qualities at 90° are conceptually and statistically independent, and qualities 180° apart are conceptual and statistical opposites. While the circular model itself is a continuum without beginning or end (Carson, 1996), any segmentalization of the IPC perimeter to identify lower-order taxa is potentially useful within the limits of reliable discriminability. The IPC has been segmentalized into sixteenths (Kiesler, 1983), octants (Wiggins, Trapnell, & Phillips, 1988), and quadrants (Carson, 1969).

Dispositional IPC models of interpersonal traits, values, and problems describe the distinctive consistencies of the individual across interpersonal situations that are assumed to give rise to healthy and disturbed interpersonal relations (Wiggins, 1997). Thus, we can use IPC models to describe a patient's typical ways of relating to others and refer to their "interpersonal style" (Pincus & Gurtman, 2003). Behavioral IPC models can be used for transactional analyses of interpersonal situations, including ongoing psychotherapy sessions. This level of analysis dovetails with new views of personality consistency and intraindividual variability of behavior. IPC models can be used to evaluate patients' "if-then" behavioral signatures, that is, generally consistent interpersonal patterns within specific interpersonal situations that recur over time (Fournier, Moskowitz, & Zuroff, 2008; Mischel & Shoda, 1995). Finally, because interpersonal situations also occur within the mind, these models can describe the patient's typical ways of encoding new interpersonal information, schematic processing of that information, and their mental representations of self and others. The use of IPC models for case conceptualization is referred to as **interpersonal diagnosis** (Leary, 1957; Wiggins, Phillips, & Trapnell, 1989).

HIGHLIGHT BOX 9.1

INTERPERSONAL PROBLEMS AND PSYCHOTHERAPY

The Inventory of Interpersonal Problems (IIP, Horowitz et al., 1988) was initially created to measure the recurrent themes identified in the presenting complaints of patients beginning outpatient psychotherapy. Interpersonal problems take two forms. One type of interpersonal problem is a chronic behavioral inhibition — an adaptive interpersonal behavior that is hard for the person to do (*It's hard for me to say "no" to other people*). A second type of interpersonal problem is a chronic behavioral excess — a maladaptive interpersonal behavior that the person does too much (*I try to control others too much*). Alden et al. (1990) demonstrated that patients' interpersonal problems conformed well to the interpersonal circle model and developed the IIP-C. This instrument exhibits sensitivity to clinical improvement across psychodynamic, cognitive, and pharmacological treatments (Horowitz et al., 1988; Markowitz et al., 1996; Vittengl, Clark, & Jarrett, 2003) and is widely used in psychotherapy research.

Research suggests patients' problematic interpersonal styles can differentially impact psychotherapy outcome and process. Tracey (1993) noted that friendly submissive behaviors are thought to be complementary to the typical behaviors of a therapist, which are likely to be friendly-dominant; therefore hostile dominance is expected to conflict with the process and goals of psychotherapy. The psychotherapy research using the IIP-C mostly confirms this prediction. For example, friendly submissive problems are associated with therapeutic alliance formation, whereas hostile dominant problems impede alliance formation (Muran, Segal, Samstag, & Crawford, 1994). Gurtman (1996) found that therapists rated patients with friendly and friendly submissive problems as more suitable for psychotherapy than patients with hostile

---

HIGHLIGHT BOX 9.1   (*continued*)

---

problems. He also found that therapists rated patients with friendly dominant and friendly submissive problems as exhibiting greater clinical improvement than patients with hostile dominant and hostile submissive problems. Horowitz, Rosenberg, and Bartholomew (1993) observed that exploitable interpersonal problems were the most treatable symptoms in brief psychodynamic psychotherapy. Similarly, Horowitz, Rosenberg, and Kalehzan (1992) found that patients with affiliative interpersonal distress communicated more clearly about others than did hostile patients and thus were better candidates for expressive (or psychodynamic) treatment. While most research suggests patients with hostile interpersonal problems will be more difficult to treat, the therapies were not explicitly focused on treating interpersonal functioning. What this research does suggest is that hostile and hostile dominant interpersonal problems may make treatments for any disorder more difficult because they directly interfere with the therapeutic alliance.

However, hostile dominant interpersonal problems are not untreatable. Maling, Gurtman, and Howard (1995) examined the change of interpersonal problems in response to varying "doses" (or number of sessions) of psychotherapy. They found that overly controlling interpersonal problems actually changed readily in psychotherapy, with 45% of the patients experiencing significant improvement around session 4, and they appeared to improve progressively as a dose-dependent function. In contrast, self-effacing interpersonal problems appeared almost intractable to psychotherapy over the course of 38 sessions. Patients with cold interpersonal problems related to detached behaviors initially appeared intractable; however, they seemed to improve progressively after the seventeenth session.

McLemore and Benjamin (1979) argued that interpersonal functioning is an essential component of the diagnostic process, in addition to the assessment of symptoms. They pointed out that quite often the most useful aspects of psychiatric diagnoses are psychosocial in nature and that most diagnoses of "functional mental disorders" are made on the basis of observed interpersonal behavior. Psychotherapy research using the IIP-C demonstrates that interpersonal behavior is relevant to case conceptualization, treatment planning, and understanding of the therapeutic process.

Structural Analysis of Social Behavior (SASB)

A second prominent descriptive model in the interpersonal tradition is structural analysis of social behavior (SASB, Benjamin, 1974, 1979, 1984, 1996, 2000). SASB is a complex three-plane model that operationally defines interpersonal and intrapsychic interactions (see Figure 9.3). The dimensions underlying SASB include interdependence (i.e., enmeshment-differentiation on the vertical axis), affiliation (i.e., love-hate on the horizontal axis), and interpersonal focus (i.e., parent-like transitive actions toward others represented by the top plane, child-like intransitive reactions to others represented by the middle plane, and introjected actions directed toward the self represented by the bottom plane). The unique multiplane structure of SASB also incorporates Sullivan's concept of introjection — that is, the expected impact of interpersonal situations

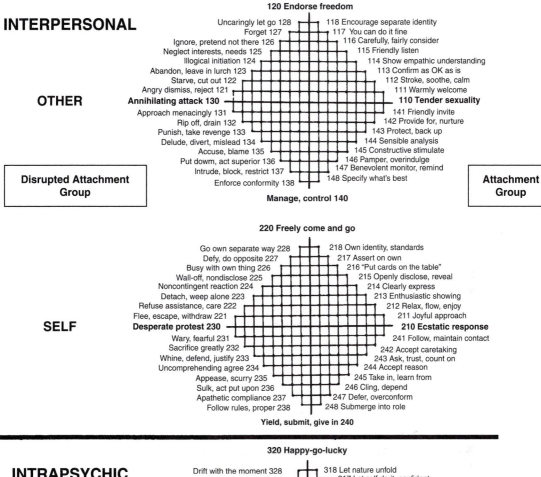

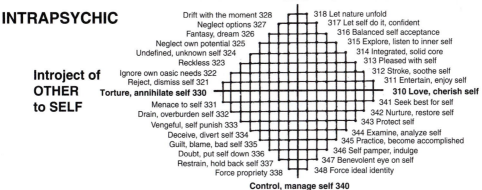

FIGURE 9.3 The Structural Analysis of Social Behavior full model. From Benjamin, L.S. (1979). Structural analysis of differentiation failure. *Psychiatry: Journal for the Study of Interpersonal Processes, 42,* 1–23. Copyright William Alanson Psychiatric Foundation.

on the self-concept — by proposing a third corresponding plane that reflects how one relates to self.

By separating transitive and intransitive behaviors into two planes, controlling and autonomy-granting are opposite interpersonal actions while submitting and autonomy-taking are opposite interpersonal reactions (Lorr, 1991). Dominance and submission are placed at comparable locations on different planes to reflect the fact that they are complementary positions rather than opposites. Thus, SASB expands interpersonal description by including taxa reflecting friendly and hostile differentiation (e.g., affirming, ignoring) not defined within the IPC structure as well as describing the introjected relationship with self. Although the vertical dimensions and complexity of SASB set it apart from the IPC, the same assumptions are applicable. Interpersonal behaviors located along the perimeters of the SASB planes represent blends of the basic

dimensions with the same spatial relations among points on each plane.

To complete the description, we note that attachment concepts have been incorporated into the SASB structure (Benjamin, 1993, 1996, 2003; Florsheim, Henry, & Benjamin, 1996; Henry, 1994). Boxes in Figure 9.3 denote that interpersonal behaviors reflecting secure attachment are on the right side of the planes (attachment group — AG), while interpersonal behaviors reflecting insecure attachment are on the left side of the planes (disrupted attachment group — DAG). Using this expanded taxonomy, SASB fully describes the interpersonal situation — that is, a real or internalized relationship rather than the individual differences or behaviors of a single interactant. Despite these differences, we view the IPC and SASB models as highly convergent in many respects, and they should be viewed as complementary approaches rather than mutually exclusive competitors (e.g., Pincus & Ansell, 2003; Pincus, Gurtman, & Ruiz, 1998; see Box 9.2).

HIGHLIGHT BOX 9.2

PSYCHOTHERAPY RESEARCH USING SASB

Benjamin's SASB model has been used extensively in psychotherapy research because it provides a descriptive language for interpersonal and intrapsychic processes, uses reliable self-report (Benjamin, 2000) and observer-coding (Benjamin & Cushing, 2000) assessment methodologies, and adheres to strong theoretical principles that aid clinicians and researchers in understanding psychopathology and the mechanisms of therapeutic change (Henry, 1996). In this section, we highlight some of the important psychotherapy studies using SASB (see Constantino, 2000, for a full review).

In a series of seminal studies, Henry, Strupp, and colleagues used SASB-based methods and found that positive and negative psychotherapy outcomes could be differentiated by the nature of interpersonal transactions in the therapeutic relationship (e.g., Bedics, Henry, & Adkins, 2005; Henry, Schacht, & Strupp, 1986, 1990; Hilliard, Henry, & Strupp, 2000; Talley, Strupp, & Morey; 1990). Compared to therapists in low-change cases, therapists in high-change cases engaged in significantly more affiliative control (e.g., helping and teaching behaviors) and affiliative autonomy granting (e.g., affirming and understanding) while exhibiting significantly less hostile control (e.g., blaming the client). Therapists and patients in high-change cases demonstrated significantly greater positive complementarity (i.e., exchanges marked by reciprocal affiliative and/or autonomy enhancing processes) and less negative complementarity (i.e., exchanges marked by reciprocal hostile and/or controlling processes) than in low-change cases. The results of these studies have been replicated by different groups of investigators in three different countries (Coady, 1991a, 1991b; Harrist, Quintana, Strupp, & Henry, 1994; Hildenbrand, Hildenbrand, & Junkert-Tress, 1994; Svartberg and Stiles, 1992).

SASB has also been used to investigate mechanisms of change in particular forms of psychotherapy. Shearin and Linehan (1992) examined four therapist-patient dyads using the SASB Intrex questionnaire to test several change hypotheses in dialectical behavior therapy for borderline personality disorder (DBT, Linehan, 1993). They wanted to investigate whether the hallmark technique of DBT (i.e., balancing of change and acceptance) would be more effective than pure change or pure acceptance techniques in reducing parasuicidal behavior in borderline patients. In SASB language, the dialectical behavior of the therapist would be represented by concurrent controlling, nurturing, and autonomy-granting behaviors (Constantino, 2000). Therapist behavior in this study was rated on the Intrex from both the therapist and client perspectives. Shearin and Linehan (1992) found that decreased parasuicidal behavior was significantly associated with client

ratings of therapists as concurrently instructing, controlling, and autonomy granting, as well as warm and understanding. Shearin and Linehan noted that the use of SASB provided valuable input for clinicians about helpful versus hindering interpersonal patterns in DBT sessions.

Finally, Greenberg and Foerster (1996) used SASB to examine mechanisms of change in emotion-focused therapy, specifically the moment-to-moment interpersonal and intrapsychic processes of the empty-chair technique (Greenberg, 1984). They found that SASB coding successfully captured the fine-grained processes involved in the empty-chair events. Their results showed that patients who were able to "work through" an important affect-laden conflict during the empty-chair event were more likely to be coded with "self-assertion, self-affirmation, or understand other" than were clients whose conflict remained unresolved.

As reviewed above, Benjamin's (1974) SASB model has shown considerable versatility and utility in the investigation of therapist-patient dynamics, therapy process, and client improvement. SASB is a complex system that provides a theoretically and empirically rigorous approach to the study of psychotherapy process and outcome. Given the demonstrated clinical utility of the SASB model, continued research using SASB is necessary to further our understanding about the mechanisms of change in psychotherapy.

Interpersonal Reciprocity and Transaction

Interpersonal behavior is not emitted in an isolated vacuum; rather it is reciprocally influential in ongoing human transaction. The notion of reciprocity in human relating has

been reflected in a wide variety of psychological concepts (Pincus & Ansell, 2003). Within the interpersonal tradition, these have typically been referred to in terms of adaptive and maladaptive transaction cycles (Kiesler, 1991) or self-fulfilling prophecies (Carson, 1982). If we assume that an interpersonal situation involves two or more people relating to each other in ways that bring about social and self-related learning, this implies that something more is happening than mere random activity. Reciprocal relational patterns create an interpersonal field (Wiggins & Trobst, 1999) in which various transactional influences impact both interactants as they integrate, negotiate, or disintegrate the interpersonal situation. Within this field, interpersonal behaviors tend to pull, elicit, invite, or evoke "restricted classes" of responses from the other, and this is a continual dynamic transactional process. Thus, the interpersonal tradition emphasizes "field regulatory" processes in addition to "self-regulatory" and "affect regulatory" processes (Mitchell, 1988; Pincus, 2005a).

Sullivan (1948) initially conceived of reciprocal processes in terms of basic conjunctive and disjunctive forces that lead to integration or disintegration of the interpersonal situation. Later, he formally presented his "theorem of reciprocal emotions," which stated that "integration in an interpersonal situation is a process in which (1) complementary needs are resolved (or aggravated); (2) reciprocal patterns of activity are developed (or disintegrated); and (3) foresight of satisfaction (or rebuff) of similar needs is facilitated" (Sullivan, 1953b, p. 129). While this theorem was a powerful interpersonal assertion, it lacked specificity, and "the surviving general notion of complementarity was that actions of human participants are redundantly interrelated (i.e., have patterned regularity) in some manner over the sequence of transactions" (Kiesler, 1983, p. 198).

Leary's (1957) "principle of reciprocal interpersonal relations" further specified the basis for patterned regularity of interpersonal behavior, stating, "interpersonal reflexes tend (with a probability greater than chance) to initiate or invite reciprocal interpersonal responses from the 'other' person in the interaction that lead to a repetition of the original reflex" (p. 123).

Learning in interpersonal situations takes place, in part, because social interaction is reinforcing (Leary, 1957). Carson (1991) referred to this as an interbehavioral contingency process where "there is a tendency for a given individual's interpersonal behavior to be constrained or controlled in more or less predictable ways by the behavior received from an interaction partner" (p. 191).

Reciprocal Interpersonal Patterns

Both the IPC and SASB provide conceptual anchors and a lexicon to systematically describe the patterned regularity of reciprocal interpersonal processes. The most central of these processes is referred to as interpersonal **complementarity** (Kiesler, 1983). Interpersonal complementarity occurs when there is a match between the field regulatory goals of each person, that is, reciprocal patterns of activity evolve where the interpersonal needs of both persons are met in the interpersonal situation, leading to stability and likely recurrence of the pattern. Carson (1969) first proposed that complementarity could be defined via the IPC based on the social exchange of status and love as reflected in reciprocity for the vertical dimension (i.e., dominance pulls for submission; submission pulls for dominance) and correspondence for the horizontal dimension (friendliness pulls for friendliness; hostility pulls for hostility). Given the continuous nature of the circular model's descriptions of behavior, the principles of reciprocity and correspondence can be employed to specify complementary points along the entire IPC perimeter. The principles of complementarity also hold for SASB. On this model, complementary behaviors are described by matching points on the two interpersonal planes. The complement of point 140 — Manage, control is point 240 — Yield, submit. The complement of point 111 — Warmly welcome is point 211 — Joyful approach.

While complementarity is neither the only reciprocal interpersonal pattern that can be

TABLE 9.2 Reciprocal Interpersonal Patterns Defined by the IPC and SASB Models

Reciprocal Patterns — Interpersonal Circle

Complementarity	Reciprocity on Dominance, Correspondence on Nurturance
Example:	Arrogant Vindictiveness (BC) → Social Avoidance (FG)
Acomplementarity	Reciprocity on Dominance *or* Correspondence of Nurturance (but not both)
Example:	Arrogant Vindictiveness (BC) → Arrogant Vindictiveness (BC)
Anticomplementarity	Neither Reciprocity on Dominance nor Correspondence on Nurturance
Example:	Warm Gregariousness (NO) → Arrogant Vindictiveness (BC)

Reciprocal Patterns — Structural Analysis of Social Behavior (Predictive Principles)

Complementarity	Corresponding Points across Other (Transitive) and Self (Intransitive) Planes
Example:	Put down, act superior (Point 136) → Sulk, act put upon (Point 236)
Similarity	Corresponding Points on Other (Transitive) or Self (Intransitive) Planes
Example:	Go own separate way (Point 228) → Go own separate way (Point 228)
Opposites	Opposing Points on Other (Transitive) or Self (Intransitive) Planes
Example:	Approach menacingly (Point 131) → Warmly welcome (Point 111)
Antithesis	Opposite of the Complementary Point
Example:	Cling, depend (Point 246) → Ignore, pretend not there (Point 126)

described using these models (see Table 9.2 for a summary) nor a proposed universal law of interaction, empirical studies consistently find support for its probabilistic predictions (e.g., Gurtman, 2001; Markey, Funder, & Ozer, 2003; Tracey, 1994). Complementarity is most helpful if considered a common baseline for the field regulatory pulls and invitations of interpersonal behavior. Used this way, chronic deviations from complementary reciprocal patterns may be indicative of pathological functioning. The patterned regularity in human transaction directly affects the outcomes of interpersonal situations. Complementary reciprocal patterns are considered to promote relational consistency, that is, such interpersonal situations are mutually reinforcing and recurring. Patterns that moderately deviate from complementarity are less stable and instigate negotiation toward or away from greater complementarity. This can be used by therapists to select interpersonal responses that may invite/pull for new patient behaviors within the therapeutic relationship. Finally, highly noncomplementary patterns are the most unstable and lead to avoidance, escape, and disintegration of the interpersonal situation (i.e., disrupted interpersonal relations).

Interpersonal Transaction Cycles

If we regard interpersonal behavior as influential or "field regulatory," there must be some basic goals toward which our behaviors are directed. Sullivan (1953b) viewed the self-system to be a dynamism that is built up from the positive reflected appraisals of significant others, allowing for relatively anxiety-free functioning and high levels of felt security and self-esteem. The self-system becomes relatively stable over time due to the self-perpetuating influence it has on awareness and organization of interpersonal experience (input) and on the field regulatory influences of interpersonal behavior (output). Sullivan proposed that both our perceptions of others' behaviors toward us and our enacted behaviors are strongly affected by our self-concept. When we interact with others, a proximal interpersonal field is created where behavior serves to present and define our self-concept and negotiate the kinds of interactions and relationships we seek from others. Sullivan's (1953b) theorem of reciprocal emotion and Leary's (1957) principle of reciprocal interpersonal relations have led to the formal view that what we attempt to regulate in the interpersonal field are the responses of the other. "Interpersonal behaviors, in a relatively unaware, automatic, and unintended fashion, tend to invite, elicit, pull, draw, or entice from interactants restricted classes of reactions that are reinforcing of, and consistent with, a person's proffered self-definition" (Kiesler, 1983, p. 201; see also Kiesler, 1996). To the extent that individuals can mutually satisfy their needs for interaction that exhibit congruence with their self-definitions (i.e., complementarity), the interpersonal situation remains integrated. To the extent this fails, negotiation or disintegration of the interpersonal situation is more probable.

What is likely obvious to the reader at this point is that psychotherapists may need to avoid responding to patients in complementary ways to avert reinforcing their maladaptive relational patterns and to inject a new interpersonal influence into the therapeutic transaction. For example, a patient treated by the first author would become highly enraged when she felt misunderstood. At these times her face would flush red, and she would curse at me and physically threaten to smash things in my office. Her intense hostility evoked complementary hostility from me, and I had the impulse to chastise her behavior and threaten to end treatment if it continued. Instead, I offered a more nurturing response and calmly said, "I can see that something I've done or not done today has made you feel very angry with me. Could you tell me more about this?" When she was questioned like this, the blood would drain from the patient's face; she would visibly

relax and begin telling me (in a therapeutically constructive way) how I messed up.

Interpersonal complementarity (or any other reciprocal pattern) should not be conceived of as some sort of stimulus-response process based solely on overt behavioral actions and reactions (Pincus, 1994). Interpersonal theorists have proposed a variety of intrapsychic processes that mediate individuals' perceptions of the interpersonal situation (input) and their overt reactions to others (output). A comprehensive account of the contemporaneous interpersonal situation must somehow bridge the gap between the proximal interpersonal situation and the internal interpersonal situation of mental representation (e.g., Pincus, 2005a; Pincus & Ansell, 2003; Safran, 1992). Kiesler's (1986, 1988, 1991, 1996) **interpersonal transaction cycle** is the most widely applied framework to describe the relations among proximal and internal interpersonal situations within the interpersonal tradition. He proposed that the basic components of an interpersonal transaction are (1) person P's covert experience of person Q, (2) person P's overt behavior toward person Q, (3) person Q's covert experience in response to Person P's action, and (4) person Q's overt behavioral response to person P. These four components are part of an ongoing transactional chain of relational events cycling toward integration, further negotiation, or disintegration. Within this process, overt behavioral output serves the purpose of regulating the proximal interpersonal field via elicitation of complementarity overt responses in the other. An interpersonal transaction is adaptive when the interbehavioral contingencies mutually satisfy the interpersonal needs of both interactants, that is, interpersonal input and output are relatively contingent upon each other.

An interpersonal transaction becomes maladaptive when person P relies on a limited class of interpersonal behaviors, reducing the potential for mutual complementary interbehavioral contingency and thus limiting person Q to a restricted class of responses complementary to person P's narrow repertoire. The impact of person Q's complementary responses is to confirm or validate person P's covert experiences of self, other, and relationship and thus escalate person P's repetition of the rigid, and often extreme, interpersonal behaviors that began the cycle. Kiesler points out that the initial complementary responses may feel mutually satisfying and the interpersonal situation remains integrated. However, as the transaction recycles, the rigidity and extreme behaviors of person P will have an aversive impact on person Q. If the relationship cannot satisfy the interpersonal needs of *both* people, either disintegration or negative affect or both are likely (Kiesler et al., 1997). If person Q cannot disintegrate the situation, the transaction cycles to "impasse — locked into a recurrent enactment of the cycle of maladaptive self-fulfilling prophecy and behavior" (Kiesler, 1986, p. 59).

Psychotherapy with personality disordered patients provides a clear example (Pincus, 2005a). Therapists generally attempt to work in the patient's best interest and promote a positive therapeutic alliance. Patients who are generally free of personality pathology typically enter therapy hoping for relief of their symptoms and are capable of experiencing the therapist as a potentially helpful and benign expert. Thus, the overt (proximal) and covert (internal) interpersonal situations are consistent with each other, and the behaviors of therapist and patient are likely to develop into a complementary reciprocal pattern (i.e., a therapeutic alliance in which the therapist exhibits helpful, friendly dominance and the patient exhibits receptive, friendly submissiveness). Despite psychotherapists taking a similar stance with personality disordered patients, the beginning of therapy is often quite rocky as the patients tend to view the therapists with suspicion, fear, contempt, and the like. The covert (internal) interpersonal situation is not consistent with the overt (proximal) interpersonal situation, and the patient and therapist likely begin

treatment by experiencing noncomplementary reciprocal patterns requiring further negotiation of the therapeutic relationship. To return to Sullivanian concepts momentarily, therapeutic relationships of this nature are much more likely to occur with patients whose social learning histories are markedly dysfunctional or traumatic, leading them to experience many interpersonal situations as anxiety provoking. Under such conditions, patients exhibit disturbed interpersonal relations via employment of rigid security operations and a tendency toward parataxic distortion of the current situation.

Interpersonal Psychotherapies

The interpersonal tradition in clinical psychology is an integrative nexus reflected in multiple therapeutic approaches employing a variety of relational, cognitive, behavioral, and interpretive techniques. In the following section, we describe five interpersonal psychotherapies that share the features listed in Table 9.1. They differ in their use of specific intervention techniques and the degree to which they focus on interpersonal behavior within the therapeutic relationship or interpersonal behavior in relationships external to the therapy (see Table 9.3).

Interpersonal Metacommunication

Blending Sullivan's (1953) interpersonal theory with the principles of communication theory, Kiesler's (1982, 1988, 1996) interpersonal metacommunication (IM) approach to psychotherapy considered the relationship between patient and therapist to be the central component of the therapeutic process. He wrote that "every event or intervention that occurs within psychotherapy does so with some aspect of the relationship serving either as its direct mechanism or its immediate context" (Kiesler, 1996, p. 217). In IM there are two halves to every relationship: the first half, which consists

TABLE 9.3 Intervention Approaches Employed Across Interpersonal Psychotherapies

Interventions	Interpersonal Psychotherapies				
	IM	CIT	IPT	IRT	CIITx
Focus on Therapist-Patient Relationship	♦	♦		♦	♦
Focus on External Relationships		♦	♦	♦	♦
Cognitive Therapy Techniques	♦	♦	♦	♦	♦
Behavioral Techniques		♦	♦	♦	♦
Interpretive Techniques				♦	♦

of the verbal and nonverbal evoking messages sent by an encoder (patient) to a decoder (therapist), and the second half, which consists of the messages that are registered covertly by the decoder (therapist) in response to the encoder's (patient's) messages. Kiesler referred to this second half of the relationship as **impact messages**, or the emotional, cognitive, and fantasy responses that are elicited in the therapist in response to the patient's verbal and nonverbal evoking messages. Many people are not directly attuned to their covert experience of impact messages; however, like Sullivan, Kiesler stresses that the therapist must become facile at attending to and identifying these highly automatic interpersonal events as they occur in session.

The interventions of IM target the recurrent and thematic relationship issues that occur between patient and therapist. In the initial sessions of psychotherapy, the patient unknowingly enacts his or her maladaptive transaction cycle (MAC, i.e., their particular repetitive self-defeating cycle of maladaptive interpersonal behavior) with the therapist. In response, the therapist experiences covert impact messages that generate automatic and often complementary patterns of responding to the patient. Because impact messages are registered covertly, the therapist may not initially be aware of how he or she is responding to the patient, which often results in the continued enactment of the MAC between patient and therapist. For example, if a depressed patient continually sends evoking messages that are unassured and submissive, the therapist's automatic complementary response may be to offer advice or instruction. However, this response by the therapist simply reinforces the MAC and confirms or validates the patient's expectancies, cognitions, or fantasies about self and other. An essential component of IM asserts that the therapist must quickly become aware of his or her covert impact messages and then must disengage from providing the automatic complementary response to the patient as soon as possible (Kiesler, 1982, 1988, 1996).

Kiesler referred to the initial phase of therapy as the "hooked" stage, where the therapist continually responds to the patient in ways that are automatic and complementary and that reinforce the patient's MAC. Kiesler observed that it is difficult for the therapist to avoid this "hooking" by patients because they are adept at maintaining their maladaptive transactional style and expect complementary responses from significant others. It is important to note that Kiesler recognized the need for the therapist to be "hooked" by the patient's transactional style because it facilitates the early formation of the therapeutic alliance and allows the therapist to make an interpersonal diagnosis.

The IM therapist should begin a process of self-reflection as soon as the therapeutic relationship is formed, in order to begin the "unhooked" or disengaged stage of treatment. He maintained that the therapist should begin to question his or her experience of the patient by asking questions such as "What is this patient trying to evoke in me?" or "What am

I feeling when I am with this patient?" and suggested that use of the Impact Message Inventory (IMI, Kiesler & Schmidt, 1993), a self-report measure examining the experience of impact messages, could help to guide the therapist's process of self-exploration in early sessions (Kiesler, 1996). Once the therapist has become aware of his or her impact messages, then the therapist is in a position to stop responding to the patient in complementary ways. In the example provided above, the therapist who feels pulled to offer advice or instruction to the submissive patient would now withhold this automatic complementary response and shift to a more asocial response such as silence, reflection of content or feeling, or a comment about the transactional style of the patient (Kiesler, 1996). By responding in an asocial manner, the therapist begins to disrupt the patient's MAC and elicits interpersonal uncertainty in the patient. Beier (1966) termed this "beneficial uncertainty" because the patient can now begin to work with the therapist to explore and understand maladaptive patterns.

A second response strategy would be to provide the anticomplementary response to the patient's evoking message. By using the anticomplementary response, the therapist is exerting the greatest amount of pressure on the patient to change his or her rigid interpersonal behavior. However, Kiesler cautioned that this type of response can often be viewed as hostile or rejecting by the patient and should not be initiated early in treatment or before the working therapeutic alliance is firmly established. Benjamin (1996, 2003) recommends following the Shaurette principle of graded asocial responding by the therapist to slowly and sequentially modify the patient's interpersonal behaviors.

One of the most powerful asocial responses is therapeutic metacommunication. According to Kiesler (1988, 1996), metacommunication occurs when the patient's pattern of verbal and nonverbal interaction styles becomes the topic of communication between patient and therapist in session. Kiesler (1988) stated that therapeutic metacommunication refers to "any instance in which the therapist provides to the patient verbal feedback that targets the central, recurrent, and thematic relationship issues occurring between them in their therapy sessions" (p. 39). Rather than simply confirming the patient's maladaptive expectations, feelings, and fantasies about relationships, the therapist opens up dialogue about the covert transactional process that is occurring in the therapeutic relationship. In providing metacommunicative feedback, the therapist may make impact disclosures, where he or she "reveals to patients their inner covert reactions which they experience as directly evoked by the patients' recurrent behaviors during psychotherapy" (Kiesler, 1988, pp. 1–2). The intent of therapeutic metacommunication is to provide feedback to the patient about his or her maladaptive interpersonal behaviors and use the context of the therapeutic relationship to explore the patient's central interpersonal problems.

Kiesler outlined several important principles of therapeutic metacommunication. First, the therapist must provide feedback in a manner that is confrontational as well as supportive and protective of the patient's self-esteem. As indicated earlier, Sullivan (1953a, 1953b) believed that threats to the self-system can create high levels of anxiety for patients; accordingly, effective delivery of metacommunicative feedback must take place within a safe and supportive working therapeutic alliance. Second, the therapist should offer the metacommunicative feedback in a manner that facilitates exploration within session. Because the purpose of the feedback is to help the patient understand and change his or her maladaptive patterns, it should be provided as a tentative hypothesis so that the therapist and patient can collaboratively explore and modify the therapist's feedback. The therapist should also be prepared to explore his or her own contributions to the patient-therapist transactional cycle; therapeutic metacommunication is two-sided, with both participants examining their contributions to the relationship. Similarly, if the therapist maintains an affiliative and collaborative relationship with the patient, then the patient will actually hear, incorporate, and respond to the feedback rather than walling off or distancing from the therapist. Finally, and importantly, the therapist cannot simply point out his or her impact messages; rather, the therapist must pinpoint specific instances in the therapeutic relationship when the patient's action elicited these responses and make hypotheses about the covert experiences of the patient that may have precipitated maladaptive patterns and behaviors.

Through therapeutic metacommunication, the patient begins to identify and understand his or her basic maladaptive transactional pattern with others, which is the first step toward healthier, more adaptive interpersonal patterns. Sullivan (1953b) noted that "one achieves mental health to the extent that one becomes aware of one's interpersonal relations" (p. 207). By addressing the therapeutic relationship directly, the therapist models for the patient a more adaptive way of communicating with significant others, thus changing the patient's MAC (Kiesler, 1996).

Cognitive-Interpersonal Therapy

In the early 1980s, Jeremy Safran and colleagues extended Kiesler's IM approach to develop an integrative psychotherapy that synthesizes cognitive therapy with principles emerging from the interpersonal tradition. The cognitive-interpersonal therapy (CIT) approach places particular emphasis on the role that the therapist plays as a participant observer in the therapeutic process and indicates that the therapist's own feelings can provide important clues for how to explore the therapeutic relationship. The central goal of the cognitive-interpersonal approach is to identify and modify the key dysfunctional cognitive structures and interpersonal patterns in a patient's life (Marcotte & Safran, 2002; Safran, 1990a, 1990b; Safran & Segal, 1990).

Safran and colleagues extended the concept of self-schema (e.g. Markus, 1977) to include the **interpersonal schema**, which is a "generic representation of self-other interactions that is abstracted from interpersonal experience" (Safran & Segal, 1990, p. 66). The interpersonal schema reflects the cognitive, affective, and interpersonal processes that are integrated to maintain relatedness. As a generic representation, the interpersonal schema holds the goals and "if-then" contingencies that regulate the maintenance of relatedness and facilitates the anticipation of future interactions (Marcotte & Safran, 2002; Safran, 1990a; Safran & Segal, 1990).

A **cognitive-interpersonal cycle** is created by expectancies about interactions that are driven by interpersonal schemas. These cycles reflect the stable influence of a learned relational style that can be either adaptive or maladaptive for maintaining relatedness. Because interpersonal schemas and cognitive-interpersonal cycles are at the center of an individual's motivation for relatedness, they can often be detected by identifying points of reference in the patient's behavior. These points of reference are referred to as **interpersonal markers** because they serve as indicators of key cognitive and interpersonal processes that influence the patient's interactions with others (Safran, 1990b). Interpersonal markers function to elicit affective or behavioral responses in others, such as the therapist. For example, a therapist may feel distracted or bored in session whenever the patient moves away from affect and begins to intellectualize. This affective response of boredom in the therapist is a signal for the corresponding behavior in the patient.

Identifying and tracking these interpersonal markers enable the therapist to clarify the patient's way of encoding and reacting to interpersonal experiences.

Once the therapist has identified a significant interpersonal marker, the therapist should begin therapeutic metacommunication with the patient. Awareness of interpersonal schemas and cycles increases as the therapist continually draws the patient's attention to the relevant marker as it occurs on different occasions in the therapeutic relationship. As the patient gains the ability to recognize his or her markers, homework assignments to monitor their appearance between sessions help the patient to increase self-monitoring and begin to change their automatic relational styles. By responding to the patient's interpersonal markers in a new and therapeutic manner, the therapist also provides new interpersonal experiences that help to disconfirm the patient's dysfunctional interpersonal schemas (Marcotte & Safran, 2002; Safran, 1990a, 1990b; Safran & Segal, 1990).

Interpersonal Psychotherapy

Interpersonal psychotherapy (IPT) is a time-limited treatment for adult outpatients with major depression that was developed by Klerman, Weissman, and colleagues in the 1970s and was also based on Sullivan's interpersonal theory (see Klerman, Weissman, Rounsaville, & Chevron, 1984, for a full review). IPT assumes that life events influence the manifestation of psychopathology and strives to find the connection between current life events and the onset of symptoms in order to help patients understand and cope with their depression. The overall strategy of IPT is to resolve an interpersonal problem (e.g., deal with grief, a role dispute or role transition, or an interpersonal deficit) so that patients will improve their life situation and simultaneously relieve their symptoms (Weissman & Markowitz, 2002).

IPT is an eclectic therapy, using techniques developed in various psychotherapies. It overlaps to some degree with psychodynamic psychotherapies and cognitive-behavioral therapies; however, it is not the specific techniques of IPT but rather its overall goals and strategies that make it a unique and coherent treatment approach (Weissman & Markowitz, 2002). The strategies of IPT include an *opening question* that leads the patients to provide information about their mood and life events; a *communication analysis* that involves a re-creation of recent affectively charged life circumstances; an *exploration of the patient's wishes and options* to achieve those wishes in particular interpersonal situations; a *decision analysis* that helps the patient to decide which options to employ in meeting their interpersonal goals; and *role playing* to help the patient rehearse tactics for real life. Using these strategies, the therapist repeatedly helps the patient to link life events to current mood and symptoms. IPT focuses on the patient's current social context and attempts to intervene in the specific symptoms associated with depression rather than addressing enduring aspects of personality (Weissman & Markowitz, 2002).

IPT is a manualized treatment that typically lasts about 12 to 16 weeks and has three phases. The first phase usually lasts from one to three sessions and includes diagnostic evaluation and psychiatric history. During this initial phase, the IPT therapist reviews the patient's symptoms, diagnoses the patient as depressed according to psychiatric criteria, educates the patient about depression and therapy, and links the patient's depressive symptoms to current interpersonal relationships and current life events. The therapist and patient identify a particular interpersonal problem area that will become the focus of treatment, such as grief, role disputes or role transitions, or interpersonal deficits. If the patient agrees to treatment and is willing to work on current relationships and life events to alleviate his or her depressive symptoms, then therapy enters the middle phase.

Each session in the middle phase of treatment begins with an opening question, such as "How have things been since we last met?" in order to focus the patient on the current interpersonal events that may be linked to his or her depressed mood. The therapist then pursues strategies specific to the chosen interpersonal problem area. For example, if the therapist and patient are working on a role dispute (e.g., a conflict with a significant other), the therapist may begin by exploring the patient's wishes and fears about the conflicted relationship. The focus of this exploration is on the "here and now" and helps the patient to clarify the nature of the relationship, the nature of the dispute, how the dispute may be maintaining the depressed mood, and what options may exist for resolving the current conflict. By exploring how the patient can change his or her current interpersonal situation, the therapist demonstrates to the patient that options for change exist, thereby giving the patient hope. The therapist also facilitates the development of skills that may allow the patient to resolve the current conflict that is underlying the depressed mood. In particular, the IPT therapist often uses role playing to help patients practice and rehearse how to communicate their interpersonal needs and goals to their significant others. IPT therapists continually encourage patients to test the skills learned in therapy with their significant others in order to improve their current interpersonal situation, consolidate treatment gains, and alleviate their depressive symptoms. Throughout treatment, IPT therapists take an active, supportive, and hopeful stance in order to counter the patient's depressive affect. As patients begin to use these skills in their daily life and resolve their interpersonal problem area, then their depressive symptoms will be alleviated.

The final phase of IPT lasts about three to four sessions. The goal of these final sessions is to support the patient's newly regained sense of competence by recognizing and consolidating treatment gains. The therapist also helps the patient to anticipate and develop ways of identifying and countering depressive symptoms that could arise in the future. Compared to traditional psychodynamic treatment, IPT deemphasizes termination. Termination is viewed as a graduation; the patient has now gained the skills to resolve his or her interpersonal problems and alleviate depressed mood (Weissman, Markowtz, & Klerman, 2000; Weissman & Markowitz, 2002).

Interpersonal Reconstructive Therapy

Benjamin (1993, 1996, 2003) advanced both interpersonal theory and therapy by expanding conceptions of how and why social learning catalyzes into recurrent interpersonal schemas and patterns. Interpersonal behavior patterns are learned (or internalized) in three ways referred to as **interpersonal copy processes** linked to **important persons and their internalized representations (IPIRs).** These processes, coupled explicitly to the SASB model, identify the nature of interpersonal learning in child development (see Table 9.4). Identification refers to learning to treat others as you have been treated by IPIRs. Recapitulation refers to continuing to behave as if the IPIR is still present and in control — a notable source of parataxic distortions in current interpersonal situations. Introjection refers to

TABLE 9.4 Interpersonal Copy Processes

Copy Process	Interpersonal Behavior	SASB Plane
Identification	*Treat others as you were treated by IPIRs.*	Transitive Actions
Recapitulation	*Act as if IPIRs are still present and in control.*	Intransitive Reactions
Introjection	*Treat self as you were treated by IPIRs.*	Intrapsychic

learning to treat yourself as you were treated by IPIRs.

In addition, Benjamin's developmental learning and loving theory (DLL) proposed that the evolutionary goal of achieving attachment to caretakers promotes interpersonal learning, catalyzing copy processes in the service of attachment formation. In normative developmental environments, this leads to adaptive social learning that promotes positive interpersonal schemas and relational expectancies characterized by the secure attachment (AG) elements of the right side of the SASB model. In dysfunctional or toxic developmental environments, attachment formation will require maladaptive social learning that promotes negative interpersonal schemas and relational expectancies characterized by the disrupted attachment (DAG) elements of the left side of the SASB model (Pincus, Dickinson, Schut, Castonguay, & Bedics, 1999).

Interpersonal reconstructive therapy (IRT) was originally designed for personality disorders (Benjamin, 1996) and related intractable cases who had not responded to other forms of treatment (Benjamin, 2003). More recently, it has been extended to the treatment of anger, anxiety, and depression (Benjamin, in preparation). IRT begins with a DLL case formulation whereby the therapist assesses the patient's symptoms, interpersonal problems, and history to identify the patient's IPIRs. The SASB model is explicitly used to describe recurrent interpersonal patterns and to link symptomatic and interpersonal dysfunction to IPIRs via interpersonal copy processes. In most cases, patient presentations exhibit a mix of identifications, introjections, and tendencies to recapitulate old patterns in the service of maintaining loyalty and attachment to the IPIRs' rules and expectations of the patient. Once a case formulation has been consensually understood, IRT works through five therapeutic steps: (1) collaborating; (2) learning what the interpersonal patterns are, where they are from, and what they are for (all

from a DLL perspective); (3) blocking maladaptive patterns; (4) enabling the will to change; and (5) learning new patterns.

IRT utilizes all forms of therapeutic intervention to promote these steps as guided by the therapeutic core algorithm or "rules of engagement." The first rule is *work from a baseline of accurate empathy* established by focusing on the patient in a friendly way. In SASB terms, the therapist is enacting transitive friendly behaviors toward the patient with moderate amounts of interdependence (i.e., AG). The second rule is to *support the growth-oriented part of the patient more than the regressive part of the patient*. As Benjamin (2003) notes, "One part presents for treatment and wishes to become better adjusted, while the other wants to continue to demonstrate the problem behaviors, affects, and cognitions consistent with perceived rules and values of the IPIRs" (p. 22). While it is often the case that the regressive part of the patient is more dominant early in treatment, the therapist must form an alliance with the growth-oriented part of the patient. The third rule is to *relate every intervention to the case formulation*. This rule allows IRT to incorporate interpretive techniques that connect and explore current symptoms and relational experiences with their developmental antecedents. The fourth rule is to *seek concrete illustrative details about input, response, and impact on the self*. In other words, employ the SASB model to articulate the details of the relevant interpersonal situations associated with the patient's history and current problems. The fifth rule is to *explore patterns in terms of affect, behavior, and cognition*. Insight and new social learning are promoted when all three aspects of experience are activated and integrated. Intellectual understanding of the case conceptualization alone is insufficient to promote change. The final rule is to explicitly *relate any interventions to the goals of the current step in therapy*, continually reminding the patient of the sequence and goals of treatment.

IRT, like all interpersonal psychotherapies, incorporates diverse forms of intervention organized around specific interpersonal conceptions of personality, psychopathology, and change processes. While the therapeutic relationship itself is a vehicle for change, the IRT therapist is also a teacher; Benjamin offers several "speeches" for therapists to deliver to encourage patient insight, remind patients of the limits of therapy, enhance the will to change, and learn new ways of relating. Thus, IRT utilizes all the treatment strategies listed in Table 9.3 and is among the most integrative of the interpersonal psychotherapies.

Contemporary Integrative Interpersonal Therapy

The most recent development in IPT is contemporary integrative interpersonal therapy (CIITx), based on the expansion of Benjamin's DLL and copy process theories and integration of Sullivanian theory with an object relations–based understanding of personality structure (Pincus, 2005a; Pincus & Ansell, 2003; Pincus & Gurtman, 2006; Pincus et al., in press). Because the approach is quite new, we only briefly cover the basics here. CIITx extends the **catalysts of internalization** beyond attachment, suggesting that interpersonal copy processes are evoked in relation to a number of important developmental achievements (or failures) and traumatic learning experiences across the life span (see Table 9.5). Case conceptualization proceeds via articulating the interpersonal situations and mental representations of self and other associated with relevant developmental catalysts. Importantly, generalization of social learning occurs through the development of **regulatory metagoals**. The emerging developmental achievements and the coping demands of traumas listed in Table 9.5 all have significant implications for emotion regulation, self-regulation, and field regulation. This further contributes to the generalization of interpersonal learning to new interpersonal situations by providing a

TABLE 9.5   Catalysts of Interpersonal Learning

Developmental Achievements	Traumatic Learning
Attachment	Early Loss of Attachment Figure
Security	Childhood Illness or Injury
Separation/Individuation	Physical Abuse
Positive Affects	Sexual Abuse
Gender Identity	Emotional Abuse
Resolution of Oedipal Issues	Parental Neglect
Self-esteem	
Self-confirmation	
Mastery of Unresolved Conflicts	
Identity Formation	

small number of superordinate psychological triggers to activate internal interpersonal situations. These parataxic distortions are identified in the therapeutic relationship and are associated with their regulatory metagoals and developmental antecedents via a sequence of clarifying, confronting, and interpretive interventions. In CIITx, the therapeutic relationship is both a vehicle for change and a context for all therapeutic interventions employed. Like IRT, the focus is on linking present symptoms and interpersonal problems to past social learning and then engaging the patient's will to change via new social learning in and out of therapy.

CIITx proposes that the larger the range of proximal interpersonal situations that can be entered in which the person exhibits anxiety-free functioning (little need for emotion regulation) and maintains self-esteem (little need for self-regulation), the more adaptive the personality. When this is the case, there is no need to activate mediating internal interpersonal situations, and the person can focus on the proximal situation, encode incoming interpersonal input without distortion, respond in adaptive ways that facilitate interpersonal relations (i.e., meet the interpersonal needs of self and other), and establish complementary patterns of reciprocal behavior by fully participating in the proximal interpersonal field. The individual's current behavior will exhibit relatively strong contingency with the proximal behavior of the other and the normative contextual press of the situation. Adaptive interpersonal functioning is promoted by relatively trauma-free development in a culturally normative facilitating environment that has allowed the person to achieve most developmental milestones in normative ways, leading to full capacity to encode and elaborate incoming interpersonal input without bias from competing psychological needs.

In contrast, when the individual develops in a traumatic or nonnormative environment, significant nonnormative interpersonal learning around basic motives such as attachment, individuation, and gender identity may be internalized and associated with difficulties with self-regulation, emotion regulation, and field regulation. Disturbed interpersonal relations are reflected in a large range of proximal interpersonal situations that elicit anxiety (activating emotion regulation strategies), threaten self-esteem (activating self-regulation strategies), and elicit dysfunctional behaviors (nonnormative field regulation strategies). When this is the case, internal interpersonal situations are activated, and the individual is prone to exhibit various forms of parataxic distortion as his or her interpersonal learning history dictates. Thus the perception of the proximal interpersonal situation is mediated by internal experience, incoming interpersonal input is distorted, behavioral responses (output) disrupt interpersonal relations (i.e., fail to meet the interpersonal needs of self and other), and relationships tend toward noncomplementary

patterns of reciprocal behavior. The individual's current behavior will exhibit relatively weak contingency with the proximal behavior of the other. In the psychotherapy context, this can be identified by a preponderance of acomplementary and anticomplementary cycles of transaction between therapist and patient (Kiesler, 1988).

TRAINING

Because interpersonal psychotherapeutic approaches are integrative and typically not identified with a single school of intervention, training is often embedded and implicit (e.g., Strupp & Binder, 1984) as well as acquired through formal training programs. Among the best sources of information for advanced training is the Society for Interpersonal Theory and Research (SITAR), a scientific society founded in 1997 that brings together clinicians, researchers, and theorists associated with the interpersonal tradition (www.sitarsociety.org). Lorna Smith Benjamin (www.psych.utah.edu/people/faculty/benjamin/) routinely holds IRT workshops and continues to train IRT therapists in her clinic at the University of Utah Neuropsychiatric Hospital. Aaron Pincus (www.personal.psu.edu/alp6/) provides CIITx training through the doctoral program in clinical psychology at Pennsylvania State University. IPT training coordinated by the International Society for Interpersonal Psychotherapy (ISIPT) is readily available via professional workshops and conferences, and training courses conducted at university centers in the United States, Canada, Europe, Asia, and New Zealand (www.interpersonalpsychotherapy.org/). Finally, for those interested in interpersonal psychoanalysis, training is coordinated by the William Alanson White Institute of Psychiatry, Psychoanalysis, and Psychology in New York City (http://www.wawhite.org/home/home.htm).

THOUGHT QUESTIONS

9.1. Because the therapeutic relationship is considered to be a real relationship between patient and therapist, the interpersonal therapist must be willing to explore his or her own contributions to the relationship as well as share his or her own covert impact messages with the patient. What are some potential challenges you may encounter when sharing your reactions with a patient, and how would you address these challenges using interpersonal principles?

9.2. Many of the principles of the interpersonal tradition were developed by observing group psychotherapy. As a group therapist, how might you use the interpersonal circle, interpersonal communications, and the interpersonal transaction cycle to identify, understand, and explore group process?

9.3. Describe how the interpersonal circle may be helpful for case conceptualization and treatment planning when you are working with a personality disordered patient.

9.4. Imagine you are the therapist working with a suicidal patient who consistently sends you the message that you are to blame for his or her psychological difficulties. First, describe your impact messages in reaction to this patient. Second, describe your automatic complementary response to this patient. Third, describe the asocial response to this patient that may be most beneficial.

9.5. Therapists using the interpersonal tradition understand that by responding to a patient in an asocial manner (rather than providing the automatic complementary response), they are increasing the patient's anxiety and uncertainty. As an interpersonal therapist, how can you create "beneficial uncertainty" in the patient while still maintaining a working alliance?

Glossary

Catalysts of internalization: Important developmental achievements (or failures) and traumatic learning processes that stimulate the internalization of interpersonal experiences.

Cognitive-interpersonal cycle: The stable influence of an interpersonal schema that can be either adaptive or maladaptive for maintaining relatedness.

Complementarity: Reciprocal patterns of activity that evolve when the interpersonal needs of both persons are met in the interpersonal situation, leading to stability and likely recurrence of the pattern.

Dynamisms: Relatively consistent and complex learned patterns of interpersonal experience.

Impact messages: The emotional, cognitive, and fantasy responses that are elicited in the therapist in response to the patient's interpersonal communications.

Important persons and their internalized representations (IPIRs): Benjamin's concept of mental representations of self and other.

Interpersonal circle/interpersonal circumplex: A two-dimensional geometric representation of individual differences that is organized around the axes of Dominance and Nurturance.

Interpersonal communication: The verbal and nonverbal messages that are sent from the encoder (patient) to the decoder (therapist) to elicit a reciprocal response that confirms or validates the automatic self-presentation of the encoder.

Interpersonal copy processes: Benjamin's concept of how interpersonal experiences are internalized.

Interpersonal diagnosis: Use of patient symptoms, interpersonal behavior, and the interpersonal circle in case conceptualization and treatment planning.

Interpersonal markers: Points of reference in a patient's behavior that serve as indicators of key cognitive and interpersonal processes that are influencing the patient's interactions with others.

Interpersonal psychoanalysis: A psychoanalytic treatment that is based on Sullivan's interpersonal theory of psychiatry.

Interpersonal schema: A generic representation of self-other interactions that is abstracted from interpersonal experience.

Interpersonal situation: The experience of a pattern of relating self with other associated with varying levels of anxiety (or security) in which learning takes place that influences the development of self-concept and social behavior.

Interpersonal theory of psychiatry: Sullivan's paradigm-shifting and highly generative theory of psychiatry, which emphasized the importance of the relationship and broke away from traditional Freudian psychoanalytic theory.

Interpersonal tradition: A paradigm in clinical psychology and psychiatry that integrates interpersonal theory with empirical research using the interpersonal circle.

Interpersonal transaction cycle: Kiesler's framework for describing the basic components of an interpersonal transaction; these components include (1) person P's covert experience of person Q; (2) person P's overt behavior toward person Q; (3) person Q's covert experience in response to person P's action; and (4) person Q's overt behavioral response to person P.

Parataxic distortion: The immediate, often maladaptive, application of learned relational patterns in the covert interpretation of a present relationship.

Participant observer: Ability of the therapist to actively engage in a real relationship with the patient while also acutely observing the patient's interpersonal communications.

Personification: Sullivan's concept of mental representations of self and other.

Regulatory metagoals: Self-, affect-, and field-regulatory goals associated with developmental achievements (or failures) and traumatic learning processes that activate internalized interpersonal situations and learned patterns of interpersonal behavior.

Security operations: Mechanisms that serve to perpetuate and protect the self-system by minimizing anxiety via activation or inhibition of certain behaviors.

Self-system: A cumulative repertoire of dynamisms that protects an individual from anxiety and maintains interpersonal security.

References

Alden, L. E., Wiggins, J. S., & Pincus, A. L. (1990). Construction of circumplex scales for the Inventory of Interpersonal Problems. *Journal of Personality Assessment, 55,* 521–536.

Anchin, J. C. (1982). Interpersonal approaches to psychotherapy: summary and conclusions. In J. C. Anchin & D. F. Kiesler (Eds.), *Handbook of interpersonal psychotherapy* (pp. 313–330). New York: Pergamon Press.

Anchin, J. C. & Kiesler, D. J. (1982). *Handbook of interpersonal psychotherapy.* New York: Pergamon Press.

Bedics, J. D., Henry, W. P., & Atkins, D. C. (2005). The therapeutic process as a predictor of change in patients' important relationships during time-limited psychotherapy. *Psychotherapy: Theory, Research, Practice, Training, 42,* 279–284.

Beier, E. G. (1966). *The silent language of psychotherapy: social reinforcement of unconscious processes.* Chicago: Aldine.

Benjamin, L. S. (1973). A biological model for understanding the behavior of individuals. In J. Westman (Ed.), *Individual differences in children* (pp. 215–241). New York: Wiley.

Benjamin, L. S. (1974). Structural analysis of social behavior. *Psychological Review, 81,* 392–425.

Benjamin, L. S. (1979). Structural analysis of differentiation failure. *Psychiatry, 42,* 1–23.

Benjamin, L. S. (1984). Principles of prediction using Structural Analysis of Social Behavior (SASB). In R. A. Zucker, J. Arnoff, & A. J. Rabin (Eds.), *Personality and the prediction of behavior* (pp. 121–173). New York: Academic Press.

Benjamin, L. S. (1993). Every psychopathology is a gift of love. *Psychotherapy Research, 3,* 1–24.

Benjamin, L. S. (1996). *Interpersonal diagnosis and treatment of personality disorders* (2nd ed.). New York: Guilford Press.

Benjamin, L. S. (2000). *Intrex user's manual.* Salt Lake City: University of Utah.

Benjamin, L. S. (2003). *Interpersonal reconstructive therapy.* New York: Guilford Press.

Benjamin, L. S. (2005). Addressing interpersonal and intrapsychic components of personality during psychotherapy. In S. Strack (Ed.), *Handbook of personology and psychopathology* (pp. 417–441). New York: Wiley.

Benjamin, L. S. (in preparation). *Interpersonal reconstructive therapy for anger, anxiety, and depression.* Washington, DC: American Psychological Association.

Benjamin, L. S. & Cushing, G. (2000). *Manual for coding social interactions in terms of structural analysis of social behavior.* Salt Lake City: University of Utah.

Blatt, S. J., Auerbach, J. S., & Levy, K. N. (1997). Mental representations in personality development, psychopathology, and therapeutic process. *Review of General Psychology, 1,* 351–373.

Carson, R. C. (1969). *Interaction concepts of personality.* Chicago: Aldine.

Carson, R. C. (1982). Self-fulfilling prophecy, maladaptive behavior, and psychotherapy. In J. C. Anchin & D. F. Kiesler (Eds.), *Handbook of interpersonal psychotherapy* (pp. 64–77). New York: Pergamon Press.

Carson, R. C. (1991). The social-interactional viewpoint. In M. Hersen, A. Kazdin, & A. Bellack (Eds.), *The clinical psychology handbook* (pp. 185–199). New York: Pergamon Press.

Carson, R. C. (1996). Seamlessness in personality and its derangements. *Journal of Personality Assessment, 66,* 240–247.

Castonguay, L. G. & Beutler, L. E. (2006). Principles of therapeutic change: a task force on participants, relationships, and technique factors. *Journal of Clinical Psychology, 62,* 631–638.

Chapman, A. H. (1978). *The treatment techniques of Harry Stack Sullivan.* Northvale, NJ: Jason Aronson.

Coady, N. F. (1991a). The association between client and therapist: interpersonal process and outcomes in psychodynamic psychotherapy. *Research on Social Work Practice, 1,* 122–138.

Coady, N. F. (1991b). The association between complex types of therapist interventions and outcomes in psychodynamic psychotherapy. *Research on Social Work Practice, 1,* 257–277.

Coffey, H. S., Freedman, M. B., Leary, T. F., & Ossorio, A. G. (1950). Community service and social research — group psychotherapy in a church setting. *Journal of Social Issues, 6,* 1–65.

Constantino, M. J. (2000). Interpersonal process in psychotherapy through the lens of the structural analysis of social behavior. *Applied & Preventative Psychology, 9,* 153–172.

Florsheim, P., Henry, W. P., & Benjamin, L. S. (1996). Integrating individual and interpersonal approaches to diagnosis: the structural analysis of social behavior and attachment theory. In F. Kaslow (Ed.), *Handbook of relational diagnosis* (pp. 81–101). New York: Wiley.

Fournier, M. A., Moskowitz, D. S., & Zuroff, D. C. (2008). Integrating dispositions, signatures and the interpersonal domain. *Journal of Personality and Social Psychology, 94,* 531–545.

Freedman, M. B., Leary, T., Ossorio, A. G., & Coffey, H. S. (1951). The interpersonal dimension of personality. *Journal of Personality, 20,* 143–161.

Gifford, R. (1991). Mapping nonverbal behavior on the interpersonal circle. *Journal of Personality and Social Psychology, 61,* 279–288.

Golding, S. L. (1978). Toward a more adequate theory of personality: psychological organizing principles. In H. London (Ed.), *Personality: a new look at metatheories* (pp. 69–95). Washington, DC: Hemisphere.

Greenberg, J. R. & Mitchell, S. A. (1983). *Object relations in psychoanalytic theory.* Cambridge, MA: Harvard University Press.

Greenberg, L. S. (1984). A task analysis of interpersonal conflict resolution. In L. N. Rice & L. S. Greenberg (Eds.), *Patterns of change: intensive analysis of psychotherapy process* (pp. 67–123). New York: Guilford Press.

Greenberg, L. S. & Foerster, F. (1996). Task analysis exemplified: the process of resolving unfinished business. *Journal of Consulting and Clinical Psychology, 64,* 439–446.

Gurtman, M. B. (1996). Interpersonal problems and the psychotherapy context: the construct validity of the Inventory of Interpersonal Problems. *Psychological Assessment, 5,* 241–255.

Gurtman, M. B. (2001). Interpersonal complementarity: integrating interpersonal measurement with interpersonal models. *Journal of Counseling Psychology, 48,* 97–110.

Harrist, R. S., Quintana, S. M., Strupp, H. H., & Henry, W. P. (1994). Internalization of interpersonal process in time-limited dynamic psychotherapy. *Psychotherapy, 31,* 49–57.

Henry, W. P. (1994). Differentiating normal and abnormal personality: an interpersonal approach based on the structural analysis of social behavior. In S. Strack & M. Lorr (Eds.), *Differentiating normal and abnormal personality*. New York: Springer.

Henry, W. P. (1996). Structural analysis of social behavior as a common metric for programmatic psychopathology and psychotherapy research. *Journal of Consulting and Clinical Psychology, 64*, 1263–1275.

Henry, W. P., Schacht, T. E., & Strupp, H. H. (1986). Structural analysis of social behavior: application to the study of interpersonal process in differential therapy outcome. *Journal of Consulting and Clinical Psychology, 54*, 27–31.

Henry, W. P., Schacht, T. E., & Strupp, H. H. (1990). Patient and therapist introject, interpersonal process, and differential psychotherapeutic outcome. *Journal of Consulting and Clinical Psychology, 58*, 768–774.

Hilldenbrand, G., Hilldenbrand, B., & Junkert-Tress, B. (1994, July). *Dropping out of therapy: analysis of cyclic maladaptive pattern and interpersonal process in prematurely terminated dynamic psychotherapy*. Paper presented at the annual meeting of the Society for Psychotherapy Research, York.

Hilliard, R. B., Henry, W. P., & Strupp, H. H. (2000). An interpersonal model of psychotherapy: linking patient and therapist developmental history, therapeutic process, and types of outcome. *Journal of Consulting and Clinical Psychology, 68*, 125–133.

Horowitz, L. M. (1979). On the cognitive structure of interpersonal problems treated in psychotherapy. *Journal of Consulting and Clinical Psychology, 47*, 5–15.

Horowitz, L. M. (2004). *Interpersonal foundations of psychopathology*. Washington, DC: American Psychological Association.

Horowitz, L. M., Rosenberg, S. E., Baer, B. A., Ureno, G., & Villasenor, V. S. (1988). Inventory of Interpersonal Problems: psychometric properties and clinical applications. *Journal of Consulting and Clinical Psychology, 56*, 885–892.

Horowitz, L. M., Rosenberg, S. E., & Bartholomew, K. (1993). Interpersonal problems, attachment styles, and outcome in brief dynamic therapy. *Journal of Consulting and Clinical Psychology, 61*, 549–561.

Horowitz, L. M., Rosenberg, S. E., & Kalehzan, B. M. (1992). The capacity to describe other people clearly: a predictor of interpersonal problems in brief dynamic psychotherapy. *Psychotherapy Research, 2*, 37–51.

Horowitz, L. M. & Vitkus, J. (1986). The interpersonal basis of psychiatric symptoms. *Clinical Psychology Review, 6*, 443–469.

Kiesler, D. J. (1966). Some myths of psychotherapy research and the search for a paradigm. *Psychological Bulletin, 65*, 110–136.

Kiesler, D. J. (1979). An interpersonal communication analysis of relationship in psychotherapy. *Psychiatry, 42*, 299–311.

Kiesler, D. J. (1982). Interpersonal theory for personality and psychotherapy. In J. C. Anchin & D. J. Kiesler (Eds.), *Handbook of interpersonal psychotherapy* (pp. 3–23). New York: Pergamon Press.

Kiesler, D. J. (1983). The 1982 interpersonal circle: a taxonomy for complementarity in human interactions. *Psychological Review, 90*, 185–214.

Kiesler, D. J. (1985). *The 1982 interpersonal circle: acts version*. Unpublished manuscript, Virginia Commonwealth University, Richmond.

Kiesler, D. J. (1986). The 1982 interpersonal circle: an analysis of DSM-III personality disorders. In T. Millon & G. L. Klerman (Eds.), *Contemporary directions in psychopathology: toward the DSM-IV* (pp. 571–598). New York: Guilford Press.

Kiesler, D. J. (1988). *Therapeutic metacommunication: therapist impact disclosure as feedback in psychotherapy*. Palo Alto, CA: Consulting Psychological Press.

Kiesler, D. J. (1991). Interpersonal methods of assessment and diagnosis. In C. R. Snyder & D. R. Forsyth (Eds.), *Handbook of social and clinical psychology* (pp. 438–468). New York: Pergamon Press.

Kiesler, D. J. (1996). *Contemporary interpersonal theory and research: personality, psychopathology, and psychotherapy*. New York: Wiley.

Kiesler, D. J., Goldston, C. S., & Schmidt, J. A. (1991). *Manual for the Check List of Interpersonal Transactions — revised (CLOIT-R) and the Check List for Psychotherapy Transactions — revised (CLOPT-R)*. Richmond: Virginia Commonwealth University.

Kiesler, D. J. & Schmidt, J. A. (1993). *The Impact Message Inventory: form IIA octant scale version*. Palo Alto, CA: Mind Garden.

Kiesler, D. J., Schmidt, J. A., & Wagner, C. C. (1997). A circumplex inventory of impact messages: an operational bridge between emotion and interpersonal behavior. In R. Plutchik & H. Contes (Eds.), *Circumplex models of personality and emotions* (pp. 221–244). Washington, DC: American Psychological Association.

Klerman, G. L., Weissman, M. M., Rounsaville, B. J., & Chevron, E. S. (1984). *Interpersonal psychotherapy of depression*. New York: Basic Books.

LaForge, R. (2004). The early development of the interpersonal system of personality (ISP). *Multivariate Behavioral Research, 39*, 359–378.

LaForge, R., Freedman, M. B., & Wiggins, J. S. (1985). Interpersonal circumplex models: 1948–1983. *Journal of Personality Assessment, 49*, 613–631.

LaForge, R., Leary, T. F., Naboisek, H., & Coffey, H. S. (1954). The interpersonal dimension of personality: II. An objective study of repression. *Journal of Personality, 23*, 129–153.

LaForge, R. & Suczek, R. F. (1955). The interpersonal dimension of personality: III. An interpersonal check list. *Journal of Personality, 24*, 94–112.

Leary, T. (1957). *Interpersonal diagnosis of personality*. New York: Ronald Press.

Leary, T. & Coffey, H. S. (1955). Interpersonal diagnosis: some problems of methodology and validation. *Journal of Abnormal and Social Psychology, 50,* 110–124.

Levenson, E. A. (2006). Fifty years of evolving interpersonal psychoanalysis. *Contemporary Psychoanalysis, 42,* 557–562.

Linehan, M. M. (1993). *Cognitive behavioral treatment for borderline personality disorder.* New York: Guilford Press.

Lionells, M., Fiscalini, J., Mann, C. H., & Stern, D. B. (1995). *Handbook of interpersonal psychoanalysis.* Hillsdale, NJ: Analytic Press.

Locke, K. D. (2000). Circumplex scales of interpersonal values: reliability, validity, and applicability to interpersonal problems and personality disorders. *Journal of Personality Assessment, 75,* 249–267.

Locke, K. D. (2006). Interpersonal circumplex measures. In S. Strack (Ed.), *Differentiating normal and abnormal personality* (2nd ed., pp. 383–400). New York: Springer Publishing.

Lorr, M. (1991). A redefinition of dominance. *Personality and Individual Differences, 12,* 877–979.

Maling, M. S., Gurtman, M. B., & Howard, K. (1995). The response of interpersonal problems to varying doses of psychotherapy. *Psychotherapy Research, 5,* 63–75.

Marcotte, D. & Safran, J. D. (2002). Cognitive-interpersonal psychotherapy. In F. L. Kaslow (Ed.), *Comprehensive handbook of psychotherapy:* vol. 4: *Integrative/eclectic* (pp. 272–293). Hoboken, NJ: Wiley.

Markey, P. M., Funder, D. C., & Ozer, D. J. (2003). Complementarity of interpersonal behaviors in dyadic interactions. *Personality and Social Psychology Bulletin, 29,* 1082–1090.

Markowitz, J. C., Friedman, R. A., Miller, N., Spielman, L. A., Moran, A., & Kocsis, L. (1996). Interpersonal improvement in chronically depressed patients treated with desipramine. *Journal of Affective Disorders, 41,* 59–62.

Markus, H. (1977). Self-schemata and processing information about the self. *Journal of Personality and Social Psychology, 35,* 63–78.

McLemore, C. W. & Benjamin, L. S. (1979). Whatever happened to interpersonal diagnosis? *American Psychologist, 34,* 17–34.

Mischel, W. & Shoda, Y. (1995). A cognitive-affective system of personality: reconceptualizing situations, dispositions, dynamics, and invariance in personality structure. *Psychological Review, 102,* 246–268.

Mitchell, S. A. (1988). The intrapsychic and the interpersonal: different theories, different domains, or historical artifacts? *Psychoanalytic Inquiry, 8,* 472–496.

Moskowitz, D. S. (1994). Cross-situation generality and the interpersonal circumplex. *Journal of Personality and Social Psychology, 66,* 921–933.

Muran, J. C., Segal, Z. V., Samstag, L. W., & Crawford, C. E. (1994). Patient pretreatment: interpersonal problems and therapeutic alliance in short-term cognitive therapy. *Journal of Consulting and Clinical Psychology, 62,* 185–190.

Norcross, J. C. (2002). *Psychotherapy relationships that work: therapist contributions and responsiveness to patients.* New York: Oxford University Press.

Pincus, A. L. (1994). The interpersonal circumplex and the interpersonal theory: perspectives on personality and its pathology. In S. Strack & M. Lorr (Eds.), *Differentiating normal and abnormal personality* (pp. 114–136). New York: Wiley.

Pincus, A. L. (2005a). A contemporary integrative interpersonal theory. In M. Lenzenweger & J. F. Clarkin (Eds.), *Major Theories of Personality Disorder* (2nd ed., pp. 282–331). New York: Guilford Press.

Pincus, A. L. (2005b). The interpersonal nexus of personality disorders. In S. Strack (Ed.), *Handbook of Personology and psychopathology.* New York: Wiley.

Pincus, A. L. & Ansell, E. B. (2003). Interpersonal theory of personality. In T. Millon & M. Lerner (Eds.), *Handbook of psychology.* vol. 5: *Personality and social psychology* (pp. 209–229). New York: Wiley.

Pincus, A. L., Dickinson, K. A., Schut, A. J., Castonguay, L. G., & Bedics, J. (1999). Integrating interpersonal assessment and adult attachment using SASB. *European Journal of Psychological Assessment, 15,* 206–220.

Pincus, A. L. & Gurtman, M. B. (2003). Interpersonal assessment. In J. S. Wiggins (Ed.), *Paradigms of personality assessment* (pp. 246–261). New York: Guilford Press.

Pincus, A. L. & Gurtman, M. B. (2006). Interpersonal theory and the interpersonal circumplex: evolving perspectives on normal and abnormal personality. In S. Strack (Ed.), *Differentiating normal and abnormal personality* (2nd ed., pp. 83–111). New York: Springer Publishing.

Pincus, A. L., Gurtman, M. B., & Ruiz, M. A. (1998). Structural Analysis of Social Behavior (SASB): circumplex analysis and structural relations with the interpersonal circle and the five-factor model of personality. *Journal of Personality and Social Psychology, 74,* 1629–1645.

Pincus, A. L., Lukowitsky, M. R., & Wright, A. G. C. (in press). The interpersonal nexus of personality and psychopathology. In T. Millon, R. F. Kreuger, & E. Simonsen (Eds.), *Contemporary directions in psychopathology: towards DSM-V and ICD-11.* New York: Guilford Press.

Pincus, A. L. & Wiggins, J. S. (1990). Interpersonal problems and conceptions of personality disorders. *Journal of Personality Disorders, 4,* 342–352.

Safran, J. D. (1990a). Towards a refinement in cognitive therapy in light of interpersonal theory: I. theory. *Clinical Psychology Review, 10,* 87–105.

Safran, J. D. (1990b). Towards a refinement in cognitive therapy in light of interpersonal theory: II. practice. *Clinical Psychology Review, 10,* 107–121.

Safran, J. D. (1992). Extending the pantheoretical applications of interpersonal inventories. *Journal of Psychotherapy Integration, 2,* 101–105.

Safran, J. D. & Segal, Z. V. (1990). *Interpersonal process in cognitive therapy*. New York: Basic Books.

Schmidt, J. A., Wagner, C. C., & Kiesler, D. J. (1999). Psychometric and circumplex properties of the octant scale Impact Message Inventory (IMI-C): a structural evaluation. *Journal of Counseling Psychology, 46*, 325–334.

Shearin, E. N. & Linehan, M. M. (1992). Patient-therapist ratings and relationship to progress in dialectical behavior therapy for borderline personality disorder. *Behavior Therapy, 23*, 730–741.

Stern, D. N. (1985). *The interpersonal world of the infant*. New York: Basic Books.

Stern, D. N. (1988). The dialectic between the "interpersonal" and the "intrapsychic": with particular emphasis on the role of memory and representation. *Psychoanalytic Inquiry, 8*, 505–512.

Strupp, H. H. & Binder, J. L. (1984). *Psychotherapy in a new key: a guide to time-limited dynamic psychotherapy*. New York: Basic Books.

Sullivan, H. S. (1948). The meaning of anxiety in psychiatry and life. *Psychiatry, 11*, 1–13.

Sullivan, H. S. (1953a). *Conceptions of modern psychiatry*. New York: Norton.

Sullivan, H. S. (1953b). *The interpersonal theory of psychiatry*. New York: Norton.

Sullivan, H. S. (1954). *The psychiatric interview*. New York: Norton.

Sullivan, H. S. (1956). *Clinical studies in psychiatry*. New York: Norton.

Sullivan, H. S. (1962). *Schizophrenia as a human process*. New York: Norton.

Sullivan, H. S. (1964). *The fusion of psychiatry and social science*. New York: Norton.

Svartberg, M. & Stiles, T. C. (1992). Predicting patient change from therapist competence and patient-therapist complementarity in short-term anxiety provoking psychotherapy: a pilot study. *Journal of Consulting and Clinical Psychology, 60*, 304–307.

Talley, P. F., Strupp, H. H., & Morey, L. C. (1990). Matchmaking in psychotherapy: patient-therapist dimensions and their impact on outcome. *Journal of Consulting and Clinical Psychology, 58*, 182–188.

Thompson, C. (1952). Sullivan and psychoanalysis. In P. Mullahy (Ed.), *The contributions of Harry Stack Sullivan* (pp. 101–116). Northvale, NJ: Jason Aronson.

Tracey, T. J. G. (1993). An interpersonal stage model of the therapeutic process. *Journal of Counseling Psychology, 40*, 396–409.

Tracey, T. J. G. (1994). An examination of complementarity of interpersonal behavior. *Journal of Personality and Social Psychology, 67*, 864–878.

Tracey, T. J. G. & Hays, K. (1989). Therapist complementarity as a function of experience and client stimuli. *Psychotherapy: Theory, Research, Practice, Training, 26*, 462–468.

Trobst, K. K. (2000). An interpersonal conceptualization and quantification of social support transactions. *Personality and Social Psychology Bulletin, 26*, 971–986.

Vittengl, J. R., Clark, L. A., & Jarrett, R. B. (2003). Interpersonal problems, personality pathology, and social adjustment after cognitive therapy for depression. *Psychological Assessment, 15*, 29–40.

Weissman, M. M. & Markowitz, J. C. (2002). Interpersonal psychotherapy for depression. In I. H. Gotlib & C. L. Hammen (Eds.), *Handbook of depression* (pp. 404–421). New York: Guilford Press.

Weissman, M. M., Markowitz, J. C., & Klerman, G. L. (2000). *Comprehensive guide to interpersonal psychotherapy*. New York: Basic Books.

White, M. J. (1952). Sullivan and treatment. In P. Mullahy (Ed.), *The contributions of Harry Stack Sullivan* (pp. 117–151). Northvale, NJ: Jason Aronson.

Wiggins, J. S. (1979). A psychological taxonomy of trait descriptive terms: the interpersonal domain. *Journal of Personality and Social Psychology, 37*, 395–412.

Wiggins, J. S. (1982). Circumplex models of interpersonal behavior in clinical psychology. In P. C. Kendall & J. N. Butcher (Eds.), *Handbook of research methods in clinical psychology* (pp. 183–221). New York: Wiley.

Wiggins, J. S. (1995). *Interpersonal Adjective Scales: professional manual*. Odessa, FL: Psychological Assessment Resources.

Wiggins, J. S. (1996). An informal history of the interpersonal circumplex tradition. *Journal of Personality Assessment, 66*, 217–233.

Wiggins, J. S. (1997). Circumnavigating Dodge Morgan's interpersonal style. *Journal of Personality, 65*, 1069–1086.

Wiggins, J. S., Phillips, N., & Trapnell, P. D. (1989). Circular reasoning around interpersonal behavior: evidence concerning some untested assumptions underlying diagnostic classifications. *Journal of Personality and Social Psychology, 56*, 296–305.

Wiggins, J. S., Trapnell, P. D., & Phillips, N. (1988). Psychometric and geometric characteristics of the revised Interpersonal Adjectives Scales (IAS-R). *Multivariate Behavioral Research, 23*, 17–30.

Wiggins, J. S. & Trobst, K. K. (1999). The fields of interpersonal behavior. In L. Pervin & O. P. John (Eds.), *Handbook of personality: theory and research* (pp. 653–670). New York: Guilford Press.

Behavior Therapy and Behavior Analysis: Overview and Third-Generation Perspectives

John P. Forsyth
University at Albany, State
University of New York

Sean C. Sheppard
University at Albany, State
University of New York

OUTLINE

OVERVIEW

Suffering is endemic to the human condition. There is no way to escape this simple fact. You've seen it in your life. We've see it in ours. And we routinely face it day in and day out in psychotherapy.

The people who seek help from a mental health professional often do so because they are suffering and more importantly because their lives are not working. In short, their suffering, unlike the physical, emotional, and psychological pain experienced by millions of people around the world, is linked with patterns of action and inaction that get in the way of living a whole, dignified, and purposeful life. Wrapping your head around this point can be hard to do, but it is vitally important that you do it.

We do not know what sparked your interest in clinical psychology, but we would venture a guess that if you really looked closely, your motivations for advanced study would boil down to a statement like this: "I want to help people … I want to help alleviate human suffering." Knowing, as you probably do, that good intentions do not always translate into good outcomes, you are likely reading this book because you are vested in learning *how* to be helpful. In short, the task you face is in learning how to translate good intentions into practical actions that make a difference.

The charge of clinical psychology is to understand, prevent, and alleviate various forms of suffering. The charge of clinical science and practice is to do that in a way that is durable, efficient, transportable, with high quality and preferably low cost, and in a way that upholds human dignity, scientific credibility, and accountability (Hayes, Barlow, & Nelson-Gray, 1999). **Behavior therapy** is no different in this regard.

Our overarching goal is to introduce you to the science and practice of behavior therapy — a term we will use broadly to refer to a range of behavior therapies, including cognitive and cognitive-behavior therapies. The scope of behavior therapy and **behavior analysis** is vast, and many excellent resources are available outlining its philosophical and conceptual roots (O'Donohue & Kitchener, 1999; Skinner, 1974; Zuriff, 1985), its history and development (Forsyth & Sabsevitz, 2002), its link with basic and applied branches of science (O'Donohue, 1998; Skinner, 1953), and of course the many efficacious intervention technologies (or behavior therapies) that have emerged as products of this work (see O'Donohue, Fisher, & Hayes, 2003).

Given space constraints, we simply cannot do justice to behavior therapy in a single chapter without leaving something out. To help you round out your professional development, we have included in Table 10.1 a list of what we consider some excellent books that have shaped our thinking. The list is not inclusive, but it is a start. We recommend that you spend some time with this material if you are interested in really wrapping your head around this approach.

Our intention in this chapter is to be intensely pragmatic. As you will see, behavior therapy and its cousin, **behavior analysis**, are ways of understanding and treating basic and applied problems using a scientific perspective with two eyes fixed squarely on practical utility. This approach has its own unique way of talking too, and that talk is built on somewhat esoteric-sounding technical terms from the basic science (e.g., positive reinforcement, matching law, extinction, discriminative stimulus, transformation of function, verbal behavior).

We won't bog you down with the technical jargon here; however, we do encourage you to spend some time learning how to talk the talk, behaviorally speaking. If you do that, you will acquire a level of depth and flexibility in your clinical work, and this will help you to work more effectively with your clients, particularly

TABLE 10.1   Building Your Intellectual Foundation in Behavior Therapy

1. O'Donohue, W. & Kitchener, R. (Eds.) (1999). *Handbook of behaviorism*. New York: Academic Press.

2. Skinner, B. F. (1953). *Science and human behavior*. New York: The Free Press.

3. Skinner, B. F. (1974). *About behaviorism*. New York: Vintage Books.

4. Hayes, S. C., Hayes, L. J., Reese, H., & Sarbon, T. R. (Eds.) (1993). *Varieties of scientific contextualism*. Reno, NV: Context Press.

5. Sidman, M. (1988). *Tactics of scientific research: evaluating experimental data in psychology*. Boston, MA: Authors Cooperative.

6. O'Donohue, W. (Ed.) (1998). *Learning and behavior therapy*. Boston, MA: Allyn & Bacon.

7. Ramnerö, J. & Törneke, N. (2008). *ABCs of human behavior: behavioral principles for the practicing clinician*. Oakland, CA: New Harbinger, Context Press.

8. Hayes, S. C., Barnes-Holmes, D., & Roche, B (Eds.) (2001). *Relational frame theory: a post-Skinnerian account of human language and cognition*. New York: Kluwer Academic/Plenum.

9. Spiegler, M. D. & Guevremont, D. C. (2003). *Contemporary behavior therapy* (4th ed.). Belmont, CA: Wadsworth-Thompson Learning.

10. Nelson, R. O. & Hayes, S. C. (Eds.) (1986). *Conceptual foundations of behavioral assessment*. New York: Guilford Press.

11. Dougher, M. J. (Ed.) (2000). *Clinical behavior analysis*. Reno, NV: Context Press.

    Hersen, M. (Ed.) (2002). *Clinical behavior therapy: adults and children*. New York: Wiley.

12. O'Donohue, W., Fisher, J. E., & Hayes, S. C. (2003). *Cognitive behavior therapy: applying empirically supported techniques in your practice*. New York: Wiley.

13. Hayes, S. C., Follette, V. M., & Linehan, M. M. (2004). *Mindfulness and acceptance: expanding the cognitive-behavioral tradition*. New York: Guilford Press.

Note: This list is not exhaustive. It represents some good foundational resources to begin the process of exploration and discovery about behavior therapy. Many of these works link to other published works that we think are useful reads too. We highly recommend reading original sources, which will give you a level of depth and sophistication that is impossible to get from secondary sources.

when tried-and-true interventions require innovation on your part or are not working as expected, or when there are no empirically supported interventions available to provide you with guidance. In short, the technical terms point to ways of predicting and influencing behavior, and knowing them will help you use scientific know-how to make a difference. This simple formula, in turn, paved the way for behavior therapy's many successes and has yielded an impressive array of efficacious intervention technologies for a wide range of problems.

To set a context for the discussion, we briefly review the history and development of behavior therapy (O'Donohue & Kitchener, 1999; Zuriff, 1985) across three generations, and we follow with a discussion of some of its core assumptions and defining features. As will be seen, behavior therapy comprises a shared set of working conceptual assumptions and values that help frame answers to basic research and applied questions, and ultimately what behavior therapists do when attempting to alleviate an increasingly wide range of human suffering in individuals, couples, groups, organizations, communities, and so on. As you read on, be mindful that behavior therapy is not one thing, but many things. The look and feel of contemporary behavior therapy (see Hayes, Follette, & Linehan, 2004) might even surprise you.

FIRST- AND SECOND-GENERATION BEHAVIOR THERAPY

Behavior therapy was conceived in a psychotherapeutic climate that was more than ready for it but not quite ready to embrace it. At the time of behavior therapy's formal inception in the early 1950s, psychiatrists ruled the roost with regard to mental health care, and psychologists often played second fiddle to them. Psychiatrists, many of whom were trained in medicine first, looked to classic psychoanalysis, or what was then the predominant Freudian or neo-Freudian psychoanalytic framework, for their clinical inspiration.

Treatment was largely nondirective, insight focused, and fixed on unearthing unconscious processes and early childhood experiences that were thought to underlie most forms of human suffering. Therapy was long term, often taking years, not weeks, and the disease model of the etiology, diagnosis, and treatment of psychological disorders served as the prevailing conceptual framework. Treatment was also driven more by hunch and clinical intuition than by science and data. Accountability, or treatment decisions supported and guided by scientific evidence, was virtually nonexistent.

Controversy mounted regarding the efficacy of psychotherapy in general (Eysenck, 1952). For instance, Eysenck reviewed the limited treatment outcome literature at the time and concluded that insight-oriented psychotherapy was equivalent to no treatment at all — a conclusion that has since been shown to have been overstated (Cartwright, 1955; Luborsky, 1954; Smith & Glass, 1977). Still, his article was a catalyst for a more serious evaluation of the benefits of traditional psychotherapy and efforts to develop more effective alternatives. All of this occurred at a time when public mistrust about psychotherapy, including social stigma about psychological disorders, was at an all-time high. Something had to change, and the pioneers of behavior therapy were poised to offer a new approach that would forever revolutionize mental health care.

Early Roots in Behaviorism

Early behavior therapy owes much of its development to a brand of behaviorism first outlined by John B. Watson (1913) in his now classic behavioral manifesto "Psychology as a Behaviorist Views It." Here, it is important to be mindful that pre-Watsonian psychology was a science of mental life, with its chief method being introspection.

Watson (1913) turned that view on its head and argued that psychology is and should be a purely objective experimental branch of natural science whose theoretical goal is the prediction and control of behavior and whose chief methods are direct observation and measurement of behavior. In so doing, Watson tried to provide a coherent rationale to legitimize behavioral methods that had been in use since the 1870s with animals and humans, chiefly the associative conditioning work of Pavlov and his colleagues.

Most importantly, Watson defined psychology as a science of behavior and limited its subject matter to directly observable and verifiable events, namely, *observable* behaviors. Mind was ruled out, more or less by fiat, as ethereal and unnecessary for psychology as a science. In short, Watson maintained that one could understand the mind and what people do by understanding relations between antecedent environmental stimuli (S) and reflexive or elicited behavioral responses (R), a view now familiar to many as an early form of stimulus-response, or S-R, psychology.

Watson's relatively short career in psychology and as an academic was influential. He can be credited for bringing the work of Russian physiologist Ivan Pavlov, and particularly

Pavlov's work on the conditioned reflex, to American psychology and proselytizing its theoretical and applied importance. By the early 1920s, Watson and Rosalie Rayner (Watson & Rayner, 1920) had demonstrated the acquisition of conditioned fear of a white rat in the now classic case study of Little Albert, and the subsequent generalization of such fear to other white furry objects. This demonstration was derived from conditioning procedures set forth originally by Pavlov, procedures that came to be known as Pavlovian or classical conditioning in the United States and abroad.

By 1924, Mary Cover Jones went on to demonstrate how fears could be treated via social imitation (now known as modeling) and exposure to a feared stimulus without anticipated negative consequences; this procedure extends basic knowledge of classical conditioning principles, such as extinction via nonreinforced exposure, to the applied realm. With this successful demonstration, the seeds of what would become behavior therapy were planted.

Although it took about 25 years for Watson's ideas and those of his followers to catch on, by the early 1930s, Watsonian behaviorism — sometimes referred to as **methodological behaviorism** — and its variants had taken center stage within American psychology and early behavior therapy through the 1970s. Psychology had ceased to be the science of mental life and had become the science of publicly observable behavior.

Limiting a science of behavior to actions occurring outside the skin was both a blessing and a curse for first- and second-generation behavior therapy. As you read on, see if you can detect why this might be so.

First-Generation Behavior Therapy

Behavior therapy emerged during the early 1950s through the tenacious and somewhat independent efforts of several pioneers, including Joseph Wolpe and his students Arnold

Lazarus and Stanley Rachman in South Africa; the experimental and clinical work of Monty B. Shapiro and Hans J. Eysenck at the Maudsley Hospital in London, England; and the studies of Andrew Salter, Ogden R. Lindsley, and Burrhus F. Skinner in the United States.

Each of these individuals was united by a shared interest in the extrapolation of experimental findings and learning principles from laboratory research with animals to explain human behavior, and predominantly — with the exception of Lindsley and Skinner — the development and amelioration of neurotic anxiety (Wolpe, 1958). Behavior therapy was, in many respects, based on extrapolation of laws and principles of behavior, much as engineers rely on the laws and principles of physics to guide their work.

The early pioneers shared a sense of unity, a common purpose, and a revolutionary passion for behavioral science itself and what that science could offer individuals, groups, and society at large. Many of the founding members had one foot planted in the laboratory and one in the clinic, and they moved between both nimbly and with grace. The early behavior therapists understood varieties of behaviorism, behavior theory, and behavior principles and how to put them to use creatively to achieve pragmatic purposes. Early behavior therapy entailed a behavioral core, which was reflected in a rigorous scientific approach aimed at developing a science of human behavior and use of that knowledge to achieve therapeutic goals.

This simple formula, linking behavioral science with practical application, proved enormously successful. In the ensuing years, data supporting the efficacy of behavior therapy began to mount at a rapid rate. Soon others increasingly joined the behavioral inner circle and rallied together to promote a rigorous experimental epistemology with regard to treatment development and analysis of therapeutic processes and outcomes, and against what was perceived as conceptually rich, but empirically weak and practically inert, competing approaches to psychotherapy and behavior change (e.g., analytic, gestalt, humanistic views). A classic example of such objections is Freud's (1909) case of Little Hans (see Highlight Box 10.1).

Behavior therapy began to grow, and with that growth came concern about the nature and meaning of the term *behavior therapy*, a term first coined in 1953 by Ogden Lindsley, Burrhus F. Skinner, and Harry Solomon in a monograph describing the application of operant procedures in a psychiatric hospital setting (Skinner, Solomon, & Lindsley, 1953). By 1958, Arnold Lazarus offered an explicit definition of behavior therapy as the application of objective, laboratory-derived therapeutic techniques to the treatment of neurotic patients. One year later, Hans Eysenck would define behavior therapy more broadly as the application of modern learning theory to the treatment of psychiatric disorders.

The definition of what constitutes behavior therapy would continue to undergo substantial revision in the decades to follow such that the conceptual foundations of behavior therapy — rooted in behaviorism, learning theory, and principles of learning — would be replaced by the more general affiliation of behavior therapy with psychological science, empiricism, a data-driven approach to treatment, and a specific brand of therapy or therapeutic techniques. The dissolution of behavior therapy's link with behavioral principles and theory began in earnest in the 1960s and, in many respects, has not recovered since.

Challenges to First-Generation Behavior Therapy

First-generation behavior therapy was an enormously successful experiment in many ways. That success owes a debt to maintaining a link between basic behavioral science and its practical application. This work, in turn, transformed psychotherapy from being a drawn-out and ill-specified process to one that was direct, evidence based, time limited, and problem focused.

The task of behavior therapy, in turn, became one of identifying problem behaviors, developing hypotheses about maintaining factors, and subsequently testing those hypotheses as a function of carefully timed intervention strategies. During this period, behavior therapists more or less couched intervention tactics in terms of broadly applicable learning principles, namely from two lines of work: (1) principles of operant conditioning, or what came to be known as behavior modification (Skinner, 1953), and (2) associative or classical conditioning, particularly with anxiety (Wolpe, 1958). These principles, in turn, guided the development of interventions, and early behavior therapists went to great pains to evaluate the effectiveness of their interventions empirically. This basic approach, linking basic science with clinical application and empirical evaluation, became a hallmark of early behavior therapy and a feature of most behavior therapies, remaining so even today.

That said, there were problems that began to emerge as behavior therapy expanded. Behavior therapies proved quite successful in settings that could be controlled (e.g., hospitals, schools, prisons), who with populations had limited verbal repertoires (e.g., young children and people with developmental disabilities), or for problems that were relatively circumscribed and fit well within a direct conditioning framework (e.g., specific phobias) (Yates, 1970). In short, the early and most dramatic successes of behavior therapy were limited largely to populations in controlled environments and, more importantly, persons with restricted verbal abilities.

Owing much to Watson and neobehavioral conceptions, early behavior therapists also tended to define behavior narrowly, namely as observable behavior. Interventions, in turn,

HIGHLIGHT BOX 10.1

BEHAVIORAL OBJECTIONS TO FREUD'S CASE OF LITTLE HANS

Little Hans was a 5-year-old boy with an extreme fear of horses (or hippophobia). Freud (1909) first learned of the child through the child's father who was a good friend and follower of Freud's ideas. Hans's father wrote to Freud explaining his concerns about Hans as follows: Hans is afraid that a horse will bite him in the street, and this fear seems somehow connected with him having been frightened by a large penis. For instance, the mother had, at times, reprimanded Hans for masturbation. She also threatened to call a doctor to "cut off his widdler" if he kept doing that. The father went on to provide Freud with extensive details of conversations with Hans, and together they tried to understand what the boy was experiencing and undertook to resolve his phobia of horses.

Though Freud only saw the child once in person, he deduced from written and verbal reports (mostly provided by Hans's father) that Hans was in the phallic stage and was suffering from an Oedipus complex (i.e., the boy wished to marry his own mother, and to do that he would first need to do away with his own father). Freud thought that during the phallic stage, most young boys develop an intense sexual love for their mothers. Because of this, Hans saw his father as a rival and wanted to get rid of him. Yet, Hans's father was far bigger and stronger, and so Hans developed a fear that he would be found out and that his father would castrate him. Because it is impossible to live with castration-threat anxiety, the young boy developed a mechanism for coping with it. In short, Hans displaced his Oedipal fears onto the horse.

The horse thus became a symbol of the father and the psychic conflict. Hans's phobic fear and avoidance, in turn, were wrapped in fanciful interpretations with sexual overtones. For instance, horses passing in and out of a gate were interpreted as feces passing through the anus (i.e., anal stage); horses with black spots around the mouth were similarly interpreted as being symbolic of the father's mustache. Loaded carts became symbolic of pregnant women, and this was related to Hans's anxiety over the birth of his newborn sibling and fears that his mother would soon become pregnant again, and not by Hans's own doing.

Early behavior therapists questioned Freud's account, and it was flatly undermined (Bandura, 1969; Wolpe & Rachman, 1960) with a far simpler explanation of Hans's phobic fear and his agoraphobic avoidance behavior (i.e., fear of leaving the home). Hans had, in fact, witnessed a terrible accident involving a horse-drawn cart falling over, along with cries and screams of the riders and passersby. Hans had learned to fear horses, in large part, because he had a traumatic conditioning history with respect to horses. This fear, in turn, fit well with classical fear conditioning principles regarding fear acquisition and stimulus generalization.

Behavior therapists later went on to show that complex psychoanalytic theorizing was unnecessary by demonstrating how simple contingencies could yield behavior that would occasion fantastic psychoanalytic interpretations (e.g., Ayllon, Haughton, & Hughes, 1965). Unconscious exploration and resolution were put aside in favor of getting people like Hans and others out of the house, going to school, and engaging in more functional behaviors (cf. Hayes, 2004).

were largely about changing problematic behavior directly, and this may have contributed to a certain narrowing of vision (Hayes, 2004) in two key respects.

First, behavior therapy rejected ideas from other traditions that were clinically rich and of deep concern to most people. Often, people come to therapy struggling with who they are, what they want out of life, wishing to find a way to live well, and how to find a way to engage important areas of their lives with painful aspects of their private experiences and histories. Moreover, early behavioral accounts did not address broader clinical concerns that are often the main reasons that clients come into therapy, namely, quality-of-life issues (e.g., intimacy, relationships, connection with others, meaning, purpose, values, spirituality, health and wellness) and why it is so hard to be human (cf. Hayes, 2004), that is, early behavior therapy tended to define treatment targets narrowly in terms of problem behavior change and/or alleviation of conditioned emotional distress, and it assumed more or less wrongly that such changes would generalize broadly to other important life areas.

Second, conditioning accounts did not deal adequately with human language and cognition. Watson rejected it out of hand, whereas Skinner (1957) focused greatly on it but implied that it was largely unimportant in the prediction and influence of behavior. This stance, in turn, was unfortunate given that Skinner's "radical behaviorism" was radical precisely because it restored a scientific analysis of thoughts, feelings, and other private events. Yet, few behavior analysts followed Skinner's lead at the time and continued to maintain that a scientific analysis of private events, though possible, was unnecessary to understand animal and human behavior. Yet, with highly verbal adults, it quickly became apparent that language and verbal behavior not only are important but also may play a functional role in adaptive and maladaptive behavior. Collectively, these issues set the stage for second-generation cognitive and cognitive-behavior therapy.

Second-Generation Behavior Therapy Goes Cognitive

By the 1960s, the behavioral revolution in mental health care was on its way to being won, and behavior therapy was considered a viable alternative framework to the prevailing psychiatric medical model of human suffering. Most behavior therapists shared a common, though by no means uniform, learning theory orientation and interest in a general behavioral approach. Yet, many were attracted to the promise of behavior therapy mostly for its pragmatic approach and its empiricism, particularly as applied to treatment development and implementation and to data-driven outcomes assessment.

Behavior therapy underwent substantial growth during the tumultuous 1960s, and with that growth came increasing diversification, internal dissent, and self-critical evaluation. During this period, it was common for behavior therapy to be wrongly associated with sterilization programs applied to black retarded persons, insulin shock therapy applied to psychotic patients in institutionalized settings (and without their consent), the use of coercive procedures such as punishment or shock to control behavior, and general charges of manipulation and dehumanization. Even within psychology, behavior therapy was often viewed as mechanistic, in an inhumane cold-hearted sense. It was the decade of oversimplification with regard to behavior theory and behavioral principles, grandiose claims regarding the effectiveness of behavior therapy, and intolerance from within and from without (Franks, 1997).

Behaviorism, as the conceptual core of behavior therapy, was gradually replaced by more pluralistic views, and behavior therapy came to be defined within much broader biopsychosocial models. Such models emphasized empiricism and changing behavior directly through the application of general psychological principles, not necessarily behavioral principles (Goldfried & Davison, 1976, 1994). Early behavioral approaches, grounded as they were in principles of learning and behavior theories, were increasingly viewed as too narrow and simplistic to account for complex human behavior, a view that persists somewhat to this day.

This issue came to a head as behavior therapists began to work with highly verbal adults in outpatient settings. There was no viable behavioral account of language and cognition at the time, and similarly no viable cognitive science on which to address the role of language and cognition in behavior therapy. Thus behavior therapists looked elsewhere to fill the cognitive gap. Interest in providing a more flexible and adequate account of the role of cognition and emotion led behavior therapists to embrace meditational principles, mechanistic computer metaphors, and commonsense talk about the role of thinking and feeling in human action.

What followed was an expanded view of behavior therapy, one in which cognition and emotion were addressed in a more direct and central way. For instance, in the late 1960s and early 1970s basic psychological research had rekindled study of cognitive processes, paving the way for newer models (e.g., social learning; see Bandura, 1969) and treatment procedures. Interestingly, many of the so-called cognitive interventions during this time emerged from the creativity and clinical insights of their originators, not from basic research in cognitive science. Examples here include Albert Ellis's rational emotive therapy (see Ellis, 1962; now called rational emotive behavior therapy) and Aaron T. Beck's cognitive therapy (Beck, 1964, 1970). Yet, these approaches had great appeal and served, in part, to foster more ecumenical strands of behavior therapy that were increasingly becoming more popular, particularly the **social learning** approach (Bandura, 1969), multimodal therapy (a version of technical eclecticism, Lazarus, 1989), cognitive therapy (Beck, 1976), and eventually the perspective known as **cognitive-behavior therapy** (Meichenbaum, 1977).

By the mid-1960s, behavior therapy had grown a belly and the song, bell, and hammer of the early days were replaced by increasing pluralism, numerous heterogeneous treatment procedures with different theoretical rationales, and open debate about the conceptual basis and methodological requirements of behavior therapy. Without a common enemy, behavior therapists increasingly began to debate among themselves about the very nature of behavior therapy and what constituted an adequate definition. The ensuing two decades were characterized by increasing interest in cognitive theory and therapy and by a weakened link with behavioral principles and theory. Few behavior therapists turned to behavioral science for their clinical inspiration. Clinical scientists and practitioners were increasingly drawn to behavior therapy for its empiricism, not for its behaviorism. Cognitive conceptualizations and cognitive-behavioral therapy became the rule, and principle-driven behavior therapy the increasing exception.

Behavior therapists began to incorporate empirical methods and concepts from experimental and social psychology, and psychological science more generally. Treatment development and implementation proliferated; numerous doctoral-level behavior therapy training programs were now well established. Behavior therapists' identity as empiricists disappeared as other approaches to therapy began to undertake clinical trials. It gradually became apparent that empiricism could be exported to any approach, not just behavior therapy. In a way, behavior therapy at the turn of the twenty-first century is nothing more than the embodiment of the conceptually neutral **scientist-practitioner model** of clinical psychology.

SHARED ASSUMPTIONS AND VALUES OF FIRST- AND SECOND-GENERATION BEHAVIOR THERAPY

Both the first and second generations of behavior therapy share some common assumptions. Some of these are philosophical, others conceptual, and still others procedural. Here we outline those assumptions and their role in defining what behavior therapists do. Some are unique to behavior therapy, whereas others are shared by empirical wings of clinical psychology and psychological science more generally.

Mechanistic Philosophy

Early forms of behavioral thinking were predominantly mechanistic, and so too was behavior therapy. A mechanistic philosophy takes as its goal the identification of essential building blocks that compose the fundamental structure. The parts are viewed as primary from which the whole is derived. Watson's original S-R reflex thesis was mechanistic, as were the S-R learning theories that predominated psychology through the middle part of the twentieth century. Mechanistic models, emphasizing meditational links between stimulus-response, were in vogue until the 1960s when they were replaced by the equally mechanistic computer metaphors and information processing models from cognitive psychology.

Central to this view is that the parts of the machine reflect an objective reality awaiting discovery and that the goal of any analysis is to elucidate principles, foundational laws, and theories that can be used to categorize the parts, relations among parts, and forces that together explain the functioning of the machine. Truth is based, in large part, on correspondence between an objective reality awaiting discovery and the belief in the presumed underlying mechanisms or structures, many of which are hypothesized but not observed directly.

For instance, a depressogenic self-schema is inferred from negative self-referential statements such as "I am worthless." When uttered by a patient, that statement is used as evidence to support the operation of the depressogenic self-schema based on correspondence between it (the statement), other statements or behaviors, and the presumed underlying structure of depressive thinking (schemas). This approach leads naturally to targeting and challenging the thinking patterns directly in order to modify the dysfunctional or inappropriate underlying structure. This is exactly what many strands of cognitive therapy aim to do. Beck (1993) articulates this view quite nicely when he states:

> Although there have been many definitions of cognitive therapy, I have been most satisfied with the notion that cognitive therapy is best viewed as the application of the cognitive model of a particular disorder with the use of a variety of techniques designed to modify the dysfunctional beliefs and faulty information processing characteristic of each disorder. (p. 194)

Contemporary behavior therapy, including much of psychology, has not liberated itself entirely from mechanistic thinking, examples of which include talk of stimulus and response as immutable events with fixed properties; conceptualizing of emotion as a loosely organized system of partially independent relations between verbal-cognitive, physiological, and overt-motoric behavioral responses (Lang, 1968); symptom-focused and diagnosis-driven treatments, most of which are eliminative in nature (i.e., the symptoms are the problem, and thus one must identify, reduce, or eliminate the symptoms to ameliorate suffering and restore life functioning); and theoretical views that treat cognition as something other than behavior and give it causal status in explaining the origins, maintenance, and treatment of psychopathology and suffering.

Added to this list would be a focus only on the topography of behavior, not its function or relation to contextual determinants; on model building, and particularly models that speak of "structures" (= parts) and their relations to account for normal and abnormal behavior; and on most nomothetic approaches that treat the group as the unit of analysis and then make inferences from the functioning of groups to the individual case.

Most people cringe at the thought of calling their scientific activity mechanistic. Yet, mechanism is neither good nor bad. It just is. These assumptions guide scientific activity and frame problems in certain ways. The point is to recognize mechanistic thinking when you confront it, including its assets and liabilities. Most mechanistic thinking has roots in early forms of behavioral thinking, particularly the writings of John B. Watson, and in the mediational and more cognitive neobehaviorists such as Clark Hull, Edward Tolman, Edwin Guthrie, O. B. Mower, but *not* Burrhus F. Skinner and applied behavior analysis.

Emphasis on First-Order Change Strategies

Mechanism naturally leads to what we and others call first-order change strategies (Hayes, 2004), or a tendency to target problematic psychological and behavioral content directly. In the first generation, such first-order targets often took the form of direct behavior change strategies, many of which tended to be eliminative (e.g., exposure) and directed at excesses or deficits in covert (e.g., anxiety, fear, anger) and overt (e.g., avoidance) motor behavior. For instance, exposure therapy is based largely on extinction principles, with the goal being attenuation of excess emotional behavior via successive nonreinforced exposures.

The transition to the second-generation cognitive approaches was made easier by this first-order change agenda (Hayes, 2004). Methodological behaviorism allowed one to study inferred private events and processes and remain a behaviorist as long as the events or

processes have measurable and operational referents, preferably anchored in terms of environmental factors (Franks & Wilson, 1974). As such, cognitive interventions were devised to identify, target, and change "problematic" or "dysfunctional" thoughts, irrational schemas or beliefs, or deficit information processing using procedures to detect, correct, test, dispute, or replace them (Beck, 1993).

The first-order change agenda also fits well within the medical model. In fact, most empirically supported psychosocial interventions build on a model of first-order change, where syndromes are identified and where symptoms are targeted and corrected as a means of life restoration. This direct change agenda also helped pave the way for many of behavior therapy's successes over the years, as it tends to lend itself to objective and replicable empirical analyses. This feature has distinguished behavior therapies from other forms of psychotherapy that tend to be more indirect, process focused, and long term.

Mixed Conceptualizations of Behavior

Two very different conceptualizations of behavior have permeated first- and second-generation behavioral thinking. The traditional mechanistic view, owing much to John B. Watson, holds that behavior is what can be observed directly. This view, in turn, leads to a sort of dualism: behavior is what can be seen and objectively observed by others, whereas that which cannot be objectively observed by others is not behavior. As an example, walking would be considered behavior, but thinking about walking would not. This view creates obvious problems, particularly when dealing with how to talk about events occurring within the skin, such as thoughts, emotions, and beliefs.

As we have seen, the solution to this conundrum offered in the 1960s was to incorporate cognitive and social learning conceptualizations to address the world beneath the skin and to restrict behavioral conceptualizations for behavior that can be observed. This solution, in turn, created its own set of problems — a sort of conceptual dualism — for now cognition and emotion were considered something other than behavior and thus required a unique conceptual system to account for them. Behavior, in turn, would continue to be conceptualized as overt motor acts to be explained in terms of operant and respondent learning principles.

Such distinctions contributed, in part, to the view that behaviorism and a science of learning are of limited conceptual value in explaining human behavior. After all, a great deal of human behavior and suffering cannot be observed directly and occurs only privately to an audience of one — the individual experiencing the private events — but this fact alone does not preclude an adequate behavioral account of such events. This is precisely the point Skinner made throughout his writings, but unfortunately he also suggested that an operant analysis of language and cognition added nothing new to the prediction and influence of behavior. Worse yet, many took Skinner to mean that private events such as thinking, feeling, problem solving, and remembering were unimportant, and they failed to see that Skinner's ideas represented a radical departure from those of Watson and other neobehaviorists and cognitivists.

The good news is that a post-Skinnerian analysis of language and cognition is well underway (see Hayes, Barnes-Holmes, & Roche, 2001), and this work is greatly transforming the look and feel of contemporary behavior therapy an area we will dive into shortly.

Abnormal Behavior Is Learned Behavior

The behavioral view of abnormal behavior is predicated on the notion that life experience gives rise to normal behavior and an adaptive range of functioning just as life experience can produce maladaptive behavior and human suffering. To explain "normal" and "maladaptive" behavior in any absolute sense is somewhat contrary to the conceptual view of those calling themselves behavior therapists. Rather, the same principles of learning that result in functional behavior (e.g., positive reinforcement) also can produce dysfunctional behavior. Dysfunctional and functional behavior are a matter of degree, not of kind.

Maladaptive, abnormal, and dysfunctional in this sense represent complex learning, most likely attributable to deficit or inappropriate environmental contingencies. Abnormality is more than constellations of symptoms as outlined in the *Diagnostic and Statistical Manual of Mental Disorders, 4th ed.* (APA, 2000); abnormality reflects, at the core, learning processes that are either excessive or deficit and that otherwise interfere with a person's ability to live a full and valued life. This view of abnormal behavior has survived more or less intact and leads directly to behavior change efforts that attempt to modify deficit and inappropriate environmental contingencies and behaviors that maintain and promote problems in living.

The assumption that abnormal behavior is learned, and constrained somewhat by biological factors, means that one is not to blame for one's problems. This conception is also optimistic in the sense that if one learned to behave in a given way, then one can also learn to think and behave differently and hence get a different outcome in his or her life following treatment. Therapy, therefore, is viewed as a means to construct and teach more adaptive repertoires and to deconstruct problematic behaviors that contribute to ongoing suffering. The pragmatic leanings of behavior therapists further constrain the analysis to the present context where the variables controlling problematic behavior can be identified and influenced directly.

Focus on the Present

All behavior has a history. Yet, the problems clients present with are problems occurring in the now, meaning the present. Here, you may be tempted to say, "Sure, but what about a horrific past, such as a difficult childhood, abuse, or trauma ... surely that's important?" It may be, but behavior therapists do not assume that going into the past is always important or necessarily helpful. Even a disturbing memory of a painful past event is still a memory happening now.

The reasons for a present focus are largely pragmatic and strategic. Behavior is thought to be lawful in the sense that it is occurring for some reason. Those reasons, or determinants of behavior, have much to do with current conditions or contingencies supporting the problem behavior. This view, by the way, is the basis for virtually all psychosocial intervention strategies, for if we did not believe that interventions would make a reliable difference in our clients' behavior (i.e., behavior is lawful in a sense), then it would not be worth the time, money, or effort offering psychotherapy. Treatment, therefore, is a powerful means to alter contingencies supporting problematic behaviors while introducing new and more functional forms of learning.

The more strategic reasons for conceptualizing problems in the present have to do with making a difference. Problems happening now are amenable to change efforts now. Behavior therapists, in turn, can focus on helping their clients make meaningful changes in what they do now in order to get a different outcome in their lives. This view is simply an acknowledgment that a painful past, or a future that has yet to be, is not subject to direct change efforts. The distress or problems linked with responding to the future in the present or the past in the present are subject to change.

Both therapist and client work in the now, and that is the place where changes can be made. In fact, your life and the lives of your clients are lived in the now because that is the only place we are. And what we do now adds up to what most people call a life that was lived

well. So, those now moments count and add up for good or for ill.

Active, Experiential, and Empirical

Behavior therapies also tend to be active, in the sense that they involve teaching clients new skills, new ways of relating with their environment and their social world. Therapists and clients work together in a collaborative relationship to identify problems that can and ought to be changed, and they follow that up with a set of specific goals and a treatment plan to achieve those goals. Those goals, in turn, are often framed in an action language (what you will do) versus an inaction language (what you will not do). This approach, sometimes referred to as passing the Dead Man's Test (Lindsley, 1968), can be quite helpful in identifying potential vital targets for therapeutic change. Let's have a look (see Highlight Box 10.2).

Although all psychotherapies involve a verbal exchange between a client and therapist, behavior therapies tend to wrap that verbal exchange in specific concrete actions that clients can do in order to alleviate their suffering and foster a broader range of functioning. At times, such changes may be supported by the therapist outside of therapy (in vivo) or by enlisting the help of other people (e.g., teachers, parents, a spouse, or friends) in the client's natural environment.

This approach demands that clients engage in specific actions to get a different outcome in their lives. Many of those actions are prescribed and practiced outside the therapy hour in the clients' natural environment via homework, or what we prefer to call experiential life-enhancement exercises (Eifert & Forsyth, 2005). This ought to make sense to you. After all, problematic ways of thinking, feeling, and relating with others and the world are problems in the clients' everyday life, and thus changes must be enacted there. In our work,

HIGHLIGHT BOX 10.2

THE DEAD MAN'S TEST

This test is rather simple and can be useful in helping you and your clients decide when you have identified a useful target for intervention. Useful targets for intervention involve *actions* and *movements*, or something that a dead person could not do.

A helpful mantra here goes like this: "If a dead man can do it, it ain't behavior, and if a dead man can't do it, then it is behavior" (Malott & Suarez, 2003, p. 9). Ideally, you want to frame your interventions in terms of actions that people can do, or do differently.

To avoid failing the Dead Man's Test, watch for statements that refer to the following:

a state of being lacking movement and action (be happy, less depressed)
a completely internal event (e.g., feel less anxious, worry less)
stopping a behavior (e.g., talking, hitting, drinking) without building in an alternative/ constructive replacement
the sheer passage of time (e.g., I just need to ride it out or get a bit older)
metaphorical talk (e.g., absorb, transcend, digest, understand, figure out)

These and other areas often fail the test because a dead person could perform them as well as or better than a live person. So, instead, focus on what a person can do and only ask your clients to do something that a living person could do.

Doing entails action and movement and does not mean that you ignore other experiences or insights that your client may report along the way. It is just that you are not focused on narrow targets but on actions that the client could do to get a different outcome in his or her life. For instance, instead of focusing on helping your client to stop smoking or gain more willpower, a therapist might instead ask: "If you were not spending your time and money on cigarettes, what would you be doing instead? Or if smoking wasn't such a problem for you, then you'd be doing what?" In addition, if your client speaks of wanting to be calmer, or less depressed, or happier, you could ask this question: "If those were to happen, how would I or others know ... what would you be doing differently?" The answers to these and other questions will often pass a Live Person's Test, and that test tends to matter greatly within and outside of therapy.

---

we tend to avoid using the word *homework*, in large part because of its historic and largely negative connotations (e.g., "I will be evaluated," "I have do it," and "If I don't do it, then I will get in trouble") and the implication that it is being done for the therapist (much like you would do homework for a teacher) and not for the client him- or herself.

All of this work is grounded in science and an explicit empirical approach. Behavior therapists tend to prefer forms of empirical evaluation and approach assessment and treatment

as a hypothesis-testing and problem-solving enterprise (see Kaholokula and Haynes in this volume). The empirical leanings of behavior therapy were present from day one and have since expanded with the availability of a broad array of evidence-based psychosocial interventions for a wide range of problems (Task Force on Promotion and Dissemination of Psychological Procedures, 1995).

Applying interventions with demonstrated efficacy, including empirical evaluation of client progress and outcomes, is a hallmark of behavior therapy. Ongoing empirical evaluation, coupled with an idiographic approach, also positions behavior therapists to change course as the data dictate. This evidentiary approach can help guide decisions regarding case conceptualization, treatment priorities, progress or obstacles to change, and eventually decisions regarding treatment termination or need for additional services. This work, in turn, dovetails nicely with increasing interest in accountability in mental health care and efforts to show that psychotherapy is effective when applied outside a research context by front-line practitioners at the local level (Hayes et al., 1999).

THIRD-GENERATION (OR "THIRD-WAVE") BEHAVIOR THERAPY

Behavior therapy has evolved over the years in ways that are progressive, expansive, and, for some traditionalists, a bit alarming. We devote the remainder of this chapter to discussing the progressive science and innovative features of the third-generation behavior therapies (Hayes et al., 2004), with specific emphasis on acceptance and commitment therapy (or ACT, said as one word; Hayes, Strosahl, & Wilson, 1999). ACT, as will be seen, provides a good example of linking behavioral science with practical application and offers a new model of psychological health and suffering that points to new intervention strategies.

To set a context for this work, it is helpful to briefly define the shared features of third- or new-wave behavior therapies as follows:

> Grounded in an empirical, principle-focused approach, the third wave of behavioral and cognitive therapy is particularly sensitive to the context and functions of psychological phenomenon, not just their form, and thus tends to emphasize contextual and experiential change strategies in addition to more direct and didactic ones. These treatments tend to seek the constructions of broad, flexible, and

effective repertoires over an eliminative approach to narrowly defined problems, and to emphasize the relevance of the issues they examine for clinicians as well as clients. The third wave reformulates and synthesizes previous generations of behavioral and cognitive therapy and carries them forward into questions, issues, and domains previously addressed primarily by other traditions, in hopes of improving both understanding and outcomes. (Hayes et al., 2004, pp. 5–6)

This definition is a mouthful, but if you look closely, you will see that the third wave retains many features that made behavior therapy so successful while also expanding it into clinically interesting areas that were rejected, underdeveloped, or previously ignored by the previous generations. Below we briefly outline several lines of work supporting the third wave.

Sea Changes Setting Up the Third Wave

Challenges to First-order Cognitive Change

Several anomalies emerging from behavior therapy itself helped to set the stage for this work (cf. Hayes, 2004). For instance, research began to mount questioning the notion that direct cognitive change was necessary and critical for clinical improvement. With depression, for example, a large component analysis (Gortner, Gollan, Dobson, & Jacobson, 1998; Jacobson et al., 1996) showed that "there was no additive benefit to providing cognitive interventions in cognitive therapy" (Dobson & Khatri, 2000, p. 913). In fact, since cognitive interventions were introduced into behavior therapy, there has been very little evidence showing that change in cognition mediates clinical outcome (Burns & Spangler, 2001; Longmore & Worrell, 2006; Robins & Hayes, 1993). More commonly, we find cognitive changes occurring prior to the delivery of the putative cognitive interventions (Haubert & Dobson, 2007; Ilardi & Craighead, 1994).

From a practical perspective, the cognitive approach is intriguing and points to the importance of helping clients develop a different relation to their thoughts and evaluations. At a conceptual level, however, the cognitive view appeals to one behavior (e.g., particular thoughts or beliefs) in order to explain another behavior (e.g., other thoughts, verbalizations, overt actions, avoidance). In the process, virtually all of these accounts fail to recognize that behavior is a dependent variable that is itself in need of explanation.

This perspective also sets up a conceptual and practical dilemma that is not easy to get around, that is, if we were to accept core beliefs and faulty schema as explanations, then we still need to answer the crucial question of how one dependent variable can cause another, including how a dependent variable can be measured and then talked about as an independent variable (Forsyth, Lejuez, Hawkins, & Eifert, 1996; Skinner, 1953).

The contemporary behavior analytic account, by contrast, tends to treat such events as behavior-behavior relations that are situated in and within a context (Hayes & Brownstein, 1986). This stance has allowed behavior analysts to study events that people experience within the skin (e.g., thinking and feeling) and directs attention away from problematic private content as the problem. Instead, it focuses on contextual variables and processes of which such behavior-behavior relations are a function.

For instance, what contexts support relations among the thought "I am a loser" and social withdrawal and feelings of sadness? Is there a way to alter the functions and contexts supporting such relations without changing the form of the private content, such that one can have the thought "I am a loser" as just a thought and engage in social activities even when sad? It turns out there are some powerful ways to do just that. A core feature of third-wave behavior therapists is a focus on contextual variables that can be influenced directly and a deemphasis on altering the form or frequency of private events directly. This approach resolves the problematic situation of elevating cognitions to

causal status without ignoring their importance in psychopathology.

Emotion Regulation and Human Suffering

Work from emotion and cognitive science began pointing to the paradoxical and potentially iatrogenic effects of first-order change efforts. Fitting broadly within the realm of emotion regulation (Gross, 1998a, 1998b), this work suggests that direct efforts to avoid, minimize, escape from, or suppress unpleasant thoughts and feelings is effortful and does little to change the quality or form of the psychological and emotional experience (Forsyth, Eifert, & Barrios, 2006). Actually, just the opposite tends to occur. The emotion or thought becomes stronger and more salient, resulting in increased sympathetic nervous system activity (e.g., peripheral vasoconstriction, cardiovascular and electrodermal response; see Gross, 1998a; Gross & Levenson, 1993, 1997; Karekla, Forsyth, & Kelly, 2004; Richards & Gross, 1999) and a range of undesired psychological content in the suppressor, and interestingly also in those interacting with him or her (see Butler & Gross, 2004, for a review).

Several other independent lines of research suggest that attempts to suppress and control unwanted thoughts and feelings can result in more (not less) unwanted thoughts and emotions (Clark, Ball, & Pape, 1991; Gold & Wegner, 1995; Lavy & van den Hout, 1990; Wegner, Schneider, Carter, & White, 1987; Wegner, Schneider, Knutson, & McMahon, 1991; Wegner & Zanakos, 1994; see also Purdon, 1999, for a review). Moreover, emotion suppression has been shown to impair memory and problem solving (e.g., Baumeister, Bratslavsky, Muraven, & Tice, 1998; Richards & Gross, 1999, 2000), contribute to suffering and pain (Cioffi & Holloway, 1993; Gross & Levenson, 1997; McCracken, 1998; McCracken, Spertus, Janeck, Sinclair, & Wetzel, 1999), increase distress and restrict life functioning (Marx & Sloan, 2002), diminish contact with meaningful and valued life activities, and reduce overall quality of life (see Hayes, Luoma, Bond, Masuda, & Lillis 2006, p. 11, for a summary of outcome studies and quality-of-life measures used in studies). In short, down regulation of emotional and physical pain tends to amplify the pain and pulls people out of activities that they would otherwise wish to do.

Although emotion or thought regulation is part of what we all engage in now and then (e.g., putting on a smile when you would rather cry), it can become toxic when it is applied rigidly and inflexibly (Bonanno et al., 2004) and, as a consequence, gets in the way of more vital activities (Forsyth et al., 2006). This inflexibility and narrowing of behavioral options, in turn, are a common experience of many people seeking psychotherapy services for emotional problems (Hayes et al., 1996).

More practically, this work suggests that first-order change efforts directed at changing the form, frequency, or intensity of thoughts and feelings can play into the very system that brings people to therapy while further establishing the functional importance of regulation and struggle as a means to alleviate suffering (Blackledge & Hayes, 2001). Riding on this line of research, newer third-wave behavior therapies tend to focus on strategies that undermine the emotion regulation agenda itself while teaching skills to help people move with painful aspects of their histories in the service of valued ends. We'll have more to say about this in a moment with ACT.

From Mechanistic to More Functional Philosophical Foundations

Lastly, changes in the philosophy of science have weakened the mechanistic foundations of first- and second-generation behavior therapies, and in their place we are witnessing a resurgence of interest in more contextual approaches. These approaches, and there are several (Hayes, Hayes, Reese, & Sarbin, 1993), tend to focus on actions in context and adopt a pragmatic truth criterion known as successful working.

Therapists operating within functional contextualism, for instance, tend to focus on the whole event, are sensitive to how context can influence the nature and function of the whole event (e.g., experience of depression), and specify goals that tend to be larger than symptom alleviation (e.g., living well). This approach is the basis of ACT and leads to a view of human suffering wherein problems are historically and contextually situated, where the targets for change tend to be broadly construed, where interventions are more constructive than eliminative, and where the focus is on doing what works. Unlike more mechanistic strands of behavior therapy, contextualists make no ontological claims about an objective reality awaiting discovering. Rather, the goals are more humble and pragmatic in that what is true is what works (truth with a small t), given the goals of the analysis.

These philosophical assumptions, in turn, have allowed third-generation behavior therapists to move into areas that are more experiential, holistic, existential, and even humanistic while retaining the empirical and scientific foundations of behavior therapy writ large. For instance, a behavior therapist operating within this framework may freely adopt a gestalt open-chair procedure if the purposes of that exercise are clearly specified in the context of therapeutic goals. In short, the approach works for the purposes to which it is being put. Workability, in turn, reflects the pragmatic leanings of those operating within functional contextualism, and doing what works hinges on specifying up front what one is working toward (i.e., a clear a priori statement of an analytic goal; Hayes, 1993). In treatment, this means that therapist and client specify the goals of treatment and evaluate whether or not they have been met, with eyes on broad functional changes over narrow symptom-focused or topographic changes.

More broadly, this contextual view seeks scientific understanding with precision (i.e., specific terms apply to the analysis), scope (i.e., principles apply to a range of phenomena), and depth (i.e., terms and principles span other levels of analysis, such as biology, sociology, and psychology). Functional contextualists, in turn, value prediction and influence (one goal, not two), and this goal comports well with the interests of therapists in making a difference in their clients' lives. To achieve that kind of influence requires successful manipulation of events, and only contextual variables can be manipulated directly (Hayes & Brownstein, 1986). Scientific work that does not point to contextual variables that are subject to direct influence is viewed as holding little practical value (e.g., studies that do not point to potent variables that a therapist could influence directly to achieve meaningful change in a client's behavior). Unfortunately, a good part of psychological science tends to fail this pragmatic test, emphasizing prediction but not "how to" influence.

Other Influential Factors

The third wave of behavior therapy also coincided with a weakening of the syndrome-based medical model that characterized treatment targets of the first two waves. It turns out that many pharmacologic (e.g., antidepressants) and psychosocial (e.g., exposure, relaxation, cognitive therapy, mindfulness) treatments work for dissimilar disorders, suggesting (a) that psychiatric diagnoses have little clinical utility and (b) that clinicians ought to look more closely at transdiagnostic commonalities at the level of process (Barlow, Allen, & Choate, 2004; Markon, Krueger, & Watson, 2005; Watson, 2005). Moreover, research began to show that it was possible to alter the function of thought and emotion without changing its form (e.g., using mindfulness, metacognitive interventions), and increasingly researchers and clinicians alike began to pay attention to broader indices of psychological health and wellness, such as quality of life and factors that may transform human pain into

psychological suffering (Eifert & Forsyth, 2005; Hayes et al., 1999).

Collectively, the above lines of work, coupled with innovation and more heuristic models of suffering and change (Hayes, 2004), paved the way for newer third-wave developments. For the remainder of this chapter, we will briefly outline the main features of acceptance and commitment therapy and how it differs from more traditional cognitive-behavioral therapies.

What Is ACT?

ACT is a third-wave behavior therapy that has its roots in clinical behavior analysis while also honoring contributions of the first and second waves of behavior therapy. It is an *approach* (not merely an intervention) that is based on a post-Skinnerian account of language and cognition known as relational frame theory (RFT, see Hayes, Barnes-Holmes, & Roche, 2001). RFT, in turn, builds on the inadequacies of early behavioral and cognitive accounts of language and cognition while expanding that analysis into directions that have traditionally been reserved for less empirical wings of clinical psychology. To better understand RFT, we strongly encourage you to check out the free online RFT tutorial at www.contextualpsychology.org/rft_tutorial.

Based in functional contextualism, ACT also focuses on places where language and cognition get in the way of more vital value-guided actions. In short, ACT is about fostering psychological flexibility in the service of valued ends. This is accomplished in treatment using a variety of experiential, metaphorical, and indirect (i.e., second-order change) methods to alter the functions of language and cognition (not their form per se) while undermining excessive thought and emotion regulation in places where it does not work and gets in the way of effective action.

ACT teaches clients that it is okay to have whatever unwanted thoughts and feelings their minds and bodies come up with. Rather than struggling with these thoughts and feelings, clients learn new ways of relating to them as experiences to be had. In the process, therapist and client work together to accomplish two major goals: (1) fostering acceptance of unwanted thoughts and feelings whose occurrence or disappearance clients cannot control, and (2) commitment and action toward living a life consistent with clients' values. This is why ACT is about both acceptance and change. For instance, as applied to anxiety disorders, ACT is used to help clients learn to accept and live with their unwanted thoughts, worries, bodily sensations, and other feelings just as they are and to take charge and move their lives in directions that they value (see Eifert & Forsyth, 2005; Forsyth & Eifert, 2007).

The ACT acronym also nicely captures the three core steps or themes of this approach: accept thoughts and feelings, choose directions, and take action:

1. *Accept thoughts and feelings:* Accept and embrace your thoughts and feelings, particularly the unwanted ones (anxiety, pain, guilt, inadequacy). The idea is for clients to accept what they already have anyway and end their struggle with unwanted thoughts and feelings by not attempting to eliminate or change them, by not acting upon them, and by ultimately letting them go. Through various mindfulness exercises, clients learn to live with their critical evaluative mind.

2. *Choose directions:* This step is about helping clients choose directions for their lives by identifying and focusing on what "really matters" and what they value in life ("What do you want your life to stand for?"). It is about helping clients to discover what is truly important to them and then making an important choice. It is about choosing to go forward in directions that are uniquely theirs and accepting what is inside them,

what comes with them, and what accompanies them along the way.

3. *Take action:* This step is about committed action and involves taking steps toward realizing valued life goals. It is about making a commitment to action and changing what can be changed. The therapist encourages clients to behave in ways that move them forward in the direction of their chosen values. In this stage of ACT, clients learn that there is a difference between them as a person, the thoughts and feelings they have about themselves, and what they do with their lives. We will describe this process in detail as it is fundamental to ACT work, regardless of the clinical presenting problem.

The philosophy of ACT is somewhat similar to the serenity creed that many people love: accept with serenity what you cannot change, have the courage to change what you can, and develop the wisdom to know the difference. Most people find that it is much easier to agree with the serenity creed than to do what it says. The reason is that often people simply do not know what they can change and what they cannot change. As a result, they do not know how to apply this profound statement in their daily lives, and they become frustrated with it. ACT teaches people to put the serenity creed into action.

ACT accepts the ubiquity of human suffering and does not seek to reduce pain or to produce a particular positive feeling. It is not about producing quick fixes or using culturally sanctioned feel-good formulas and methods to reduce suffering. ACT seeks instead to reduce suffering by increasing people's vitality and ability to do what they want to do with their lives. This is what the ACT approach is all about: accept and have what there is to be had (anxiety, anger, joy, memories, the whole package) while also staying committed to doing what needs to be done to live a fulfilled, rich life guided by chosen values. People can choose to do things they enjoy and value regardless of what it is that they think or feel. Emotional and psychological pain need not be a barrier to a life lived well. Unfortunately, people seeking out the services of a mental health professional often see painful thoughts and feelings as barriers to living well and have made many efforts to reduce, minimize, or avoid that pain so that they can be happy and live well.

A Concise ACT Analysis of Human Suffering

From an ACT perspective, human suffering is primarily the result of normal human language processes being applied where they do not work, that is, just as we use language to solve problems in the world around us, we can also readily apply the same tactics to our own pain. And we can do so rigidly and inflexibly, even at significant cost.

The rub, though, is that we cannot readily problem-solve ourselves out of our own pain. And we cannot entirely escape, avoid, or control it either. As we described in regard to findings from emotion regulation research, these efforts may work well enough in the short term in that they buy people a brief honeymoon from the pain and its source. This acute relief makes it more likely that we will struggle and avoid the next time. However, in the long term, such strategies tend to amplify the pain and restrict lives.

Human beings also tend to see the world through their own thoughts and not the process of thinking itself, and this tendency is established and maintained by powerful social contingencies. One of the interesting and fundamental properties of language and cognition is that it is relational, meaning that it is symbolic in the sense that words can, through social convention, be established to mean (or stand for) something. For instance, if I say "lemon," it is likely that you can see it in your mind's eye and perhaps imagine some of its tart properties. Yet, thinking lemon does not make you a lemon, right? You are not that thought. If you think you are, then we might wonder whether you might suffer from a psychotic disorder.

This experiential point is often lost on people suffering with their emotional and psychological pain. Thus, for someone with severe depression, the thought "I am worthless" is not just a thought like "lemon." It is an unacceptable thought, linked with the self (I am . . .). Worthless is also linked with other thoughts too. So, we might associate worthless with garbage, and thus the person may think of him- or herself as garbage. Now, what do you do with a worthless piece of garbage? You throw it out, right? Suicide, or the purposeful taking of one's own life to escape pain and suffering, is one of several potentially disastrous outcomes of this process. It follows from key elements of the ACT model of psychopathology. In the next section, we outline the ACT model of psychopathology and describe a couple of the key targets for intervention as well as some therapeutic alternatives that flow from them.

The ACT Model of Psychopathology and Targets for Change

From the ACT perspective, the primary source of human suffering and psychopathology is psychological inflexibility, or a narrowing of behavioral options. Such inflexibility is thought to emerge when individuals use language and cognition in inappropriate situations and in ineffective or problematic ways (Luoma, Hayes, & Walser, 2007). The interaction of six core processes (e.g., experiential avoidance, cognitive fusion, lack of values) are thought to create and feed psychological inflexibility, and these processes further serve as specific targets for intervention (see Figure 10.1). It is beyond the scope of this chapter to fully describe these processes, but we will illustrate a few that we

ACT Model of Psychopathology

ACT Targets of Intervention

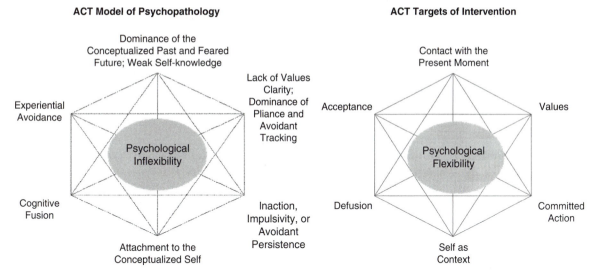

FIGURE 10.1   ACT model of psychopathology linked with ACT targets of intervention. Within the ACT research and clinical community, these illustrations are referred to as the Hexaflex model (adapted from Hayes et al., 2006). Notice that points on the left figure (pathological process) correspond to those on the right (intervention process). The intersecting lines show how different process elements tend to be linked with one another both in feeding human suffering and in its successful alleviation. You can find the Hexaflex model online at www.contextualpsychology.org (see also Hayes et al., 2006; Luoma et al., 2007).

believe are central to the approach, including some treatment alternatives that flow from them.

Experiential Avoidance

This process, itself a form of *excessive* thought and emotion regulation, refers to efforts to escape or avoid unpleasant private events or the circumstances that might occasion them, even when such efforts result in significant psychological harm (Hayes et al., 1996, 1999). Experiential avoidance, in turn, is greatly amplified by culture and is enabled via language. For instance, nonverbal species will avoid and escape a source of pain and threat in the environment, in part because of a past history of learning with respect to threat. This also makes evolutionary sense. What they will not do is struggle to avoid and escape from their own pain. Humans, though, can turn these adaptive actions on its host and thus struggle with and

attempt to avoid psychological, physical, and emotional hurt. As we saw early on, this not only is effortful but tends not to work well.

To illustrate, go ahead and try not to think about a *pink elephant*. Try really hard. Give yourself a few moments with this and then continue reading. Were you able to do it? Most people have a hard time doing it, in part because trying not to think about it is itself a thought of it. That said, you may have been clever here and perhaps used distraction by thinking about something that is clearly not a pink elephant. Yet, how did your mind know that the distracter is not a pink elephant? To distract, your mind needs to make a comparison — this is not that. And as soon as it does that, you are right back thinking about the thing you are not supposed to think about. Similar processes are at work when people attempt to avoid aversive thoughts and emotions (e.g., pain, anxiety, sadness). This, by the way, illustrates why distraction tends to be an ineffective way to manage and control thoughts and feelings.

Now, we can step this process up. Take a moment to think about the most shameful thing you have ever done. Notice here that your pain can be brought to mind anytime and anywhere just with this verbal prompt. Now, let's call that shameful thing "star." You are doing your best to not think this, and then you happen to walk into a situation where this comes to mind: Twinkle, twinkle, little ___. Don't think what comes next. You must not think about what comes next. What happens? What if you thought that your life hinged on not thinking "star"? What do you suppose people would do in this situation?

The point here is that a good deal of human suffering is fed by excessive struggle and avoidance, largely focused on thoughts, memories, images, emotions, and physical pain. With language, we can amplify this pain and buy into the products of our mind and fail to see the difference between thinking and its products. Within ACT, experiential avoidance is identified and targeted experientially via mindful acceptance strategies (Baer, 2003). The finger trap exercise depicted in Highlight Box 10.3 illustrates one of several mindful acceptance strategies.

The finger trap exercise is powerful precisely because it provides direct experience with our instinctive and often well-intentioned solutions to our problems and shows us how often these turn out not to be solutions at all. These so-called solutions may create even bigger problems than the ones they were designed to address.

Cognitive Fusion

Cognitive fusion refers to the tendency for humans to fail to see thoughts for what they are — just thoughts. Instead, we tend to treat

---

HIGHLIGHT BOX 10.3

ACCEPTANCE AS AN ALTERNATIVE TO EXPERIENTIAL AVOIDANCE

Acceptance literally means "to take what is offered." This taking does not mean wallowing or passive resignation. Rather, it means acknowledging experiences just as they are while persisting in the direction of valued ends. This can be difficult, in part, because the natural and more automatic tendency is to avoid, escape, suppress, or act on the unacceptable urges and impulses, that is, we tend to pull out from our pain rather than leaning into it and letting it be.

Acceptance counters this tendency by teaching skills to lean into experience just as it is (not as our minds say it is) rather than pulling out from our experiences. It is vital and active, and it requires a willingness to do something radically different

than before. This skill is taught throughout ACT interventions for a wide range of problems, using a variety of experiential methods. One powerful experiential metaphor is the Chinese Finger Cuffs activity.

A Chinese finger trap is a tube of woven straw about five inches long and half an inch wide. First, you must slide both index fingers into the straw tube, one finger at each end. If you attempt to pull the fingers out, the tube catches and tightens, causing discomfort. The only way to regain some freedom and space to move is to push the fingers in *first* and *then* slide them out. The purpose of this exercise is to let clients experience how doing something seemingly counterintuitive

HIGHLIGHT BOX 10.3   *(continued)*

("leaning into one's anxiety") may be a better solution than persisting with the same old solutions that have not worked.

The Chinese finger trap is a metaphor for moving *toward* suffering in order to lessen it and heal from it. We have adapted this exercise from the metaphor described by Hayes, Strosahl, and Wilson (1999), who present the metaphor to clients in verbal form and in research showing that allowing clients to act out the metaphor more experientially can be powerful (see Eifert & Heffner, 2003). This experiential component is in line with the action-oriented nature of behavior therapy and could serve to enhance the credibility and effectiveness of the metaphor. Following the exercise, give clients an extra finger trap to take home.

The goal of this exercise is to let clients discover that attempting to reduce and control essentially uncontrollable sensations, though understandable and seemingly logical (like pulling out of the finger trap), only creates more problems: the harder you pull, the more the trap tightens, resulting in less room to move and even more discomfort. In contrast, doing something counterintuitive, such as pushing the fingers *in* rather than *out* and leaning into the discomfort, effectively ends the struggle. It gives the client more space to move and do other things. Doing the exercise together with the client is a good way to illustrate that we are all in this boat together and that clients are not alone in the way they attempt to deal with their struggles.

Give clients a finger trap and use one yourself. First, ask the clients to slide in both index fingers, one finger at each end of the tube. After you fully insert your fingers, ask clients to try and get out of the finger trap. They are likely to do so by attempting to pull their fingers out. If they do that, ask them what they notice. They will experience

and report some discomfort as the tube squeezes their fingers and reduces circulation. They might also voice some worry that they might be stuck inside the finger trap for the rest of the session. They may experience some confusion because pulling out of the tube seems the most obvious, natural way to escape. Yet it doesn't work, and they are definitely stuck if they simply just go on pulling. Use the following dialogue as an example of how to individualize this exercise to specific client responses, suggestions, and comments as you and the client work through the exercise.

Therapist: Pulling out is a very natural and seemingly logical reaction to free yourself from the finger trap, but what happens when we do that? [Hold up your finger trap and encourage the client to try pulling out again.]

Client: It doesn't work. I'm stuck.

Therapist: I notice that too. Our fingers only get caught more tightly, creating more discomfort and less room to move.

Client: So how do we get out of here?

Therapist: Perhaps getting out is not the main issue. The good news is that there *is* an alternative that does work, insofar as it gives you some space and room to move. To get there, however, you have to approach this situation differently. What could that be?

Client: I am not quite sure. There has to be some kind of trick that will do it and get me out of here. Perhaps I need to pull in a different way.

Therapist: Okay, why don't you go ahead and do that and see what happens.

Client: It doesn't work either. I am still stuck.

Therapist: So am I. Let me give you a hint. We have to do something that goes against the grain and doesn't seem

HIGHLIGHT BOX 10.3   (continued)

to make sense at first. Instead of pulling out, we could push our fingers *in*. Let us try that instead and see what happens [Therapist models gently leaning into the tube.]

Client: Well, I can move now, but I still can't get out of the trap. I'm still in it.

Therapist: So am I. We might not get out of the trap, but as you noticed, pushing the fingers in definitely gave you more space to move around. It seems like leaning into the tube gave us more wiggle room. What if we didn't need to get out of the finger trap at all? What if we just created some more space for us to have what we have, to experience what there is to be experienced?

Client: That sounds weird and scary — and I don't like it.

Therapist: I understand that you do not like and would want to get away from things that scare you like your [insert some of client's worst fears]. But what happens when you keep on pulling away from what you have? The harder you pull away from your anxiety, the more the trap tightens, and the more stuck you are. Trying to get rid of your anxiety, trying to reduce it when it's there, trying not to have it come back when it happens to be gone — what has all this pulling and controlling done to your life? Has it created more space for you to do what really matters to you, or has it taken over more and more of your life?

Client: Well, what I have done certainly hasn't helped much or solved any problems. So tell me, what should I do instead?

Therapist: I am not quite sure, but when you look at these finger traps, pulling away doesn't seem to work, does it? Yet doing something counterintuitive, pushing your fingers *in* rather than *out*, has given you space and new options to make moves. Perhaps doing something that goes against the grain is a way of getting yourself unstuck from where you are with your life right now. What could you do that would go against the grain?

them as equivalent to their direct and socially established referents. With fusion, language, rules, stories we tell about ourselves and our lives, and evaluations of our experience (really more thoughts) tend to dominate over direct and more experiential contingencies, and in a way people live more in their heads than in the world of raw experience. This process can manifest itself in many ways.

For instance, some people fuse their sense of self with "being right," "looking smart," "being loved," "never making a mistake," and the stories they tell about their past. All humans are susceptible to fusion. In fact, wars have been fought through this very process. This, in turn, can lead to a narrowing of behavioral options. Thus, if you buy into "being right," you may act in ways to defend that sense of rightness or avoid situations and experiences where you might be wrong, even at significant cost to you. See Highlight Box 10.4 for one of several exercises designed to undermine fusion and to teach defusion (see also Forsyth & Eifert, 2007; Hayes et al., 1999).

HIGHLIGHT BOX 10.4

UNDERMINING FUSION WITH DEFUSION

Defusion strategies are designed to teach clients to acknowledge thoughts as thoughts, feelings as feelings, urges as urges, memories as memories, and so on, without engagement, without struggle. Distinguishing a person's thoughts from who they are gives people perspective, and they become more able to notice when their mind is serving them well or not.

Many ACT-relevant exercises, ranging from mindfulness practice (e.g., noticing the breath, taking your mind for a walk) to more metaphorical strategies, can be employed. Here, we describe one exercise that has been used for difficult private content. We call it *concretizing your thoughts* (see also Hayes et al., 1999).

In this exercise, the therapist writes the client's urge, worry, or other unwanted thought on an index card. Then the therapist puts the card in the client's hand and asks the client to push the card. The client is asked to increase the strength of the push. When the client pushes harder to make the urge or thought "go away," the friction causes the card to stay in the palm of the client's hand. Then the therapist asks the client to simply put the card in the client's lap and leave it alone, sit there, and do nothing. The therapist asks the client to look at the card and its corresponding text and notice the difference in effort between "pushing" the urge away compared to simply letting it be.

This can be repeated for any number of thoughts, urges, or feelings. Normally, we would ask the client to continue this activity at home. When difficult private content shows up, simply write it on an index card or piece of paper. Then just *notice* it. A moment ago the thought seemed really heavy, but now it is out and revealed for what it is — a bunch of letters, a bunch of words. Clients are encouraged to hold and notice the thoughts on the cards and to carry them in their pocket or bag throughout the day. The activity is useful in teaching (a) that the client is not their thoughts, (b) that thoughts can be observed and noticed without acting on them, (c) that clients can move with the thoughts and do something else, and (d) that although clients may not choose to experience challenging thoughts, clients can choose what to do with them.

We should add here that therapists are human beings and are not immune to fusion processes. For instance, when you first start seeing clients, you may be preoccupied with thoughts about "being helpful" or your "sense of credibility" and "avoiding making a mistake." You might even find yourself stuck with the discomfort of not knowing what to say or do, and so to resolve that, you say or do this or that when it is not in the best interest of the client. You may even fill painful silence with chatter, thus rescuing yourself and your client from the unease.

The point here is that fusion can, at times, pull us out of the immediate present moment and result in insensitivity to the experiences that are afforded to us. With fusion, we fail to see that our verbal constructions of the world are not the world, and we respond more to the products of our mind than to direct experience. Defusion can be a powerful way to gain space and more response options.

ACT in Practice

In practice, none of this unfolds in a step-by-step linear fashion. Rather, ACT in practice tends to be more like a dance, where therapist and client move back and forth between acceptance and mindfulness processes on the one hand and commitment and behavior change processes on the other. The larger goal is to undermine processes that feed psychological inflexibility while promoting psychological flexibility (Hayes et al., 1999, 2004). This work can be challenging for client and therapist alike, and thus it is important to spend time with the core competencies (see Strosahl, Hayes, Wilson, & Gifford, 2004) entailed in the ACT therapeutic stance (see Highlight Box 10.5).

It is also equally important to apply ACT concepts in your own life. The reason is simple and has to do with practicing what we preach. Regardless of the brand of therapy you practice, you ought to use the techniques and strategies when you encounter difficulties in your life so that you understand (a) how to apply them, (b) how well they work and for what purpose, and (c) what the challenges as well as expected benefits are of applying them.

There is another reason for practicing what we preach, and that has to do with being genuine in therapy. If you are recommending that a client do something that you think is helpful, you ought to have a strong sense that it is helpful. You also ought to be willing to use that

---

HIGHLIGHT BOX 10.5

THE ACT THERAPEUTIC STANCE

In ACT, the therapeutic stance is crucial to creating a meaningful and useful therapeutic relationship, namely one that fosters the client's development of psychological flexibility. The ACT therapeutic stance stems from the core assumption that suffering is endemic to the human condition. In other words, we're all in the same soup together – therapists and clients alike struggle with worry, pain, sadness, guilt, and so on.

The implication here is that you have to begin applying the ACT model of language and human functioning to your own professional and personal life. This can be a bit challenging and anxiety provoking at times, but it can be helpful to remember why we are involved in this profession in the first place: to alleviate human suffering and help individuals find ways to live more meaningful and vital lives.

So how do you as a therapist go about creating an ACT-consistent therapeutic stance? One important way is by modeling psychological flexibility yourself. If you find yourself reacting emotionally to a client's story about a traumatic event in his or her past, you might say something like "I notice that I am feeling upset by your story." You can also foster psychological flexibility in clients by encouraging them to stay present with whatever painful experience they are having. You, as a therapist, can practice this in-the-moment presence too. Watch for places where you are being pulled to do something that is in the service of being right, looking smart, appearing helpful, or not making a mistake or places where you say and do something in session to alleviate the discomfort you are experiencing or to rescue the client from his or her own discomfort. These and other tactics are common with new therapists (and some seasoned ones too) and again illustrate places where we can get stuck just like our clients.

HIGHLIGHT BOX 10.5 (*continued*)

When a client struggles with any problematic thought or feeling, it can be tempting to provide information or tools about how to "fix" the problem. From the ACT perspective, it's more important to be willing to experience your own discomfort at not being able to solve your clients' problems. Remember, it's not clients' emotions and thoughts that are the enemy; it's the struggle with these thoughts and feelings that is potentially harmful.

If you are faced with a situation in session that you aren't sure how to handle or that brings up your own issues (and this will surely happen!), remember the basic premise that you and the client are both human beings with the same sorts of problems, desires, goals, and dreams. Your job as an ACT therapist is not to argue with clients or persuade them to "see the light." It's your job to help them find more workable ways to live well and in accordance with their values without wallowing in, drowning in, or needlessly struggling with forms of emotional and psychological pain that will show up now and then.

In sum, the ACT therapeutic stance in session means approaching clients with a sense of equality, honesty, openness, compassion, vulnerability, and a genuine interest in helping them find more useful ways to live in accordance with their values.

---

intervention for yourself. The research literature will help you answer this question, but it will only take you so far. Think how you learned to ride a bike and you will quickly connect with the limits of written or oral forms of knowledge and the importance of learning by doing and direct experience. No book, article, or movie will teach you to ride. You have to do it and do it over and over again. The same is true about developing competence in ACT or any other form of therapy.

ACT Research Support and Criticisms

There is now a growing basic and applied research base showing that ACT is effective for a broad range of problems (Hayes et al., 2004). This work includes both effectiveness and efficacy studies in diverse areas such as anxiety, stress, depression, substance use disorders, chronic pain, diabetes, epilepsy, eating disorders, and some of the more serious problems that we know of, namely, psychosis (see Hayes et al., 2004). Additional work is ongoing on the basic research end, including work in RFT and experimental psychopathology. Newer work even shows that training in ACT and mindfulness tends to improve therapist effectiveness for a wide range of clients and clinical problems (e.g., Grepamair et al., 2007; Lappalainen et al., 2007; Strosahl, Hayes, Bergan, & Romano, 1998).

This kind of breadth is unusual in the current mental health care climate, where the tendency has been to develop and test treatments matched to specific disorders. ACT, by contrast, is a model of processes that feed many forms of human suffering. If the model is correct, then areas where those processes show up ought to be amenable to ACT interventions. Thus, it is not surprising that ACT is working for such a broad range of problems that are linked to the model. If you look closely, you will see that many forms of psychopathology are linked in one way or another to excessive experiential avoidance and cognitive fusion and the narrowing effects of both in terms of activities that matter to people. What ACT seems to do is give people the freedom to make choices and take action in important life areas and to risk the pain and joys that may come when they take steps in directions of their chosen values.

We should add here that ACT is just beginning to be subjected to criticism from within the behavior therapy community (Arch & Craske, in press; Hofmann & Asmundson, 2008; Öst, 2008). The criticisms, and there are several, tend to reflect unfamiliarity with the basic philosophical, theoretical, and science foundations of ACT. Some have claimed, mostly in unpublished forms, that ACT is a cult, that it offers nothing new, that it is proselytized as a way of life, that it is a fad, that it is based in Buddhist thought, and on and on. People here seem to be speaking at odds and fail to see that ACT is a part of behavior therapy — it is a model, not merely a treatment technology. As such, ACT must be evaluated in terms of its own goals and objectives, not standards and objectives held by other scientific areas (Hayes, in press).

Some of the criticisms are more substantive, however. ACT has yet to reach the level of an empirically supported psychosocial intervention by conventional standards (e.g., large randomized clinical trials patterned on the FDA model of psychotherapy treatment development established with the Division 12 Task Force Criterion, 1995). Yet, it is well on its way to doing that. The ACT community of scientists and practitioners has resisted following the more traditional FDA model of treatment development and instead has focused on establishing empirically supported principles of change (Hayes, in press) — principles that are broad in scope, are precise, have depth, retain a link between the more basic and applied branches of science, and can be disseminated and tested readily for a wide range of problems. This approach, interestingly

enough, is exactly what helped pave the way for behavior therapy's early successes.

SUMMARY AND CONCLUSIONS

When viewed historically, behavior therapy has been an enormously successful experiment. Its success, in turn, is based in large part on approaching clinical science with at least one eye on practical utility. This approach paved the way for many effective intervention technologies for a wide range of problems. The growth and expansion of behavior therapy through the first two generations and into its present form represent characteristics of a progressive science.

The challenges and limitations of first- and second-wave behavior therapy are being met by the third-generation approaches. These approaches, in turn, (a) are grounded in an empirical, principle-focused approach, (b) employ contextual and experiential as well as direct change strategies, (c) aim to construct more effective and flexible repertoires over the elimination of narrowly defined problems, (d) emphasize the relevance of the topics they examine for practitioners as well as their clients, (e) integrate and synthesize work from previous generations, (f) address questions and domains previously reserved for other traditions, and (g) improve our understanding of processes and outcomes. This work, in turn, is yielding an expanded and richer view of psychological health and human suffering and a clinical science more adequate to the human condition.

We end here as we began. We are all in the business of understanding, preventing, and alleviating human suffering while promoting human dignity and vitality. The clinical prize here is a life, one that does not disavow normal pain and hardship but creates space to move with that pain in the service of valued ends. For a time behavior therapy has been in the business of helping people to think and feel better in order to live better. With the third wave, the view has been tipped on its head. The focus is now on helping people to live well with whatever they may think or feel. This is the secret to creating a life — we do it by what we spend our time doing, one small step at a time.

The task we face as scientists and practitioners is serious business. We have come a long way and still have a long way to go. It is now your turn. You are the next generation. What will you do?

Glossary

Behavior analysis: An integrated basic and applied branch of psychology concerned with the prediction and control (influence) of behavior via identification and manipulation of consequences that follow behavior. This view is grounded in the philosophy of science known as radical behaviorism. The applied branch of behavior analysis is often used synonymously with behavior modification, and terms such as applied behavior analysis. Clinical behavior analysis is a newer branch of behavior analysis most closely affiliated with outpatient psychotherapy.

Behavior Therapy: Comprises the systematic application of operant and respondent learning principles and contemporary learning theory for the purposes of scientific understanding and the alleviation of human suffering in therapy. This approach values objectivity and demands that rigorous empirical standards of proof be applied to treatment development and ongoing evaluation of psychosocial treatment outcomes.

Cognitive-Behavior Therapy: A branch of behavior therapy that considers cognition as something other than behavior, and therefore requiring a unique conceptual system and procedures to account for it. Cognition is said to mediate or cause other behavior, and faulty cognitive processes are believed to contribute to the etiology, maintenance, and treatment of abnormal behavior. Traditional behavior therapists, who hold to the monistic assumption that cognition is behavior, regard the hyphenated term "cognitive-behavioral" as a redundancy.

Methodological Behaviorism: Is a normative theory about the scientific conduct of psychology and claims that psychology should concern itself with the observable behavior of organisms (human and nonhuman animals), not mental events such as thoughts, feelings, and other similar private constructions. The reason is that private events fail to meet the criterion of public agreement. In this view, reference to mental events adds nothing to explaining the variables controlling behavior. Mental events are private entities which, given the necessary publicity of science, do not form proper objects of empirical study. Methodological behaviorism is at the core of John B. Watson's (1878–1958) behaviorism, *not* Burrhus F. Skinner's (1904–1990) radical behaviorism.

Scientist-Practitioner Model: Originated out of the 1949 conference in Boulder, Colorado. The model stipulated a framework for training clinical psychologists such that clinical psychologists should be (a) producers of scientific knowledge, (b) consumers of scientific knowledge, and (c) evaluators of knowledge via data-driven outcomes assessment in their work with those they serve.

Social Learning: A theory, developed by Albert Bandura, proposing that the influence of environmental events on the acquisition and regulation of behavior is largely determined by cognitive processes. Expectancies and vicarious learning play a central role and the person is viewed as an agent and an object of environmental influences.

References

American Psychiatric Association (2000). *Diagnostic and statistical manual of mental disorders* (4th ed.), text revision. Washington, DC: Author.

Arch, J. & Craske, M. G. (in press). Need Article Title. *Clinical Psychology: Science and Practice.*

Ayllon, T., Haughton, E., & Hughes, H. B. (1965). Interpretation of symptoms: fact or fiction. *Behavior Research and Therapy, 3,* 1–7.

Baer, R. A. (2003). Mindfulness training as a clinical intervention: a conceptual and empirical review. *Clinical Psychology: Science and Practice, 10,* 125–143.

Bandura, A. (1969). *Principles of behavior modification.* New York: Holt, Rinehart, & Winston.

Barlow, D. H., Allen, L. B., & Choate, M. L. (2004). Toward a unified treatment for emotional disorders. *Behavior Therapy, 35,* 205–230.

Baumeister, R. F., Bratslavsky, E., Muraven, M., & Tice, D. (1998). Ego depletion: is the active self a limited resource? *Journal of Personality and Social Psychology, 74,* 1252–1265.

Beck, A. T. (1964). Thinking and depression: II. Theory and therapy. *Archives of General Psychiatry, 10,* 561–571.

Beck, A. T. (1970). Cognitive therapy: nature and relation to behavior therapy. *Behavior Therapy, 1,* 184–200.

Beck, A. T. (1976). *Cognitive therapy for emotional disorders.* New York: International Universities Press.

Beck, A. T. (1993). Cognitive therapy: past, present, and future. *Journal of Consulting and Clinical Psychology, 61,* 194–198.

Blackledge, J. T. & Hayes, S. C. (2001). Emotion regulation in Acceptance and Commitment Therapy. *JCLP/In session: Psychotherapy in Practice, 57,* 243–255.

Bonanno, G. A., Papa, A., LaLande, K., Westphal, M., & Coifman, K. (2004). The importance of being flexible: the ability to both enhance and suppress emotional expression predicts long-term adjustment. *Psychological Science, 15,* 482–487.

Burns, D. D. & Spangler, D. L. (2001). Do changes in dysfunctional attitudes mediate changes in depression and anxiety in cognitive behavioral therapy? *Behavior Therapy, 32,* 337–369.

Butler, E. A. & Gross, J. J. (2004). Hiding feelings in social contexts: out of sight is not out of mind. In P. Philippot & R. S. Feldman (Eds.), *The regulation of emotion* (pp. 101–126). Mahwah, NJ: Erlbaum Associates.

Cartwright, D. E. (1955). Effectiveness of psychotherapy: a critique of the spontaneous remission argument. *Journal of Counseling Psychology, 2,* 290–296.

Cioffi, D. & Holloway, J. (1993). Delayed costs of suppressed pain. *Journal of Personality and Social Psychology, 64,* 274–282.

Clark, D. M., Ball, S., & Pape, D. (1991). An experimental investigation of thought suppression. *Behaviour Research and Therapy, 29,* 253–257.

Dobson, K. S. & Khatri, N. (2000). Cognitive therapy: looking backward, looking forward. *Journal of Clinical Psychology, 56,* 907–923.

Eifert, G. H. & Heffner, M. (2003). The effects of acceptance versus control contexts on avoidance of panic-related symptoms. *Journal of Behavior Therapy and Experimental Psychiatry, 34,* 293–312.

Eifert, G. H. & Forsyth, J. P. (2005). *Acceptance and Commitment Therapy for anxiety disorders: a practitioner's treatment guide to using mindfulness, acceptance, and value-based behavior change strategies.* Oakland, CA: New Harbinger.

Ellis, A. (1962). *Reason and emotion in psychotherapy.* New York: Lyle Stuart.

Eysenck, H. J. (1952). The effects of psychotherapy: an evaluation. *Journal of Consulting Psychology, 16,* 319–324.

Eifert, G. H. & Heffner, M. (2003). The effects of acceptance versus control contexts on avoidance of panic-related sysptoms. *Journal of Behavior and Experimental Psychiatry, 34,* 293–312.

Forsyth, J. P. & Eifert, G. H. (2007). *The mindfulness and acceptance workbook for anxiety: a guide to breaking free from anxiety, phobias, and worry using Acceptance and Commitment Therapy.* Oakland, CA: New Harbinger.

Forsyth, J. P., Eifert, G. H., & Barrios, V. (2006). Fear conditioning research as a clinical analog: what makes fear learning disordered? In M. G. Craske, D. Hermans, & D. Vansteenwegen (Eds.), *Fear and learning: basic science to clinical application* (pp. 133–153). Washington, DC: American Psychological Association.

Forsyth, J. P., Lejuez, C., Hawkins, R. P., & Eifert, G. H. (1996). A critical evaluation of cognitions as causes of behavior. *Journal of Behavior Therapy and Experimental Psychiatry, 27,* 369–376.

Forsyth, J. P. & Sabsevitz, J. (2002). Behavior therapy: historical perspective and overview. In M. Hersen & W. Sledge (Eds.), *Encyclopedia of psychotherapy,* vol. 1 (pp. 259–275). New York: Elsevier.

Franks, C. M. (1997). It was the best of times, it was the worst of times. *Behavior Therapy, 28,* 389–396.

Franks, C. M. & Wilson, G. T. (1974). *Annual review of behavior therapy: theory and practice.* New York: Brunner/Mazel.

Freud, S. (1909). Analysis of a phobia in a five year old boy. In *Standard edition, 10,* 3–147.

Gold, D. B. & Wegner, D. M. (1995). Origins of ruminative thought: trauma, incompleteness, nondisclosure, and suppression. *Journal of Applied Social Psychology, 25,* 1245–1261.

Goldfried, M. R. & Davison, G. C. (1976). *Clinical behavior therapy.* New York: Wiley.

Goldfried, M. R. & Davison, G. C. (1994). *Clinical behavior therapy, expanded edition.* New York: Wiley.

Gortner, E. T., Gollan, J. K., Dobson, K. S., & Jacobson, N. S. (1998). Cognitive-behavioral treatment for depression: relapse prevention. *Journal of Consulting and Clinical Psychology, 66,* 377–384.

Grepamair, L., Mitterlehner, F., Loew, T., Bachler, E., Rother, W., & Nickel, M. (2007). Promoting mindfulness in psychotherapists in training influences the treatment results of their patients: a randomized, double-blind, controlled study. *Psychotherapy and Psychosomatics, 76*, 33–338.

Gross, J. J. (1998a). The emerging field of emotion regulation: an integrative review. *Review of General Psychology, 2*, 271–299.

Gross, J. J. (1998b). Antecedent — and response-focused emotion regulation: divergent consequences for experience, expression, and physiology. *Journal of Personality and Social Psychology, 74*, 224–237.

Gross, J. J. & Levenson, R. W. (1993). Emotional suppression: physiology, self-report, and expressive behavior. *Journal of Personality and Social Psychology, 64*, 970–986.

Gross, J. J. & Levenson, R. W. (1997). Hiding feelings: the acute effects of inhibiting negative and positive emotion. *Journal of Abnormal Psychology, 106*, 95–103.

Haubert, L. C. & Dobson, K. S. (2007). Treatment of depression and mechanisms of change: strengthening the links among theory, research, and practice. *Clinical Psychology: Science and Practice, 14*, 247–251.

Hayes, S. C. (1993). Goals and varieties of scientific contextualism. In S. C. Hayes, L. J. Hayes, H. W. Reese, & T. R. Sarbin (Eds.), *The varieties of scientific contextualism* (pp. 11–27). Reno. NV: Context Press.

Hayes, S. C. (2004). Acceptance and Commitment Therapy, Relational Frame Theory, and the third wave of behavioral and cognitive therapies. *Behavior Therapy, 35*, 639–666.

Hayes, S. C. (in press). Climbing our hills: a beginning conversation of the comparison between ACT and traditional CBT. *Clinical Psychology: Science and Practice*.

Hayes, S. C., Barlow, D. H., & Nelson-Gray, R. O. (1999). *The scientist practitioner: research and accountability in the age of managed care* (2nd ed.). Boston, MA: Allyn & Bacon.

Hayes, S. C., Barnes-Holmes, D., & Roche, B. (2001). *Relational frame theory: a post-Skinnerian account of human language and cognition*. New York: Kluwer.

Hayes, S. C. & Brownstein, A. J. (1986). Mentalism, behavior-behavior relations, and a behavior-analytic view of the purposes of science. *The Behavior Analyst, 9*, 175–190.

Hayes, S. C., Follette, V. M., & Linehan, M. M. (2004). *Mindfulness and acceptance: expanding the cognitive-behavioral tradition*. New York: Guilford Press.

Hayes, S. C., Hayes, L. J., Reese, H. W., & Sarbin, T. R. (Eds.) (1993). *Varieties of scientific contextualism*. Reno, NV: Context Press.

Hayes, S. C., Luoma, J. B., Bond, F. W., Masuda, A., & Lillis, J. (2006). Acceptance and Commitment Therapy: model, process, and outcomes. *Behaviour Research and Therapy, 44*, 1–25.

Hayes, S. C., Strosahl, K., & Wilson, K. G. (1999). *Acceptance and Commitment Therapy: an experimental approach to behavior change*. New York: Guilford Press.

Hayes, S. C., Wilson, K. G., Gifford, E. V., Follette, V. M., & Strosahl, K. (1996). Experiential avoidance and behavioral disorders: a functional dimensional approach to diagnosis and treatment. *Journal of Consulting and Clinical Psychology, 64*, 1152–1168.

Hofmann, S. G. & Asmundson, G. J. (2008). Acceptance and mindfulness-based therapy: new wave or old hat? *Clinical Psychology Review, 28*, 1–16.

Ilardi, S. S. & Craighead, W. E. (1994). The role of non-specific factors in cognitive-behavior therapy for depression. *Clinical Psychology: Science and Practice, 1*, 138–156.

Jacobson, N. S., Dobson, K. S., Truax, P. A., Addis, M. E., Koerner, K., Gollan, J. K., Gortner, E., & Prince, S. E. (1996). A component analysis of cognitive-behavioral treatment for depression. *Journal of Consulting and Clinical Psychology, 64*, 295–304.

Jones, M. C. (1924). A laboratory study of fear: the case of Peter. *Pedagogical Seminar, 31*, 308–315.

Karekla, M., Forsyth, J. P., & Kelly, M. M. (2004). Emotional avoidance and panicogenic responding to a biological challenge procedure. *Behavior Therapy, 35*, 725–746.

Lang, P. J. (1968). Fear reduction and fear behavior: problems in treating a construct. In J. M. Schlien (Ed.), *Research in psychotherapy*, vol. 3 (pp. 90–102). Washington, DC: American Psychological Association.

Lappalainen, R., Lehtonen, T., Skarp, E., Taubert, E., Ojanen, M., & Hayes, S. C. (2007). The impact of CBT and ACT models using psychology trainee therapists: a preliminary controlled effectiveness trial. *Behavior Modification, 31*(4), 488–511.

Lavy, E. H. & van den Hout, M. A. (1990). Thought suppression induces intrusions. *Behavioural Psychotherapy, 18*, 251–258.

Lazarus, A. A. (1989). *The practice of multimodal therapy*. Baltimore, MD: Johns Hopkins University Press.

Lindsley, O. R. (1968, March). *Training parents and teachers to precisely manage children's behavior*. Address presented at the C.S. Mott Foundation Children's Health Center.

Longmore, R. & Worrell, M. (2006). Do we need to challenge thoughts in cognitive behaviour therapy? *Clinical Psychology Review, 27*, 173–187.

Luborsky, L. (1954). A note on Eysenck's article: "The effects of psychotherapy: an evaluation." *British Journal of Psychology, 45*, 129–131.

Luoma, J. B., Hayes, S. C., & Walser, R. (2007). *Learning ACT: an Acceptance & Commitment Therapy Skills-Training Manual for Therapists*. Oakland, CA: New Harbinger & Context Press.

Malott, R. W. & Suarez, E. A. T. (2003). *Principles of behavior*. New York: Prentice Hall.

Markon, K. E., Krueger, R. F., & Watson, D. (2005). Delineating the structure of normal and abnormal personality:

an integrative hierarchical approach. *Journal of Personality and Social Psychology*, 88, 139–157.

Marx, B. P. & Sloan, D. M. (2002). The role of emotion in the psychological functioning of adult survivors of childhood sexual abuse. *Behavior Therapy*, 33, 563–577.

McCracken, L. M. (1998). Learning to live with pain: acceptance of pain predicts adjustment in persons with chronic pain. *Pain*, 74, 21–27.

McCracken, L. M., Spertus, I. L., Janeck, A. S., Sinclair, D., & Wetzel, F. T. (1999). Behavioral dimensions of adjustment in persons with chronic pain: pain-related anxiety and acceptance. *Pain*, 80, 283–289.

Meichenbaum, D. (1977). *Cognitive-behavior modification: an integrative approach*. New York: Plenum.

O'Donohue, W. (Ed.) (1998). *Learning and behavior therapy*. New York: Allyn & Bacon.

O'Donohue, W., Fisher, J. E., & Hayes, S. C. (2003). *Cognitive behavior therapy: applying empirically supported techniques in your practice*. New York: Wiley.

O'Donohue, W. & Kitchener, R. (Eds.) (1999). *Handbook of behaviorism*. New York: Academic Press.

Öst, L. G. (2008). Efficacy of the third wave of behavior therapies: a systematic review and meta-analysis. *Behaviour Research and Therapy*, 46, 296–321.

Purdon, C. (1999). Thought suppression and psychopathology. *Behaviour Research and Therapy*, 37, 1029–1054.

Richards, J. M. & Gross, J. J. (1999). Composure at any cost? the cognitive consequences of emotion suppression. *Personality and Social Psychology Bulletin*, 25, 1033–1044.

Richards, J. M. & Gross, J. J. (2000). Emotion regulation and memory: the cognitive costs of keeping one's cool. *Journal of Personality and Social Psychology*, 79, 410–424.

Robins, C. J. & Hayes, A. M. (1993). An appraisal of cognitive therapy. *Journal of Consulting and Clinical Psychology*, 61, 205–214.

Skinner, B. F. (1953). *Science and human behavior*. New York: The Free Press.

Skinner, B. F. (1957). *Verbal behavior*. New York: Appleton-Century-Crofts.

Skinner, B. F. (1974). *About behaviorism*. New York: Vintage Books.

Skinner, B. F., Solomon, H. C., & Lindsley, O. R. (1953, November 30). *Studies in behavior therapy: status report I.* Waltham, MA: Metropolitan State Hospital.

Smith, M. L. & Glass, G. V. (1977). Meta-analysis of psychotherapy outcome studies. *American Psychologist*, 32, 752–760.

Strosahl, K. D., Hayes, S. C., Bergan, J., & Romano, P. (1998). Assessing the field effectiveness of Acceptance and Commitment Therapy: an example of the manipulated training research method. *Behavior Therapy*, 29, 35–64.

Strosahl, K. D., Hayes, S. C., Wilson, K. G., & Gifford, E. V. (2004). An ACT primer: core therapy processes, intervention strategies, and therapist competencies. In S. C. Hayes & K. D. Strosahl (Eds.), *A practical guide to acceptance and commitment therapy* (pp. 34–58). New York: Springer.

Task Force on Promotion and Dissemination of Psychological Procedures (1995). Training in and dissemination of empirically-validated psychological treatments. *The Clinical Psychologist*, 48(1), 3–23.

Watson, D. (2005). Rethinking the mood and anxiety disorders: a quantitative hierarchical model for DSM-V. *Journal of Abnormal Psychology*, 114, 522–536.

Watson, J. B. (1913). Psychology as a behaviorist views it. *Psychological Review*, 20, 158–177.

Watson, J. B. & Rayner, R. (1920). Conditioned emotional reactions. *Journal of Experimental Psychology*, 3, 1–14.

Wegner, D. M., Schneider, D. J., Carter, S. R., & White, T. L. (1987). Paradoxical effects of thoughts suppression. *Journal of Personality and Social Psychology*, 53, 5–13.

Wegner, D. M., Schneider, D. J., Knutson, B., & McMahon, S. R. (1991). Polluting the stream of consciousness: the effect of thought suppression on the mind's environment. *Cognitive Therapy and Research*, 15, 141–152.

Wegner, D. M. & Zanakos, S. (1994). Chronic thought suppression. *Journal of Personality*, 62, 615–640.

Wolpe, J. (1958). *Psychotherapy by reciprocal inhibition*. Stanford, CA: Stanford University Press.

Wolpe, J. & Rachman, S. (1960). Psychoanalytic "evidence": a critique based on Freud's case of Little Hans. *Journal of Nervous and Mental Disease*, 131, 135–148.

Yates, A. J. (1970). *Behavior therapy*. New York: Wiley.

Zuriff, G. E. (1985). *Behaviorism: a conceptual reconstruction*. New York: Columbia University Press.

Cognitive-Behavioral Therapy: Breadth, Range, and Diversity

William C. Oakley
Midwestern University

Arthur Freeman
Governors State University

OUTLINE

"Revolutions are not made; they come. A revolution is as natural a growth as an oak. It comes out of the past. Its foundations are laid far back."— Wendell Phillips

THE COGNITIVE REVOLUTION: AN INTRODUCTION

If one were to perform a data search using the PsycINFO database and type the key term "cognitive therapy," limiting the publication criteria to end in 1970, only 10 articles would be found under this condition, and none would be found using the search term "cognitive-behavioral therapy." Since that time, however, the literature on this therapy has grown exponentially, with some considering its implementation to have been a revolution in the therapeutic milieu. Today, cognitive therapy is widely accepted as an empirically supported, cost-effective psychotherapy for many disorders and psychological problems. In those early days it was important to clearly spell out what cognitive therapy was and what it was not. Now, 30 years later, it may even be more important to distinguish cognitive therapy from other noncognitive therapies, and also among the many offshoots of the original work. It is important for the reader to observe that throughout this chapter we will use the terms *cognitive therapy* (CT) and *cognitive-behavioral therapy* (CBT) interchangeably. The term CBT is more of a general term for a broad array of approaches that have been conceptualized by clinicians in the field over the past three decades. The reasoning for the abundance of therapeutic approaches under the auspices of CBT is not so much due to an underlying disagreement of the foundation of CBT but rather can be reframed and understood more fully as attempts to continually research and broaden our understanding of humans through a CBT lens.

An Overview of CBT

Many students beginning their academic study of, and practice in, the myriad applications of psychotherapy can be bombarded by several different theoretical forms of psychotherapy at the same time. Keeping this in mind, it is important for the reader to understand that CBT, as with most forms of psychotherapy, is more than a set of techniques to be used during therapy sessions. CBT is a comprehensive perspective on how to conceptualize human behavior and psychopathology. At its core, CBT emphasizes the role of cognitions/thoughts in the etiology and maintenance of psychopathology and how emotions and behaviors are a result of our cognitions. Throughout the process of therapy there is a therapeutic collaboration in which the therapist strives to engage clients during all phases of treatment.

In the course of the therapeutic sessions, the client takes an **active** role describing their current difficulties and is considered the expert of their own life. The therapist, on the other hand, is **directive** and helps the client become aware of cognitive distortions that cause psychological distress. Further, the therapist's expertise in research-based techniques is utilized to assist the client in developing specific interventions. Because of both skills deficits and emotional problems, the therapy work often takes on a **psychoeducational** focus. Additionally, during the session the client and therapist engage in a process known as **collaborative empiricism**. Within this perspective, clients are encouraged to develop a scientific perspective in which they make objective interpretations of data collected during therapeutic activities. The client-therapist collaboration generates hypotheses for clients to test during individualized in-session work and through structured **homework** assignments. As a result, cognitive behavior therapy is **problem-oriented** (as opposed to focused on vague complaints) and **solution-focused** (to help the client reach closure and develop sustainable coping skills).

In CBT, there are three levels of cognitions that the therapist attempts to access during therapy: automatic, intermediate beliefs, and the **dynamic** level of the core beliefs or schema (See Fig. 11.1). Automatic thoughts are spontaneous rapid beliefs that are often outside of our immediate awareness but can be brought to attention easily. They represent our internalized commentary of experienced events. In contrast, intermediate beliefs include attitudes and assumptions in rules and expectations that people make about the world. At the cognitive core are schemas, or the central ideas of self that individuals hold that underlie the more manifest automatic cognitions. Schemas are also reflected in the content of immediate beliefs and are often described as global, overgeneralized, and absolute (Beck, 1995). The three levels of cognition can be compared to a piece of fruit, with the outer layer of skin representing the automatic beliefs a person experiences. Just underneath the skin are the intermediate beliefs a person holds, and beneath that, at the very center, reside the core schemas that form the foundation of how a person understands one's self and the world.

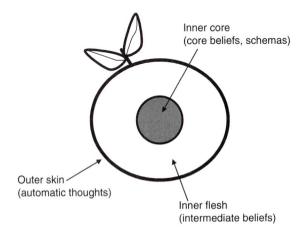

FIGURE 11.1 The three levels of cognitive therapy.

The Cognitive Revolution

As Wendell Phillips eloquently proposed, revolutions are not just formed out of the mind of one individual with their own unique ideas. Revolutions are founded on the work of many individuals throughout political, scientific, academic, social, and philosophical discord. The cognitive revolution was no exception, taking place in many locations at the same time, and involved a number of subject areas beyond the therapeutic milieu, including the studies of memory, language, imagery, and attention. In fact, the cognitive revolution could be considered a counterrevolution in psychology, which brought the mind back into psychology, going beyond the behaviorist assertion at the time that psychology could qualify as a science only by restricting itself to the study of observable behavior (Miller, 2003). It is an important point to note that there were many individuals who contributed to the cognitive revolution that did not even receive training in the field of psychology. It was the work of individuals such as Noam Chomsky (a linguist), who demonstrated the ineffectiveness of Skinner's simple learning model of language, Allen Newell (a computer scientist) and Herbert Simon (an economist), who studied artificial intelligence and the psychology of human cognition, and many others who provided critical ideas in the early cognitive literature (Campbell, 1999). For the purposes of this chapter, however, the focus will be on the development of the revolution's applied cousin, cognitive therapy.

The notion of revolutions synthesizing ideas from the past holds true for the cognitive revolution in psychotherapy, with a centuries-old foundation dating back to antiquity. In a letter Sir Isaac Newton wrote to fellow English scientist Robert Hooke regarding his life work in the field of physics, he stated: "If I have seen further, it is by standing on the shoulders of giants." What Newton may be referring to is the fact that modern researchers owe much of their current base of knowledge to what scientists and researchers developed before them. What was true for Newton is true of the two most celebrated cognitive-behavioral theorists and therapists, Drs. Albert Ellis and Aaron T. Beck, who stood on the shoulders of many giants, including George Kelly, Alfred Korzybski, Immanuel Kant, B.F. Skinner, Albert Bandura, Jean Piaget, and others.

The initial portion of this chapter will describe pertinent philosophical perspectives that have influenced the development of CBT and how each of these philosophical foundations has found their way into the actual practice of cognitive therapy. This will be followed by a general overview of how behaviorism and the social cognitive theory have influenced CBT. Finally, there will be a review of a few key CBT therapeutic models used today along with a highlight of the similarities and differences between the forms of cognitive therapy described.

PHILOSOPHICAL UNDERPINNINGS OF CBT

Stoicism

One of the roots of CBT can be dated back to the first-century traditions of the Stoic philosophers (Stumpf, 1994). In some respects the Stoics could be thought of as the first psychotherapists. The Stoic philosopher Epictetus of the first century said, "I cannot escape death, but cannot I escape the dread of it?" (Stumpf, 1994). The Stoics believed that humans cannot control all events, but we can control our attitude toward what happens to and around us. For the Stoics, the achievement of knowledge was a major topic of discussion. They believed that all knowledge enters the mind through the senses. Since all knowledge is knowledge of sense-objects, truth is simply the correspondence of impressions and perceptions to things. Concepts are merely ideas in the mind, abstracted from gathered

information, and possess no reality outside one's consciousness. Further, words express thoughts, which are predicated on the impact of some object in the mind. Thus, there is no universally grounded criterion of truth because it is based, not on reason, but on *feeling*. Additionally, from birth, the mind develops its store of ideas and percepts through repeated exposure to people and experiences in the world (Stumpf, 1994).

Because sensations are the foundation of knowledge according to the Stoics, they are also the source of illusion and cognitive errors. Epictetus commented, "What upsets people is not things themselves but their judgments about the things.... So when we are thwarted or upset or distressed, let us never blame someone else but rather ourselves, that is, our own judgments" (Epictetus, 1983, p. 13). To the Stoics, human rationality was not only the ability to reason but the ability to create a structure and order of nature.

Constructivism

From a CBT perspective, the Stoic's philosophic stance can be considered one of the foundational mindsets that the CBT therapist embraces in the therapeutic session. Like the Stoics, CBT acknowledges that events happen in our lives: Individuals fail tests, they get divorced, they can be assaulted, earthquakes can occur, etc. The therapist, however, does not focus a client's attention on the event, nor is the therapist necessarily concerned with what the event was. What *is* of concern is the meaning of the event to the client. Thus, an important therapist role is to constructively assist the client in understanding that although life events may not always be under one's control, a person's attitudes and reactions generally are. Constructivism has been vital to the practice of CBT because it asserts that individuals do not simply react to events; rather, they are goal-directed, purposive, and active, and they adapt (Reinecke & Freeman, 2003). This viewpoint is empowering and encourages clients to consider how they should go about constructing and changing their lives. Second, the CBT therapist focuses on how the client organizes and interprets information. The client's presentation at any point in time reflects the summation of a client's efforts to make sense of and survive unique life circumstances.

Constructivism can be thought of as a major philosophical context within which cognitive therapy is done (Anderson, 1990; Mahoney, 2003, 2007). Constructivism is founded on the premise that humans actively construct their own reality and focuses on how language builds, maintains, and changes each individual's worldview. It proposes that an individual's conceptions of knowledge are derived from a meaning-making search in which the individual engages in a process of constructing individual interpretations of their experiences (Applefield, Huber, & Moallem, 2000). Its foundation can be traced as far back as Eastern philosophy. Buddha (560–477 B.C.E.) opened his book of spiritual reflections, *Dhammapada*, with:

> We are what we think.
> All that we are arises with our knowledge.
> With our thoughts we make the world. (Byrom, 1976)

Constructivism as a systematic meta-theory can be traced to the work of Immanuel Kant (Mahoney, 1988). Kant believed that the main ability of the mind was to structure thought in such a way as to synthesize and unify our experiences (Stumpf, 1994). The mind then makes various kinds of judgments to interpret the world through means of categories (Mahoney, 2003). The beliefs become templates for understanding one's experience. Kant postulated that an individual has no direct access to external reality and can develop knowledge only by using categories to organize experience (Stumpf, 1994). Our knowledge of experience is not fixed; it is constructed by the individual through their own experience of the world (Stumpf, 1994).

Mahoney (2003) stated that constructivist theorists share five basic themes: (1) the active agency of the human beings; (2) the importance of order or meaning in human experience; (3) the centrality of an embodied identity, or self, in the organization of experiencing; (4) an immersion in social and symbolic networks; and (5) a lifelong developmental unfolding.

Active Agency

Humans are not just reactive to their environments but are proactive participants in their lives as well (Mahoney, 2007). This goes against the determinist view held by Freud and Skinner, who believed humans are driven by internal or environmental forces with humans as relatively passive pawns in a mechanical universe (Mahoney, 2007). In contrast, constructivism argues that our choices influence who we are and how we respond in a broad range of life situations (Mahoney, 2003). Constructivism does not assume that the individual has total control over his environment (i.e., it may not be possible to change the direction of the wind, but it is possible to change the way that our sails are positioned). However, it is optimistic in the human ability to adapt and change the way one thinks about one's environment.

Ordering Processes

Ordering processes refer to how individuals categorize events and how emotions are related to categorization. As Kant wrote, humans organize information into categories to establish and maintain order in our environment, which is essential to our existence. Central to our cognitive organization of the world are our emotions. From a constructivist perspective, emotions serve a critical role for directing attention, shaping perceptions, organizing memory, and motivating active engagement (Mahoney & Granvold, 2005). Over time, our emotions contribute to our flexibility in adapting to new challenges and deepen our capacities to relate to one another (Mahoney, 2007). Essentially, what we call personality is a characteristic way of organizing our style toward the world and our response to the perceived order within it. In time, these reactions become automatic and form the root structure of stereotypical thinking and feeling (Mahoney & Granvold, 2005).

Self

Among the most powerful contrasts that an individual establishes is the differentiation of the self from the non-self (Mahoney, 2003). The self becomes the primary tool and reference point for the management and organization of one's world. Each person's perspective of the world is then relative to a hierarchically self-organized system of postulated beliefs that the individual holds (Raskin, 2007). Through the self, constructions are experienced cognitively, emotionally, bodily, socially, interpersonally, and intrapersonally (Butt, 1998; Chiari & Nuzzo, 2004; Faidley & Leitner, 1993; Mahoney & Marquis, 2002; Watts & Phillips, 2004). Therefore, the world is experienced in a unique manner for each person, with constructivism recognizing the uniqueness of each individual (Mahoney, 2007).

Social and Symbolic Relatedness

Although we individually construct our personal realities, we do so within a cultural context that shapes both the way we process information and the interpretation of the results (Raskin, 2007). The individual cannot be separated from their support systems and the environment (Mahoney, 2007), and there is a delicate interplay between the two (Raskin & Bridges, 2004). Even the words used in this chapter are symbols that are read, processed, and formulated to create an understanding of what is being stated. Much of this understanding is then dependent on one's personal history, interactions with professors, familiarity with the concepts, breadth of vocabulary, sophistication in psychological and philosophical constructs, etc. (Mahoney, 2003).

Lifelong Development

Constructivism formulates that we are in a continuous process of change. In technical terms, it is called dynamic dialectical development (Mahoney, 2007). Mahoney and Granvold (2005) define dynamic dialectical development as: "complex flows among essential tensions (contrasts) that are reflected in patterns and cycles of experiencing that can lead to episodes of disorder (disorganization) and, under some circumstances, the reorganization (transformation) of core patterns of activity, including meaning-making and both self- and social relationships" (p. 75). Thus, our developmental lives are characterized by cycles and spirals of experiencing (Mahoney & Granvold, 2005). This change process occurs whether it is desired or not.

THE DEVELOPMENT OF CONTEMPORARY COGNITIVE THERAPY

George Kelly—Personal Construct Psychology

From Kant, we move to the Dust Bowl and Great Depression. Psychologist George Kelly felt that he had an obligation to relieve the suffering that was occurring all around him among the families in the west-central part of Kansas, and he decided to open a rural clinic. Kelly was formally trained in psychoanalysis but questioned its effectiveness after many of his patients failed to improve (Fransella & Neimeyer, 2005). Kelly observed that although individuals would listen to his interpretations, his formulations were most effective when they were relevant to the person's specific difficulties and when the person was provided with a different way of looking at the problem (Fransella & Neimeyer, 2005). These experiences led Kelly to develop a philosophy of "constructed alternativism." He believed that although there is one true reality, reality is always experienced from a personal perspective (i.e., an alternative construction). Thus, reality is accessed only indirectly and is mediated by an individual's constructions (Raskin, 2001). Each individual continually makes meaning out of the world and develops an understanding of it (Epting & Paris, 2006). Kelly stated: "Events do not tell us what to do, nor do they carry their meanings engraved on their backs for us to discover. For better or for worse, we ourselves create the only meanings they will ever convey during our lifetime" (Kelly, 1970, p. 3).

In 1955, his two-volume work *The Psychology of Personal Constructs* expanded to include a theory of psychopathology entirely based on cognitive processing. According to Kelly, anxiety, depression, anger, and paranoia are consequences of the individual's "construction of reality." Kelly theorized that individuals create bipolar dimensions of meaning, or personal constructs, which they use to make sense of their experiences and to anticipate consequences (Raskin, 2001). Further, Kelly believed that individuals differ in the content of their constructs, the degree to which their constructs are open to disconfirmation, and the degree to which information might be assimilated to a construct. Individuals also differ in the complexity and differentiation of their personal constructs. As a result, Kelly began to listen to what his clients had to say, taking it at face value, and paid attention to content for its own sake, rather than as a symbol for some underlying meaning (Jankowicz, 1987).

Kelly's personal construct theory is specifically comprised of a postulate, which is elaborated through 11 corollaries. His postulate states: "A person's processes are psychologically channelized by the ways in which he anticipates events" (Kelly, 2003, p. 7). This postulate is grounded in the understanding of his notion of constructed alternativism. His 11 corollaries include (Kelly, 2003):

1. Construction Corollary: *A person anticipates events by constructing their replications*. Essentially, constructs are generalizations and patterns about the world based on past experience. An individual creates generalizations to make predictions about the course of prospective events by referencing past observations. This can be viewed as inductive reasoning.

2. Individuality Corollary: *Persons differ from each other in their constructions of events*. This is the foundation of his theory and is the reason it is called a personal construct theory, with constructs being uniquely experienced by individuals. Kelly (1955) postulated that individuals both experience and interpret events differently depending upon their unique frame of reference.

3. Organization Corollary: *Each person characteristically evolves, for his convenience in anticipating events, a construction system embracing ordinal relationships between constructs*. Each of us organizes our constructs in different ways by giving them an order of importance. Kelly (1955) ranges this order from most important, or superordinal, to subordinal, or secondary.

4. Dichotomy Corollary: *A person's construction system is composed of a finite number of dichotomous constructs*. Constructs are viewed by Kelly as bipolar, with each person having a limited, or finite, number of constructs they commonly use. For example, to understand the construct "strong," we must also have an understanding of the alternative construct "weak." However, another individual's opposite to "strong" might be "small." With this assertion Kelly emphasizes that constructs are reference axes that are used in an effort

to make some sense out of what is occurring (Kelly, 2003).

5. Choice Corollary: *A person chooses for himself that alternative in a dichotomized construct through which he anticipates the greater possibility for the elaboration of his system.* Kelly theorized that individuals make choices that align themselves in terms of their constructs. Sometimes individuals will choose to validate existing constructs; other times individuals may choose to extend an existing construct. An individual will use one pole of a construct more than another to guide their perceptions and behaviors, preferring the one that offers the most reliable predictions. For example, an individual who is guarded around others may come in contact with someone who provides them an unexpected positive act. As a result, either they can construct this event as "the person is trying to get something" or they could expand their construct by including "not everyone is out for themselves." This is similar to Piagetian acts of accommodation and assimilation.

6. Range Corollary: *A construct is convenient for the anticipation of a finite range of events only.* Few constructs are applicable to all situations that transpire; therefore a construct has what Kelly calls a range of convenience. Since each individual has a unique level of experience, their ability to apply a construct to a range of events will vary.

7. Experience Corollary: *A person's construction system varies as he successively construes the replications of events.* As the individual experiences events in their lives, they can develop alternative constructs depending on the result of their experience.

8. Modulation Corollary: *The variation in a person's construction system is limited by the permeability of the constructs within*

whose ranges of convenience the variants lie. Essentially, the ability of an individual to alter their constructs depends on how rigid or flexible their thinking is. The modulation corollary suggests the levels of allowing new elements of experience to be admitted into its range of convenience are subject to change through experience. Thus for a concrete or impermeable construct, there will be a resistance to its modification regardless of our experience.

9. Fragmentation Corollary: *A person may successively employ a variety of construction subsystems that are inferentially incompatible with each other.* Although individuals can appear to act in ways that seem inconsistent, they may not be seen as inconsistent to the individual. This can depend on the situation that is presented to the individual. For example, a judge in the courtroom may present as stern with an accused individual but at home may be understanding with his children when they make a mistake.

10. Commonality Corollary: *To the extent that one person employs a construction of experience that is similar to that employed by another person, his processes are psychologically similar to those of the other person.* Individuals can think and act in similar ways if their experiences have caused them to develop similar constructs. Although no two people are the same, and it is impossible to have the exact same perspective and constructs, similar constructions frequently occur. For example, two individuals who are graduating from the same doctoral program in clinical psychology can both experience relief, since they don't have to write any more papers, and joy from having obtained the goal they both set out to accomplish.

11. Sociality Corollary: *To the extent that one person construes the construction processes of another, he may play a role in a social process with the other person.* Relationships are based on mutual understanding. An individual is able to communicate with others to the extent that he or she can actively interpret and apprehend others' constructions. Social interactivity reflects an attempt to understand another person's construction in order to have meaningful interactions.

These corollaries form the foundation of Kelly's personality theory. Although his theory is considered to be the forerunner of cognitive psychotherapy (Jankowicz, 1987), Kelly was ambivalent in its use as a cognitive theory:

> There is also the question of whether or not it is a cognitive theory. Some have said that it was; others have classed it as existential. Quite an accomplishment; not many theories have been accused of being both cognitive and existential! But this, too, is all right with me. As a matter of fact, I am delighted. (Kelly, 2003, p. 8)

Later, Kelly became more and more puzzled that his personal construct theory was considered a cognitive theory and set out to write another short book clarifying his position (Cote, 1995).

Alfred Korzybski—General Semantics

Although Kelly's contribution highlighted unique ways in which individuals make meaning of their world, other contributors focused on the role language played in creating personal realities. After all, if thoughts represent internalized language, then the content of one's thoughts, and the effects of one's thoughts, may be understood in terms of linguistic rules.

Alfred Korzybski was the originator of general semantics and believed that human suffering is both a function of life events and linguistic representations of those events. Korzybski's early years were spent as an artillery officer during World War I, an experience that left him with an important observation (Dawes, 2007). He came to the conclusion that although there were continued advancements in the understanding of nature in the scientific community, the non-scientific community was failing to solve the social and political problems of the world (Postman, 2003). As a case in point, he described that when an engineer builds a bridge, it functions normally as designed, but when politicians create a treaty or government, human suffering often results (Bourland, 1989). Korzybski did not believe that it was a coincidence that engineers were more successful than politicians. He concluded that the discrepancy between the two was attributable to the structure of the languages used by the different professions. He postulated that engineers and scientists use mathematics in its language, which has a structure that is similar to a constructed bridge. On the other hand, the politician uses a static structure of language that does not represent well dynamic human socioeconomic issues (Bourland, 1989).

Korzybski defined general semantics as a way of thinking based on the belief that science and mathematics represent human thinking at its best, with progress in human relationships only accomplished through conscious time-binding (Caro, 2004). In his papers, *Time-Binding: The General Theory*, Korzybski classified humans as time binders in the sense that we have the ability to accumulate knowledge and transfer what we know to the future (Korzybski, 1965). We create the binding of time through symbols or representations, which are generated by our capacity of mental abstraction. Korzybski defined mental abstracting as the continuous activity of selection, omission, and organizing reality in order to experience it in a coherent patterned manner (Postman, 2003). Additionally, he believed that our ability to abstract and use symbols is largely dependent on the cultural and semantic language used in the environment. Symbols are constructions and only stand for things—they are the same as the things they represent (Caro, 2004). This sentiment is captured in Korzybski's now famous remark, "The map is not the territory," meaning that our abstractions and constructions of reality are derived from something, or are a reaction to it, but it is not the thing itself.

Korzybski's work with general semantics has had several important implications with regard to language vis-à-vis CBT. First, the way in which a CBT therapist speaks to patients is vital to a successful therapy. The therapist needs to structure language during the session to fit with the client's reality. Second, during therapy sessions the CBT therapist needs to be aware of the language that is used by the client. In fact, Albert Ellis, one of the founding theorists in the CBT movement, was greatly influenced by Korzybski's work and credits Korzybski for drawing Ellis's attention to the overgeneralizations clients often make during therapy (Ellis, 2007).

Behaviorism

Cognitive-behavioral therapy also grew out of a growing dissatisfaction with the limitations inherent in a strictly behavioral approach to clinical problems (Meichenbaum, 1993a). Early behavioral approaches did not directly investigate the role of cognition and cognitive processes in the development or maintenance of emotional disorders because they were considered covert and not directly measurable.

CBT does not reject learning theory so much as expanding upon it to include clinical applications of extensive research into the role of cognitions in the development of psychological disorders. Thus, the "consequences" for behavior in CBT are subjectively defined with rates of behavior determined by an individual's interpretation of consequences. Processing of environmental stimuli, rather than the stimuli themselves, is the driving force behind a person's response.

Mahoney (2000) emphasized four contributions that the behavioral movement had on cognitive therapy and therapy in general:

1. Emphasis on agency and the activity of the organism;
2. Emphasis on contrast and directionality;
3. Emphasis on the wisdom of working with small steps in the direction of desired change; and
4. Emphasis on accountability and the evidence of experience.

Further, behaviorism highlighted the need to do more than simply talk about a problem (Mahoney, 2000). For example, behaviorists were not satisfied with just talking about an individual's fear of elevators. Instead, therapy involved riding an elevator and having the patient actively participate in the change process. The contrast and directionality emphasis of behaviorists refers to their emphasis on structure and clarity within therapy sessions. Along with structure and clarity, behaviorists recognized the need for small incremental steps during the change process. This can be seen with their use of chaining, fading, and shaping techniques. Finally, and perhaps most importantly, it was the scientific rigor that behaviorists championed that has contributed greatly to the current practice of clinical psychology.

Albert Bandura—Social Cognitive Theory

Beginning in the 1960s and 1970s, Albert Bandura, a clinical psychologist, focused his work on how individuals learned and behaved. At the time, the predominant theory of learning posited that responses were elicited, or evoked, directly by stimuli (Bandura, 1977). Learning theory, in his view, relied too much on a limited range of principles derived from animal and human studies that involved only one organism (Grusec, 1992). Bandura believed that there were more covert processes at work, specifically the individual's cognitions. In 1963, Bandura and Walters, in their text *Social Learning and Personality Development*, proposed that observational learning, or modeling, was the major way that children acquire new behaviors and modify old ones (Parke & Clarke-Stewart, 2003). In this work and others, Bandura expanded upon the behavioral learning model, which emphasized how the environment impacts overt behavior, by theorizing how the environment additionally impacts covert processes or cognition (Bandura, 1989). Bandura termed the shared relationship among cognition, behavior, and environment *reciprocal determinism.* In 1986, he relabeled his approach as "social cognitive theory" to reflect the influence information processing theory had on his views (Grusec, 1992).

The main contribution Bandura has made to the development of cognitive theory was to elaborate the roles of modeling and self-efficacy in learning. Bandura identified three types of reinforcers of behavior: direct reinforcement, vicarious reinforcement, and self-reinforcement (Bandura, 1977). Direct reinforcement coincides with Skinner's notion of reinforcement, which is directly experienced by the learner, usually through a physical reward or consequence. Bandura, however, went one step further and suggested that individuals learn through vicarious, or nonmaterial, reinforcement. Reinforcement, in this instance, occurs as a consequence of observing the actions of another individual. According to Bandura, through observational learning, an individual learns which behaviors are likely to lead to reward and which behaviors are likely to result in punishment. Self-reinforcement, in contrast, cognitions relating to satisfaction or displeasure with one's own behavior has the effect of self-regulating behavior (Bandura, 1971). In this case, the reinforcing cognitions are under an individual's control and can moderate an individual's behavior, effectively ceding to cognitive processing properties of behavioral control that were formerly thought to only exist in the environment (Bandura, 1989).

An individual's judgment as to his or her ability to successfully perform a behavior is called self-efficacy (Bandura, 1989). Bandura (1994)

defined self-efficacy as: "people's beliefs about their capabilities to produce designated levels of performance that exercise influence over events that affect their lives" (p. 2). Bandura (1993) thought that an individual's self-efficacy produces effects through four major processes: cognitive, motivational, affective, and selection. With regard to cognitive processes, human behavior is regulated by forethought embodying recognized goals. Appraisal of one's ability to perform a task or action determines, in part, subsequent performance (Stajkovic & Luthans, 1998). Motivational processes are governed by the expectation that behaviors will produce certain outcomes, the level of effort necessary to achieve the outcome, and the degree of necessary perseverance (Bandura, 1993). Affective processes are mediated by beliefs an individual has in their own coping capacities, which also determine how much stress and depression they may experience subsequent to threatening or difficult situations. Finally, self-efficacy also influences a person's selection of environments. People avoid activities and situations that exceed their self-perceived coping capacities or abilities. For example, a person who is perfectly capable of communicating in a small group situation may enthusiastically avoid speeches to large groups for fear of a catastrophic social or professional failure.

INFLUENTIAL CBT THERAPIES

Albert Ellis—Rational Emotive Behavior Therapy

Albert Ellis is known as the "grandfather" of the cognitive therapy movement and founded rational emotive behavior therapy (REBT) in 1955. Originally rational therapy, the name was changed to rational emotive therapy in 1961 and to its current name in 1993 (Ellis, 1999). The changes in the name, however, did not reflect substantive changes in theory. Ellis's approach to psychological treatment has from its inception emphasized the interaction of the emotional and behavioral aspects of human disturbance while stressing its cognitive component. Ellis called the interdependent interaction between these forces the ABCs of REBT (Dryden & Ellis, 2001). A stands for the activating event or adversity, B refers to the belief system or the way an event or the activating event is evaluated, and C refers to the subsequent consequences that stem from our beliefs or B; these consequences can take the form of emotions, behaviors, or cognitions. REBT also acknowledges that there are healthy negative feelings such as sadness and grief when one suffers a great loss and unhealthy negative feelings such as serious panic and depression (Ellis, 1994). As therapy progresses, two additional sections are added to the model: D, disputing, and E, effective beliefs. The therapist must dispute (D) the irrational belief of the client in order for them to ultimately develop effective (E) rational beliefs, creating an A-B-C-D-E model (Morris, 1975).

According to Ellis, the root of psychological dysfunction results from the human tendency to make devout, dogmatic, and absolutistic evaluations about the self, others, and social transactions (Dryden & Ellis, 2001). Faulty thinking leads to incorrect inferences that are made on the basis of inadequate information. Because the individual places irrational absolutistic demands on the self, others, and the world, the role of the therapist is to collaborate with the client to rationally evaluate beliefs and suggest alternative interpretations (Ellis, 1993). It is important to note that the words *rational* and *irrational* in REBT are used contextually to describe behaviors and beliefs that either aid or hinder an individual's goal achievement. REBT's view of the person is optimistic in that humans have the capacity to replace irrational thinking with nondogmatic and more rational beliefs (Dryden & Ellis, 2001).

The replacement of irrational beliefs with rational ones is accomplished through the use of the scientific method. The therapist helps the client to view their beliefs as hypotheses that require testing. Ellis called this process *disputing*. For example, if an individual was spurned when asking a prospective love interest on a date, the irrational belief that "I'm unlovable" may develop. In this case, the therapist might challenge the validity of the belief by querying the patient for supporting evidence. Disputing a belief has the effect of generating alternative explanations that are less absolute in their condemnation. The therapist and client can then create more effective philosophies, emotions, and behaviors that the client can use outside the therapy session. However, verbally disputing irrational beliefs does not suffice in the REBT therapeutic process. Patients also perform shame-attacking exercises that encourage clients to engage in tasks that may make them feel foolish or embarrassed. For example, a therapist might have a client go to a gas station and ask the attendant if they are able to purchase gas there. Although the question is admittedly absurd, and the patient will feel foolish for asking it, the reality is that the client will come to understand that any embarrassment is merely transitory.

Ellis's REBT model has been used successfully for anger management (Ellis & Lange, 1994; Ellis & Tafrate, 1997; Wilde, 2001), sexual abuse (Moeller & Steel, 2002), substance abuse (Ellis, McInerny, DiGiuseppe, & Yeager, 1988; Ellis & Velten, 1992), couples problems (Ellis & Crawford, 2000; Ellis, Sichel, Yeager, DiMattia, & DiGiuseppe, 1989), depression (Ellis, 1987; Hauck & McKeegan, 1997; Macavei, 2005), pain management (Blackburn, 2001), and anxiety (Cowan & Brunero, 1997; Warren, 1997).

Aaron T. Beck—Cognitive Therapy

Aaron T. Beck is a major pioneer in the development of cognitive therapy: He has published more than 450 articles and authored or coauthored 17 books in the field. His main contribution to the cognitive movement was his observation that negative moods and behaviors are usually the result of distorted thoughts and beliefs, not of unconscious forces as proposed in Freudian theory (Beck, 1976). Beck was educated as a psychiatrist and later completed psychoanalysis and psychoanalytic training and, as a result, began his career in the medical model of psychoanalysis. Early in his career he conducted experiments to test and verify the psychoanalytic concept of depression (i.e., that depression was a result of anger turned inward). Beck sought evidence of the psychoanalytic hypothesis by analyzing the dreams of depressed inpatients on the psychiatry unit of Philadelphia General Hospital. In reviewing their dreams, he hoped to detect a theme of hostility. However, he found no support for the psychoanalytic hypothesis and instead found that the dreams of depressed patients were characterized by themes of loss, emptiness, and failure (Leahy, 1996). Over the course of time, Beck came to realize that the way that patients viewed themselves was at the core of the way they felt about themselves (Bloch, 2004).

According to Beck, the source of an individual's depression is distorted information processing (DeRubeis, Tang, & Beck, 2001). Beck emphasizes that the underlying cognitive structures that organize the patient's experiences, or schemata, are at the core of their distortions (DeRubeis et al., 2001). He proposes that the negative thinking characteristic of depression is brought on by what he called a *negative cognitive shift* (Beck, 1991). The shift occurs as a result of a change in *cognitive* organization such that positive information relevant to the individual is filtered out, the effect of which is to make negative self-relevant information more readily available (Beck, 1991). Beck conceptualizes depression in terms of a cognitive triad: negative thoughts about self, the future, and the world (Beck, Rush, Shaw, & Emery, 1979; Freeman, Pretzer, Fleming, & Simon, 2003).

Ultimately, Beck believes that by changing a person's automatic thoughts, the therapist will be able to eventually restructure the core schemata. According to DeRubeis and colleagues (2001), the role of the therapist is to teach the client three questions while they learn the methods of cognitive therapy: (1) *What is the evidence for and against the belief?* (2) *What are alternative interpretations of the event or situation?* and (3) *What are the real implications if the belief is correct?*

Although Beck's model of cognitive therapy was based on his work with depression, it has been subsequently applied to cases of anxiety (Beck, Emery, & Greenberg, 1985; Freeman & Simon, 1989), panic disorder (Beck, 1987), marital conflict (Baucom & Epstein, 2004; Beck, 1989), personality disorders (Beck, Freeman, Davis, & Associates, 2004), suicide (Freeman & Reinecke, 1994; Weishaar & Beck, 1992), substance abuse (Wright, Beck, Newman, & Liese, 1993), schizophrenia (Henriques & Beck, 2000), bipolar disorder (Alford & Beck, 2006), and stress management (Pretzer & Beck, 2007).

Arnold A. Lazarus—Multimodal Therapy

Arnold Lazarus was born and raised in South Africa and received his doctorate in clinical psychology at the University of Witwatersrand in Johannesburg in 1960. While still a graduate student, it was Lazarus who introduced the terms *behavior therapy* and *behavior therapist* to the literature (Lazarus, 1958). During the early 1970s Lazarus decided to focus his attention on an already expanding field of behavioral therapy by incorporating cognitive aspects in his 1971 book, *Behavior Therapy and Beyond* (Lazarus, 1971). Lazarus did not stop there in the development of his therapeutic style and created an integrated model he called multimodal therapy (MT) (Lazarus, 1989). Over the years, Lazarus came to the conclusion that therapists should utilize therapeutic strategies that are empirically supported (Lazarus &

Shaughnessy, 2002). His use of multiple methods in MT is defined as technical eclecticism (Lazarus, 1997). Technical eclecticism refers to the process of utilizing clinical strategies and techniques derived from two or more theoretical orientations regardless of origin while maintaining a nonredundant, unified theoretical focus (Stricker & Gold, 2003). The unified theory that Lazarus used was Bandura's social cognitive theory (Lazarus & Shaughnessy, 2002).

Lazarus and Abramovitz (2004) explained that the various forms of "behavior therapy" and "cognitive-behavior therapy" are *trimodal* because they address problems within affective, behavioral, and cognitive domains. MT, on the other hand, employs seven different modalities. In addition to evaluating affect, behavior, and cognition, MT emphasizes the need to take account of sensory responses, mental images, interpersonal factors, and biological considerations, leading to a seven-point approach that the therapist utilizes (behavior, affect, sensation, imagery, cognition, interpersonal relationships, and drugs/biological factors), which gives the mnemonic BASIC ID (Lazarus, 1973). Lazarus's BASIC ID is used not only during the initial interview stage of therapy but also as a way of directing intervention (Lazarus & Shaughnessy, 2002). Lazarus and Abramovitz (2004) suggest that a multimodal assessment include the following range of questions:

B: (Behavior) What is this individual doing that is getting in the way of his or her happiness or personal fulfillment (self-defeating actions, maladaptive behaviors)? What does the client need to increase and decrease? What should he/she stop doing and start doing?

A: (Affect) What emotions (affective reactions) are predominant? Is the client angry, anxious, depressed, or a combination thereof, and to what extent (e.g., irritation versus rage, sadness versus profound melancholy)? What is the source of negative affect — cognitions, images, interpersonal conflicts? How does the person respond (behave) when feeling a certain way? It is important to look for interactive processes—what impact do various behaviors have on the person's affect, and vice versa? How does this influence each of the other modalities?

S: (Sensation) Are there specific sensory complaints (e.g., tension, chronic pain, tremors)? What feelings, thoughts, and behaviors are connected to these negative sensations? What positive sensations (e.g., visual, auditory, tactile, olfactory, and gustatory delights) does the person report? This includes the individual as a sensual and sexual being. When required, the enhancement or cultivation of erotic pleasure is a viable therapeutic goal.

I: (Imagery) What fantasies and images are predominant? What is the person's "self-image"? Are there specific success or failure images? Are there negative or intrusive images (e.g., flashbacks to unhappy or traumatic experiences)? How are these images connected to ongoing cognitions, behaviors, affective reactions, and the like?

C: (Cognition) Can we determine the individual's main attitudes, values, beliefs, and opinions? What are the person's predominant *shoulds*, *oughts*, and *musts*? Are there any predominant dysfunctional beliefs or irrational ideas? Are there any automatic thoughts that undermine his or her functioning?

I: (Interpersonal Relationships) Interpersonally, who are the significant others in this individual's life? What does he or she want, desire, expect, and receive from them, and what does he or she, in turn, give to and do for them? What relationships give him/her particular pleasures and pains?

D: (Drugs/Biological Factors) Is this person biologically healthy and health-conscious? Does he or she have any medical complaints or concerns? What relevant details pertain to diet, weight, sleep, exercise, or alcohol and drug use?

Lazarus suggests that patients are bothered by a number of specific problems that are best dealt with by a number of specific treatments. Therefore, the therapist must have a host of skills and techniques available in his or her repertoire (Roberts, Jackson, & Phelps, 1980). Therapist empathy and patient insight are not enough. MT posits that behavior change is facilitated by matching specific techniques to the problems for which they are best suited. Examples include coaching, training, rehearsing, directive role playing, desensitization, or didactic learning. Thus, treatment is customized for each client and focuses on as many BASIC ID modalities as needed (Lazarus & Abramovitz, 2004; Lazarus & Shaughnessy, 2002). MT has been shown to be an effective form of therapy for anorexia nervosa (O'Keefe & Castaldo, 1985), agoraphobia (Lazarus, 1986), performance anxiety (Lazarus & Abramovitz, 2004), depression (Brunell, 1990; Lazarus, 1974), and obsessive compulsive behaviors (Beaty, 1979).

Donald Meichenbaum—Self Instructional Training and Stress Inoculation Training

Donald Meichenbaum is a prominent researcher in the cognitive-behavioral therapy movement and continues to be an integral contributor to the development of the therapeutic approach. Meichenbaum grew up in New York City and recalled that his entire research career had its origins in the interactions he had at the family dinner table (Meichenbaum, 1993b). One of his major influences growing up was his mother. He explained in a chapter entitled "A Personal Journey of a Psychotherapist and His Mother" that his mother would not only describe an incident in her life but also explain feelings and thoughts she had before, during, and after the incident (Meichenbaum, 1993b). In addition to the influence of his mother, he based his therapeutic work on a constructivist narrative perspective that postulated, as we saw earlier, that the human mind is a product of the personal meanings individuals create though the use of story. According to Meichenbaum, the role of the therapist is to be a co-constructivist, helping clients alter and reinterpret their life stories (Meichenbaum, 1993a).

Growing up in New York, Meichenbaum also observed that it was not unusual for New Yorkers to talk to themselves as an adaptive skill to maneuver through the city safely (Meichenbaum, 2003). As a result, throughout his career he has incorporated the analysis of client self-talk and encouraged change in self-talk for therapeutic effect. Meichenbaum's observations lead him to remark that CBT is a form of "New York therapy" (Meichenbaum, 2003). Meichenbaum was so interested in the self-talk of individuals that he later completed his dissertation on teaching schizophrenics to talk to themselves in an adaptive coherent fashion (Meichenbaum & Cameron, 1973). Later he took a position at the University of Waterloo, where he taught hyperactive children and aggressive children to talk to themselves in a more productive fashion through modeling and didactic activities (Meichenbaum & Goodman, 1971). These research experiences were the foundation of what he called self instructional training. He believed that an individual's self-instructions mediate changes in behavior (Rokke & Rehm, 2001). Additionally, he reasoned that maladaptive self-statements contribute to a person's problems and the task of the therapist is to assist the patient in developing more adaptive thoughts. In addition to its use with schizophrenics and children with ADHD, this approach has been used for social anxiety

(Craighead, Kimball, & Rehak, 1979), impulsiveness (Kendall & Finch, 1978), learning disabilities (Graham & Wong, 1993), fear (Vallis, & Bucher, 1986), and behavioral disorders (Yeo, Wong, Gerken, & Ansley, 2005).

Meichenbaum has also been involved in the development of stress prevention and reduction, creating an approach he called stress inoculation training (SIT). Essentially, SIT exposes clients to mild forms of stress in a controlled environment in order to bolster coping mechanisms and foster client confidence in his or her repertoire of coping skills (Meichenbaum, 2007). Meichenbaum compared the use of SIT to when an individual goes to the doctor to get a vaccination. (Vaccinations are purposeful infections delivered in a controlled manner that induce immunity to further infection.) The therapist then assists the client in developing skills to better evaluate and respond to stress cognitively, emotionally, and behaviorally (Rokke & Rehm, 2001). Therapeutic exercises include rehearsal of coping behaviors with the therapist and implementation of new skills in daily routines. The therapist also assists the client in recognizing the changeable and unchangeable aspects of stressful situations. SIT has been used for anger management (Novaco, 1977b), pain (Turk, Meichenbaum, & Genest, 1983), anxiety disorders (Holcomb, 1986; Rapee, 1987), depression (Novaco, 1977a), rape (Veronen & Kilpatrick, 1983), public speaking anxiety (Jaremko, 1980), and social anxiety (Jaremko, 1983).

Steven C. Hayes—Acceptance and Commitment Therapy

Acceptance and Commitment Therapy (known as "ACT"—pronounced as one word, not the initials) is a form of cognitive-behavioral therapy developed by Steven Hayes. ACT is an empirically based approach that views many maladaptive behaviors as produced by unhealthy attempts to avoid or suppress thoughts, feelings, or bodily sensations (Hayes, Wilson, Gifford, Follette, & Strosahl, 1996). ACT is founded on functional contextualism and includes the following components: a focus on the whole event, an understanding of the nature and function of the event within a context, and a pragmatic truth criterion (Zettle & Hayes, 2002). Functional contextualism has a philosophical view similar to that of constructivism but offers a more coherent philosophical foundation to build an empirical science of learning and instruction (Fox, 2006). Essentially, cognitions, feelings, and impulses are products of the interaction between an individual and his or her context, with context encompassing both the actual contextual variables and the personal learning history (Hummelen & Rokx, 2007). For example, consider the rather straightforward event of tying your shoes. Tying your shoes involves more than just the shoes or a person or the shoelaces or the floor or the motions with your hands to tie the laces. This action is an amalgamation of all these elements, with the objects used and the behaviors completed defining and characterizing the process. Therefore, our everyday understanding of an event, such as tying our shoes, includes an understanding of the behavior or action and its current context, or setting, as an integrated whole (Fox, 2006). From a theoretical standpoint, ACT is based on Relational Frame Theory (RFT). According to RFT, human language and cognition are the learned and contextually controlled abilities to subjectively relate events through interactions with the environment (Blackledge, 2007).

Psychopathology can then be viewed as the dysfunctional links between emotion, cognition, and behavior produced by cognitive fusion and experiential avoidance (Zettle & Hayes, 2002). Cognitive fusion is defined as the tendency of verbal/cognitive events to dominate other modes of behavior regulation. Thus, behavior is guided more by relatively inflexible verbal networks than by contacted environmental contingencies (Zettle & Hayes, 2002). As a result, thoughts and language have an enormous influence on our behavior (Harris, 2006). The term *experimental avoidance* refers to the observation that humans avoid certain private experiences that are construed as negative (such as particular feelings, memories, behavior predispositions, or thoughts) by suppressing them (Hayes & Wilson, 1993). Paradoxically, avoidance increases the frequency of aversive thoughts, especially in the physical or emotional contexts associated with the suppression (Hayes & Gifford, 1997). People who frequently use these coping strategies have poorer clinical outcomes because the more they allow their behavior to be determined by the control and avoidance of inner processes, the less they will be inclined to make behavior choices that accord with their own goals (Hummelen & Rokx, 2007).

To alter this cycle of suppression, ACT focuses on increasing clients' willingness to be exposed to unpleasant private events (Bach & Hayes, 2002). In order to accomplish this task, the ACT therapist helps clients to distinguish between circumstances in which direct behavioral change is possible (*commitment*) and those in which psychological *acceptance* is a more viable alternative (Zettle & Hayes, 2002). ACT works to change the client's acceptance of his or her symptoms in order to permit development of more adaptive behavior (Bach & Hayes, 2002). Instead of insisting that clients eliminate undesirable private events, ACT therapists use metaphors, paradoxes, and experiential exercises to illustrate the contribution of language or self-statements to a client's problems (Zettle & Hayes, 2002). Cognitive defusion techniques are used to help clients understand that undesirable thoughts are not binding realities (Blackledge, 2007). Hayes, Strosahl, and Wilson (1999) define cognitive defusion as "disrupt[ing] ordinary meaning functions of language such that the ongoing process of framing events relationally is evident in the moment and competes with

the stimulus products of relational activity" (p. 74). The goal of using cognitive defusion techniques is to teach clients to identify and abandon internally oriented control strategies; accept the presence of difficult thoughts or feelings; learn to notice the occurrence of private experiences without struggling with them, arguing with them, or taking them to be literally true; and to focus on overt behaviors that produce valued outcomes (Bach & Hayes, 2002). For example, the ACT therapist might instruct the client to simply observe the thought with detachment or repeat it over and over, out loud, until it becomes just a meaningless sound (Harris, 2006).

If the theory behind ACT is correct, therapy should produce decreased symptom believability in the client, increase acceptance of his or her symptoms, and promote positive behavioral change (Bach & Hayes, 2002). ACT has been used in the treatment of pain (Dahl & Lundgren, 2006; Hayes et al., 1999), depression (Zettle, 2007; Zettle & Hayes, 2002), posttraumatic stress disorder (Batten, Orsillo, & Walser, 2005; Blackledge, 2004), parents of children with autism (Blackledge & Hayes, 2006), workplace conflicts (Bond & Hayes, 2002), anger (Eifert, McKay, & Forsyth, 2006), and anxiety (Forsyth & Eifert, 2008).

Marsha Linehan—Dialectical Behavior Therapy

Marsha Linehan developed dialectical behavior therapy (DBT) initially to help suicidal and self-mutilating patients (Linehan, 1987) and later applied it more specifically to individuals with borderline personality disorder (BPD) and parasuicidal tendencies (Linehan, 1993a, 1993b). DBT integrates behavioral and cognitive treatment principles along with dialectical philosophy and Zen Buddhism (Robins, Ivanoff, & Linehan, 2001). Cognitively, it focuses on identifying maladaptive thinking styles and automatic thoughts through the use of chain analyses and self-monitoring diaries, education, role playing, and problem-solving strategies (Sneed, Balestri, & Belfi, 2003). DBT is also founded on dialectical philosophy. The dialectical component in DBT reflects its emphasis on synthesizing apparent polarities, or oppositions, in the client's worldview (Robins & Koons, 2004). Additionally, Zen principles and practices are taught to patients, including the importance of being mindful of the moment, seeing reality without delusion, accepting reality without judgment, letting go of attachments that cause suffering, and finding a middle way (Robins & Koons, 2004).

The treatment of BPD is based on a biosocial theory positing that the central problem of those with BPD is emotional dysregulation or biological vulnerability to experience emotions more intensely. Further, individuals with BPD have difficulty modulating emotional intensity and often come from invalidating environments (Robins & Koons, 2004). Accordingly, the DBT therapist provides a validating environment and modifies maladaptive behaviors by supplanting them with adaptive skills that help foster more positive emotions and relationships. Newly learned skills are reinforced, and enhanced, and efforts are made to encourage generalization to all relevant environments (Swenson, Sanderson, Dulit, & Linehan, 2001). According to Reynolds and Linehan (2002), DBT can be applied in any setting as long as five treatment functions are addressed: (1) help patients develop a new skill set, (2) address motivational obstacles to using the new skills, (3) help patients generalize the skills to their daily lives, (4) keep therapists motivated and skilled in treating a difficult-to-treat population, and (5) structure the environment in a manner that will promote and reinforce patient's and therapist's capabilities.

The skill sets are taught in a group format and the skills-training manual covers four sets of skills: mindfulness, distress tolerance, emotion regulation, and interpersonal effectiveness (assertiveness) (Linehan, 1993b). These four skills are taught in two different ways: a set of *what* skills (what to do) and a set of *how* skills (how to do it). The emotional regulation and interpersonal effectiveness modules teach skills to address change in order to improve current life situations, while core mindfulness and distress tolerance skills focus on the acceptance of reality and the here and now (Wisniewski & Kelly, 2003). Individual therapy emphasizes application of newly acquired skills and addresses motivational obstacles in utilizing the skills. Skill generalization beyond the therapy setting is facilitated by telephone coaching between sessions (Robins & Koons, 2004). The purpose of these telephone sessions is to have the patient call the therapist prior to engaging in high-priority target behaviors such as self-injuring, drug or alcohol consumption, staying in bed, or other problem behaviors (Robins & Koons, 2004). Due to the challenging treatment that this population entails, enhancement of therapist's capabilities and motivation to treat patients is maintained through weekly consultation with a team of therapists who are involved with the DBT treatment (Reynolds & Linehan, 2002). Finally, in order to change a client's passive approach to problem solving, the therapist advises the client on better ways to interact with the environment (Swales, Heard, & Williams, 2002) or meets with family members to restructure the environment (Reynolds & Linehan, 2002).

DBT has been found to be successful for the treatment of BPD (Koons et al., 2001; Linehan, Armstrong, Suarez, Allmon, & Heard, 1991; Linehan, Heard, & Armstrong, 1993; Linehan et al., 1999, 2002, 2006; Turner, 2000; Verheul et al., 2003). In addition, it has demonstrated efficacy for chronically depressed older adults (Lynch, Morse, Mendelson, & Robins, 2003), the treatment of binge-eating disorder (Telch, 1997; Telch, Agras, & Linehan, 2001) and bulimia nervosa (Safer, Telch, & Agras, 2001). DBT has been examined for a variety of clinical problems in several uncontrolled or nonrandomized trials (e.g., Bohus et al., 2000; Koons, Chapman, Betts,

HIGHLIGHT BOX 11.1

CASE EXAMPLE

Gerald, age 41, called for an appointment for therapy at the behest of his mother with whom he had lived up until 5 years ago. He is employed as a computer programmer for a large aerospace firm. His mother, with whom he speaks daily, has emphasized that unless Gerald starts dating and gets a girlfriend, he will never marry, and never have children, thereby denying her of any grandchildren. When he called the therapist, he stated the reason for his visit involved some "social problems."

He appeared 3 days later for his appointment. He wore an unpressed suit, a shirt whose collar was far too large and that was partly untucked from his pants, a tie that was improperly fixed, and pants that were so long the cuffs were worn by his walking on them. He needed a haircut, and his sideburns were trimmed at unequal length.

He was a graduate of a large technical university, completing his 4 years with a GPA of 4.0. He had worked for the same company since college and routinely refused promotions and the accompanying salary increases, preferring his more simple job and responsibility. He was a member of Mensa and belonged to a crossword club that met monthly. He proudly noted that he could complete the *New York Times* weekend puzzle within minutes, using a pen. Gerald had no friends and spent his evenings either alone or at his mother's home for dinner twice a week. To make sure that Gerald ate well, his mother would shop for frozen dinners that he would take home and microwave. When at home, Gerald would either watch a movie on cable or surf the Internet, researching arcane ideas.

From a cognitive-behavioral perspective, Gerald's problems could be conceptualized as deficits in motivation and social skills/abilities. He made numerous self-statements that were, in fact, reasonably accurate (e.g., "I'm not good with people," "I don't know what to say to others," "People think that I'm a dork," and "I disappoint my mother"). There were other beliefs that were more conditional and available for restructuring (e.g., "I could never learn to talk to a woman," "No woman would ever want me," or "My mother will never be happy with what I do").

By using a combination of cognitive and behavioral interventions, each of these beliefs and their consequent feelings and behaviors were challenged. Treatment started with behavioral interventions that addressed his skills deficits. The therapist hypothesized that as his skills increased, so would his motivation, provided Gerald came in contact with significant events and experiences that gave him pleasure. Thus, as his skills increased, the focus of therapy would shift to a more cognitive focus. As his presenting symptoms became less severe, he was open to the cognitive work involved in exploring his automatic thoughts ("I'll fail") and his core schema ("I will always be alone except for my mother").

Gerald's therapy lasted for a total of 43 sessions. These included individual therapy, group therapy, and pharmacotherapy. The pharmacotherapy was used initially to help Gerald deal with his overwhelming social anxiety. Medication was discontinued after about 7 weeks.

Gerald started taking notes on how other men dressed. He tried dressing "as if" he was *not* a dork and assessed the reactions of coworkers. In all cases, the reaction was positive, encouraging Gerald to continue. He started dating a woman, Elise, in his crossword puzzle club, which became a physical relationship, though without sex.

When Gerald terminated therapy, he looked and sounded far different. His mother, however, sounded the same. He and Elise had planned several day trips and even an overnight weekend. He was not sure if he would ever give his mother a grandchild, but he appeared satisfied with the changes in his life.

O'Rourke, & Robins, 2006; Rathus & Miller, 2002).

SUMMARY

Dobson and Dozois (2001) emphasized that all CBT therapies share three fundamental propositions: (1) cognitive activity affects behavior, (2) cognitive activity may be monitored and altered, and (3) desired behavior change may be affected through cognitive change. In point of fact, there are far more CBT variants than those discussed here, including treatments that focus on schema (Young, Klosko, & Weisher, 2003), mindfulness (Segal, Williams, & Teasdale, 2002), problem solving (D'Zurilla & Nezu, 2001), interpersonal processes (Safren & Segal, 1990), and emotion (Safren, 1998). The CBT model has been applied to virtually every client population, every age group, and every clinical problem. We cannot, within the limits of the present chapter, review all extant models. Nor can we, from our perspective, make judgments in terms of which CBT model is "best." The reader is, we hope, intrigued by the breadth, range, and diversity of cognitive-behavioral therapy.

Cognitive-behavioral therapy has roots in philosophy, psychodynamic psychotherapy, and behavioral traditions. Our goal in this chapter has been to offer the reader the broad range, variety, emphases, foci, and interventions of the diverse CBT models. From a model that was initially limited in its application, CBT has been applied to every clinical population, with every clinical problem, and in every clinical setting. The future of CBT is limited only by the vision and creativity of the next generation of psychologists.

THOUGHT QUESTIONS

What is the role of the CBT therapist and client in the therapeutic milieu? What characteristics are clients perceived to possess in therapy?

What are the three levels of cognition and how are they different?

What is the Stoic perspective on the human experience?

How has CBT incorporated a Stoic perspective into therapy sessions?

What is constructivism? Describe the five basic themes of the philosophy.

What elements of constructivistic thought have been integrated into a CBT session?

What did George Kelly propose was the cause of psychopathology?

What precipitated the development of general semantics?

How has behaviorism influenced CBT?

How does Albert Ellis view psychopathology? What is the ABCs model, and how is it used in the therapeutic process? Give an example.

What is the cognitive triad, and how does Aaron Beck view psychopathology?

What does BASIC ID stand for, and how does it apply to the therapeutic process?

According to Donald Meichenbaum, what is the role of self-talk for clients? How is stress inoculation training similar to getting a vaccination?

How does Steven Hayes view psychopathology? How does avoidance of emotion contribute to psychopathology? How does Marsha Linehan theorize that borderline personality disorder

develops? What processes are required in order for a treatment to be defined as DBT?
What do all CBT therapies have in common?

Glossary

ABC Model: sequence of antecedents, behavior, and consequences theorized by Albert Ellis in which difficulties stem from beliefs, not events.

Acceptance and Commitment Therapy: a form of cognitive-behavioral therapy developed by Steven Hayes that views many maladaptive behaviors as produced by unhealthy attempts to avoid or suppress thoughts, feelings, or bodily sensations.

Automatic thoughts: maladaptive thoughts that arise without conscious deliberation and can be easily brought to the attention of the individual.

BASIC ID: a pneumonic for the seven (behavior, affect, sensation, imagery, cognition, interpersonal relationships, and drugs/biological factors) different modalities that the multimodal therapist assesses in the client throughout the treatment process.

Cognitive-behavioral therapy: a general term for a broad array of approaches that have been conceptualized by clinicians that aim to change the cognitions leading to psychological problems.

Cognitive defusion: techniques used to help clients understand that undesirable thoughts are not binding realities and accept the presence of their difficult thoughts or feelings.

Cognitive distortions: thoughts that an individual has which perpetuate psychological distress.

Cognitive fusion: the tendency of an individual to get overinvolved with their thoughts and language, resulting in an influence over their behavior.

Cognitive revolution: a movement that emphasized the study of internal thought processes and involved a number of subject areas beyond the therapeutic milieu, including the studies of memory, language, imagery, and attention.

Cognitive therapy: an approach to psychotherapy created by Aaron Beck that seeks to modify faulty thinking of clients to produce changes in the client's feelings and behaviors.

Cognitive triad: a term which explains that negative thoughts are about the self, the world, and the future.

Collaborative empiricism: a perspective in which clients are seen as scientists who are able to make objective interpretations and the client-therapist collaboration is used to generate hypotheses with clients testing them through individualized homework assignments.

Constructed alternativism: a philosophy espoused by George Kelly which theorizes that there is one true reality, but reality is accessed only indirectly, being experienced from one or another perspective, or alternative construction.

Constructivism: a philosophy which postulates that humans actively construct their own reality and how language builds, maintains, and changes each individual's worldview.

Dialectical behavior therapy: an approach to psychotherapy created by Marsha Linehan that integrates behavioral and cognitive treatment principles along with dialectical philosophy and Zen Buddhism.

Dialectical philosophy: originated by Hegel, it is a philosophy based on a fundamental worldview concerning the nature of reality as composed of interrelated parts that cannot be defined without reference to the system as a whole and reality as composed of opposites.

Direct reinforcement: a type of reinforcement that is directly experienced by the learner in response to stimuli.

Experimental avoidance: the observation that humans avoid certain private experiences that are construed as negative, such as particular feelings, memories, behavioral predispositions, or thoughts, by suppressing them.

Functional contextualism: a philosophical view that explains an individual's everyday understanding of an event in terms of the interaction between an individual and his or her context, with context encompassing both the actual contextual variables as well as the personal learning history.

General semantics: an educational discipline created by Alfred Korzybski that deals with the study of how we perceive, construct, evaluate, and communicate our life experiences taking into account knowledge of biology, chemistry, neurology, psychiatry, anthropology, and physics.

Intermediate beliefs: the attitudes an individual has and the assumptions and rules/ expectations that individuals make.

Irrational belief: a quality of thinking that hinders an individual's goal achievement.

Multimodal therapy: a cognitive-behavioral approach to psychotherapy founded by Arnold Lazarus that emphasizes the need to take into account seven different modalities in the treatment of clients, which are behavior, affect, sensation, imagery, cognition, interpersonal relationships, and drugs/biological factors.

Rational belief: quality of thinking that promotes an individual's attainment of personal goals.

Rational emotive behavior therapy: a cognitive approach to psychotherapy created by Albert Ellis which emphasizes that human disturbance is determined by how an individual constructs their view of reality through their evaluative beliefs and philosophies about adversities.

Reciprocal determinism: the dynamic interaction of cognition, behavior, and environment in the process of behavior.

Relational frame theory: theorizes that human language and cognition is the learned and contextually controlled ability to subjectively relate events through interactions with the environment.

Schema: central ideas or core beliefs that underlie many of an individual's automatic cognitions and usually are reflected in immediate beliefs.

Self-efficacy: an individual's beliefs about their capabilities to produce designated levels of performance can influence the result of the actual level of performance.

Self instructional therapy: a form of cognitive psychotherapy created by Donald Meichenbaum which emphasizes an individual's internal dialogue directly influences their behavior and feelings.

Self-reinforcement: self-regulation of behavior through cognitions of satisfaction or displeasure for behavior measured by whether their personal performance meets their self--prescribed demands.

Self-talk: an internal dialogue an individual has when they are thinking to themselves.

Shame-attacking exercises: a strategy used in REBT that encourages clients to perform strange tasks regardless of feeling foolish or embarrassed in order to help them see that they can still function if perceived as foolish.

Social cognitive theory: Albert Bandura's theory to explain how individuals acquire and maintain certain behavioral patterns, expanding the theory of behavioral reinforcement to include the processes of learning through modeling and self-efficacy.

Stoicism: a philosophy that believes humans cannot control all events but can control their attitude toward what happens to and around them.

Stress inoculation training: a form of cognitive psychotherapy created by Donald Meichenbaum that exposes clients to mild forms of stress, in a controlled environment, to bolster coping mechanisms and foster client confidence in his or her repertoire of coping skills.

Technical eclecticism: the process of utilizing clinical strategies and techniques derived from two or more theoretical orientations regardless of origin while maintaining a nonredundant, unified theoretical focus.

Time-binding: a term used by Alfred Korzybski to describe human progress in which the transmission of knowledge and abstractions is passed on through time.

Vicarious reinforcement: a type of reinforcement in which an individual observes the consequences of the behavior of another individual.

References

Alford, B. A. & Beck, A. T. (2006). Psychotherapeutic treatment of depression and bipolar disorder. In D. Evans (Ed.), *The physician's guide to depression and bipolar disorders*. Washington, DC: American Psychiatric Association.

Anderson, W. T. (1990). *Reality isn't what it used to be*. New York: Harper & Row.

Applefield, J. M., Huber, R., & Moallem, M. (2000). Constructivism in theory and practice: toward a better understanding. *High School Journal, 84,* 35–54.

Bach, P. & Hayes, S. C. (2002). The use of acceptance and commitment therapy to prevent the rehospitalization of psychotic patients: a randomized controlled trial. *Journal of Consulting and Clinical Psychology, 70,* 1129–1139.

Bandura, A. (1971). Vicarious and self-reinforcement processes. In R. Glaser (Ed.), *The nature of reinforcement* (pp. 228–278). New York: Academic Press.

Bandura, A. (1977). Self-efficacy: Toward a unifying theory of behavioral change. *Psychological Review, 84,* 191–215.

Bandura, A. (1989). Social cognitive theory. In R. Vasta (Ed.), *Annals of child development,* vol. 6. *Six theories of child development* (pp. 1–60). Greenwich, CT: JAI Press.

Bandura, A. (1993). Perceived self-efficacy in cognitive development and functioning. *Educational Psychologist, 28,* 117–148.

Bandura, A. (1994). Self-efficacy. In V. S. Ramachaudran (Ed.), *Encyclopedia of human behavior* (vol. 4, pp. 71–81). New York: Academic Press.

Bandura, A. & Walters, R. H. (1963). *Social learning and personality development*. New York: Holt, Rinehart & Winston.

Batten, S. V., Orsillo, S. M., & Walser, R. D. (2005). Acceptance and mindfulness-based approaches to the treatment of posttraumatic stress disorder. In S. M. Orsillo & L. Roemer (Eds.), *Acceptance and mindfulness-based approaches to anxiety: conceptualization and treatment*. New York: Springer.

Baucom, D. H., & Epstein, N. (1990). *Cognitive behavioral marital therapy*. New York: Brunner/Mazel.

Beaty, D. T. (1979). A multimodal approach to multiple obsessive-compulsive behaviours. *South African Journal of Psychology, 9,* 27–29.

Beck, A. T. (1976). *Cognitive therapy and the emotional disorders*. New York: International Universities Press.

Beck, A. T. (1987). Cognitive approaches to panic disorder: Theory and therapy. In S. Rachman & J. Maser (Eds.), *Panic: Psychological perspectives* (pp. 91–109). Hillside, NJ: Lawrence Erlbaum Associates.

Beck, A. T. (1989). Cognitive marital therapy. *The Harvard Medical School Mental Health Letter, 6,* 4–6.

Beck, A. T. (1991). Cognitive therapy: A 30-year retrospective. *American Psychologist, 46,* 368–375.

Beck, A. T., Davis, D. D., & Freeman, A. (2004). *Cognitive therapy of personality disorders* (2nd Ed.). New York: Guilford Press.

Beck, A. T., Emery, G., & Greenberg, R. L. (1985). *Anxiety disorders and phobias: A cognitive perspective*. New York, NY: Basic Books.

Blackburn, J. (2001). Anger, chronic pain and rational emotive behavior therapy. *The Rational Emotive Behaviour Therapist, 9,* 23–28.

Blackledge, J. T. (2004). Functional contextual processes in posttraumatic stress. *International Journal of Psychology and Psychological Therapy, 4,* 443–467.

Blackledge, J. T. (2007). Disrupting verbal processes: cognitive defusion in acceptance and commitment therapy and other mindfulness-based psychotherapies. *The Psychological Record, 57,* 555–576.

Blackledge, J. T. & Hayes, S. C. (2006). Using acceptance and commitment training in the support of parents of children diagnosed with autism. *Child & Family Behavior Therapy, 28*, 1–18.

Bloch, S. (2004). A pioneer in psychotherapy research: Aaron Beck. *Australian and New Zealand Journal of Psychiatry* 38, 855–867.

Bohus, M., Haaf, B., Stiglmayr, C., Pohl, U., Bohme, R., & Linehan, M. (2000). Evaluation of inpatient dialectical behavior therapy for borderline personality disorder — a prospective study. *Behaviour Research and Therapy, 38*, 875–887.

Bond, F. & Hayes, S. C. (2002). ACT at work. In F. Bond & W. Dryden (Eds.), *Handbook of brief cognitive behaviour therapy* (pp. 117–140). Chichester, England: Wiley.

Bourland, D. D. (1989). To be or not to be: E-prime as a tool for critical thinking. *ETC: A Review of General Semantics, 61*, 546–557.

Brunell, L. F. (1990). Multimodal treatment of depression: a strategy to break through the "strenuous lethargy" of depression. *Psychotherapy in Private Practice, 8*, 13–23.

Butt, T. (1998). Sociality, role, and embodiment. *Journal of Constructivist Psychology, 11*, 105–116.

Byrom, T. (1976). *Dhammapada: the sayings of the Buddha.* Boston: Shambhala Publications.

Campbell, R. L. (1999). Ayn Rand and the cognitive revolution in psychology. *Journal of Ayn Rand Studies, 1*, 107–134.

Caro, I. (2004). General semantics theory: its implications for psychotherapy. *ETC: A Review of General Semantics, 61*, 308–326.

Chiari, G. & Nuzzo, M. L. (2004). Steering personal construct theory towards hermerneutic constructivism. In J. D. Raskin & S. K. Bridges (Eds.), *Studies in meaning 2: bridging the personal and social in constructivist psychology* (pp. 51–65). New York: Pace University Press.

Cote, R. L. (1995). *George Kelly: The theory of personal constructs and his contributions to personality theory.* (ERIC Document Reproduction Service No. ED 397368).

Cowan, D. & Brunero, S. (1997). Group therapy for anxiety disorders using rational emotive behavior therapy. *Australian and New Zealand Journal of Mental Health Nursing, 6*, 164–168.

Craighead, W. E., Kimball, W. H., & Rehak, P. J. (1979). Mood changes, physiological responses, and self-statements during social rejection imagery. *Journal of Consulting and Clinical Psychology, 47*, 385–396.

Dahl, J. C. & Lundgren, T. L. (2006). *Living beyond your pain: using acceptance and commitment therapy to ease chronic pain.* Oakland, CA: New Harbinger.

Dawes, M. (2007). As I see it: a personal overview of general semantics. *ETC: A Review of General Semantics, 64*, 144–146.

DeRubeis, R. J., Tang, T. Z., & Beck, A. T. (2001). Cognitive therapy. In K. S. Dobson (Ed.), *Handbook of cognitive-behavioral therapies* (2nd ed., pp. 349–392). New York: Guilford Press.

Dobson, K. S. & Dozois, D. J. A. (2001). Historical and philosophical basis of the cognitive and behavioral therapies. In K. S. Dobson (Ed.), *Handbook of cognitive behavioral therapy.* New York: Guilford Press.

Dryden, W. & Ellis A. (2001). Rational emotive behavior therapy. In K. S. Dobson (Ed.), *Handbook of cognitive-behavioral therapies* (2nd ed., pp. 295–348). New York: Guilford Press.

D'Zurilla, T. J. & Nezu A. M. (2001). Problem-solving therapies. In K. S. Dobson (Ed.), *Handbook of cognitive behavior therapies* (pp. 211–245). New York: Guilford Press.

Eifert, G. H., McKay, M., & Forsyth, J. P. (2006). *Act on life not on anger: the new acceptance and commitment therapy guide to problem anger.* Oakland, CA: New Harbinger.

Ellis, A. (1987). A sadly neglected cognitive element in depression. *Cognitive Therapy and Research, 11*, 121–145.

Ellis, A. (1993). Reflections on rational-emotive therapy. *Journal of Consulting and Clinical Psychology, 61*, 199–201.

Ellis, A. (1994). *Reason and emotion in psychotherapy.* Secaucus, NJ: Birch lane.

Ellis, A. (1999). Why rational emotive therapy to rational emotive behavior therapy. *Psychotherapy, 36*, 154–159.

Ellis, A. (2007). General semantics and rational-emotive therapy: 1991 Alfred Korzybski Memorial Lecture. *ETC: A Review of General Semantics, 64*, 301–319.

Ellis, A. & Crawford, T. (2000). *Making intimate connections: Seven guidelines for great relationships and better communication.* Atascadero, CA: Impact Publishers.

Ellis, A. & Lange, A. (1994). *How to keep people from pushing your buttons.* New York: Citadel.

Ellis, A., McInerny, J. F., DiGiuseppe, R., & Yeager, R. J. (1988). *Rational-emotive therapy with alcoholics and substance abusers.* Needham, MA: Allyn & Bacon.

Ellis, A. & Tafrate, C. (1997). *How to control your anger before it controls you.* New York: Kensington.

Ellis, A., Sichel, J. L., Yeager, R. J., DiMattia, D., & DiGiuseppe, R. (1989). *Rational-emotive couples therapy.* Needham, MA: Allyn & Bacon.

Ellis, A. & Velten, E. (1992). *When AA doesn't work for you: rational steps for quitting alcohol.* New York: Barricade Books.

Epictetus. (1983). *Handbook of Epictetus.* Indianapolis, IN: Hackett.

Epting, F. R. & Paris, M. E. (2006). A constructive understanding of the person: George Kelly and humanistic psychology. *The Humanistic Psychologist, 34*, 21–37.

Faidley, A. F. & Leitner, L. M. (1993). *Assessing experience in psychotherapy: personal construct alternatives.* Westport, CT: Praeger.

Forsyth, J. P. & Eifert, G. H. (2008). *The mindfulness & acceptance workbook for anxiety: a guide to breaking free from anxiety, phobias, and worry using Acceptance and Commitment Therapy.* Oakland, CA: New Harbinger.

Fox, E. J. (2006). Constructing a pragmatic science of learning and instruction with functional contextualism. *Educational Technology Research & Development, 54*, 5–36.

Fransella, F. & Neimeyer, R. A. (2005). George Alexander Kelly: the man and his theory. In F. Fransella (Ed.), *The essential practitioner's handbook of personal construct psychology*. New York: Wiley.

Freeman, A. & Reinecke, M. (1994). *Suicide*. New York: Springer.

Freeman, A., Pretzer, J., Fleming, B., & Simon, K. M. (1990). *Clinical applications of cognitive therapy*. New York: Plenum.

Freeman, A., Simon, K. M., Beutler, L. E., & Arkowitz, H. (Eds.) (1989). *Comprehensive handbook of cognitive therapy*. New York: Plenum Press.

Graham, L. & Wong, B. L. (1993). Comparing two modes of teaching a question-answering strategy for enhancing reading comprehension: didactic and self-instructional training. *Journal of Learning Disabilities, 26*, 270–279.

Grusec, J. E. (1992). Social learning theory and developmental psychology: the legacies of Robert Sears and Albert Bandura. *Developmental Psychology, 28*, 776–786.

Harris, R. (2006). Embracing your demons: an overview of acceptance and commitment therapy. *Psychotherapy in Australia, 12*, 2–8.

Hauck, P. A. & McKeegan, P. (1997). Using REBT to overcome depression. In J. Yankura and W. Dryden (Eds.), *Using REBT with common psychological problems: a therapist's casebook* (pp. 44–73). New York: Springer.

Hayes, S. C., Bissett, R., Korn, Z., Zettle, R. D., Rosenfarb, I., Cooper, L., & Grundt, A. (1999). The impact of acceptance versus control rationales on pain tolerance. *The Psychological Record, 49*, 33–47.

Hayes, S. C. & Gifford, E. V. (1997). The trouble with language: experiential avoidance, rules, and the nature of verbal events. *Psychological Science, 8*, 170–173.

Hayes, S. C., Strosahl, K. D., & Wilson, K. G. (1999). *Acceptance and commitment therapy: an experiential approach to behavior change*. New York: Guilford Press.

Hayes, S. C. & Wilson, K. G. (1993). Some applied implications of a contemporary behavior analytic account of verbal behavior. *The Behavior Analyst, 16*, 283–301.

Hayes, S. C., Wilson, K. W., Gifford, E. V., Follette, V. M. & Strosahl, K. (1996). Experiential avoidance and behavioral disorders: a functional dimensional approach to diagnosis and treatment. *Journal of Consulting and Clinical Psychology, 64*, 1152–1168.

Henriques, G. R. & Beck, A. T. (2000). Cognitive approaches to schizophrenia: overview of theory, practice, and research. *Complexity and Change, 9*, 30–39.

Holcomb, W. R. (1986). Stress inoculation therapy with anxiety and stress disorders of acute psychiatric patients. *Journal of Clinical Psychology, 42*, 864–872.

Hummelen, J. W. & Rokx, T. A. (2007). Individual-context interaction as a guide in the treatment of personality disorders. *Bulletin of the Menninger Clinic, 71*, 42–55.

Jankowicz, A. D. (1987). Whatever became of George Kelly? *American Psychologist, 42*, 481–487.

Jaremko, M. (1980). The use of stress inoculation training in reduction of public speaking anxiety. *Journal of Clinical Psychology, 36*, 735–738.

Jaremko, M. (1983). Stress inoculation training for social anxiety with emphasis on dating anxiety. In D. Meichenbaum & M. Jaremko (Eds.), *Stress reduction and prevention*. New York: Plenum.

Kelly, G. A. (1955). *The psychology of personal constructs: a theory of personality*. New York: W.W. Norton & Company.

Kelly, G. A. (1970). A brief introduction to personal construct theory. In D. Bannister (Ed.), *Perspectives in personal construct theory* (pp. 1–29). London: Academic Press.

Kelly, G. A. (2003). A brief introduction to personal construct theory. In F. Fransella (Ed.), *International Handbook of Personal Construct Psychology*. Hoboken, NJ: John Wiley and Sons, Inc.

Kendall, C. & Finch, A. J. (1978). A cognitive-behavioral treatment for impulsivity: a group comparison study. *Journal of Consulting and Clinical Psychology, 46*, 110–117.

Koons, C., Chapman, A. L., Betts, B., O'Rourke, B., & Robins, C. J. (2006). Dialectical behavior therapy adapted for the vocational rehabilitation of significantly disabled mentally ill adults. *Cognitive and Behavioral Practice, 13*, 146–156.

Koons, C., Robins, C. J., Tweed, J. L., Lynch, T. R., Gonzelez, A. M., Morse, J. Q., et al. (2001). Efficacy of dialectical behavior therapy in women veterans with borderline personality disorder. *Behavior Therapy, 32*, 371–390.

Korzybski, A. (1965). *Time-binding: the general theory (two papers 1924–1926)* (4th ed.). Lakeville, CT: Institute of General Semantics.

Lazarus, A. A. (1958). New methods in psychotherapy: a case study. *South African Medical Journal, 32*, 660–664.

Lazarus, A. A. (1971). *Behavior therapy and beyond*. New York: McGraw-Hill.

Lazarus, A. A. (1973). Multimodal behavior therapy: treating the "basic id." *Journal of Nervous and Mental Disease, 156*, 404–411.

Lazarus, A. A. (1974). Multimodal behavioral treatment of depression. *Behavior Therapy, 5*, 549–554.

Lazarus, A. A. (1986). Treating agoraphobia: behavioral/multimodal perspectives. *Psychotherapy in Private Practice, 4*, 11–23.

Lazarus, A. A. (1989). *The practice of multimodal therapy*. Baltimore: Johns Hopkins University Press.

Lazarus, A. A. (1997). *Brief but comprehensive psychotherapy: the multimodal way*. New York: Springer.

Lazarus, A. A. & Abramovitz, A. (2004). A multimodal behavioral approach to performance anxiety. *Journal of Clinical Psychology: In Session, 60*, 831–840.

Lazarus, A. A. & Shaughnessy, M. F. (2002). An interview with Arnold A. Lazarus. *North American Journal of Psychology, 4*, 171–181.

Leahy, R. L. (1996), *Cognitive therapy: Basic principles and application.* Northvale, NJ: Aronson.

Linehan, M. M. (1987). Dialectical behavior therapy: a cognitive-behavioral approach to parasuicide. *Journal of Personality Disorders, 1*, 328–333.

Linehan, M. M. (1993a). *Cognitive-behavioral treatment of borderline personality disorder.* New York: Guilford Press.

Linehan, M. M. (1993b). *Skills training manual for treating borderline personality disorder.* New York: Guilford Press.

Linehan, M. M., Armstrong, H. E., Suarez, A., Allmon, D., & Heard, H. L. (1991). Cognitive behavioral treatment of chronically parasuicidal borderline patients. *Archives of General Psychiatry, 48*, 1060–1064.

Linehan, M. M., Comtois, K. A., Murray, A. M., Brown, M. Z., Gallop, R. J., et al. (2006). Two-year randomized controlled trial and follow-up of dialectical behavior therapy vs. therapy by experts for suicidal behaviors and borderline personality disorder. *Archives of General Psychiarty, 63*, 757–766.

Linehan, M., Dimeff, L., Reynolds, S., Comtois, K., Shaw-Welch, S., Heagerty, P., et al. (2002). Dialectical behavior therapy versus comprehensive validation plus 12 step for the treatment of opioid dependent women meeting criteria for borderline personality disorder. *Drug and Alcohol Dependence, 67*, 13–26.

Linehan, M. M., Heard, H. L., & Armstrong, H. E. (1993). Naturalistic follow-up of a behavioral treatment for chronically parasuicidal borderline patients. *Archives of General Psychiatry, 50*, 971–974.

Linehan, M., Schmidt, H., Dimeff, L., Craft, C., Kanter, J., & Comtois, K. (1999). Dialectical behavior therapy for patients with borderline personality disorder and drug-dependence. *The American Journal of Addictions, 8*, 279–292.

Lynch, T. R., Morse, J., Mendelson, T., & Robins, C. (2003). Dialectical behavior therapy for depressed older adults: a randomized pilot study. *American Journal of Geriatric Psychiatry, 11*, 33–45.

Macavei, B. (2005). The role of irrational beliefs in the rational emotive behavior theory of depression. *Journal of Cognitive and Behavioral Psychotherapies, 5*, 73–81.

Mahoney, M. J. (1988). Constructive metatheory I: basic features and historical foundations. *International Journal of Personal Construct Psychology, 1*, 299–315.

Mahoney, M. J. (2000). Behaviorism, cognitivism, and constructivism: reflections on persons and patterns in my intellectual development. In M. R. Goldfried (Ed.), *How therapists change: personal and professional reflections* (pp. 183–200). Washington, DC: American Psychological Association.

Mahoney, M. J. (2003). *Constructive psychotherapy: a practical guide.* New York: Guliford Press.

Mahoney, M. J. (2007). Constructive complexity and human change processes. *Nebraska Symposium on Motivation, 52*, 245–273.

Mahoney, M. J. & Granvold, D. K. (2005). Constructivism and psychotherapy. *World Psychiatry, 4*, 74–77.

Mahoney, M. J. & Marquis, A. (2002). Integral constructivism and dynamic systems in psychotherapy processes. *Psychoanalytic Inquiry, 22*, 794–813.

Meichenbaum, D. (1993a). Changing conceptions of cognitive behavior modification: retrospect and prospect. *Journal of Consulting and Clinical Psychology, 61*, 202–204.

Meichenbaum, D. (1993b). The personal journey of a psychotherapy and his mother. In G. B. Brannigan & M. R. Merrens (Eds.), *The undaunted psychologist: adventures in research* (pp. 189–201). Philadelphia: Temple University Press.

Meichenbaum, D. (2003). Cognitive–behavior therapy: folktales and the unexpurgated history. *Cognitive Therapy & Research, 27*, 125–129.

Meichenbaum, D. (2007). Stress inoculation training: a preventative and treatment approach. In P. M. Lehrer, R. L. Woolfolk, & W. S. Sime, *Principles and practice of stress management* (3rd ed.). New York: Guilford Press.

Meichenbaum, D. & Cameron, R. (1973). Training schizophrenics to talk to themselves: a means of developing attentional controls. *Behavior Therapy, 4*, 515–534.

Meichenbaum, D. & Goodman, J. (1971). Training impulsive children to talk to themselves: a means of developing self-control. *Journal of Abnormal Psychology, 77*, 115–126.

Miller, G. A. (2003). The cognitive revolution: a historical perspective. *TRENDS in Cognitive Sciences, 7*, 141–144.

Moeller, A. T. & Steel, H. R. (2002). Clinically significant change after cognitive restructuring for adult survivors of childhood sexual abuse. *Journal of Rational-Emotive & Cognitive Behavior Therapy, 20*, 49–64.

Morris, K. T. (1975). The perls of perversion. *Personnel and Guidance Journal, 54*, 91–93.

Novaco, R. (1977a). Stress inoculation: a cognitive therapy for anger and its application to a case of depression. *Journal of Consulting and Clinical Psychology, 45*, 600–608.

Novaco, R. (1977b). A stress inoculation approach to anger management in the training of law enforcement officers. *American Journal of Community Psychology, 5*, 327–346.

O'Keefe, E. J. & Castaldo, C. (1985). Multimodal therapy for anorexia nervosa: an holistic approach to treatment. *Psychotherapy in Private Practice, 3*, 19–29.

Parke, R. D. & Clarke-Stewart, K. A. (2003). Developmental Psychology. In D. K. Freedheim (Ed.), *Handbook of psychology: history of psychology* Hoboken, NJ: Wiley.

Postman, N. (2003). Alfred Korzybski. *ETC: The Journal of General Semantics, 60*, 354–361.

Pretzer, J. & Beck, A. T. (2007). Cognitive approaches to stress and stress management. In P. M. Lehrer, R. L. Woolfolk, & W. E. Sime (Eds.), *Principles & practice of stress management* (3rd ed.). New York: Guilford Press.

Rapee, R. (1987). The psychological treatment of panic attacks: Theoretical conceptualization and review of evidence. *Clinical Psychology Review, 7*, 427–438.

Raskin, J. D. (2001). The modern, the postmodern, and George Kelly's personal construct psychology. *American Psychologist, 56*, 368–369.

Raskin, J. D. (2007). Assimilative integration in constructivist psychotherapy. *Journal of Psychotherapy Integration, 17*, 50–69.

Raskin J. D. & Bridges S. K. (Eds.) (2004). *Studies in meaning 2: Bridging the personal and social in constructivist psychology*. New York: Pace University Press.

Rathus, J. H. & Miller, A. L. (2002). Dialectical behavior therapy adapted for suicidal adolescents. *Suicide and Life Threatening Behavior, 32*, 146–157.

Reinecke, M. A. & Freeman, A. (2003). Cognitive therapy. In A. S. Gurman & S. B. Messer (Eds.), *Essential psychotherapies*. New York: Guilford Press.

Reynolds S. K. & Linehan, M. M. (2002). Dialectical behavior therapy. In M. Hersen & W. Sledge (Eds.), *Encylopedia of Psychotherapy*. New York: Academic Press.

Roberts, T. K., Jackson, L. J., & Phelps, R. (1980). Lazarus' multimodal therapy model applied in an institutional setting. *Professional Psychology, 11*, 150–156.

Robins, C. J., Ivanoff, A. M., & Linehan, M. M. (2001). Dialectical behavior therapy. In W. J. Livesley (Ed.), *Handbook of personality disorders: theory, research, and treatment*. New York: Guilford Press.

Robins, C. J. & Koons, C. R. (2004). Dialectical behavior therapy for severe personality disorders. In J. Magnavita (Ed.), *Handbook of personality disorders*. New York: Wiley.

Rokke, P. D. & Rehm, L. P. (2001). Self-management therapies. In K. S. Dobson (Ed.), *Handbook of cognitive behavior therapies*. New York: Guilford Press.

Safer, D. L., Telch, C. F., & Agras, W. S. (2001). Dialectical behavior therapy for bulimia nervosa: a case study. *International Journal of Eating Disorders, 30*, 101–106.

Safren, J. D. (1998). *Widening the scope of cognitive therapy: the therapeutic relationship, emotion, and the process of change*. Northvale, NJ: Jason Aronson.

Safren, J. D. & Segal, Z. V. (1990). *Interpersonal process in cognitive therapy*. New York: Basic Books.

Segal, Z. V., Williams, J. M. G., & Teasdale, J. (2002). *Mindfulness-based cognitive therapy for depression: a new approach to preventing relapse*. New York: Guilford Press.

Sneed, J. R., Balestri, M., & Belfi, B. J. (2003). The use of dialectical behavior therapy strategies in the psychiatric emergency room. *Psychotherapy: Theory, Research, Practice, Training, 40*, 265–277.

Stajkovic, A. D. & Luthans, F. (1998). Self-efficacy and work-related performance: a meta-analysis. *Psychological Bulletin, 124*, 240–261.

Stricker, G. & Gold, J. (2003). Intergrative approaches to psychotherapy. In A. S. Gurman & S. B. Messer (Eds.), *Essential Psychotherapies: Theory and Practice* (2nd ed.). New York: Guilford Press.

Stumpf, S. E. (1994). *Philosophy history and problems* (5th ed.). New York: McGraw-Hill.

Swales, M., Heard, H. L., & Williams, J. M. (2002). Linehan's dialectical behavior therapy (DBT) for borderline personality disorder: overview and adaptation. *Journal of Mental Health, 9*, 7–23.

Swenson, C. R., Sanderson, C., Dulit, R. A., & Linehan, M. M. (2001). The application of dialectical behavioral therapy for patients with borderline personality disorder on inpatient units. *Psychiatric Quarterly, 72*, 307–324.

Telch, C. F. (1997). Skills training treatment for adaptive regulation in a woman with binge-eating disorder. *International Journal of Eating Disorders, 22*, 77–81.

Telch, C. F., Agras, W. S., & Linehan, M. M. (2001). Dialectical behavior therapy for binge eating disorder. *Journal of Consulting and Clinical Psychology, 69*, 1061–1065.

Turk, D. C., Meichenbaum, D., & Genest, M. (1983). *Pain and behavioral medicine: a cognitive-behavioral perspective*. New York: Guilford Press.

Turner, R. (2000). Naturalistic evaluation of dialectical behavior therapy–oriented treatment for borderline personality disorder. *Cognitive and Behavioral Practice, 7*, 413–419.

Vallis, T. M. & Bucher, B. (1986). Individual difference factors in the efficacy of covert modeling and self-instructional training for fear reduction. *Canadian Journal of Behavioural Science, 18*, 146–158.

Verheul, R., van den Bosch, L. M. C., Koeter, M. W. J., de Ridder, M. A. J., Stijnen, T., & van den Brink, W. (2003). Dialectical behavior therapy for women with borderline personality disorder. *British Journal of Psychiatry, 182*, 135–140.

Veronen, L. J. & Kilpatrick, D. G. (1983). Stress management for rape victims. In D. Meichenbaum & M. Jaremko (Eds.), *Stress Prevention and management: a cognitive behavioral approach*. New York: Plenum.

Warren, R. (1997). REBT and generalized anxiety disorder. In J. Yakura & W. Dryden (Eds.), *Using REBT with common psychological problems: a therapist's casebook*. New York: Springer.

Watts, R. E. & Phillips, K. A. (2004). Adlerian psychology and psychotherapy: a relational constructivist approach. In J. D. Raskin & S. K. Bridges (Eds.), *Studies in meaning*

2: Bridging the personal and social in constructivist psychology. New York: Pace University Press.

Weishaar, M. E. & Beck, A. T. (1992). Clinical and cognitive predictors of suicide. In R. W. Maris, A. L. Berman, J. T. Maltsberger, & R. I. Yufit (Eds.), *Assessment and Prediction of suicide.* New York: Guilford Press.

Wilde, J. (2001). Interventions for children with anger problems. *Journal of Rational-Emotive & Cognitive Behavior Therapy, 19,* 191–197.

Wisniewski, L. & Kelly, E. (2003). The application of dialectical behavior therapy to the treatment of eating disorders. *Cognitive and Behavioral Practice, 10,* 131–138.

Wright, F. D., Beck, A. T., Newman, C. F., & Liese, B. F. (1993). Cognitive therapy of substance abuse: theoretical rationale. In L. S. Onken, J. D., Blaine, & J. J. Boren (Eds.), *Behavioral treatments for drug abuse and dependence.* NIDA Research Monograph 137. Rockville, MD: National Institutes of Health.

Yeo, L. S., Wong, M., Gerken, K., & Ansley, T. (2005). Cognitive-behavioral therapy in a hospital setting for children with severe emotional and/or behavior disorders. *Child Care in Practice, 11,* 7–22.

Young, J. E., Klosko, J. S., & Weisher, M. E. (2003). *Schema therapy: a practitioner's guide.* New York: Gilford.

Zettle, R. (2007). *ACT for depression: A clinician's guide to using acceptance and commitment therapy in treating depression.* Oakland, CA: New Harbinger.

Zettle, R. D. & Hayes, S. C. (2002). Brief ACT treatment of depression. In F. Bond & W. Dryden (Eds.), *Handbook of brief cognitive behaviour therapy.* Chichester, England: Wiley.

12

Existential and Humanistic Psychotherapies[1]

Robert Smither
Rollins College

> Everything can be taken from a man but one thing; the last of the human freedoms—to choose one's attitude in any given set of circumstances, to choose one's own way.
>
> Viktor Frankl
> *Man's Search for Meaning*

Despite their very important differences, existential and humanistic psychotherapies share many assumptions about human responsibility, the critical nature of the relationship between therapist and client, and what is ultimately important in life. But the most significant commonality—

and the quality that most sets them apart from the other therapeutic approaches described in this book—is their primary focus on the client's ability to *choose*. Both existential and humanistic psychotherapies categorically reject the idea that human behavior is controlled by either unconscious motivations or conditions in the client's environment. No matter what a person's history or current situation, that person can choose, at any moment, to rise above any limiting factors and determine what his or her future will be.

Most existential and humanistic therapists do not make detailed diagnoses or give specific advice on handling a client's personal problems. From both the existential and humanistic

---

[1]The author wishes to thank Angela Bishop and Judith Provost for their assistance with this chapter.

perspectives, the client alone knows the answers he or she is seeking. Because each person who comes for therapy is a unique human being, the therapist cannot rely upon a formula or program for creating change. Rather, the therapist uses existential and humanistic principles to help the client resolve the issues that brought him or her to therapy. In other words, the existential therapist has the goal of assisting the client's growth of awareness rather than trying to change the client's inner world (Greenberg, Safran, & Rice, 1989).

Existential and humanistic psychology are known as the "Third Force" (Maslow, 1962)—an alternative to Freudian psychoanalysis and behaviorism. Many of the ideas of existential and humanistic psychotherapy have their origin in existential philosophy. This chapter first considers some of the major ideas of existentialism and then looks at how those ideas influenced the development of existential therapy. The second half of the chapter considers the major humanistic approach—the client-centered therapy of Carl Rogers—as well as the assumptions and practices of Gestalt therapy.

EXISTENTIAL PSYCHOTHERAPY

Major Ideas of Existential Philosophy

Existential psychotherapy was first developed by Ludwig Binswanger in the middle of the twentieth century, but its roots lie in the philosophical writings of Søren Kierkegaard (1813–1815), Jean-Paul Sartre (1905–1980), Martin Heidegger (1889–1976), and others. Although the general goal of existential philosophy is to understand what it means to be human, its proponents addressed questions about many other aspects of life as well. Some of the ideas most relevant to existential psychotherapy include the following.

Existence precedes essence. From an existential perspective, an individual's behavior cannot

be attributed to innate qualities. People are not born selfish, pessimistic, or hostile. Rather, selfish, pessimistic, or hostile people have chosen to behave in that way, and they are also free to choose to be generous, optimistic, or accepting. From an existential perspective, people have the ability to *create* themselves, that is, a person exists first and then chooses his or her essence, not the other way around, as many other psychological theories would argue.

Existentialists believe, for example, that a person cannot reasonably blame his or her choice to avoid social interaction on the personal quality of introversion. Even if the person's introversion has a genetic base, he or she still has the choice of acting in an introverted or extroverted manner. This choice is important because, to some degree, it defines—and either expands or limits—that person's experiences of the world and the people in it.

Most people who enter therapy feel that their choices in life (i.e., the actions that are open to them) are constrained by a variety of factors, such as family history or responsibilities, job and career considerations, or their social environment. From an existential perspective, however, believing they have no choice is an illusion that is psychologically harmful to individuals. People may not like the consequences associated with those choices, but every action they take reflects a decision on their part. A person is not forced to stay in an unhappy marriage because of the children, for example; staying is that person's choice.

Existentialists also believe that only two aspects of life limit a person's choices. The first is death. From an existential perspective, no human has a choice about continuing to exist. Death comes to ourselves, our friends, and our family, and that realization is—or should be—an important psychological issue for everyone (Yalom, 1980). Although society does its best to deny death by promoting the concept of youth, the knowledge that someday they will no longer exist creates anxiety that most people are unwilling to face.

The second factor limiting our choices is what Heidegger (1927) called *facticity*—the concrete details of life that may proscribe certain actions, such as our age, gender, or race. For example, an older client may profoundly regret his youthful decision to get married rather than accept a scholarship to play football in college. Irrespective of his regret, the facticity of the client's situation—his diminished physical abilities—is a fact that makes the possibility of a career as a professional athlete unlikely.

Freedom and responsibility. Because humans are not limited by their essence, they have the freedom to define their lives through their choices. The choices may not be appealing, but they are always there. As existential psychotherapist Viktor Frankl (1963) pointed out, even the concentration camp prisoner who faces torture is free to choose how to react to the situation.

But along with the freedom to choose comes responsibility for one's choices. From an existential perspective, it is not honest to attribute either the good or bad aspects of one's life to other people or situations. A distant and uncaring mother, an alcoholic father, or the experience of a natural catastrophe, for example, can have a profound effect on an individual. But the individual chooses what that effect will be. In the words of existential psychiatrist Irvin Yalom: "the individual is entirely responsible for—that is, is the author of—his or her own world, life design, choices, and actions" (Yalom, 1980).

Whatever may have happened in the past, the person's reaction in the present represents a choice he or she has made. Existentialists believe people should attend to the present and be moving toward the future rather than focusing on what has happened before. From an existential perspective, people should always be seen as becoming something new—*emerging,* in the words of existential therapist Rollo May (1958)—rather than simply being the culmination of what has happened before.

The importance of authenticity. Refusing to accept responsibility for one's decisions and blaming one's current situation on the past are examples of inauthenticity, or what Sartre (1953) called bad faith. Attributing one's failure to establish a long-term romantic relationship to a "dysfunctional family," but doing nothing about that failure, would be an example of living in bad faith. The opposite of living in bad faith is to live authentically, which is living in accordance with one's deepest beliefs, values, and goals (Jacobsen, 2007).

Bad faith also occurs when people ignore not only their personal problems but the larger issues of life as well. Focusing on acquiring more and more possessions while ignoring the hungry people in the world and working long hours while ignoring family problems would be other examples of living in bad faith. From an existential perspective, facing life honestly is important on the levels of both ethics and mental health.

Life has no inherent meaning. As the French writer Albert Camus (1955), Viktor Frankl (1963), and other existentialist writers point out, there is no universal principle or guiding force in the world that gives life meaning. Because of this, each person must find his or her own meaning. In Frankl's system of psychotherapy, finding a meaning is the key factor in psychological health.

The belief that life has no inherent meaning carries another important psychological implication. Because there is no guiding force or order to what happens in the world, existentialists recognize that many important life events are unpredictable. Because any of us could at any moment be accidentally killed, suffer great personal tragedy, or be diagnosed with a terminal disease, it is important to keep our focus on the important issues of life such as meaning, death, and existence.

Phenomenology. Phenomenology refers to the method of existentialists and existential therapists, which is to approach life without preconceived ideas and to try and experience phenomena directly. Because people cannot know what someone else's experiences mean to that person, any interpretation or judgment we make regarding someone else's experience may be incorrect or even harmful. From an existential perspective, this is a particular danger of relying on psychoanalytic interpretations or using conditioning as an explanatory principle. Attributing a client's anxiety to an attachment disorder or inappropriate reinforcements, for example, is describing phenomena in terms that are meaningful to the therapist, but perhaps not to the client. From an existentialist perspective, this practice of attaching the therapist's labels can be quite harmful, resulting in misinterpretation or negation of an experience that is important to the client. Existential, as well as humanistic, therapists believe that each problem must be considered from the view of the patient rather than the therapist's personal theoretical orientation (Walsh & McElwain, 2001).

To summarize, the existential principles underlying existential psychotherapy are that people create their identities through the choices they make; that every situation—other than death and facticity—holds the possibility of an alternative choice; and that people are responsible for the choices they make. Furthermore, it is the present and the future that are important, and the past should not be allowed to define either. Because life has no inherent meaning or guiding power, each person must find his or her own meaning, and because we could cease to exist at any time, we should make every effort to live our lives authentically. Finally—and very important for both existential and humanistic psychotherapies—because no person can truly know the experiences of another, the experiences of each client should be approached without preconceived notions or judgments.

Because of its emphasis on issues such as responsibility, meaning, and death, some people have labeled existentialism a gloomy philosophy that allows little room for human happiness. In a lecture given in 1946 entitled *Existentialism Is a Humanism*, Sartre (1989) rejected this idea, arguing that existentialism is simply about looking at the world honestly and taking action to improve it.

Most existential psychotherapists would agree with Sartre—the important questions of life are profound, but they are not necessarily depressing. In *Man's Search for Meaning*, a book about his concentration camp experiences and his system of psychotherapy, Frankl (1963) argued that all people must face the "tragic triad" of life—pain, guilt, and death—and that suffering is unavoidable. Nonetheless, Frankl argued, pain, guilt, and death are bearable if a person approaches life's challenges with what he called "tragic optimism," or a drive to make the best of any situation. Using tragic optimism, people can manage, and perhaps rise above, whatever tragedies befall them. Frankl based this belief on his observations of human behavior in the concentration camps.

Existential Psychotherapy

The first application of existential principles to psychotherapy is usually attributed to the Swiss psychiatrist **Ludwig Binswanger** (1881–1966), who studied under Carl Jung and was a lifelong friend of Sigmund Freud. In his book *Foundations and Knowledge of Human Existence* (1942), Binswanger made the observation that the ways by which people live in the world and interact with others occur on three levels. When people act at the level of the *Umwelt*, the lowest mode of existence, they focus on their own satisfactions, treating others as objects rather than people. In general, people living at the level of the Umwelt lack self-awareness.

In the *Mitwelt*, people focus largely on interpersonal relations, acting toward others in one of four modes. In the *anonymous mode*, people respond to others in terms of roles, much as a bureaucrat reacts to an individual with a problem without considering that person's uniqueness. In the *mutual mode*, people treat others in an open, honest, and accepting way, which Binswanger considered the ideal form of human relationship. The *singular mode* refers to narcissistic and self-oriented behaviors, such as masturbation or suicide, and the *plural mode* refers to formal types of relationships, such as those between people riding a bus or seated together in a movie theater.

According to Binswanger, the highest level of existence is the *Eigenwelt*, where people are self-aware and self-actualizing. People who act at the level of the Eigenwelt are able to interpret phenomena in the world in terms of their personal meaning to each individual. For example, a person operating at the level of the Eigenwelt is able to take each personal experience and determine its meaning outside of the judgments of societal norms or expectations. In the Eigenwelt, things in the world are experienced in terms of one's personal development (Hogan, 1976).

Binswanger also observed that despite the fact that most people feel their lives must have a purpose, they usually don't know what that purpose is. Rather than developing a meaning for life that is unique to them—a key criterion of mental health in existential psychotherapy—most people unthinkingly join a religion, participate in politics, or become neurotic rather than make the authentic choices recommended by the existential philosophers.

The Viennese psychiatrist **Viktor Frankl** (1905–1997) is one of the most influential existential therapists. Frankl called his method of working with patients *logotherapy*, a term created from the Greek word *logos*, defined as "meaning." No matter what a person's situation, Frankl argued, he or she needs to find a meaning in life. Otherwise, life will be empty and the person will be at risk for neurosis and psychological suffering. In a famous passage, Frankl described his views on finding meaning:

> It did not really matter what we expected from life, but rather what life expected from us. We needed to stop asking about the meaning of life, and instead to think of ourselves as those who were being questioned by life—daily and hourly. Our answer must consist, not in talk and meditation, but in right action and in right conduct. Life ultimately means taking the responsibility to find the right answer to its problems and to fulfill the tasks which it constantly sets for each individual. (Frankl, 1963, p. 122)

According to Frankl, there are three ways to discover meaning in life. First, we can create or accomplish something that has significance to ourselves or others. Second, we can go through meaningful experiences, such as working for the benefit of people who need our help, appreciating works of art, or loving another person. Finally, meaning also comes from encountering suffering. As mentioned earlier, Frankl felt that suffering is an unavoidable part of the human experience and that suffering the loss of loved ones, experiencing failure, or simply being in unhappy situations can also give meaning to life.

Frankl introduced the technique of *paradoxical intention*, a form of brief therapy that is also used by modern behavioral therapists (e.g., O'Hanlon, 2000). In this approach, Frankl wrote, "the phobic patient is invited to intend, even if only for a moment, precisely that which he fears" (1963). For example, Frankl describes treating a young physician who was afraid of being embarrassed by his perspiration. Whenever the physician started to sweat, Frankl advised, he was to try and sweat as much as possible, regardless of the consequences. The physician agreed to follow Frankl's suggestion, but the next time he started sweating and tried to perspire more, he could not. By trying to do the thing he feared most, Frankl wrote, the physician was relieved of a phobia that had bothered him for four years. Frankl also used paradoxical intention to treat cases of stuttering, obsessive compulsive disorder, and insomnia.

In the United States, **Rollo May** (1909–1994) added to the growing interest in existential psychology by serving as a co-editor of *Existence* (May, Angel, & Ellenberger, 1958), an influential collection of essays written by existential psychotherapists. Early in his career,

May had studied psychoanalysis at the William Alanson White Institute and received a PhD in clinical psychology from Columbia University.

In *Man's Search for Himself* (May, 1954), May identified four stages of psychological development. *Innocence*, the stage of infancy, is characterized by actions taken without regard for their consequences for others. During *rebellion*, children struggle for independence. In the *ordinary* stage, adults conform and adapt to traditional values. In the *creative* stage, however, the person lives authentically—he or she faces life honestly and pursues a personal meaning that is not based in conformity or fears of what others might think.

Another concept associated with May is the *existential neurosis*. This refers to the anxiety and emptiness felt, for example, by a person who has achieved worldly success in terms of home, career, and possessions. In many cases, the person who has worked hard to acquire all the things expected to bring happiness feels no satisfaction with these accomplishments and questions the meaning of his or her life. Highlight Box 12.1 describes a case of existential neurosis.

HIGHLIGHT BOX 12.1

THE CASE OF C.

As an undergraduate, C. earned A's in all her science courses, so she was naturally drawn to a career in medicine. Aside from the status and financial rewards associated with being a physician, C. was also attracted by the fact that people from her geographic area had high rates of cancer and that she might be able to help the community by becoming an oncologist.

C. did well in medical school, but after two years of residency, she became unhappy with the long hours and the work of an oncologist. In fact, the demands of her career left her no time to consider what in life might make her happy. After a hard day at the hospital, C. had little energy to do more than sit at home watching TV and eating. In fact, eating junk food was one source of pleasure for C., and over several months she gained a considerable amount of weight. The weight gain further contributed to her unhappiness.

This unhappiness eventually led to an attempted suicide and admission to an inpatient psychiatric unit. At the unit, C. was given antidepressants and taught how to avoid or change negative cognitions that might arise. At the time of her discharge, C. no longer felt depressed, but she had a vague sense of emptiness and anxiety because the therapy had not addressed her unhappiness with her work and home life.

In the months after her discharge, C. became attracted to Kabbalah, a mystical branch of Judaism that addresses questions of human existence, such as a person's true identity and reason for being on earth. C. became an enthusiastic practitioner of Kabbalah, but eventually the attraction faded and the depression returned. Despite her therapy and medication, C. realized she still had a job she hated, no close friends, no romantic relationship, and no activities she loved doing.

According to Keshen (2006), C.'s life was characterized by the use of what he calls *purposive substitutes*, or activities that substitute for authentic attitudes or behaviors. Relying on purposive substitutes rather than facing life's big questions can be an indication of existential neurosis. Although C. chose her career partly because it offered the opportunity to help others, she later chose a number of destructive and avoidant behaviors when her career became a disappointment. Working long hours, overeating, and looking to the Kabbalah for answers

---

HIGHLIGHT BOX 12.1   (*continued*)

all served to avoid addressing C.'s existential neurosis.

In this example, the existential therapist would be less interested in factors in C.'s past that caused her depression or identifying new behaviors that might distract C. from that depression. Rather, the therapist would want to help C. expand her awareness as to how she currently avoids addressing the question of meaning or purpose in her life. Another goal of the therapy would be for C. to understand that although her problems are the result of unsatisfactory choices in the past, she has the potential to make new choices that can bring a greater sense of satisfaction with her life. In other words, C. must accept responsibility for her behavior in the present while looking for a reason or purpose that will give her life meaning.

Finally, psychiatrist and group therapist **Irvin Yalom** (1931–) is one of the most influential modern existential theorists. His book *Existential Psychotherapy* (Yalom, 1980) defines the existential orientation as "a dynamic approach to therapy which focuses on the concerns that are rooted in the individual's existence." According to Yalom, psychological conflicts arise from confronting the problems of existence, of which four are paramount in importance. Yalom defines these sources of existential anxiety as follows:

Death: anxiety caused by the inevitability of death (Highlight Box 12.2 describes Yalom's ideas about the importance of death in a person's life and psychotherapy);

Freedom: anxiety caused by being responsible for the choices a person makes as well as the conditions of one's life;

Isolation: anxiety resulting from the recognition that "each of us enters existence alone and must depart from it alone"; and

Meaninglessness: anxiety caused by the fact that life has no inherent meaning and each person must find his or her own meaning (Yalom, 1980).

HIGHLIGHT BOX 12.2

EXISTENTIAL PSYCHOLOGY AND DEATH ANXIETY

As mentioned in the text, existential psychologists such as Irvin Yalom consider four issues to be critical in any person's life: freedom, isolation, meaningless, and death. From an existential perspective, therapy that does not consider questions of existence is unlikely to be successful in addressing anything more than superficial issues.

Of particular interest to Yalom is the question of death, which is probably not a topic that comes up in most therapeutic interactions. Although Freud introduced the idea of death as an instinct in *Beyond the Pleasure Principle* (1955), existential therapists approach the topic in terms of how the fear of death affects our behavior as both children and adults. Despite the human preference to

<hr>

HIGHLIGHT BOX 12.2   (*continued*)

deny the pervasiveness of death fears, Yalom (1980) believes that a plan for therapy can actually be constructed around raising a client's awareness of death. His assumptions about death's role in psychotherapy are as follows:

1. The fear of death plays a major role in our internal experience; it haunts as does nothing else; it rumbles continuously under the surface; it is a dark, unsettling presence at the rim of consciousness.
2. The child, at an early age, is pervasively preoccupied with death, and his or her

major developmental task is to deal with terrifying fears of obliteration.

3. To cope with these fears, we erect defenses against death awareness, defenses that are based on denial, that shape character structure, and that, if maladaptive, result in clinical syndromes. In other words, psychopathology is the result of ineffective modes of death transcendence.
4. Lastly, a robust and effective approach to psychotherapy may be constructed on the foundation of death awareness.

<hr>

Yalom's approach focuses strongly on the client's view of the present. Events in the past have contributed to the way in which the client faces the ultimate concerns of existence, but the past, overall, is "not the most useful area for therapeutic exploration. The future-becoming-present is the primary tense of existential therapy" (Yalom, 1980).

The Existential View of Mental Health

From an existential perspective, most psychological problems can be traced to a person's anxieties about the questions of existence. Often unconsciously, people worry about death, the meaning of their lives, or their isolation from others. These concerns can create unhealthy behaviors and lead to psychological disorders such as depression, paranoia, or alcoholism. Usually, however, the person with the disorder does not recognize its source. He or she attributes psychological problems to stressors at work, unhappy family relationships, or even physical symptoms such as chemical imbalances. From an existential perspective, allowing

external factors to define an individual's values and behavior is known as being in a state of *fallenness* (Moustakas, 1994). Rather than face the anxieties that existential questions can create, the person experiencing fallenness typically looks for distractions such as new accomplishments, possessions, or relationships. Because the person is not dealing with the real source of his or her anxiety, however, satisfaction from these distractions is likely to be transitory. At some point, the person may seek psychotherapy.

In existential psychotherapy, patients are challenged to examine their values and to identify areas of their lives where they may not be acting authentically. The basic goal of existential psychotherapy is to expand the client's awareness of his or her uniqueness, choose goals, and move toward decisive action to achieve those goals (May, 1969), that is, the therapist helps the client examine aspects of his or her life such as career, relationships, or aging to determine how the client really feels about such issues. Although the therapist helps the client with pressing problems—the impending breakup of a relationship, for example—these problems are always explored within the context of the bigger questions of human existence (Kiser, 2007). The therapist does not have the goal of alleviating the client's suffering, because suffering is unavoidable. Rather, the therapist helps the client channel the suffering into more productive ways of facing life's challenges (Fernando, 2007).

Existential therapists are, of course, phenomenological in their approach. The therapist recognizes that his or her personal interpretation of the client's situation may be incorrect, so the therapist is careful to avoid imposing interpretations or meanings on the client's experiences. At the same time, the therapist also tries to interact authentically with the client. From the existential perspective, the therapist and client are two real people encountering each other, not simply an expert who uses psychological techniques to solve another person's problems.

Although the therapist avoids interpreting the client's experiences, he or she is likely to point out choices the client makes and encourage the client to take responsibility for what happens in the present and the future. A cold and demanding father may have undermined a client's sense of self-esteem, for example, but the father is not responsible for the client's actions in the present. The patient has the ability to choose what to do, and blaming current actions on the past is usually a form of inauthenticity. In the words of Rollo May:

> I propose that *the purpose of the psychotherapy is to set people free*. Free, as far as possible from symptoms . . . free from compulsions. . . . But, most of all, I believe that the therapist's function should be to help people become free to be aware of and to experience their possibilities. (May, 1981)

Because of the nature of the questions addressed in existential psychotherapy, the therapy can be lengthy. Furthermore, an individual's attitudes toward meaning and death are rarely resolved once and for all. A client's feelings about these issues may change as his or her life experiences change. But the existential therapist will consider therapy successful if the client expands his or her awareness, takes responsibility for choices, recognizes that important philosophical issues affect everyday matters, and moves toward finding a meaning for his or her life. It is important to note, however, that existential therapy is not considered successful if the client merely achieves insight into his or her problems. Existential therapists believe that real change results in action (Yalom, 1980).

Evaluating Existential Psychotherapy

Existential psychotherapy has several unique features that complicate the evaluation of its effectiveness. First, the existential emphasis on phenomenology and the uniqueness of each person makes evaluation based on traditional statistical methods almost impossible. Since existentialists believe there is no underlying human nature or universal law of behavior, they tend to react negatively to nomothetically derived information based on group means, standardized scores, or statistical hypothesis testing. Furthermore, existential therapists regard the issues that their patients confront—death, meaninglessness, and isolation, for example—as far too complex to lend themselves to traditional methods of evaluation. Finally, despite its distinguished intellectual history, existential psychotherapy has not become part of mainstream psychotherapy (Cooper, 2003; Keshen, 2006), so few researchers outside its proponents have written much about either its efficacy or effectiveness.

Nonetheless, researchers have provided support for some of the beliefs that are the foundation of existential psychotherapy. For example, research supports the importance of the therapist recognizing the client's subjective view in the therapy process (e.g., Strupp, 1996; Walsh,

Perucci, & Severns, 1999). This is particularly important because the client's view may differ from the view of the therapist and may affect the course and outcome of the therapy (Walsh & McElwain, 2001),

Along the same lines, other research (Rice & Greenberg, 1984; Walsh, Perucci, & Severns, 1999) supports the existential notion that successful psychotherapy should be considered in terms of diverse goals rather than specific behavioral changes, that is, the course of psychotherapy in general consists of many small but significant changes that impact the client's life. Success in therapy should also be considered in terms of these smaller goals and not only from the perspective of a final outcome.

Finally, the concepts of authenticity and awareness have also been found to be relevant to the success of psychotherapy (Jones, Parke, & Pulos, 1992; Lietaer, 1992). In other words, research shows that successful therapy occurs when clients explore their inner worlds, integrate denied emotions or experiences, and act on new possibilities.

Overall, the existential approach to psychotherapy has not been evaluated in the way that most therapies are evaluated. This is not a problem for most existential therapists, however, because they believe that no matter how robust the research design, it cannot fully capture the process of dealing with the problems of human existence.

HUMANISTIC PSYCHOTHERAPY

Despite the overlap between most of the values of existential and humanistic psychotherapies, the humanistic approach clearly has its origin in psychology rather than philosophy. The major humanistic theorists—Abraham Maslow and Carl Rogers—adopted many ideas first proposed by the existentialists, but humanistic psychology had already established itself before

Rollo May brought existentialism to the United States in the 1950s. Rogers had published *Counseling and Psychotherapy* in 1942, and Maslow's *Motivation and Personality* appeared in 1954.

From a theoretical perspective, humanistic psychotherapy's greatest difference from existential psychotherapy is its generally more optimistic approach to life's issues. Whereas existential psychotherapy aims at finding meaning and accepting life's unavoidable tragedies, humanistic psychology emphasizes the unique qualities of resourcefulness, the capacity for constructive change, resilience, self-awareness, and uniqueness (Cain, 2001). A particularly distinct feature of humanistic psychotherapy is its focus on self-actualization and the realization of human potential. This difference is apparent from the Articles of Association of the American Association of Humanistic Psychologists:

> Humanistic psychology . . . stands for the respect for the worth of persons, respect for differences of approach, open-mindedness as to acceptable methods, and interest in exploration of new aspects of human behavior. . . . [I]t is concerned with topics having little place in existing theories and systems: e.g., love, creativity, self, growth, organism, basic need-gratification, self-actualization, higher values, being, becoming, spontaneity, play, humor, affection, naturalness, warmth, ego-transcendence, objectivity, autonomy, responsibility, meaning, fair play, transcendental experience, peak experience, courage, and related concepts. (American Association of Humanistic Psychologists, 1962)

A second important difference between existential and humanistic psychotherapies relates to the interaction between the client and the therapist. Although both approaches emphasize the need for the therapist to respect the client's phenomenological world, humanistic psychotherapy puts special emphasis on the actual interpersonal relationship between the therapist and the client. In fact, this relationship is key to the success of humanistic therapy. Humanistic psychologists believe that an individual's inability to solve his or her problems—which is the reason for seeking professional help—originates in flawed interpersonal relationships from the past. Because of this, the humanistic psychotherapist takes special precautions not to convey any kind of evaluation or judgment other than his or her warm acceptance of the client as a person (Rogers, 1957).

Humanistic therapists usually trace the beginning of their orientation to the work of **Otto Rank** (1884–1939), Freud's collaborator and secretary of the Vienna Psychoanalytic Society. Although trained as a psychoanalyst, Rank eventually broke with Freud, developing his own therapeutic approach, which he called *will therapy* (Rank, 1978). Rank argued that therapy should focus on the client's present situation rather than events from the past and on his or her conscious choices rather than unconscious motivations. Rank also felt patients and therapists should have a more equal relationship and that therapy could be shorter than the many years that psychoanalysis usually required. Although Rank's innovative views on therapy were denounced by the psychoanalytic establishment and overlooked for many years, his theories were later resurrected by Rollo May (1953) and Carl Rogers (1942).

Another important influence on the growth of humanistic psychotherapy came from the German neurologist and psychiatrist **Kurt Goldstein** (1878–1965). From his work with brain-damaged patients, Goldstein concluded that the most basic drive of every organism is "to actualize, as much as possible, its individual capacities, its 'nature,' in the world" (1939). This drive to actualize—to reach a higher level of functioning—can actually create anxiety, but this anxiety is not a problem for healthy individuals. According to Goldstein, only sick organisms focus solely on tension reduction.

Goldstein's book, *The Organism* (1939), had an important impact on **Abraham Maslow**, who dedicated *Toward a Psychology of Being* (1968) to Goldstein. In particular, Maslow (1959) used Goldstein's concept of self-actualization to develop his theory of human needs, placing self-actualization at the highest level of human functioning. Although Maslow was not a psychotherapist, he helped found the American Association of Humanistic Psychologists in 1962 and the Division of Humanistic Psychology (Division 32) within the American Psychological Association.

From a purely therapeutic perspective, however, the most important contributions to humanistic psychotherapy came from **Carl Rogers** (1902–1987), creator of *client-centered therapy*. Although Rogers started his career with the intention of becoming a minister, he later concluded that he could not work in a field where he would be required to believe a specific doctrine (Rogers, 1961). Eventually Rogers studied psychology at Columbia University. From his early experiences in psychotherapy, Rogers began to realize

> that it is the *client* who knows what hurts, what directions to go, what problems are crucial, what experiences have been deeply buried. It began to occur to me that unless I had a need to demonstrate my own cleverness and learning, I would do better to rely upon the client for the direction of movement in the process. (Rogers, 1961)

Rogers's comment reflects the fundamental premise of client-centered therapy: that the client is the person who knows his or her situation best and that meaningful change comes about most effectively when the client directs the therapy. Rogers's point of view came to be known as client-centered therapy or CCT, which evolved from his earlier version of nondirective therapy (Bozarth, Zimring, & Tausch, 2001). In *Counseling and Psychotherapy*, Rogers (1942) identified three conditions for the therapeutic setting that are most helpful to clients.

First, the therapist should keep his or her focus on the emotions connected with what a client says rather than the specific content of the client's words. Second, the therapist must be accepting of the feelings expressed by the client, and third, the therapist may only clarify what the client has expressed, that is, in terms of communication, the therapist does not suggest, interpret, evaluate, or do anything other than accept the words or actions of the client at face value. Rogers's approach, which gives almost total control of the course of the therapy to the client, sharply contrasted with the approach of psychoanalysis—where the analyst offers interpretations of the client's experiences—the main therapeutic alternative at the time.

Rogers eventually modified his views of the therapeutic situation, and in 1951 he published *Client-centered Therapy*, which encouraged therapists to move beyond simply addressing a client's immediate problem toward a broader understanding of the client's worldview. Rogers continued to believe that the client always knows the best way to solve the problem, but if the therapist understands how the client sees the world, then the client may be able to address new problems that could bring about personality change. Rogers (1964) created the term *fully functioning person* to describe a state of optimal mental health. The fully functioning person experiences greater openness to experience, sensitivity and acceptance of others, and more profound interpersonal relationships.

In contrast with nondirective therapy, the client-centered technique is much more than the therapist not making comments or suggesting courses of action for the client. Rather, the main goal of the therapist is to provide a supportive environment where the client feels free to explore his or her feelings without the fear of being judged. Only in this kind of environment, Rogers believed, could the client restore the ability to make personally meaningful choices that he or she had lost over time. In other words, the goal of the therapy is to help the client recapture the ability to evaluate accurately his or her life experiences.

Rogers (1951) argued that although people are born with an innate ability to choose what is best for them—a quality he called the *organismic*

valuing process—this ability is lost as a child matures. As infants encounter different aspects of the world, they make a judgment as to their personal value for that aspect. A child may learn, for example, that he or she values or enjoys experiences such as being held, chasing the family cat, or fighting with a younger sibling.

This natural process of learning one's values is undermined, however, when the child eventually realizes that what he or she values may not be what other, more powerful people value. Over time, the child learns that others' opinions of him or her may depend on what values the child chooses. This causes anxiety, which leads the child to drop the organismic valuing process and begin to introject the values of parents, teachers, and other authority figures. The reason a person comes to therapy, Rogers wrote, is because a lifetime of denying one's own values has caused the person to lose touch with his or her valuing process. The person no longer recognizes his or her best course of action. The goal of humanistic psychotherapy is to restore the client's ability to make value judgments without fear of disapproval or experiencing a threat to his or her sense of self-worth.

In a 1957 article, Rogers identified what he considered key concepts for change in the therapeutic situation. First, the client comes into therapy in a state Rogers called *incongruence*. Incongruence reflects a difference between a client's self-image and his or her actual experience. A client who is an outstanding performer at his job and who has many friends, for example, may feel incongruence because of his lack of success in romantic relationships. Feelings of incongruence create anxiety for the client and are usually the motivation to seek therapy.

Second, in the therapeutic setting, the therapist acts as a real person, and not in a role such as "expert" or "solution provider." The therapist honestly presents his or her own perceptions of what the client is experiencing, as well as what the therapist experiences within him- or herself while interacting with the client.

Third—and critical to the success of the therapy—the therapist offers the client what Rogers called *unconditional positive regard*. Rogers (1957, p. 98) defined unconditional positive regard as "a caring for the client as a *separate* person, with permission to have his own feelings, his own experiences." This means that no matter what the client says or does, the therapist always conveys a warm acceptance of the client as a person. The therapist recognizes that his or her understanding of the phenomenological world of the client is limited, so the therapist does not act in a way or say anything that would suggest an evaluation, judgment, or categorization of the client. Because of their recognition of each client's uniqueness, most humanistic psychologists take a negative view of formal diagnoses and psychological assessments that place clients into broad categories (e.g., Friedman & MacDonald, 2006; Honos-Webb & Leitner, 2001; Siebert, 2000).

Fourth, the therapist feels *empathy* for the client's situation: "To sense the client's anger, fear, or confusion as if it were your own, yet without your own anger, fear, or confusion getting bound up in it" (Rogers, 1957, p. 99). In client-centered therapy, the client's emotions are more important than the content of his or her communications. The goal of the therapist is to facilitate the expression of those emotions that, theoretically, will help the client realize the solution to his or her problem.

Finally, in order for the client-centered method to work, the client must sense the therapist's unconditional positive regard and empathy. Only then will he or she feel free to explore the feelings of incongruence without fear of being judged by another person.

On the surface, client-centered therapy seems easy to do—the therapist simply expresses no judgments, either positive or negative, but merely reflects what the client is saying while, at the same time, conveying his or her feelings of positive regard. Furthermore, the therapist need not offer any insightful interpretations or clever solutions to the client's problems. This is a misunderstanding of client-centered therapy, however. In the therapeutic setting, the therapist, like the client, must use his or her emotions, rather than intellect, to help the client work toward solutions. This requires an intense focus on the part of the therapist that can be much more demanding than simply offering suggestions or interpretations to change behavior.

To summarize, client-centered therapy evolved from being simply nondirective to emphasizing the importance of the relationship between the client and the therapist. By respecting the client's phenomenological world and providing both unconditional positive regard and empathy, the client-centered therapist creates an environment where the client will discover solutions within him- or herself.

Gestalt Therapy

Over the years, the humanistic approach to psychotherapy came to include a wide variety of theories and practices, not all of which would have been acceptable to the founders of the field. Although quite different from client-centered therapy, Gestalt therapy is usually considered one of the most influential humanistic psychotherapies.

In terms of therapist-client interaction, Gestalt therapy—in which the therapist constantly challenges the client's assertions—differs greatly from client-centered therapy. Yet Gestalt therapy also emphasizes many of the values underlying humanistic—and existential—psychology: a belief in each person's uniqueness, freedom of choice, responsibility, the human tendency toward growth, the importance of a phenomenological approach in understanding others, and empathy. Gestalt therapists also believe that it is the client who holds the answers to the questions he or she is addressing. In the words of one gestalt therapist: ". . . even when [the client] is stuck, he is more capable of finding his solutions than anyone else" (Greenwald, 1976).

Frederich Perls (1893–1970) is generally considered the founder of Gestalt therapy. Perls originally trained as a psychoanalyst with Wilhelm Reich, whose emphasis on the importance of the body influenced the formulation of Gestalt therapy. Perls's first book, *Ego, Hunger, and Aggression* (1947), used Freud's instinct theory as the basis of his psychotherapeutic approach, but Perls eventually abandoned the psychoanalytic approach altogether. *Gestalt Therapy Verbatim* (1969) is probably Perls's best-known work.

From a Gestalt perspective, people's behavior is motivated by fulfilling biological and social needs. Unfortunately, the behaviors needed to fulfill these needs often get codified into roles that remove an individual from how he or she actually feels and limits his or her choices of action. For example, a wife may downplay her feelings of ambition and competitiveness with her husband because she feels expressing those feelings may deprive her of her husband's love and acceptance. The wife has sacrificed her true feelings for a social role that she feels is expected of her.

The goal of Gestalt therapy is to increase the client's awareness of parts of him- or herself as well as how the client relates to others. The Gestalt therapist begins by helping the client understand how he or she feels at that very moment, irrespective of what has happened in the past. In many cases, adherence to social roles is so rigid that the client cannot see alternative ways to behave or even recognize how he or she really feels about a situation.

According to Gestalt theory, awareness of feelings will help the client see the limitations of adhering strictly to social roles. As the client talks about his or her situation, the Gestalt therapist—in contrast with the client-centered therapist—is likely to take a confrontational approach. Perls often used unconventional behavior—such as the time he crawled across the floor at a workshop and invited Abraham Maslow to stop pontificating, get out of his chair,

and come down to Perls's level (Schwartz, 1996)—to make a point. For example, Perls categorized the communications people use in therapy—and life—as "chicken shit," "bull shit," and "elephant shit." Chicken shit refers to inconsequential small talk; bull shit consists of contradictions, lies, and attempts to avoid the truth; and elephant shit is communication about grandiose plans or intellectualizing that avoids the reality of emotions in the present. Another of Perls's well-known aphorisms that reflects gestalt therapy's emphasis on feelings over intellect is "Leave your mind and come to your senses."

Although Gestalt therapy can be practiced with individual clients, Perls originally emphasized the importance of group therapy. Over the years, Gestalt therapists developed a number of techniques for facilitating group interaction, and two of the most famous are the *two-chair method* and the *empty-chair method*, which can also be used with individual clients (Greenberg, Rice, & Elliott, 1993). The two-chair method, which is done with a single client, addresses conflict within an individual regarding unresolved events in the past with a person important in the individual's life. The goal of the therapeutic technique is to move a client from his or her original decision and adopt a decision that is more satisfying (Goulding & Goulding, 1997).

One chair represents the actual experience of a situation by a client; the other represents criticisms or evaluations of the experience. For example, in one chair, a client may talk about his or her depression around a longstanding unhappy marriage, but in the chair representing evaluation, the client might speak from the perspective of his or her parents' negative view of divorce or possible guilt about divorce's impact on children.

As the client moves from chair to chair, expressing his or her feelings and then taking the role of criticizing those feelings, memories and emotions about related situations are likely to emerge. Identifying these emotions is key to relieving at least some of the tension around the situation. As the client experiences more profound emotions, the critical perspective on the situation represented by the other chair may become more tolerant of the client's feelings (Strumpfel & Goldman, 2001). On the other hand, the client may also find the critical aspect unyielding. In these situations, the therapist will recommend that the client think of a friend or family member who would be more accepting and mentally put that person into the empty chair (Goulding & Goulding, 1997).

The empty-chair method addresses a client's needs that have not been met or emotions that have not been expressed. For example, a client may harbor lingering resentment toward her dead mother who she felt always favored her sister. Using the empty-chair method, the client states her feelings to her mother, whom she imagines sitting in the empty chair. The goal of this method is to increase the client's self-confidence with regard to her mother, as well as to create greater tolerance for the mother's behavior. Another form of the empty-chair method is called "saying goodbye," in which the client holds onto a relationship that no longer exists that prevents further development (Tobin, 1976). The client places the person in the empty chair and then plays the role of saying goodbye as well as the person's reaction to the client's goodbye. For clients who suffer from diseases or problematic physical conditions, the Gestalt therapist may recommend the client place the disease in the empty chair and speak directly to it (Kellogg, 2004). Highlight Box 12.3 describes a two-chair approach to dealing with sexual abuse.

HIGHLIGHT BOX 12.3

THE EMPTY-CHAIR METHOD AND CHILDHOOD SEXUAL ABUSE

One use of the empty-chair method is to address individuals from a client's past who have abused the client. When the emotions connected with the abuse are more than the client can tolerate, this approach allows the client to call his or her adult self or the therapist into the therapeutic setting to help confront the abuser. Goulding and Goulding (1997) developed the following empty-chair method for dealing with childhood sexual and physical abuse.

1. The client describes an abuse scene from the perspective of an outside observer.
2. The client and the therapist discuss the scene to clarify the details.
3. An empty chair is then brought in for the abused "child," and the client and abused child have a two-chair dialogue about the experience.

4. In the next step, the child relives the traumatic scene, telling the story as he or she experienced it. If this is emotionally overwhelming, the client may include a protective figure as support (such as the therapist, an adult version of the client, or even an armed protector), and the client is allowed to leave the scene at any time.
5. The abuser is then put in the empty chair and confronted. In this scenario, the perpetrator is *not* allowed to change. He or she is not allowed to apologize or promise to behave differently. This is because the goal is to have the patient change. The patient then clearly says how he or she will live a satisfying life that is created in defiance of what the abuser did.

Statements that indicate that the client is moving beyond the abuse and taking a new approach to life may include "I know there are people in the world I can trust," "Everyone is not like you," "I enjoy sex today despite what you did," or "My life is happy; I do not feel guilty about what you did."

(Cited in Kellogg, 2004.)

Evaluating Humanistic Psychotherapy

Aside from being the creator of client-centered therapy, Carl Rogers occupies a unique position in psychology because of his efforts researching the effectiveness of psychotherapy in general (Kirschenbaum & Jourdan, 2005). Nonetheless, humanistic psychotherapy, like existential psychotherapy, starts from assumptions that greatly complicate quantitative evaluation. The phenomenological basis, the difficulty of operationalizing concepts such as meaning and isolation, and a general distrust of measurement have probably hindered the scientific evaluation of the effectiveness of both these approaches (Patterson & Joseph, 2007).

Despite the fact that the popularity of the client-centered approach has declined somewhat, the field remains active. In a review of articles related to humanistic psychotherapies between 1987 and 2004, for example, researchers found 777 articles on Rogers or client-centered therapy and 620 articles on Perls or Gestalt therapy (Kirshenbaum & Jourdan, 2005). Similarly, more than 200 centers, mostly in Europe, are dedicated to researching and practicing the principles of client-centered therapy (Kirschenbaum & Jourdan, 2005). In contrast with attitudes about client-centered therapy, however, one survey of psychotherapists found that most expected the practice of Gestalt therapy to decline over time (Norcross, Hedges, & Prochaska, 2003).

One particular problem with evaluating humanistic—as well as existential—approaches to therapy is their emphasis on subjective experience. Some researchers have argued that the medical model used in other forms of therapy (i.e., identification of a symptom followed by its treatment) does not fit well with the humanistic emphasis on the interpersonal context of psychotherapy. In contrast, the humanistic approach would probably consider reducing or eliminating symptoms to be less important than the client realizing how to make an authentic assessment of the symptom and deciding what he or she wants to do about it.

In a review of research that specifically focused on the outcomes of humanistic psychotherapy, Levitt, Stanley, Frankel, and Raina (2005) found that the measures typically used for this kind of assessment—including the Beck Depression Inventory, State-Trait Anxiety Inventory, Symptom Checklist, and Personal Orientation Inventory—were designed to assess qualities not specifically connected to the values of humanistic psychology. Rather than focusing on personal growth, interpersonal interaction, or the client taking responsibility for his or her situation, the measures used to evaluate humanistic outcomes typically focused on physical symptoms and psychopathology, which are not the main focus of humanistic approaches to psychotherapy.

Yet other research suggests that Rogers's greatest impact may be less on the specific techniques of therapy than on the conditions necessary for change in *any* psychotherapeutic setting. An early review of studies on the effectiveness of psychotherapy in general concluded:

These studies taken together suggest that therapists or counselors who are accurately empathic, nonpossessively warm in attitude, and genuine are indeed effective. Also, these findings seem to hold with a wide variety of therapists and counselors, regardless of their training or theoretic orientation, and with a wide variety of clients or patients. (Truax & Mitchell, 1976)

These results have been supported by subsequent reviews of the conditions necessary for psychotherapy success (e.g., Blatt, Zuroff, Quinlan, & Pilkonis, 1996; Bohart, Elliott, Greenberg, & Watson, 2002; Bozarth et al., 2001; Orlinsky, Grawe, & Parks, 1994; Sexton & Whiston, 1994). Bozarth et al. (2001) concluded that the single best predictor of success in psychotherapy is how the client perceives the empathy of the therapist at the end of the second session.

In a review of the impact of Carl Rogers's contributions, Kirschenbaum and Jourdan (2005) stated:

Although relatively few therapists describe themselves as primarily client-centered in their orientation, client-centered principles permeate the practice of many, if not most, therapists. Various schools of psychotherapy increasingly are recognizing the importance of the therapeutic relationship as a means to, if not a core aspect of, therapeutic change. (p. 48)

In many respects, existential and humanistic psychotherapies stand outside the mainstream of modern psychotherapeutic practice. This makes their effectiveness difficult to assess through traditional models. But, as suggested earlier, existential and humanistic psychotherapists recognize that their theoretical approach and methods, as well as the issues they address, do not easily fit into standard evaluative paradigms. For many existential and humanistic therapists, demonstrating the effectiveness of their approach through standard scientific methodologies is probably not a matter of great concern.

THOUGHT QUESTIONS

1. Existential and humanistic psychotherapists object in principle to the therapist offering interpretations of the experiences of the client. Are there *any* situations in existential or humanistic psychotherapy where an interpretation from the therapist might be appropriate?
2. In contrast with other schools of psychotherapy, existential and humanistic therapists regard events from the past as far less important than the present or the future. Can the past really be unimportant in addressing a client's issues? Can therapy be successful without addressing concerns from the past?
3. Because existential and humanistic psychologists work from the assumption that only the client knows the answers he or she is seeking, what would be the proper response to a client who has a pressing concern, such as thoughts of suicide?
4. Given the kinds of issues addressed in existential psychotherapy and the field's distrust of quantitative evaluation of outcomes, how can an existential psychotherapist know if a particular client's therapy is successful?
5. In your view, what kind of client would be best suited for existential therapy? In what situations would client-centered therapy be more appropriate? Under what conditions might Gestalt therapy be appropriate?
6. Which do you feel is a more accurate perception: existential psychology's tragic view of life or humanistic psychology's optimistic view?
7. Do you agree with Yalom that therapy should begin with a recognition of the client's fear of death?

Glossary

anonymous mode: a way of responding to other people in terms of roles rather than as unique individuals.

authenticity: a way of living in accordance with one's deepest beliefs, values, and goals.

bad faith: a way of living in which the person acts contrary to his or her actual beliefs or ignores facts he or she doesn't want to confront.

bull shit: in gestalt psychology, contradictions, lies, and attempts to avoid the truth.

chicken shit: in gestalt psychology, inconsequential small talk.

client-centered therapy: an approach to psychotherapy developed by Carl Rogers that emphasizes the roles of the client in directing the therapy and the therapist in providing a supportive therapeutic environment.

creative stage: in Rollo May's system of existential therapy, the stage where adults face life honestly and pursue a personal meaning.

Eigenwelt: in existential psychology, the highest level of existence, where people are aware and self-actualizing.

elephant shit: in gestalt psychotherapy, grandiose communication that avoids the reality of emotions in the present.

empathy: the ability to feel a client's emotions.

empty-chair method: a technique in gestalt therapy designed to address a client's needs that have not been met or emotions that have not been expressed.

existential neurosis: neurosis characterized by having achieved worldly success accompanied by feelings of emptiness.

facticity: in existentialism, the concrete details of life that limit a person's actions.

fallenness: in existential psychology, the state of allowing external factors to define an individual's values and behavior.

fully functioning person: an optimal state of mental health characterized by openness, acceptance of others, and deeper interpersonal relationships.

incongruence: the difference between a person's self-image and his or her experiences.

innocence: in Rollo May's system of existential therapy, the stage where the infant has no regard for others.

logotherapy: the system of psychotherapy developed by Viktor Frankl based on a person discovering a meaning for his or her life.

Mitwelt: in existential psychology, the level of existence that is focused on living with other people.

mutual mode: in existential psychology, a way of responding to others based on openness, honesty, and acceptance.

ordinary stage: in Rollo May's system of existential therapy, the stage where adults conform and accept traditional values.

organismic valuing process: in humanistic psychology, the process by which the developing child determines the experiences that he or she values.

paradoxical intention: a therapeutic technique developed by Frankl in which a phobic patient tries to create the situation he or she fears.

phenomenology: an approach to life based on avoiding preconceived ideas and experiencing phenomena directly.

rebellion: in Rollo May's system of existential therapy, the stage where the child struggles for independence.

self-actualization: the state of achieving one's highest potential.

tragic optimism: the drive to make the best of any situation.

tragic triad: three great issues of life identified by Viktor Frankl: pain, guilt, and death.

two-chair method: a gestalt therapy technique that addresses past conflicts with a person important in the client's life.

Umwelt: in existential psychology, the lowest level of existence, where a person treats others as objects rather than people.

unconditional positive regard: in humanistic psychotherapy, an attitude of warm acceptance of and respect for the client as a person.

will therapy: a system of therapy developed by Otto Rank emphasizing a focus on the present, conscious choices, and greater equality between therapist and client.

References

American Association of Humanistic Psychologists (1962). *Articles of association*. Alameda, CA: Association for Humanistic Psychology.

Binswanger, L. (1942). *Foundations and knowledge of human existence*. Zurich: M. Niehaus.

Blatt, S. J., Zuroff, D. C., Quinlan, D. M., & Pilkonis, P. A. (1996). Interpersonal factors in brief treatment of depression: further analyses of the National Institute of Mental Health Treatment of Depression Collaborative Research Program. *Journal of Consulting and Clinical Psychology, 64*, 162–171.

Bohart, A. C., Elliott, R., Greenberg, L. S., & Watson, J. C. (2002). Empathy. In J. C. Norcross (Ed.), *Psychotherapy relationships that work: therapist contributions and responsiveness to patients*. New York: Oxford University Press.

Bozarth, J. D., Zimring, F. M., & Tausch, R. (2001). Client-centered therapy: the evolution of a revolution. In D. J. Cain & J. Seeman (Eds.), *Humanistic psychotherapies*. Washington, DC: American Psychological Association.

Cain, D. J. (2001). Defining characteristics, history, and evolution of humanistic psychotherapies. In D. J. Cain & J. Seeman (Eds.), *Humanistic psychotherapies*. Washington, DC: American Psychological Association.

Camus, A. (1955). *The myth of Sisyphus*. New York: Vintage.

Cooper, M. (2003). *Existential psychotherapies*. London: Sage.

Fernando, D. M. (2007). Existential theory and solution-focused strategies: integration and application. *Journal of Mental Health Counseling, 29*, 226–242.

Frankl, V. (1963). *Man's search for meaning*. New York: Washington Square.

Freud, S. (1955). Beyond the pleasure principle. In J. Strachey (Ed. and Trans.). *The standard edition of the complete works of Sigmund Freud*, Vol. 18. London: Hogarth.

Friedman, H. L. & MacDonald, D. A. (2006). Humanistic testing and assessment. *Journal of Humanistic Psychology, 46*, 510–529.

Goldstein, K. (1939). *The organism*. New York: American Book.

Goulding, M. M. & Goulding, R. (1997). *Changing lives through redecision therapy*. New York: Grove.

Greenberg, L. S., Rice, L. N., & Elliott, R. (1993). *Facilitating emotional change*. New York: Guilford.

Greenberg, L. S., Safran, J., & Rice, L. (1989). Experiential therapy: its relation to cognitive therapy. In A. Freeman, K. M. Simon, L. E. Beutler, & H. Arkowitz (Eds.), *Comprehensive handbook of cognitive therapy*. New York: Plenum.

Greenwald, J. A. (1976). The ground rules in Gestalt therapy. In C. Hutcher & P. Himelstein (Eds.), *The handbook of Gestalt therapy*. New York: Aronson.

Heidegger, M. (1927). *Being and time*. Albany: State University of New York.

Hogan, R. (1976). *Personality theory: the personological tradition*. Englewood Cliffs, NJ: Prentice-Hall.

Honos-Webb, L. & Leitner, L. (2001). How using the DSM causes damage: a client's report. *Journal of Humanistic Psychology, 41*, 36–54.

Jacobsen, B. (2007). Authenticity and our basic existential dilemmas. *Existential Analysis, 18*, 288–296.

Jones, E. E., Parke, L. A., & Pulos, S. M. (1992). How therapy is conducted in the private consulting room: a multidimensional description of brief psychodynamic treatment. *Psychotherapy Research, 2*, 16–30.

Kellogg, S. (2004). Dialogical encounters: contemporary perspectives on "chairwork" in psychotherapy. *Psychotherapy: Theory, Research, Practice, Training, 41*, 310–320.

Keshen, A. (2006). A new look at existential psychotherapy. *American Journal of Psychotherapy, 60*, 285–299.

Kirschenbaum, H. & Jourdan, A. (2005). The current status of Carl Rogers and the person-centered approach. *Psychotherapy: Theory, Research, Practice, Training, 42*, 37–51.

Kiser, S. (2007). Become who you are: integrating the conceptions of will and being in the psychotherapeutic theory of Rollo May. *Journal of Humanistic Psychology, 47*, 151–159.

Levitt, H. M., Stanley, C. M., Frankel, Z., & Raina, K. (2005). An evaluation of outcome measures used in humanistic psychotherapy research: using thermometers to weigh oranges. *The Humanistic Psychologist, 33*, 113–130.

Lietaer, G. (1992). Helping and hindering processes in client-centered/experiential psychotherapy. In S. G. Toukmanian & D. L. Rennie (Eds.), *Psychotherapy process research: paradigmatic and narrative approaches*. Newbury Park, CA: Sage.

Maslow, A. H. (1954). *Motivation and personality*. New York: Harper & Row.

Maslow, A. H. (1959). Psychological data and value theory. In A. H. Maslow (Ed.), *New knowledge in human values*. New York: Harper & Brothers.

Maslow, A. H. (1962). Some basic propositions of a growth and self-actualization psychology. In A. W. Combs (Ed.), *Perceiving, behaving, becoming: a new focus for education*. Washington, DC: Association for Supervision and Curriculum Development.

Maslow, A. H. (1968). *Toward a psychology of being*. New York: Van Nostrand Reinhold.

May, R. (1953). *Man's search for himself*. New York: W. W. Norton.

May, R. (1958). The origins and significance of the existential movement in psychology. In R. May, E. Angel, & H. Ellenberger (Eds.), *Existence: a new dimension in psychiatry and psychology*. New York: Simon & Schuster.

May, R. (1969). *Love and will*. New York: W. W. Norton.

May, R. (1981). *Freedom and destiny*. New York: W. W. Norton.

May R., Angel, E., & Ellenberger, H. (Eds.) (1958). *Existence: a new dimension in psychiatry and psychology*. New York: Simon & Schuster.

Moustakas, C. (1994). *Existential psychotherapy and the interpretation of dreams*. Northvale, NJ: Aronson.

Norcross, J. C., Hedges, M., & Prochaska, J. O. (2003). The face of 2010: a Delphi poll on the future of psychotherapy. *Professional Psychology: Research and Practice, 33*, 316–322.

O'Hanlon, B. (2000). *Do one thing different*. New York: Harper Paperbacks.

Orlinsky, D. E., Grawe, K., & Parks, B. K. (1994). Process and outcome in psychotherapy: *Noch einmal*. In S. L. Garfield & A. E. Bergin (Eds.), *Handbook of psychotherapy and behavior change* (4th ed.). New York: Wiley.

Patterson, T. G. & Joseph, S. (2007). Person-centered personality theory: support from self-determination theory and positive psychology. *Journal of Humanistic Psychology, 47*, 117–139.

Perls, F. (1947). *Ego, hunger, and aggression*. London: Allen & Unwin.

Perls, F. (1969). *Gestalt therapy verbatim*. Lafayette, CA: Real People Press.

Rank, O. (1978). *Will therapy*. New York: W. W. Norton.

Rice L. N. & Greenberg L. S. (Eds.) (1984). *Patterns of change: intensive analysis of psychotherapy process*. New York: Guilford.

Rogers, C. R. (1942). *Counseling and psychotherapy*. Boston: Houghton Mifflin.

Rogers, C. R. (1951). *Client-centered therapy*. Boston: Houghton Mifflin.

Rogers, C. R. (1957). The necessary and sufficient conditions of therapeutic personality change. *Journal of Consulting Psychology, 21*, 95–103.

Rogers, C. R. (1961). *On becoming a person*. Boston: Houghton Mifflin.

Rogers, C. R. (1964). Toward a modern approach to values: the valuing approach in the mature person. *Journal of Abnormal and Social Psychology, 68*, 160–167.

Sartre, J.-P. (1953). *Existential psychoanalysis*. New York: Philosophical Library.

Sartre, J.-P. (1989). Existentialism is a humanism. In W. Kaufmann (Ed.), *Existentialism from Dostoevsky to Sartre*. New York: Meridian.

Schwartz, T. (1996). *What really matters*. New York: Bantam.

Sexton, T. L. & Whiston, S. C. (1994). The status of the counseling relationship: an empirical review, theoretical implications, and research directions. *The Counseling Psychologist, 22*, 6–78.

Siebert, A. (2000). How non-diagnostic listening led to a rapid "recovery" from paranoid schizophrenia: what is wrong with psychiatry? *Journal of Humanistic Psychology, 401*, 34–58.

Strumpfel, U. & Goldman, R. (2001). Contacting Gestalt therapy. In D. J. Cain & J. Seeman (Eds.), *Humanistic psychotherapies*. Washington, DC: American Psychological Association.

Strupp, H. H. (1996). The tripartite model and the *Consumer Reports* study. *American Psychologist, 51*, 1017–1024.

Tobin, S. A. (1976). Saying goodbye in Gestalt therapy. In C. Hatcher & P. Himelstein (Eds.), *The handbook of Gestalt therapy*. New York: Aronson.

Truax, C. B. & Mitchell, K. M. (1976). Research on certain therapist interpersonal skills in relation to process and outcome. In A. E. Bergin & S. L. Garfield (Eds.), *Handbook of psychotherapy and behavior change*. New York: Wiley.

Walsh, R., Perucci, A., & Severns, J. (1999). What's in a good moment: a hermeneutic study of psychotherapy values across levels of psychotherapy training. *Psychotherapy Research, 9*, 304–326.

Walsh, R. A. & McElwain, B. (2001). Existential psychotherapies. In D. J. Cain & J. Seeman (Eds.), *Humanistic psychotherapies*. Washington, DC: American Psychological Association.

Yalom, I. (1980). *Existential psychotherapy*. New York: Basic Books.

Child, Family, and Couples Therapy

George C. Tremblay
Antioch University,
New England

Megan Phillips
Antioch University,
New England

OUTLINE

HIGHLIGHT BOX 13.1

MEET JOSHUA AND HIS FAMILY

Ten-year-old Joshua arrived at the clinic with his father, Robert, and his stepmother, Emily. Joshua's fifth-grade teacher and the school guidance counselor encouraged Robert to consult a mental health professional about Joshua's increasingly oppositional behavior, which has recently escalated to outright refusal to engage in some classroom work. The teacher expressed concern that Joshua's academic performance and relationships with adults and peers are all

---

HIGHLIGHT BOX 13.1 *(continued)*

suffering declines this year. She knows that Joshua's family has experienced some recent turmoil, and she hopes that speaking with a therapist about it may help Joshua recover his former high level of functioning.

Joshua is the oldest of two children born to Robert and his first wife, Joan. Robert and Joan were divorced 2 years ago, and Joshua and his 6-year-old brother, Will, initially moved with their mother to live with her parents in a neighboring town. Robert had remained in the family's home, and he and Joan had been able to negotiate a flexible visitation schedule to coparent the boys. About a year and a half after the divorce, two events challenged the adaptations this family had made to their separation. First, Robert remarried, and although his relationship with Emily had been gradually introduced to the boys, the marriage inserted Emily into their lives on a more formal and permanent basis. What was formerly their home became also her home, and her relationship with the children subtly shifted from benign, caring adult to quasi-parent, with some unclear level of authority. Second, Joan began attending nursing school full-time, and the decision was made to switch the boys' primary residence to Robert's home. Although the boys had been able to remain in the same school throughout the shifting family circumstances, adapting to a new stepparent and to greater separation from their mother had been stressful for all concerned. Will showed few outward indications of strain, warming readily to Emily and continuing to enjoy his time at school, though he often cried briefly when leaving his mother's home. Joshua, by contrast, became indiscriminately irritable, never more so than on the days when he had to return from weekend visits with his mother. Robert and Emily were increasingly at odds about how to manage Joshua's behavior, with Emily wanting Robert to exercise his authority more assertively to support firmer boundaries and respectful behavior toward her. Under this strain, both Emily and Robert feel insufficiently understood and supported. They maneuver tensely around each other during the week, their expectation of intimacy and nurturance from their young relationship is suffering, and weekend breaks from the demands of parenthood no longer provide sufficient refuge to recover. For her part, Joan wanted very much for her sons to experience a tranquil home while she was engaged in these 2 years of intensive professional training. Although she had maintained that she wished Robert and his new wife all the best, it was hard for her not to have doubts about their competence in the face of Joshua's distress.

Where Does the Problem Just Described "Reside"?

Is this a child behavior problem, because the referral was precipitated by Joshua's oppositional behavior in school? Is it a family problem, because its emergence seems to have coincided with shifts in family structure? Is it a couple problem, because Robert and Emily might benefit from assistance in strengthening their relationship in the face of these stressors? The answer, of course, is yes, it is all of those. In this chapter, we will discuss how and why one might intervene at any of these levels to address problems that "reside" at the intersections of family relationships. In so doing, we'll periodically return to the case of Joshua and his family.

INTRODUCTION: WHAT'S UNIQUE ABOUT CHILD, FAMILY, AND COUPLES WORK?

You may have noticed that this is the only chapter in this book defined by a clinical population's demographic parameters. Why does this clinical population uniquely warrant a chapter of its own? In another hint at the distinctiveness of work involving children in particular, clinicians tend to very clearly claim or disclaim membership among the "kid people" (i.e., professionals who work with children). We begin, then, with some reflections concerning how clinical psychologists approach work with children, families, and couples differently from intervention with individual adults. For this introductory discussion, we refer to features common to all work discussed in this chapter, for which we will adopt the label *family work* for expediency, reasoning that couples are small families, and children always imply families.

Family work forces systemic thinking. A system is an organized collection of parts that perform a function. The parts are connected by feedback loops so that each part responds to changes in other parts, often to support homeostasis, or the maintenance of a steady state. Systems have emergent properties—characteristics that emerge only from their interaction and not from any of the component parts in isolation. To view families as systems is to highlight the extent to which family members always behave in response to one another, serve functions larger than any one member, collectively are likely to resist change, and generate emergent properties. A family's achievements and problems reflect contributions from all members.

All humans are embedded in social systems, of course, but a therapist working with one adult typically has no direct contact with the client's social systems, whereas the psychologist who works with families must engage directly with multiple members of surrounding systems (parents, partners, family members, school personnel, etc.). These members are all stakeholders in the therapy, with varying motivation to participate. Children, for example, are rarely instrumental in bringing a mental health problem to the attention of a professional, and the initiative to engage in couples work often resides more with one partner than the other. Whose voice will be heard, how the problem will be defined, how responsibility for both causes and solutions to the problem will be allocated—all of these are matters that the therapist helps to negotiate.

The therapist who engages with multiple stakeholders is often less inclined to conceptualize problems as residing within individuals and more inclined and able to attend to interactions between individuals, or between individuals and larger systems (children and schools, or couples and their families or cultures of origin). Problems may arise, for example, from differing role expectations—gender roles, student roles, childrearing roles—shaped by divergent familial or cultural histories. The *Diagnostic and Statistical Manual of Mental Disorders* (American Psychiatric Association [APA], 2000), our dominant nomenclature for describing problems within individuals, includes very few codes that address problems within systems (V-codes for problems in role functioning and relationships).

Family work highlights developmental considerations. Developmental factors are most obvious in the treatment of children, given that problems often arise from a misalignment of children's behavior and adults' expectations. A child who inserts himself clumsily into a group of playmates without waiting for his turn is displaying behavior likely to be regarded as normative and acceptable for a 4-year-old but as a potential manifestation of ADHD for a 9-year-old. Parents or other caregivers of 4-year-olds will experience intense frustration if their expectations are calibrated for 9-year-olds, and indeed research has shown that adults who hold developmentally unrealistic expectations are at greater risk of responding punitively to children (Azar, Robinson, Hekimian, & Twentyman, 1984). Thus, assessment of developmental expectations is commonplace in child and family work. Assessment can be as informal as eliciting descriptions of what the parent regards as problematic versus appropriate child behavior, or it may involve a standardized measure such as the Parent Opinion Questionnaire (Azar et al., 1984). Unrealistic expectations become a target for psychoeducational intervention, typically in the form of information about normative child development and encouragement to adopt realistic goals and provide effective supports for children's behavior.

Less obviously, developmental considerations are also implicated in couples work, because partners' satisfaction is a function of what they expect from their relationship, and these expectations tend to evolve over time. Although the normative trend is from naïve idealism toward acceptance and negotiation of limitations, partners in even healthy relationships may experience dyssynchrony in the rate or direction of that trajectory. This experience can be reflected in a sense of having "grown apart." Again, explicit assessment of expectations is warranted.

Family work complicates the therapeutic alliance while also offering unique opportunities for in vivo assessment, modeling, and practice. All theoretical orientations recognize the central role of a trusting therapeutic relationship in helping clients to contemplate change (Safran & Muran, 2000). Demonstrating credibility and compassion is complicated when the therapist must navigate among the sometimes competing agendas of multiple clients. When clients are entrenched in opposing views of the problem, each naturally wants the therapist to validate his or her perspective. The couples or family therapist attempts to earn the trust of all parties by acknowledging their experience, creating safe conditions for difficult conversations, and supporting meaningful

changes in and out of session. In so doing, the therapist has an opportunity to directly model the validation of seemingly incompatible perspectives and to invite clients to join him or her in practicing this skill. Acknowledgment of competing needs and capacity to discuss them are central to coping effectively with interpersonal challenges.

All of the perspectives just described—systemic, developmental, interpersonal—can be useful in work with individual adults, but they are unavoidably central to the work described in this chapter. In what follows, we will devote separate sections to work with children, couples, and families, using the case of Joshua and his family (see Highlight Box 13.1) to illustrate different modes of intervention. We will discuss some of what we see as the central issues unique to each mode, identify some of the more fruitful theories associated with each mode, and offer a few more specific empirically supported strategies or techniques. Our goal is to offer the reader a sufficient glimpse of this domain to encourage and guide further exploration.

WORKING WITH CHILDREN

Central Issues

Who is the focus of therapy? When presented with a troubled child, a therapist must choose between intervening directly with the child and supporting one or both parents as the intervention agent(s). The unique potency of the parent-child relationship makes it a potentially efficient and compelling route for achieving widespread and enduring improvements in the child's rearing environment. On the other hand, the therapist who engages with the child gains direct access to the child's experience and the opportunity to develop a new nurturing relationship. Any of the following factors may come into play in this strategic decision:

- The clinician's *theoretical orientation*. With their emphasis on situational determinants of behavior, social learning theorists have a strong tradition of working with parents and/or schools to reshape how the child's environment responds to his or her behavior. Dynamically oriented therapists have a more extensive tradition of direct interaction with young children.
- Age of the child. The older the child is, the greater the likelihood that the clinician or youth him- or herself will prefer to work directly together (see Highlight Box 13.2 on negotiating a therapeutic contract with children).
- Parents' level of functioning. Acting in a therapeutic role requires, at minimum, the capacity to distinguish one's own needs from the child's. Highly distressed parents can be so preoccupied with their own unmet needs as to be unable to perceive or attend to the child's needs.
- Complexity of intervention needed. If the optimal intervention for the child requires

technical skills that are not feasible to teach to parents (for example, trauma-focused cognitive behavioral treatment; Cohen, Mannarino, & Deblinger, 2006), this would mitigate in favor of direct interaction between professional and child.

Multiple informants. The default for clinicians working with adults is to assume the client to be a sufficient informant, unless there is another referral agent with whom the referral question must be negotiated or another health-care provider with whom treatment should be coordinated. It is much more common for child therapists to seek input from parents, teachers, guidance counselors, or other treatment providers concerning the child's capacities and challenges. This difference in practice emerges partly because adults are the arbiters of children's functioning in various settings—so we want to engage them directly in the assessment—and partly because children have less capacity than adults for insight and description. Conducting and documenting these collateral

---

HIGHLIGHT BOX 13.2

INFORMED CONSENT AND CONFIDENTIALITY WITH CHILDREN

With a few exceptions (state-specific regulations that permit adolescents to seek treatment for substance use, unwanted pregnancy, or other threats to health without the knowledge of a parent), children are not legally empowered to consent to treatment. Their parents or legal guardians consent on their behalf, are entitled to be fully informed about all treatment activities and conversations, and have access to any resulting clinical documentation. Minors, therefore, have no broad legal right to confidentiality.

In most instances, of course, it is helpful to negotiate children's *assent* (willingness) to engage in treatment, which implies a developmentally

appropriate explanation of treatment goals and plan. A therapist wishing to facilitate some semblance of confidentiality for the child must negotiate such explicitly with the consenting adult. We recommend explaining to the adult why some degree of confidentiality would facilitate successful therapy in a given situation and seeking a consensus about the scope of information that could be kept between the therapist and child and information that would need to be divulged to the adult. We further recommend that this discussion happen in the presence of the child, so that he or she is exposed to all the nuances of the conversation and can decide what to reveal in therapy

---

HIGHLIGHT BOX 13.2   (*continued*)

accordingly. Finally, throughout this discussion, we join with the parent by supporting his or her responsibility for being informed and concerned, and we join with the child by indicating our collective commitment to bring to parents any

information that reaches beyond the negotiated confidentiality zone. Therapists should be advised that no legal standing would likely be accorded to any such agreement—parents will still retain the right to demand all clinical documentation.

---

communications can be a time-consuming—and often poorly compensated—activity.

Theories and Techniques

Much of the child therapy practiced in the United States today traces its origins to either *attachment* or *cognitive-behavioral/social learning* theories. Attachment theory (Ainsworth & Bowlby, 1991) combines an ethological perspective on the survival functions of imprinting on a primary caregiver with a psychoanalytic tradition that posits an innate drive among humans to form relationships (object relations; cf. Winnicott, 1988). The attachment theorist believes that children's relationships with early caregivers serve as a prototype for all subsequent interactions. Within the context of these early relationships, children develop capacities for regulating their own arousal, coping with affect (their own and others'), estimating and coping with risk, and a whole host of other competencies that support successful engagement with the world. From an attachment perspective, the therapist's role is to invite the child into a relationship characterized by interest, responsiveness, confidence, and tolerance. The expectation is that the therapy relationship can serve as a corrective experience to problems in managing any of the aforementioned activities, essentially reshaping the child's internal relationship prototype and leaving him or her better equipped to cope with intrapersonal and interpersonal experience.

Research from an attachment perspective has been influential in shaping our understanding of child development (e.g., Fonagy, Gergely, & Target, 2007) and has contributed to empirically supported interventions for children (parent-child interaction therapy; Herschell, Calzada, Eyberg, & McNeil, 2002) and couples (emotion-focused couple therapy; Greenberg & Johnson, 1988, to be discussed later in this chapter).

Social learning theory emerged out of the behavioral tradition, sharing common roots in the shaping of behavior by experience, but focused particularly on how we are influenced by the behavior of others in our environment. The social learning theorist assumes that patterns emerge in children's behavior for functional reasons, that is, these patterns "work" to bring about desirable outcomes for the child. Some of these desirable outcomes are in the form of rewards (parent buys candy when the child throws a tantrum in the grocery store checkout line), but many problematic behavior patterns are reinforced, instead, by escape from aversive situations (child's resistance when asked to perform a chore results in the parent performing the chore, or child's expression of somatic pain results in being excused from an unwelcome occasion; cf. Patterson, 1975). From this functional analytic perspective, the therapist's task is to identify outcomes that both the parent and child regard as desirable, negotiate a behavioral "contract" that will provide a reliable and mutually acceptable means for attaining those outcomes, and coach parents and/or children in implementing the contract. Along the way, parents and children are helped to recognize situational triggers for distress or conflict and to prepare for those eventualities. Child behavior management interventions with parents, teachers, and other caregivers, based on this social learning/functional analytic perspective, have accumulated an impressive record of empirical support (Hershell, McNeil, & McNeil, 2004; Kazdin, 2005). Adaptations for engaging older children in negotiating conflict with their parents have also demonstrated effectiveness (Robin & Foster, 1989).

Sample Interventions

Returning to the case of Joshua and his family, let us imagine two of many potential interventions that might emerge from the theoretical frameworks presented. Both scenarios are designed to target Joshua's distress, but one does so through the parents, whereas the other does so through direct engagement with Joshua. Both assume that assessment has suggested a functional relationship between Joshua's family distress and decrements in his social and academic functioning at school. In the parent intervention scenario, the therapist and all adults involved—Robert, Emily, and Joan—have identified the process of transitioning the children between households as laden with chaos, sadness, stress, and risk for hostility among all concerned. The therapist has proposed to work with just the three adults, to see if they can negotiate a transition process that will be predictable in time and form, smoothly coordinated among all adults involved, and structuring and reassuring for the children. The process begins with psychoeducation concerning the impact of divorce on families, and especially the importance of adults being able to distinguish between their needs surrounding detachment from a former spouse and their children's best interests in remaining attached to both parents. Subsequently, the therapist attempts to

engage the adults in a shared problem-solving approach to minimize stress and conflict. Success in this highly focused intervention would establish a precedent for coparenting in this family. Building on that initial success, the therapist would then help the adults identify other situational precipitants for Joshua's (and/or Will's) distress and again attempt to structure the environment to support more adaptive coping behavior. If the adults can be guided through a few successful repetitions of this pattern, the therapist hopes that they will generalize it to new sources of distress as they arise and that they will be primed to seek and utilize therapeutic support again if they encounter a situation that exceeds their capacities.

In our hypothetical child intervention scenario, the therapist aims to help Joshua articulate his experience surrounding his parents' separation, develop a realistic understanding of what the future might hold (his parents are not going to reunite, but he will be able to maintain relationships with both of them, and he may come to regard a third parent as more of a benefit than an intrusion), and devise effective strategies for pursuing successful interactions at home and school. The cognitive (labeling affect, making attributions for the separation, developing hopes for the future) and behavioral (coping strategies) elements of this treatment plan are core ingredients in many empirically supported interventions with children (Kendall et al., 2003; Ollendick & Davis, 2004). This strategy is simultaneously an attachment intervention, to the extent that the therapist reliably demonstrates attention, caring, and responsiveness to the child, who is likely to be feeling disregarded in the wake of a family restructuring that clearly was not driven by his preferences. It is worth noting that the cognitive and behavioral elements of this intervention are largely dependent on direct discussion of the relevant material, whereas the attachment elements may not be. This invites consideration of attachment-oriented interventions for children who either lack the capacity for verbally mediated exchange or are initially resistant (Straus, 1999). Although minimally verbal interventions with children, particularly play therapy, have been widely practiced, there remains controversy about whether they have yet demonstrated effectiveness. Critics assert that such methods have rarely been subject to robust empirical evaluation, so their effectiveness must be considered unknown at this time (Ollendick & Davis, 2004). Supporters contend that there is now a sufficient evidence base to establish play techniques as effective (Bratton, Ray, Rhine, & Jones, 2005; Leblanc & Ritchie, 2001).

WORKING WITH FAMILIES

Central Issues

Indications: when to treat as a "family case"? This decision can be shaped by both philosophical and pragmatic considerations. Family therapists who are philosophically committed to a systemic understanding of behavior will intervene in ways that target systemic roles or communication patterns for change. Even if only a single family member is attending therapy sessions, these therapists will be seeking to influence systems-level processes by inviting that individual to try new ways of engaging with the system. From a pragmatic perspective, having multiple family members participate in therapy can be an efficient way to influence the behavior of the entire system. This is particularly true when family roles and communication patterns are centrally implicated in the presenting problem. Classic indications for family therapy include high levels of conflict within the family or between the family and external systems (school, police), problems accompanying a recent shift in family structure, isolated or *scapegoated* members, and persistent role struggles (for example, what authority should a stepparent or eldest child exercise?).

Many matters that have been covert and perhaps regarded as untouchable, such as substance abuse by a family member, may be productively made overt and available for examination. We often find that clinicians first being introduced to family work hesitate to address topics that might trigger conflict or discomfort, but of course it is with these issues that the family most needs to develop the capacity to engage effectively. The therapist must find a balance between exposing or provoking levels of conflict that may undermine the family's safety or motivation and *colluding* with the temptation to leave difficult matters unnamed. Perhaps the only contraindication for working with multiple family members is conflict at a level that threatens the safety of family members during or subsequent to sessions.

Nontraditional family configurations. The latter half of the twentieth century in the United States saw a dramatic reduction in the proportion of children residing with two married, biological parents. Rates of divorce, stepfamilies, blended families, single parenthood, and same-sex parents have all escalated dramatically over the past two generations. It is not necessary to assert that these nontraditional configurations are inherently problematic in order to observe that they have access to fewer culturally sanctioned "scripts" for how they are supposed to operate. A stepparent, for example, cannot assume the same legitimate authority that a biological parent takes for granted, yet he or she may perceive pressure from the spouse or from the community to exercise parental responsibilities. Same-sex parents operate under constant threat of prejudicial treatment or active discrimination. Any circumstance that requires families to negotiate roles without the support of suitable cultural models is stressful, and stress undermines coping. Therapists attempting to assist nontraditional families must be prepared to share a heightened level of challenge surrounding role definition.

Stressful life events: when "normal" parenting and family communication skills just aren't enough. Events that disrupt family structures (divorce, parental death) and/or reduce the availability of caregivers (health problems or military service, for example) are known to place families at risk for adjustment difficulties and more serious mental health problems (Gibbs, Martin, Kupper, & Johnson, 2007; Malia, 2007; Rutter, 1999; Tremblay & Israel, 1998). Families experiencing highly stressful events may benefit from intervention, not to correct "deficits" but to enhance skills beyond levels that would suffice for coping with normal circumstances. Where the family was functioning well prior to the stressful event, such relatively low-intensity interventions as coaching through problem solving (D'Zurilla & Nezu, 2001), connecting children and parents with sources of social support, or helping them advocate within the systems in which they function (health care, legal, employment, extended family, etc.) may be enough to help them regain their footing.

Theories and Techniques

The term *family therapy* encompasses a broad array of practices, united only by the assumption that many problems are best understood to reside in family systems rather than in individuals. Hazelrigg, Cooper, and Borduin (1987) proposed a superordinate classification of family therapy approaches as embracing either pragmatic or aesthetic goals. Pragmatic goals address behavioral outcomes and alleviation of presenting problems. An aesthetic approach prioritizes instead the achievement of a valued therapeutic process and actually regards rapid symptom relief as a potential threat to the family's motivation and focus for change.

HIGHLIGHT BOX 13.3

RECOMMENDATIONS FOR HELPING FAMILIES COPE WITH HIGH-CONFLICT DIVORCE

Jay Lebow (2005) recommends the following foci for work with divorced families:

- Create a **solution-oriented focus:** build commitment to prioritize children's needs, undermine investment in blaming the other parent, support flexibility.
- Promote **disengagement skills** between parents and separation of Mom's house and Dad's house. Help children avoid being pulled into parental conflict.
- Establish **reliable, rule-driven methods of communication:** Minimize the need for coordination between households.
- **Negotiation:** when hostility precludes mediated conversation between parents,

therapist may resort to shuttle diplomacy, or individual meetings with each parent to reach compromise.
- **Reattribution:** new ways of thinking about recurring problems.
- **Work with children** to help them cope with and insulate themselves from conflict.
- **Build parent-child understandings** about how to make child's life work better in each household.
- **Work with the judicial system** to help the court understand the needs of the family, and help the therapist prepare the family for upcoming proceedings.

Aesthetic approaches tend to be *humanistic* or *psychodynamic* in nature; Bowenian family therapy, for example, focuses on differentiation of self from "triangulated" family relationships (Nichols & Schwartz, 1995). Perhaps in part owing to the challenges of measuring such constructs as differentiation or triangulation (Hazelrigg et al., 1987), aesthetic models have not been strongly represented in the empirical literature (Sexton & Alexander, 2002). Several pragmatic approaches, however, have accumulated substantial empirical support, particularly for various manifestations of parent-child conflict (Sexton & Alexander, 2002), but also for schizophrenic behavior (Gingerich & Bellack, 1995). *Antisocial behavior* in families has prompted some of the most intensive and successful treatment research, with multisystemic therapy (MST, Henggeler, Schoenwald, Borduin, Rowland, & Cunningham, 1998) and functional family therapy (FFT, Alexander & Parsons, 1973) each having demonstrated significant and lasting reductions in delinquent behavior and family conflict, now replicated across multiple sites (Sexton & Alexander, 2002).

Sample Interventions

The family we introduced at the outset of this chapter is not exhibiting delinquent or seriously undercontrolled behavior, so intensive intervention along the lines of MST is not warranted. Further, Robert and Joan have demonstrated the capacity to communicate and negotiate well on behalf of their children, which offers more latitude for joint problem solving than exists with conflict-ridden divorce situations (see Highlight Box 13.3). Several of the demonstrably effective elements of empirically supported pragmatic family therapies (Sexton & Alexander, 2002) could be applied to their concerns. The intervention might address issues similar to those in the parent-only option that was proposed earlier in the

chapter, with the notable exception that the children would be present and engaged in the treatment as well. Like the parent intervention, following an initial assessment (one or two sessions) to elicit various perspectives on the family's strengths and challenges, this family approach would likely begin with psychoeducation about the experience and impact of divorce in families. The psychoeducational phase typically offers both adults and children an experience of validation of their struggles and a greater understanding of others' distress. Joshua and Will would hear how difficult it can be for caring parents to relinquish some control over their children's environment and nurturance, Robert and Joan would learn about the pressure children often experience to "choose sides," Emily might come to better understand Joshua's reluctance to welcome even a compassionate "intruder" into the family, and Robert might become more sensitized to the ambiguity inherent in Emily's role. If family members better understand each other's struggles, they may be less inclined to attribute hostile intent to others' actions and consequently be more willing to engage in joint problem solving. The therapist might build on this opportunity to engage in collective problem solving around stressful scenarios for Joshua and other family members. It may be, for example, that the children would be reassured by some reliable one-on-one time with each parent, perhaps on the evening of their return from the other parent's house (a high-stress time for Joshua). The therapist might encourage Robert and Joan to help prepare the children for transitions to the other parent's home by coaching with positive statements about their time with the other parent and planning some activity the children can look forward to upon their return. Clearly, in this case, there is also some work to be done in negotiating Emily's parenting responsibilities and authority. Perhaps, with the therapist's help, this family arranges for Robert to retain much of the disciplinary role, Robert and Emily to present a united front concerning their expectations for the children, and Emily to have some defined supportive role as well (perhaps she's particularly effective at helping Joshua with homework, or she picks the children up from after-school care). All of these interventions are designed to reduce distress and increase support for all family members. It may be that this is sufficient to restore Joshua's former high functioning at school, or it may be that additional measures will be necessary.

WORKING WITH COUPLES

There is growing demand for couples work and evidence for its effectiveness. Concerns related to intimate relationships are the most commonly presented problem in the practice of psychotherapy, and over the past decades, couples therapy has grown in its popularity as a treatment for distress in close relationships (Johnson & Lebow, 2000). The negative effects of marital conflict on children have been widely recognized, as have potential links between relationship distress and depression, anxiety, and general health in adults (Johnson, 2003). Some have suggested that decreases in positive social connection and a sense of belonging have contributed to the growth of anxiety in our culture (e.g., Twenge, 2000), a phenomenon that is often acted out in intimate relationships. Within this context, the public's growing acceptance and use of couples therapy, and increasing research and practitioner interests, have resulted in a proliferation of models and uses for couples treatment (Johnson & Lebow, 2000). In general, couples therapy has been found to be about as effective for alleviation of relationship distress as individual psychotherapy is for distress related to individual problems (Jacobson & Addis, 1993; Johnson & Lebow, 2000).

Central Issues

All couples work is "in vivo." One advantage of couples over individual work is that interpersonal issues and patterns can be viewed directly as they are enacted in the therapist's office, offering salient avenues for direct intervention. The interpersonal nature of couples treatment naturally pulls for a direct focus on immediate behaviors and their consequences in the therapy room. The forms of couples therapy that we examine in detail next encourage live enactment of typical behaviors and practice of new, more effective ones between partners in session. Most approaches to couples work therefore assume pathology to lie between, rather than within, individuals, though as we address here, individual pathology can certainly play a large role in couple distress (Budman & Gurman, 1988).

Managing neutrality and bias. The couples therapist must provide a safe environment for both partners to risk authentic expression and new ways of interacting. A central ingredient of that safe environment is the therapist's capacity to ally equally—or at least alternately—with both partners. For this reason, many therapists will not engage in couples work with a dyad if they have previously worked individually with one of the partners for any extended period of time, in order to maintain a credible posture of neutrality. A related issue is managing the therapist's investment in a particular outcome of the therapy. Couples therapists must hold hope for the couple and coach them through the communication process, while entrusting the outcome to the couple's best judgment of their well-being rather than the therapist's wishes. Successful couples therapists are able to establish and maintain a *working alliance* with both partners, even though the two are likely to hold very divergent points of view (Friedman & Lipchick, 1999), while ultimately remaining allied with the relationship itself as well.

Facing emotional disengagement and reactivity. Many couples wait too long to enter into treatment: couples in active, but not extremely severe, conflict actually have a better prognosis for improvement in relationship satisfaction than those in which at least one partner has become emotionally disengaged over time, resulting in distance and estrangement within the relationship (Jacobson & Addis, 1993). On the other end of the spectrum, we find couples engaged in communicative patterns of high emotional reactivity and intensity, and the therapist is faced with the challenge of helping the couples to manage such affect in a way that moves them out of their conflict while supporting their needs to express themselves and be heard (Friedman & Lipchick, 1999).

Addressing gender roles and power imbalances. Couples work is inherently political, in that there are often unspoken assumptions made in intimate relationships related to gender role expectations and power balance. Couples for whom expectations and needs are highly disparate (e.g., a highly independent husband paired with a wife craving closeness and intimacy) tend to benefit less from marital therapy (Jacobson, Follette, & Pagel, 1986). It is often up to the therapist to help a couple make these polarized needs explicit and address them openly. *Feminist theory* has done much over the years to address differences in power and privilege between men and women, encouraging couples therapists to help partners examine unspoken assumptions about how decisions are made, how tasks are divided, and what roles each member of the dyad should play in relation to the other (Rampage, 2002).

Working with same-sex couples. Much of the literature on working with couples assumes heterosexual partners, although 72% of therapists report that at least 10% of their cases involve lesbians or gay male clients (Green & Bobele, 1994). Couples therapists need to be knowledgeable about and prepared to discuss tasks specific to same-sex couples without assuming that these specific issues are what is bringing the couples to therapy. Such challenges might include dealing with homophobia, feeling tension within families of origin, locating social supports, and having questions about boundaries and commitment within the relationship. Same-sex couples in distress may be seeking treatment for issues faced in any intimate relationship, as well as the specific challenges mentioned earlier. Homosexual couples may wonder whether heterosexual therapists can truly understand their issues, and such therapists would be well served by a willingness to explore these concerns openly with their clients. Many therapists report feeling unprepared to deal with issues specific to same-sex partners and would benefit from additional training in assessing and working with such couples (Green & Mitchell, 2002).

Possible contraindications and complications for couples therapy. Questions sometimes arise as to the appropriateness of conducting couples therapy in situations where there is ongoing physical aggression or substance abuse. *Intimate partner violence* is a widely recognized problem, with 30% of couples reporting at least one instance of violence within the course of their marriages (Straus & Gelles, as cited in Holtzworth-Munroe, Meehan, Rehman, & Marshall, 2002). Although general rates of women abusing men have been shown to be about equal to those for men abusing women (Felson & Cares, 2005), physical aggression by men against women in intimate relationships tends to be more severe and criminally oriented and results in more injury. Reciprocal violence between partners (DiLillo, Giuffre, Tremblay, & Peterson, 2001) and violence within same-sex relationships are also quite common, with 28% of gay males and 25% of lesbian couples reporting instances of physical aggression (Bailey, 1996). There is debate within the field as to whether it is appropriate to engage in couples work when there is continued physical aggression. On the one hand, conjoint therapy may inappropriately diffuse the responsibility for violence in a relationship and expose the target of that violence to retaliation for disclosures in session. Conversely, conjoint couples work may enhance the possibility that interventions are adopted outside of the therapy hour, provide space for heated discussions that might have ended in violence elsewhere, and better address situations in which violence is reciprocated (Holtzworth-Munroe et al., 2002). Theories of intimate partner violence have traditionally used a heterosexual model, and so it is important for the therapist working with same-sex partners to attempt a nonheterosexist point of view when working with these couples (Bailey, 1996). As with many areas of psychological intervention, it is important for the therapist to conduct a thorough assessment of the situation (and in this case, establish a reliable safety plan for those being abused) before deciding to offer treatment.

Substance abuse can also complicate the course of therapy with couples. One of the major goals of the work is often abstinence, or at least a reduction in use, by at least one partner. In support of this goal, the therapist can find him- or herself unequally aligned with the nonabusing partner, upsetting the therapeutic alliance. Therapists need to find some way of allying with the substance-abusing partner, which can present a particularly difficult challenge in the face of the relational distress and self-destruction that are often witnessed in such substance-abusing environments (Epstein & McCrady, 2002).

Evidence points to an integral role of interpersonal relationships in the development and maintenance of individual psychopathology. Strong associations have been found between couple and family functioning and psychological issues such as anxiety, depression, suicidality, borderline personality disorder, substance abuse, and sexual dysfunction (Fruzzetti & Iverson, 2004). However, there may be circumstances in which individual work is recommended instead of or conjointly with couples therapy, such as when one partner's level of psychopathology is extreme enough that there is not space enough within a couples therapy session to give it the attention it warrants. The systemically oriented couples therapist may struggle with a desire to understand an individual's pathology in the context of the larger relationship when in some circumstances a partner may actually require more intensive individual work in order to have his or her treatment needs met.

Theories and Techniques

Empirically supported treatments. To date there are two major approaches to couples therapy that have accumulated substantial empirical support—*behavioral couples therapy* and *emotion focused therapy* for couples. In addition to significant research foundations, both have strong theoretical bases with manualized treatment guides (Byrne, Carr, & Clark, 2004) and so have received much attention in the literature.

Behavioral couples therapy. Behavioral couples therapy (BCT), also known as behavioral marital therapy (BMT, Jacobson & Margolin, 1979), was developed using a social learning model that incorporates ideas from *behavior exchange* and *reinforcement theory*, as well as *cognitive, social,* and *developmental psychology* (Jacobson, 1981). Essentially, BCT assumes that couples tend to become engaged in negatively reinforcing interactions and works to help them (1) increase positive interactions through *behavior exchange training* and (2) enhance *problem-solving* and *communication skills*. In behavior exchange training, the therapist helps the couple plan for behavioral changes designed to increase the frequency of mutually reinforcing, pleasing activities (e.g., going on a date, taking a walk together). Communication and problem-solving skills help the couple to engage in such conversations outside of the therapy room. Interventions are focused on present-day issues in the relationship that are within a couple's awareness and often include homework assignments for outside the therapy hour (Baucom, Shoham, Mueser, Daiuto, & Stickle, 1998; Byrne et al., 2004). Rather than focusing on individual characteristics, personal history, or differences between partners, BCT highlights exchanges between the partners and environmental and social conditions that are created by and that reinforce such interactions (Jacobson, 1981).

Emotion focused therapy for couples. Emotion focused therapy (EFT) integrates *systemic, experiential,* and *attachment theories* to understand couple distress. Drawing upon *systems theory,* EFT proposes that each partner's *intrapsychic* experience both supports and is supported by cycles of interaction between the partners. The negative interactional cycles that exist between two people are reciprocally determined and so in some ways take on lives of their own. *Circular causality,* articulated by family systems theory, proposes that behaviors are linked together in a circular chain: "partner A nags because partner B withdraws while partner B withdraws because partner A nags" (Greenberg & Johnson, 1988, p. 33). Attachment theory, introduced earlier in this chapter in the context of children's relationships with adults, proposes that emotional disconnection in couple relationships leads to separation anxiety and circular patterns such as pursue-withdraw, mutual withdrawal, or mutual attack (Greenberg & Johnson, 1988). Emotions such as anger, resentment, frustration, or irritation are signposts for underlying fears, yearnings, and needs in response to threats to strong connection with and trust toward a partner. Emotions, generated in the here and now within the therapy session, are considered vital information that signifies how and why partners interact with each other in often rigid,

determined ways. In sessions, through a series of nine explicit steps, the therapist works to coax the expression of emotion to explore and reframe these feelings as attachment needs (Johnson & Greenman, 2006).

Sample Interventions

Let's explore in more depth how these empirically supported approaches to couples therapy might look in practice with our hypothetical case scenario. We'll suppose that Robert, the biological father, and Emily, the stepmother, present to us requesting couples therapy to help them manage the stressors impacting their relationship, including tensions surrounding Joshua. For now, we'll focus on two major strategies drawn from EFT and BCT, as discussed earlier.

Identifying maladaptive interactional cycles and expressing underlying emotional needs through EFT. As a first step in the therapeutic process, the EFT couples therapist explores conflicts in the relationship and assesses ways in which these conflicts may express underlying attachment needs, such as dependence/independence and connection/separateness between the partners. When Emily speaks of her desire for Robert to establish firmer boundaries with Joshua, and Robert disagrees, the therapist thinks of this as an incongruity between their respective needs for dependence and connection, with Emily seeking more than Robert may desire. This helps the therapist to identify and formulate how each partner is seeking to have attachment needs met through his or her current behavior.

Next, the therapist helps Robert and Emily to identify the ways they engage in maladaptive cycles of interaction as a result of these unfulfilled attachment needs. He or she might reframe Emily's requests of Robert as attempts to feel that he is supporting and being sensitive to her as his partner, and Robert's withdrawal as a response to what he experiences as intrusive opinions and requests. This may take the form of a classic pursue-withdraw cycle, in which Emily attempts to get her needs met by Robert, he recoils from such demands, and she, in turn, pursues him further. By helping the couple to identify this cycle, the therapist is beginning a process of deescalation of their maladaptive pattern (Johnson & Greenman, 2006).

Once these maladaptive patterns are explicit, the therapist would coach Robert and Emily to express the previously unacknowledged attachment needs that underlie these cycles of behavior. The therapist would work with each partner to help him or her recognize and accept the emotional needs of the other. This may take the form of Emily expressing her need to feel more supported by Robert as a parental figure in the home and thus feel more accepted and loved by him. Robert may express to Emily that her criticisms of his parenting feel like an unloving rejection of him, and thus he may need to hear more encouraging and supportive expressions from her. The EFT therapist works to achieve the expression of emotion in the moment by reflecting emotional responses made by each partner, attempting to validate and normalize each partner's experience, asking evocative questions, and bringing attention back to critical interpersonal events (Johnson & Greenman, 2006).

As therapy progresses, the therapist would continue to assist Robert and Emily in finding new and more productive ways to express these wishes, leading to new solutions for the handling of conflict and disappointment related to not having one's emotional needs met. Using a technique such as rehearsal, the couple works to establish new ways of interacting, and the therapist aids them in the consolidation of successful changes. For example, the EFT therapist would identify critical emotional events in the couple's development. If Robert were to verbally validate Emily's needs and refrain from emotionally distancing himself in response to them (withdrawer reengagement), the therapist would point this out and reflect the emotions that Robert expresses in order to help nurture the creation of a secure bond between them. The therapist may even model this behavior for Robert (e.g., "I can see that you need to feel more involved in taking care of Joshua and that you feel closer to me when we work together") and ask him to rehearse it in session. Similarly, the therapist might coach Emily through the process of blamer softening, in which requests for changes in Robert's behavior are made without aggression but instead reflect Emily's underlying emotional needs (e.g., "I feel more involved and loved when we can talk about Joshua's behavior and work together on solutions"). Near the end of therapy, consolidation is enhanced through the therapist's attempts to specify gains made over the course of treatment and to help the couple to create a verbal narrative of their successes and emotional journey (Greenberg & Johnson, 1988; Johnson & Greenman, 2006).

Behavior exchange, communication, and problem-solving training in BCT. Behavior exchange training with Robert and Emily would take early advantage of opportunities for reinforcement of positive behaviors, which cleverly makes use of preexisting strengths and resources within their relationship. In this way, early steps toward change are both positively reinforcing and relatively painless, paving the way for later, more intensive work. We might ask Robert and Emily to identify occasions on which one of them felt more support and intimacy from the other. We would then provide an opportunity for each partner to practice asking the other to increase the frequency of these positive behaviors. We would encourage Robert and Emily to do this in simple, straightforward ways and deflect complicated, conflict-generating requests for further exploration later in therapy. This *communication training* will create a foundation for the couple to engage in more effective problem-solving behaviors when tensions and conflicts arise. As their therapists, we could model effective communication

HIGHLIGHT BOX 13.4

TRAINING AND PROFESSIONAL DEVELOPMENT CONSIDERATIONS

Here, we identify some of the choices that lie along the career path of an aspiring clinician seeking to work with children, families, and/or couples. Although you must decide for yourself what information you would need to evaluate the options at each choice point, we encourage you to find some way to get closer to where the work of interest to you is happening. Seek a job or volunteer opportunity at an agency that provides clinical services, or just ask a clinical professional in a role that interests you what his or her worklife is like—most of us are happy to talk about what we do.

Choice of terminal degree. Chapter 1 of this book outlines distinctions in training and professional opportunities, between master's- and doctoral-level degrees, and between PsyD and PhD degrees. For the kind of work described in this chapter, a master's degree in clinical social work and a master's or doctoral degree in clinical psychology or marriage and family therapy (MFT) are all potentially suitable credentials.

Generalist versus specialized training. All doctoral programs in clinical psychology seeking accreditation from the American Psychological Association must commit to providing "broad and general" training, but some offer specialized elective concentrations (sometimes called "tracks") in clinical child or family psychology. Even within programs that do not offer designated concentrations, students can develop focused proficiencies through selection of academic (paper topics), clinical (practicum or volunteer), and research (dissertation or research assistantship)

experiences. Master's programs similarly vary in their degree of specialization, and MFT programs are obviously oriented to the type of work described in this chapter.

Predoctoral internship year and postdoctoral opportunities. At the doctoral level and beyond, these represent further opportunities for intensive clinical training, following either a generalist or specialty model. Many of these sites hold membership in the Association of Psychology Postdoctoral and Internship Centers (APPIC), which maintains an online directory (http://www.appic.org/directory/4_1_directory_online.asp; retrieved February 5, 2008), searchable by populations served, treatment modalities, or specialty areas.

Practice settings. Some of the settings in which child and family clinicians can be found include schools, where they often fulfill a substantial psychoeducational assessment function; primary medical care settings, which are often the first place parents will bring concerns about a child's behavior; community mental health clinics, which provide a wide array of services, often to the most needy segments of the population; and private practice, where the entrepreneurial clinician may shape his or her competencies to suit his or her interests or to fit a market niche.

Membership in professional associations. These memberships provide access to like-minded colleagues, networking opportunities, specialty journals or newsletters, and conferences and other continuing education. Many associations offer deep discounts and a welcoming culture for

---

HIGHLIGHT BOX 13.4   *(continued)*

student members and represent a rich venue for socialization into the profession. Among the associations that might be of interest to child and family clinicians are the American Psychological Association's Divisions 37 (Child and Family Policy and Practice), 43 (Family Psychology),

53 (Clinical Child and Adolescent Psychology), and 54 (Pediatric Psychology); the Association for Behavioral and Cognitive Therapies (ABCT); the American Association for Marriage and Family Therapy; and your local state and regional psychological associations.

---

strategies by engaging in a role-play exercise with them, speaking to one partner as we assume the role of the other. Then Robert and Emily would practice these new skills, with us giving feedback to help each partner master them as their own.

Problem-solving training. Interpersonal problems tend to surface in vague terms (e.g., "You're not parenting well" or "You never listen to me") and under duress, such that the listener feels attacked, defensive, and unlikely to fully perceive the needs of the other. Problem-solving training encourages a collaborative atmosphere in which partners work together to identify problems and consider potential solutions. A therapist would coach Robert and Emily to begin with positive comments such as appreciation, to be specific and brief in identifying the problem, to share the emotional impact of the problem on the speaker, and to acknowledge one's own role in the problem (Jacobson, 1981). Further guidelines for problem-solving communication include talking about only one problem at a time, paraphrasing comments made by the other partner to check one's understanding before responding, steering clear of verbal abuse and aggression, and avoiding inferences about the other partner's motivations, feelings, or attitudes.

THOUGHT QUESTIONS

From the Introduction

- What advantages might the therapist gain by working with more than one client in the room? What are some of the challenges that might be presented by this arrangement?
- Think of an example of a problem that could be construed as either located in an individual or located in a system— how might these different ways of understanding the problem influence your choice of interventions?

From Working with Children

- When collecting collateral information from multiple informants in child assessment, how might a therapist understand different stories emerging from different informants—does this mean that one informant is more "accurate" than another, that different informants have access to different—but equally (real)— aspects of the child, or that children are actually different in various settings?
- Using attachment theory as a guide, in what ways might the therapeutic relationship with a child affect how he or

she interacts with other important people in his or her life?

- Imagine that you are a social learning theorist seeking to understand Joshua's pattern of irritable behavior upon returning from visits with his mom. What sort of information would you seek to develop your hypothesis about why this pattern persists?
- What coparenting strategies can you imagine for Joshua's biological parents to consider?

From Working with Families

- What case might you make for treating Joshua's difficulties from a family therapy perspective?
- How might a therapist help to create safe conditions for open exploration of conflict among family members when there is a potential for hostility or high levels of discord?
- Can you imagine how a therapist might integrate both aesthetic and pragmatic goals in the course of family therapy? Do you believe this is possible or desirable?
- How might a therapist encourage children to express themselves in family sessions if they appear uncomfortable?

From Working with Couples

- As the couple's therapist, how might you go about introducing and engaging in a role-play exercise with the couple?
- In assessing this family, why might we recommend couples treatment for Robert and Emily?
- What advantages or disadvantages could there be in using a couples therapy format for the treatment of substance abuse by one partner?
- How can a couples therapist work to maintain a sense of neutrality in his or her work? What advantages and disadvantages do you see in this type of stance?
- What benefits are there in allowing clients time away from therapy to consolidate gains and changes on their own?
- In what ways do decreases in positive connection and sense of belonging in society potentially affect dynamics between couples? For example, how does this affect expectations of each partner for fulfillment of his or her needs by the other?

Glossary

Antisocial behavior: behavior that demonstrates disregard for the rights or welfare of others.

Attachment theory: a theory emphasizing the functions of an early caregiving relationship for a developing child, and the enduring influence of that relationship on an individual's perception and negotiation of his or her emotional and other psychological needs.

Behavioral couples therapy: an approach to couple treatment that focuses on behavioral principles such as reinforcement theory, utilizing techniques such as behavior exchange and the development of communication and problem-solving skills.

Behavior exchange theory: an aspect of behavioral psychology emphasizing the ability of one person's actions to reinforce another's.

Circular causality: a concept from family systems theory that emphasizes the reciprocal reinforcement of interactions between individuals.

Cognitive-behavioral theory: a theory that emphasizes the role of cognitive processes in shaping how humans respond to events in their environment.

Cognitive psychology: a branch of psychology focusing on information-processing functions such as perception, attention, memory, attribution, language, and problem solving.

Colluding: in a clinical context, when the therapist acts in a way that functions to support a client's maladaptive behavior pattern, as if by unspoken agreement with the client.

Communication training: a technique used in behavioral couples therapy to develop skills for verbal interaction between partners, often including modeling, role play, and feedback by the therapist.

Contradindication: any element of a clinical presentation that makes a particular intervention inadvisable.

Developmental psychology: a branch of psychology focusing on mental, emotional, behavioral, and physiological changes in humans throughout the life span.

Emotion focused therapy: an integrative model of treatment that, when applied to couples, emphasizes maladaptive interactional patterns, the expression of emotions, and underlying attachment needs of each partner.

Empirically supported treatments: techniques of therapeutic intervention that have been shown, through rigorous empirical investigation, to be effective for treating particular symptoms.

Experiential therapy: a form of therapy that emphasizes an individual's cognitive and emotional experience in the present moment.

Feminist theory: a school of thought that emphasizes women's life issues and roles in political, social, psychological, and other domains.

Humanistic theory: an understanding of human behavior that is primarily concerned with conscious experience, choice, and seeking of meaning and that resists attempts to reduce human experience to component elements.

Intimate partner violence: also referred to as domestic abuse or spousal abuse; the attempt by one partner to gain power over another through the use of psychological or physical force.

Intrapsychic: pertaining to a person's internal cognitive and emotional experience, as distinct from interpersonal (between persons) dynamics or behaviors.

Problem-solving training: a technique used in behavioral couples therapy that coaches partners through the identification and management of interpersonal conflicts in collaborative solution-focused ways.

Psychodynamic theory: an understanding of human behavior that focuses on the role of unconscious processes in human development and personality and that prioritizes insight as the goal of therapy.

Reinforcement: any consequence of a behavior that increases the probability that the behavior will be repeated.

Scapegoating: when one member of a system is blamed for problems to which others have contributed.

Social learning theory: a theory focused on the ways in which humans learn from their observations of, and interactions with, others.

Social psychology: a branch of psychology focusing on how social contexts influence the behavior of individuals and groups.

Theoretical orientation: an approach to understanding human experience that shapes what the therapist regards as important dimensions of assessment, how the therapist makes sense of the client's experience, and what interventions the therapist contemplates.

Working alliance: a relational stance developed between a therapist and client(s), often characterized by mutual understanding, collaboration, and positive regard, which becomes a tool for therapeutic change in the client.

References

Ainsworth, M. D. S. & Bowlby, J. (1991). An ethological approach to personality development. *American Psychologist, 46*, 331–341.

Alexander, J. F. & Parsons, B. V. (1973). Short term behavior interventions with delinquent families: impact on family process and recidivism. *Journal of Abnormal Psychology, 81*, 219–225.

American Psychiatric Association (2000). *Diagnostic and statistical manual of mental disorders* (4th ed., text revision). Washington, DC: Author.

Azar, S. T., Robinson, D. R., Hekimian, E., & Twentyman, C. T. (1984). Unrealistic expectations and problem-solving ability in maltreating and comparison mothers. *Journal of Consulting and Clinical Psychology, 52*, 687–691.

Bailey, G. R. (1996). Treatment of domestic violence in gay and lesbian relationships. *Journal of Psychological Practice, 2*, 1–8.

Baucom, D. H., Shoham, V., Mueser, K. T., Daiuto, A. D., & Stickle, T. R. (1998). Empirically supported couple and family interventions for marital distress and adult mental health problems. *Journal of Consulting and Clinical Psychology, 66*, 53–88.

Bratton, S. C., Ray, D., Rhine, T., & Jones, L. (2005). The efficacy of play therapy with children: a meta-analytic review of treatment outcomes. *Professional Psychology: Research and Practice, 36*, 376–390.

Budman, S. H. & Gurman, A. S. (1988). *Theory and practice of brief therapy*. New York: Guilford.

Byrne, M., Carr, A., & Clark, M. (2004). The efficacy of behavioral couples therapy and emotionally focused therapy for couple distress. *Contemporary Family Therapy, 26*, 361–387.

Cohen, J. A., Mannarino, A. P., & Deblinger, E. (2006). *Treating trauma and traumatic grief in children and adolescents.* New York: Guilford.

DiLillo, D., Giuffre, D., Tremblay, G. C., & Peterson, L. (2001). A closer look at the nature of intimate partner violence reported by women with a history of child sexual abuse. *Journal of Interpersonal Violence, 16*, 116–132.

D'Zurilla, T. J. & Nezu, A. M. (2001). Problem solving therapies. In K. Dobson (Ed.), *Handbook of cognitive-behavioral therapies.* New York: Guilford.

Epstein, E. E. & McCrady, B. S. (2002). Couple therapy in the treatment of alcohol problems. In A. S. Gurman & N. S. Jacobson (Eds.), *Clinical handbook of couple therapy* (pp. 597–628). New York: Guilford.

Felson, R. B. & Cares, A. C. (2005). Gender and the seriousness of assaults on intimate partners and other victims. *Journal of Marriage and Family Therapy, 67*, 1182–1195.

Fonagy, P., Gergely, G., & Target, M. (2007). The parent-infant dyad and the construction of the subjective self. *Journal of Child Psychology and Psychiatry, 48*, 288–328.

Friedman, S. & Lipchik, E. (1999). A time-effective, solution-focused approach to couple therapy. In J. M. Donovan (Ed.), *Short-term couple therapy* (pp. 325–359). New York: Guilford.

Fruzzetti, A. E. & Iverson, K. M. (2004). Mindfulness, acceptance, validation, and "individual" psychopathology in couples. In S. C. Hayes, V. M. Follette, & M. M. Linehan (Eds.), *Mindfulness and acceptance* (pp. 168–191). New York: Guilford.

Gibbs, D. A., Martin, S. L., Kupper, L. L., & Johnson, R. E. (2007). Child maltreatment in enlisted soldiers' families during combat-related deployments. *Journal of the American Medical Association, 298*, 528–535.

Gingerich, S. L. & Bellack, A. S. (1995). Research-based family interventions for the treatment of schizophrenia. *The Clinical Psychologist, 48*, 24–27.

Green, R. J. & Mitchell, V. (2002). Gay and lesbian couples in therapy: homophobia, relational ambiguity, and social support. In A. S. Gurman & N. S. Jacobson (Eds.), *Clinical handbook of couple therapy* (pp. 546–568). New York: Guilford.

Green, S. K. & Bobele, M. (1994). Family therapists' response to AIDS: an examination of attitudes, knowledge, and contact. *Journal of Marital and Family Therapy, 20*, 349–367.

Greenberg, L. S. & Johnson, S. M. (1988). *Emotionally focused therapy for couples.* New York: Guilford.

Hazelrigg, M., Cooper, H. M., & Brown, C. M. (1987). Evaluating the effectiveness of family therapies: an integrative review and analysis. *Psychological Bulletin, 101*, 428–442.

Henggeler, S. W., Schoenwald, S. K., Borduin, C. M., Rowland, M. D. & Cunningham, P. B. (1998). *Multisystemic treatment of antisocial behavior in children and adolescents.* New York: Guilford.

Herschell, A. D., Calzada, E. J., Eyberg, S. M., & McNeil, C. B. (2002). Parent-Child Interaction Therapy: new directions in research. *Cognitive and Behavioral Practice, 9*, 9–16.

Herschell, A. D., McNeil, C. B., & McNeil, D. (2004). Clinical child psychology's progress in disseminating empirically supported treatments. *Clinical Psychology: Science and Practice, 11*, 267–288.

Holtzworth-Munroe, A., Meehan, J. C., Rehman, U., & Marshall, A. D. (2002). Intimate partner violence: an introduction for couple therapists. In A. S. Gurman & N. S. Jacobson (Eds.), *Clinical handbook of couple therapy* (pp. 441–465). New York: Guilford.

Jacobson, N. S. (1981). Behavioral marital therapy. In A. S. Gurman & D. P. Kniskern (Eds.), *Handbook of family therapy* (pp. 556–591). New York: Brunner/Mazel.

Jacobson, N. S. & Addis, M. E. (1993). Research on couples and couple therapy: what do we know? where are we going? *Journal of Consulting and Clinical Psychology, 61*, 85–93.

Jacobson, N. S., Follette, V. M., & Pagel, M. (1986). Predicting who will benefit from behavioral marital therapy. *Journal of Consulting and Clinical Psychology, 54*, 518–522.

Jacobson, N. S. & Margolin, G. (1979). *Marital therapy: strategies based on social learning and behavior exchange principles.* New York: Brunner/Mazel.

Johnson, S. M. (2003). The revolution in couple therapy: a practitioner-scientist perspective. *Journal of Marital and Family Therapy, 29*, 365–384.

Johnson, S. M. & Greenman, P. S. (2006). The path to a secure bond: emotionally focused couple therapy. *Journal of Clinical Psychology: In Session, 62*, 597–609.

Johnson, S. & Lebow, J. (2000). The "coming of age" of couple therapy: a decade review. *Journal of Marital and Family Therapy, 26*, 23–38.

Kazdin, A. (2005). *Parent management training: treatment for oppositional, aggressive, and antisocial behavior in children and adolescents.* New York: Oxford University Press.

Leblanc, M. & Ritchie, M. (2001). A meta-analysis of play therapy outcomes. *Counseling Psychology Quarterly, 14*, 149–163.

Lebow, J. L. (2005). Integrative family therapy for families experiencing high-conflict divorce. In J. Lebow (Ed.), *Handbook of clinical family therapy.* Hoboken, NJ: Wiley.

Malia, J. (2007). A reader's guide to family stress literature. *Journal of Loss and Trauma, 12*, 223–243.

Nichols, M. P. & Schwartz, R. C. (1995). *Family therapy: Concepts and methods* (3rd ed.). Boston: Allyn & Bacon.

Ollendick, T. H. & Davis, T. E. (2004). Empirically supported treatments for children and adolescents: Where to from here? *Clinical Psychology: Science and Practice, 11*, 289–294.

Patterson, G. R. (1975). *Families: Applications of social learning to family life.* Champaign, IL: Research Press.

Rampage, C. (2002). Working with gender in couple therapy. In A. S. Gurman & N. S. Jacobson (Eds.), *Clinical handbook of couple therapy* (pp. 533–545). New York: Guilford.

Robin, A. & Foster, S. (1989). *Negotiating parent-adolescent conflict: a behavioral-family systems approach.* New York: Guilford.

Rutter, M. (1999). Resilience concepts and findings: implications for family therapy. *Journal of Family Therapy, 21*, 119–144.

Safran, J. D. & Muran, C. J. (2000). *Negotiating the therapeutic alliance: a relational treatment guide.* New York: Guilford.

Sexton, J. L., & Alexander, J. F. (2002). Family-based, empirically supported interventions. *Counseling Psychology, 30*, 238–261.

Straus, M. (1999). *No-talk therapy for children and adolescents.* New York: W.W. Norton.

Tremblay, G. C. & Israel, A. C. (1998). Children's adjustment to parental death. *Clinical Psychology: Science and Practice, 5*, 424–438.

Twenge, J. M. (2000). The age of anxiety? birth cohort change in anxiety and neuroticism. *Journal of Personality and Social Psychology, 79*, 1007–1021.

Winnicott, D. W. (1988). *Human nature.* New York: Schocken Books.

14

Clinical Health Psychology

Heather D. Hadjistavropoulos
University of Regina

Gordon J. G. Asmundson
University of Regina

OUTLINE

CLINICAL HEALTH PSYCHOLOGY

Mac is a 50-year-old male executive with high blood pressure. He has significant difficulties managing stress at work and at home. He is concerned about being at increased risk for cardiovascular disease.

Brenda, a 22-year-old university student, was in a car accident 3 years ago. The car accident resulted in multiple injuries. Over the past 3 years, she has gained 35 pounds and no longer participates in the physical activities she used to enjoy.

Larry is a 60-year-old man. He suffers from adult-onset diabetes and has difficulties adhering to treatment recommendations.

Raymond is a 30-year-old patient with AIDS who is experiencing difficulties coming to terms with his recent diagnosis and the social stigma that he is feeling.

Sara is a 75-year-old woman who is suffering from metastasized terminal breast cancer. She is seeking services for depression in part related to her concern that her husband will not be able to cope with her impending death.

Craig is a 45-year-old male laborer who experienced a significant back injury at work. He underwent surgery but continues to have significant pain with many activities. He is concerned with the impact the injury is having on his mood and ability to return to work.

Dale is a 30-year-old construction worker. He was punched in the jaw by a coworker following a disagreement at work. He subsequently experienced jaw pain and headaches. Within a few days, he began to experience significant anxiety, believing he had suffered a head injury. Despite negative investigations and reassurance to the contrary, he continues to be concerned that he has a head injury. He has decided to change health-care providers and seek a second opinion.

All of the foregoing cases depict individuals who could benefit from the services of a clinical health psychologist. In this chapter, it is our goal to introduce you to the profession of clinical health psychology and provide you with information on how these clients may be helped by clinical health psychologists. In doing so, some representative topics within the area will be presented and the interested reader will be directed to additional learning resources (e.g., organizations, Web sites, journals, programs).

As most graduate students in psychology likely know, health psychology is the subdiscipline of psychology devoted to understanding health and illness. What is most striking about the area of health psychology is that, although well known today as a significant and growing subfield of psychology, the discipline itself is relatively young. The American Psychological Association (APA), in fact, only formed the division of Health Psychology (Division 38) in

1978. There are many definitions of *health psychology*, but among the most common is one articulated by Matarazzo (1980), who stated that it is the discipline of psychology devoted to "the promotion and maintenance of health, the prevention and treatment of illness, the identification of etiologic and diagnostic correlates of health, illness and related dysfunction, and the improvement of the health care system and health policy formation" (p. 815).

Clinical health psychology, as the name suggests, is a subdiscipline of clinical psychology (described in previous chapters as the discipline of psychology focused on mental health) and health psychology. Although basic health psychology research is important, clinical health psychology focuses on applying or translating knowledge from clinical psychology and health psychology into practices that promote health, treat illness or disability, and improve the health-care system (Belar, 1997). In the cases described earlier, the clinical health psychologist might work with Mac, Brenda, and Larry on lifestyle issues to promote health and with Raymond, Sara, and Craig on various disease management strategies to improve coping with illness and disability. The clinical health psychologist would likely assist Dale with health anxiety in order to decrease distress and, equally importantly, reduce unnecessary health care utilization.

Fundamental to the work of the clinical health psychologist is the **biopsychosocial model** of health. Although widely accepted today, the biopsychosocial model was only formally introduced in the late 1970s by George Engel (1977). Prior to this, the biomedical model of health and illness had dominated conceptualizations of health for hundreds of years. In the biomedical model, disease was understood and explained by physiological processes alone, and health was considered to be physical in nature. The **biopsychosocial model,** in contrast, views both health and illness as a function of biological (e.g., genetic predisposition), psychological (e.g., beliefs, emotions, behaviors), and social (e.g., social support, relationships) variables that interact and ultimately determine where an individual falls on a health/illness continuum, with health and illness at one end and illness at the other end (Taylor, 1990). In this model, clinical health psychologists have an important role to play in promoting health and treating illness or disability.

Like other areas of clinical psychology, clinical health psychologists not only frequently engage in clinical practice but also teach and conduct research. Whereas some clinical health psychologists focus on one particular area (e.g.,

one specific disease or condition), others work with a wide variety of patient concerns. Clinical health psychologists work in a number of different environments, ranging from universities to various health-care settings. The latter may include primary care, hospital-based care, rehabilitation, and long-term care.

There are numerous noteworthy clinical health psychologists who can serve to illustrate the roles and important contributions of clinical health psychologists. In Highlight Box 14.1, the career activities of two clinical health psychologists are described; they serve as great

HIGHLIGHT BOX 14.1

One way for students to identify leaders in the field of clinical health psychology is to visit the APA Health Psychology Division (38) Web site to view the recipients of the Division award for Outstanding Contributions to Health Psychology, as well as the Career Service Award and Timothy B. Jeffrey Award in Clinical Health Psychology (http://www.health-psych.org/awards.php). In this highlight box, we highlight the career activities of two clinical health psychologists.

In 2007, **Janice Kiecolt-Glaser, PhD**, Professor of Psychiatry and Psychology at Ohio State University and the S. Robert Davis Chair of Medicine, was the recipient of the Award for Outstanding Contributions to Health Psychology. This award emphasizes contributions to research, although Dr. Kiecolt-Glaser is also known for her significant contributions to teaching, administration, and public service.

Dr. Kiecolt-Glaser received her PhD in Clinical Psychology at the University of Miami in 1976, notably at about the same time that clinical health psychology was first officially recognized by APA. After finishing her degree, she completed a postdoctoral fellowship at the University of Rochester, School of Medicine. With this

background, Dr. Kiecolt-Glaser went on to become a leader in the field of psychoneuroimmunology. To support her research, she has actively applied for and has been successful in obtaining continuous funding from the **National Institutes of Health**. She has authored more than 200 articles, chapters, and books. Her research has been published in the highest-impact journals in the field. As an indicator of how successful she has been in disseminating her findings, she is listed in the Institute for Scientific Information as among the world's most highly cited authors.

Although too extensive to describe, Dr. Kiecolt-Glaser's research is notable in many ways. She has carried out extensive research on older adults and their caregivers, and this work has improved our understanding of psychological and biological processes involved in health conditions, including cancer. She has been at the forefront of research on stress, demonstrating the important health consequences of stress, including its impact on depression, immune dysregulation, slower wound healing, impaired vaccine responses, and accelerated age-related changes in IL-6, a cytokine that has been linked to some cancers, cardiovascular disease, and

HIGHLIGHT BOX 14.1   (*continued*)

arthritis. She has also ventured into examining the impact of personal relationships on immune and endocrine function, the ability of omega-3 supplementation to alter mood and inflammation, and the ability of mind-body interventions such as yoga to modulate endocrine and immune responses. As a concrete example of her research, with caregivers, she found that stress has a long-term impact and that changes in immune system function exist several years or more after caregiving has ended (Kiecolt-Glaser, Preacher, MacCallum, Atkinson, Malarkey, & Glaser, 2003). Many students of psychology will have learned by now how bad marriages not only can reduce quality of life but can also be bad for your health. This knowledge, in part, can be attributed to research by Dr. Kiecolt-Glaser, who demonstrated that married couples with more hostile interactions report decreased wound healing and increased IL-6 production (Kiecolt-Glaser et al., 2006).

One of the reasons we have chosen to highlight the work of Dr. Kiecolt-Glaser is that her research is exemplary of how clinical health psychologists can systematically and progressively work toward understanding the interplay between psychological, social, and biological processes.

Another individual whom we would like to highlight for her work in the area of clinical health psychology is **Suzanne Bennett Johnson, PhD.** In 2007, Division 38 of APA awarded Dr. Bennett Johnson the Career Service Award. Like Dr. Kiecolt-Glaser, Dr. Suzanne Bennett Johnson stands out as an exemplary clinical health psychologist. She obtained her PhD in Clinical Psychology at the State University of New York at Stony Brook in 1974. She then completed an internship in clinical psychology and a postdoctoral fellowship in clinical child psychology at the University of Florida. Since that time, she has held numerous prestigious research appointments, including

the titles of Distinguished Professor and Director of the Center for Pediatric Psychology and Family Studies at the University of Florida and Robert Wood Johnson Health Policy Fellow in the office of Senator Clinton. She is currently the Chair of the Department of Medical Humanities and Social Sciences at Florida State University.

Dr. Bennett Johnson is an award-winning psychologist for her research on type 1 diabetes, with some of her current research efforts focused on clinic-based adherence intervention for diabetes. Her honors are too diverse to mention but have been from organizations including APA and the American Diabetes Association. Her research has received national funding by the National Institute of Health Research continually since 1980 and has been published in highly regarded journals. She is an editor of a major textbook in health psychology (Johnson, Perry, & Rozensky, 2002). Furthermore, she is the recipient of several awards for mentorship. Her mentoring spirit is illustrated in articles she published in *American Psychologist*, where she describes opportunities for prevention in health-care settings (Johnson, 2003), and the *Journal of Clinical Psychology in Medical Settings*, where she provides insights into challenges faced by clinical health psychologists in health research and health care (Johnson, 2004).

Dr. Bennett Johnson is particularly known, however, for her contributions to public service. Dr. Bennett Johnson was on the first organizing committee that sought to establish the initial standards for training in health psychology. She has served on numerous committees for Division 38 and has also taken on the role of President of the Division. She was a member of the American Board of Clinical Health Psychology, which is responsible for examination standards and the

---

HIGHLIGHT BOX 14.1   *(continued)*

awarding of diplomas in Clinical Health Psychology. Outside of clinical health psychology, she has also served on numerous editorial boards and grant review committees. What is important for graduate students to understand is that it is only because of people like Dr. Bennett Johnson that clinical health

psychology can advance. Disciplines advance only when individuals step up and pave the way for future clinical health psychologists, doing things like being actively involved in training, disseminating research, advocating for the profession, and setting practice standards.

---

examples of the contributions future clinical health psychologists can aspire to and demonstrate the diverse roles clinical health psychologists can take on.

BEHAVIORAL MEDICINE AND PSYCHOSOMATIC MEDICINE

Health psychology is a term often used interchangeably with the term *behavioral medicine*, but strictly speaking, health psychology is a subfield of psychology and often a subcomponent of behavioral medicine. *Behavioral medicine*, on the other hand, is a term used to refer to an interdisciplinary field with diverse health professionals who typically integrate behavioral principles and medical sciences (Straub, 2007). Like health psychology, the focus of behavioral medicine is on either preventing illness or assisting people who suffer from illness or disease. Historically, behavioral medicine focused on learned behaviors that contribute to health and disease, but it has since expanded beyond learning to examine a broad range of biopsychosocial variables.

Yet another term that is often associated with health psychology is *psychosomatic medicine*. Psychosomatic medicine began initially as the study of illness behavior that may be caused by psychological factors. Over time it has broadened to include psychosocial factors

involved in illness (Straub, 2007). The area has historical roots with Freud and psychiatry and, like behavioral medicine, is an interdisciplinary field. To assist the reader in learning more about health psychology, behavioral medicine, and psychosomatic medicine, Highlight Box 14.2 describes key organizations and journals related to these fields.

IMPORTANCE OF HEALTH PSYCHOLOGY

Numerous factors have contributed to the emergence and growth of health psychology. As noted by Matarazzo (1982), however, the greatest reason for the emergence of health psychology has likely been the decreased prevalence of acute infectious diseases, such as tuberculosis and influenza, and the increased prevalence of preventable disorders, such as cardiovascular disease, cancer, and diabetes. Research evidence showing that modifying behaviors such as smoking, diet, and sedentary lifestyles can prevent disease and improve quality of life and death rates and that general negative affective style is associated with a broad range of diseases has created a demand for clinical health psychologists (Taylor, 1990). Combining this knowledge of lifestyle disorders with the substantial increase in health-care costs (Smith & Suls, 2004), it is surprising that

HIGHLIGHT BOX 14.2

The Health Psychology Division (Division 38) of the APA is by far the most developed group for health psychology. Information on the Division can be obtained from the following Web address: **http://www.health-psych.org/**. This group is interested in basic and clinical research, education, and service activities that integrate biomedical information and psychological knowledge about health and illness. There are several special-interest groups within the division, such as groups on aging, women, and minority health issues. The Division publishes the quarterly newsletter *The Health Psychologist* and the journal *Health Psychology*. A recent initiative put forward in 2006 by the editorial board of *Health Psychology* and that is likely of great interest to graduate students is publication of a regular series of evidence-based reviews followed by a clinician's comment on the review. The review is meant to provide up-to-date evidence on a topic, and the clinician's comment is designed to aid in the application of the research to clinical practice.

As noted in Highlight Box 14.1, the Division highlights the contributions of clinical health psychologists each year. Students will be interested to know that they are also eligible for research awards. Currently there are five awards valued at $1,200. Two awards are given in the area of general health psychology, one award is given in child health psychology, and two additional awards are reserved for students conducting research on health disparities. Full-time graduate students are eligible for the awards and must submit information on the aims, background, and methods of the research proposed.

There are also other organizations that are relevant to clinical health psychology, although not as specific or developed as Division 38 of APA. In the United States, the Society of Behavioral Medicine (**http://www.sbm.org/**), for instance, is a multidisciplinary organization of clinicians, educators, and scientists who promote the study of behavior, biology and the environment, and the application of knowledge to health of not only individuals, but families, communities, and populations. The organization publishes the *Annals of Behavioral Medicine*.

Also relevant to health psychology is the American Psychosomatic Society (**http://www.psychosomatic.org/**), which publishes *Psychosomatic Medicine*. The American Psychosomatic Society is a group of academics and clinicians interested in the understanding of the interaction of mind, brain, body, and social context in promoting health and contributing to disease.

In Canada, unfortunately, the Health Psychology Section of the Canadian Psychological Association (http://www.cpa.ca) is not nearly as active, and little information on health psychology is available on the Web site. The Division of Health Psychology of the British Psychological Society (http://www.health-psychology.org.uk/) and the European Health Psychology Association (**http://www.ehps.net/800/index.html**) have more extensive information that may be of interest to graduate students interested in international experiences.

---

there has not been even further growth in clinical health psychology. Perhaps even more astonishing, given the prevalence of disorders related to lifestyle, is that clinical health psychology is not even more available to the public than it currently is. The research evidence highlighted in this chapter would, in fact, support clinical health psychology as an essential service rather than the adjunct service that it presently is. Patients routinely see family physicians on a yearly basis to monitor health status; quite possibly as important might be an annual visit to a clinical health psychologist!

REPRESENTATIVE AREAS OF PRACTICE

Students who seek advanced training in clinical health psychology can expect to learn about many areas, including strategies for promoting health and preventing illness (e.g., managing stress, weight, substance use), strategies for managing chronic and life-threatening illness (e.g., cardiovascular disease, chronic pain, diabetes, cancer, HIV, AIDS), and strategies for improving the quality of health-care services (e.g., fostering active participation in health

care and appropriate utilization of health-care services). Obviously, a chapter like this can only hope to introduce the reader to the area. Drawing on our own area of expertise, we provide further detail in a number of common areas of practice. Given that the focus of this chapter is on clinical health psychology, we have focused on applied aspects of health psychology rather than basic research findings or public health. We also selected topics that are common to many of the health conditions that clinical health psychologists treat and that represent areas where clinical health psychologists have had significant success in improving the lives of patients with medical conditions. Given these limits to the chapter, the interested reader is directed to Highlight Box 14.3, which describes several books that focus exclusively

HIGHLIGHT BOX 14.3

Below we list a number of the most recent comprehensive books on the topic of clinical health psychology.

Belar, C. D. & Deardoff, W. W. (1995). *Clinical health psychology in medical settings: a practitioner's guidebook* (2nd ed.). Washington, DC: APA.

This book, although a bit older, is highly appropriate for clinical graduate students. Rather than dividing chapters by disease states or health issues, the authors discuss topics that are relevant across conditions, such as general information on assessment and intervention strategies and ethical issues.

Boyer, B. A. & Paharia, M. I. (2007). *Comprehensive handbook of clinical health psychology*. Hoboken, NJ: Wiley.

This is an edited book that begins by reviewing theoretical models of health psychology and then covers various health problems (e.g., obesity,

tobacco addiction), diseases (cardiovascular diseases, cancer, diabetes), and special topics (e.g., pediatric psychology, pain management).

Camic, P. M. & Knight, S. J. (2004). *Clinical handbook of health psychology: a practical guide to effective interventions* (2nd ed.). Cambridge, MA: Hogrefe & Huber.

The first section of this edited book covers how to carry out an effective initial clinical interview and assessment. The main section then turns to the most common medical conditions, covering pathophysiology, medical treatment, common psychological referral issues, psychological assessment, psychological treatment, and professional and practice issues. The final section examines special topics, such as social support, spirituality, alternative health methods, and risk reduction in minority populations.

HIGHLIGHT BOX 14.3   (*continued*)

Gatchel, R. J. & Oordt, M. S. (2003). *Clinical health psychology and primary care: practical advice and clinical guidance for successful collaboration.* Washington, DC: APA.

This book is unique in that it offers practical advice on how to set up a primary care health psychology practice and collaborate with physicians on common health complaints. Chapters are organized by conditions and describe biopsychosocial strategies that can be used by psychologists.

Kennedy, P. & Llewelyn, S. (2006). *The essentials of clinical health psychology.* Hoboken, NJ: Wiley.

This edited book covers not only various medical conditions but some common topics of practical concern (e.g., tele-health, caregiving, working with patients with cognitive impairment).

Nikcevic, A. V., Kuczmierczyk, A. R., & Bruch, M. (2006). *Formulation and treatment in clinical health psychology.* New York: Routledge.

This edited text covers key biopsychosocial information, assessment procedures, and empirically based treatment strategies for various health problems. This book takes a unique approach in providing a general approach to case formulation and using case studies to demonstrate the link between case formulation, treatment planning, and outcome.

---

on clinical health psychology and provide in-depth coverage of the vast areas of clinical health psychology.

BIOPSYCHOSOCIAL ASSESSMENT

The cornerstone of practicing as a clinical health psychologist is conducting a comprehensive biopsychosocial assessment to evaluate the patient's problem. This is accomplished through interviewing, using appropriate assessment tools either specifically for use with certain medical populations or adapted for use with medical populations, reviewing available medical documentation, and, when applicable, consulting with other health professionals involved in care.

Interviewing. In addition to covering psychological and social information as typically asked by clinical psychologists, clinical health psychologists also ask questions about: (a) the patient's health difficulties (e.g., nature, duration, severity, course, diagnosis, prognosis, treatment); (b) the impact of health difficulties on all aspects of life (e.g., self-care, housework, yard work, work, school, leisure, sleep, mood, cognition, relationships, community involvement, finances); (c) the ability of the patient to predict, cope with, and control health difficulties; (d) risk factors for physical illness, injury, or disability (e.g., weight, smoking, substance use); (e) difficulties with adherence to care recommendations; and (f) the psychosocial impact of medical care. To illustrate questions unique to a biopsychosocial interview, Highlight Box 14.4 contains some of the core questions that are asked when conducting a biopsychosocial interview.

Testing. Questionnaires are often used to add to the information gleaned from the interview and can address various areas, such as psychopathology, physical symptoms, disability, social support, and coping (for a more extensive review, see Belar & Deardorff, 1995). The nature of the questionnaires varies depending on the

HIGHLIGHT BOX 14.4

Sample Introduction

Sometimes people wonder why they have been asked to see a clinical health psychologist. My role today is to learn about the health difficulties you have been experiencing. What most health professionals have come to understand is that health difficulties can have a significant impact on our mood, relationships, and ability to function. Our mood, beliefs, attitudes, relationships, and daily activities can also have an impact on our health problems. Today, I am going to ask you lots of questions about your health, mood, relationships, and daily activities in an attempt to better understand your situation and assist in your care. Some of the questions I will ask may be similar to what other health professionals have asked you about, while other questions may be unique.

Sample Questions

- Can you tell me about the health difficulties you have been having?
- How long have you had these difficulties?
- What is your understanding of what has caused these problems? Of your diagnosis?
- Can you tell me how this problem has changed over time?
- Is the problem constant or sporadic?
- How severe is this problem in your own opinion?
- What impact does this problem have on your activities (self-care, housework, yardwork, work, recreational activities)?
- What impact does this problem have on your sleep (duration, quality, early waking, waking with pain, sleep hygiene)?
- What has been the impact of your health problems on your mood (sadness, anxiety, irritability, restlessness)? Has it ever been so bad that you feel you don't want to live

or you would consider harming yourself in any way?
- What impact has your health had on your concentration or attention?
- What has been the impact of your difficulties on your relationships? How have people in your life responded to your health condition (e.g., sympathy, support, withdrawal, hostility, anxiety)? Are you experiencing any difficulties in your relationships that you feel are impacting your current health condition?
- Do you belong to certain community, cultural, religious, or recreational groups? What kind of support do you receive from these groups? What has been the impact of your health on your activities with these groups?
- Are you currently working or going to school? How is your work or schooling been impacted by your health difficulties? How is your health impacted by your work or schooling? What future plans do you have related to work or school?
- Have you experienced any financial difficulties related to your health difficulties?
- Do you have any concerns with health coverage related to your health difficulties?
- What makes your health problem worse, in your opinion? What makes it better?
- How much control do you feel you have over your health problem?
- What do you do to attempt to manage this problem?
- What kind of medication are you taking?
- What kind of health professionals have you seen to assess these difficulties? What kind of diagnostic procedures have you undergone? Did you experience any difficulties with respect to these procedures (e.g., anxiety, side effects)?

HIGHLIGHT BOX 14.4 *(continued)*

- What kind of treatment have you received for your health difficulties? In your opinion, has there been a treatment that has not been helpful or made your condition worse?
- Have you had any problems with your health-care providers or health-care experiences that have concerned you (e.g., change in providers, errors in care, delays in care, clarity of information)?
- Have you had any difficulties following the medical advice that you have been given?

- Do you have any problems with weight (underweight, overweight)?
- Are you a smoker (e.g., age of onset, how much, frequency, attempts to quit)?
- What are your experiences with alcohol (e.g., age of onset, how much, frequency, impairment as a result, treatment)?
- Do you use any other substances (e.g., what, age of onset, how much, frequency, impairment as a result, treatment)?

---

patient group; there is no one battery of questionnaires that is used with all patients. Some clinical health psychologists use broadband measures, such as the Minnesota Multiphasic Personality Inventory-2 (MMPI-2, Butcher, Dahlstrom, Graham, Tellegen, & Kaemmer, 1989). This 567-item measure can be used to assess the impact of the health condition on emotional functioning but also has been used to examine emotional factors contributing to the development of health conditions, differentiate between functional and organic conditions, predict compliance with medical treatment, screen for organ transplants, or determine appropriateness for treatment (Arbisi & Butcher, 2004). Some strengths of the MMPI-2 for use with medical patients include its provision of an estimate of response bias in the assessment (e.g., openness, candor) and standardized objective measure of psychological adjustment, as well as degree of somatization (Arbisi & Butcher, 2004). Given the length of the measure and concerns about overpathologizing normal responses to medical illness, other clinicians use briefer measures such as the Brief Symptom Inventory (BSI, Derogatis, 1993),

which consists of 53 items to screen for psychopathology. The Hospital Anxiety and Depression Scale (HADS, Zigmond & Snaith, 1983) is also commonly used; this is a 14-item validated questionnaire (e.g., Bjelland, Dahl, Haug, & Neckelmann, 2002) with equally balanced subscales screening for anxiety and depression in general medical settings. The HADS avoids using certain physical items (e.g., weight loss, pain) to assess anxiety and depression since these symptoms may reflect physical problems. The Mini-Mental State Examination (MMSE, Folstein, Folstein, & McHugh, 1975) is a common method of screening for clients' cognitive functioning. It evaluates orientation, attention, recall, and language use. It requires less than 10 minutes to administer and provides a reliable and valid measure of cognitive functioning.

Other questionnaires used by clinical health psychologists are designed to help understand the health condition. As an example, the 36-item Short Form Health Survey (SF-36, Ware & Sherbourne, 1992) is a useful measure of patient functioning and quality of life that can be used with diverse medical conditions. Other common measures used with diverse medical patients include the Psychosocial Adjustment to Illness Scale (PAIS, Derogatis & Derogatis, 1990), which assesses adjustment to a chronic medical condition; the Millon Behavioral Health Inventory (MBHI, Millon, Green, & Meagher, 1982), which assesses basic coping styles as well as feelings and perceptions that may aggravate disease or increase susceptibility to disease; and the Social Readjustment Rating Scale (SRRS, Holmes & Rahe, 1967) or one of the many checklists that have been adapted from this original measure (Scully, Tosi, & Banning, 2000). The SRRS consists of 43 positive and negative events commonly reported as stressful (e.g., death of a spouse, marriage, retirement, vacation), with each event weighted for degree of stress. Review of research on the measure reveals strong relationships between exposure to stressful life events and psychological and physiological symptoms associated with stress (Scully et al., 2000).

Also of considerable value in the practice of clinical health psychology is the use of patient diaries (Belar & Deardorff, 1995). Diaries help the clinical health psychologist gain further information about a patient; variable information can be collected at different time periods using different methods (e.g., completion of forms versus open-ended report) depending on the patient. Diaries might be kept of symptoms (e.g., nature, frequency, duration, severity), behaviors (e.g., diet, exercise, activity), thoughts, or emotions. They are useful for learning about relationships among these variables as well as learning about antecedents to and consequences of physical symptoms.

In practice, some clinical health psychologists may also take psychophysiological measurements, such as heart rate, skin temperature, blood pressure, and respiratory activity. This information can be of potential value for understanding the medical condition and for monitoring psychological interventions over time (e.g., changes in blood pressure). To collect this information,

however, the psychologist must have the expertise and the equipment and also be aware of potential measurement problems (Belar & Deardorff, 1995).

Case formulation. The purpose of a thorough interview combined with test results and appropriate medical evaluation and consultation is to yield evidence for a case formulation, or shared understanding of the presenting condition that will guide treatment. Case formulation is regarded as the bridge between research and practice. Central to the case formulation is to describe the presenting problem (including diagnosing mental health disorders using the *Diagnostic and Statistical Manual* of the APA if appropriate) and use research to consider the cognitive, affective, behavioral, environmental, and sociocultural variables contributing to and maintaining the patient's concerns. The formulation enables the psychologist to specify treatment goals and associated interventions that have the potential to assist the patient. Specific treatment interventions will depend on both the condition being treated and the primary factors that influence it. The case formulation will also involve consideration of a patient's personal strengths and challenges that will facilitate treatment or alternatively pose a barrier to intervention.

One challenge in case formulation is to appropriately consider sociocultural issues in the conceptualization of problems. As discussed by Yali and Revension (2004), this requires extensive knowledge of how individual variables such as age, ethnicity, culture, religion, socioeconomic status, and sexual orientation affect not only vulnerability to illness but health beliefs and behaviors (e.g., perception of symptoms, help-seeking behaviors, relationships with health-care professionals). Sociocultural variables may also influence the interventions that will be acceptable to and also effective for patients (Nicassio, Meyerowitz, & Kerns, 2004). The clinical health psychologist needs to be aware of how these sociocultural variables may come into play in the patient's problems and take these into consideration when specifying treatment goals and interventions. This is consistent with culturally competent practice—the ability to understand and respect how cultural differences affect beliefs, interpersonal relationships, and behavior and to use this knowledge effectively in assessment, diagnosis, and treatment (Whaley & Davis, 2007). It is also consistent with the guidelines APA has developed for providers of psychological services to culturally diverse populations (APA, 2003).

DEPRESSION

Not surprisingly, many patients with chronic health conditions experience high rates of depression. In a recent study by Egede (2007), the 12-month prevalence of major depression was calculated for adults with various chronic conditions. Approximately 9% of patients with diabetes mellitus and coronary artery disease were depressed; rates were higher in other conditions, with depression found in 11% of patients with a history of stroke, 15% of patients with chronic obstructive pulmonary disease, and 17% of patients with end-stage renal disease. In this study, major depression was also found to be associated with significant increases in health-care utilization, lost productivity, and functional disability.

Katon, Lin, and Kroenke (2007) recently completed a systematic review of the effect of anxiety and depressive comorbidity in patients with chronic medical illnesses. They examined 31 studies involving 16,922 patients. Patients with chronic medical illness and comorbid depression or anxiety were compared to those with chronic medical illness alone. They found significantly higher numbers of medical symptoms among patients with comorbid depression, even when controlling for severity of medical disorder. Two treatment studies they reviewed also showed that improvement in

depression was associated with decreased somatic symptoms. They concluded that accurate diagnosis of comorbid depressive and anxiety disorders in patients with chronic medical illness is essential to optimizing the management of disease.

Various factors have been linked to depression in medical patients. Low levels of optimism and perceived control, changes in self-image, perceived threat to life goals, disease-related fears, avoidant coping, and lack of social support have all been associated with poor adjustment to chronic disease (Friedman & Silver, 2007; Mohr et al., 1999). Clinical health psychologists use many of the same strategies for managing depression in medical patients as are used with depressed nonmedical patients, with a predominant focus on cognitive-behavioral treatment strategies. Common practices used by clinical health psychologists include altering dysfunctional cognitions related to depression and developing adaptive behavioral coping strategies.

A recent systematic review of meta-analyses on cognitive-behavioral interventions (Butler, Chapman, Forman, & Beck, 2006) showed that this treatment is highly effective for depression and that effects are maintained for substantial periods (e.g., 12 months), with relapse rates half those of pharmacotherapy (DeRubeis & Crits-Christoph, 1998). Similarly, cognitive-behavioral therapy also has been found to be efficacious when applied to various medical conditions, such as cancer (Antoni et al., 2001), multiple sclerosis (Mohr, Boudewyn, Goodkin, Bostrom, & Epstein, 2001), and chronic pain (Turner, Mancl, & Aaron, 2006).

HEALTH BEHAVIORS

Clinical health psychologists are increasingly involved in assisting individuals in altering health habits, engaging in behaviors that promote health, and discontinuing behaviors that increase risk of illness. Health habits are difficult to change in that they are firmly established and often automatic in nature. They can also vary considerably depending on patient background. Gottlieb and Green (1984), for instance, found that health behaviors are significantly better among younger, more affluent, better educated people under low levels of stress and with higher levels of social support. It is evident that clinical health psychologists have an important contribution to make in this area, as knowledge alone about health-promoting behaviors (e.g., weight loss, exercising) and health-risk behaviors (e.g., smoking, abusing alcohol or drugs) does not necessarily motivate individuals to change their behaviors.

There are a number of conceptualizations of health behavior that guide the work of the clinical health psychologist. The health belief model, for instance, suggests that decisions about health behavior are based on four interacting factors, including perceptions of susceptibility to a health problem, perceived severity of a health threat, perceived benefits and barriers to particular health behaviors, and environmental influences encouraging the health behavior (Rosenstock, 1974). Another influential conceptualization is the theory of planned behavior (Ajzen, 1985). This theory suggests that the best way to predict whether a health behavior will occur is to measure a person's behavioral intention. It suggests that behavioral intentions are influenced by (a) attitudes toward the behavior, (b) perceptions of whether other people are performing the behavior in question, and (c) perceived behavioral control or expectation of success in controlling the behavior. Also relevant to the work of clinical health psychologists assisting individuals with health behavior changes is the transtheoretical model (Prochaska, DiClemente, & Norcross, 1992). The model contends that people progress through five stages in altering health-related behaviors, including precontemplation, contemplation, preparation, action, and maintenance. This model recognizes that people move back and forth through the stages in a nonlinear fashion. It is useful to clinical health psychologists in that it helps them consider the stage of change the individual is at (e.g., precontemplation, contemplation, action, maintenance) and tailor interventions to the identified stage (e.g., consciousness raising for those in the contemplation stage, substituting alternative behaviors for the negative health behavior for those in the action stage, reinforcement for those in the maintenance stage).

Common to the foregoing conceptualizations is the idea that beliefs influence behavior; therefore, clinical health psychologist work with patients to identify and challenge beliefs that may be a barrier to engaging in health-promoting behaviors. Behavioral strategies are also common and diverse in nature and can include (a) self-monitoring of the behavior of interest to assess the frequency of the behavior and antecedents and consequences of the behavior, (b) stimulus control procedures (e.g., controlling the environment), (c) self-control procedures (e.g., controlling how the person engages in the problematic health behavior), (d) contingency contracting (e.g., setting reasonable goals and reinforcing behavior when goals are met), (e) modeling of behavior, (f) relaxation training, and (g) use of aversive techniques (e.g., making alcohol aversive through pairing with Antabuse, a drug that produces nausea and vomiting). At other times, clinical health psychologists focus on cognitive-behavioral strategies for managing mood (such as depression described earlier), as negative emotions are often linked to poor health behaviors (e.g., Brandon, Copeland, & Saper, 1995). Clinical health psychologists often work collaboratively with other health-care providers. In the case of smoking, for instance, clinical health psychologists may work with physicians who prescribe nicotine replacement therapies. In the case of weight loss, clinical health psychologists frequently work alongside a nutritionist and or exercise therapist.

Among the most common health behaviors that clinical health psychologists treat is obesity. As noted by Wadden, Brownell, and Foster (2002), obesity has reached epidemic proportions, with as many as 27% of adults being obese and an additional 34% being overweight. Furthermore, they note that although research has shown that genetics predispose some individuals to obesity, much of the problem is attributable to environments that discourage physical activity while encouraging poor dietary habits (e.g., the consumption of high-fat, high-sugar foods). They propose that the management of obesity requires a two-pronged approach. Cognitive-behavioral, pharmacologic, and surgical interventions are needed for individuals who are already obese. Public policy initiatives, however, are needed to prevent the development of obesity. In practice, clinical health psychologists most commonly use a cognitive-behavioral approach in the treatment of obesity, including self-monitoring, exercising control over eating, increasing activity, adding exercise, controlling self-talk, addressing self-image, problem-solving, and having social support (e.g., Cooper, Fairburn, & Hawker, 2003). Although variability exists in how treatment is delivered, this type of treatment is very effective for adults in both the short term and longer term (Brownell & Wadden, 1992). This approach also appears to be effective with children. Wilfley and colleagues (2007), for instance, recently performed a meta-analysis to evaluate the efficacy of weight loss treatments specifically for children. The meta-analysis focused on 14 randomized controlled trials comparing pediatric lifestyle interventions to no treatment or information/education-only controls. The authors concluded that lifestyle interventions for pediatric patients who are overweight are efficacious in the short term, with some evidence of long-term outcomes. Further research, however, is still needed on the ideal length and intensity of treatment and also on how to best address the broader social context contributing to childhood obesity (Saelens & Liu, 2007).

MEDICAL ADHERENCE

The management of many health conditions involves complex, intrusive, and unpleasant treatment plans. Adherence to these treatment plans has a significant impact on patient health; thus, development of interventions to aid with adherence has been a subject of considerable study. The care that clinical health psychologists provide to patients with diabetes serves as a good example. Diabetes is a chronic condition that individuals must manage throughout their lives. The management varies depending on the severity of the condition but most often involves monitoring blood glucose levels and food intake (e.g., following a meal plan) and, in many cases, also involves insulin administration (orally or by injections). Noncompliance with insulin administration and dietary recommendations has been reported to occur in the vast majority of patients (Kurtz, 1990). Aikens and Wagner (1998) further estimate that 13% of patients with diabetes who are referred to psychologists are referred for failure to adhere to their diabetes management regimen. Interventions with patients follow from assessment and case formulation but commonly involve identifying and modifying dysfunctional health beliefs that may contribute to nonadherence, enhancing motivation to adhere to treatment recommendations, problem-solving to overcome barriers to compliance, and fostering social support to assist with compliance. These types of interventions are reported to have considerable success (e.g., Aikens & Wagner, 1998).

Motivational interviewing (MI), a patient-centered method that seeks to improve an individual's motivation to change problematic behaviors and promote treatment adherence in medical settings, has been the subject of recent research (Knight, McGowan, Dickens, & Bundy, 2006). Knight and colleagues systematically reviewed the effectiveness of MI interventions in medical settings. Although they found many limitations with quality of the research (e.g., small sample sizes, inadequate validation of questionnaires, poorly defined therapy), they reported that the majority of studies with diverse patient conditions (e.g., diabetes, asthma, hypertension, heart disease) found positive results for effects of MI on adherence.

STRESS

There are very few patients with health problems who cannot benefit from stress management. This is, in our opinion, a topic that is appropriate to address with all patients, including those with and without significant health problems. Research and scholarly work on stress date back to at least the 1930s when Walter Cannon introduced the term *stress*, noting that a number of variables, such as lack of oxygen and emotional experiences, resulted in physiological changes in the body (Straub, 2007). In his research, he also identified the body's "fight or flight" reaction to stressful events. Following this research, Hans Selye also studied the stress response and noted its topographical similarity across diverse stressors along with its potentially negative health consequences in cases of chronic stress response (Straub, 2007).

Stress has been defined in two different ways. At times, it is defined as an event. Examples include major life events (death, marriage, retirement), daily hassles (e.g., traffic, line-ups), environmental conditions (e.g., noise, crowding, pollution), and job-related circumstances (e.g., overload, role conflict, role ambiguity, lack of control) (Straub, 2007). Stress is also defined as a negative emotional response to events such as those just described. This response involves biochemical, physiological, cognitive, and behavioral changes directed toward altering the event or accommodating its effects (Baum, 1999). As such, stress can be defined as a response that occurs when "environmental demands tax or exceed the adaptive capacity of an organism, resulting in psychological and biological changes that may place a person at risk for disease" (Cohen, Kessler, & Gordon, 1995, p. 3).

Core to the study of stress is knowledge that what is stressful is largely based on perception, such that events appraised as negative, uncontrollable, unpredictable, or ambiguous are typically experienced as stressful. In this case, a distinction is made between primary and secondary appraisal. In primary appraisal, the individual assesses whether an event is benign, irrelevant, or a potential threat or challenge; in secondary appraisal, the individual assesses the coping resources available for meeting the challenge (Taylor, 1990). Given the fast-paced lives that many of us lead, juggling work and educational responsibilities with leisure and family pursuits, it is often the case that our coping resources are challenged and that we find ourselves feeling "stressed out."

The stress response has both indirect and direct effects on health (Baum, 1999). Stress has indirect effects on health in that it often results in an increase in unhealthy behaviors and a decrease in healthy behaviors. Directly, stress results in physiological changes that, when persistent or chronic, increase vulnerability to many disorders, including cancer, heart disease, diabetes, arthritis, headaches, asthma, digestive disorders, and anxiety and depression. The body's response to stress, for instance, involves the brain and nervous system, the endocrine glands and hormones, and the immune system (Straub, 2007). Kiecolt-Glaser and colleagues (Kiecolt-Glaser, McGuire, Robles, & Glaser, 2002) have found that, when exposed to stress, individuals experience declines in certain indicators of immune activity. One hypothesis is that immunosuppression is part of the body's natural response to stressors. Another hypothesis, however, is that it is an aftereffect of the stress response. Regardless of the reason, the stress response exacerbates many diseases whose central feature is excessive inflammation, such as autoimmune, rheumatologic, and cardiovascular diseases.

Also relevant to the area of stress is the concept of coping. *Coping* has been defined as cognitive and/or behavioral attempts to manage events, either internal or external, that are appraised by the individual as overwhelming (Lazarus & Folkman, 1987). Clinical health psychologists often differentiate between coping strategies that are problem-focused, meaning they are designed to solve a problem, and emotion-focused, meaning they are designed to help the individual tolerate the problem (Lazarus & Folkman, 1987). There is also strong evidence for psychological and physical benefits of social support. Individuals with social support have greater adherence to medical regimens (DiMatteo, 2004) and adjust better to stressful events, recover from illness faster, and have reduced risk of mortality from diseases (Uchino, Cacioppo, & Kiecolt-Glaser, 1996); in short, they generally cope better.

To address stress, clinical health psychologists often (a) provide psychoeducation on stress (e.g., much like the information presented in the preceding paragraphs); (b) assist in the reduction or elimination of dysfunctional coping strategies, such as smoking, drinking, and gambling; (c) promote healthy coping strategies to regulate emotional and physiological states, such as relaxation, time management, problem solving, social support, and optimism; and (d) use cognitive-behavioral therapy to assist patients in how they interpret events and their ability to manage and respond to the event (e.g., perceptions of control and self-efficacy) (Carroll, 1992). These strategies have been shown to be effective for a diverse range of conditions and in a variety of settings (e.g., Conrad & Roth, 2007; Kraag, Zeegers, Kok, Hosman, & Abu-Saad, 2006; Richardson & Rothstein, 2008).

PAIN MANAGEMENT

Our own clinical work also often involves the use of cognitive-behavioral treatment for the management of pain. Contemporary models of pain recognize that it is a complex perceptual experience that is determined by sensory as well as psychological (e.g., thinking, emotions, behaviors) and social influences (Asmundson & Wright, 2004). Although once used only as a last resort, cognitive-behavioral treatment for pain management is now common, especially for conditions such as low back pain, headaches, and arthritis.

Cognitive-behavioral interventions (e.g., Thorn, 2004) are most commonly used in collaboration with a multidisciplinary team, especially involving attention to medication management (e.g., elimination of medication or substitution of non-opioid for opioid analgesics) and exercise and occupational therapy to work on reconditioning and patient fears about certain movements.

Hadjistavropoulos and Williams (2004) describe the core components of cognitive-behavioral intervention for pain as follows:

a. Education on the nature of acute versus chronic pain, the role of psychological and social factors in the pain experience, and the rationale for pain management.
b. Identification of short- and long-term goals and how to achieve these goals.
c. Skills acquisition and rehearsal of behavioral strategies such as relaxation and activity pacing.
d. Contingency management, such as having patients and significant others self-reinforce desired behaviors.
e. Cognitive therapy involving various attention diversion methods (see Fernandez & Turk, 1989), problem-solving strategies, and cognitive restructuring (e.g., identification and challenging of catastrophizing cognitions).
f. Generalization and maintenance in which patients anticipate and plan for setbacks.

In practice, there is wide variability in the delivery of the foregoing components. For example, treatment can be provided in groups or individually. Groups have the advantage that they allow patients to share experiences and result in decreased isolation. Treatment also can be on an outpatient basis, which provides opportunities for generalizability of the techniques to the usual environment, or on an inpatient basis, which allows for intensive treatment for those with more severe disability.

In a recent meta-analysis of randomized controlled trials examining psychological interventions for chronic low back pain, Hoffman, Papas, Chatkoff, and Kerns (2007) found positive effects of psychological interventions for pain intensity, pain-related interference, health-related quality of life, and depression. Cognitive-behavioral treatment was specifically found to be efficacious. Multidisciplinary approaches that included a psychological component were also noted to have positive short-term effects on pain interference and positive long-term effects on return to work.

Another recent meta-analysis was conducted by Dixon, Keefe, Scipio, Perri, and Abernethy (2007), who examined efficacy of psychosocial interventions for arthritis pain and disability. They focused on 27 randomized controlled trials. Psychosocial interventions resulted in significantly lower pain, disability, and psychological distress than did standard medical care. Pisetsky (2007) provided a commentary on the findings, discussing differences that may be needed in treatment, depending on whether the patient presents with rheumatoid arthritis (RA) versus osteoarthritis (OA). RA is a systemic disease, whereas OA is primarily a degenerative process. Although both involve pain, there are many differences between the two conditions that may result in variation in whether psychosocial interventions are used. As an example, the medication available to RA patients is much more extensive than that for OA, which may result in greater likelihood of psychosocial interventions used with OA than RA, even though data support the efficacy of psychosocial interventions in both.

HEALTH ANXIETY

Our inclusion of health anxiety in this chapter reflects the fact that it is one of our primary areas of clinical and research interest; nevertheless, understanding health anxiety is an extremely important topic for clinical health psychologists. *Health anxiety* is a dimensional construct that is characterized by lack of concern about one's health at one end of the continuum and excessive anxiety about health on the other (Asmundson, Taylor, & Cox, 2001). It is most commonly associated with hypochondriasis but is also found in other clinical conditions and among individuals with varying medical conditions. Although health anxiety is often equated with hypochondriasis, to meet the diagnostic criteria for hypochondriasis individuals also need to demonstrate an excessive preoccupation with fears of having a serious disease despite lack of medical evidence (following appropriate medical evaluation) and reassurance (APA, 2000).

The cognitive-behavioral model of health anxiety is predominant in the literature (Salkovskis & Warwick, 1986). Although other models have been proposed (e.g., psychodynamic), it is the cognitive model that has received the brunt of empirical support (Asmundson et al., 2001; Taylor & Asmundson, 2004). The model holds that dysfunctional beliefs derived from past experience lead to the experience of health anxiety, which itself is a function of beliefs about severity of illness, vulnerability to illness, ability to cope with illness, and adequacy of resources for dealing with illness. These beliefs oftentimes vary as a function of culture (for more detailed discussion, see Taylor & Asmundson, 2004). People with excessive health anxiety are overly attentive to information related to illness and biased in their interpretation of illness-related information in a catastrophic and personally threatening manner. To cope with excessive health anxiety, people sometimes make efforts to avoid illness or, if not possible, persistently seek out reassurance of good health via symptom checking or medical attention. Avoidance and excessive reassurance exacerbate health anxiety in the long run (Warwick & Salkovskis, 1990) and, unfortunately, lead to other maladaptive behaviors. More specifically, people with excessive health anxiety are more likely to misinterpret bodily sensations as painful, to use palliative coping, to take medications, to miss work, and to have significantly increased health care utilization (Hadjistavropoulos & Hadjistavropoulos, 2003).

Given the evidence, in our clinical practice we attend to health anxiety on a routine basis, whether working with patients who have a known chronic condition or those who do not. Taylor and Asmundson (2004) provide a number of interview questions and detail self-report measures that are helpful in understanding the extent to which health anxiety may be having negative effects on a person's life. As a quick screen, the 14-item dichotomous (yes/no) response version of the Whiteley Index (Pilowsky, 1967) can be used; scores equal to or greater than 8 are indicative of excessive health anxiety.

There are a number of options for addressing health anxiety. First, it is possible that education regarding health anxiety may be helpful; this is a good place to start and may resolve health anxiety. For those who are open to psychological intervention (this itself may require intervention, such as application of MI techniques), cognitive-behavioral treatments have been developed and supported by research evidence (Taylor & Asmundson, 2004; Taylor, Asmundson, & Coons, 2005). Such approaches involve (a) education on the worry about illness and its cognitive, behavioral, physiological, and affective components; (b) encouraging patients to develop coping thoughts and challenge maladaptive negative thoughts about illness (e.g., an inability to cope with the worst-case scenario); (c) reduction of checking and reassurance seeking; (d) exposure to illness worries through narratives related to their anxious thoughts about illness; (e) addressing avoidance of illness-related worries; (f) establishment of personal goals; and often (g) behavioral stress management as described earlier. Clinical health psychologists, however, should be aware that Enns, Kjernisted, and Lander (2001) have reviewed a variety of pharmacological alternatives that have been used in the treatment of extreme health anxiety and concluded that pharmacological approaches (e.g., involving serotonergic medications) can also be helpful.

Another way that clinical health psychologists can be helpful in the treatment of health anxiety is by working with medical providers. Clinical health psychologists can help other health-care professionals understand that patients with excessive health anxiety have a tendency to repeatedly seek the same information. In these cases, it is helpful to work with providers to determine what constitutes necessary information and to minimize provision of unnecessary and harmful reassurance. Warwick (1992) recommends that providers work on (a) listening so that the patient feels understood, (b) answering specific questions about fears, (c) using simple terminology and clear explanations, and (d) providing consistent statements. If willing, clinical health psychologists can review medical feedback that is provided to patients, identifying areas where the health-care communication could be improved.

CLINICAL PRACTICE CHALLENGES

The preceding review may give the impression that the work of a clinical health psychologist is relatively straightforward and without challenges. This can certainly be the case, but quite often there are clear challenges to working as a clinical health psychologist. First and foremost, to effectively work with patients, clinical health psychologists must have a comprehensive understanding of the medical condition(s) that the patient is faced with. Lack of understanding of a medical condition limits one's ability to assist and can be a substantial barrier to building of a therapeutic relationship with a patient. Second, more often than not, before providing assessment and treatment, considerable education must be provided to patients on the role of psychology in medical conditions and how psychologists can be of assistance. Because patients are often focused on physical symptoms, discussing emotional or social difficulties can be difficult for some patients. Patients are actually not the only ones who are in need of this education; many healthcare providers also require education about the role of psychology in the treatment of medical conditions. Third, the clinical health psychologist must determine limits to confidentiality within a team environment. It is often assumed who psychological information on patients should be shared completely among providers; however, this needs to be negotiated with the patient. Fourth, in some health-care environments, there is also a hierarchy in terms of who is ultimately responsible for the care of the patient. Ultimate responsibility at times rests with the physician (e.g., determining admission, discharge, treatment), and differences in opinion on how to work with patients can emerge. Fifth, a challenge faced in clinical practice pertains to written reports; reports need to be succinct and jargon free, which can be contrary to other reports that psychologists are accustomed to providing in other treatment settings. Finally, treatment of patients in the hospital can also present challenges in terms of the physical environment where care is provided. In contrast to an office setting, patients sometimes need to be seen in hospital rooms, where they may be clothed in hospital attire, where there may be a lack of privacy, and where interruptions by staff and visitors are frequent.

FUTURE DIRECTIONS IN CLINICAL HEALTH PSYCHOLOGY

There are many exciting opportunities for the aspiring clinical health psychologist to conquer. Some of these opportunities are outlined below and are drawn from a 2004 volume of *Health Psychology* (volume 23, no. 2), which was devoted to the future of health psychology. The eager student is encouraged to review this special issue.

Evaluation of the biopsychosocial model and the need for transdisciplinary research. As described earlier, the biopsychosocial model is the cornerstone of health psychology. Health psychologists have contributed to an improved understanding of this model, collecting considerable evidence to support relationships among biological, psychological, and social processes. Suls and Rothman (2004) emphasize, however, that our understanding of this model is far from complete, and there is significant room for improvement in the extent to which the medical community embraces psychosocial issues in practice and also in the extent to which health psychologists adequately consider nonpsychosocial variables in their research and practice. They emphasize that the biopsychosocial model is a "work in progress." There is a need for more sophisticated studies that allow for multilevel, multisystem, and multivariate study of health. Transdisciplinary collaboration is of utmost importance, and educational and funding institutions need to take an active role in facilitating collaboration.

Changing demographics. As noted by Smith, Orleans, and Jenkins (2004), the population is rapidly becoming ethnically diverse and older;

as such, we need to develop conceptual models, research methods, and applications that are sensitive to these groups. For example, as the population lives longer, addressing preventable risk factors for disease is even more important to ensure that longer lives are also quality lives. Furthermore, as the population increases in cultural diversity, the ability to understand this diversity and be culturally competent in providing services is also of utmost importance (Yali & Revenson, 2004).

Knowledge translation. With increased evidence supporting psychosocial interventions to improve health behaviors and manage chronic disease, we have seen an increased role for health psychology in health care. That said, there remain significant limits to the extent to which these interventions are used in routine clinical practice (Nicassio et al., 2004). This means that there is a need to focus on ensuring research is appropriately disseminated and effectively translated into practice.

Cost-effectiveness and public relations. A further direction for clinical health psychologists will be to continue to demonstrate the cost-effectiveness of clinical health psychology. While past research has demonstrated the value of clinical health psychology, we have paid less attention to research on cost-effectiveness. Furthermore, research that has been carried out in this area (e.g., Kaplan & Groessel, 2002) has not necessarily had the impact that clinical health psychologists would hope (e.g., increased public access to clinical health psychologists). In this regard, considerably more effort needs to be turned to public relations through marketing of clinical health psychology and addressing institutional barriers to bringing clinical health psychology to the public (e.g., insurance coverage).

Incorporating new technologies. There are enormous opportunities in clinical health psychology to better use technology to advance the field. We still have much to learn about the use of online treatment programs, self-help chat rooms, computerized assessment, computer-based adherence strategies (e.g., email), and interactive computer programs. Saab et al. (2004) also discuss the importance of keeping up with rapid advances in technologies (e.g., using information technology to monitor patient progress) and studying the psychosocial impact of new health technologies (e.g., genetic testing, organ and tissue transplants) on patients.

Attention to worldwide health disparities. The application of clinical health psychology in nonindustrialized parts of the world is also developing. As summarized by Lyons and Chamberlain (2006), it is estimated that about 90% of the global burden of disease is carried by the developing world, which has access to only 10% of the world's resources for health. To illustrate, although life expectancy has increased worldwide (from 56 to 63 years), over the past 30 years life expectancy has declined in 18 countries in Africa. We can only hope that one day clinical health psychology will be able to make a greater contribution in nonindustrialized parts of the world, helping to reduce health discrepancies and increase the span of healthy life for all.

TRAINING TO BE A CLINICAL HEALTH PSYCHOLOGIST

Assuming we have piqued your interest in clinical health psychology, you may be wondering how to obtain training in this area. There are initiatives in progress that we suspect will result in greater standardization of training in the future. (In March 2007, the Board of Directors of APA Division 38 held a summit to examine the standards of graduate curriculum and training in clinical health psychology. The summit resulted in the APA Division 38—Tempe Summit Report, which is posted on the APA Web site.) At present, however, there is wide variability in the training that clinical health psychologists obtain. Clinical health psychologists typically obtain a doctoral degree (PhD or PsyD) in clinical or counseling psychology. As part of their degree, they then take coursework, conduct research, and/or obtain clinical training in health psychology. Following completion of primary training, psychologists then declare competency to practice in this area if they (a) are registered or licensed for independent practice of clinical or counseling psychology, (b) have some background in clinical health psychology, and (c) work with individuals on issues related to health and illness.

For students who have a strong interest in obtaining formal training in clinical health psychology, Division 38 of the APA has a directory on their Web site (http://www.health-psych.org/) of doctoral programs that offer at least some coursework and research experiences in health psychology. It is worth noting, however, that this information is voluntarily provided by educational institutions, and as such, there are likely more institutions offering training than are listed on the Web site. Increasingly, there are programs that are standardizing their training in clinical health psychology. In Highlight Box 14.5, we describe two programs, one in Canada and one in the United States, that illustrate how this is accomplished.

By far the greatest training in clinical health psychology comes from the predoctoral internship. The purpose of a predoctoral internship program is to offer training to senior PhD-level clinical psychology students, most often through a full-year, full-time program. Through supervised experience with a variety of patient populations and presenting problems, the fundamental goal is to transition the student toward independent practice as a professional psychologist. For a list of predoctoral internships with major or minor rotations

---

HIGHLIGHT BOX 14.5

Health Psychology Doctoral Diploma Program, Department of Psychology, York University, Toronto, Ontario, Canada

Web site: http://www.yorku.ca/health/psyc/research/health/

The Clinical Program at York University follows the scientist-practitioner model, emphasizing the development of research skills and clinical skills through a combination of coursework, research, and clinical experiences. Clinical experiences are obtained through a department-run psychology clinic or in the community.

This PhD-level graduate diploma program is intended to promote competency in health psychology and to be complementary to the student's program in psychology. The requirements of the Health Psychology Diploma Program for clinical psychology students include:

1. Completion of a PhD dissertation focused on health psychology. Health psychology research at York University covers a broad range of topics, such as cancer care, cardiovascular disease, diabetes, eating disorders, HIV/AIDS, pain, stress, and coping.

HIGHLIGHT BOX 14.5 *(continued)*

2. Two major health psychology research projects outside of the PhD dissertation.
3. Coursework
   a. At least two graduate-level health psychology half courses or one full-year course;
   b. At least one biomedical half course relevant to the student's research.
4. Health Psychology Colloquium—consistently attended for two years.
5. Pre-doctoral Internship must involve significant clinical training in health psychology.

Department of Clinical and Health Psychology, College of Public Health and Health Professions, University of Florida, Gainesville, Florida

Web site: http://chp.phhp.ufl.edu/programs/doctoral/index.html#requirements

The Clinical Psychology Program at the University of Florida also follows the scientist-practitioner model and involves a combination of coursework, research experiences, and clinical experiences obtained both in the community and in the Department of Clinical and Health Psychology Clinic.

In addition to general clinical psychology training, students develop an area of concentration as part of their program of studies. Clinical health psychology is one of the areas of concentration.

The goal of concentrated study in clinical health psychology is to provide the student with an understanding of the relationships among psychosocial factors, physical illness, and health. Concentration typically involves:

1. Conducting research in the area of clinical health psychology. Current areas of research in the department include chronic pain, smoking cessation, treatment of obesity, psychosocial oncology, and psychological evaluations for organ transplantation and donation (e.g., heart, liver, bone marrow).
2. Enrolling in a two-semester core seminar in health psychology/medical psychology and selecting from other appropriate courses in clinical health psychology.
3. Attending a series of conferences, rounds, seminars, workshops, and colloquia related to clinical health psychology.
4. Completing an advanced clinical placement with inpatient and outpatient medical populations resulting in training in inpatient consultation/liaison and outpatient assessment and treatment. There is incredible access to diverse patient populations in the associated health-care facilities and community, as well as extensive opportunities to collaborate with other health professionals.

in health psychology, students can examine the Association of Psychology Postdoctoral and Internship Centers (APPIC) Web site (http://www.appic.org/directory/search_dol_internships.asp). Based on our search of this Web site, there are more than 100 internships in the United States and Canada with a major rotation

in health psychology. In Highlight Box 14.6, we provide an overview of two predoctoral internships that stand out as offering major training in clinical health psychology.

As evidence of the increased attention given to clinical health psychology, we also note that it is now possible to obtain board certification

HIGHLIGHT BOX 14.6

Psychology Department, Queen Elizabeth II Health Sciences Centre (QEII), Halifax, Nova Scotia, Canada

Web site: http://www.cdha.nshealth.ca/default.aspx?page=DocumentRender&doc.Id=1578

The QEII provides primary-level health-care services to the nearly 400,000 residents in the region. It is also a regional medical center providing a number of specialized tertiary care services to residents throughout Nova Scotia and the Atlantic Provinces, with approximately 1,000 beds and a broad range of ambulatory care programs. The QEII is the main teaching facility for Dalhousie University.

The Department of Psychology provides a wide range of psychological services to medicine, physical medicine and rehabilitation, mental health, and geriatric services, including inpatient, day patient, outpatient, and consultation services. Specific psychological services have been developed for cardiology and cardiac rehabilitation, geriatrics (inpatient, outpatient, and day hospital programs), HIV, medical rehabilitation (inpatient and outpatient programs), organ transplantation, otolaryngology, pain management, mental health, neuropsychology, stroke, surgical epilepsy, traumatic brain injury, and sleep medicine.

In 2008–2009 the QEII will offer three full-time, funded predoctoral internship positions.

Veterans Affairs Palo Alto Health Care System (VAPAHCS)

Web site: http://www.palo-alto.med.va.gov/MentalHealth/PsychologyTraining.asp.

The VAPAHCS is part of a national network of facilities operated by the Department of Veterans Affairs to provide comprehensive health care to individuals who have served in the armed forces. The VAPAHCS is a combined neuropsychiatric, general medical, and surgical facility, with three inpatient facilities at Palo Alto, Menlo Park, and Livermore and six outpatient clinics in San Jose, Capitola, Monterey, Stockton, Modesto, and Sonora. Comprehensive health care is provided in areas of medicine, surgery, psychiatry, rehabilitation, neurology, oncology, dentistry, geriatrics, and extended care. The health-care facilities operate 897 inpatient beds, including three nursing homes and a 100-bed homeless domiciliary, and more than 50 primary care and specialty outpatient clinics. In addition to basic medical and mental health care programs, this VA has a variety of specialized regional programs, including a Polytrauma Rehabilitation Center; a Spinal Cord Injury Center; a Comprehensive Rehabilitation Center; the Western Region Blind Rehabilitation Center; the National Center for PTSD; a Women's Trauma Recovery program; a Homeless Veterans Rehabilitation program; a Geriatric Research, Educational, and Clinical Center; and a Mental Illness Research, Education, and Clinical Center. The VAPAHCS is affiliated with the Stanford University School of Medicine.

There are opportunities for training in psychological and neuropsychological assessment and for training in interventions with adults and families in geriatric settings, medically based settings including primary care as well as inpatient and outpatient mental health settings, and substance abuse settings.

For 2008–2009, VAPAHCS will offer 14 funded internship placements. At least 4 of the 14 positions emphasize clinical health psychology /behavioral medicine experience.

in clinical health psychology through the American Board of Professional Psychology (see http://www.abpp.org/certification/abpp_certification_clinical_health.htm). This board serves the public by overseeing the certification of psychologists competent to deliver high-quality services in various specialty areas of psychology, including clinical health psychology. To obtain certification in clinical health psychology, the psychologist must be licensed for independent practice, have 2 years of supervised practice in the area, submit work samples, and undergo a lengthy exam relevant to the area. The board contends that the best way for a psychologist to represent himself or herself as a specialist is to obtain this certification. In the United States, clinical health psychologists are increasingly taking this step.

SUMMARY

We opened this chapter with a number of brief vignettes describing a variety of people with various concerns and conditions that may be well served by intervention by a clinical health psychologist. Our attention then turned to defining the area, highlighting select areas of practice, and summarizing future challenges. Turning your attention back to Mac, Brenda, Larry, and the others, you should now have a general understanding of how the clinical health psychologist might help these individuals. We hope that we have provided you with a basic understanding of the steps that one must take to become a clinical health psychologist—and, more important, we hope that you take up the challenge!

THOUGHT QUESTIONS

1. What are the primary roles of a clinical health psychologist?
2. How does clinical health psychology differ from behavioral medicine? How does it differ from psychosomatic medicine?
3. The biopsychosocial model is of particular relevance to clinical health psychologists. What are the key elements of the model? How does culture factor into the model?
4. The authors suggest that an adequate medical evaluation and/or consultation needs to be considered in case formulation. Why do you think this is an important consideration? How do you think "adequacy" is established by the clinical health psychologist?
5. Clinical health psychologists can deal with a variety of presenting problems, whether in research or practice, for which a significant component includes general medical conditions. To what degree do clinical health psychologists need to be knowledgeable of body systems, disease, disease-related processes, and biomedical interventions?
6. Should clinical health psychology be a routine service that patients seek out on an annual basis in much the same way as they routinely see physicians and dentists?

Glossary

Behavioral medicine: a term used to refer to an interdisciplinary field with diverse health professionals who typically integrate behavioral principles and medical sciences.

Biopsychosocial model: a model that views both health and illness as a function of biological (e.g., genetic predisposition), psychological (e.g., beliefs, emotions, behaviors), and social (e.g., social support, relationships) variables that interact and ultimately determine where an individual falls on the health continuum, with illness at one end and health and wellness at the other end.

Coping: cognitive and/or behavioral attempts to deal with events, either internal or external, that are appraised by the individual as overwhelming.

Health anxiety: a dimensional construct that is characterized by lack of concern about one's health at one end of the continuum and excessive anxiety about one's health on the other.

Health psychology: a subdiscipline of psychology devoted to the promotion and maintenance of health; the prevention and treatment of illness; the identification of etiologic and diagnostic correlates of health, illness, and related dysfunction; and the improvement of the health-care system and health policy formation.

Pain: a complex perceptual experience that is determined by sensory as well as psychological (e.g., thinking, emotions, behaviors) and social influences.

Psychosomatic medicine: an interdisciplinary study of illness behavior that may be caused by psychological factors and psychosocial factors involved in illness.

Stress: either an event that is stressful (e.g., death of loved one) or an emotional response that occurs when environmental demands tax or exceed the adaptive capacity of an organism, resulting in psychological and biological changes that may place a person at risk for disease.

References

Aikens, J. E. & Wagner, L. I. (1998). Diabetes mellitus and other endocrine disorders. In P. Camic & S. Knight (Eds.), *Clinical handbook of health psychology* (pp. 191–225). Seattle, WA: Hogrefe & Huber.

Ajzen, I. (1985). From intensions to actions: a theory of planned behavior. In J. Kuhl & J. Beckman (Eds.), *Action-control: From cognition to behavior* (pp. 11–39). Heidelberg, Germany: Springer.

American Psychiatric Association (2000). *Diagnostic and statistical manual of mental disorders* (4th ed., Text Revision). Washington, DC: Author.

American Psychological Association (2003). *Guidelines for providers of psychological services to ethnic, linguistic, and culturally diverse populations.* Retrieved March 24, 2008 from http://www.apa.org/pi/oema/guide.html

Antoni, M. H., Lehman, J. M., Kilbourn, K. M., Boyers, A. E., Culver, J. L., & Alferi, S. M. (2001). Cognitive behavioral stress management intervention decreases the prevalence of depression and enhances benefit finding among women under treatment for early-stage breast cancer. *Health Psychology, 20,* 20–32.

Arbisi, P. A. & Butcher, J. N. (2004). Relationship between personality and health symptoms: Use of the MMPI-2 in medical assessments. *International Journal of Clinical and Health Psychology, 4,* 571–595.

Asmundson, G. J. G. & Wright, K. D. (2004). Biopsychosocial approaches to pain. In T. Hadjistavropoulos & K. D. Craig (Eds.), *Pain: Psychological perspectives* (pp. 13–34). Mahwah, NJ: Lawrence Erlbaum Associates.

Asmundson, J. G., Taylor, S., & Cox, B. (2001). *Health anxiety: clinical and research perspectives on hypochondriasis and related conditions.* New York: Wiley.

Baum, A. (1999). Health psychology: mapping biobehavioral contribution to health and illness. *Annual Review of Psychology, 50,* 137–163.

Belar, C. D. (1997). Clinical health psychology: a specialty for the 21st century. *Health Psychology, 16,* 411–416.

Belar, C. D. & Deardorff, W. W. (1995). *Clinical health psychology in medical settings: a practitioner's guidebook* (2nd ed.). Washington, DC: APA.

Bjelland, I., Dahl, A. A., Haug, T. T., & Neckelmann, D. (2002). The validity of the Hospital Anxiety and Depression Scale: an updated literature review. *Journal of Psychosomatic Research, 52,* 69–77.

Boyer, B. A. & Paharia, M. I. (2007). *Comprehensive handbook of clinical health psychology.* Hoboken, NJ: Wiley.

Brandon, T. H., Copeland, A. L., & Saper, Z. L. (1995). Programmed therapeutic messages as a smoking treatment adjunct: reducing the impact of negative affect. *Health Psychology, 14,* 41–47.

Brownell, K. D. & Wadden, T. A. (1992). Etiology and treatment of obesity: understanding a serious, prevalent, and refractory disorder. *Journal of Consulting and Clinical Psychology. Special Issue: Behavioral Medicine: An Update for the 1990s, 60,* 505–517.

Butcher, J. N., Dahlstrom, W. G., Graham, J. R., Tellegen, A., & Kaemmer, B. (1989). *MMPI-2 manual for administration and scoring.* Minneapolis: University of Minnesota Press.

Butler, A. C., Chapman, J. E., Forman, E. M., & Beck, A. T. (2006). The empirical status of cognitive behavioral therapy: a review of meta-analyses. *Clinical Psychology Review, 26,* 17–31.

Camic, P. M. & Knight, S. J. (2004). *Clinical handbook of health psychology: a practical guide to effective interventions* (2nd ed.). Cambridge, MA: Hogrefe & Huber.

Carroll, D. (1992). *Health psychology: stress, behavior and disease.* New York: Routledge.

Cohen, S., Kessler, R. C., & Gordon, L. U. (1995). Conceptualizing stress and its relation to disease. In S. Cohen, R. C., Kessler, & L. U. Gordon (Eds.), *Measuring stress: a guide for health and social scientists* (pp. 3–28). New York: Oxford University Press.

Conrad, A. & Roth, W. T. (2007). Muscle relaxation therapy for anxiety disorders: it works but how? *Journal of Anxiety Disorders, 21,* 243–264.

Cooper, Z., Fairburn, C. G., & Hawker, D. M. (2003). *Cognitive-behavioral treatment of obesity: a clinician's guide.* New York: Guilford.

Derogatis, L. R. (1993). *BSI Brief Symptom Inventory. Administration, scoring, and procedures manual* (4th ed.). Minneapolis, MN: National Computer Systems.

Derogatis, L. R. & Derogatis, M. F. (1990). *The Psychosocial Adjustment to Illness Scale (PAIS & PAIS-SR): administration, scoring, and procedures manual II.* Baltimore: Clinical Psychometric Research.

DeRubeis, R. J. & Crits-Christoph, P. (1998). Empirically supported individual and group psychological treatments for adult mental disorders. *Journal of Consulting and Clinical Psychology, 66,* 37–52.

DiMatteo, M. R. (2004). Social support and patient adherence to medical treatment: a meta-analysis. *Health Psychology, 23,* 207–218.

Dixon, K. E., Keefe, F. J., Scipio, C. D., Perri, L. M., & Abernethy, A. P. (2007). Psychological interventions for arthritis pain management in adults: a meta-analysis. *Health Psychology, 26,* 241–250.

Egede, L. E. (2007). Major depression in individuals with chronic medical disorders: prevalence, correlates and association with health resource utilization, lost productivity and functional disability. *General Hospital Psychiatry, 29,* 409–416.

Engel, G. (1977). The need for a new medical model: a challenge for biomedicine. *Science, 196,* 129–136.

Enns, M. W., Kjernisted, K., & Lander, M. (2001). Pharmacological management of hypochondriasis and related disorders. In G. J. G. Asmundson, S. Taylor, & B. J. Cox (Eds.), *Health anxiety: clinical and research perspectives on hypochondriasis and related disorders* (pp. 298–323). New York: Wiley.

Fernandez, E. & Turk, D. C. (1989). The utility of cognitive coping strategies for altering pain perception: a meta-analysis. *Pain, 38,* 123–135.

Folstein, M. F., Folstein, S. E., & McHugh, P. R. (1975). "Mini-mental state:" A practical method for grading the cognitive state of patients for the clinician. *Journal of Psychiatric Research, 12,* 189–198.

Friedman, H. S. & Silver, R. C. (Eds.) (2007). *Foundations of health psychology.* New York: Oxford University Press.

Gatchel, R. J. & Oordt, M. S. (2003). *Clinical health psychology and primary care: practical advice and clinical guidance for successful collaboration.* Washington, DC: APA.

Gottlieb, N. H. & Green, L. W. (1984). Life events, social network, life-style, and health: an analysis of the 1979 National Survey of Personal Health Practices and Consequences. *Health Education Quarterly, 11,* 91–105.

Hadjistavropoulos, H. D. & Hadjistavropoulos, T. (2003). Relevance of health anxiety to chronic pain: recommendations for assessment and treatment. *Pain and Headache Reports, 7,* 98–104.

Hadjistavropoulos, H. D. & Williams, A. (2004). Psychological interventions, and chronic pain. In T. Hadjistavropoulos & K. D. Craig (Eds.), *Pain psychological treatment perspectives.* Mahwah, NJ: Lawrence Erlbaum Associates.

Hoffman, B. M., Papas, R. K., Chatkoff, D. K., & Kerns, R. D. (2007). Meta-analysis of psychological interventions for chronic low back pain. *Health Psychology, 26,* 1–9.

Holmes, T. H. & Rahe, R. H. (1967). The Social Readjustment Rating Scale. *Journal of Psychosomatic Research, 14,* 213–218.

Johnson, S. B. (2003). Prevention opportunities in health care settings. *American Psychologist, 58,* 475–481.

Johnson, S. B. (2004). Integrating behavior into health research and health care: one psychologist's journey. *Journal of Clinical Psychology in Medical Settings, 11,* 91–99.

Johnson, S. B., Perry, N. W., & Rozensky, R. (Eds.) (2002). *Handbook of clinical health psychology,* vol. I: *Medical disorders and behavioral applications.* Washington, DC: APA Press.

Kaplan, R. M. & Groessel, E. J. (2002). Applications of cost-effectiveness methodologies in behavioral medicine. *Journal of Consulting and Clinical Psychology, 70,* 482–493.

Katon, W., Lin, E. H. B., & Kroenke, K. (2007). The association of depression and anxiety with medical symptom burden in patients with chronic medical illness. *General Hospital Psychiatry, 29,* 147–155.

Kennedy, P. & Llewelyn, S. (2006). *The essentials of clinical health psychology.* Hoboken, NJ: wiley.

Kiecolt-Glaser, J. K., Loving, T. J., Stowell, J. R., Malarkey, W. B., Lemeshow, S., Dickinson, S. L., et al. (2006). Hostile marital interactions, proinflammatory cytokine production, and wound healing. *Archives of General Psychiatry, 62,* 1377–1384.

Kiecolt-Glaser, J. K., McGuire, L., Robles, T. F., & Glaser, R. (2002). Psychoneuroimmunology: psychological influences on immune function and health. *Journal of Consulting and Clinical Psychology. Special Issue: Behavioral Medicine and Clinical Health Psychology, 70,* 537–547.

Kiecolt-Glaser, J. K., Preacher, K. J., MacCallum, R. C., Atkinson, C., Malarkey, W. B., & Glaser, R. (2003). Chronic stress and age-related increases in the proinflammatory cytokine IL-6. *Proceedings of the National Academy of Sciences of the United States of America, 100,* 9090–9095.

Knight, K. M., McGowan, L., Dickens, C., & Bundy, C. (2006). A systematic review of motivational interviewing in physical health care settings. *British Journal of Health Psychology, 11,* 319–332.

Kraag, G., Zeegers, M. P., Kok, G., Hosman, C., & Abu-Saad, H. H. (2006). School programs targeting stress management in children and adolescents: a meta-analysis. *Journal of School Psychology, 44,* 449–472.

Kurtz, M. (1990). Adherence to diabetes regimens: empirical status and clinical applications. *Diabetes Educator, 16,* 50–56.

Lazarus, R. S. & Folkman, S. (1987). Transactional theory and research on emotions and coping. *European Journal of Personality, 33,* 141–169.

Lyons, A. C. & Chamberlain, K. (2006). *Health psychology: a critical introduction.* New York: Cambridge University Press.

Matarazzo, J. D. (1980). Behavioral health and behavioral medicine: frontiers for a new health psychology. *American Psychologist, 35,* 807–817.

Matarazzo, J. D. (1982). Behavioral health's challenges to academic, scientific and professional psychology. *American Psychologist, 37,* 1–14.

Millon, T., Green, C. J., & Meagher, R. B. (1982). *Millon Behavioral Health Inventory manual* (3rd ed.). Minneapolis, MN: Interpretive Scoring Systems.

Mohr, D. C., Boudewyn, A. C., Goodkin, D. E., Bostrom, A., & Epstein, L. (2001). Comparative outcomes for individual cognitive-behavior therapy, supportive-expressive group psychotherapy, and sertraline for the treatment of depression in multiple sclerosis. *Journal of Consulting and Clinical Psychology, 69,* 942–949.

Mohr, D. C., Dick, L. P., Russo, D., Pinn, J., Boudewyn, A. C., Likosky, W., et al. (1999). The psychosocial impact of multiple sclerosis: exploring the patient's perspective. *Health Psychology, 18,* 376–382.

Nicassio, P. M., Meyerowitz, B. E., & Kerns, R. D. (2004). The future of health psychology interventions. *Health Psychology, 23,* 132–137.

Nikcevic, A. V., Kuczmierczyk, A. R., & Bruch, M. (2006). *Formulation and treatment in clinical health psychology.* New York: Routledge.

Pilowsky, I. (1967). Dimensions of hypochondriasis. *British Journal of Psychiatry, 113,* 89–93.

Pisetsky, D. S. (2007). Clinician's comment on the management of pain in arthritis. *Health Psychology, 26,* 657–659.

Prochaska, J. O., DiClemente, C. C., & Norcross, J. C. (1992). In search of how people change: Applications to addictive behaviors. *American Psychologist, 47,* 1102–1114.

Richardson, K. M. & Rothstein, H. R. (2008). Effects of occupational stress management intervention programs: a meta-analysis. *Journal of Occupational Health Psychology, 13,* 69–93.

Rosenstock, I. M. (1974). Historical origins of the health belief model. *Health Education Monographs, 2,* 1–8.

Saab, P. G., McCalla, J. R., Coons, H. L., Christensen, A. J., Kaplan, R., Johnson, S. B., et al. (2004). Technological and medical advances: implications for health psychology. *Health Psychology, 23,* 142–146.

Saelens, B. E. & Liu, L. (2007). Clinician's comment on treatment of childhood overweight meta-analysis. *Health Psychology, 26,* 533–536.

Salkovskis, P. M. & Warwick, H. M. C. (1986). Morbid preoccupation, health anxiety and reassurance: a cognitive behavioral approach to hypochondriasis. *Behavior Research and Therapy, 24,* 597–602.

Scully, J. A., Tosi, H., & Banning, K. (2000). Life event checklists: revisiting the social readjustment rating scale after 30 years. *Educational and Psychological Measurement, 60,* 864–876.

Smith, T. W., Orleans, C. T., & Jenkins, C. D. (2004). Prevention and health promotion: decades of progress, new challenges, and an emerging agenda. *Health Psychology, 23,* 126–131.

Smith, T. W. & Suls, J. (2004). Introduction to the special section on the future of health psychology. *Health Psychology, 23,* 115–118.

Straub, R. (2007). *Health psychology: Biopsychosocial approach* (2nd ed.). New York: Worth.

Suls, J. & Rothman, A. (2004). Evolution of the biopsychosocial model: prospects and challenges for health psychology. *Health Psychology, 23,* 119–125.

Taylor, S. & Asmundson, G. J. G. (2004). *Treating health anxiety: a cognitive-behavioral approach.* New York: Guilford.

Taylor, S., Asmundson, G. J. G., & Coons, M. J. (2005). Current directions in the treatment of hypochondriasis. *Journal of Cognitive Psychotherapy, 19,* 291–310.

Taylor, S. E. (1990). Health psychology: the science and the field. *American Psychologist, 45,* 40–50.

Thorn, B. E. (2004). *Cognitive therapy for chronic pain: a step-by-step guide.* New York: Guilford.

Turner, J. A., Mancl, L., & Aaron, L. A. (2006). Short- and long-term efficacy of brief cognitive-behavioral therapy for patients with chronic temporomandibular disorder pain: a randomized, controlled trial. *Pain, 121,* 181–194.

Uchino, B. N., Cacioppo, J. T., & Kiecolt-Glaser, J. K. (1996). The relationship between social support and physiological processes: a review with emphasis on underlying mechanisms and implications for health. *Psychological Bulletin, 119,* 488–531.

Wadden, T. A., Brownell, K. D., & Foster, G. D. (2002). Obesity: responding to the global epidemic. *Journal of Consulting and Clinical Psychology. Special Issue: Behavioral Medicine and Clinical Health Psychology, 70,* 510–525.

Ware, J. E. & Sherbourne, C. D. (1992). The MOS 36-item Short-Form Health Survey (SF-36). *Medical Care, 30,* 473–483.

Warwick, H. (1992). Provision of appropriate and effective reassurance. *International Review of Psychiatry, 4,* 76–80.

Warwick, H. M. C. & Salkovskis, P. M. (1990). Hypochondriasis. *Behavior Research and Therapy, 28,* 105–117.

Whaley, A. L. & Davis, K. E. (2007). Cultural competence and evidence-based practice in mental health services: a complementary perspective. *American Psychologist, 62,* 563–574.

Wilfley, D. E., Tibbs, T. L., Van Buren, D. J., Reach, K. P., Walker, L. H., & Epstein, L. H. (2007). Lifestyle interventions in the treatment of childhood overweight: a meta-analytic review of randomized controlled trials. *Health Psychology, 26,* 521–532.

Yali, A. M. & Revenson, T. A. (2004). How changes in population demographics will impact health psychology: incorporating a broader notion of cultural competence into the field. *Health Psychology, 23,* 147–155.

Zigmond, A. S. & Snaith, R. P. (1983). The Hospital Anxiety and Depression Scale. *Acta Psychiatrica Scandinavica, 67,* 361–370.

Pharmacotherapy and Psychotherapy

Brett Deacon
University of Wyoming

OUTLINE

WHY PHARMACOTHERAPY IS IMPORTANT IN CLINICAL PSYCHOLOGY

Compared to the other chapters in this volume, this one may seem a bit out of place. What is a chapter on *pharmacotherapy*, or medication treatment, doing in a clinical psychology textbook? Of what relevance are psychotropic medications to those who practice psychotherapy?

It is true that the vast majority of clinical psychologists do not currently prescribe medication (see the later discussion of a notable exception), and as such this chapter does not cover topics related to the practice of prescribing such as selecting appropriate medications, avoiding drug interactions, and monitoring adverse effects. However, clinical psychologists frequently treat patients who have been prescribed medication. In fact, the majority of treatment-seeking patients in community settings have at least one psychotropic medication prescription (e.g., Stein et al., 2004), which means that many patients who present for psychotherapy will do so in the context of ongoing pharmacotherapy.

Both psychotherapy and pharmacotherapy are generally effective treatment modalities (Nathan & Gorman, 2002), and much has been written about the relative merits of these approaches. Research has demonstrated several unique benefits of some psychological treatments relative to pharmacotherapy, including greater desirability and acceptability to patients (e.g., Deacon & Abramowitz, 2005), superior durability of clinical improvements after treatment is discontinued (e.g., Hollon et al., 2005), and favorable long-term cost-effectiveness (e.g., Gould, Otto, & Pollack, 1995). Psychotherapy is also devoid of the often troublesome side effects associated with many psychotropic medications. On the other hand, taking medication involves much less effort, and often costs less in the short term, than attending psychotherapy sessions. Pharmacotherapy is also a particularly attractive option in settings where patients have difficulty accessing empirically supported psychotherapies, which is to say virtually everywhere. While proponents of psychotherapy and pharmacotherapy will doubtless continue to debate the pros and cons of these treatment modalities, the important point for our purposes is that many patients who seek psychotherapy are also taking medications. *Combined treatment* is thus the norm in many areas of clinical psychology, and clinicians who are ignorant of the issues that arise when their clients are taking medications may find themselves at a disadvantage in the therapy office.

This chapter will begin with a review of the major classes of psychotropic medications. Next, the general effectiveness of pharmacotherapy, both alone and in combination with psychotherapy, will be discussed. Last, a number of potential complications pharmacotherapy

may pose for the practice of psychotherapy are detailed. By no means exhaustive, this chapter is intended to introduce students of clinical psychology to the issues involved when working with patients who are either considering or undergoing pharmacotherapy.

MAJOR CLASSES OF PSYCHOTROPIC MEDICATIONS

Most psychotropic medications may be divided into four major classes (National Institute of Mental Health, 2008). These include antianxiety medications, antidepressant medications, antimanic medications (also known as neuroleptics), and antipsychotic medications (sometimes called "mood stabilizers"). Commonly used medications within each drug class, and their potential side effects, are summarized in Table 15.1. Note that this section does not describe some psychotropic medications such as methylphenidate (Ritalin), disulfiram (Antabuse), and naltrexone (Revia) that do not fit into these major drug classes.

Antianxiety Medications

Antianxiety medications (also known as anxiolytics) are commonly used in the treatment of anxiety-related problems such as panic disorder. Benzodiazepines are the most popular category of antianxiety drugs and include medicines such as diazepam (Valium) and alprazolam (Xanax). These sedative medications often relieve anxiety symptoms in a relatively rapid fashion. Like other sedatives (e.g., alcohol), benzodiazepines' side effects can include drowsiness and loss of coordination. Longer-term risks include abuse, tolerance, dependence, and withdrawal symptoms. The drugs may be taken regularly or on an as-needed basis to cope with anxiety in certain situations (e.g., flying, having a panic attack). Despite the increasing use of SSRIs in the treatment of anxiety

TABLE 15.1   Common Psychotropic Medications and Their Side Effects

Drug Class	Examples		Potential Side Effects (Varies by Specific Medication)
	Trade Name	Generic Name	
Antianxiety	Ativan	lorazepam	Drowsiness, loss of coordination, fatigue, confusion, dependence, abuse, withdrawal
	BuSpar	buspirone	
	Klonopin	clonazepam	
	Valium	diazepam	
	Xanax	alprazolam	
Antidepressant	Effexor	venlafaxine	Dry mouth, sexual dysfunction, constipation, dizziness, drowsiness, increased heart rate, headache, nausea, agitation, suicidality
	Lexapro	escitalopram	
	Nardil	phenelzine	
	Paxil	paroxetine	
	Prozac	fluoxetine	
	Tofranil	imipramine	
	Zoloft	sertraline	
Antimanic	Depakote	valproic acid	Drowsiness, weakness, nausea, fatigue, hand tremor, thirst, increased urination, weight gain, gastrointestinal problems
	Lamictal	lamotrigine	
	Lithane	lithium carbonate	
	Neurontin	gabapentin	
	Tegretol	carbamazepine	
	Topamax	topiramate	
Antipsychotic	Clozaril	clozapine	Drowsiness, rapid heartbeat, dizziness, weight gain, decreased libido, tardive dyskinesia
	Geodon	ziprasidone	
	Haldol	haloperidol	
	Risperdal	risperidone	
	Seroquel	quetiapine	
	Thorazine	chlorpromazine	
	Zyprexa	olanzapine	

Note: Source: National Institute of Mental Health (2008).

disorders, benzodiazepines remain a popular pharmacotherapy and are still the most commonly used drugs in the treatment of panic disorder (Bruce et al., 2003). Other medications sometimes used to relieve anxiety symptoms include buspirone (BuSpar) and beta-blockers such as propranolol (Inderal).

Antidepressant Medications

Antidepressants are the most commonly prescribed medications *of any kind* (National Institute for Health Care Management, 2002) and are often used to treat mood, anxiety, and numerous other mental disorders. There are three major types of antidepressants:

(a) tricyclics, (b) monoamine oxidase inhibitors (MAOIs), and (c) selective serotonin reuptake inhibitors (SSRIs). Tricyclic antidepressants such as imipramine and amitriptyline were considered first-line pharmacotherapies for depression from the 1960s to the 1980s (NIMH, 2008). MAOIs such as phenelzine were also introduced during this period and have been used primarily for individuals who fail to respond to other antidepressants. Despite their effectiveness MAOIs are somewhat undesirable owing to their tendency to interact with tyramine (a substance found in some foods and beverages including cheeses, pickles, and wine), which necessitates dietary restrictions. SSRIs like fluoxetine (Prozac), sertraline (Zoloft), and paroxetine (Paxil) are also effective but have fewer side effects than tricyclics and MAOIs and have displaced these older antidepressants as the first-line pharmacotherapies for most mental disorders for which these drugs are used. One notable exception to their generally favorable side-effect profile is that SSRIs increase the risk of suicidality. Findings from placebo-controlled clinical trials indicate that depressed patients taking SSRIs attempt suicide more than twice as often as those taking placebo (Fergusson et al., 2005), a fact that prompted the United States Food and Drug Administration (FDA) to issue a public health advisory in 2004 and place a "black box" warning on all SSRI medications warning consumers of the increased risk of suicidality.

SSRI medications have become immensely popular in the decades since their inception. To illustrate, during the 10 years following the FDA's approval of Prozac, the first SSRI, the percentage of depressed patients who received a prescription medication increased from 37.3% in 1987 to 74.5% in 1996 (Olfson et al., 2002). By the end of this period, more than half of treatment-seeking depressed outpatients were prescribed an SSRI, and fewer were participating in psychotherapy.

Antimanic Medications

Antimanic medications are typically used in the treatment of bipolar disorder. Lithium was the first such agent and has a large body of literature supporting its beneficial effects on mood swings associated with mania and depression (NIMH, 2008). Lithium is useful both as an acute treatment for manic symptoms and as a maintenance treatment to prevent or minimize the recurrence of manic and depressive symptoms. Other popular "mood-stabilizing" drugs in this class include the anticonvulsants valproic acid (Depakote) and carbamazepine (Tegretol). Antimanic drugs may produce marked side effects including drowsiness, nausea, and weight gain. Recent years have seen an extraordinary increase in the number of children and adolescents diagnosed with bipolar disorder and treated with psychotropic medications (Moreno et al., 2007). From 1994–1995 to 2002–2003, the number of outpatient physician visits for bipolar disorder among young people increased by a factor of more than 40 (that's 4,000%!) and nine out of ten were prescribed a mood stabilizer, antipsychotic, or antidepressant medication. Time will tell if this trend reflects improved detection and treatment of true cases of bipolar disorder or rampant misdiagnosis and overmedication.

Antipsychotic Medications

Psychotic disorders like schizophrenia are usually treated with antipsychotic medications, also known as neuroleptics. Introduced in the 1950s, drugs such as haloperidol and chlorpromazine were the first to provide psychotic patients with relief from symptoms such as hallucinations and paranoid thoughts (NIMH, 2008). Today, "atypical antipsychotics" such as risperidone (Risperdal) and olanzapine (Zyprexa) are most often used as first-line pharmacotherapies for schizophrenia. These medications are somewhat effective in reducing the severity of psychotic symptoms in both the short term and longer term, but they do not "cure" the disorder. Antipsychotic medications often have pronounced side effects such as drowsiness and weight gain, and long-term use of these medications may cause tardive dyskinesia, a difficult-to-reverse neurological disorder characterized by involuntary movements usually involving the jaw and mouth. One reason for the popularity of the atypical antipsychotics is their lower risk of tardive dyskinesia in comparison with older antipsychotics. However, even atypical antipsychotics are characterized by considerable problems with refusal and noncompliance among many schizophrenic patients who have difficulty tolerating their adverse effects. In the United States, antipsychotic medications have been prescribed with increasing frequency in recent years, particularly for children and adolescents. Olfson, Blanco, Liu, Moreno, and Laje (2006) reported that the estimated number of outpatient physician visits among patients younger than 21 years of age that included a prescription antipsychotic changed from approximately 201,000 in 1993 to 1,224,000 in 2002—an increase of over 600%.

EFFECTIVENESS OF PHARMACOTHERAPY AND COMBINATION TREATMENTS

Like psychotherapy, pharmacotherapy is effective in the treatment of a broad range of psychological problems. A comprehensive review of the efficacy of pharmacotherapy for different mental disorders is beyond the scope of this chapter and could easily fill a volume larger than this textbook. Readers interested in the efficacy of specific drugs for specific mental disorders might begin by familiarizing themselves with Nathan and Gorman's (2002) *Guide to Treatments That Work* (2nd edition).

There is clear scientific evidence that psychotropic medications are effective treatments for schizophrenia, bipolar disorder, attention-deficit hyperactivity disorder (ADHD), depression, and anxiety disorders among other mental health problems (Nathan & Gorman, 2002). Indeed, psychotropics are effective for such a broad range of disorders that it requires some effort to generate a list of problems for which they do not convey some benefit (personality disorders, for example, might be prominently featured on such a list). This is not to say that pharmacotherapy is a panacea, or that it obviates the need for psychotherapy. Despite their established efficacy in producing symptom relief for many mental disorders, psychotropic medications suffer from numerous problems, including (a) a tendency to reduce, rather than eliminate, psychological symptoms, (b) frequent and sometimes serious adverse effects, (c) high relapse rates upon discontinuation, (d) high long-term financial cost, especially for newer and more expensive medications, (e) an unclear mechanism of action that is almost certainly more complex than the popular but unscientific "correcting a chemical imbalance in the brain" theory (Lacasse & Leo, 2005), and (f) the frequent failure to outperform pill placebo in clinical trials for some common clinical disorders such as depression. A related problem is that owing to the considerable influence of the drug industry over scientific journals and organized medicine (Angell, 2004; Pachter, Fox, Zimbardo, & Antonuccio, 2007), available information about the safety and efficacy of psychotropic medications is often biased (see Highlight Box 15.1).

A particularly important issue for practicing psychologists is to understand when their patients are likely to benefit from the combination of pharmacotherapy and psychotherapy. A general rule of thumb is to consider referring patients for pharmacotherapy if they have

HIGHLIGHT BOX 15.1

To determine the effectiveness of a particular treatment, clinicians, patients, and other interested parties naturally look to the published literature. If the results of peer-reviewed, scientific studies consistently demonstrate the benefits of a treatment, we confidently assume that it works. Unfortunately, recent research suggests that this assumption may be overly naïve in the case of psychotropic medications owing to the influence of *publication bias*.

Publication bias refers to the greater likelihood that studies with positive (i.e., statistically significant) findings will be published than studies reporting nonsignificant results. Authors may be hesitant to submit studies with null findings for publication, and journal editors may be unenthusiastic about publishing them. In the case of psychotropic medications, publication bias decreases the likelihood of publication for clinical trials in which the active drug was no more effective than placebo and facilitates the publication of studies demonstrating a statistically significant advantage of the drug over placebo. Publication bias is commonplace in all scientific disciplines and undoubtedly plagues the psychotherapy literature as well (Vevea & Woods, 2005). However, the potential for this bias in the pharmacotherapy literature is especially high because psychotropic medications can be immensely profitable, in some cases accounting for billions of dollars in annual sales (Lacasse & Leo, 2005). Pharmaceutical companies might be tempted to suppress the results of negative clinical trials and promote findings from positive trials in order to maximize the apparent effectiveness of their products for marketing purposes. As a result, the published literature might not be the unbiased and accurate source of information about psychotropic medications many assume it to be.

One creative method scientists have used to circumvent publication bias in the antidepressant medication literature has been to obtain the results of industry-sponsored clinical trials from the FDA using the Freedom of Information Act. Because the FDA requires drug companies to submit the results of every clinical trial as part of the licensing process, the FDA database is free from any publication bias. In 2000, Khan et al. reported the first meta-analysis of the effectiveness of antidepressant medications using clinical trials data obtained from the FDA (Khan, Warner, & Brown, 2000). The authors calculated the degree of improvement in depressive symptoms across all clinical trials conducted for seven newer generation antidepressants such as Prozac and Zoloft in the treatment of adult depression. Patients receiving placebo improved, on average, 76% as much as those taking antidepressants, a finding described as "less-than-impressive" by the authors.

A more in-depth examination of the FDA antidepressant clinical trials database was conducted by Kirsch, Moore, Scoboria, and Nicholls (2002). Their analysis of six newer generation antidepressants yielded the provocative finding that slightly more than half of all clinical trials submitted to the FDA failed to produce a statistically significant advantage of the antidepressant over placebo. Moreover, patients receiving placebo experienced 82% as much improvement in depressive symptoms as those taking antidepressants, a difference that falls below the level necessary for *clinical significance* (NICE, 2004). In other words, the degree of improvement produced by antidepressants was indistinguishable from that produced by placebo in a practical sense. A recent follow-up study of these same data (Kirsch et al., 2008) demonstrated that patients with extremely severe depression did

HIGHLIGHT BOX 15.1 *(continued)*

in fact obtain a clinically significant benefit of newer generation antidepressant medications over placebo; however, this was the result of a lower placebo response rather than a stronger drug response. The relative benefits of these medications decreased along with the severity of depression to the point where patients with mild-to-moderate depressive symptoms improved to the same degree regardless of whether they had taken an antidepressant or a sugar pill. These results are important because the vast majority of individuals who take antidepressants probably do not have extremely severe depressive symptoms, which suggests the benefits they derive from SSRIs are mostly or even entirely due to the placebo effect.

Two studies have directly measured the extent to which publication bias inflates the apparent effectiveness of antidepressant medications. In the first report of its kind, Melander, Ahlqvist-Rastad, Meijer, and Beermann (2003) investigated this issue among five newer generation antidepressants approved for the treatment of depression in Sweden prior to 2000. Similar to the United States FDA, the Swedish drug regulatory authority requires that drug companies submit the results of all clinical trials regardless of the outcome. The authors assessed publication bias by comparing the results from the 42 trials submitted to the Swedish government with the published studies that were based on data from these same trials. In this manner, the authors were able to directly compare the *actual* versus *apparent* efficacy of these medications. Exactly half of the trials drug makers submitted to the Swedish government yielded a statistically significant advantage of the antidepressant over placebo on the primary dependent measure. Whereas 90.5% of the positive submitted trials were published, only 28.6% of the negative trials were published. Of interest, the same positive

trials were often published more than once—five times, in fact, for three trials of Paxil. Not surprisingly, the apparent effectiveness of antidepressants was markedly higher in the published studies than in the trials submitted for government approval.

More recently, Turner and colleagues (Turner, Matthews, Linardatos, Tell, & Rosenthal, 2008) obtained clinical trials data from the FDA for 12 newer generation antidepressants approved for the treatment of depression between 1987 and 2004. Similar to Melander et al. (2003), the authors identified published versions of the trials submitted to the FDA. Although only 51% of the 74 trials submitted to the FDA demonstrated a statistically significant advantage of the drug over placebo, 94% of the published trials did so. All but one of the 38 positive FDA trials were published. Conversely, only 14 (39%) of negative antidepressant trials were published, 11 of which were falsely characterized as positive in the published report. Improvement in depressive symptoms for the 12 antidepressants was between 11% and 69% ($M = 32\%$) higher in the published literature than in the original trial results submitted to the FDA.

Figure 15.1 combines the results of Melander et al. (2003) and Turner et al. (2008) to graphically depict the extent to which antidepressant trials conducted by drug companies are selectively published based on whether they obtained positive or negative findings. The studies just reviewed suggest that because of publication bias, antidepressant medications appear substantially more effective in the published literature than they actually are. In response to this observation, some have expressed concern that prescribers are making treatment decisions without access to all the facts about these medications (Carey, 2008). An additional concern is the lack of respect shown to patients who enroll in a clinical trial in order to contribute to science, only to see their

HIGHLIGHT BOX 15.1   (*continued*)

results suppressed because they conflict with the goals of the pharmaceutical company's marketing department. Others have responded that drug companies should not be blamed for the fact that journal editors are hesitant to publish the results

of negative clinical trials, and that the aforementioned research findings run contrary to the experience of countless depressed patients, and their prescribers, who have observed the beneficial effects of antidepressant medications.

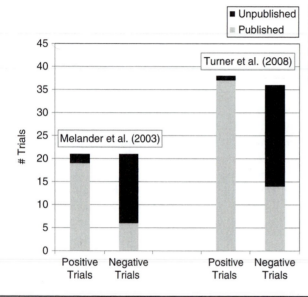

FIGURE 15.1 Selective publication of industry-sponsored antidepressant trials as a function of whether or not the trials obtained a statistically significant advantage of the antidepressant over placebo ("positive trials") or no advantage over placebo ("negative trials").

failed to benefit from an adequate course of psychotherapy. However, are there circumstances under which certain patients in psychotherapy should also be taking medication as a matter of course? In other words, for what clinical problems is the combination of pharmacotherapy and psychotherapy expected to be more effective than psychotherapy alone?

The treatment of schizophrenia provides a clear example of a context in which combined treatment is more effective than either pharmacotherapy or psychotherapy alone (American Psychiatric Association, 2004). Although effective in reducing the severity of

hallucinations and delusions, antipsychotic medications have little impact on the interpersonal and functional problems experienced by people with schizophrenia. Psychological interventions that include social skills training, assertiveness training, cognitive therapy, relapse prevention, medication management, family education, and/or vocational rehabilitation are helpful adjuncts to pharmacotherapy (Barlow & Durand, 2006). In particular, the combination of such psychotherapies and antipsychotic medication appears to prevent and delay relapse more effectively than pharmacotherapy alone.

There is considerable evidence for the effectiveness of behavior therapy involving parent training and/or classroom interventions in the treatment of ADHD in children and adolescents (Brown et al., 2008). Pharmacotherapy, however, is a much more prevalent treatment, with stimulant drugs such as methylphenidate (Ritalin) being by far the most commonly utilized intervention for ADHD (Olfson, Gameroff, Marcus, & Jensen, 2003). This diagnosis has become increasingly popular in recent years (Olfson et al., 2003), and stimulants are prescribed to more than 4 out of every 100 children age 6 to 14 years (Olfson, Marcus, Weissman, & Jensen, 2002). Fortunately, these drugs have well-established efficacy in the treatment of ADHD (Brown et al., 2008). Their effects are most pronounced on the *symptoms* of ADHD such as inattention and impulsivity, whereas behavior therapy is especially useful in improving ADHD-related *functional impairments* (e.g., social skills, classroom performance). Accordingly, the additive effects of stimulant medications and behavior therapy appear more beneficial, at least in the short term, than either treatment alone (e.g., MTA Cooperative Group, 1999). An additional advantage of combined treatment is that the benefits of stimulant medications may be achieved with lower doses, which reduces the risk of side effects. However, it is important to note that the beneficial effects (as opposed to the side effects) of stimulant medications gradually fade over time, which makes combination treatment less attractive as a long-term treatment (Brown et al., 2008).

In the case of depression, the evidence for the superiority of combined treatment over psychotherapy alone is less clear. Whereas some systematic reviews (e.g., Pampallona, Bollini, Tibaldi, Kupelnick, & Munizza, 2004) have suggested that combination treatment is somewhat more effective than antidepressant pharmacotherapy alone, the superiority of combined treatment over psychotherapy alone is less consistent and appears to be somewhat context-dependent.

To illustrate, a meta-analysis by de Maat, Dekker, Schoevers, and de Jonghe (2007) found a significant advantage of combined treatment only for patients with severe chronic depression. On the basis of the available evidence from randomized controlled trials, Pettit, Voelz, and Joiner (2001) recommended that combined treatment be considered the preferred strategy for individuals with severe depression while acknowledging that the potential benefits of adding antidepressant pharmacotherapy to psychotherapy should be balanced with the greater risk of adverse effects and higher financial cost of doing so.

Comprehensive reviews of the anxiety disorder treatment literature (Deacon, 2007; Foa, Franklin, & Moser, 2002; Otto, Smits, & Reese, 2005; Schmidt, Koselka, & Woolaway-Bickel, 2001) have converged on the conclusion that combined treatment is not more effective than cognitive-behavioral therapy (CBT) alone. In the treatment of most anxiety disorders, the combination of pharmacotherapy and CBT produces the same outcome as CBT alone. In contrast, some studies of panic disorder treatment (e.g., Barlow, Gorman, Shear, & Woods, 2000) have simultaneously reported evidence for a short-term advantage and long-term disadvantage of combined treatment relative to CBT alone. Of interest is the observation that studies comparing the augmentation of CBT with pharmacotherapy versus pill placebo almost always find the same degree of benefit (Deacon, 2007), suggesting that whatever mild advantages psychotropic medications sometimes confer on CBT are attributable to the psychological aspects of pill taking and not the pharmacological effects of antianxiety medications. Overall, it appears that two different but effective treatment modalities do not combine to produce a uniquely powerful result for patients with anxiety disorders. Whereas this conclusion is valid with respect to conventional psychotropic medications, a notable and exciting exception to this trend has recently emerged (see Highlight Box 15.2).

HIGHLIGHT BOX 15.2

Because psychotherapy and pharmacotherapy are believed to work via different mechanisms (e.g., belief change vs. change in brain structure and function), they are often delivered together in the hope that patients will receive the major benefits of both, leading to greater improvement than when either treatment is delivered by itself. Unfortunately, decades of research on combined treatments have failed to produce clear evidence of an advantage of combined treatment over psychotherapy alone for most common clinical problems. In general, it appears that drugs and psychotherapy do not synergistically combine to produce uniquely beneficial therapeutic effects. This observation suggests that medications and psychotherapy typically work through different mechanisms that do not complement each other.

An important and exciting exception to this trend has recently emerged in the treatment of anxiety disorders. In contrast to the usual method of attempting to augment CBT with drugs thought to have specific antianxiety effects, researchers have examined the effects of combining CBT with D-cycloserine (DCS), a medication that has no antianxiety effect per se but that appears to enhance learning and facilitate fear extinction. An FDA-approved treatment for tuberculosis for over 20 years, DCS has also been shown in animal studies to enhance the neural learning process underlying fear extinction (e.g., Ledgerwood, Richardson, & Cranney, 2003), highlighting its potential as a "cognitive enhancer" with the ability to facilitate the learning that takes place when patients directly face their fears in exposure therapy. DCS is fundamentally different from other psychotropic medications because its sole purpose is to enhance the effects of psychotherapy.

In the first clinical study of DCS in humans, Ressler et al. (2004) randomly assigned 27 adults with acrophobia (fear of heights) to receive two sessions of virtual reality exposure combined with either pill placebo, 50 mg of DCS, or 500 mg of DCS. A single pill of DCS or placebo was ingested 2 to 4 hours prior to both exposures. All three groups had equivalent levels of fear during the first exposure session. However, during the second exposure session, 1 week later, and at 3-month follow-up, patients who had received either dose of DCS were less afraid during virtual acrophobic exposures than were placebo patients. The beneficial effects of DCS extended beyond the virtual world, as patients receiving DCS reported fewer real-world acrophobic symptoms than patients receiving placebo at each assessment. The substantial benefits conveyed by DCS in this study are rather remarkable. Is it possible that simply taking a pill of DCS prior to conducting an exposure makes that much difference in what patients learn from this experience?

Numerous studies have independently replicated the beneficial effects of DCS reported by Ressler et al. (2004). For example, Wilhelm et al. (2008) compared the effectiveness of DCS versus pill placebo in augmenting exposure-based CBT for 23 patients with obsessive compulsive disorder. Study participants took a tablet of either DCS (100 mg) or placebo one hour prior to each of 10 exposure therapy sessions. The longer duration of treatment in this study, unlike the two-session intervention used by Ressler et al. (2004), more closely approximates the actual length of treatment in real-world practice. Those patients receiving DCS improved more quickly by mid-treatment and had markedly fewer obsessions and compulsions at post-treatment and a 1-month follow-up assessment than patients receiving placebo. The DCS group also had significantly fewer symptoms of depression.

At the time of this writing, seven clinical trials have examined the effects of combining CBT with

DCS in the treatment of social phobia, panic disorder, and obsessive compulsive disorder (see Norberg, Krystal, & Tolin, 2008). All but one (Storch et al., 2007) found clear evidence that DCS facilitates exposure therapy. Compared to placebo, DCS yielded statistically significant and moderately large benefits at both post-treatment and follow-up assessments in these studies (Norberg et al., in press). The effects of DCS appear to vary according to the dose (lower is better) and timing of DCS administration (shortly before exposure is better), and its benefits appear most pronounced early in therapy. It is possible that the effects of DCS are time-limited, with the greatest benefits obtained during initial exposure sessions and the effects diminishing gradually over time and repeated administrations of DCS.

The combination of DCS and exposure-based CBT represents a novel and revolutionary method of combining pharmacotherapy and psychotherapy. Rather than the usual (and often unsuccessful) additive approach, DCS augmentation is based on an interactive approach in which the medication is intended to specifically target the theorized neural mechanism through which exposure-based CBT works. Further positive research findings in this area could fundamentally change the manner in which prescribers and psychotherapists work together to treat anxious patients. This new type of collaboration would necessitate increased coordination between prescribers and psychotherapists and require a major change in the way prescribers think about the goals and process of pharmacotherapy.

CLINICAL ISSUES ASSOCIATED WITH COMBINED TREATMENTS

Conveying an Integrated Treatment Rationale

A central task in the early stages of psychotherapy is to communicate a compelling treatment rationale to the patient (Addis & Carpenter, 2000). This process includes discussion of factors that led to the development of the problem, maintaining factors, and the pros and cons of available treatment options. Under ideal circumstances, the treatment rationale logically integrates the conceptualization and treatment of the problem and instills hope that the treatment will be effective. Research demonstrates that patients who agree with the treatment rationale are more engaged in treatment and have better outcomes (Addis & Jacobson, 1996, 2000).

Using the example of anxiety disorder treatment, CBT approaches (e.g., Clark, 1999) emphasize the role of inaccurate beliefs and avoidance behaviors in the development and maintenance of anxiety symptoms. Accordingly, the treatment rationale in CBT typically emphasizes the importance of learning more accurate ways of thinking and directly facing one's fears via exposure in order to correct inaccurate beliefs and facilitate fear extinction. In contrast, biological approaches to anxiety typically emphasize the causal role of neurotransmitter dysregulation (e.g., Krystal, Deutsch, & Charney, 1996; Pigott, 1996), and the rationale for pharmacotherapy often emphasizes the correction of biochemical imbalances.

Although each approach has some validity, they can easily appear incongruous to the patient whose treatment providers did not attempt to integrate them. Confusion is likely to result when patients in combined treatment receive a reductionistic, biologically based treatment rationale from their prescriber and a purely psychological rationale from their psychotherapist. A "chemical imbalance" explanation appears incompatible with the notion that anxiety symptoms are caused by fully modifiable psychological factors. A one-sided cognitive-behavioral explanation leaves no room for the possible contribution of biological dysfunction. CBT may appear ineffective as a treatment for biochemically induced symptoms, whereas pharmacotherapy may appear unnecessary to treat a problem caused by problematic cognitions and behaviors. Such an atmosphere may foster poor medication adherence and/or inadequate compliance with the requirements of CBT such as self-directed exposure homework tasks.

To avoid these potential pitfalls, clinical psychologists (and ideally, prescribers) should convey an integrated rationale that acknowledges the role of biology but emphasizes the need to develop durable anxiety management strategies. Biological factors (e.g., genetics, neurotransmitter dysregulation) may be described as one of many variables that contribute to anxiety disorders. These factors may increase an individual's vulnerability to anxiety in general, and as such they are legitimate targets for intervention via pharmacotherapy. However, biological factors alone are insufficient for the development of an anxiety disorder. The content of the patient's inaccurate threat-related beliefs, as well as their persistence over time, is best viewed as the product of psychological and environmental processes that may be modified by cognitive-behavioral procedures (Foa & Kozak, 1986). According to this integrated model, pharmacotherapy may facilitate recovery by producing symptom relief, while the task of directly modifying problematic cognitive and behavioral responses is targeted with CBT.

This integrated model seems to be accepted by most patients. Occasionally, individuals will express skepticism that CBT will benefit them

based on the belief, often reinforced by prescribers, that their symptoms are caused entirely by a chemical imbalance. In such instances it may be helpful to inform patients that CBT is often more effective than pharmacotherapy alone (Schmidt et al., 2001) and produces changes in brain function (e.g., Schwartz, Stoessel, Baxter, Martin, & Phelps, 1996). The latter observation may be especially useful in correcting the pervasive but incorrect assumption that symptoms attributed to faulty brain chemistry can only be improved with pharmacotherapy.

Managing Context Effects

Under some circumstances, the biological and/or psychological effects of taking a medication may interfere with a patient's ability to benefit from psychotherapy. *Context effects* represent such a circumstance. The occurrence of state-dependent learning, in which individuals are better able to subsequently recall information learned in a particular context (e.g., while intoxicated) when in that context, provides a nonclinical example of this phenomenon. Recent research suggests that the process of psychotherapy is fertile ground for potentially problematic context effects (see Powers, Smits, Leyro, & Otto, 2007, for a review).

The learning that takes place during treatment for an anxiety disorder, for example, is partially dependent on the context in which the learning occurs. The spider-phobic patient who spends a psychotherapy session holding a spider, for example, does so in a specific context that may include (among other things) the office where the session took place, the presence of the therapist, the physical characteristics of the spider, and the internal state associated with having consumed several cups of coffee prior to the session. Therapists should not assume that learning in one context will fully generalize to different contexts. To illustrate, Mystkowski, Mineka, Vernon, and Zinbarg (2003) found that spider-phobic participants who were exposed to a spider while under the influence of caffeine experienced more fear when retested without caffeine than when retested in their original caffeinated state. The following clinical vignette provides another example of the influence of context in learning during psychotherapy.

Susan was a 70-year-old woman whose life was severely restricted by the irrational fear of losing bowel control in public. Susan participated in several sessions of cognitive-behavioral therapy during which she engaged in activities that triggered this fear (e.g., briskly walking, riding a bus). Despite experiencing a large reduction in anxiety during each session, Susan's fear of losing bowel control remained strong and unchanged for 3 consecutive weeks. In discussing this paradox with the author, Susan revealed that she had taken a tablet of prescription-strength antidiarrheal medication prior to each session in order to prevent herself from having an accident. Susan reluctantly agreed to abstain from her medication before the next session. One week later, she accompanied the therapist to a fast-food restaurant and ate a cheeseburger before walking around a crowded shopping mall for 45 minutes. Although she experienced intense anxiety during the exposure, Susan's fear gradually dissipated and she reported a significant improvement in her fear of losing bowel control 1 week later.

Susan's response to psychotherapy illustrates the importance of context in fear reduction. Her failure to benefit from initial sessions was most likely a product of the context in which her learning occurred. Susan had acquired conditional learning (i.e., "I won't lose bowel control provided that I take antidiarrheal medication") that failed to generalize to contexts in which this condition did not apply. It was not until learning took place in a new context that Susan experienced significant improvement.

How is Susan's case relevant to combined treatment? The use of pharmacotherapy during psychotherapy introduces a number of potential contexts and conditions that may, like Susan's use of antidiarrheal medication, interfere with learning when a change in context occurs. One such context is the internal state created by the pharmacological effects of the medication. For example, internal cues associated with the context of the popular antidepressant imipramine include dry mouth, sweating, and increased heart rate (Mavissakalian, Perel, & Guo, 2002). A large randomized controlled trial of combined treatment for panic disorder with imipramine (Barlow et al., 2000) provides powerful evidence of an internal context effect. Following imipramine discontinuation, patients in combined treatment (who had previously responded quite well) experienced a marked increase in their panic symptoms. The most likely explanation for this finding is that learning that occurred in the internal context created by imipramine did not generalize to the new context in which the pharmacological effects of the medication were absent. Practically speaking, the context effect of internal drug state increases the risk of relapse after patients discontinue their medication.

Medications are especially likely to interfere with learning in psychotherapy when they are used as a *safety behavior*. This phenomenon is observed when patients take benzodiazepine medications on an as-needed basis to avert or cope with perceived threat. When used in this manner, these medications may acquire in the minds of their users the power to prevent the very catastrophes that psychotherapy seeks to disconfirm. To illustrate, the author assessed a 35-year-old woman with panic disorder who described an intense fear of suffocation during her panic attacks. When asked why she continued to fear this consequence despite its failure to occur in over 100 previous attacks, she responded that only by taking Xanax during each attack had she managed to prevent suffocation. This case exemplifies two problematic cognitive effects of using medications as safety aids. First, patients are effectively prevented from learning that their inaccurate threat-related beliefs are mistaken. Second, these beliefs may actually be strengthened based on the notion that the nonoccurrence of catastrophe constitutes a "near-miss" that was achieved only through the power of the medication (Salkovskis, 1991). Beyond the deleterious effects on cognition, the use of medications in this manner may interfere with improvement during psychotherapy by strengthening escape behavior (i.e., taking a pill to short-circuit increasing anxiety), effectively preventing patients from learning that high anxiety in the presence of fear cues will eventually dissipate without the use of safety behaviors. Discouraging the use of medications as safety behaviors sometimes requires psychologists to educate well-meaning prescribers who coach patients to use their pills in this manner.

When working with patients who are taking benzodiazepines, psychotherapists should be vigilant for the possibility that the medication is serving as a safety behavior. It may be wise to ask patients to refrain from this form of medication use, particularly prior to and during psychotherapy sessions. Of importance, research suggests that safety aids merely need to be available—not utilized—in order for them to interfere with learning during CBT (Powers, Smits, & Telch, 2004). In other words, a tablet of Xanax may interfere with the benefits of psychotherapy to the same extent regardless of whether it is ingested or kept in the patient's pocket. Learning during psychotherapy may be most robust when therapists ensure that it takes place in the absence of internal (e.g., the physiological effects induced by a psychotropic medication) and external (e.g., in the office with the therapist) contexts that might impede its generalization.

Collaborating with Prescribers

It is often helpful for clinical psychologists to work directly with prescribers to facilitate the integration of psychotherapy and pharmacotherapy. The failure of prescribers and psychotherapists to collaborate may result in the rigid delivery of two seemingly incompatible treatment modalities, leaving it up to the unfortunate patient to determine which competing approach to follow. Ideally, the prescribing physician and psychologist present an integrated treatment rationale that leaves room for the role of both psychotherapy and pharmacotherapy. However, as discussed earlier, this ideal may not reflect the clinical reality in which therapists and physicians often present a one-sided psychological or biological rationale. A related problem occurs when well-meaning prescribers instruct patients to use their medications in ways that directly contradict the process of psychotherapy; for example, panic disorder patients are sometimes instructed to carry fast-acting benzodiazepine medications on their person and ingest them at the first sign of a panic attack. It is especially important that clinical psychologists consult with prescribers in these circumstances in order to properly coordinate the treatment rationale and plan.

The informed consent process in combined treatment should include discussion of the possibility of relapse upon medication discontinuation. Patients who plan on taking medication for the foreseeable future are usually willing to accept this risk. However, individuals who wish to discontinue their medication in the near future may express concern about their prognosis. For such individuals, it is often useful to taper off medications during ongoing psychotherapy so the therapist can assist the patient in managing withdrawal symptoms and coping with other effects associated with discontinuing pharmacotherapy. Prescribers should be involved in the process of deciding whether or not, and how, to taper the patient's medication. Because withdrawal symptoms and other adverse effects may occur during drug discontinuation, this process should always occur under the supervision of an adequately trained prescriber.

Many prescribers are eager to learn about effective psychotherapies and are willing to consider prescribing medications in a circumspect manner, or not at all, when effective nonpharmacological treatment options are available. Proactive psychotherapists may have the opportunity to educate prescribers, particularly those with little mental health training, about how to optimally integrate pharmacotherapy and psychotherapy. The use of DCS to augment exposure-based CBT for anxiety disorders, for example, provides an excellent example of an area where the well-informed clinical psychologist can educate prescribers about their potential role in coordinating effective combination treatment. Therapists who foster collaborative relationships with prescribers may avoid the aforementioned problems associated with combined treatment and facilitate consistently better outcomes for their patients.

PRESCRIPTIVE AUTHORITY FOR PSYCHOLOGISTS

For the past several decades, the American Psychological Association (APA) and state psychological associations throughout the United States have engaged in a coordinated and aggressive effort to promote legislation securing specially trained psychologists the right to prescribe psychotropic medications. Psychologists in Louisiana and New Mexico have already won the right to prescribe, and similar legislation is considered in numerous other states each year. Prescriptive authority is such an important priority of the APA that clinical psychologists are assessed additional membership fees in order to facilitate lobbying and related efforts in this area. Not surprisingly, physician organizations, particularly the American Psychiatric Association, are vehemently opposed to this practice and have worked to defeat legislation granting prescriptive authority to psychologists. Intense battles have been waged in state legislatures across the country and will likely continue into the foreseeable future.

The pursuit of prescription privileges is a controversial and even polarizing issue in clinical psychology (see Chapter 21). From the outset, this movement has been driven largely by practitioners, including those who dominate leadership positions within APA, and the support of scientists and academicians is likely somewhere between equivocal (Fagan et al., 2004) and nonexistent (Society for a Science of Clinical Psychology, 2001). Although the APA has never fully surveyed its membership on this issue, the largest survey of APA members (Frederick/Schneiders, 1990) revealed that 30% strongly supported prescriptive authority, 38% favored it, and the rest were unsure or opposed. A more recent meta-analysis of 17 surveys revealed a lack of consensus among psychologists (Walters, 2001). Notably, there may be more support for collaboration with psychiatrists and other prescribers than full, independent prescriptive authority for psychologists (Tatman, Peters, & Greene, 1997). However, the APA has devoted relatively little attention to the idea of enhancing patient care via improved collaborations with prescribers and has instead focused its energy and considerable resources on securing independent prescriptive authority for psychologists.

Regardless of the degree of support for prescriptive authority among APA members, the question of whether or not psychologists should prescribe medications should probably not be decided by the results of opinion polls. A great deal has been written both in defense of and in opposition to prescriptive authority for psychologists; interested readers might begin by familiarizing themselves with an APA book on this subject edited by Sammons,

Paige, and Levant (2003), as well as the Society for a Science of Clinical Psychology (SSCP) Task Force statement on prescribing privileges (2001). A brief sampling of questions raised in this debate includes the following: (a) Does prescribing represent a natural evolution in the practice of psychology? (b) What degree of training is sufficient to ensure prescriber competency and patient safety? (c) Will mental health consumers benefit from prescriptive authority for psychologists? (d) How will psychologists resist the influence of the pharmaceutical industry that has so profoundly affected psychiatry?

The major arguments in favor of prescriptive authority for psychologists concern its alleged safety, consistency with the practice and training of psychologists, and potential benefits to mental health consumers (Sammons et al., 2003). Advocates of prescribing argue that by expanding their clinical options, psychologists can provide a greater range of effective treatments to a larger population of mental health consumers. The vast majority of psychiatrists do not practice psychotherapy, thus making prescribing psychologists uniquely qualified to provide combined treatment. All graduates from APA-accredited psychology programs receive some training in biopsychology and many routinely work closely with medical professionals in the study and treatment of mental disorders. The Department of Defense's Psychopharmacology Demonstration Project, in which ten psychologists received intensive training including 700 hours of didactic and bedside instruction, showed that psychologists can prescribe competently and safely (American College of Neuropsychopharmacology, 1998). Prescriptive authority for psychologists might also increase patient access to mental health care, especially in underserved areas where psychiatrists are sparse. Less often advertised, but nonetheless important, motives for attaining prescriptive authority are protecting psychology's status in the mental health arena and

increasing the economic opportunities available to psychologists.

Critics of this movement (e.g., Robiner et al., 2002; SSCP, 2001) cite concerns about the adequacy of available training programs, effects on the core identity of psychology, the questionable benefits to patients, and its diversion from encouraging more collaborative relationships with existing prescribers. Most psychology students have little undergraduate training in the biological and physical sciences (Robiner et al., 2003), and many APA-accredited programs require only a single graduate course in the biological bases of behavior (which may or may not have anything to do with pharmacology). Compared to other prescribing professions, the typical training of psychologists is far less medical and they are inadequately prepared for prescribing in the absence of advanced, rigorous instruction. The training received by graduates of the Department of Defense's Psychopharmacology Demonstration Project was far more intensive than that proposed by the APA and mandated in states where psychologists can legally prescribe, and as such the moderate success of this program cannot be used as evidence for the validity of current training models. Regarding the actual benefits to patients, one concern is that only a small minority of psychologists are likely to devote several years and tens of thousands of dollars, all of it following their graduate training and without compensation, to complete the training required to prescribe. In addition, the geographical distribution of psychologists largely follows that of psychiatrists, and few psychologists completing the required prescriber training are likely to relocate to rural areas in order to assist underserved patients. A related concern is that due to economic pressures and incentives, prescriptive authority could lead psychologists away from practicing in their primary areas of expertise and toward prescribing. It is not clear how prescribing psychologists will be able to resist the economic and pharmaceutical industry influences that have ushered psychiatry into the era of 15-minute medication checks, though valiant efforts have been conducted to develop guidelines aimed at protecting the profession in this regard (Antonuccio, Danton, & McClanahan, 2003; Pachter et al., 2007).

Students of clinical psychology are often curious about the degree of training necessary to be able to prescribe. At present, graduate clinical psychology programs are not designed to prepare students to prescribe medications. What level of additional training is necessary for a psychologist living in a state with prescriptive authority to take advantage of this option? In New Mexico, the first state to grant prescriptive authority to psychologists, psychologists must complete at least 450 hours of didactic educational instruction in neuroscience, pharmacology, psychopharmacology, pathophysiology, physical and laboratory assessment, and clinical pharmacotherapeutics following completion of their degree requirements (NAMI, 2002). This training may require prerequisite undergraduate courses in the physical sciences (e.g., biochemistry, human anatomy, and physiology), many of which psychologists have not taken (Robiner et al., 2003). Following this instruction, the psychologist must complete a 400+-hour clinical practicum in which at least 100 patients are seen under the supervision of a psychiatrist or other physician. Psychologists must then pass a national certification examination testing their knowledge of pharmacology in the treatment of mental disorders. At this point, psychologists may apply for a 2-year conditional prescription certificate, which permits them to prescribe under the supervision of a physician. Psychologists who successfully complete the 2-year supervision process are subsequently allowed to independently prescribe providing they maintain ongoing collaborative relationships with their patients' other physicians.

While this degree of pharmacology training may appear quite rigorous to students of clinical psychology, critics of prescriptive authority for psychologists (e.g., Robiner et al., 2003) have observed that it falls far short of that received by medically oriented prescribers. Whether or not this puts patient safety in jeopardy has been a matter of debate. Some advocates of prescriptive authority contend that prescribing is a relatively basic activity, comparable in the words of former APA president Patrick DeLeon to "learning how to use a desk-top computer" (Roan, 1993, as cited in Robiner et al., 2002). In some cases, the process of choosing an appropriate drug for a specific clinical problem (e.g., an SSRI for depression) may be relatively straightforward. As a counterpoint, consider the words of one psychologist turned psychiatrist (Kingsbury, 1992):

> The effect of medications on the kidney, the heart, and so forth is important for the use of many medications. Managing these effects is often crucial and has more to do with biochemistry and physiology than with psychology. I was surprised to discover how little about medication use has to do with psychological principles and how much of it is just medical. (p. 5)

Despite the many unresolved issues in the debate over prescriptive authority for psychologists, several things seem relatively certain at this point. First, despite the absence of a clear consensus among its membership, the APA will continue to pursue a state-by-state strategy to secure prescription privileges for psychologists throughout the United States. Second, the chasm between clinically oriented and scientifically oriented psychologists (Tavris, 2003) will deepen as each group digs in its heels over this issue. Third, the antipathy between organized psychiatry and psychology will escalate as psychology continually attempts, and occasionally succeeds, in encroaching on psychiatry's turf. Perhaps more than any other contemporary issue, the pursuit of prescription privileges has the strongest potential to shape the future of clinical psychology. Will the coming decades see fundamental changes in the training and practice of clinical psychology marked by an increasing emphasis on pharmacotherapy? How might this affect the uphill battle to improve graduate training in psychological science and discourage the widespread use of pseudoscientific psychotherapies among practicing psychologists (Lilienfeld, Lynn, & Lohr, 2003)?

SUMMARY

Issues related to pharmacotherapy are of substantial importance in clinical psychology. Psychotropic medications are ubiquitous in our society and are used far more often than psychotherapy in the treatment of most mental disorders. Many patients who seek psychotherapy are already taking one or more drugs and may have been told by their prescriber that their symptoms are caused by biological factors. In some cases, concurrent pharmacotherapy may have no discernible effect on the process and outcome of psychotherapy. In other cases, psychotropic medications may improve patient outcomes relative to psychotherapy alone or, alternatively, may interfere with the effectiveness of psychotherapy. Psychologists who are knowledgeable about these contexts, and who forge collaborative relationships with their patients' prescribers, are best able to navigate the complexities that exist when psychotherapy patients are taking medications. The profession is entering a new era in which qualified practitioners in some states are able to prescribe medications. Regardless of how widespread this practice becomes, it constitutes perhaps the strongest evidence for the importance of pharmacotherapy in contemporary clinical psychology.

THOUGHT QUESTIONS

1. Is it important for clinical psychologists to be informed about pharmacotherapy? Why or why not? What degree of knowledge about pharmacotherapy is sufficient?
2. National trends indicate that psychotropic medications have been prescribed with much greater frequency in recent years, especially for children and adolescents. Is this a good or bad thing? What factors might be responsible for this trend?
3. What would you say to patients who express skepticism that psychotherapy will benefit them because their mental disorder is caused by a "chemical imbalance"?
4. Under what circumstances should clinical psychologists consider actively collaborating with their patient's prescriber? What benefits might such collaboration offer?
5. Are you in favor of prescriptive authority for psychologists? Why or why not?
6. As a result of the prescription privileges for psychologists movement, do you think clinical psychology training programs will increasingly emphasize pharmacotherapy training? What might be the advantages and disadvantages to this change?
7. To what extent does publication bias influence our knowledge about psychotropic medications? What steps would you recommend to reduce the influence of publication bias in the scientific literature?

8. Assuming the beneficial effects of D-cycloserine in the augmentation of exposure therapy are replicated in future studies, should clinical psychologists routinely work with prescribers when treating patients with anxiety disorders? What barriers, if any, might hinder efforts to collaborate with prescribers to coordinate this unusual method of combining pharmacotherapy and psychotherapy?

Glossary

Antianxiety medications: also known as anxiolytics; medications commonly used to treat anxiety-related disorders; includes class of sedative drugs called benzodiazepines.

Antidepressant medications: medications commonly used to treat depression and related affective disorders; includes selective serotonin reuptake inhibitors, tricyclics, and monoamine oxidase inhibitors.

Antimanic medications: medications commonly used to treat bipolar and related disorders; includes lithium and anticonvulsants often referred to as "mood stabilizers."

Antipsychotic medications: medications commonly used to treat schizophrenia and related disorders; includes older "conventional" antipsychotics and newer "atypical" antipsychotics.

Clinical significance: degree of improvement considered to be meaningful in a practical sense, such as producing a noticeable difference in an individual's life or altering how a clinician treats a patient.

Combined treatment: concurrent treatment with psychotherapy and medication.

Context effect: when learning and recall are influenced by internal or external cues present when learning was acquired.

Pharmacotherapy: treatment with medication.

Publication bias: greater likelihood that studies obtaining statistically significant results will be published than studies failing to obtain statistically significant results.

Safety behavior: action designed to avert or cope with a perceived threat.

References

Addis, M. E. & Carpenter, K. M. (2000). The treatment rationale in cognitive behavioral therapy: psychological mechanisms and clinical guidelines. *Cognitive and Behavioral Practice, 7,* 147–156.

Addis, M. E. & Jacobson, N. S. (1996). Reasons for depression and the process and outcome of cognitive-behavioral psychotherapies. *Journal of Consulting and Clinical Psychology, 64,* 1417–1424.

Addis, M. E. & Jacobson, N. S. (2000). A closer look at the treatment rationale and homework compliance in cognitive therapy for depression. *Cognitive Therapy and Research, 24,* 313–326.

American College of Neuropsychopharmacology (1998, May) *Final report: DoD prescribing psychologists: external analysis, monitoring, and evaluation of the program and its participants.* Nashville, TN: Author.

American Psychiatric Association (2004). Practice guideline for the treatment of patients with schizophrenia. *American Journal of Psychiatry, 154,* 1–63.

Angell, M. (2004). *The truth about the drug companies: how they deceive us and what to do about it.* New York: Random House.

Antonuccio, D. O., Danton, W. G., & McClanahan, T. M. (2003). Psychology in the prescription era: building a firewall between marketing and science. *American Psychologist, 58,* 1028–1043.

Barlow, D. H. & Durand, V. M. (2006). *Abnormal psychology: an integrative approach* (4th ed.). Belmont, CA: Thomson Wadsworth.

Barlow, D. H., Gorman, J. M., Shear, M. K., & Woods, S. W. (2000). Cognitive-behavioral therapy, imipramine, or their combination for panic disorder: a randomized controlled trial. *Journal of the American Medical Association, 283,* 2529–2536.

Brown, R. T., Antonuccio, D. O., DuPaul, G. J., Fristad, M. A., King, C. A., Leslie, L. K., et al. (2008). *Childhood mental health disorders.* Washington, DC: American Psychological Association.

Bruce, S. E., Vasile, R. G., Goisman, R. M., Salzman, C., Spencer, M., Machan, J. T., et al. (2003). Are benzodiazepines still the medication of choice for patients with panic disorder with or without agoraphobia? *American Journal of Psychiatry, 160*, 1432–1438.

Carey, B. (2008, January 17). Antidepressant studies unpublished. *New York Times*. Retrieved March 20, 2008, from http://www.nytimes.com/2008/01/17/health/17depress.html?_r=1 &oref=slogin.

Clark, D. M. (1999). Anxiety disorders: why they persist and how to treat them. *Behaviour Research and Therapy, 37*, S5–S27.

de Maat, S. M., Dekker, J., Schoevers, R. A., & de Jonghe, F. (2007). Relative efficacy of psychotherapy and combined therapy in the treatment of depression: a meta-analysis. *European Psychiatry, 22*, 1–8.

Deacon, B. J. (2007). The effect of pharmacotherapy on the effectiveness of exposure therapy. In D. C. Richard & D. Lauterbach (Eds.), *Comprehensive handbook of the exposure therapies* (pp. 311–333). New York: Academic Press.

Deacon, B. J. & Abramowitz, J. S. (2005). Patients' perceptions of pharmacological and cognitive-behavioral treatments for anxiety disorders. *Behavior Therapy, 36*, 139–145.

Fagan, T. J., Ax, R. K., Resnick, R. J., Liss, M., Johnson, R. T., & Forbes, M. R. (2004). Attitudes among interns and directors of training: who wants to prescribe, who doesn't, and why. *Professional Psychology: Research and Practice, 35*, 345–356.

Fergusson, D., Doucette, S., Glass, K. C., Shapiro, S., Healy, D., Hebert, P., & Hutton, B. (2005). Association between suicide attempts and selective serotonin reuptake inhibitors: systematic review of randomized controlled trials. *British Journal of Medicine, 330*, 646–653.

Foa, E. B., Franklin, M. E., & Moser, J. (2002). Context in the clinic: how well do cognitive-behavioral therapies and medications work in combination? *Biological Psychiatry, 10*, 987–997.

Foa, E. B. & Kozak, M. J. (1986). Emotional processing of fear: exposure to corrective information. *Psychological Bulletin, 99*, 20–35.

Frederick/Schneiders, Inc. (1990, December). *Survey of American Psychological Association members*. Washington, DC: Author.

Gould, R. A., Otto, M. W., & Pollack, M. H. (1995). A meta-analysis of treatment outcome for panic disorder. *Clinical Psychology Review, 8*, 819–844.

Hollon, S. D., DeRubeis, R. J., Shelton, R. C., Amsterdam, J. D., Salomon, R. M., O'Reardon, J. P., et al. (2005). Prevention of relapse following cognitive therapy vs. medications in moderate to severe depression. *Archives of General Psychiatry, 62*, 417–422.

Khan, A., Warner, H. A., & Brown, W. A. (2000). Symptom reduction and suicide risk in patients treated with placebo in antidepressant clinical trials: an analysis of the Food and Drug Administration database. *Archives of General Psychiatry, 57*, 311–317.

Kingsbury, S. J. (1992). Some effects of prescribing privileges. *Professional Psychology: Research and Practice, 23*, 3–5.

Kirsch, I., Deacon, B. J., Huedo-Medina, T. B., Scoboria, A., Moore, T. J., & Johnson, B. T. (2008). Initial severity and antidepressant benefits: a meta-analysis of data submitted to the FDA. *PLoS Medicine, 5*, 0260–0268.

Kirsch, I., Moore, T. J., Scoboria, A., & Nicholls, S. S. (2002). The emperor's new drugs: an analysis of antidepressant medication data submitted to the U.S. Food and Drug Administration. *Prevention and Treatment, 5*, article 23.

Krystal, J. H., Deutsch, D. N., & Charney, D. S. (1996). The biological basis of panic disorder. *Journal of Clinical Psychiatry, 57*(suppl. 6), 23–31.

Lacasse, J. & Leo, J. (2005). Serotonin and depression: a disconnect between the advertisements and the scientific literature. *PLoS Medicine, 2*(12), e395.

Ledgerwood, L., Richardson, R., & Cranney, J. (2003). Effects of D-cycloserine on extinction of conditioned freezing. *Behavioral Neuroscience, 117*, 341–349.

Lilienfeld, S. O., Lynn, S. J., & Lohr, J. M. (Eds.) (2003). *Science and pseudoscience in clinical psychology*. New York: Guilford.

Mavissakalian, M., Perel, J., & Guo, S. (2002). Specific side effects of long-term imipramine management of panic disorder. *Journal of Clinical Psychopharmacology, 22*, 155–161.

Melander, H., Ahlqvist-Rastad, J., Meijer, G., & Beermann, B. (2003). Evidence b(i)ased medicine selective reporting from studies sponsored by pharmaceutical industry: review of studies in new drug applications. *British Medical Journal, 326*, 1171–1173.

Moreno, C., Laje, G., Blanco, C., Jiang, H., Schmidt, A. B., & Olfson, M. (2007). National trends in the outpatient diagnosis and treatment of bipolar disorder in youth. *Archives of General Psychiatry, 64*, 1032–1039.

Multimodal Treatment of ADHD Cooperative Group (1999). 14-month randomized clinical trial of treatment strategies for attention-deficit/hyperactivity disorder. *Archives of General Psychiatry, 56*, 1073–1086.

Mystkowski, J. L., Mineka, S., Vernon, L. L., & Zinbarg, R. E. (2003). Changes in caffeine states enhance return of fear in spider phobia. *Journal of Consulting and Clinical Psychology, 71*, 243–250.

Nathan, P. E. & Gorman, J. M. (2002). *A guide to treatments that work* (2nd ed.). New York: Oxford University Press.

National Alliance on Mental Illness (2002). *Prescribing privileges task force report and recommendations to the NAMI board of directors*. Retrieved March 20, 2008 from http://www.nami.org/Content/ContentGroups/Policy/Prescribing_Privileges_Task_Force_Report_and_Recommendations_to_the_NAMI_Board_of_Directors.htm.

National Institute for Clinical Excellence (2004). *Depression: management of depression in primary and secondary care.* Clinical practice guideline No. 23. London: Author.

National Institute for Health Care Management (2002). *Prescription drug expenditures in 2001.* Washington, DC: Author.

National Institute of Mental Health (2008). *Medications.* Retrieved March 20, 2008 from http://menanddepression. nimh.nih.gov/health/publications/medications/complete-publication.shtml.

Norberg, M. M., Krystal, J. H., & Tolin, D. F. (2008). A meta-analysis of D-cycloserine and the facilitation of fear extinction and exposure therapy. *Biological Psychiatry, 63,* 1118–1126.

Olfson, M., Blanco, C., Liu, L., Moreno, C., & Laje, G. (2006). National trends in the outpatient treatment of children and adolescents with antipsychotic drugs. *Archives of General Psychiatry, 63,* 679–685.

Olfson, M., Gameroff, M. J., Marcus, S. C., & Jensen, P. S. (2003). National trends in the treatment of attention deficit hyperactivity disorder. *American Journal of Psychiatry, 60,* 1071–1077.

Olfson, M., Marcus, S. C., Druss, B., Elinson, L., Tanielian, T., & Pincus, H. A. (2002). National trends in the outpatient treatment of depression. *Journal of the American Medical Association, 287,* 203–209.

Olfson, M., Marcus, S. C., Weissman, M. M., & Jensen, P. S. (2002). National trends in the use of psychotropic medications by children. *Journal of the American Academy of Child and Adolescent Psychiatry, 41,* 514–521.

Otto, M. W., Smits, J. A. J., & Reese, H. E. (2005). Combined psychotherapy and pharmacotherapy for mood and anxiety disorders in adults: review and analysis. *Clinical Psychology: Science and Practice, 12,* 72–86.

Pachter, W. S., Fox, R. E., Zimbardo, P., & Antonuccio, D. O. (2007). Corporate funding and conflicts of interest: a primer for psychologists. *American Psychologist, 62,* 1005–1015.

Pampallona, S., Bollini, P., Tibaldi, G., Kupelnick, B., & Munizza, C. (2004). Combined pharmacotherapy and psychological treatment for depression: a systematic review. *Archives of General Psychiatry, 61,* 714–719.

Pettit, J. W., Voelz, Z. R., & Joiner, T. E. (2001). Combined treatment for depression. In M. T. Sammons & N. B. Schmidt (Eds.), *Combined treatments for mental disorders: a guide to psychological and pharmacological interventions* (pp. 131–160). American Psychological Association.

Pigott, T. A. (1996). OCD: where the serotonin selectivity story begins. *Journal of Clinical Psychiatry, 57*(suppl. 6): 11–20.

Powers, M. B., Smits, J. A. J., Leyro, T. M., & Otto, M. W. (2007). Translational research perspectives on maximizing the effectiveness of exposure therapy. In D. C. S.

Richard & D. L. Lauterbach (Eds.), *Handbook of the exposure therapies* (pp. 109–126). Academic Press.

Powers, M. B., Smits, J. A. J., & Telch, M. J. (2004). Disentangling the effects of safety-behavior utilization and safety-behavior availability during exposure-based treatment: a placebo-controlled trial. *Journal of Consulting and Clinical Psychology, 72,* 448–454.

Roan, S. (September 7, 1993). Tug-of-war over prescription powers; health: Pharmacists, nurses, and other non-doctors want the authority to prescribe drugs. Others insist only physicians have the training to do so safely. *Los Angeles Times,* Part E, 1, 6.

Ressler, K. J., Rothbaum, B. O., Tannenbaum, L., Anderson, P., Graap, K., Zimand, E., et al. (2004). Cognitive enhancers as adjuncts to psychotherapy: use of D-cycloserine in phobic individuals to facilitate extinction of fear. *Archives of General Psychiatry, 61,* 1136–1144.

Robiner, W. N., Bearman, D. L., Berman, M., Grove, W. M., Colón, E., Armstrong, J., et al. (2002). Prescriptive authority for psychologists: a looming health hazard? *Clinical Psychology: Science and Practice, 9,* 231–248.

Robiner, W. N., Bearman, D. L., Berman, M., Grove, W. M., Colón, E., Armstrong, J., et al. (2003). Prescriptive authority for psychologists: despite deficits in education and knowledge? *Journal of Clinical Psychology in Medical Settings, 3,* 211–221.

Salkovskis, P. M. (1991). The importance of behaviour in the maintenance of anxiety and panic: a cognitive account. *Behavioural Psychotherapy, 19,* 6–19.

Sammons M., Paige R., & Levant R. F. (Eds.) (2003). *The evolution of prescribing psychology: a history and guide.* Washington, DC: American Psychological Association.

Schmidt, N. B., Koselka, M., & Woolaway-Bickel, K. (2001). Combined treatments for phobic anxiety disorders. In M. Sammons & N. B. Schmidt (Eds.), *Combined treatment for mental disorders: a guide to psychological and pharmacological interventions* (pp. 81–110). Washington, DC: American Psychological Association.

Schwartz, J. M., Stoessel, P. W., Baxter, L. R., Martin, K. M., & Phelps, M. E. (1996). Systematic changes in cerebral glucose metabolic rate after successful behavior modification treatment of obsessive-compulsive disorder. *Archives of General Psychiatry, 53,* 109–113.

Society for a Science of Clinical Psychology (2001). Task Force statement on prescribing privileges (RxP). Retrieved March 20, 2008 from http://wwwmspp.net/SSCPscript-priv.htm.

Stein, M. B., Sherbourne, C. D., Craske, M. G., Means-Christensen, A., Bystritsky, A., Katon, W., et al. (2004). Quality of care for primary care patients with anxiety disorders. *American Journal of Psychiatry, 161,* 2230–2237.

Storch, E. A., Merlo, L. J., Bengtson, M., Murphy, T. K., Lewis, M. H., Yang, M. C., et al. (2007). D-Cycloserine does not enhance exposure-response prevention therapy in obsessive-compulsive disorder. *International Clinical Psychopharmacology*, *22*, 230–237.

Tatman, S. M., Peters, D. B., & Greene, A. L. (1997). Graduate students' attitudes toward prescription privileges training. *Professional Psychology: Research and Practice*, *28*, 515–517.

Tavris, C. (2003). The widening scientist-practitioner gap: a view from the bridge. In S. O. Lilienfeld, S. J. Lynn & J. M. Lohr (Eds.), *Science and pseudoscience in clinical psychology* (pp. ix–xviii). New York: Guilford.

Turner, E. H., Matthews, A. M., Linardatos, E., Tell, R. A., & Rosenthal, R. (2008). Selective publication of antidepressant trials and its influence on apparent efficacy. *New England Journal of Medicine*, *358*, 252–260.

Vevea, J. L. & Woods, C. M. (2005). Publication bias in research synthesis: sensitivity analysis using a priori weight functions. *Psychological Methods*, *10*, 428–443.

Walters, G. D. (2001). A meta-analysis of opinion data on the prescription privilege debate. *Canadian Psychology*, *42*, 119–125.

Wilhelm, S., Buhlmann, U., Tolin, D. F., Meunier, S. A., Pearlson, G. D., Reese, H. E., et al. (2008). Augmentation of behavior therapy with D-cycloserine for obsessive-compulsive disorder. *American Journal of Psychiatry*, *165*, 335–341.

Empirically Supported Treatments and Comparative Psychotherapy Outcome Research

Matteo Bertoni
Pacific Graduate School
of Psychology

Elaine Gierlach
Pacific Graduate School
of Psychology
Larry E. Beutler
Pacific Graduate School of
Psychology

Satoko Kimpara
Pacific Graduate School
of Psychology

OUTLINE

INTRODUCTION

After three decades of emerging acceptance as a legitimate "treatment" for behavioral disorders, by 1992 psychotherapy was in danger of having its role marginalized in the health-care system. During the debate about the implementation of a national health-care plan in the United States, a lack of reliable data on cost control, effectiveness, and specificity of effects placed psychotherapy at risk for being excluded from health-care plans. In contrast to psychotherapy, psychopharmacological treatments had earned a place in psychiatric practice guidelines by virtue of the presumed differential cost of medications and research evidence that suggested equivalent effects with psychotherapy (Beutler, 1998, 2000). Unlike medications, whose effects seemed to be relatively specific to depression, anxiety, and thought disorder, psychotherapy had failed to prove that it was more than a general treatment whose many labels masked common and similar effects. Thus, both the varieties of psychotherapy and the diverse professionals who practiced them were considered to be interchangeable, leading both to recommendations that emphasized medication over "talk" therapies and to the downgrading of doctoral-level psychotherapists in favor of those who were less expensive (Beutler, 1998).

In reality, research in psychotherapy had already proven wrong Eysenck's (1952) conclusion that behavior therapy was more effective than psychotherapy and, in its place, had concluded that all psychological interventions were essentially equivalent. Even among scholarly professionals who were increasingly challenging the so-called Dodo bird verdict (i.e., "All have won and all must have prizes"; Luborsky, Singer, & Luborsky, 1975, p. 995), it was largely conceded that no one model of psychotherapy was uniquely effective for any particular condition. Many therapies were effective for almost any given condition, and conversely,

any condition could be affected by multiple different therapeutic approaches. Indeed, most systems of procedures used in clinical practice lacked a solid basis of support based on empirical research (Beutler, Williams, Wakefield, & Entwhistle, 1995).

In the mid-1990s, the emerging body of evidence that suggested that psychological interventions were at least as effective as pharmacological interventions in terms of cost and effects (e.g., Barlow et al., 1994; Evans et al., 1992) had not yet risen to sufficient salience to be more than a curiosity. Likewise, the accumulating evidence that would eventually reveal that drug companies were inflating the positive effects of antidepressants by withholding negative findings from publication (Carey, 2008; and see Chapter 15) was still more than a decade away. In an environment in which scientific and clinical communities did not agree with one another about which treatments were effective and with whom, the judicial system inserted its own, non–empirically based standards by which to judge when malpractice had been committed and thereby to assess the validity of claims against mental health clinical procedures. By leaving the resolution of complex matters of treatment effects to the court system, and particularly to case law, treatments were recommended based on what were most popular or familiar. Thus, the court decided that effective practice could be determined by a standard of "common practice" and thereby put aside the need to evaluate actual and observed effects of various psychotherapies.

In an effort to offset some of the problems with such a subjective criterion of effectiveness, the court adopted a second principle—the principle of the respectable minority (Beutler, 1998). This latter principle asserted that a treatment which did not achieve widespread or "common" use could be considered valid if a group of practitioners of sufficient numbers to be called a "respectable minority" was to vouch for the veracity of the procedure being used.

In practice, the number of individuals required to practice the minority procedure in order for it to place the practice above the "malpractice" line was ruled to be at least five (Beutler, Bongar, & Shurkin, 1998). Noticeably, both the criterion of "common practice" and that of "respectable minority" lacked the evidentiary foundations of scientific study. They also lacked consideration of whether the procedures were safe, thus leaving the door open for the dissemination and practice of questionable and controversial interventions. Many such treatments soon became newsworthy, ranging from soon-to-be-refuted interventions such as recovered memory therapies, past lives therapies, rebirthing therapies, and various forms of demon expulsion therapies. Dramatic incidents of the failures of psychotherapy were introduced to the public via television, raising questions about the legitimacy of psychology and psychotherapy as scientific disciplines.

THE DEFINITION AND IDENTIFICATION OF EMPIRICALLY VALIDATED TREATMENTS

To lend greater credibility to psychotherapies and to reduce the confusion that had been generated by the reliance on unscientific and "non-empirical" criteria of what is effective (i.e., legal criteria based on "common practice" and "respectable minority" opinion), the Society for Clinical Psychology (Division 12 of the American Psychological Association) established a Task Force on the Promotion and Dissemination of Psychological Procedures (1995), charged with the duty of reviewing available literature and identifying interventions that were grounded in sound scientific research. The Task Force eventually evolved into a standing committee of the Society and is now called the Committee on Science and Practice, where the initial work is periodically updated and corrected.

Permuting the concept of evidence-based medicine on the principle that the quality of patient care is improved when practitioners use treatments with empirical support (Sackett, Richardson, Rosenberg, & Haynes, 2000), the Task Force first selected a set of criteria by which to identify the presence of adequate scientific evidence. They drew on the criteria previously established by the U.S. Food and Drug Administration (FDA) to demonstrate the efficacy of medications. These criteria required that at least two independent studies using a randomized clinical trial (RCT) design reached similar conclusions that demonstrated that a targeted treatment was more effective than either a no-treatment or placebo control/comparison condition. The results of the reviews conducted by major figures in the field were published in two annual reports (Chambless et al., 1996; Chambless, 1998), including a well-documented description of the inclusionary criteria used by the Task Force. In the initial report, the empirically supported treatments (ESTs), defined as "clearly specified psychological treatments shown to be efficacious in controlled research with a delineated population" (Chambless & Hollon, 1998, p. 7), consisted a list of 25 treatments (Chambless et al., 1996). Ultimately, Oxford University Press published a volume directly derived from the Task Force results named *A Guide to Treatment That Works* (Nathan & Gorman, 1998, 2002), which is now in its second edition and has been enormously influential in the field.

The Task Force initiated a plethora of similar reports on "empirically supported" treatments (ESTs), with overlapping lists of ESTs now identifying at least 143 manualized treatments (108 for adults and 35 for children or adolescents) that have been found to be efficacious or probably efficacious for 51 different categories of DSM-IV-TR *conditions (Beutler, Moleiro, & Talebi, 2002; Chambless & Ollendick, 2001).*

The Task Force's original inclusion criteria (Chambless et al., 1996) were strongly criticized for being too narrow and exclusive. The leaders of the Task Force, Chambless and Hollon (1998), subsequently embraced some of the critiques and suggestions made by the clinical and scientific communities. They opened the acceptable methodology to include well-designed and replicated single case studies, emphasized the importance of the two supporting studies also being consistent with the preponderance of other evidence about the efficacy of the targeted treatment, and began to emphasize the role of "empirical support" rather than "empirical validation" (Chambless, 1996). Within this context, however, the role of the Task Force remained quite similar. The members reviewed the literature on psychotherapy treatment efficacy, but nominally addressed the broader concepts of effectiveness and efficiency as well (Seligman, 1995).

The Task Force continued to view RCT designs as the methods of choice and emphasized that this level of control provided the most reliable form of scientific evidence in support of the role of causality and the reduction of sources of potential bias (Lachin, Matts, & Wei, 1988). They argued that this design provided the best hope of reducing the role of confounding variables or chance in order to allow scholars to make proper inferences on treatment efficacy (Chambless et al., 1994) (see Highlight Box 16.1).

The selection of the particular treatments that were considered and then evaluated by the Task Force and subsequent committees was conducted by nomination of either a Task Force member or by interested groups and organizations. In undertaking the review, the Task Force guidelines emphasized the importance of having the results of one study replicated by another research group or in another setting in order to reduce bias and reduce the likelihood of spurious results that are applicable only in a very narrow location or setting (Chambless & Hollon, 1998). The choice to favor studies that provided a written manual to guide the treatments was somewhat automatic, given the necessity to control for the implementation of specific techniques both session to session (or phase to phase) as well as general construct and theory. A high degree of either competence or adherence to the technique employed was considered, in order to ensure adequate consistency between the procedure and the actual clinical implementation (Chambless et al., 1996). Strict training and supervision in the techniques were deemed particularly important, mainly because they minimized therapist variability and therefore controlled therapist effects in a better fashion than in naturalistic studies, where differences among more- and less-talented and experienced providers influence the therapy outcome (Crits-Christoph et al., 1991). Finally, investigator allegiance (preference and expertise that favor the results of comparative studies) was noted, but it was assumed that this effect allegiance would be balanced out across studies (Chambless & Hollon, 1998).

Of particular interest to the Task Force was the way to achieve a resolution of studies that produced conflicting results, not an uncommon event in psychotherapy research. The Task Force suggested evaluating the methodological rigor, the quantity of studies pointing in one direction versus the other, and considering both the preponderance of available evidence and the results of meta-analyses of multiple studies as a final determiner of reliable conclusions in the most difficult cases. In the ideal condition, in order for a treatment to be deemed as efficacious, it would be supported by at least two independent randomized studies that converged on the same conclusions that were not offset by conflicting data. The supporting studies along with a meta-analytic review of the extant literature on the given population and treatment were included as reference in the Task Force reports.

CRITIQUING THE DEFINITION AND IDENTIFICATION OF EMPIRICALLY SUPPORTED TREATMENTS

The original Task Force report elicited an outpouring of critiques and comments, both substantial and conceptual (e.g., Drozd & Goldfried,

---

HIGHLIGHT BOX 16.1

The original Task Force on the Promotion and Dissemination of Empirically Validated Treatments (1995) required that a listed treatment must have demonstrated its superiority to either a no-treatment control condition or a treatment-as-usual comparison using a randomized clinical trial design. Such a design applied to psychosocial treatment, attempted to mirror as much as possible the double-blind study design of pharmacological therapies (Lachin et al., 1988). That is, these studies first identify a group of patients who have the same reliably determined and specific disorder (e.g., major depressive disorder). Then, these patients are randomly assigned to two or more well-defined and structured treatments, along with a control condition. Symptoms of the defining disorder are then measured before, during, and at the end of treatment and at follow-up.

However, modifications to this general design are necessary to accommodate psychological procedures. For example, it is impossible to keep the patient and therapist blind to what is being done in the sessions, as is done by using similarly appearing placebo and active pills in drug studies. Likewise, the ingredients of a psychological treatment are difficult to keep constant (Garfield, 1996).

To address these concerns, great effort was made to eliminate therapist factors and non-diagnostic patient differences. Care was taken to train therapists in all treatments to act the same way as one another and to apply the treatments in a very systematic and structured manner. Likewise, the use of a placebo control was usually replaced with the use of either (1) a nontreatment or waiting list condition, (2) a treatment-as-usual condition, or (3) an alternative treatment that emphasizes the establishment of hope and trust in the clinician rather than in the techniques that are used (Butler et al., 1991).

1996; Fay & Lazarus, 1993; Garfield, 1996). The preponderance and most vociferous of these were those generated by practitioners of non-declared EST techniques or scientific groups that supported long-term noncognitive or nonbehavioral approaches to treatment. Indeed, the majority of the literally hundreds of treatments available to practitioners (Beutler, 1991) were not on the list of accepted ESTs, and the omission of many of the most widely practiced of these was perceived by their advocates as threatening the future of clinical practice, financial security, and preferred research directions, despite the Task Force's efforts to assuage these concerns (Chambless et al., 1998; Chambless & Hollon, 1998). While the Task Force sought to distinguish between treatments that were omitted because no research had been conducted and those for whom research had produced negative findings by emphasizing that the absence of a given treatment on the designation list was not sufficient reason to cease its use, the fears of practitioners persisted. Moreover, clinical and counseling psychology training programs began to use the EST list to make decisions about what should be taught in graduate courses, raising concerns among practitioners all the more about whether students were being adequately taught to conduct psychotherapy. Critics of the EST movement (e.g., Bohart, 2006; Duncan & Miller, 2006; Lambert & Barley, 2002; Silverman, 1996; Westen, Novotny, & Thompson-Brenner, 2004a) focused on the role of nontechnical factors associated with the skill of the therapist, the quality of the relationship, and the non representativeness of the research used to support various treatments.

Not only the data but also the pragmatics of following the recommendations and the assumptions and methods utilized by the Task Force were scrutinized (e.g., Lambert & Barley, 2002; Westen et al., 2004a, 2004b). The issues raised included a critique of purported methodological flaws and limitations in the collection and interpretation of supporting data. The issues further highlighted the wide differences of viewpoints that exist among scientists and practitioners, and even among scientists themselves, regarding the relative value of internal and external validity and the pragmatics of basing a workable practice on the EST version of clinical science.

In spite of the many critiques of randomized clinical trial designs, the Division 12 Task Force persisted in asserting that RCTs were necessary and sufficient to ensure internal validity and causal agency of the treatments tested in regard to the outcomes. It showed itself to be very reluctant to open the doors to consider research based on alternative research designs in order to address related clinical questions as such designs were to be reserved to address questions other than those of empirical validity (e.g., Silverman, 1996).

Affirming that the clinical change observed in clinical trials is caused by the procedures advocated by a given treatment model (internal validity) is only one piece of the puzzle required to answer the question of the nature of research-based practice. To comprehensively identify what practices and factors have achieved reliable research support requires that one consider and scrutinize the utility and effectiveness of treatments as they are practiced by real clinicians on real patients, in real or actual clinical practice, without the constraints that are necessitated in an RCT research design and with a full array of complex interactions among multiple variables that are present in the "real world." Quasi-experimental and nonexperimental designs are required in order to systematically study the role of variables that are associated with treatment but which cannot be randomly assigned—

variables such as those embodied in the style of the therapist, in the personality and demographics of the patient, and in the environment in which people live and work. Critics argued that these factors were endemic parts of the treatment, but the Division 12 Task Force summarily rejected this perspective. Although the Task Force acknowledged the value of reviewing studies that used such methodologies (Hollon, 1996), they did not consider these variables to be central to the questions related to specific treatments. They subordinated the scope of these non-RCT studies to simply supporting evidence of treatments that must be defined by the use of RCTs (Chambless & Hollon, 1998) (see Highlight Box 16.2).

This latter point of view contrasted with the emphasis of some critics on the relative merits of statistical and clinical significance (e.g., Jacobson & Truax, 1991). Being able to predict an outcome at a level that is too low to notice in practice is not a persuasive finding in assuring either scholars or the public that a given treatment is likely to be of value. For example, most head-to-head comparisons of different psychotherapies have produced inconsequential differences in outcomes, making "no difference" the most usual and valid conclusion regarding differential effects (Beutler, 2002). To the degree that there are differences among outcomes for different treatment models, most are inconsequential relative to factors such as patient demographics, the environment in which they live, quality of treatment relationship, and the like. The lack of well-designed studies and long-term studies and insufficient follow-up data on short-term changes also raise questions about whether results, if they are obtained, are sufficiently reliable and durable to recommend any given treatment above any or all others (Stricker et al., 1999; Westen, Novotny, & Thompson-Brenner, 2004a).

Furthermore, early suggestions to use sequential manuals to approach comorbid and multi-symptomatic cases (e.g., Wilson, 1998) seemed too simplistic and not clinically valid (Westen, Novotny, & Thompson-Brenner 2004a).

HIGHLIGHT BOX 16.2

One critique of the nature of EST findings that has been particularly salient and frequent is that the sampling procedure used in RCT studies is so narrow as to preclude the complex problems and patients that are usually treated in clinical settings (Silverman, 1996; Westin, 2006). While interesting, this critique may be exaggerated. Stirman and DeRubeis (2006) have systematically compared those in controlled research studies and those patients in different practice arenas. They conclude that patients in controlled trial studies have been at least as severely impaired and complex as those in conventional practice. Inclusion criteria frequently allow for patients with comorbid conditions, severe social disturbances, and very chronic problems.

The way in which the participants are selected for an RCT study and the methods of evaluating changes are often substantially different from what happens in typical clinical practice. To ensure appropriateness to a research protocol, individuals are usually first screened and then interviewed keeping eligibility and exclusionary criteria in mind, ensuring that pretreatment data are collected. Outcome data are usually symptom-focused with assessment at different times during the course of treatment. Outcome is some function of change from pretest to the end of the defined protocol (Westen, Novotny, & Thompson-Brenner, 2004a). In contrast, in clinical practice a broader collection of biological, psychological, and/or social information is obtained, and treatments may be assigned to occur in tandem or sequentially. Efforts to apply a sequential treatment to research patients in order to address these concerns (e.g., Wilson, 1998) are often seen as too simplistic and inflexible (Westen et al., 2004b). Change is assessed over time in clinical practice, but with the recognition that the relevance of these changes may vary over time. For example, at different points of treatment, symptomatic, interpersonal, and intrapersonal processes are of more or less relevance, and these factors may require different treatments.

Another problem that EST research (and psychotherapy research in general) is facing resides in the current scarcity and narrowness of studies and established ESTs on underserved populations, with elements that are largely underrepresented in research. These include such factors as poverty, language and cultural barriers (e.g., Bernal & Scharron-del-Rio, 2001), older age, and particular settings such as rural environments or community-based centers. This lack of breadth may further diminish the applicability in those specific clinical areas and settings.

Length of treatment and the exclusive use of manualized treatments were other elements of RCT studies that have raised vivid discussions about the generalizability of findings. Detractors of ESTs have pointed out that the Task Force privileged short-term cognitive and behavioral techniques, largely because these studies are more prevalent in the literature. Unfortunately, such qualities of research may be at variance with usual practice and may have skewed the definition of what "empirical validation" means in favor of short-term interventions.

Supporters of the effort to define a finite list of ESTs have observed that one would be justified in privileging short-term therapies if research were able to show that such interventions produce comparable results to longer alternatives (Crits-Christoph, Wilson, & Hollon, 2005). However, in most instances, the decision is made because a particular duration of treatment is imposed by a granting agency, not by research evidence of its value, and by the ability to better control attrition and other confounding variables that is offered by this methodological decision.

The exclusive use of samples on the basis of their compliance with a homogeneous DSM disorder is another concern that has serious implications for the nature of the EST movement. It also has implications for the nature of the treatments that are then translated to training manuals. Beutler, Moleiro, and Talebi (2002) have observed that a common diagnosis may hide a great deal of personal but relevant heterogeneity. Manuals, however, focus on the criteria of the diagnostic category and may take little account of nondiagnostic variability such as lifestyle, environment, personal styles, and interpersonal sensitivity. Even then, these authors observe that a substantial amount of time is required to master the newly minted manualized treatment, which systematically and intentionally strengthens the tendency to ignore these nondiagnostic factors. Since the complexity of patients that goes unrecognized or unacknowledged may result in a proportion of patients who do not respond well to the defined EST, a clinician who is devoted to the EST view would logically be in the position of learning and applying a second treatment model for each diagnostic group with which he or she works. In an EST world, therefore, clinicians would be required to learn from 6 to 70 different treatment manuals to be considered effective and competent, each requiring a year or more of practice and each of which might become obsolete at any moment (Beutler, 2002; Westen, Novotny, & Thompson-Brenner, 2004a). Such an extended training program seems simply impracticable.

The range of these concerns with the methodology, with nondiagnostic factors, with therapist characteristics, and with relationship factors that are independent of the therapy

model used, and the corresponding failure of the Division 12 Task Force to address these issues satisfactorily, gave rise to another Task Force with a broader mission.

EMPIRICALLY SUPPORTED RELATIONSHIPS

The Division of Psychotherapy (Division 29) Task Force contested the importance given to "specific" factors of psychotherapy by the Division 12 Task Force. This Task Force concluded that other factors are more responsible for therapeutic change than the particular techniques and model used, and it argued that identifying these general or "common factors" that are embedded in all therapies to one degree or another was key to understanding the efficacy of psychotherapy. The role of "common factors" in psychotherapy has shifted from being considered as both necessary and sufficient conditions for change (e.g., Rogers, 1957) to being considered a characteristic that interacts with other variables and that are characteristic of psychotherapies that focus on emotional expression and insight. Historically, many different—but not always interrelated—concepts fell under the general definition of "common factors," and in the context of the Division 29 review, these factors included such things as client motivation, role preparation, cooperation, collaboration, role engagement, openness, expressiveness, experiencing, and positive affect (e.g., Castonguay, 2002). Particularly important in the Division 29 deliberation was the role of the therapeutic relationship, a component that both is more predictive of change than any specific model of intervention and was relegated to a mere supporting role in EST research.

The movement to give favor to defining the nature of the "empirically supported relationships" (ESRs) over the qualities of the therapeutic model has observed that studies which have compared different treatments often yield equivocal effects, and in these studies, most clients are found to improve regardless of the treatment techniques or model used. Through an intensive and exhaustive review of research literature, which included both naturalistic and quasi-experimental studies, the ESR Task Force identified elements of the therapeutic relationship that they identified as either "probably effective" or "promising" or of unknown importance. Among the effective or promising variables identified, the therapeutic alliance, therapist empathy, therapist positive regard, therapist genuineness, patient resistance, goal consensus and collaboration, level of functional impairment, and group cohesion rose to prominence (Norcross, 2002). Among these, the most consistent effect was attributed to the therapeutic alliance, which alone was estimated to account for 10–20% of the total variance in therapeutic outcome research (Beutler et al., 2003; Horvath & Symonds, 1991; Wampold, 2001). This level of effect is at least as strong and perhaps more so than that attributed to specific treatment effects (Luborsky et al., 2002).

A major contribution of the Division 29 Task Force was the identification of the particular participant factors that are associated with change. This was an important contribution particularly because it addressed the concerns of those who believed that patients themselves were the main agents of change in psychotherapy. Such advocates argued that patients bring their own biases, expectations, and filters into therapy and that these factors determine the nature of the therapeutic equation (Bohart, 2006). Patient characteristics identified by the Task Force, such as the severity of distress and functional impairment (Norcross, 2002), and later others such as diagnosis, demographic variables, personality factors, and interpersonal factors (Clarkin & Levy, 2004) have been estimated to account for 25–30% of the therapy outcome (Norcross & Lambert, 2006), suggesting them to be more important than therapeutic model and procedures.

Before one takes these comparative estimates of contribution as conclusive, it is important to observe that some of the same criticisms are relevant for ESR conclusions as they are for conclusions from EST research. The correlational methods on which most ESR research relies do not allow for clear determinations of cause-and-effect relationships. Additionally, patient factors such as levels of distress and symptom manifestations are transient by nature and often change within a single session, making them difficult to monitor in any reliable fashion (Clarkin & Levy, 2004). Finally, neither approach addresses the possibility that some therapist-patient pairs work better than other patient-therapist pairs, and that the effectiveness of a given pair interacts with the power of different treatments. Factors that are embodied in all effective treatments may be a product of the unique personality or style of the therapist; the expectations, hopes, and fears that each client brings to the table; and the fit of the interventions to the patient's proclivities (Beutler et al., 2002). Ultimately, as Lambert and Barley (2002, p. 21) have suggested, "It is difficult to conceptually differentiate between therapist variables (interpersonal style, attributes), facilitative conditions (empathy, warmth, positive regards), and the client-therapist relationship (therapeutic alliance, working endeavor)." Perhaps the most significant critique of the ESR movement is that it is at least as unbalanced as the EST movement in the relevance it assigns to certain types of variables. Whereas the EST movement virtually ignored therapeutic relationship qualities, the ESR movement virtually ignores the technique- and theory-based interventions that the therapist uses. Furthermore, the ESR Task Force failed to articulate how to translate the findings on effective therapy components into specific guidelines for therapists to implement in treatment. Essentially, focusing on any one component of therapy outcome to the exclusion of others is missing the bigger picture. The question is not which component is more important, because all have been deemed necessary, but rather how to best integrate the separate components into tangible recommendations on how to best effect change in psychotherapy. The movements for integration of factors soon followed.

PRINCIPLES OF CHANGE THAT WORK: AN INTEGRATIVE APPROACH

By themselves, treatment factors and relationship factors each explain only a fraction of the variance among psychotherapy outcomes. Treatment factors account for up to 10% of the total variance (e.g., Luborsky et al., 2002), relationship factors account for about 20% (Wampold, 2001), and participant factors contribute the most to treatment outcome, accounting for 25–30% of the total variance (Norcross & Lambert, 2006). However, in a response to the debate regarding which factor or factors are most important, research has suggested that the integration of factors can prospectively account for more than any additive combination of them.

Indeed, one study (Beutler et al., 2002) that contrasted preselected patient, therapy, and relationship factors found that more than 70% of observed changes in depressive symptoms were predicted from the combination of these research-informed factors. Even more notable, this predictive power rose to over 90% when one inserted a measure of how well the treatment "fit" the patient's intake characteristics.

The study was based on a small sample of clients with co-occurring depression and chemical dependence problems that were randomly assigned to three different treatments. Using hierarchical multiple regression procedures, the authors were able to parse out the contribution of multiple factors and to see how strong were their predictive validity, especially at the 6-month follow-up mark (Beutler et al., 2003). Although the results of other studies are not so optimistic, there is a consistent trend indicating that psychotherapy is more than any of these factors (treatment, participants, or relationships) alone. Effective psychotherapy constitutes an amalgamation of all of these factors in some harmonious relationship with one another. The challenge for clinicians lies in knowing what factors work together, when they should be activated, and how to do that.

In 2005, the American Psychological Association (APA) created a Presidential Task Force on Evidence-Based Practice (Levant, 2005). This Task Force was charged with determining the basis on which a clinician is to decide when a treatment is effective. The Task Force concluded that evidence-based practice of psychology (EBPP) should be based on a clinical judgment that incorporates not only the findings of scientific literature but also therapist experience and expertise and patient preferences. To many scientist-scholars, the equating of sound research findings with the illusiveness of clinical judgment and values posed a threat to the effort to reach a conclusion that would advance the field (Beutler, 2004). The Presidential Task Force, for example, urged clinicians to incorporate "the best available research with clinical expertise in the context of patient characteristics, culture, and preference" (Levant, 2005, p. 5).

This definition of EBPP suffers from two major concerns: (1) the committee placed unfounded confidence in the subjective clinical judgments of clinicians, ignoring the very real possibility that most clinicians are not in a position to either know what constitutes the "best research" or accurately to judge the value of their own "clinical expertise"; and (2) the committee failed to provide specific guidelines for how actually to integrate treatment, therapist, and patient variables into a workable treatment plan. Therefore, in an effort to address these concerns and develop a concrete mechanism for integrating these various factors into treatment guidelines, a joint work group was appointed by the presidents of the Society for Clinical Psychology (Division 12 of APA) and the North American Society for Psychotherapy Research (NASPR) (Castonguay & Beutler, 2006).

The Joint Task Force on the Establishment of Effective Principles of Psychotherapy sought to answer two main questions: (1) What is known about the nature of the therapy participants, relationships, *and* treatment procedures that will tend to induce positive effects across treatment models and orientations? (2) How do the factors that are related to these domains work together synchronously to enhance and optimize change? The Joint Task Force was charged with reviewing the empirical literature and identifying specific optimizing factors that characterized treatment interventions, relationship qualities, and participant variables without being tied to any particular theoretical orientation. The result was a list of research-derived principles or working statements that could be used to guide the clinician. These broadly based, empirically supported principles could then collectively be used as guidelines for a particular patient's treatment.

The members of this Task Force were broken into 12 groups. Pairs of senior scholars and their associates reviewed all available literature on the role of one variable domain (treatment factors, relationship factors, or participant factors) within one particular problem area (depression, anxiety, personality disorder, or substance use). From this review, members were asked to extract a set of principles that describe the conclusion that can be reached by the preponderance of available evidence. These guiding principles of change were each associated with a particular domain and problem area and cut across theoretical orientations.

Once each author group had reviewed the pertinent literature and had derived a list of principles that they believed described the state of knowledge, one member from each these subgroups then attended a joint working group whose mission was to compile a final list of empirically supported principles. These principles were of two types. One list of principles defined relationships and connections that were (1) common across all disorders, and another list defined relationships that (2) were unique to one of the problem areas. Each set of principles defined the conditions that were associated with measurable and reliable improvement.

A total of 61 principles were ultimately delineated by the Joint Task Force and separately constituted 26 "common" (i.e., were true for the treatment of most of the conditions studied) and 35 "unique" (i.e., were true of treating one or another of the different disorders) guiding statements to direct change efforts. Each principle addressed a factor of the treatment, the relationship, the participant, or an interaction that had been empirically demonstrated to be associated with effective treatment outcomes. For example, five principles defined qualities of the patient/client that contributed to change across conditions. These principles included:

1. Clients with a high level of impairment are less likely to benefit from therapy than those with a better level of functioning at pretreatment.
2. Clients who have been diagnosed with a personality disorder are less likely to benefit from treatment than those who have not.
3. Clients who face financial and/or occupational difficulties may benefit less from treatment than those who do not.
4. Clients who experienced significant interpersonal problems during their early development may have difficulty responding to psychotherapy.
5. Client's expectations are likely to play a role in treatment outcome.

Other principles defined aspects of an effective therapist. These therapist qualities included compassion and flexibility (e.g., "Therapists should relate to their clients in an empathic way") as well as specific therapist technical skills (e.g., "Therapists should use relational interpretations quite sparingly"). They also suggested that the influence of therapist qualities was seldom unique and separate either from patient or treatment compatibility.

Principles related to the treatment suggested ways to optimally structure the session (e.g., "Therapeutic change may be facilitated by, or even require, intense therapy if a personality disorder or severe problem is present"), whereas those that identified interactions among factors provided ways to tailor interventions to fit the characteristics of the individual (e.g., "Therapeutic change is greatest when the directiveness of the intervention is either inversely correspondent with the patient's current level of resistance or authoritatively prescribes a continuation of the symptomatic behavior").

Eleven of the 61 principles addressed the quality of a productive therapeutic relationship, and all but 2 of these suggested that their influence occurred regardless of the type of disorder being treated. The importance of fostering a collaborative alliance was emphasized (e.g., therapeutic change is greatest when the therapist is skillful and provides trust, acceptance, acknowledgment, collaboration, and respect for the patient within an environment that both supports risk and provides maximal safety).

Taken altogether, the 61 principles of therapeutic change identified by the Joint Task Force confirmed that the extensive research literature of clinical judgment and patient preferences can be condensed into cross-cutting principles that if followed could objectify a research-informed system of integrating treatment, relationship, and participant factors. They also emphasized the cross-cutting role of the therapeutic relationship but, equally, emphasized that there are treatment qualities that have

distinguishing and unique impacts on different kinds of patients. Indeed, the importance of fitting the treatment to the particular patient and that patient's problem was an important and consistent finding. Finally, the results suggested that a principle-based treatment plan, at least as much as a theory-based one, could provide clinicians with a tangible way to apply multiple variables and decisions to psychotherapy.

EMPIRICALLY SUPPORTED TREATMENTS AND EVIDENCE-BASED PRACTICE AT WORK: THE EXAMPLE OF TREATING VICTIMS OF MASS DISASTER AND TERRORISM

As we have suggested, there are at least three conceptual models that provide meaningful ways of applying research-based and research-informed treatment. The most widely known is based on identifying treatments that work better than a no-treatment control group based on randomized clinical trial research.

The second approach to research-based practice emphasizes quasi-experimental and naturalistic research and the identification of participant and relationship variables that contribute to effective change. A treatment from this perspective would take care to assign a given patient to a particular type of therapist and would guide the therapist in how to develop and maintain the therapeutic relationship, following observed and empirically derived correlations between certain patient and therapist characteristics, the nature of the working relationship, and treatment outcomes.

The third model of research-based practice is one that integrates the previous two, incorporating information that derives both from research on participant and relationship factors and from research that defines strategies and procedures that work. It begins, as we have noted, with an

---

HIGHLIGHT BOX 16.3

In this discussion, we have intentionally excluded using the illustration of a treatment that derives from the APA Presidential Task Force on Research-Based Practice. We have done this because this latter Task Force was more concerned with defining what the basis of practice should be than either how to implement it or how to ensure that it works. Thus, the proposal from this Task Force emphasized giving attention to patient values, research, and clinician expertise. However, without some method of measuring these things and without some guidelines in how to incorporate them and balance among them, it leaves little that can be translated into a practical treatment.

---

extraction of principles of effective treatment for different kinds of problems, basing these principles upon available research evidence. It then uses these principles, both those that are common to different disorders and symptoms and those that are uniquely suited for ameliorating specific symptoms and problems, to construct a treatment plan. This plan is founded in research evidence and addresses the integration of participant factors, relationship factors, treatment factors, and the fit of the treatment to the patient (see Highlight Box 16.3).

The first and third of these models of research-based practice have been applied to the problem of treating victims of mass disaster and trauma. In this section we will illustrate the application of evidence-based practices from these two perspectives, using the example of a treatment for the psychological consequences of a mass trauma such as natural disaster or a major terrorist attack. This practical example will allow us to consider the complex interactions and applications of research and clinical findings by integrating them into a workable treatment.

Empirically Supported Treatments for ASD and PTSD

Acute stress disorder (ASD) and posttraumatic stress disorder (PTSD) are the usual conditions to which ESTs for victims of mass trauma are addressed. These disorders share a variety of symptoms, with differences in the temporal length in which the symptoms are experienced and the lassitude of criteria necessary for the diagnosis, with PTSD having the more stringent and narrow criteria.

The EST approach begins with the anticipated or observed set of symptoms and a reliably established diagnosis. Then, a treatment is selected that has been validated and tested on similar patients with similar diagnoses. The treatment to be used is selected from a list of those that have been found to be effective based on a series of specific studies or that are referenced as effective from meta-analytic review of qualified studies. In either case, the studies have been subjected to randomized clinical trial research designs. Such reviews are available through a variety of professional sources, including: (a) the International Societies of Posttraumatic Stress Studies (ISTSS); (b) the American Psychiatric Association; (c) the U.S. National PTSD Center; (d) the UK National Institute for Clinical Excellence (NICE); (e) the Australian Center for Posttraumatic Mental Health; and (f) the Israel Center for the Treatment of Psychotrauma (ICTP).

The treatment favored by these various groups may differ. For example, the U.S. National PTSD Center has emphasized the value of applying its Psychological First Aid (PFA) program (2nd edition) within hours and days of subsequent mass disasters (Brymer et al., 2006). On the other hand, ISTSS guidelines have emphasized the use of cognitive therapy models, prolonged exposure therapies, and pharmacological interventions for both ASD and PTSD (Bryant et al., 2007; Brymer et al., 2006; Foa, Keane, & Friedman, 2000; ICTP, 2007; NICE, 2005; Ursano et al., 2004). Cognitive therapy attempts to intervene through a program of education, exercises, homework assignments, and self-monitoring a patient's automatic thought processes, feelings, and behaviors. Exposure therapies, in contrast, emphasize the role of extinction and confrontation of avoided and feared situations associated with the trauma. Prolonged exposure (PE) uses visualization and direct exposure to these situations, in which the stimulation is maintained until a decline in affective arousal and fear is noted (see Highlight Box 16.4).

The American Psychiatric Association's Practice Guidelines (2004) recommended pharmacological interventions as the first-line of treatment; however, at the twenty-third annual ISTSS meeting, Elginga (2007) found that pharmacological regulation of the HPA axis for veterans in acute states was not effective, suggesting that recommendations based solely on EST evidence may not be sufficiently flexible or attentive to other factors.

Few ESTs have been specifically developed for the initial period following a trauma in which most people experience acute stress disorder (ASD). Randomized clinical trial studies are difficult to implement during this immediate phase, and outcomes are difficult to assess because they are often confounded with the effects of post-trauma changes in the environment. However, Bryant and colleagues (Bryant, Sackville, Dang, Moulds, & Guthrie, 1999) have provided some relatively strong evidence that applications of cognitive control strategies to reduce fear and practice in evaluating one's response and behavior are effective in relieving many ASD symptoms. For example, a randomized controlled study between prolonged exposure therapy (PE) and supportive counseling (SC) for 45 patients with acute levels of stress (Bryant et al., 1999) demonstrated that SC was more effective (with some exceptions) than PE both at post-treatment and 6 months after treatment. In any case, Foa, Keane, and Friedman (2000) recommended avoiding the use of exposure or debriefing-based treatment with people in acute states due to the possibility of unnecessarily increasing their agitation.

Unfortunately, there are many factors that seem to limit the effectiveness of these structured treatments and suggest the need for a more flexible alternative. A comorbid personality disorder (PD) (Bisson, McFarlane, & Rose, 2000), premorbid negative self-appraisals (Bryant & Guthrie, 2007), prior exposure to violence or trauma, and the

---

HIGHLIGHT BOX 16.4

Less well established or accepted alternatives to cognitive and exposure therapy are also sometimes used. One of the most controversial of these, but one in which a good deal of research has been conducted, is eye movement desensitization and reprocessing (EMDR). This approach to treatment initiates bilateral eye movements or other bilateral stimulation (e.g., tapping) while the patient focuses on the traumatic event (Sikes & Sikes, 2008). The mechanism of action is uncertain in this approach, but some evidence suggests that it is relatively effective in reducing anxiety, panic, and obsessive thoughts associated with traumatic events (ICTP, 2007; NICE, 2005).

absence of a social support system (Castonguay & Beutler, 2006; Housley & Beutler, 2006), for example, have a generally negative impact on the recovery rates of victims in acute states. Likewise, other nondiagnostic variables play a significant role in how symptoms manifest and how treatment may be implemented (e.g., Brady, 2001; Zlotnick, Zimmerman, Wolfsdorf, & Mattia, 2001). The influence of such variables suggests a need to look beyond patient diagnosis to nondiagnostic participant and relationship factors and to modify the recommended treatments in ways that address these variables. Within the EST methods, for example, some success has been achieved by adding supportive counseling and psychoeducation (Bryant et al., 2007; Brymer et al., 2006; Ursano et al., 2004), but the rationale and effectiveness of these efforts are still not clearly established.

While existing ESTs may demonstrate that there are significant and effective treatments for ASD and PTSD, and thereby may provide useful guidelines for clinicians in Western civilizations, few randomized clinical studies have been conducted among clients in African and Eastern countries. These considerations are among those that have led to the development of alternative methods of applying research-based practices. We turn now to an illustration of the application of empirically informed principles of therapeutic change to the treatment of victims of mass trauma and terrorism.

Empirically Informed Principles for Treating Victims of Mass Disaster and Terrorism

One of the first differences that one is likely to notice between the applications of ESTs and those of empirically informed principles is that the latter approach does not start with nor is it focused on a particular diagnosis. Next, one is likely to notice that the latter approach is not based on a single theoretical model of how symptoms develop or change. Whereas ESTs are grounded in a theory of psychopathology, empirically

informed principles are extracted and applied independently of a model of symptom development or change—the principles are empirical observations rather than theoretical constructs.

The advantage of using a system that eschews adherence either to a specific theoretical model or to a particular diagnostic group is that the treatment is much more closely dependent on the problem rather than the assumed pattern of symptoms and causes that are "usually" present. For example, an EST model makes the assumption that a mass trauma will result in an elevated risk of PTSD and, on the basis of this assumption, has evolved treatments that address panic, anxiety, flashbacks, and the like. But, if non-PTSD symptoms predominate, such as depression or chemical abuse, the treatment is no longer viable; whereas, in the application of research-informed principles, the intervention is flexible enough to step outside of the theoretical model of symptom development or change in order to address the symptoms from a different perspective. Although clinicians may value this kind of flexibility or eclecticism, in practice, it is not an easy transition to make when one is trying to adhere to a consistent model of treatment.

It is quite possible that what is considered to be "true" from one theoretical view of problem development or symptom change is considered to be quite "untrue" from another. Critical incident stress debriefing (CISD; Mitchell, 1983), for example, has been the most widely used treatment for exposed individuals during the acute postincident period. This approach is based loosely on a model of stages of stress reduction in which denial is broken down so that reconciliation and recovery can follow (see Highlight Box 16.5).

However, empirical evidence has demonstrated that this is a model that does not work well in practice for those in acute stages of exposure. While the theory directs the clinician to encourage the victim to reexperience, discuss, and describe his/her reactions to the traumatic event, there is good reason to think that doing so may actually impede the activation

---

HIGHLIGHT BOX 16.5

CISD (Mitchell, 1983) and critical incident stress management (CISM) (Everly & Mitchell, 1999) usually: (1) is composed of a single session within a 24- to 72-hour window following a traumatic incident; (2) is mandated for first responders; (3) requires the patient to re-create the event, followed by a group discussion of emotional and cognitive reactions and symptoms; and (4) entails an effort to normalize one's symptoms. However, despite the fact that recipients and providers of CISD report positive experiences with the intervention, its effectiveness has come under scrutiny (Bisson, Jenkins, Alexander, & Bannister, 1997; Litz & Gray, 2004; Rose, Wessely, & Bisson, 1998; Rose, Bisson, & Wessely, 2001), with the conclusion that it may, in some cases, impede the natural recovery process and *increase* the likelihood of PTSD.

---

of the individual's normal resiliency (Bisson, Jenkins, Alexander, & Bannister, 1997; Litz & Gray, 2004).

It is unclear at the present time why a well-developed theory such as that on which CISD is based does not yield more positive effects. Is it, as some suppose, because thinking about the immediately past trauma produces more trauma, because it is too short in duration, or maybe because it is often delivered as a mandated intervention? Until research is able to clarify why the reduced effects occur in such interventions, it is probably unwise to continue their practice.

One thing is clear about the level of effectiveness attributable to any treatment: Namely, the variability among individuals' levels of personal resilience, their coping styles, levels of social support, and many other variables complicates our ability to observe and predict the pattern of natural response and recovery. Thus, a single, clear evolution or unfolding of single or uniform psychopathological response is the exception, rather than the rule, following a traumatic event. Recently, research has focused on the study of individual resiliency and capacity to restore a psychological balance among those who have been exposed to trauma (Bonanno, 2004) and has confirmed the observation that the substantial majority of such individuals will not develop

an enduring psychological disorder in spite of acute suffering immediately following the event.

Perhaps as few as 20% of those who have been directly exposed to even a severe traumatic event will develop a psychopathological condition, and, among these, PTSD may be much less frequent than major depression and chemical abuse (Housley & Beutler, 2006). By giving the greatest attention to the predictors of symptom development and outcome rather than to the model of change and the symptoms of the expected disorders, research-informed principles of treatment can be used effectively before a full-blown diagnostic condition has evolved. A clinician can maintain a synchronized and consistent treatment by first applying common principles that alert us to who is most at risk for short- and long-term problems, and then by applying treatments whose applications cut across a variety of relevant disorders, and finally by applying specific principles of change as the patients' unique difficulties become manifest. Principles can allow a clinician to move within and across these three stages of treatment in order to maintain treatment coherence and integrity as the patient changes across time.

In the immediate aftermath of the trauma, most people have similar short-term reactions that are typically seen as ASD. Most of these will dissipate over the course of 3 to 6 months, however, leaving the individual indistinguishable from those who have not been so exposed. If one then knows, by relying on sound principles of change, what factors pose risks and signals for the evolution of a more prolonged condition that does not dissipate, a clinician can be poised to respond in a timely fashion as the patient's problems evolve (Housley & Beutler, 2006). It may not be until 8 to 10 weeks after the evoking trauma that one can begin to tell whose symptoms will consolidate into diagnostically stable groupings and whose will disappear. At this point, major depression, chemical abuse, and anxiety disorders appear among vulnerable individuals. If one knows the principles of treatment that are associated with ameliorating risk and identifying the type of problem most likely to occur, then treatment need not wait until this amount of time passes.

The Palo Alto Medical Reserve Corps (PAMRC) is a disaster mental health organization developed in 2003 with the mission of developing an evidence-based disaster mental health intervention to serve as an alternative to psychological debriefing. The PAMRC succeeded in fulfilling this mission and subsequently published a manual of the intervention entitled *Treating Victims of Mass Disaster and Terrorism* (Housley & Beutler, 2006). The PAMRC currently dedicates its efforts to training and educating mental health professionals and other first responders in this treatment model.

The PAMRC's three-stage model was developed using empirically based principles identified by the Society for Clinical Psychology (Division 12 of the American Psychological Association) and the North American Society for Psychotherapy Research Task Force (Castonguay & Beutler, 2006). The application of the principles are illustrated with interventions extracted directly from randomized trial research on trauma intervention, giving the PAMRC's three-stage model a sound

empirical foundation in both principles and practices.

The three stages are separated temporally, with the first stage beginning immediately following a disaster, the second stage initiated 2 to 4 weeks post-trauma, and the third stage given 1 to 3 months after the disaster. This modular approach was designed as a way to triage so that only those most at risk for developing future problems are administered all three stages.

The first stage incorporates Psychological First-Aid (PFA), the new recognized alternative to PD (Litz & Gray, 2004). PFA was developed by the U.S. National Center for Post-traumatic Stress Disorder and the National Child Traumatic Stress Network, and the field operations guide is currently in its 2nd edition (PFA, 2006). PFA is an evidence-informed practical intervention for treating victims immediately following a traumatic incident. Techniques include assisting with basic physical needs such as food and shelter, teaching coping and problem solving, stabilizing overwhelmed victims, collecting information to be used in triaging, enhancing social support, and linking with supportive services. These techniques satisfy humanitarian desires to help without risking retraumatization. The PAMRC emphasizes the fact that even though many people exposed to traumatic incidents will experience transient stress symptoms, most will go on to recover through natural processes and will not develop more serious psychopathology (Housley & Beutler, 2006). However, individuals who continue to experience lasting problems after stage 1 are followed to stage 2.

The Task Force principles (Castonguay & Beutler, 2006) guide the informal assessment used to determine whether individuals require follow-up treatment after stage 1. Individuals that meet any of the following five criteria should be followed to stage 2: (1) history of a personality disorder or severe psychiatric disorder, (2) multiple symptoms of distress that impair current functioning and hamper reality testing, (3) lack of stable social support, (4) history of interpersonal difficulties, and (5) history of prior exposure to violence.

The second stage is an anxiety management stage using cognitive-behavioral therapy (CBT) techniques. Research has found CBT more effective than supportive counseling in reducing symptoms of ASD and other early posttrauma symptoms (Bryant, Harvey, Dang, Sackville, & Basten, 1998; Bryant et al., 1999). Specific techniques relating to CBT for ASD include creating a supportive and collaborative environment, communicating a basis for treatment, providing psychoeducation about patient-specific ASD symptoms, identifying and assessing thoughts, cognitive restructuring, homework, and anxiety management (Bryant et al., 1998). The principles guiding stage 2 focus on the quality of the therapeutic relationship, the therapist's interpersonal skills, and the therapist's clinical skills. For example, a principle related to the quality of the therapeutic relationship states, "Therapists should attempt to facilitate a high degree of collaboration with clients during therapy" (Housley & Beutler, 2006, p. 26). Individuals who continue to experience persistent symptoms after stage 2 are followed to stage 3, which resembles typical psychotherapy for trauma.

The PAMRC's third stage offers two alternative interventions: a supportive model and an exposure-based model. Practitioners choose a model based upon the client's characteristics identified by the Task Force (Castonguay & Beutler, 2006) and the presenting problem. Individuals with an internalizing coping style are indecisive, engage in self-inspection, overcontrol, and tend to have low self-esteem. Therefore, it is more effective to begin with supportive techniques before exposure with individuals with an internalizing coping style (Housley & Beutler, 2007). Designing treatment to begin with monitoring symptoms and psychoeducation in a supportive environment enhances self-esteem and parallels the internalizer's natural tendency to

be insight-oriented and self-aware. Individuals with externalizing coping styles are characterized as being impulsive and socially gregarious and blame others for their problems. Externalizers tend to benefit from treatment designed to reduce symptoms through direct behavioral change and building new skills. Therefore, the exposure-based model is most effective with externalizing individuals.

In addition to the Task Force principles suggesting empirically supported treatment techniques, they also alert therapists to some of the challenges that may arise. For example, a unique principle identified for anxiety disorders (including PTSD) states: "Psychotherapy for anxiety is less likely to be successful if the client has low internal attributions of control or high negative self-attribution. Thus, rigid externalizing or internalizing coping styles are negative prognostic indicators" (Housley & Beutler, 2006, p. 29). While most people fall along the internalizing-externalizing coping style continuum, individuals at either extreme will have a difficult time developing adequate perceived levels of control to make necessary changes. Stage 3 also uses the Task Force principles to assist practitioners in determining which techniques and interventions are effective for other post-trauma conditions. An example of a unique principle for depression and substance abuse that could be applied to posttrauma disorders is: "In dealing with the resistant patient, the therapist's use of directive therapeutic interventions should be planned to inversely correspond with the patient's manifest level of resistant traits and states" (Housley & Beutler, 2006, p. 29). Therefore, the research suggests that using relatively fewer directive interventions with more resistant patients is associated with better therapy outcomes.

Although the PAMRC three-stage model as a whole has not been tested in a randomized controlled trial, all elements of the model are based on empirically supported and field-tested principles. The three-stage model is intended to educate and prepare mental health professionals to treat the short-term and long-term psychological consequences of disaster. For a complete overview of the PAMRC's three-stage model, please refer to the training manual (Housley & Beutler, 2006) (see Highlight Box 16. 6).

SUMMARY

In this chapter we have attempted to introduce the reader to the complex concept of research-informed (or research-based) practice. There are several different views of what constitutes the most effective way of identifying a research foundation for practice. Some approaches, indeed the most widely recognized approach to this problem (ESTs), concentrate only on the research that bears on the techniques, procedures, and theoretical model that are used by the clinician. Other approaches are broader, focusing on the quality of the therapeutic relationship (ESRs) or the underlying principles that drive the assignment of particular participants, procedures, relationships, and contexts of treatment (ESPs). Although opinions vary as to which alternative is better, it

is clear that they differ in the breadth of the constructs that they address and include within the definition of treatment. EST models emphasize conscious interventions that are under the therapist's control, whereas ESRs emphasize more abstract and stylistic concepts related to participants and relationships, and ESPs combine the foregoing and suggest that psychotherapy includes methods, people, and relationships. The last approach, which admittedly is the one to which the current authors adhere, is unique in also addressing how well the treatment and patient and therapist fit one another to produce both a good working relationship and a predictable change.

We have illustrated the use of a principle-based approach to practice by describing applications to the treatment of victims of mass trauma. The application of empirically supported treatments was contrasted with the application of empirically informed principles. Although both approaches illustrate the use of techniques, even similar techniques, the ESP approach takes a broader view of the impact of trauma rather than narrowing the treatment to a specific disorder. This latter approach also grounds the procedures used in principles of practice rather than in a

---

HIGHLIGHT BOX 16.6

It must be noted that we have not addressed the extension of research-based practice to training (Woody, Weisz, & McLean, 2005). While both APA and the Canadian Psychological Association (CPA) now require continuing education (CE) instructors to identify the degree of empirical support for treatments they teach (Woody et al., 2005), graduate programs still give little note of research evidence in practice. Surveys confirm that graduate students received training in fewer than ten ESTs (Woody et al., 2005). This result is consistent with the suggestion (Beutler, 2000) that it is impractical to learn and master the many manualized treatments that would be necessary to follow an EST guideline in the limited amount of time available in training programs. Furthermore, even if time were available, the reliance on intensive supervision as a teaching method has achieved poor results (e.g., Holloway & Neufeldt, 1995; Stein & Lambert, 1995).

theory of pathology and change. Thus, cognitive ESTs view the development and change of symptoms through a lens of causality that is specific to cognitive theory, whereas the ESP approach we illustrated identifies only the conditions that should be present to foster change without assuming a particular causal role. In practice, this is a major difference and gives the clinician much more flexibility to choose a theory from which to operate without sacrificing the reliance on research evidence.

We believe that the future of psychotherapy will be preserved only if practitioners are willing to accept the social salience and ethical responsibility of adhering to some form of scientific practice base. To do otherwise means that the only criteria of worth are the clinician's goodwill, sincerity, and belief. But this subjective standard is weak as a method of assessing the effects of a treatment. It places psychotherapy on a plane that is no more reliable that that based on witchcraft, magic, astrology, and bloodletting, all of which share this same subjective basis of knowledge. For centuries, humankind has struggled to rise above a subjective standard that identifies truth with one's vaules and intentions, rather than objective evidence of effects. Accepting such a standard now would be a giant step backward.

That is not to say that there is no place for subjectivity in psychotherapy. Indeed there is. There are many schools of thought that emphasize the importance of the subjective experiences of the patient and of the therapist. Indeed, the importance that the therapeutic relationship has in facilitating outcomes is, in part, because the therapist is able to resonate with the subjective experiences of the patient. But it is in the realm of assessing that elusive concept of improvement that subjective judgment ceases to provide as much benefit as might be hoped. To the degree that we can, we must set aside the potential biases that exist within our subjective judgments of value and worth and adopt objective tools when it comes to defining what works. These tools can, however, be applied equally well to assessing changes in the patient's own subjective experience, emotions, thoughts, values, and biases and to assessing mere changes in behavior. We are best served when we reserve our own subjectivity for aspects of intervention that are not so closely bound to evaluating a patient's level of change, but in helping us develop, feel, and express the experience that is that of the patient and is, thereby, an important if not necessary ingredient of evoking change in our patients. This line between subjective and objective may be difficult for some to comprehend, but it is a distinction that we must keep in our minds and in our practices to be effective and ethical.

Glossary

Common factors: 26 of the 61 principles identified by the Joint Task Force. Common factors are principles found to be true across all disorders studied.

Division 12—Society for Clinical Psychology: division of the American Psychological Association that focuses on the integration of the science, theory, and practice of psychology. Division 12 examines many elements of human behavior including intellectual, emotional, biological, psychological, social, and behavioral aspects.

Division 29—Psychotherapy: division of the American Psychological Association that focuses on studying, understanding, and educating others about psychotherapy.

Empirically supported relationships (ESRs): term given by the Division 29 Task Force to qualities of the therapeutic relationship deemed to be more important than treatment factors—therapeutic alliance, therapist empathy, therapist positive regard, therapist genuineness, patient resistance, goal consensus and collaboration, level of functional impairment, and group cohesion rose to prominence.

Empirically supported treatments (ESTs): name given to treatments deemed empirically valid in producing positive outcomes in randomized controlled studies with specific populations. The movement to identify ESTs stemmed from the desire to prove psychotherapy was a scientifically based treatment and to identify which elements of treatment were important for specific disorders.

Evidence-based practice (EBPP): term given by the 2005 APA Presidential Task Force in an attempt to expand the definition of an EST by including therapist experience and expertise and patient preferences.

Evidence-informed principle: broad-based statements identified by the Joint Task Force (made up of Division 12 and North American Society for Psychotherapy Research) that include treatment, relationship, and participant recommendations to assist clinicians in guiding treatment.

North American Society for Psychotherapy Research (NASPR): a regional chapter of the Society for Psychotherapy Research (SPR)—an international multidisciplinary scientific organization.

Palo Alto Medical Reserve Corps (PAMRC): a disaster mental health organization developed in 2003 with the mission of developing an evidence-based disaster mental health intervention to serve as an alternative to psychological debriefing. The PAMRC published a manual of the intervention entitled *Treating Victims of Mass Trauma and Terrorism* (Housley & Beutler, 2006). The PAMRC currently dedicates its efforts to training and educating mental health professionals and other first responders in this treatment model.

Psychological First-Aid (PFA): an evidence-informed practical intervention for treating victims immediately following a traumatic incident developed by the U.S. National Center for Post-traumatic Stress Disorder and the National Child Traumatic Stress Network. This intervention is meant for first responders and mental health professionals.

Randomized clinical trials (RCTs): an experimental design in which patients are randomly assigned to either a group that will receive an experimental treatment or one that will receive a comparison treatment or placebo.

Unique factors: 35 of the principles identified by the Joint Task Force. Unique factors are principles found to be true for a specific disorder such as depression, anxiety, substance use, and personality disorder.

References

Barlow, D. H. (1994). Psychological interventions in the era of managed competition. *Clinical Psychology: Science and Practice, 1*, 109–122.

Bernal, G. & Scharron-del-Rio, M. R. (2001). Are empirically supported treatments valid for ethnic minorities? Toward an alternative approach for treatment research. *Cultural Diversity and Ethnic Minority Psychology, 7*, 328–342.

Beutler, L. E. (1991). Have all won and must all have prizes? Revisiting Luborsky et al.'s verdict. *Journal of Consulting and Clinical Psychology, 59*, 226–232.

Beutler, L. E. (1998). Identifying empirically supported treatments: what if we didn't? *Journal of Consulting and Clinical Psychology, 66*, 113–120.

Beutler, L. E. (2000). David and Goliath: when empirical and clinical standards of practice meet. *American Psychologist, 55*, 997–1007.

Beutler, L. E. (2002). The dodo bird really is extinct. *Clinical Psychology: Science and Practice, 9*, 30–34.

Beutler, L. E. (2004). The empirically-validated treatments movement: a scientist-practitioner's perspective. *Clinical Psychology: Science and Practice, 11*, 225–229.

Beutler, L. E., Bongar, B., & Shurkin, J. L. (1998). *Am I crazy or is it my shrink?* New York: Oxford University Press.

Beutler, L. E., Malik, M., Alimohamed, S., Harwood, T. M., Talebi, H., Noble, S., et al. (2003). Therapist variables. In M. J. Lambert (Ed.), *Handbook of psychotherapy and behavior change* (5th ed., pp. 227–306). New York: Wiley.

Beutler, L. E., Moleiro, C., Malik, M., Harwood, T. M., Romanelli, R., Gallagher-Thompson, D., et al. (2003). A comparison of the Dodo, EST, and ATI indicators among co-morbid stimulant dependent, depressed patients. *Clinical Psychology and Psychotherapy, 10*, 69–85.

Beutler, L. E., Moleiro, C., & Talebi, H. (2002). How practitioners can systematically use empirical evidence in treatment selection. *Journal of Clinical Psychology, 58*, 1199–1212.

Beutler, L. E., Williams, R. E., Wakefield, P. J., & Entwistle, S. R. (1995). Bridging scientist and practitioner perspectives in clinical psychology. *American Psychologist, 50*, 984–994.

Bisson, J. I., Jenkins, P. L., Alexander, J., & Bannister, C. (1997). Randomized controlled trial of psychological debriefing for victims of acute burn trauma. *British Journal of Psychiatry, 171*, 78–81.

Bisson, J. I., McFarlane, A., & Rose, S. (2000). *Psychological debriefing*. Northbrook, IL: The International Society for Traumatic Stress Studies.

Bohart, A. A. (2006). The active client. In J. C. Norcross, L. E. Beutler, & R. F. Levant (Eds.), *Evidence-based practices in mental health* (pp. 218–226). Washington, DC: American Psychological Association.

Bonanno, G. A. (2004). Loss, trauma, and human resilience: Have we underestimated the human capacity to thrive after extremely aversive events? *American Psychologist, 59*, 20–28.

Brady, K. T. (2001). *Gender differences in PTSD*. Lecture presented to the 154th Annual Meeting of the American Psychiatric Association. New Orleans, LA.

Bryant, R. A., Creamer, M., Devilly, G., McFarlane, A., Matthews, L., Doran, C., et al. (2007, February). *Australian guidelines for the treatment of adults with Acute Stress Disorder and Posttraumatic Stress Disorder: Practitioner guides*. Australian Government: Australian Centre for Posttraumatic Mental Health.

Bryant, R. A. & Guthrie, R. M. (2007). Maladaptive self-appraisals before trauma exposure predict posttraumatic stress disorder. *Journal of Consulting and Clinical Psychology, 75*(5):812–815.

Bryant, R. A., Harvey, A. G., Dang, S. T., Sackville, T., & Basten, C. (1998). Treatment of acute stress disorder: a comparison of cognitive-behavioral therapy and supportive counseling. *Journal of Consulting and Clinical Psychology, 66*(5):862–866.

Bryant, R. A., Sackville, T., Dang, S. T., Moulds, M., & Guthrie, R. (1999). Treating acute stress disorder: an evaluation of cognitive behavior therapy and supportive counseling techniques. *American Journal of Psychiatry, 156*(11):1780–1786.

Brymer, M., Jacobs, A., Layne, C., Pynoos, R., Ruzek, J.,Steinberg, A., et al. (2006, July). *National Child Traumatic Stress Network and National Center for PTSD, Psychological First Aid: Field Operations Guide* (2nd ed.). Retrieved from http://www.nctsn.org and www.ncptsd.va.gov (January 7, 2008).

Carey, B. (2008, January 17). Antidepressant studies published. *New York Times*. Retrieved February 2008 from http://www.nytimes.com/2008/01/17/health/17depress.html?ei= 5070&en=bff3cb16e49ff5f.

Castonguay, L. G. (2002). Controlling is not enough: the importance of measuring the process and specific effectiveness of psychotherapy treatment and control conditions. *Ethics and Behavior, 12*, 31–42.

Castonguay, L. G. & Beutler, L. E. (2006). *Principles of therapeutic change that work*. New York: Oxford University Press.

Chambless, D. L., Baker, M. J., Baucom, D. H., Beutler, L. E., Calhoun, K. S., Crits-Christoph, P., et al. (1988). Update on empirically validated therapies, II. *The Clinical Psychologist, 51*, 3–16.

Chambless, D. L. & Hollon, S. (1998). Defining empirically supported therapies. *Journal of Consulting and Clinical Psychology, 66*, 7–18.

Chambless, D. L. & Ollendick, T. H. (2001). Empirically supported psychological interventions: controversies and evidence. *Annual Review of Psychology, 52*, 685–716.

Chambless, D. L., Sanderson, W. C., Shoham, V., Johnson, S. B., Pope, K. S., Crits-Christoph, P., et al. (1996). An update on empirically validated therapies. *The Clinical Psychologist, 49*, 5–14.

Clarkin, J. F. & Levy, K. N. (2004). The influence of client variables on psychotherapy. In M. J. Lambert (Ed.), *Handbook of psychotherapy and behavior change* (5th ed., pp. 194–226). New York: Wiley.

Crits-Christoph, P., Baranackie, K., Kurcias, J. S., Beck, A. T., Carroll, K., Perry, K., et al. (1991). Meta-analysis of therapist effects in psychotherapy outcome studies. *Psychotherapy Research, 1*, 81–91.

Crits-Christoph, P., Wilson, G. T., & Hollon, D. D. (2005). Empirically supported psychotherapies: Comment on Westen, Novotny, and Thompson-Brenner (2004). *Psychological Bulletin, 131*, 412–417.

Drozd, J. E. & Goldfried, M. R. (1996). A critical evaluation of the state-of-the-art in psychotherapy outcome research. *Psychotherapy, 33*, 171–180.

Duncan, B. L. & Miller, S. D. (2006). Treatment manuals do not improve outcomes. In J. C. Norcross, L. E. Beutler, & R.F. Levant (Eds.), *Evidence-based practices in mental health* (pp. 140–149). Washington, DC: American Psychological Association.

Elginga, B. (2007, November). *HPA axis regulation in veterans with and without PTSD*. Lecture presented to the Twenty-third Annual Meeting of the International Societies for Posttraumatic Stress Studies, Baltimore.

Evans, M. D., Hollon, S. D., DeRubeis, R. J., Piasecki, J. M., Grove, W. M., Garvey, M. J., et al. (1992). Differential relapse following cognitive therapy and pharmacotherapy for depression. *Archives of General Psychiatry, 49*, 802–808.

Everly, G. & Mitchell, J. (1999). *Critical incident stress management (CISM): a new era and standard of care in crisis intervention* (2nd ed.). Ellicott City, MD: Chevron.

Eysenck, H. J. (1952). The effects of psychotherapy: an evaluation. *Journal of Consulting and Clinical Psychology, 60*, 659–663.

Fay, A. & Lazarus, A. A. (1993). On necessity and sufficiency in psychotherapy. *Psychotherapy in Private Practice, 12*, 33–39.

Foa, E. B., Keane, T. M., & Friedman, M. J. (2000). *Effective treatments for PTSD: practice guidelines from the international society for traumatic stress studies.* New York: Guilford.

Garfield, S. L. (1996). Some problems associated with "validated" forms of psychotherapy. *Clinical Psychology: Science and Practice, 3*, 218–229.

Hollon, S. D. (1996). The efficacy and effectiveness of psychotherapy relative to medications. *American Psychologist, 51*, 1025–1030.

Holloway, E. L. & Neufeldt, S. A. (1995). Supervision: its contributions to treatment efficacy. *Journal of Consulting and Clinical Psychology, 63*, 207–213.

Horvath, A. O. & Symonds, B. D. (1991). Relation between working alliance and outcome in psychotherapy: a meta-analysis. *Journal of Counseling Psychology, 38*, 139–149.

Housley, J. & Beutler, L. E. (2006). *Treating victims of mass disaster and terrorism.* Cambridge, MA: Hogrefe & Huber.

Jacobson, N. J. & Truax, P. (1991). Clinical significance: a statistical approach to defining meaningful change in psychotherapy research. *Journal of Consulting and Clinical Psychology, 59*, 12–19.

Lachin, J. M., Matts, J. P., & Wei, L. J. (1988). Randomization in clinical trials: conclusions and recommendations. *Controlled Clinical Trials, 9*, 365–374.

Lambert, M. J. & Barley, D. E. (2002). Research summary on the therapeutic relationship and psychotherapy outcome. In J. C. Norcross (Ed.), *Psychotherapy relationships that work: therapist contributions and responsiveness to patients* (pp. 17–32). New York: Oxford University Press.

Levant, R. F. (2005). *Report of the 2005 Task Force on Evidence-Based Practice.* Retrieved December 31, 2007 from http://www.apa.org/practice/ebpreport.pdf.

Litz, B. & Gray, M. (2004). Early intervention for trauma in adults: framework for first aid and secondary prevention. In B. Litz (Ed.), *Early intervention for trauma and traumatic loss.* New York: Guilford.

Luborksy, L., Rosenthal, R., Diguer, L., Andrusyna, T. P., Berman, J. S., Levitt, J. T., et al. (2001). The dodo bird verdict is alive and well — mostly. *Clinical Psychology: Science and Practice, 9*, 2–12.

Luborsky, L., Singer, B., & Luborsky, L. (1975). Comparative studies of psychotherapy. *Archives of General Psychiatry, 32*, 995–1008.

Mitchell, J. (1983). When disaster strikes ... the critical incident stress debriefing process. *Journal of Emergency Medical Services, 8*, 36–39.

Nathan P. E. & Gorman. J. M. (Eds.) (1998). *A guide to treatments that work.* New York: Oxford University Press.

Nathan P. E. & Gorman, J. M. (Eds.) (2002). *A guide to treatments that work* (2nd ed.). New York: Oxford University Press.

Norcross J. C. (Ed.) (2002). *Psychotherapy relationships that work: therapist contributions and responsiveness to patient needs.* New York: Oxford University Press.

Norcross, J. C. & Lambert, M. J. (2006). The therapy relationship. In J. C. Norcross, L. E. Beutler, & R. F. Levant (Eds.), *Evidence-based practices in mental health* (pp. 208–218). Washington, DC: American Psychological Association.

Psychological First Aid: Field Operations Guide (2nd ed., Electronic Version). (2006). National Child Traumatic Stress Network & National Center for Posttraumatic Stress Disorder, UCLA.

Rogers, C. R. (1957). The necessary and sufficient conditions of therapeutic personality change. *Journal of Consulting Psychology, 22*, 95–103.

Rose, S., Bisson, J., & Wessely, S. (2001). Psychological debriefing for preventing posttraumatic stress disorder (PTSD) (Cochrane Review). *The Cochrane Library 3.* Oxford: Update Software.

Rose, S., Wessely, S., & Bisson, J. (1998). Brief psychological interventions ("debriefing") for trauma-related symptoms and prevention of posttraumatic stress disorder (Cochrane Review). In *The Cochrane Library 2.* Oxford: Update Software.

Sackett, D. L., Richardson, W. S., Rosenberg, W., & Haynes, R. B. (2000). *Evidence-based medicine: how to practice and teach EBM* (2nd ed.). New York: Churchill Livingstone.

Seligman, M. E. P. (1995). The effectiveness of psychotherapy: the Consumer Reports Study. *American Psychologist, 50*, 965–974.

Sikes, C. & Sikes, V. (2003). EMDR: why the controversy? *Traumatology, 7(3),* 169–181.

Silverman, W. H. (1996). Cookbooks, manuals, and paint-by-numbers: psychotherapy in the 90's. *Psychotherapy, 33*, 207–215.

Stein, D. M. & Lambert, M. J. (1995). Graduate training in psychotherapy: are therapy outcomes enhanced? *Journal of Consulting and Clinical Psychology, 63*, 182–196.

Stricker, G., Abrahamson, D. J., Bologna, N. C., Hollon, S. D., Robinson, E. A., & Reed, G. M. (1999). Treatment guidelines: the good, the bad, and the ugly. *Psychotherapy, 36*, 69–79.

Stirman, S. W. & DeRubeis, R. J. (2006). Research patients and clinical trials are frequently representative of clinical practice. In J. N. Norcross, L. E. Beutler, & R. Levant (Eds.), *Evidence based practices in mental health: debate and dialogue on the fundamental questions* (p. 3, 403). Washington, DC: American Psychological Press.

Task Force on Promotion and Dissemination of Psychological Procedures (1995). Training in and dissemination of empirically-validated treatments: report and recommendations. *The Clinical Psychologist, 48*, 3–23.

The Israel Center for the Treatment of Psychotrauma (ICTP) (2007). *Trauma and PTSD*. Retrieved January 2008 from http://www.traumaweb.org.

UK National Institute for Clinical Excellence (NICE) (2005). *Post-traumatic stress disorder (PTSD): the management of PTSD in adults and children in primary and secondary care*. London: Author.

Ursano, R. J., Bell, C., Pfeferbaum, B., Eth, S., Pynoos, R. S. Friedman, M., et al. (2004). *American Psychiatric Association Practice Guidelines: Practice guidelines for the treatment of patients with acute stress disorder and posttraumatic stress disorder*. Arlington, VA: American Psychiatric Association.

Wampold, B. E. (2001). *The great psychotherapy debate: models, methods, and findings*. Hillsdale, NJ: Lawrence Erlbaum Associates.

Westen, D., Novotny, C. M., & Thompson-Brenner, H. (2004a). The empirical status of empirically supported psychotherapies: assumptions, findings, and reporting in controlled clinical trials. *Psychological Bulletin, 130*, 631–663.

Westen, D., Novotny, C. M., & Thompson-Brenner, H. (2004b). EBP ≠ EST: Reply to Crits-Christoph, et al. (2005) and Weisz, et al. *Psychological Bulletin, 131*, 427–433.

Westin, D. I. (2006). Patients and treatments in clinical trials are not adequately representative of clinical practice. In J. N. Norcross, L. E. Beutler, & R. Levant (Eds.), *Evidence based practices in mental health: debate and dialogue on the fundamental questions* (pp. 161–171). Washington, DC: American Psychological Press.

Wilson, T. G. (1998). The clinical utility of randomized controlled trials. *International Journal of Eating Disorders, 24*(1):13–29.

Woody, S. R., Weisz, J., & McLean, C. (2005). Empirically supported treatments: 10 years later. *Clinical Psychologist, 58*, 5–11.

Zlotnick, C., Zimmerman, M., Wolfsdorf, B. A., & Mattia, J. I. (2001). Gender differences in patients with posttraumatic stress disorder in a general psychiatric practice. *American Journal of Psychiatry, 158*, 1923–1925.

Program Evaluation and Clinical Psychology

John M. Houston
Rollins College

Erin Krauskopf
Rollins College

David C. S. Richard
Rollins College

Julia Humphrey
Rollins College

OUTLINE

Program evaluation provides a vital tool for developing, implementing, and assessing interventions in clinical psychology. Although practitioners differ in the way they define program evaluation, Chen (2005) provides a useful applied perspective that defines the purpose of program evaluation as "the application of evaluation approaches, techniques, and knowledge to systematically assess and improve the planning, implementation, and effectiveness of programs" (p. 3). This specification of its aim reflects the expanding scope of program evaluation beyond its original meaning of evaluating a program's outcomes, as well as highlighting several features that make this type of assessment activity particularly important and challenging.

Clinical psychologists are likely to encounter program evaluation in any of a variety of occupational activities. For example, clinical supervisors are frequently asked to evaluate the effectiveness of supervisees' therapy skills. Clinicians administering employee assistance programs may be asked to evaluate the effectiveness of group smoking cessation interventions in reducing work absenteeism. Health psychologists may be asked to assess the effect a staff training program has on patient satisfaction with care in a long-term residential home. In short, program evaluation is relevant to clinical psychology anytime one is interested in developing an intervention, monitoring program implementation, or assessing program outcomes.

Program evaluation possesses several distinctive characteristics that reflect its unique theoretical development and applied focus. Program evaluation draws on techniques and principles developed by researchers and practitioners from a number of disciplines within the social and health sciences. This interdisciplinary orientation represents one of the major strengths of the field and provides evaluators with a rich array of theories and strategies. However, the resulting diversity of theoretical perspectives also tends to generate a proliferation of terms describing similar, but actually distinct, activities. Consequently, the terminology used in program evaluation can be a source of confusion, particularly to those new to the field. Another distinctive feature of program evaluation stems from the pragmatic approach evaluators take in applying research methodology. Unlike highly controlled laboratory experiments where everything but the independent variable is held constant, program evaluations necessarily occur within social environments that are fluid and often subject to change. To deal with the complexity caused by such dynamic social environments, the process of planning, implementing, and completing a program evaluation demands a broad set of technical and social problem-solving skills.

Clinical psychologists have a special stake in program evaluation because many interventions relate directly to the development or delivery of mental health services. Information generated from program evaluation is particularly useful in informing researchers and practitioners about the effectiveness of strategies involved in the assessment, diagnosis, and treatment of psychological issues. Often, program evaluation provides valuable information about the practical effectiveness, or ecological validity, of interventions originally developed in the laboratory. At a broader social level, the findings of program evaluation can play a vital role in helping clinical psychologists advocate for public policy and health-care practices that will successfully address mental health problems.

At its most fundamental level, program evaluation involves accurately describing the current state of an intervention and comparing it to some criteria. Although this description and comparison may seem like a simple task that inevitably occurs in all interventions, the following example shows that this is not always the case.

THE NECESSITY OF MEANINGFUL EVALUATION

Since 1972, 447,400 students in California and 1.7 million students nationwide have attended the Narconon Drug Abuse Prevention program (NDAP). Designed to supplement a school's drug abuse prevention education curriculum, the NDAP program is provided at no charge by Narconon International, a drug prevention network that includes 120 organizations in 39 countries. The NDAP program consists of eight 30- to 45-minute presentations for elementary, middle, and high school classrooms. The sessions include general drug information, while focusing specifically on tobacco, alcohol, and marijuana, and the negative effects of drug use on the body and mind. The program also makes available drug use prevention videos, booklets, student worksheets, and training workshops for teachers.

Beginning in June 2004, a series of articles in *The San Francisco Chronicle* reported that key parts of the Narconon program were based on the Church of Scientology's beliefs about drugs and raised questions about the scientific accuracy of the program. These articles influenced a number of California school districts to bar the Narconon program from classrooms and caused the California Superintendent of Public Schools to request an independent evaluation of the program. Narconon officials acknowledged that Narconon's antidrug program is based on the research and writing of L. Ron Hubbard, founder of the Church of Scientology, but insisted that the program is nonsectarian and provides a science-based curriculum. Furthermore, they welcomed the opportunity to provide evaluators with more information about the program.

At the request of the California Department of Education (CDE), an evaluation team composed of medical doctors, psychologists, and health education experts initiated a review of the NDAP program. Following written procedures and research-based evaluation forms discussed with CDE and Narconon, the evaluation team assessed Narconon's drug prevention materials in terms of medical/scientific accuracy, developmental appropriateness, and teaching methods.

The program evaluation report, completed in January 2005, revealed a number of troubling features of the NDAP program. With regard to medical and scientific accuracy, the program evaluation found that "some drug-related information presented in the NDAP and supplementary resources provided to schools—although aligned with the Narconon drug rehabilitation methodology—does not reflect accurate, widely accepted medical and scientific evidence" (Wood, 2005, p. 1). Examples of inaccurate information include such statements as "drugs burn up vitamins and nutrients," "drug-activated vitamin deficiency results in pain which prompts relapse," and "small amounts of drugs stored in fat are released at a later time causing the person to reexperience the drug effect and desire to use again." The report noted that inaccurate and misleading information about drugs is problematic because it may confuse students, discredit the school's drug prevention program, and generate distrust toward educators.

The report also pointed out problems in the developmental appropriateness of the program. More specifically, the presentation scripts used for elementary, middle, and high school classes were virtually the same and lacked attention to the developmental characteristics and cognitive levels of students. In addition, the report expressed concern about using ex-addicts as presenters and using scare tactics that research has shown to be ineffective and possibly counterproductive. A final problem identified in the report focused on the lack of standardization in the program due to insufficient instructional direction and the flexible approach presenters are encouraged to adopt. Shortly after receiving the report, the State Superintendent urged all California schools to drop the Narconon anti-drug program.

The story of the NDAP program although extreme, illustrates several key concepts common to all program evaluations. First, a program evaluation must have a clearly defined purpose and scope, with specific and answerable *evaluation questions*. In the case of the NDAP evaluation, the evaluators limited the scope, of the evaluation to the program's medical/scientific accuracy, developmental appropriateness, and teaching methods. After determining the purpose of the evaluation, the evaluation team was then able to develop such logical questions as "Does the program reflect accurate, widely accepted medical and scientific evidence?" "Does the program present material in an effective way for students at different cognitive levels and ages?" and "Are the teaching methods consistent with approaches which have demonstrated effectiveness in the scientific literature?" Questions that lay outside the scope of the evaluation, such as "Does the program prevent drug abuse?" and "Is the program being used as a vehicle to promote beliefs espoused by Scientology?" were not investigated or discussed in the program evaluation report.

As with most evaluations, the purpose of the NDAP evaluation was determined by the *evaluation sponsor* (the CDE), which requested and funded the evaluation. Often the evaluation sponsor consults with key *stakeholders*—the individuals, groups, or organizations that have a significant interest in the effectiveness of the program—before finalizing the specific purpose of the evaluation. Stakeholders in the NDAP evaluation included the *target participants* (students), the *program sponsor* (Narconon), parents, educators, and state and local officials. Once the evaluation questions were identified, the evaluators then selected an appropriate evaluation plan and research methods to meet the needs of the evaluation and ensure the results are relevant to stakeholders. Based on the findings of the report, school officials and educators around the state were able to make informed decisions about whether to invite Narconon presenters into classrooms. The fact that an intervention as large as the Narconon antidrug program operated for so long without systematic evaluation shows the urgent need for such evaluation, and the rapidity with which evaluation results were able to influence public policy attests to the power of a carefully planned and executed program evaluation.

MODELS FOR UNDERSTANDING PROGRAM EVALUATION

Since program evaluations can address a broad range of questions, the evaluation process can be quite simple and straightforward or dauntingly complex and arcane. In keeping with the variety of questions driving evaluations, program evaluation incorporates a constellation of distinct but interrelated activities. This potentially confusing aspect of program evaluation comes about, at least in part, because a number of very different types of assessment efforts may be termed in the literature as "program evaluation." In spite of such a wide range, program evaluations tend to progress in a relatively predictable fashion through a series of stages (Rossi, Lipsey, & Freeman, 2004). Several practitioners have proposed models that identify the different stages in a program's development along with the corresponding research approaches best suited for each stage. For example, Scriven (1967) proposed that *formative evaluation* should be used during the program's developmental phases, while *summative evaluation* is appropriate once the program reaches a more mature, stable state. As the field of program evaluation has evolved, developmental stage models have become more detailed and comprehensive.

Pancer and Westhues (1989) presented an influential developmental stage model that identifies the question to be asked, the research function, and the research techniques that apply to each of eight different program stages. Although a complete review of program evaluation models is beyond the scope of this chapter, a closer examination of this developmental stage model provides a useful overview of the entire program evaluation process and offers a point of reference for mapping changes in the field over the past two decades. The eight stages of the developmental stage model—which link program planning and evaluation activities—are described next.

Developmental Stage Model for Program Planning and Evaluation

Stage 1: Assess Social Values. According to Pancer and Westhues's model (1989), the first stage in program planning involves the determination of community values and operational definitions that constitute the criteria the community is striving to meet. Accordingly, if there is interest in improving mental health within a community, program planners should investigate what community members believe is an acceptable level of mental health. This question can be answered by conducting a values analysis using a number of research techniques including surveys, interviews, nominal groups, or the Delphi technique.

Stage 2: Assess Needs. Information collected during the values analysis can then be used to identify community standards, which in turn leads to the next evaluation question: "To what extent are those standards being met?" This question can be addressed by conducting a community needs assessment based on an examination of the desired community standards and the current community conditions. The gaps between the desired and current conditions highlight problematic areas that need attention. A variety of approaches can be used to conduct a needs assessment and range from

social indicators derived from existing data bases, such as hospital admissions and socioeconomic status (e.g., Hall & Royce, 1987), to comprehensive strategies like the Developing Individual Services in the Community (DISC) Framework utilizing stakeholder conferences (Smith, 1998).

Stage 3: Determine Goals. Based on the findings from the needs assessment stage, program evaluation planning then focuses on the question "What do we need to change in order to meet the standards we have established?" To address this question, a general program goal as well as several specific goals must be established. During this goal-setting process, the types of changes the program is intended to bring about must be stated as measurable goals. These goals must then be prioritized by importance and assessed for congruence with stakeholders' values. Potentially useful research techniques for goal setting include surveys, interviews, Q-sorts, and rating procedures with program staff, administrators, and stakeholders.

Stage 4: Design Program Alternatives. The establishment of goals leads to a new question for program planners: "What kind of service activities could be used to produce the changes desired?" Pancer and Westhues (1989) argue that this stage requires the design of program alternatives in which at least two different program models must be proposed along with the major service activities embedded in each proposed model. The key research activity for this stage of program development involves program logic analysis and careful consideration of the theory of the program. The *program theory* is generally defined as the logic that connects the program's activities to the intended outcomes and the rationale for "why it does what it does" (Rossi et al., 2004). By systematically exploring the causal set of assumptions linking the program's activities with its intended effects, program planners can identify the types of intervention activities that would be most likely to produce the desired outcomes.

Literature reviews covering relevant theories and empirical studies can provide a useful framework for considering plausible approaches and promising program elements. Techniques drawn from the problem-solving and decision-making literature designed to increase possible courses of action, such as the analysis of metaphors and concept maps (Novak, 1998), are also useful during this stage of program development.

Stage 5: Selection of Alternative. Once an adequate number of program alternatives have been generated, program planners are faced with the question "Which program alternatives should be selected?" The nature of this question necessarily shifts the emphasis of the planning process from theoretical concerns to practical considerations such as financial feasibility, cost-effectiveness, political support, and administrative capacity. Not surprisingly, the type of analysis required and the research methods employed during the selection of program alternatives differ significantly from those used in previous developmental stages. Financial feasibility must be explored through consultations with potential funding sources. Cost-effectiveness is usually analyzed using calculation of the costs and the potential outcome or forecasted benefits of each program alternative. A cost-benefit approach can also be used by assigning monetary values to outcomes and calculating the benefit-to-cost ratio. Political support can be assessed using a force-field analysis by mapping the relative strengths of political forces supporting the program and those resisting the program. If the resisting forces are equal to or greater than the political forces supporting the program, the program is not politically viable. Finally, administrative feasibility can be gauged by examining the availability of staff, space, and other resources needed to make the alternative program operational. Together, the four criteria of financial, cost-effectiveness, political, and administrative feasibility provide the basis for determining the most promising program alternative from a practical point of view.

Stage 6: Program Implementation. Following the selection of the program, planners next consider the question "How should the program be implemented?" By initiating an implementation assessment, information gathered during previous stages of the program's development is brought together to determine which tasks must be completed by specific people within a particular time frame. As the implementation plan becomes more detailed and refined, problems are often identified that require modifications or supplemental strategies in the form of training, changes in job description, and acquisition of additional resources. Project management techniques such as Gantt charts can be used to graphically represent the phases and activities of program implementation.

Stage 7: Program Operation. As the program moves from implementation to full operation, the central question becomes "Is the program operating as planned?" Although the transition from implementation to operation varies according to the nature of the program, once a stable state is reached, process evaluation can commence. At this point the evaluators can examine whether the intended amount of service is being provided as well as whether the quality of the service meets the standards specified by the program goals. A variety of research techniques such as the review of case studies, surveys, and interviews can be used to collect data on participation by the target population, delivery of the intervention as planned, and other aspects of program functioning.

Stage 8: Program Outcomes. According to Pancer and Westhues's model, the last stage in program development deals with program outcomes. During this stage the key question becomes "Is the program having the desired effects?" To assess program outcomes, either experimental or quasi-experimental designs can be used depending on the setting and nature of the program. While experimental designs involve random assignment of program participants to either a treatment or control condition, quasi-experimental designs rely on self-selection or administrative decisions to determine who will be exposed to the treatment. Although lacking random assignment, quasi-experiments can have all the other major characteristics of experiments, including comparison groups and pretest and posttest observations. Because evaluating the effects of a program requires research strategies designed to assess cause-and-effect relationships, correlational research is generally not appropriate for this stage of program evaluation.

Current Models

Although developmental stage models like Pancer and Westhues's continue to have considerable heuristic value and provide a useful overview of program evaluation, not all social or clinical interventions follow this developmental sequence. More recent models of program evaluation build on the core concepts of earlier models but offer a more comprehensive and holistic view of evaluation activities (e.g., Rossi et al., 2004; Weiss, 1998). These comprehensive models highlight the complexity of contemporary program evaluation by acknowledging the nonlinear nature of many evaluation processes and recognizing that more than one program stage can be evaluated at one time.

In one of the most comprehensive and detailed evaluation models to date, Chen (2005) proposed a holistic approach to evaluation practices that integrates a linear sequence of developmental program stages with multiple feedback pathways (see Figure 17.1). Since evaluation feedback from later stages can lead to reconsideration of earlier stages, the focus of the evaluation activities may shift accordingly. As a result, evaluation activities may progress in a dynamic and nonlinear manner along program stages. Further, the program evaluator may also be an active participant in both the development and implementation of the program—a role that is in stark contrast to the stereotypical view of program evaluators as

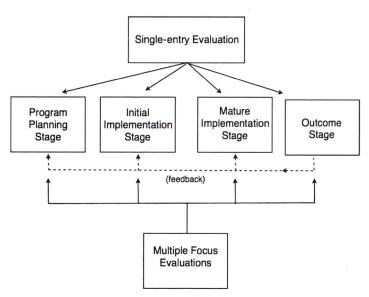

FIGURE 17.1 Comprehensive Evaluation Model. (*Source:* Adapted from Chen, H. (2005). *Practical program evaluation: Assessing and improving planning, implementation, and effectiveness.* Thousand Oaks, CA: Sage.)

independent external assessors. This approach also draws a distinction between single-entry and multiple-entry evaluation. Whereas *single-entry evaluation* focuses on a single program stage, such as the implementation of the program, *multiple-entry evaluation* addresses two or more program stages. For example, in multiple-entry evaluation the evaluator may be asked to assess both the implementation and outcome stages of an established program. Conversely, an evaluation sponsor may be dissatisfied with a program and request an evaluator to assess the mature implementation stage and identify opportunities for improvement that can then be used to facilitate the assessment of the planning stage of a revised program. Thus multiple-stage evaluation activities can also follow a nonlinear path.

AN APPLIED FRAMEWORK FOR PROGRAM EVALUATION: PRINCIPLES, ISSUES, AND PRACTICE

Over the past two decades, a number of changes have occurred in the field of program evaluation that have shaped the theory and practice of evaluation activities. The following section reviews the major components of program evaluation with special emphasis on the key principles and issues that guide successful evaluation efforts.

The Social Ecology of Evaluation

In planning and conducting a successful evaluation, the evaluator must consider a number of features that form the social ecology of the evaluation, including (1) the reasons for conducting the evaluation, (2) the vested interests of stakeholders, and (3) the relationship between the evaluator and the stakeholders. Obviously, this is a very different way of conceptualizing the research enterprise from what is typically taught at the graduate level in clinical psychology. However, understanding the differences between traditional clinical research and the applied nature of program evaluation is critical.

The need to examine the social circumstances surrounding the evaluation thoroughly before engaging in any formal evaluation activities reflects ongoing changes in the way evaluators view their duties, tasks, and responsibilities. During the early years of program evaluation, following World War II, evaluators often equated evaluation with research. Accordingly, conducting evaluations in ways consistent with accepted social scientific practices represented a key concern for evaluators. Over time, this view has evolved into a more inclusive perspective on evaluation that stresses the political nature of the evaluation process. Although research expertise remains important, evaluators must also have strong negotiation and conflict resolution skills to meet the challenges posed by multiple stakeholders and competing interests. Thus, Markiewicz (2005) asserts that the first step in effectively dealing with stakeholders is the recognition that evaluation is "an inherently political process, rather than a research opportunity" (p. 17).

Conceptualizing evaluation as a political process has several implications for evaluators. First, stakeholders may not have a background in applied research and may be more interested in the uses of the evaluation findings than the details of the methodology. Accordingly, stakeholders may need to contract the services of professionals who do possess the requisite background (e.g., clinical psychologists). Second, different stakeholders, including policy makers, service providers/practitioners, and clients, may be affected by the results in different ways. As a result, diverse groups of stakeholders may wish to initiate an evaluation for different reasons. Because the purposes of a given evaluation are often more complex than they first appear, Rossi, Lipsey, and Freeman

HIGHLIGHT BOX 17.1

TEN PRINCIPLES OF EMPOWERMENT EVALUATION

One of the distinctive features of empowerment evaluation is the concept that evaluation methods are extensions of the values associated with the principles of empowerment. Because empowerment involves individuals and communities having influence and control over the decisions that affect them, the community must determine the direction of its own evaluations. This involves community involvement and engagement in all phases of the evaluation process. Wandersman et al. (2004) identify ten principles that form the basis of all empowerment evaluation activities. These principles are:

- Improvement: empowerment evaluation promotes improvement in people, programs, organizations, and communities. Evaluators actively work to achieve positive results.
- Community ownership: evaluators assist community stakeholders to take responsibility for designing, conducting, and interpreting the results of their own evaluation.
- Inclusion: all community members are invited to participate in the evaluation process.
- Democratic participation: empowerment evaluation promotes active participation in the shared decision making and processes that foster deliberation and collaborative action.
- Social justice: empowerment evaluation values practices that empower those who have been oppressed and disenfranchised and works toward a more equitable society.
- Community knowledge: community-based experience and information are

respected and used to make decisions and understand the local context of results.
- Evidence-based strategies: empowerment evaluation promotes the use of interventions with demonstrated effectiveness that can be adapted to the needs of the local community.
- Capacity building: evaluators provide community members with opportunities to plan, implement, and evaluate their own program.
- Organizational learning: empowerment evaluation promotes learning and change through a cycle of reflection and action and the creation of a community of learners.
- Accountability: community members hold each other accountable for reaching specific and mutually agreed-upon goals or standards.

These principles are used to guide evaluation activities and to assess the quality of the empowerment evaluation. Although the extent to which specific principles are utilized will vary across empowerment evaluations, the quality tends to increase as the number of principles increases. Thus, if only a few principles are followed by the evaluators or community members, the evaluation may not be considered a fully operational empowerment evaluation.

In keeping with the values of empowerment evaluation, the ten principles were developed by a group of experienced empowerment evaluators who vigorously discussed and debated the conceptual foundations of empowerment before eventually reaching a consensus.

Source: Adapted from Wandersman, A., Snell-Johns, J., Lentz, B., Fetterman, D., Keener, D., Livet, M., et al. (2004). The principles of empowerment evaluation. In D. Fetterman & A. Wandersman (Eds.), *Empowerment evaluation principles in practice.* New York: Guilford.

(2004) argue that prospective evaluators must attempt to determine who wants the evaluation, what they want, and why they want it. To determine the rationale for the evaluation request, the evaluator may need to interview key informants, review source documents, and search the Internet. By understanding the concerns and expectations of stakeholders and the various motivations for commissioning an evaluation, the evaluator is better equipped to make strategic decisions, negotiate effective working relationships, and avoid ethical problems (see Highlight Box 17.1).

In general, evaluations are conducted for the purpose of determining a program's relevance, progress, efficiency, effectiveness, and outcomes (Adkins & Weiss, 2002). However, on occasion, other purposes and motives may be involved. In some cases, an evaluation may be commissioned to justify an administrative decision that has already been made or to placate critics and delay an unpopular decision. Under circumstances involving these kinds of hidden agendas, the evaluator is unlikely to serve a constructive purpose and should withdraw from the situation (Rossi et al., 2004).

The relationship between the stakeholders and the evaluator plays an important role in shaping the evaluation process. As previously mentioned, stakeholders are defined as the individuals, groups, or organizations that have a significant interest in the effectiveness of the program. In a study of 40 nonprofit organizations that had recently engaged in a program evaluation, Fine, Thayer, and Coghlan (2000) found that the participation of stakeholders increased satisfaction with the evaluation process and improved the design and usefulness of the evaluation. In addition, program administrators believed that high-participation evaluations were viewed as more credible by staff, board members, and funding sources. The results also indicated that most program administrators perceived stakeholder involvement as important in bringing about programmatic changes based on evaluation findings. These findings demonstrate the broad effects of soliciting input from stakeholders and making an effort to include their concerns and participation in the evaluation process.

Although every evaluation environment contains a variety of stakeholders, the evaluation sponsor holds a special position as the executive decision maker and initiator of the evaluation process. Because the evaluation sponsor usually selects the evaluator and provides the funding for the evaluation, the evaluation sponsor plays a major role in determining the evaluator-stakeholder relationship. The program evaluation literature generally identifies three types of evaluator-stakeholder relationships that influence the entire evaluation process: (1) traditional or independent evaluation, (2) participatory evaluation, and (3) empowerment evaluation. These evaluator-stakeholder relationships fall along a continuum of involvement with the program that ranges from limited interaction to zealous political advocacy.

In a *traditional* or *independent evaluation*, the evaluator functions much like a primary investigator in a funded research project. The evaluator takes responsibility for planning, conducting, and reporting the results of the evaluation. Although this approach usually involves consulting with key stakeholders and incorporating their input into the evaluation, the level of stakeholder involvement is relatively low. In contrast, significant care is exercised in applying the scientific method and maintaining methodological rigor. As with a scientific study, the evaluator makes a special effort to be objective and remain neutral toward the result of the study. Although evaluators continue to use this approach, critics of traditional evaluations point out that many of the reports generated in this manner are not used or even read (e.g., Torres & Preskill, 2001).

A *participatory evaluation* refers to any evaluation approach that actively involves stakeholders in decision making and other activities related to the planning and implementation of the evaluation (King, 1998). To foster a sense of participant ownership, a variety of group activities are built into the evaluation, such as question generation, collaborative data analysis, and a reflection session. This approach is also designed to create a team-based relationship between the evaluator and the stakeholders. The evaluator may take on the role of partner, facilitator, or coach depending on the needs of the stakeholders. Although all evaluations require some degree of interaction and contact between the evaluator and stakeholders, participatory evaluation emphasizes the active collaborative role of stakeholders throughout the entire evaluation.

In *empowerment evaluation*, the evaluator-stakeholder relationship promotes the initiative, advocacy, and self-determination of the stakeholders (Fetterman, Kaftarian, & Wandersman, 1996). In this approach the evaluator functions as a critical friend, facilitator, and evaluation expert. Rather than approaching the evaluation

---

HIGHLIGHT BOX 17.2

STRATEGIES FOR FACING ETHICAL CHALLENGES IN PROGRAM EVALUATION

Because program evaluation often involves working in a complex political environment with stakeholders who may have differing concerns and expectations, evaluators must remain alert to ethical problems throughout the course of the evaluation.

To avoid ethical problems in evaluation and effectively address them when they arise, Mathison (2005) recommends the following five steps.

First, during the contracting stage of the evaluation, the evaluator and key stakeholders should thoroughly discuss and negotiate their expectations for the evaluation. The evaluator should actively explore stakeholders' ethical concerns and point out any ethical issues that may need to be addressed. By investing time in clarifying ethical issues early in the evaluation, a number of thorny and time-consuming problems can be avoided later on.

Second, the evaluator can conduct an ethics cost-benefit analysis. This process involves comparing the ethical risks of the evaluation with the social good it is likely to produce for current and future program clients. This process is analogous to the types of analysis a university institutional review board conducts when reviewing research involving human participants. Accordingly, issues such as informed consent, assurances of confidentiality and anonymity, respect for privacy, and the use of coercion in recruiting participants must all be taken into consideration. Before proceeding with the evaluation, the evaluator must be convinced that the risks are being minimized and the benefits of the evaluation clearly exceed the risks.

Next, evaluators should review relevant professional guidelines and principles such as the *Guiding Principles* of the American Evaluation Association and the *Ethical Principles of Psychologists and Code of Conduct* developed by the American Psychological Association. These provide a general framework for ethical decision making and alert evaluators to ethical issues confronted by practitioners. However, under certain circumstances, following one guideline can lead to violating another.

HIGHLIGHT BOX 17.2   *(continued)*

When ethical dilemmas arise, the evaluator should consult with experienced colleagues and carefully consider the situation. Although colleagues may not provide a clear answer or even a convergent perspective, seeking input will increase awareness of the key issues and the possible response options. Discussions generated through consultation should help the evaluator arrive at an informed decision based on ethical reasoning.

Finally, one's own value system must be considered before deciding on a course of action. Since people tend to rank personal values by importance, our values can help us address ethical concerns when considered in conjunction with professional principles and an ethics cost-benefit analysis.

Source: Mathison, S. (Ed.). (2005). *Encyclopedia of evaluation.* Thousand Oaks, CA: Sage.

---

as a neutral researcher, the evaluator is not impartial but supports the purpose of the program and wants it to succeed. Guided by a strong set of principles, including improvement, community ownership, and inclusion (see Highlight Box 17.2), the evaluator helps participants develop a rigorous and organized approach to evaluation and clarify stakeholders' theories of change. Because this approach is grounded in work with marginalized and disenfranchised populations (Fetterman, 2001), the purpose of evaluation is to produce useful findings and to support the self-development and political influence of participants.

Program Planning and Evaluation

When evaluators are asked to help stakeholders plan and develop a program, a series of diagnostic activities must be undertaken to ensure that the planning proceeds in a logical and empirically based manner. A critical step in this process is *needs assessment*, which consists of research procedures to identify, measure, and prioritize needs within a community (Witkin & Altschuld, 1995). As previously discussed, a variety of techniques and data sources can be used to conduct a needs assessment. Once the social problem is defined, the target population and program goals must be identified.

As program planning progresses, the evaluator and stakeholders develop a *program theory*, which identifies "program resources, program activities, and intended program outcomes, and specifies a chain of causal assumption linking program resources, activities, intermediate outcomes, and ultimate goals" (Wholey, 1987, p. 78). Chen, Tseng, Ting, and Huang (2007) provide an example of how evaluation during program planning can help ensure that the program adequately addresses the needs of the target population.

The Silver Yoga Programme is an exercise program available to senior citizens in Taiwan. Research has shown that yoga is a useful addition to traditional therapy and that the incorporation of these practices into daily routines has proven to enhance the quality of life and general well-being of this target population. The three main goals of the study were (1) to develop a program based on expert consultation; (2) to evaluate the appropriateness of the program for older adults; and (3) to explore appropriate yoga practice frequency and preferences.

In phase I of this study, a printed description and video containing detailed descriptions of the program were sent to 10 experts who were asked to critique the yoga postures for clarification and feasibility on a scale of 1 to 4. These experts included 2 certified yoga instructors, 2 gerontological nurse practitioners, 2 physical therapists, 2 osteopathic doctors, and 2 physical educators/trainers, who together served as evaluators of the developing program's protocol.

The second phase of the program used 14 women age 60 to 86 years who were recruited via convenience sampling. The participants from the sample completed the four parts of the program (warmup, Hatha yoga, relaxation, and guided-imagery meditation), which lasted for 70 minutes in a senior activity center in Taiwan. Using a descriptive design with quantitative and semistructured evaluations, the women were asked to assess the program 1 month after completing it for the appropriateness of postures based on the criteria of difficulty, acceptability, feasibility, and helpfulness. With the help of the experts, evaluators, and target population, constant revision of the protocols was possible to adjust the appropriateness, safety, and suitability of the program. Because the results of the study yielded extremely high quantitative and qualitative ratings and boasted a 100% attendance rate by the participants, the implementing organization has increased validation of its ultimate goal: the incorporation of the program into the daily living activities of older adults. However, because convenience sampling limited the generalizability of these results, the authors note that the Silver Yoga Programme should be further tested with a larger sample of seniors before international proliferation.

Because the previously researched psychological benefits of yoga include alleviation of anxiety, depression, and stress and improvement in perceived self-efficacy, energy, and mood, the Silver Yoga Programme illustrates the way that physical exercise can contribute to the preservation of mental health in older populations. Embedded in the context of the program planning stage, this example provides confirmation of the need to establish sound implementation procedures prior to the delivery of an intervention. Implementation failures are often the result of poor planning and development and can be overcome using ongoing process evaluations. The Silver Yoga Programme evaluation not only was successful in establishing a feasible, manageable, and helpful protocol but also contributed to the elucidation of trouble spots that might arise in this type of exercise program.

Initial Program Implementation and Evaluation

During initial program implementation, evaluation focuses on identifying problems in bringing the program to an operationally functional state. Since programs at this stage are still developing, protocols, procedures, and rules for implementation may require fine-tuning to meet the needs of the target population of clients. Because this stage represents the point of convergence for theory and practice, a variety of programmatic concerns must also be examined including training staff, contacting potential clients, and creating service delivery procedures. Chen (2005) identifies two evaluation approaches that can be used for troubleshooting: formative evaluation and the program review/development meeting. Whereas formative evaluation involves the evaluator collecting data on potential implementation problems, the program review/development meeting is designed to build consensus among program staff about the implementation problems and possible solutions. Based on the particular characteristics of the program, a number of research methods, ranging from focus groups to structured surveys, can be used to search for problems. However, whatever type of research method is used, timely feedback to program staff is essential to prevent problems from becoming serious program flaws.

In a program designed to reduce the risk of eating disorders in college women, Franko et al. (2005) demonstrate how Internet-based technology can be used for formative evaluation and pilot testing within the same data collection process. Although a small percentage of college females are actually diagnosed with an eating disorder, an estimated 10–30% qualify as at risk for developing this disorder throughout their college years (Franko et al., 2005). Previous research has shown that prevention programs have been effective in producing significant reductions in at least one risk factor related to the development of eating disorders (Stice & Shaw, 2004). Food, Mood and Attitude (FMA) is a 2-hour CD-ROM prevention program based on pilot studies of Internet-based preventions specifically designed to decrease the risk for developing eating disorders in both low-risk and at-risk groups of college females. Its advantages include accessibility to large groups, cost-effectiveness, less laborious learning and shorter time span, and multisensory experiences, which actively engage participants (Franko et al., 2005). The FMA program theory is based on three theoretical constructs that were incorporated into the program's component parts: the dual-pathway model, interpersonal theory, and cognitive-behavioral theory. To create both the control and experimental groups and to categorize the women as low or high risk, the participants completed two screening measures, a demographic and follow-up questionnaire and a questionnaire for eating disorder diagnoses (Q-EDD), a highly validated measure. Thus, the FMA program used a quasi-experimental design focusing on both qualitative and quantitative data collection. The FMA program was designed over the course of 1 year to address the five most pertinent risk factors in

disordered eating: pressure to be thin, thin ideal internalization, body dissatisfaction, dieting, and negative affect (Franko et al., 2005). The FMA is based on an adaptive learning model in which the participant must sequentially complete learning modules relevant to eating disorders. Each of the modules addressed one of the five risk factors, was only historically and culturally appropriate, and was also highly interactive.

The efficacy study, which focuses on internal validity, was conducted using 231 first-year female students from two universities who completed a preliminary knowledge test, sociocultural attitudes toward appearance questionnaire (SATAQ), and the eating disorder examination questionnaire (EDE-Q) prior to exposure to the FMA. The researchers' use of three assessment methods to measure students' baseline attitudes regarding eating disorders illustrates the importance of selecting more than one valid assessment when studying clinical disorders. Results from the repeated-measures ANOVA revealed that both at-risk and low-risk participants in the FMA group had increased their knowledge of eating disorders relative to controls (Franko et al., 2005). Overall, the findings indicated that the FMA program was a safe, educative prevention tool for college women that positively affected social awareness of the disease. Most important, the program evaluation revealed that (1) compared with traditional ways of educating students about eating disorders, the FMA program was 82% more effective and (2) the students reported a 97% overall satisfaction rating with the program (Franko et al., 2005).

This study illustrates that the success of a program in its initial implementation stage is highly dependent on formative research and pilot testing. The use of multiple assessment measures increased the internal validity and decreased the risk of mono-method bias by providing evaluators with a rich volume of quantitative data. By surveying the target population at two universities and accruing participants across a continuum of at-risk factors, the study was able to randomly select at-risk and low-risk participants for designation into separate conditions: randomized to intervention and randomized to control intervention. This maximized the internal and external validity of the design, further allowing evaluators to determine that FMA is a cost-effective, successful, and highly accepted program among college females. This study also illustrates the way that evaluation in the initial implementation stage does not address issues of which components of FMA were most likely to be related to outcomes. As the program increases its implementation and interventions, it will move to the mature stage in which process evaluation can more precisely identify mechanisms of therapeutic action and those variables that may mediate efficacy. The example of the FMA program provides a clear depiction of the most essential parts of evaluation in the initial implementation stage: timely feedback on major implementation matters and identification of the source of problems.

Evaluating Mature Program Implementation

Once program procedures and rules of implementation become stabilized, evaluation activities shift from troubleshooting initial implementation problems to investigating more persistent implementation concerns during the mature stage of the intervention. Assessment activities at this stage are referred to as *process evaluation* and may examine either ongoing problems associated with implementation issues or how well the program was implemented. When assessing how well the actual implementation compares to the original program plan, evaluators engage in what is called *intervention fidelity evaluation*. In an evaluation of a London-based suicide prevention program, Briggs, Webb, Buhagiar, and Braun (2007) demonstrate

how a variety of research techniques can be used to assess organizational practices and outcomes 3 years after the initial implementation of the program.

Maytree is a nonmedical residential service that provides brief sanctuary for patients suffering from suicidal cognitions. Using applications of the crisis intervention theory, the program provides opportunities for relief of intense feelings that lead to suicidal thoughts through discussion, reflection, and relaxation over a 4-night period. Maytree's program theory is reliant upon a psychotherapeutic "befriending" approach, which emphasizes the need for a nonjudgmental, trusting environment in which the guest can begin the restoration of interpersonal relationships and emotional healing. By upholding a sound policy with strict limits including criteria for suitability, initial assessments, and no violence, alcohol, or drug use, the program was able to manage possible risks associated with suicidal populations. Maytree's profile of guests included both men and women between the ages of 18 and 66 with ethnically diverse backgrounds who were referred to treatment by health professionals, counselors, family, friends, and social workers. Recurrent in the guests' previous histories were mental illness, previous suicidal behavior, and disrupted social networks. Illustrating the need for intervention, the guests' total average score on the CORE (Clinical Outcomes in Routine Evaluation) pretest was 2.77, well above the 1.82 criterion for risk.[1] After admission, the guests were sorted into either the anomic or acute group. The anomic group was characterized by persistent and complex mental health problems that left patients feeling socially isolated. The acute group was characterized by increasingly severe states of depression and an enormous history of loss.

---

[1] The CORE is a 34-item questionnaire (scored on a 5-point Likert scale) that assessed four dimensions of subjective well-being for each patient.

The Maytree program was evaluated at the end of its third year of operation when the program had reached the mature stage. Aims of the study were to understand its rationale, aims, and objectives and to identify its philosophical, theoretical, and value bases. One of the evaluators was assigned to observe the interactions among guests, staff, and volunteers, providing rich qualitative data for analysis of the program's effectiveness. The process evaluation included semistructured interviews with individuals and groups (ex-guests, staff, volunteers, referrers, and trustees) and revealed that the effectiveness of the program was highly attributable to the skill and dedication of staff, the focus on "befriending," and the robustness of the entire Maytree process. The evaluation of outcomes was completed using data collected from 48 guests who stayed at Maytree during a 6-month period using pretest, posttest, and 3-month follow-up scores from the CORE. Maytree was successful at reaching its goal, which was short-term relief of suicidal thoughts and feelings.

The Maytree study also illustrates one of the challenges inherent in clinical sampling: a noncontrolled, nonrandom, self-selected sample. The condition that showed no statistical significance (posttest to follow-up) consisted of a sample of ex-guests who were able to participate in the follow-up study. It is possible that treatment effects exhibited by this group were a function of the group itself and not the intervention. It is also possible that the sample for the follow-up data comprised those who benefited most from Maytree. Further, change scores could have simply represented regression toward the mean.

Ultimately, the program evaluators were successful in discovering the source of immediate problems (lack of long-term effects) and generated data that reassured stakeholders that the program was effective in achieving its immediate goals (short-term effectiveness). The evaluators also identified positive unintended effects of the program, which included the observation that some patients received long-term benefits from Maytree's services. In identifying areas in need of improvement and areas of success, the evaluators were able to assure stakeholders that the Maytree model was ready to be exported to other localities.

Evaluating Outcomes

The evaluation of a program in the outcome stage can be complex but is essential to program success. Although the program is already firmly established at the time of the outcome stage, it is important to bear in mind that changes facilitating improvement are always warranted. However, since outcome evaluations are often rigorous, time-consuming, and expensive, measures should be taken to ensure the program is ready to be meaningfully evaluated. Wholey (1994) called this process *evaluability assessment*. An important feature of outcome evaluation is ensuring the fidelity of the program plan. Over time, a program can lose sight of the original rationale as a result of natural progression, staff turnover, and changes in training strategies. It is essential for evaluators to work with stakeholders to modify program strategies that have strayed from the original program purpose. After the evaluability and fidelity of a program have been established, evaluators can take one of three basic directions: efficacy evaluation, effectiveness evaluation, or theory-driven outcome evaluation (Chen, 2005). The main objective of all three approaches is to assess whether the program has been achieving its desired goals and whether it has the capacity to continue to do so. Efficacy evaluation is most concerned with internal validity and whether program outcomes are successful in a scientifically controlled setting. Effectiveness evaluation, on the other hand, measures the extent to which programs can be applied across settings and ecological contexts, and it primarily employs a quasi-experimental design. Theory-driven evaluation assesses the program's consistency and fidelity to the program plan while systematically pointing out weaknesses and working with stakeholders to facilitate improvement. An evaluation of a summer weekend camp by Farber and Sabino (2007) presents an example of a theory-driven outcome evaluation.

Camp Forget-Me-Not is a therapeutic summer weekend camp for grieving children in Washington, DC. The goal of the program is to aid children who have lost loved ones in coping with loss through activities in a camp setting. The literature on child grief asserts that if grief is not dealt with in a developmentally healthy way, it will have serious long-term implications for healthy growth (Brown & Goodman, 2005). Addressing death in a social context allows children to gain a better understanding of the meaning of loss. The theory-based design of the camp is constructed after a three-dimensional model of grief, which consists of educating the grief-ridden while promoting self-awareness through expression and interaction with others (Ward-Wimmer, Napoli, Brophy, & Zager, 2002). The weekend camp consists of four central activities designed to systematically improve the children's psychosocial functioning and ability to cope with grief. The activities are run by clinicians and "buddies" assigned to individual children to guide them through the weekend.

Over the course of two summers, evaluators from the Wendt Center for Loss and Healing and departments from the Catholic University of America conducted an evaluation of *Camp Forget-Me-Not*. Evaluators conducted a theory-driven evaluation of the program using both qualitative and quantitative data collection methods. Initial measures included ratings of the level of engagement in the activities filled out by clinicians and ratings of the children's psychosocial functioning completed by clinicians and buddies on the last 2 days of the camp. In addition, parents were interviewed 1 month after the camp to assess their perception of the overall camp experience and their child's psychosocial functioning.

What is notable about this evaluation is the way in which the researchers flexibly adapted measurements and aspects of the program in response to evaluation findings. During the first summer, clinicians and researchers worked together to flesh out the program rationale, develop measurement instruments, provide feedback, and make changes. This type of collaboration is representative of a participatory evaluation, where the stakeholders and evaluators work together to make changes. In addition, because information obtained through the outcome assessment provided feedback for the refinement of program planning and implementation, these assessment activities demonstrate the nonlinear nature of this evaluation. During the second summer, researchers assessed the data and made appropriate changes to both measurement instruments and camp activities. Evaluators discovered that there were discrepancies between the way the evaluator rated the level of the children's psychosocial engagement and the way parents rated their children at the 1-month follow-up. To solve this problem, evaluators implemented a pretest-posttest design. In addition to the issues with measurement techniques, the first summer of evaluation also revealed some problems with the camp curriculum. Evaluators discovered that the third camp activity, which consisted of drumming that symbolically represented paying tribute to lost loved ones, did not yield as much engagement as stakeholders and evaluators initially expected. Qualitative feedback revealed that the drumming was too overwhelming for the campers. Evaluators conferred with the clinicians (stakeholders) and decided to keep the activity but to also provide more explanation to the campers for the rationale and meaning behind drumming as a symbolic gesture (Farber & Sabino, 2007). In a follow-up study, evaluators discovered the changes made to the activity significantly improved the engagement with that activity and had no negative effects on the other camp activities. These modifications to the program again show the need for flexible methods within clinical program evaluation to facilitate beneficial change.

PROGRAM EVALUATION AND QUASI-EXPERIMENTAL DESIGNS

Because of the fluid and practical nature of evaluation environments, evaluators often use research strategies based on quasi-experimental designs instead of randomized experiments. Thus, while most program evaluation designs possess a high degree of external validity, drawing strong cause-effect conclusions is usually not possible. The basic process in estimating the effect of an intervention involves comparing outcome measures from the target participants who received the intervention with outcome measures from the target participants who did not receive or have not yet received the intervention. As with any empirically based research activity, reliable and valid measures are necessary for estimating the effect of an intervention. However, evaluators using quasi-experimental designs must also face the challenge of reducing threats to validity and selection bias caused by nonrandom assignment of participants to conditions. Although quasi-experimental designs can take on a number of different forms, Reichardt (2005) identifies four types of designs found in the program evaluation literature: before-after comparisons, interrupted time-series, nonequivalent groups, and regression-discontinuity designs.

In a *before-after comparison design*, outcomes are measured on the same target participants before the introduction of the intervention and again after sufficient exposure to the intervention. By comparing outcome measures before and after the intervention, the evaluator can estimate the effect of the intervention. Although this is a very common and simple design, it is also one of the most problematic because of its vulnerability to a variety of threats to internal validity. Specifically, because mean differences between before and after measurements may be due to causes other than the intervention, before-after comparison designs will often produce biased estimates of the intervention effect. Although the pre-post aspect of this design is a desirable feature, the absence of a control group seriously compromises attempts to draw causal inferences. Since threats to internal validity for this design can take so many forms, ranging from interfering events (history) to maturational and developmental processes, before-after comparisons should not be used for estimating intervention effects. However, before-after comparisons may have some use in providing general feedback to program administrators on routine outcome monitoring (Rossi et al., 2004).

An *interrupted time-series design* represents a strengthened form of a before-after comparison by conducting multiple observations before and after the intervention. The advantage of this design is that the multiple measures allow the evaluator to see trends in observations over time. Accordingly, the trend over time in the pretreatment observations is compared to the trend over time in posttreatment observations, and the difference between the two trends provides an estimate of the intervention effect. When an intervention has a significant immediate effect, a break or interruption occurs in the trend in the pretreatment and posttreatment observations. By observing behavior multiple times over the course of a study and across phases of intervention, an interrupted time-series design offers a way to rule out several threats to validity. For example, since the effects of maturation and statistical regression can be identified in the pretreatment trend data, these threats to validity can be modeled and removed during data analysis. The effects of history can be removed in a similar manner by adding a second time series of observation for participants who do not receive the intervention but experience the same historical events.

The *nonequivalent group design* resembles a before-after comparison design except for the addition of a nonequivalent control group that is used as a comparison group. Because participants are not randomly assigned to the intervention or control groups, these groups may different on a number of characteristics and are therefore considered nonequivalent. Since estimates of intervention effects are based on group differences on posttreatment measures, statistical procedures, such as analysis of covariance, or research design features, such as matching procedures, must be used to reduce selection bias associated with the nonequivalent control group. Aside from bias due to selection differences, other threats to validity include history and differential attrition. Consequently, evaluators must be mindful that external events may influence the outcome of treatment groups in different ways and that different types of individuals may drop out under different treatment conditions.

In a *regression-discontinuity design*, participants are assigned to treatment conditions based on cutoff scores on some continuum, such as need, merit, or other relevant selection variable. Using measured values along the continuum, participants with scores above the cutoff are assigned to one group and those with scores below the cutoff go into another group. Because the selection procedure uses scores on a specified variable, selection bias can be statistically controlled by regressing the outcome scores onto the selection variable scores. If the intervention has no effect, the regression lines will be the same for the treatment and comparison groups. However, if the intervention has a positive effect, the regression line in the treatment group will be higher than the regression line in the comparison group. Although the regression-discontinuity design generally provides a better estimate of the intervention effect than other quasi-experimental approaches, defining the selection criteria and implementing the rules for group assignment can be difficult. Consequently, despite its many positive features, the regression-discontinuity design is rarely used in program evaluation.

PROGRAM EVALUATION AND THE CLINICAL PSYCHOLOGIST

A solid understanding of issues surrounding program evaluation of community-based clinical programs is an essential skill for the developing clinical psychologist. However, despite the pressing need for skilled program evaluators, clinical psychology training programs have been slow to educate students in the essential differences between highly controlled lab-based research and the more complex situation encountered in a program evaluation. Next, we contrast research training in the classic sense with what students need to know to become competent program evaluators.

Efficacy versus Effectiveness

Most clinical graduate students, especially students in PhD programs, complete research methods courses that emphasize controlling threats to internal validity. From a practical perspective, such training makes sense given that faculty often conduct their research in highly controlled laboratory settings in order to maximize their ability to draw cause-effect conclusions from data (i.e., efficacy research). This emphasis, however, provides the clinical student with little understanding of those methods that are most appropriate for studying the effectiveness of an intervention in an applied setting. For example, most program evaluations do not have the luxury of randomization or a control group. Nonetheless, stakeholders will be interested in gauging the effectiveness of a program, and a properly trained evaluator will be able to measure outcomes while simultaneously communicating awareness of threats to the validity of conclusions. In our view, graduate training in clinical psychology should routinely include training in program evaluation. Not only is the program evaluation context an increasingly common one for clinicians hired into a variety of professional roles (e.g., administrative, hospital-based, nonprofit, consultative), but it is more frequently encountered postgraduation than the lab-based research training in which students gain experience during their graduate training.

Theoretical Questions versus Stakeholder Questions

Another key difference between classic research training and training in program evaluation centers on the manner in which research questions are posed. In lab-based research, the experimental design usually flows from a thorough review of the literature and a critical question posed by the investigator. Programmatic research is preferred in that a study's design seeks to answer questions left unresolved from a previous study. As a result, there is a potentially infinite number of questions that could be asked and designs that could be employed. In program evaluation, the number of relevant questions and corresponding designs are much smaller. Most program evaluators must answer derivations of one or more of the following questions: "Does the program work?" "How can the program improve?" "Is the program consistent with the original program theory?" and "Do program results justify continued financial support by a funding agency?" As such, program evaluation addresses questions that are of primary interest to stakeholders, not the investigator. This is a critically important distinction, because classic research training is entirely devoid of the stakeholder concept. In the classic view, research is conducted to test a hypothesis of theoretical importance. In program evaluation, empirical investigation is conducted to answer an

important question posed by a stakeholder. Which question is most relevant depends upon the program theory, the program's goals, specific stakeholder interests, and the program's stage of development. It is not that program evaluation ignores questions of theoretical interest (indeed, good programs develop from strong theory), but advancing theory is not the central purpose of program evaluation. Instead, the focus is on development, evaluation, and refinement of existing programs.

Meaningfulness and Understandability of Treatment Effects

Although clinical researchers may be interested in small effect sizes for any of a number of theoretical reasons, program stakeholders usually are not. This is because, from a cost-effectiveness standpoint, small effects for expensive programs may represent wasted resources that could be more usefully applied elsewhere. It is of little consolation to a program stakeholder to show changes in client behavior that, although statistically significant, do not represent much of a treatment effect. Thus, although classic research training emphasizes null hypothesis testing, program evaluation outcomes are more easily understood by stakeholders in terms of effect sizes since these can be easily adapted to a cost-benefit analysis (for an example, see Muntz, Hutchings, Edwards, Hounsome, & O'Céilleachair, 2004). Relatedly, the aspiring program evaluator should understand that most stakeholders do not have a background in statistics and may require clarification of the assessment plan and the subsequent results. As such, May (2004) recommends that psychologists ensure that results are presented to stakeholders in a way that is understandable, easily interpretable, and comparable to other studies with similar aims. Whereas lab-based research results are usually reported in a manner consistent with the guidelines of a relevant publication outlet (e.g., a peer-reviewed journal), program evaluation results must be reported in a way that is consistent with its intended audience (i.e., stakeholders). The single most critical task facing a program evaluator is ensuring that a program evaluation answers stakeholders' questions.

Training Matters

One of the reasons we advocate routine training in program evaluation for clinical psychology graduate students is that the average graduate is much more likely to engage in program evaluation than in highly controlled laboratory research. Further, whereas lab-based research makes an important contribution to the science of psychology, program evaluation makes equally important contributions to the practice of psychology and to policy formulation. In other words, good program evaluation can have a significant impact on the distribution of scarce public resources.

Training in program evaluation could be incorporated into both the doctoral curriculum and applied research experiences on practicum. Although many departments support clinics that provide clinical services for the local community, systematic evaluations of their effectiveness are rarely reported in the research literature. For example, Walsh and colleagues (1985) report a comprehensive evaluation of a clinic affiliated with the psychology department at the University of Montana. Their program evaluation found that the clinic needed to increase its emphasis on report writing, formalize practicum expectations of students, and more adequately train students in supervision and consultation work. In short, the department's own clinic provided the forum within which students could learn program evaluation skills. These kinds of efforts are critically needed because there is a relative dearth of literature surrounding the effectiveness of outpatient community support services. In this respect, as Speer and Newman (1996) noted some time ago, there have been more *discussions* about program evaluation than actual evaluations being done. This is surprising given that the APA has explicitly stated that expertise in program evaluation is "expected" of clinically trained psychologists (see http://www.apa.org/crsppp/clipsych.html). A more concerted effort to train developing clinical psychologists in program evaluation is consistent with the scientist-practitioner model (Hayes, Barlow, & Nelson-Gray, 2002) and with recommendations for including routine evaluation in private clinical practice (Kazdin, 1996).

SUMMARY

Program evaluation represents an important activity for clinical psychologists involved in developing, implementing, and assessing mental health interventions. Given the current practice environment in which managed care and cost containment have become prominent features, clinical psychologists have a vested interest in evaluating programs involved in the development and delivery of mental health services. Although program evaluation draws on expertise from a number of fields, clinical psychologists often have the kind of knowledge, skills, and dispositions program evaluators need to be effective. Because the social ecology of program evaluation demands many of the same interpersonal, consulting, and ethical competencies needed to establish a clinical practice, clinical psychologists, with appropriate training, are well suited to take on the role of program evaluators. Broad training in research design and multivariate statistics should also enable clinical psychologists to function effectively in the evolving field of program evaluation.

THOUGHT QUESTIONS

1. Why is program evaluation relevant to clinical psychology?
2. What are the major challenges involved in applying the scientific method to program evaluation?
3. What are some of the advantages and disadvantages of using a participatory evaluation approach?
4. What is the difference between efficacy and effectiveness? What is the relationship of each term to internal and external validity?
5. Why is it difficult to draw strong cause-effect conclusions from program evaluation results?

Glossary

Before-after comparison design: a quasi-experimental design in which outcomes are measured on the same participants before the introduction of the intervention and again after sufficient exposure to the intervention. This design is highly vulnerable to threats to internal validity.

Empowerment evaluation: an approach to program evaluation in which the evaluator-stakeholder relationship promotes initiative, advocacy, and self-determination of the stakeholder.

Evaluability assessment: an assessment procedure to determine whether a program can be meaningfully evaluated and if the evaluation is likely to contribute to improved program performance.

Evaluation questions: a set of questions that defines the issues the evaluation will investigate.

Evaluation sponsor: the person or institutional entity that serves as the initiator of the evaluation and the executive decision maker.

Formative evaluation: the evaluation activities conducted during the early phases of a program that provide developmental feedback.

Interrupted time-series design: a quasi-experimental design that represents a strengthened form of a before-after comparison by using multiple observations before and after the intervention.

Intervention fidelity evaluation: the evaluation activities that examine how well the actual implementation matches the original program plan.

Multiple-entry evaluation: an evaluation that addresses two or more program stages.

Needs assessment: the research procedures used to identify, measure, and prioritize needs within a community.

Nonequivalent group design: a quasi-experimental design similar to a before-after comparison but with the addition of a nonequivalent control group.

Participatory evaluation: any evaluation approach that actively involves stakeholders in decision making and other activities related to the planning and implementation of the evaluation.

Process evaluation: the assessment activities that focus on implementation issues once a program has reached a mature, stable stage.

Program sponsor: the person, group, or organization that requests the evaluation and provides funding and other resources to complete the process.

Program theory: a theory that defines the logic that connects the program's activities to the intended outcomes.

Quasi-experimental designs: the research approaches that closely resemble randomized experiments but lack random assignment to treatment groups. These strategies use a variety of statistical procedures and design features to reduce threats to validity.

Regression-discontinuity design: a quasi-experimental design in which participants are assigned to treatment conditions based on cut-off scores on relevant selection variables.

Single-entry evaluation: an evaluation that focuses on a single program stage.

Stakeholders: the individuals, groups, or organizations that have a significant interest in the effectiveness of the program.

Summative evaluation: the assessment activities conducted during the mature phase of a program to evaluate outcomes and the merits of a program.

Target participants: the individuals, families, or communities for whom the intervention is designed to serve.

Theory-driven outcome evaluation: a theory that assesses the accountability of a program while also considering aspects of the program that are and are not working, in an effort to facilitate improvement.

Traditional evaluation: an evaluation approach in which the evaluator takes responsibility for planning, conducting, and reporting the results of the evaluation.

References

Adkins, J. & Weiss, H. (2002). Program evaluation: a bottom line in organizational health. In J. C. Quick & L. E. Tetrick (Eds.), *Handbook of occupational health psychology* (pp. 399–416). Washington, DC: American Psychological Association.

APA Online (n. d.). Graduate education. Retrieved March 24, 2008 from http://www.apa.org/crsppp/clipsych.html.

Briggs, S., Webb, L., Buhagiar, J., & Braun, G. (2007). Maytree: a respite center for the suicidal. *Crisis, 28*(3),140–147.

Brown, E. J. & Goodman, R. F. (2005). Childhood traumatic grief: an exploration of the construct in children bereaved on September 11. *Journal of Clinical and Adolescent Psychology, 34*, 248–259.

Chen, H. (2005). *Practical program evaluation: assessing and improving planning, implementation, and effectiveness.* Thousand Oaks, CA: Sage.

Chen, K. M., Tseng, W. S., Ting, L. F., & Huang, G. F. (2007). Development and evaluation of a yoga exercise programme for older adults. *Journal of Advanced Nursing, 57*(4), 432–441.

Farber, M., & Sabatino, C. (2007). A therapeutic summer weekend camp for grieving children: supporting clinical practice through empirical evaluation. *Child and Adolescent Social Work Journal, 24*, 385–402.

Fetterman, D., Kaftarian, S., & Wanderman, A. (Eds.) (1996). *Empowerment evaluation: knowledge and tools for self-assessment & accountability.* Thousand Oaks, CA: Sage.

Fetterman, D. (2001). *Foundations of empowerment evaluation.* Thousand Oaks, CA: Sage.

Fine, A., Thayer, C., & Coghlan, A. (2000). Program evaluation practice in the nonprofit sector. *Nonprofit Management and Leadership, 10*(3), 331–339.

Franko, D., Mintz, L., Villapiano, M., Green, T., Mainelli, D. Folensbee, L., et al. (2005). Food, mood and attitude: reducing risk for eating disorder in college women. *Health Psychology, 24*(6), 567–578.

Hall, O. & Royce, D. (1985). Mental health needs assessment with social indicators: an empirical case study. *Administration in Mental Health, 15*(1), 36–46.

Hayes, S. C., Barlow, D. H., Nelson-Gray, R. O. (2002). Review of The Scientist-Practitioner: research and accountability in the age of managed care (2nd ed.). *Adolescence, 37*, 860–861.

Kazdin, A. E. (1996). Evaluation in clinical practice: an introduction to the series. *Clinical Psychology: Science and Practice, 3*, 144–145.

King, J. (1998). Making sense of participatory evaluation. *New Directions for Evaluation, 80*, 5–23.

Markiewicz, A. (2005). "A balancing act": resolving multiple stakeholder interests in program evaluation. *Evaluation Journal of Australasia, 4*(1 & 2), 13–21.

Mathison, S. (2005). Strategies for ethical practice in program evaluation. In S. Mathison (Ed.), *Encyclopedia of evaluation* (pp. 131–134). Thousand Oaks, CA: Sage.

May, H. (2004). Making statistics more meaningful for policy research and program evaluation. *American Journal of Evaluation, 25*, 525–540.

Muntz, R., Hutchings, J., Edwards, R.-T., Hounsome, B., & O'Céilleachair, A. (2004). Economic evaluation of treatments for children with severe behavioral problems. *Journal of Mental Health Policy and Economics*, 7, 177–189.

Novak, J. (1998). *Learning, creating, and using knowledge: concept maps as facilitative tools for schools and corporations.* Mahwah, NJ: Lawrence Erlbaum Associates.

Pancer, S. & Westhues, A. (1989). A developmental stage approach to program planning and evaluation. *Evaluation Review*, 13(1), 56–77.

Reichardt, C. (2005). Quasi-experimental design. In S. Mathison (Ed.), *Encyclopedia of evaluation* (pp. 351–355). Thousand Oaks, CA: Sage.

Rossi, P., Lipsey, M., & Freeman, H. (2004). *Evaluation: a systematic approach* (7th ed.). Thousand Oaks, CA: Sage.

Scriven, M. (1967). The methodology of evaluation. In R. E. Stake (Ed.), *Curriculum evaluation* (American Educational Research Association monograph series on evaluation, No. 1, pp. 39–83). Chicago: Rand McNally.

Smith, H. (1998). Needs assessment in mental health services: the DISC framework. *Journal of Public Health Medicine*, 20(2), 154–160.

Speer, D. C. & Newman, F. L. (1996). Mental health services outcome evaluation. *Clinical Psychology: Science and Practice*, 32, 105–129.

Stice, E. & Shaw, H. (2004). Eating disorder prevention programs: a meta-analytic review. *Psychological Bulletin*, 130, 206–227.

Torres, R. & Preskill, H. (2001). Evaluation and organizational learning: past, present, and future. *American Journal of Evaluation*, 22(3), 387–395.

Walsh, J. A., Wollersheim, J. P., Bach, P. J., Bridgwater, C. A., Klentz, B. A., Steblay, N. M. (1985). Program evaluation as applied to the goals of a psychology department clinic. *Professional Psychology: research and Practice*, 16, 661–670.

Wandersman, A., Snell-Johns, J., Lentz, B., Fetterman, D., Keener, D., Livet, M., et al. (2004). The principles of empowerment evaluation. In D. Fetterman & A. Wandersman (Eds.), *Empowerment evaluation principles*. New York: Guilford.

Ward-Wimmer, D., Napoli, C., Brophy, S. O., & Zager, L. (2002). *Three-dimensional grief: a model for facilitating grief groups for children* (2nd ed.). Washington, DC: Wendt Center for Loss and Healing (http://www.wendtcenter.org).

Weiss, C. (1998). *Evaluation: Methods for studying programs and policies* (2nd ed.). Upper Saddle River, NJ: Prentice Hall.

Wholey, J. (1987). Evaluability assessment: developing program theory. In L. Bickman (Ed.), *Using program theory in evaluation* (New Directions for Program Evaluation, No. 33, pp. 77–92). San Francisco: Jossey-Bass.

Wholey, J. (1994). Assessing the feasibility and likely usefulness of evaluation. In J. Wholey, H. Hatry, & K. Newcomer (Eds.), *Handbook of practical program evaluation*. San Francisco: Jossey-Bass.

Witkin, B. & Altschuld, J. (1995). *Planning and conducting a needs assessment: a practical guide*. Thousand Oaks, CA: Sage.

Wood, D. (2005). *Narconon drug abuse prevention program evaluation*. Retrieved March 20, 2008 from http://www.cde.ca.gov/ls/he/at/narcononevaluation.asp.

CHAPTER

18

Diversity Issues in Clinical Psychology

Carmela Alcàntara
University of Michigan

Kira Hudson Banks
Illinois Wesleyan University

Tiffany Haynes
University of Michigan

Erin T. Graham
University of Michigan

Karryll Winborne
University of Michigan

Laura P. Kohn-Wood
University of Michigan

OUTLINE

INTRODUCTION

Widespread attention to diversity issues in the general field of psychology and within the specific area of clinical psychology has been a relatively recent development. It has been argued that multiculturalism represents the "fourth force" in the field of psychology, following three previous forces that have influenced the field: psychoanalysis, behaviorism, and humanism (Pederson, 1999). Although there is significant room to improve our understanding of how

449

diversity influences clinical research, therapy, and training, contemporary clinical psychologists cannot afford to ignore multicultural issues in their scientific or clinical work.

For example, the current changing demographics of the United States have been well documented and hold major implications for the field of clinical psychology. It is projected that the population of non-Hispanic White Americans will shift from 69% to approximately 50% by 2050 (U.S. Census Bureau, 2004). In some states the reality of a "majority minority" already exists, particularly in specific cities. For example, Latino/as predominate the population of Miami, Florida; Asians represent a majority group in San Francisco, California; and African Americans make up a slight majority in Detroit, Michigan (U.S. Census Bureau, 2004). The American Psychological Association (APA) defines "cultural and individual diversity" as personal and demographic characteristics that include, but are not limited to, age, color, disabilities, ethnicity, gender, language, national origin, race, religion, sexual orientation, and social economic status (APA, 2000). The APA has recognized the need to be aware of cultural and individual diversity and has mandated that programs accredited by the body appropriately recruit, retain, and train psychologists to address a multicultural population (APA, 2002a) (see Highlight Boxes 18.1 and 18.2).

HIGHLIGHT BOX 18.1

APA'S EFFORTS TO INCREASE DIVERSITY IN PSYCHOLOGY

APA's efforts to increase diversity in psychology culminated with the development of the *Guidelines on Multicultural Education, Training, Research, Practice, and Organizational Change for Psychologists* (APA, 2002b). These guidelines seek to encourage the profession to become more culturally competent with the goal of attracting and retaining more minority students and thereby leading to an increased number of psychology professionals of color. The guidelines are:

Guideline #1: Psychologists are encouraged to recognize that, as cultural beings, they may hold attitudes and beliefs that can detrimentally influence their perceptions of and interactions with individuals who are ethnically and racially different from themselves.

Guideline #2: Psychologists are encouraged to recognize the importance of multicultural sensitivity/responsiveness, knowledge, and understanding about ethnically and racially different individuals.

Guideline #3: As educators, psychologists are encouraged to employ the constructs of multiculturalism and diversity in psychological education.

Guideline #4: Culturally sensitive psychological researchers are encouraged to recognize the importance of conducting culture-centered and ethical psychological research among persons from ethnic, linguistic, and racial minority backgrounds.

Guideline #5: Psychologists strive to apply culturally appropriate skills in clinical and other applied psychological practices.

Guideline #6: Psychologists are encouraged to use organizational change processes to support culturally informed organizational (policy) development and practices.

HIGHLIGHT BOX 18.2

APA INITIATIVES FOR INCREASING DIVERSITY IN THE RANKS OF CLINICIANS

Although the demographic makeup of the United States is becoming more ethnically diverse, minorities remain underrepresented in the field of psychology. As of 2004, approximately 80% of doctoral degrees in psychology were awarded to Whites (National Center for Education Statistics, 2003). However, across all disciplines, doctoral degrees are disproportionately awarded to Whites, particularly outside the social sciences. Even so, despite the popularity of psychology as an undergraduate major, in 2007 only 23% of students enrolled full-time in psychology doctoral programs were ethnic minorities (APA Center for Workforce Analysis and Research, 2007). The lack of minority representation in psychology doctoral programs has led to a paucity of people of color in the profession of psychology. Therefore, APA has taken strides to enhance diversity among psychology students and professionals.

In response to the underrepresentation of minorities in psychology, APA established the Office of Ethnic Minority Affairs (OEMA) in 1979. OEMA was founded with the goals to promote recruitment, retention, and training opportunities for ethnic minorities in psychology; increase and enhance the delivery of appropriate psychological services to ethnic minority communities; and promote the development of public policies that support the concerns of minority psychologists. Since its foundation, OEMA has implemented several programs in hopes of reaching the above goals including:

- **Job Bank Services:** This program allows employers to search a database of more than 3,000 ethnic minority psychologists in an effort to connect employers with available minority applicants.
- **Diversity Project 2000 and Beyond (DP2KB):** This program seeks to encourage ethnic minority honor students in community college settings to become professional psychologists.
- **Commission on Ethnic Minority Recruitment, Retention, and Training in Psychology (CEMRRAT2) Taskforce:** This task force seeks to increase the number of students, faculty, and professionals who are people of color. CEMRRAT2 is also influential in the implementation of APA's efforts in the areas of recruitment, retention, and training.
- **Council of National Psychological Associations for the Advancement of Ethnic Minority Interests (CNPAAEMI):** CNPAAEMI consists of the professional psychology organizations devoted to ethnic minority populations, such as the Asian Psychological Association. This task force seeks to promote the professional and career development of ethnic minority psychologists (APA Office of Ethnic Minority Affairs).

DIVERSITY ISSUES IN TRAINING

In recognition of multiculturalism as the "fourth force" or sphere of influence on the field, clinical psychology programs should incorporate explicit training for addressing multicultural issues in therapy, assessment, and research. At minimum, courses related to multicultural issues in clinical psychology should be offered as part of a comprehensive clinical psychology graduate curriculum. However, several kinds of training models for addressing diversity exist. Rather than offering one course, or a sampling of courses that focus on culture, some programs prefer to incorporate cultural training across all aspects of graduate students' experiences. This approach results in some attention to diversity issues across all graduate courses in research, psychopathology, psychotherapy, assessment, and practicum training. As such, cultural issues are not marginalized as a special topic or isolated in a single course. Another approach to multicultural training involves providing opportunities for real-world training experiences with diverse individuals in an "immersion" approach. This approach emphasizes the benefits of direct contact to refine cultural knowledge and skills, and proponents assert that experiential training is superior to didactic training methods (e.g., readings and discussion) that remain abstract in nature (Magyar-Moe et al., 2005).

Some advancements of cultural competence training models include process-oriented training models (Sue, 1998) that emphasize the importance of "shifting cultural lenses" between the cultural perspective of the therapist and that of the client (López, 1997). Lakes, López, and Garro (2006) have described a refinement of the shifting cultural lens model. This approach incorporates Kleinman's (1995) conceptualization of culture as "that which is at stake in one's local, social world" (as cited by Lakes et al., 2006) and Mattingly and Lawlor's (2001)

conceptualization of the development of shared narratives in service of intervention (as cited by Lakes et al., 2006). The authors use a clinical case example to detail the ways in which a socially based conception of culture informed the establishment of shared narratives for treatment with a Latino family caring for a son with pervasive developmental disorder. In this way, the definition and process of culturally competent care are broadened from approaches that limit conceptions of culture to group-based values and beliefs as well as enriched to include the idiosyncratic, dynamic, and therapeutically relevant aspects of culture that are specific to a given client.

Currently, however, widespread measurement and evaluation of cultural competence training models do not exist. Therefore, it is unclear how we should define and measure cultural competence in a reliable and valid way or whether increased cultural competence results in explicitly measurable outcomes, such as improved treatment outcomes or increased treatment utilization. Further, the question of whether one training approach is better than another has not been answered. In the absence of empirical evidence for the efficacy or effectiveness of training, Fouad (2006) has identified seven "critical elements of a multi-culturally infused psychology curriculum." These recommendations for graduate programs include (1) explicitly state a commitment to diversity, (2) actively make an effort to recruit graduate students from diverse populations, (3) actively make an effort to recruit and retain diverse faculty members, (4) make efforts to make the admissions process fair and equitable, (5) ensure that students gain awareness of their own cultural values and biases, knowledge of other groups, and skills to work with diverse populations, (6) examine all courses for an infusion of a culture-centered approach throughout the curriculum, and (7) evaluate students on their cultural competence on a regular basis.

The degree to which training programs can adopt and adhere to these critical elements can determine the pace of improvements in the field of clinical psychology with regard to diversity in education, practice, and research.

DIVERSITY ISSUES IN THERAPY

Cultural Competence in Treatment

Issues of diversity have been highlighted in the APA code of ethics (2002a). Ethics Principle E states:

> Psychologists are aware of and respect cultural, individual, and role differences, including those based on age, gender, gender identity, race, ethnicity, culture, national origin, religion, sexual orientation, disability, language, and socioeconomic status and consider these factors when working with members of such groups. Psychologists try to eliminate the effect on their work of biases based on those factors, and they do not knowingly participate in or condone activities of others based upon such prejudices. (p. 4)

In addition, in section 2.01, it is made clear that when these factors are essential for services, a psychologist must "have or obtain the training, experience, consultation, or supervision necessary to ensure the competence of their services, or they make appropriate referrals" (p. 5) except in emergencies. The implications of these ethical codes are that psychologists should engage in understanding issues relevant to diversity as a part of training, when delivering services, when interpreting assessment results, and in other areas such as research and teaching.

These guidelines speak to the need for *cultural competence*, which has been increasingly explored in recent literature. The concept refers to having the skills and abilities to work with clients who are culturally different, similar to how one would gain the necessary skills before administering a new assessment. An excellent resource for learning how to become culturally competent is in Sue and Sue's (2008) book *Counseling the Culturally Diverse: Theory and Practice*, 5th edition. This book provides a comprehensive examination of personal and professional topics relevant to diversity and therapy. Another resource is the *Handbook of Multicultural Counseling*, second edition (2001).

In addition, APA has developed "Guidelines on Multicultural Education, Training, Research, Practice, and Organizational Change for Psychologists" (APA, 2002b) (see Highlight Box 18.1). The main principles encourage psychologists to recognize how understanding cultural differences can enhance the treatment of all people. Two of the most important topics addressed in the guidelines include the need for psychologists to be aware of historical models, which viewed cultural difference as deficits, and the ways in which psychologists are uniquely positioned to promote social justice. For further reading, the full document can be found at http://www.apa.org/pi/multiculturalguidelines.pdf.

Even with the awareness provided through reading and coursework, clinical psychology graduate students may still feel uncomfortable with broaching the topic of diversity with clients or supervisors. That feeling is an expected part of the process. Appreciation of these issues does not automatically translate into the knowledge of how and when to bring up racial or ethnic issues in the consulting room. Inexperienced therapists could feel that by bringing an issue up, they are "making it an issue," or perhaps they just cannot see how to start the conversation. This is not uncommon. One myth that must be debunked is that talking about diversity will create problems that might not really exist—similar to the myth about talking to clients who exhibit suicidal ideation. Certainly, one would not think that the disclosure of suicidal thoughts following specific questions about suicidal ideation would be a function of the questioning itself. So, we recommend that beginning students should be willing to bring issues of racial and ethnic diversity into the room. It can be as simple as adding a question to a standard intake: "Often, I ask my clients about their racial and ethnic background because it helps me have a better understanding of who they are. Is that something you'd feel comfortable talking about?" (Cardemil & Battle, 2003, p. 279).

Several other recommendations have been made for working with clients of a different race or ethnicity, which can certainly be relevant for other areas of diversity including gender and sexual orientation or physical ability: (1) suspend preconceptions about clients' race/ethnicity and that of family members, (2) recognize that clients may be quite different from other members of their racial/ethnic group, (3) consider how racial/ethnic differences between therapist and client might affect psychotherapy, (4) acknowledge that power, privilege, and racism might affect interactions with clients, and (5) err on the side of discussion when in doubt and be willing to take risks with clients (see Cardemil & Battle, 2003, for full explanation). Again, these dynamics exist whether verbally acknowledged or not. Supervision can be helpful in navigating the layers of how diversity can influence treatment. Additionally, trainees might need to pay closer attention to resources for further study to aid growth and development in the area of cultural competence.

Individual and Cultural Factors Related to Diversity

There are several culturally relevant constructs that might be helpful in the development of cultural competence. First, group membership constructs that are relevant for one client should not lead clinicians to presume that the same constructs are relevant for all group members. This awareness reiterates the importance of being willing to talk openly with clients to generate, confirm, or disconfirm

hypotheses about culture that are relevant to the treatment process and to provide the space for diversity to be a part of the conversation if necessary.

Second, understanding and asking for clarification about a client's worldview can aid in case conceptualization. It involves overarching principles that guide and influence individuals' experiences in the world and is particularly relevant to understanding individuals of different cultures than one's own. *Worldview* refers to the way individuals understand and perceive their relationship to the world (Sue & Sue, 2008). For example, some worldviews, and hence cultures, value emotional restraint versus emotional expressiveness. Others might focus on individual rights, while another might honor collective rights and family. This construct can refer to ways of knowing or reasoning in addition to the concept of time and self.

Another construct that could prove useful in understanding racial minority clients is *racial identity*. Racial identity is conceptualized as how individuals integrate race into their understanding of who they are. It is a key variable in understanding oneself and individuals from different racial groups. There have been numerous models of racial identity development, some which examine the construct across multiple groups and others which focus specifically on one group.

The **Racial/Cultural Identity Development (R/CID) model** provides a general framework of various stages by which individuals come to understand their racial identity (Sue & Sue, 2008). The stages reflect common experiences across different groups: (1) **conformity** is marked by an alignment with dominant culture prior to individuals integrating race into their identity, (2) **dissonance** occurs when individuals encounter information or experiences that provoke the integration of race into their identity, (3) **resistance and immersion** involve rejection of mainstream values, active exploration of their own culture, and are sometimes marked by anger, (4) **introspection** brings a deeper level of personal and group understanding, and (5) **integrative awareness** adds appreciation of other cultures to the inner sense of security that has developed through the stages. Assessing where clients are in this process of integrating race into their identity can help therapists understand how clients experience the world. In addition, at times it might be useful to consider the extent to which a client has adopted values and beliefs of the host culture, or of **acculturation** (see Bowskill, Lyons, & Coyle, 2007, for a discussion of the role this construct can play).

The major criticism of general racial identity models is that they lack cultural specificity. There are experiences and values specific to racial and ethnic groups that are highly relevant when understanding identity (e.g., reservation life, slavery, internment, immigration). Therefore, when a more focused conceptualization is possible, it is important to consider group-specific racial identity models, which take into consideration culture-specific histories and constructs.

Several prominent models focus specifically on African American or Black identity (Cross, 1971; Sellers, Smith, Shelton, Rowley, & Chavous, 1997). Cross's (1971) stage model of Black identity, called "nigrescence," was a major innovation in the racial identity literature, and the R/CID model is designed using Cross's conceptualized structure. In more recent years, researchers have called for multidimensional models rather than stage models, allowing for more complex conceptualizations of identity (Sellers et al., 1997). Models capturing the specific experience of other racial and ethnic groups are still emerging, yet there exist published scales for Hispanic/Latino Americans (Ruiz, 1990) and multiracial individuals (Poston, 1990).

Racial identity development is not reserved for people of color. The development of racial identity relevant to White Americans has also been captured (Helms, 1995). Becoming aware of White privilege, the inherent benefits of being White in America, and developing a positive White identity are key elements in the consciousness-raising process. Helms (1995) believed that White Americans grow from being oblivious about race (contact status), to recognizing unequal treatment targeted at people of color (disintegration), to regressing to blaming the victim (i.e., people of color) for such treatment (reintegration). These first three stages are thought to encapsulate the abandonment of a racist identity. The following three stages involve developing a positive White identity: **pseudo-independence**, which includes beginning to engage with people of color in addition to trying to understand White privilege on an intellectual level; **immersion/emersion**, which involves focusing on what it means to be White and a personal understanding of White privilege; and **autonomy**, which includes increasing awareness of Whiteness and the personal role in perpetuating racism while decreasing feelings of guilt.

Understanding these models of racial identity development in the context of delivering services is recommended. However, self-exploration is also an important component of therapeutic cultural competence. Understanding various models of racial identity can help beginning therapists reflect on their own development with regard to race. In addition, it is useful to see racial identity models as a framework for understanding additional aspects of one's own identity. Having a more conscious awareness of oneself and beliefs, assumptions, and expectations can improve one's ability as a clinician. It helps therapists to be fully present with clients who are working to understand their own person-specific struggles and equips therapists to become quickly aware when their own worldview is clouding judgment or understanding.

HIGHLIGHT BOX 18.3

CLIENT MATCHING

Given the attention paid to cultural competence, one might wonder whether clients would fare better if they were simply matched with therapists who were similar in identity. What are your thoughts? At first glance, one might think that this idea would work. Rather than having to learn about different groups, therapists could work only with clients who are similar to them. However, assuming homogeneity of personality characteristics simply by virtue of group membership not only is hazardous but runs the risk of foreclosing meaningful clinical understanding and investigation of a person's unique circumstances.

Also, research on racial, ethnic, or linguistic (same language) "matching" of clients and therapists has been mixed. Researchers have examined the impact of matching and generally found that, for some clients, being similar to the therapist in terms of race, ethnicity, or language can affect length of treatment and reduce the likelihood of dropout after the first session (see Maramba & Hall, 2002 for review). For example, Sue and colleagues (Sue, Fujino, Hu, Takeuchi, & Zane, 1991) showed that Mexican and Asian clients are less likely to drop out, receive more services, and improve in functioning when they are ethnically and linguistically matched, in comparison to those who were not.

Racial matching of client and therapist, however, has not been shown to improve treatment outcomes for African Americans. This may be due to the fact that racial, ethnic, and linguistic matching are distal indicators of cultural competence. Research has suggested that same-race dyads could be beneficial if variables beyond simply the race of the client and therapist were examined (Thompson & Alexander, 2006). For example, introducing specific cultural adaptations to treatment may be more effective than racial matching for improving therapy outcomes for racial or ethnic minority clients (Kohn et al., 2002).

Developing cultural competence in reducing risk and alleviating the burden of psychiatric disorders is of major importance. Research on cultural competence as it relates to conducting therapy can help elucidate the skills, processes, and awareness necessary to improve therapy and intervention for diverse clients and therefore is of great practical relevance for the field. Further, culturally competent therapeutic interventions may help to offset cultural beliefs and attitudes that preclude ethnic and racial minority clients from seeking mental health treatment.

Cultural Beliefs and Attitudes about Help Seeking

Research suggests that minority patients with mental disorders are reluctant to seek help from professionals when needed. It has been noted that many Asians who experience clinical symptoms will not seek a mental health provider for alleviation of psychological distress (U.S.D.H.H.S, 2001; Zhang, Snowden, & Sue, 1998). An early study on help seeking found that when experiencing moderate levels of depression, African Americans report less willingness to seek treatment than Whites, citing fear of treatment and hospitalization (Sussman, Robins, & Earls, 1987). Mental health treatment may be avoided by racial and ethnic minorities due to a fear of labeling, particularly if treatment involves children (Spencer, Kohn, & Woods, 2002). These findings suggest that cultural beliefs and attitudes may preclude help seeking.

Others have suggested that members of minority groups prefer to utilize methods other than formal mental health treatment. Research on treatment preferences suggests that African Americans are more likely than Whites to delay or defer treatment for depression and doubt the efficacy of care for particular problems (Cooper-Patrick et al., 1997) although these differences have narrowed over time (Cooper-Patrick et al., 1999). Another study indicated that the most effective reported coping strategy for depressed South Asians and Caribbean Blacks was to engage in activities to take their minds off negative thoughts (Lawrence et al., 2006). Similarly, African Americans may prefer to utilize self-reliant and spiritual practices to cope with psychological problems (Broman, 1996; Snowden, 2001).

Some cultures may scorn individuals for seeking professional help for a mental illness. Researchers have noted that cultural stigma and disgrace are often correlated with mental illness (Akutsu, 1997) and that institutional barriers common to traditional mental health services may make it difficult for minority groups, such as Asian Americans, to acknowledge that psychological problems require professional help (Chin, 1998; Flaskerud, 1986; Uba, 1994). Less acculturated or marginalized individuals are sometimes reluctant to seek help because of social stigma and cultural mistrust (Constantine, Okazaki, & Utsey, 2004; Smart & Smart, 1995; Vega & Lopez, 2001; Whaley, 2001). Related to the help-seeking literature detailing the sources of reluctance to seek treatment among ethnic minorities are data showing lower and different rates of

actual utilization of mental health services by ethnic minorities.

Underutilization of Mental Health Services

According to *Mental Health: Culture, Race, and Ethnicity—A Supplement to Mental Health: A Report of the Surgeon General* (USDHHS, 2001), formal mental health services continued to be underused by Americans. Among Americans, however, ethnic minorities are less likely to utilize mental health services, specifically outpatient services, in comparison to White Americans (Neighbors, Bashur, Price, Selig, Donabedian, & Shannon, 1992; Snowden, 2001; USDHHS, 2001; Wells et al., 2001). Wells, Klap, Koike, and Sherbourne (2001) found that among Americans with perceived or actual clinical needs, Whites were more likely to be receiving active treatment than either Hispanics or African Americans. Further, it has been reported that African Americans underutilize outpatient mental health services (Alvidrez, 1999; Pumariega, Glover, Holzer, & Nguyen, 1998) and overuse inpatient and emergency mental health services, likely due to differences in health insurance coverage (Maynard, Ehreth, Cox, Peterson, & McGann, 1997; Scheffler & Miller, 1991). Recent data from the National Survey of American Life show that only about half of African Americans and Caribbean Blacks with serious mental illness reported using mental health services and only approximately 40% had contact with mental health care specialists (Neighbors et al., 2007).

The reasons for race and ethnic differences in the utilization of mental health services are not entirely clear. In addition to issues related to stigma, mistrust, and fear that have been cited in the help-seeking literature, some have noted that systemic barriers reduce the likelihood of utilization for ethnic minorities. For example, mental health experts note that often the problem is not initially seeking treatment but following through. Akutsu, Tsuru, and Chu (2004) found that one-third of Asian Americans who reported having had a mental health intake appointment failed to show up for their first session. Further, Diala et al. (2000) have shown that prior to using mental health services, African Americans report more positive attitudes toward seeking care in comparison to Whites; however, after utilization their attitudes toward care were less positive than those of Whites.

Other researchers cite demographic and economic factors that affect the availability and accessibility of services (Alegria et al., 2002; Dana, 2002; Melfi, Croghan, & Hanna, 1999), including the cost of psychological treatment and lack of insurance coverage (Snowden & Thomas, 2000; Vega & Lopez, 2001). In fact, when compared to White and higher SES individuals, ethnic minority and low SES individuals report experiencing more systemic barriers to using mental health services such as the lack of insurance, transportation, and time (Smedley, Stith, & Nelson, 2003; Takeuchi, Leaf, & Kuo, 1988). Instrumental barriers to mental health care may not, however, completely explain race and ethnic differences in mental health utilization. Researchers have found that even among diverse populations with equivalent levels of insurance coverage, ethnic minorities are still less likely to use outpatient mental health services compared to Whites (Padgett, Patrick, Burns, & Schlesinger, 1994; Smedley et al., 2003; Thomas & Snowden, 2002). Therefore, other factors likely explain some of the racial and ethnic variance in utilization.

For example, racial identity has been found to be a protective factor for African Americans who experience negative experiences such as

---

HIGHLIGHT BOX 18.4

DISCRIMINATION

Unfortunately, *discrimination* based on group membership continues to exist. Recent research has highlighted the ways in which discrimination has changed over the past several decades and is now less overt (e.g., being ignored/overlooked while waiting in line) than earlier forms of discrimination (e.g., lynching, being denied service at a restaurant; Dovidio & Gaertner, 1998; Harrell, 2000; Pettigrew, 1998). However, even less overt incidents may be stressful, leading to feelings of resignation and hopelessness (Harrell, 2000; NRC, 2004). Over time, accumulated and chronically stressful or discriminatory events can negatively affect mental health (DeLongis, Coyne, Dakof, Folkman, & Lazarus, 1982).

It is important to understand how discrimination might affect some clients in relation to their presenting problems or function as a stressor in their lives. How individuals experience discrimination can be influenced by racial identity and worldview. Yet the association between identity and discrimination may be complex. For example, even though being more identified with one's racial or ethnic group may increase the recognition and report of discrimination (see Highlight Box 18.2) (Neblett, Shelton, & Sellers, 2004; Operario & Fiske, 2001; Sellers, Caldwell, Schmeelk-Cone, & Zimmerman, 2003), individuals with strongly salient racial identities report experiencing fewer deleterious psychological symptoms due to discrimination experiences in comparison to those with less salient identities (Neblett et al., 2004; Sellers et al., 2003). Therefore, greater awareness of discrimination may be offset by the protective benefits of a strong sense of group membership.

discrimination (Banks & Kohn-Wood, 2007; Sellers & Shelton, 2003) (see Highlight Box 18.4) and who experience symptoms of anxiety and depression (Banks, Kohn, & Spencer, 2006). It is possible that feelings of affiliation with one's group provide a sense of pride that decreases a perceived need for help. Alternatively, individuals with a high level of racial affiliation may be less likely to utilize services that are perceived to be for those outside their racial group. Further, racial identity has been found to moderate negative experiences of discrimination, such that African Americans with highly salient racial identities who experience discrimination are less likely to utilize mental health services (Richman, Kohn-Wood, & Williams, 2007). In addition to racial identity, African Americans have been found to report more use of religious resources and engagement as coping techniques in comparison to White Americans (Ferraro & Koch, 1994; Koenig et al., 1992). African Americans demonstrate higher levels of both public and private religious behaviors than White Americans and report higher levels of religious participation (Taylor, Levin, & Joseph, 2004), including a 60% higher likelihood of engaging in prayer (Bearon & Koenig, 1990). Further, research examining the correlation between religiousness and depressive symptoms has shown that although the reasons are unclear, people who are more religious report experiencing fewer depressive symptoms (Smith, McCullough, & Poll, 2003). Individuals who attend church regularly exhibit lower rates of depression (Braam, van den Eeden, & Prince, 2001). It is possible that African Americans' increased level of religiosity is related to decreased mental health service utilization, either because of psychological relief provided by religion or activities. Racial and ethnic underutilization of services may be related to structural barriers but also to protective factors and behaviors that mitigate the need to utilize formal mental health services (Neighbors, 1985). Despite this possibility, there have been widespread efforts to increase appropriate utilization of treatment among ethnic minorities.

Efforts to Encourage Treatment Seeking among Ethnically Diverse Individuals

Racial and ethnic differences in treatment utilization have become a focus of mental health policy and led to the implementation of programs and initiatives aimed at increasing treatment use in diverse populations. The federal government has focused on transforming the mental health delivery system by reducing the barriers that currently discourage minorities from accessing mental health care. In 2001, President Bush signed the New Freedom Initiative, which seeks to promote access to community life for people with disabilities. As a part of this initiative, the New Freedom Commission on Mental Health was formed to assess the current mental health system and suggest changes that will positively affect mental health outcomes. The commission outlined six goals for fundamental change to the mental health care system including the need to improve "access to quality mental health care that is culturally competent" (The President's New Freedom Commission on Mental Health, 2003, p. 10). Under the leadership of the Substance Abuse and Mental Health Services Administration (SAMHSA), several federal programs collaborated to form an action plan to implement the commission's suggestions. The Federal Mental Health Action Agenda was born from this collaboration. This action agenda includes steps such as implementing public education campaigns, creating a strategic development plan to reduce mental health disparities, and evaluating current behavioral health training programs on the level of multicultural training received by students (Substance Abuse and Mental Health Services Administration [SAMHSA], 2006).

Building on research from the *Surgeon General's Report: Mental Health: A Report of the*

Surgeon General (DHHS, 1999), which shows that collaboration with community agencies and aggressive outreach efforts increase engagement and treatment seeking in ethnic minority communities, the Federal Mental Health Action Agenda highlighted the importance of disseminating information regarding mental illness and treatment options by using existing community services. Many mental health organizations have followed suit and implemented community-led public education programs. In an effort to encourage the acceptance and use of formal mental health services, the National Institute of Mental Health (NIMH) together with SAMHSA created a community outreach program entitled the Outreach Partnership Program. The Outreach Partnership Program aims to reduce stigma by using community organizations to deliver a mental health education and outreach program to health professionals and traditionally underserved populations in each state (National Institute of Mental Health, n.d.). Similarly, APA has also encouraged members to utilize a community education approach to reach minority groups. APA's public education campaign provides practitioners with educational materials and tools to connect with community organizations such as religious institutions, schools, and businesses in hopes of better meeting the mental health needs of minority communities (American Psychological Association, 2007). The National Alliance on Mental Illness (NAMI) has created faith-based public education programs that target minority populations. NAMI has also established a Multicultural Action Center that produces outreach manuals for each ethnic minority group. These manuals outline culturally specific guidelines for reaching out to minority clients to both provide culturally competent mental health services and encourage the use of these services (National Alliance on Mental Illness, n.d.). Additionally, the aforementioned mental health organizations

have created user-friendly Web sites that have information regarding mental illness, recognizing when to seek help, and options for treatment.

In addition to public education and outreach efforts, the action agenda also calls for collaboration between the primary care system and the mental health care system. As ethnic minorities tend to seek mental health treatment in primary care settings (DHHS, 2001), there are also efforts by SAMHSA and the U.S. Department of Health and Human Services (DHHS) to examine the possibility of integrating primary care services and mental health care services (i.e., screening individuals at risk for mental disorders in primary health clinics and coordinating follow-up with appropriate providers) (SAMHSA, 2006). By combining these two services, accessibility barriers caused by cultural factors, such as language differences, and geographic factors, such as living in remote areas, can be reduced.

By taking the steps just outlined, the federal government along with several mental health organizations has sought to remove barriers that discourage minorities from seeking mental health treatment. The removal of these barriers should transform the mental health care delivery system from a system that was historically neglectful of ethnic minorities into a system that is more tailored to the needs of ethnic minority clients, thereby increasing the utilization of mental health services and better meeting the mental health needs of ethnic minority communities.

DIVERSITY ISSUES IN RESEARCH

Cross-cultural Relevance of Diagnostic Categories

In the past 30 years, major advancements have been made in the fields of psychiatry, anthropology, and psychology in the study and understanding of mental disorders between and within geographic spheres (e.g., East/West), national economic indicators (e.g., developing/developed), socioeconomic statuses (e.g., low/high), genders (female/male), age cohorts (adolescents/adults), ethnic groups (e.g., Black Caribbean/African American), racial categories (e.g., Latinos/non-Latino Whites), and tribal regions (e.g., Southwest/Northern Plains), to provide a few examples (e.g., Alegria et al., 2004; Beals et al., 2005; Breslau, Kendler, Aguilar-Gaxiola, & Kessler, 2005a; Kleinman, 1988; Kleinman & Good, 1985; Williams et al., 2007b; World Health Organization, 2004). These cross-cultural studies have largely shown that culture does indeed influence an individual's expression, experience, and understanding of psychiatric conditions (López & Guarnaccia, 2000), although much remains unknown about the exact ways in which cultural factors modulate these relationships (for a recent conceptual attempt, see Chentsova-Dutton & Tsai, 2007). On the most basic level, it is agreed that there is evidence for a complex patterning of "abnormal behavior" across national and international contexts, but we are far from reaching a consensus about the extent to which current Western formulations of mental disorders are valid across cultures (e.g., Alarcón et al., 2002).

It should be noted at the outset that much of what we know about the cross-cultural relevance of diagnostic categories stems from research that often harbored one of two polarized methodological perspectives. On one pole is the **etic** perspective, which privileges the study of "objective" or universal constructs by drawing comparisons *between* cultures to understand phenomena theorized to be common to all humankind. On the other pole is the **emic** perspective, which aims to study within-culture constructs for the purpose of understanding concepts *within* a cultural mode (Berry, 1969; Brislin, Lonner, & Thorndike, 1973). Primarily etic or universalistic perspectives are most common in cultural psychiatric epidemiology research because of the focus on prevalence rates of Western-derived psychiatric disorders and associated symptoms. Alternatively, primarily emic perspectives are typical in anthropology, but less common in psychiatry and psychology. These perspectives usually examine cultural models of mental illness and question the blind application of diagnostic categories to particular cultural groups. Integration of etic and emic perspectives, though highly encouraged (e.g., Alarcón et al., 2002; Draguns & Tanaka-Matsumi, 2003; Guarnaccia & Rogler, 1999; Vega et al., 2007), is even less common (for recent exemplars, see Alegria et al., 2004; Beals et al., 2003; Jackson et al., 2004).

In an effort to briefly summarize the literature on the cross-cultural relevance of mental disorders, three broad conditions or categories as defined in the *Diagnostic and Statistical Manual of Mental Disorders* (4th ed., Text Revision; DSM-IV-TR; American Psychiatric Association [APA], 2000) were selected for review, namely, depression, anxiety, and schizophrenia. These disorders or categories were chosen because of the amount and type of cross-cultural research conducted about these conditions, though the literature presented is by no means exhaustive or representative. What follows is a brief review of select etic and emic cross-cultural research on depression, anxiety, and schizophrenia among adults. Examples of research that point to the cross-cultural relevance of the selected conditions while either rendering support or complicating current DSM-IV-TR conceptualizations of the selected psychiatric disorders are provided (for recent and more comprehensive reviews on adult psychopathology, see Chentsova-Dutton & Tsai, 2007; Draguns & Tanaka-Matsumi, 2003; Lee & Sue, 2001; López & Guarnaccia, 2000; Tanaka-Matsumi, 2001; for reviews on cross-cultural research on childhood psychopathology, see López & Guarnaccia, 2000; Weisz, McCarty, Eastman, Chiyasit, & Suwanlert, 1997).

Depression

The experience of depression and dysphoria occurs across cultures (e.g., Kleinman & Good, 1985). A recent etic study commissioned by the World Health Organization (WHO) and conducted by the WHO World Mental Health Survey Consortium (2004) revealed that the 12-month prevalence of mood disorders (including depression, dysthymia, and bipolar I and II) was the second highest for a disorder class, following anxiety disorders, with rates ranging from 1.7% in Shanghai to 9.6% in the United States (U.S.). These cross-national comparisons of prevalence rates for depression also demonstrate higher prevalence rates among people living in Western and Latin American cities versus those living in Eastern cities (Simon, Goldberg, VonKorff, & Ustun, 2002). Ethnic minorities living in the U.S. have been found to have a lower risk for depression or a depressive episode in comparison to non-Hispanic Whites (e.g., Beals et al., 2005; Breslau et al., 2005a). Moreover, within-group comparisons of ethnic minorities living in the U.S. have demonstrated that prevalence rates of depression vary according to generational status among those of the same descent. In particular, prevalence rates for depression were lowest among Mexican-born Mexican Americans and highest among U.S.-born Mexican Americans (Vega et al., 1998). The protective or buffering effect of nativity or generational status and ethnicity has been implicated elsewhere as well (e.g., Williams et al., 2007b).

Emic studies of depression have called into question the assumption of a universal and unitary experience of depression across cultures. Kleinman and Good's (1985) seminal edited text about the complex understanding of depression as a mood, symptom, and illness among specific cultural communities stands out as one of the early catalysts for a cultural psychiatry or cultural clinical psychology that challenged these universal presuppositions.

In this text, for example, Manson, Shore, and Bloom (1985) showed that there was no conceptual or linguistic equivalent of the syndrome of depression among the Hopi tribe of American Indians. Moreover, only one of the five illness categories provided by the participants correlated strongly with a substantive number of Western-derived depressed symptoms. The 2-week duration criterion also emerged as potentially invalid and likely inappropriate in this community.

Anxiety

Anxiety and disordered anxiety have also been shown to be prevalent across cultures with variations in expression, phenomenology, and causal attributions (e.g., Good & Kleinman, 1985; Low, 1989). Overall, international prevalence rates for anxiety disorders are the highest of any psychiatric disorder (WHO, 2004). These etic cross-national comparisons have found that 12-month prevalence of anxiety disorders (to include agoraphobia, generalized anxiety disorder, obsessive-compulsive disorder, posttraumatic stress disorder, social phobia, and specific phobia) ranged from 2.4% in Shanghai to 18.2% in the United States (WHO). Recent studies of psychiatric morbidity across ethnic groups living in the United States indicate a greater risk for a chronic course for anxiety disorders (and mood disorders) among non-Hispanic Blacks and English-speaking Hispanics versus non-Hispanic Whites (Breslau et al., 2005a). Within–ethnic group comparisons also reveal variations in prevalence rates of anxiety disorders for members categorized as Latina/o, such that 14.7% of Mexican Americans, 21.61% of Puerto Ricans, 15.71% of Cuban Americans, and 14.16% of other Latinos met criteria for a lifetime prevalence of anxiety disorder (Ortega, Feldman, Canino, Steinman, & Alegria, 2006). Similar to findings on depression, nativity or generational status also appears to moderate the experience of anxiety disorders in immigrant groups living in the United States (e.g., Karno et al., 1987).

Notably, the systematic research program (often integrating etic and emic perspectives) on **ataque de nervios** and its relationship with anxiety disorders demonstrates the ways in which our understanding of prevalence rates for anxiety disorders among Latinas/os is convoluted once we consider the meaning, function, and phenomenology of *ataques*. *Ataque de nervios* is a culture-bound syndrome characterized as an acute syndromal experience involving both typical and atypical panic symptomatology such as loss of control, screaming, crying, rage, aggressiveness, amnesia, and ensuing sense of relief (APA, 2000; Guarnaccia, De la Cancela, & Carrillo, 1989). *Ataques* are also highly comorbid with mood and anxiety disorders. Despite these high rates of comorbidity, distinct features have been found that distinguish these experiences from panic attacks and other anxiety disorders.

A Note on Somatization

The concept of somatization or the tendency to experience and express distress in somatic terms must be discussed in relation to the cross-cultural literature on depression and anxiety. Somatization is common across cultures (e.g., Kirmayer & Young, 1998). However, there are mixed results regarding the prevalence of somatization across cultures, with some studies finding support for a greater tendency to experience somatization among people in non-Western communities (e.g., Kleinman, 1977) and others finding equal prevalence rates between Western and non-Western communities (e.g., Simon, VonKorff, Piccinelli, Fullerton, & Ormel, 1999). Kirmayer and Young argue that the inconclusive results may be an artifact of different definitions of somatization and that somatization as a concept is a reflection of Western dualism that separates mind and body. Understanding the unique function of

somatization across cultural groups is then central to making sense of experiences of disordered mood and anxiety at the individual and cultural level. In the case of anxiety disorders especially, which are conceptualized as involving cognitive, somatic, and interpretive aspects, somatization as an illness style structures the very configuration of cognitions, physical symptoms, and interpretations (Good & Kleinman, 1985). The cultural variation in the configuration of the exact nature of the syndromes is then inherently problematic to the search for discrete and universal anxiety disorders.

Schizophrenia

The first major international study about the nature and course of schizophrenia was published in 1979 by the WHO's International Pilot Study on Schizophrenia (WHO, 1979). This study was followed by the Determinants of Outcomes of Severe Mental Disorder (DOSMD) study (Jablensky et al., 1992). Results coupled from these two influential studies provide support for the cross-cultural validity of the core symptoms of schizophrenia and the role of culture in shaping symptom manifestation. These results also corroborate early work with Eskimos from the Bering Sea and Egba Yorubas by Murphy (1976), which showed a universal patterning of psychotic symptoms. Moreover, these studies provided evidence that the course of schizophrenia differed across nations, with people in developing countries having a less chronic and severe course than those in developed countries. It has been proposed that the early studies sponsored by the WHO were catalysts for an interrogation of the methods, concepts, and practices used to examine the complex interactions between schizophrenia, social context, and its related constructs (López & Guarnaccia, 2000).

Emic studies on schizophrenia have found that *nervios*, a culture-bound syndrome prevalent across cultures, has been used by Mexican and Puerto Ricans to understand schizophrenia spectrum disorders (Jenkins, 1988a, 1988b; Swerdlow, 1992). These authors argue that the use of *nervios* functions to lessen the stigma associated with this condition and to facilitate continued family interaction and support. The use of *nervios* to explain schizophrenia in this case calls attention to the complicated and dialectical relationship between causal explanations and psychiatric syndromes; the links are not unidirectional, and the boundaries between the two are often blurred such that causal explanations can serve as syndromes and vice versa.

Summary

In tandem, the etic and emic studies just presented above highlight the complex ways in which depression, anxiety, and schizophrenia as either or both a state and condition can vary in prevalence rates, symptom manifestation, syndromal configuration, and meaning across cultures. It is clear, though, that the experience of psychological distress is commonly shared across countries in different spheres of the world. However, evidence about the universal patterning of these experiences across cultures is not clear-cut. Depressive and anxiety disorders may be configured differently across cultural groups and may not neatly adhere to the temporal and descriptive features included in the DSM-IV, although there are indications of a common reliance on mood and somatic descriptors. The cultural variation of somatization as an illness style, however, poses a direct challenge to the Western dualism that pervades psychiatry and informs the DSM, thereby complicating the ways in which mood and anxiety experiences are configured. In the case of schizophrenia, international studies have documented a core cluster of symptom types across cultures, but the causal explanations, symptoms, and course appear to be greatly influenced by cultural context.

A Note on Methodology

As noted at the outset, cultural psychiatric epidemiology research relies on an etic or universalistic perspective that assumes disorders look the same regardless of culture (Kleinman, 1988). This etic framework has been called into question because of the dangers of committing a **category fallacy**: imposing Western diagnostic categories on other groups in the absence of compelling empirical evidence of their validity (Kleinman, 1977). However, adoption of a strictly emic perspective is also not without costs. Strictly emic perspectives are vulnerable to extreme cultural relativism, which renders the experiences of any two cultural groups incommensurable and comparisons impossible. Most importantly, either of these two extremes could result in over- or underpathologization of individuals and groups. Proponents for an inclusive cross-cultural research agenda call for the integration of both etic and emic perspectives and the foregrounding of culture (e.g., Alarcón et al., 2002; Guarnaccia & Rogler, 1999; Vega et al., 2007). The integration of perspectives, most often conceptualized as mixing of quantitative and qualitative methods, holds methodological promise, because of its ability to triangulate around a phenomenon to find convergent, inconsistent, or contradictory results (Denzin, 1978). Allowing for these multiple types of data increases our ability to capture diversity and complexity of human experience. This integration directly disavows mere semantic translation of diagnostic instruments as sufficient to methodologically sound cross-cultural research. Instead, it is necessary that the search for conceptual equivalence or culturally meaningful equivalents of categories of experience is prioritized (Kleinman, 1988; Kleinman & Good, 1985; Rogler, 1999). Proponents of this perspective also argue against making non-Western experiences seem exotic, an accusation made about the presentation of culture-bound syndromes in the DSM as uniquely non-Western experiences, despite evidence suggestive of the existence of culture-bound syndromes (e.g., anorexia nervosa) in Euro-Western countries (Alarcón et al., 2002; Mezzich et al., 1999). Ultimately, an integrative cross-cultural research program and clinical profession take seriously the study of culture and psychopathology from both etic and emic perspectives and thereby do not privilege in a priori fashion universalistic or relativistic assumptions about the nature of disorder.

Generalizing Clinical Intervention Research to Diverse Groups

In a review of the research literature on evidence-based mental health care with ethnic minorities, Miranda, Bernal, and Lau (2005) conclude that such interventions have been clearly demonstrated to be effective for treatment of depression among African Americans and Latinos. The reviewed evidence is also promising, though much more sparse, for Asian American populations. Although mental health service delivery based on empirically supported interventions is certainly necessary, it has not been sufficient for addressing widespread disparities between ethnic minority and White clients in treatment outcomes.

One missing piece of this treatment puzzle appears to be the integration of sociocultural considerations with evidence-based intervention approaches. Research largely supports using culture to achieve insights into the reduction of racial disparities in health care (Fisher, Burnet, & Huang, 2007). A number of interventions aimed at narrowing health-care disparities between minority and nonminority racial groups were reviewed, revealing three effective intervention types. Individual-level interventions focused on self-care strategies to promote health education and positive health behavior among individual clients of color. Access interventions focused on decreasing barriers to care within communities of color. The third type of intervention focused on the health-care system itself, promoting greater cultural competence among service providers and improved quality of care to racial minority clients and communities at large.

Quality improvement (QI) programs aim to synthesize each of these intervention types into one comprehensive approach to mental health care. QI has been shown to be quite effective for improving short-term and cumulative outcomes of treatment for depression, also reducing treatment outcome disparities across ethnic groups (Wells, Sherbourne, & Miranda, 2007). In particular, evidence-based psychotherapy offered through QI programs, which additionally increased access and provided education about depression treatment to both clients and primary care professionals, resulted in significant mental health gains as well as reduction of outcome disparities. QI psychotherapy demonstrated greater effectiveness compared to both QI pharmacotherapy and usual care without the added access and educational resources of QI. Adapted care models, including QI, were also found to be more effective than community referral in the treatment of depression (Ward, 2007). Such models of intervention that provide outreach, case management, and access resources such as childcare and transportation offer clear benefits for ethnic minority women especially.

The Paradox of Mental Health Disparities

Epidemiological research on race, ethnicity, and psychiatric diagnoses has uncovered interesting and in some ways paradoxical findings. First, the Hispanic *paradox* is characterized by unexpectedly lower rates of psychiatric disorder observed among the least acculturated Mexican immigrants in comparison to more acculturated Mexican American peers (Vega et al., 1998). Specifically, community-based studies of psychiatric diagnoses showed migrant Mexican farmworkers to have the lowest rate of psychiatric disorders when compared to both native-born

Mexican Americans and non-Hispanic White Americans (Alderete, Vega, Kolody, & Aguilar-Gaxiola, 2000). Although some have argued that these findings are due to methodological problems in the study (Palloni & Morenoff, 2001) and are not replicable (Smith & Bradshaw, 2006), the possibility of the veracity of the Hispanic mental health paradox has, nevertheless, generated greater interest in the field with regard to cultural and traditional beliefs and behaviors that may confer protection from negative mental health, even among seemingly vulnerable populations (Castro & Coe, 2007; Morales, Mara, Kington, Valdez, & Exarce, 2002).

Further, evidence for additional paradoxical findings has emerged from recent national survey studies of psychiatric disorder prevalence across race and ethnicity, Specifically, despite a robust literature detailing racial disparities in physical health outcomes, it appears as though racial and ethnic minorities in the United States exhibit reduced risk for lifetime rates of some psychiatric disorders in comparison to Whites. The National Comorbidity Survey (NCS), conducted in the early 1990s, sought to determine the national prevalence of psychiatric disorders in the United States, using a complex survey design that resulted in a stratified probability sample representing the broad demographics of the country. Researchers utilized a new (at the time) instrument for assessing psychiatric diagnoses that could be administered by trained interviewers who did not have to be mental health professionals yet could still arrive at accurate diagnostic decisions. The instrument, the WHO's version of the Composite International Diagnostic Interview (WMH-CIDI) (Kessler & Ustun, 2004), is considered an updated improvement over other structured diagnostic interview tools such as the Structured Clinical Interview for DSM-IV (SCID) because of the inclusion of international and multicultural standardization norms and the ease of administration. The NCS data found lower-than-expected rates of psychiatric disorders among racial and ethnic

minorities (Breslau et al., 2005a). These findings are paradoxical because increased social adversity is typically associated with increased risk for psychiatric disorders. In fact, social disadvantage has been used to explain racial disparities in physical health outcomes whereby African Americans and Hispanics in the United States disproportionately suffer poor health and exhibit higher rates of physical health disorders in comparison to Whites.

Two additional sources of data further emphasize the paradox of "reverse" disparities with regard to mental health outcomes. Breslau, Aguilar-Gaxiola, Kendler, Su, Williams, and Kessler (2005b) examined data from the National Comorbidity Survey Replication (NCS-R) to test for variation in racial and ethnic differences across individual disorders by class of disorder. These findings show that in comparison to non-Hispanic Whites, both African Americans and Hispanics exhibit lower risk for depression, generalized anxiety disorder, and social phobia. Further, compared to Whites, Hispanics showed lower risk for dysthymia, oppositional-defiant disorder, and attention-hyperactivity disorder, whereas African Americans had lower risk for panic disorder, substance use disorders, and early-onset impulse control disorders. Breslau and colleagues found that the evidence for decreased risk for psychiatric disorders appears to begin in childhood, that lower risk for Hispanics was found only among those under age 43, and that lower risk for minorities was more pronounced among those with lower levels of education. Further evidence for lower risk for mood disorders among African Americans in comparison to Whites in the United States comes from the recent National Survey of American Life (NSAL) conducted by Jackson and colleagues (2004). In this study, lifetime prevalence rates for major depressive disorder were highest for Whites (approximately 18% of the population), followed by Caribbean Blacks (approximately 13% of the population) and African Americans (approximately 10% of the population) (Williams et al., 2007a). These emerging research findings indicate that, paradoxically, racial and ethnic minorities experience lower risk for many of the most common psychiatric disorders.

Other paradoxical findings have been found in international studies comparing psychiatric disorders across countries. For example, surveys of 14 countries including China, Japan, Mexico, Colombia, Nigeria, and France showed that the United States has the highest rate of mental illness (WHO, 2004). Further, a series of large-scale multinational studies has consistently reported that outcomes for individuals with serious mental illness who live in developing countries are significantly better than individuals living in industrialized countries (Jablensky et al., 1992; Lin & Kleinman, 1988). As stated earlier, for example, the International Pilot Study of Schizophrenia has found that individuals diagnosed with schizophrenia who live in the nations of Nigeria, India, and Colombia exhibit better functioning and fewer symptoms than similarly diagnosed individuals who live in Denmark, the United Kingdom, and the United States (Leff, Sartorius, Jablensky, Korten, & Enberg, 1992). Although some researchers have questioned these findings as methodologically flawed and nonspecific (Patel, Cohen, Thara, & Gureje, 2006), an investigation of six potential sources of bias indicates that the course and outcomes of schizophrenia in developing countries hold up under systematic scrutiny (Hopper & Wanderling, 2000). Therefore, other researchers have turned their attention to sociocultural factors that may explain differences in societal beliefs about and responses to mental illness and that influence prognosis (López & Guarnaccia, 2000). It is suggested that developing countries' values and customs, including religion and kinship structure, may minimize the stress, social stigma, and self-devaluation associated with serious mental illness in industrialized countries (Weisman, 1997). Similarly, research on family caretaking for schizophrenia

in rural areas of the United States indicates that families with few resources and minimal connection to a formal mental health care system exhibit relatively low levels of burden and high levels of tolerance toward ill family members, which may be related to fewer symptoms and better functioning among those affected with schizophrenia (Kohn-Wood & Wilson, 2005).

It is possible that data showing paradoxical findings related to mental health outcomes may be due to issues related to reporting and disclosure such that ethnic minorities or individuals from developing countries are more reluctant than others to admit they are experiencing symptoms. Popular literature, for example, suggests that African Americans are not likely to recognize psychiatric symptomatology as such, nor are they likely to tell anyone about the degree of their distress because it contradicts cultural values associated with perseverance (Danquah, 1999; Williams, 2008). Further, there is some evidence (see earlier discussion) that ethnic minority individuals or individuals from non-Western countries may tend to somaticize psychiatric symptomatology and, therefore, do not endorse psychological or emotional symptom criteria for major mental disorders. However, given converging evidence from national and international epidemiological surveys along with several community studies (Kessler et al., 1994; Seng, Kohn-Wood, & Odera, 2005; Somervell, Leaf, Weissman, Blazer, & Bruce, 1989), it appears that the paradox of better mental health outcomes among many socially disadvantaged groups could lead the field to uncover potential protective factors among ethnic minority groups that, if elucidated, could be utilized to reduce risk for psychiatric disorders across all groups of people.

SUMMARY

Increasing international globalization along with the changing demographics of many countries, including the United States, has led to increased attention to the meaning and process of cultural competence in therapy and the importance of self-awareness and identity growth of the clinician. Racial and ethnic variance in treatment seeking and utilization of services has led to multiple efforts for increasing access to and acceptance of treatment across diverse groups to close the gap between majority and minority groups in unmet need. Diversity issues in research have led to accumulated evidence about the relevance of diagnostic categories of mental illness and identified culturally distinct idioms and expressions of psychological distress, such as *ataques de nervios*, a culture-bound syndrome similar to panic attacks, characterized by loss of control, screaming, crying, rage, aggressiveness, amnesia, and ensuing sense of relief. Interestingly, epidemiological surveys on the prevalence of mental disorders find that individuals from diverse groups in the United States have lower lifetime risk of mood and anxiety disorders, and individuals with serious mental disorders living in developing countries exhibit better outcomes than those living in industrialized countries. These paradoxical findings suggest that sociocultural factors may influence the risk and course of mental disorders. Training efforts to improve skills and knowledge about diversity among clinical psychologists include coursework focused on culture as well as experiences of direct contact with diverse groups.

THOUGHT QUESTIONS

1. APA created *Guidelines on Multicultural Education, Training, Research, Practice, and Organizational Change for Psychologists* (2002) to encourage cultural competence in training and practice. However, these guidelines are aspirational in nature and are not mandatory. With empirical research showing the importance of cultural competence in training and practice settings, should APA take a stronger stance and create enforceable standards regarding multicultural education, training, research, and practice?

2. The fact that minority group members do not utilize mental health services at a rate comparable to White Americans is well documented. However, what exactly the profession should do to make mental health treatment more accessible and attractive to minority group members is not entirely clear. If you were in a position to develop programs to encourage minority group utilization of mental health services, what kinds of programs would you consider developing? What do you think are the principal barriers to utilization?

3. Given significant group differences in the way mental health services are perceived (e.g., with regard to desirability, stigmatization), what are alternative ways in which mental health services could be delivered? What are some creative ways, for example, that services could be delivered in order to minimize the effects of barriers or obstacles?

4. Cross-cultural mental health research with ethnic minorities in the United States often uses ethnicity as a proxy for culture. However, assuming that ethnicity is a meaningful marker of identity and operates similarly for everyone is unsubstantiated. What challenge does this pose to understanding research findings gleaned from psychiatric epidemiology research that only assessed ethnicity through a "check the corresponding ethnicity box" method?

Glossary

Acculturation: the extent to which an individual adopts the beliefs and values of the host culture.

Ataque de nervios: a culture-bound syndrome characterized as an acute syndromal experience involving both typical and atypical panic symptomatology such as loss of control, screaming, crying, rage, aggressiveness, amnesia, and ensuing sense of relief.

Autonomy: a developmental stage of the White racial/cultural identity model proposed by Helms (1995) that includes increasing awareness of Whiteness and one's personal role in perpetuating racism while decreasing feelings of guilt.

Category fallacy: imposing Western diagnostic categories on other groups in the absence of compelling empirical evidence of their validity.

Conformity: a developmental stage of the R/CID model that is marked by an alignment with dominant culture prior to individuals integrating race or ethnicity into their identity.

Cultural competence: the knowledge and skill base to work with clients from different backgrounds.

Discrimination: unfair treatment on the basis of group membership.

Dissonance: a developmental stage of the R/CID model that occurs when individuals encounter information or experiences that provoke the integration of race into their identity.

Emic perspective: with regard to methodological perspectives for studying culture, the emic perspective aims to study within-culture constructs for the purpose of understanding concepts *within* a particular and specific cultural milieu.

Etic perspective: with regard to methodological perspectives for studying culture, the etic perspective privileges the study of "objective" or universal constructs by drawing comparisons *between* cultures to understand phenomena theorized to be common to all humankind.

Immersion/emersion: a developmental stage of the White racial/cultural identity model proposed by Helms (1995) that involves focusing on what it means to be White and a developing personal understanding of White privilege.

Integrative awareness: a developmental stage of the R/CID model whereby one adds the appreciation of other cultures to an inner sense of security that has developed through the stages of acquiring a full actualized sense of racial/cultural identity.

Introspection: a developmental stage of the R/CID model whereby one brings a deeper level of understanding to the sense of personal and group identity.

Pseudo-independence: a developmental stage of the White racial/cultural identity model proposed by Helms (1995) that includes beginning to engage with people of color in addition to attempts to understand White privilege on an intellectual level.

Racial/cultural identity development (R/CID) model: a conceptualization of the stages of development of racial or cultural identity developed by Sue and Sue (2008).

Racial identity: how an individual conceptualizes race as a part of personal identity.

Resistance and immersion: a developmental stage of the R/CID model that involves rejection of mainstream values and active exploration of one's own culture and that is sometimes marked by anger.

Worldview: the way people understand and perceive relationship to the world.

References

Akutsu, P. D. (1997). Mental health care delivery to Asian Americans: review of the literature. In E. Lee (Ed.), *Working with Asian Americans: a guide for clinicians* (pp. 464–476). New York: Guilford.

Akutsu, P. D., Tsuru, G. K., & Chu, J. P. (2004). Predictors of non-attendance of intake appointments among five

Asian American client groups. *Journal of Consulting and Clinical Psychology*, 72, 891–896.

Alarcón, R. D., Bell, C. C., Kirmayer, L. J., Lin, K-M., Ustun, B., & Wisner, K. L. (2002). Beyond the funhouse mirrors: research agenda on culture and psychiatric diagnosis. In D. J. Kupfer, M. B. First, & D. A. Regier (Eds.), *A research agenda for DSM-V* (pp. 219–281). Washington, DC: American Psychiatric Association.

Alderete, E., Vega, W. A., Kolody, B., & Aguilar-Gaxiola, S. (2000). Lifetime prevalence of and risk factors for psychiatric disorders among Mexican migrant farmworkers in California. *American Journal of Public Health*, 90, 608–614.

Alegria, M., Canino, G., Rios, R., Vera, M., Calderon, J. Rusch, D., et al. (2002). Mental health care for Latinos: inequalities in use of specialty mental health services among Latinos, African Americans, and non-Latino Whites. *Psychiatric Services*, 53, 1547–1555.

Alegria, M., Vila, D., Woo, M., Canino, G., Takeuchi, D. Vera, M., et al. (2004). Cultural relevance and equivalence in the NLAAS instrument: integrating etic and emic in the development of cross-cultural measures for a psychiatric epidemiology and services study of Latinos. *International Journal of Methods in Psychiatric Research*, 13, 270–288.

Alvidrez, J. (1999). Ethnic variations in mental health attitudes and service use among low-income African American, Latina, and European American young women. *Community Mental Health Journal*, 35, 515–531.

American Psychiatric Association (2000). *Diagnostic and statistical manual of mental disorders* (4th ed., Text Revision). Washington, DC: Author.

American Psychological Association, Committee on Accreditation (2000). *Guidelines and principles for accreditation of programs in professional psychology*. Retrieved March 7, 2008 from http://www.apa.org/ed/gp2000.html.

American Psychological Association (2002a). *Ethical principles of psychologists and code of conduct*. Retrieved March 7, 2008 from http://www.apa.org/ethics/code2002.pdf.

American Psychological Association (2002b). *Guidelines on multicultural education, training, research, practice, and organizational change for psychologists*. Retrieved March 7, 2008 from http://www.apa.org/pi/multiculturalguidelines.pdf.

American Psychological Association (2007). *Reaching Out to Diverse Populations: Opportunities and Challenges*. Washington, D.C.: Author. Retrieved March 31, 2008, from http://www.apapractice.org/apo/insider/professional/reaching_out_to_diverse.html#.

American Psychological Association Center for Workforce Analysis and Research (2007). *Race/Ethnicity of Students Enrolled Full-Time and Part-Time in Doctoral and Master's Programs in Psychology, 2006-2007*. Washington, D.C.:

Author. Retrieved March 29, 2008, from http://research.apa.org/doctoraled16.html.

Banks, K. H., Kohn, L. P., & Spencer, M. S. (1999). (2006). An examination of the African American experience of everyday discrimination and psychological distress. *Community Mental Health Journal*, 42, 555–570.

Banks, K. H. & Kohn-Wood, L. P. (2007). The influence of racial identity profiles on the relationship between racial discrimination and depressive symptoms. *Journal of Black Psychology*, 33, 331–354.

Beals, J., Manson, S. M., Mitchell, C. M., & Spicer, P., AI-SUPERPFP Team (2003). Cultural specificity and comparison in psychiatric epidemiology: walking the tightrope in American Indian research. *Culture, Medicine, and Psychiatry*, 27, 259–289.

Beals, J., Novins, D. K., Whitesell, N. R., Spicer, P., Mitchell, C. M., Manson, S. M., et al. (2005). Prevalence of mental disorders and utilization of mental health services in two American Indian reservation populations: mental health disparities in a national context. *American Journal of Psychiatry*, 162, 1723–1732.

Bearon, L. B. & Koenig, H. G. (1990). Religious cognitions and use of prayer in health and illness. *Gerontologist*, 30, 249–253.

Berry, J. W. (1969). On cross-cultural comparability. *International Journal of Psychology*, 4, 119–128.

Bowskill, M., Lyons, E., & Coyle, A. (2007). The rhetoric of acculturation: when integration means assimilation. *British Journal of Social Psychology*, 46(4), 793–813.

Braam, A. W., van den Eeden, P., & Prince, M. J. (2001). Religion as a cross-cultural determinant of depression in elderly Europeans: results from the EURODEP collaboration. *Psychological Medicine*, 31, 803–814.

Breslau, J., Kendler, K. S., Su, M., Aguilar-Gaxiola, S., & Kessler, R. C. (2005a). Lifetime risk and persistence of psychiatric disorders across ethnic groups in the USA. *Psychological Medicine*, 35, 317–327.

Breslau, J., Aguilar-Gaxiola, S., Kendler, K. S., Su, M., Williams, D., & Kessler, R. C. (2005b). Specifying race-ethnic differences in risk for psychiatric disorder in a USA national sample. *Psychological Medicine*, 35, 1–12.

Brislin, R., Lonner, W. J., & Thorndike, R. M. (1973). *Cross-cultural research methods*. New York: Wiley.

Broman, C. L. (1996). The health consequences of racial discrimination: a study of African Americans. *Ethnicity and Disease*, 6, 148–153.

Cardemil, E. V. & Battle, C. L. (2003). Guess who's coming to therapy? Getting comfortable with conversations about race and ethnicity in psychotherapy. *Professional Psychology: Research and Practice*, 34, 278–286.

Castro, F. G. & Coe, K. (2007). Traditions and alcohol use: a mixed-methods analysis. *Cultural Diversity and Ethnic Minority Psychology*, 13, 269–284.

Chentsova-Dutton, Y. E. & Tsai, J. L. (2007). Cultural factors influence the expression of psychopathology. In S. O. Lilienfeld & W. T. O'Donohue (Eds.), *The great principles of clinical science* (pp. 375–396). New York: Routledge.

Chin, J. L. (1998). Mental health services and treatment. In L. C. Lee & N. W. S. Zane (Eds.), *Handbook of Asian American psychology* (pp. 485–504). Thousand Oaks, CA: Sage.

Constantine, M. G., Okazaki, S., & Utsey, S. O. (2004). Self-concealment, social self-efficacy, acculturative stress, and depression in African, Asian, and Latin American international college students. *American Journal of Orthopsychiatry*, 74, 230–241.

Cooper-Patrick, L., Gallo, J. J., Powe, N. R., Steinwachs, D. S., Eaton, W. W., & Ford, D. E. (1999). Mental health service utilization by African Americans and Whites: the Baltimore epidemiologic catchment area follow-up. *Medical Care*, 37, 1034–1045.

Cooper-Patrick, L., Powe, N. R., Jenckes, M. W., Gonzales, J. J., Levin, D. M., & Ford, D. E. (1997). Identification of patient attitudes and preferences regarding treatment of depression. *Journal of General Internal Medicine*, 12, 431–438.

Cross, W. E. (1971). Negro-to-Black conversion experience. *Black World*, 20, 13–27.

Dana, R. H. (2002). Mental health services for African Americans: a cultural/racial perspective. *Cultural Diversity and Ethnic Minority Psychology*, 8, 3–18.

Danquah, M. N. (1999). *Willow weep for me: a black woman's journey through depression.* New York: Random House.

DeLongis, A., Coyne, J. C., Dakof, G., Folkman, S., & Lazarus, R. S. (1982). Relationship of daily hassles, uplifts, and major life events to health status. *Health Psychology*, 1, 119–136.

Denzin, N. K. (1978). *The research act: an introduction to sociological methods.* New York: Praeger.

Diala, C., Muntaner, C., & Walrath, C. (2000). Racial differences in attitudes toward professional mental health care and the use of services. *American Journal of Orthopsychiatry*, 70, 455–464.

Dovidio, J. F. & Gaertner, S. L. (1998). On the nature of contemporary prejudice: the causes, consequences, and challenges of aversive racism. In J. Edherhardt & S. T. Fiske (Eds.), *Confronting racism: the problem and the response* (pp. 3–32). Thousand Oaks, CA: Sage.

Draguns, J. G. & Tanaka-Matsumi, J. (2003). Assessment of psychopathology across and within cultures: Issues and findings. *Behaviour Research and Therapy*, 41, 755–776.

Ferraro, K. F. & Koch, J. R. (1994). Religion and health among black and white adults: examining social support and consolation. *Journal for the Scientific Study of Religion*, 33, 362–375.

Fisher, T. L., Burnet, D. L., & Huang, E. S. (2007). Cultural leverage: interventions using culture to narrow racial disparities in health care. *Medical Care Research and Review*, 64, 243–282.

Flaskerud, J. H. (1986). The effects of culture-compatible intervention on the utilization of mental health services by minority clients. *Community Mental Health Journal*, 22, 127–141.

Fouad, N. A. (2006). Multicultural guidelines: implementation in an urban counseling psychology program. *Professional Psychology: Research and Practice*, 37, 6–13.

Good, B. J. & Kleinman, A. M. (1985). Culture and anxiety: cross-cultural evidence for the patterning of anxiety disorders. In A. H. Tuma & J. D. Maser (Eds.), *Anxiety and the anxiety disorders* (pp. 297–323). Hillsdale, NJ: Lawrence Erlbaum Associates.

Guarnaccia, P. J., De la Cancela, V., & Carrillo, E. (1989). The multiple meanings of ataques de nervios in the Latino community. *Medical Anthropology*, 11, 47–62.

Guarnaccia, P. J. & Rogler, L. H. (1999). Research on culture-bound syndromes: new directions. *American Journal of Psychiatry*, 156, 1322–1327.

Harrell, S. P. (2000). A multidimensional conceptualization of racism-related stress: implications for the well-being of people of color. *American Journal of Orthopsychiatry*, 70(1), 42–57.

Helms, J. E. (1995). An update of Helm's White and people of color racial identity models. In J. G. Ponterotto, J. M. Casas, L. A. Suzuki, & C. M. Alexander (Eds.), *Handbook of multicultural counseling* (pp. 181–191). Thousand Oaks, CA: Sage.

Hopper, K. & Wanderling, J. (2000). Revisiting the developed versus developing country distinction in course and outcome in schizophrenia: results from ISoS, the WHO collaborative followup project. *Schizophrenia Bulletin*, 26, 835–846.

Jablensky, A., Sartorius, N., Ernberg, G., Ankar, M., Korten, A., Cooper, E., Day, R., et al. (1992). Schizophrenia: manifestations, incidence and course in different cultures. *Psychological Medicine*, 20, 1–97.

Jackson, J. S., Torres, M., Caldwell, C. H., Neighbors, H. W., Nesse, R. M., Taylor, R. J., et al. (2004). The National Survey of American Life: a study of racial, ethnic and cultural influences on mental disorders, and mental health. *International Journal of Methods in Psychiatric Research*, 13, 196–207.

Jenkins, J. H. (1988a). Ethnopsychiatric interpretations of schizophrenic illness: the problem of nervios within Mexican-American families. *Culture, Medicine and Psychiatry*, 12, 301–329.

Jenkins, J. H. (1988b). Conceptions of schizophrenia as a problem of nerves: a cross-cultural comparison of Mexican-Americans and Anglo-Americans. *Social Science and Medicine*, 26, 1233–1243.

Karno, M., Hough, R. L., Burnam, A., Escobar, J. I., Timbers, D. M., Santana, F., et al. (1987). Lifetime prevalence of specific psychiatric disorders among Mexican Americans and non-Hispanic whites in Los Angeles. *Archives of General Psychiatry, 44*, 695–701.

Kessler, R. C., McGonagle, K. A., Zhao, S., Nelson, C. B., Hughes, M., Eshleman, S., et al. (1994). Lifetime and 12-month prevalence of DSM–III–R psychiatric disorders in the United States. *Archives of General Psychiatry, 51*, 8–19.

Kessler, R. C. & Ustun, T. B. (2004). The World Mental Health (WMH) Survey Initiative Version of the World Health Organization (WHO) Composite International Diagnostic Interview (CIDI). *International Journal of Methods in Psychiatric Research, 13*, 93–121.

Kirmayer, L. J. & Young, A. (1998). Culture and somatization: clinical, epidemiological, and ethnographic perspectives. *Psychosomatic Medicine, 60*, 420–430.

Kleinman, A. (1977). Depression, somatization and the "new cross-cultural psychiatry." *Social Science and Medicine, 11*, 3–10.

Kleinman, A. (1988). *Rethinking psychiatry*. New York: Free Press.

Kleinman, A. (1995). *Writing at the margin: discourse between anthropology and medicine*. Berkeley: University of California Press.

Kleinman, A. & Good, B. (1985). *Culture and depression: studies in the anthropology and cross-cultural psychiatry of affect and disorder*. Berkeley: University of California Press.

Koenig, H. G., Cohen, H. J., Blazer, F. H., Pieper, C., Meador, K. G., Shelp, F., et al. (1992). Religious coping and depression among elderly, hospitalized medically ill men. *American Journal of Psychiatry, 149*, 1693–1700.

Kohn, L. P., Oden, T. M., Muñoz, R. F., Leavitt, D., & Robinson, A. (2002). Adapted cognitive-behavioral group therapy for depressed low-income, African American women. *Community Mental Health Journal, 38*, 497–504.

Kohn-Wood, L. P. & Wilson, M. N. (2005). The context of caretaking in rural areas: family factors influencing the level of functioning of seriously mentally ill patients living at home. *American Journal of Community Psychology, 36*, 1–13.

Lakes, K., López, S. R., & Garro, L. C. (2006). Cultural competence and psychotherapy: applying anthropologically informed conceptions of culture. *Psychotherapy: Theory, Research, Practice and Training, 43*, 380–396.

Lawrence, V., Banerjee, S., Bhugra, D., Sangha, K., Turner, S., & Murray, J. (2006). Coping with depression in later life: a qualitative study of help-seeking in three ethnic groups. *Psychological Medicine, 36*, 1375–1383.

Lee, J. & Sue, S. (2001). Clinical psychology and culture. In D. Matsumoto (Ed.), *The handbook of culture and psychology* (pp. 287–305). New York: Oxford University Press.

Leff, J., Sartorius, N., Jablensky, A., Korten, A., & Ernberg, G. (1992). The international pilot study of schizophrenia: five-year follow-up findings. *Psychological Medicine, 22*, 131–145.

Lin, K. & Kleinman, A. (1988). Psychopathology and clinical course of schizophrenia: a cross-cultural perspective. *Schizophrenia Bulletin, 14*, 555–568.

López, S. R. (1997). Cultural competence in psychotherapy: a guide for clinicians and their supervisors. In C. E. Watkins (Ed.), *Handbook of psychotherapy supervision* (pp. 570–588). New York: Wiley.

López, S. R. & Guarnaccia, P. J. (2000). Cultural psychopathology: uncovering the social world of mental illness. *Annual Review of Psychology, 51*, 571–598.

Low, S. M. (1989). Gender, emotion, and nervios in urban Guatemala. In D. L. Davis & S. M. Low (Eds.), *Gender, health, and illness: the case of nerves* (pp. 23–48). New York: Hemisphere.

Magyar-Moe, J. L., Pedrotti, J. T., Edwards, L. M., Ford, A. I., Petersen, S. E., Rasmussen, H. N., et al. (2005). Perceptions of multicultural training in predoctoral internships: a survey of interns and training directors. *Professional Psychology: Research and Practice, 36*, 446–450.

Manson, S. M., Shore, J. H., & Bloom, J. D. (1985). The depressive experience in American Indian communities: a challenge for psychiatric theory and diagnosis. In A. Kleinman & B. Good (Eds.), *Culture and depression: studies in the anthropology and cross-cultural psychiatry of affect and disorder* (pp. 331–368). Berkeley: University of California Press.

Maramba, G. G. & Hall, G. C. N. (2002). Meta-analyses if ethnic match as a predictor of dropout, utilization, and level of functioning. *Cultural Diversity and Ethnic Minority Psychology, 8*, 290–297.

Mattingly, C. & Lawlor, M. (2001). The fragility of healing. *Ethos, 29*, 30–57.

Maynard, C., Ehreth, J., Cox, G. B., Peterson, P. D., & McGann, M. E. (1997). Racial differences in the utilization of public mental health services in Washington State. *Administration and Policy in Mental Health and Mental Health Services Research, 24*, 411–424.

Melfi, C. A., Croghan, T. W., & Hanna, M. P. (1999). Access to treatment for depression in a Medicaid population. *Journal of Health Care for the Poor and Underserved, 10*, 201–215.

Mezzich, J. E., Kirmayer, L. J., Kleinman, A., Fabrega, H., Parron, D., Good, B. J., et al. (1999). The place of culture in DSM–IV. *Journal of Nervous and Mental Disease, 187*, 457–464.

Miranda, J., Bernal, G., & Lau, A. (2005). State of the science on psychosocial interventions for ethnic minorities. *Annual Review of Clinical Psychology, 1*, 113–142.

Morales, L S., Mara, M., Kington, R. S., Valdez, R. O., & Exarce, J. J. (2002). Socioeconomic, cultural and behavioral factors affecting Hispanic health outcomes. *Journal of Health Care for the Poor and Underserved, 13*, 477–503.

Murphy, J. M. (1976). Psychiatric labeling in cross-cultural perspective. *Science, 191*, 1019–1028.

National Alliance on Mental Illness (n.d). Retrieved March 31, 2008 from http://www.nami.org/Hometemplate.cfm.

National Center for Education Statistics [NCES] in U.S. Department of Education (2003). *Statistical Profile of persons receiving doctor's degrees by field of study and selected characteristics.* Retrieved March 29, 2008, from http://nces.Ed.gov/programs/digest/d06/tables/dt06_301.asp.

National Institute of Mental Health (n.d.). *NIMH Outreach Partnership Program.* Retrieved March 31, 2008, from http://www.nimh.nih.gov/health/outreach/partnershipprogram/index.shtml

National Research Council (2004). *Measuring racial discrimination. Panel on methods for assessing discrimination,* Rebecca M. Blank, Marilyn Dabady, and Constance F. Citro (Eds.), Committee on National Statistics, Division of Behavioral and Social Sciences and Education, Washington, D.C.: National Academies.

Neblett, E. W., Shelton, J. N., & Sellers, R. M. (2004). The role of racial identity in managing daily racial hassles. In G. Philogene (Ed.), *Racial identity in context: the legacy of Kenneth Clark* (pp. 77–90). Washington, DC: American Psychological Association.

Neighbors, H. W. (1985). Seeking professional help for personal problems: Black Americans' use of health and mental health services. *Community Mental Health Journal, 21*, 156–166.

Neighbors, H. W., Bashur, R., Price, R., Selig, S., Donabedian, A., & Shannon, G. (1992). Ethnic minority mental health service delivery: a review of the literature. *Research in Community Mental Health, 7*, 55–71.

Neighbors, H. W., Caldwell, C., Williams, D. R., Nesse, R., Taylor, R. J., Bullard, K. M., et al. (2007). Race, ethnicity and the use of services for mental disorders: results from the National Survey of American Life. *Archives of General Psychiatry, 64*, 485–494.

Operario, D. & Fiske, S. (2001). Ethnic identity moderates perceptions of prejudice: judgments of personal versus group discrimination and subtle versus blatant bias. *Personality and Social Psychology Bulletin, 27*(5):30–37.

Ortega, A. N., Feldman, J. M., Canino, G., Steinman, K., & Alegria, M. (2006). Co-occurrence of mental and physical illness in U.S. Latinos. *Social Psychiatry and Psychiatric Epidemiology, 41*, 927–934.

Padgett, D. K., Patrick, C., Burns, B. J., & Schlesinger, H. J. (1994). Ethnicity and the use of outpatient mental health services in a national insured sample. *American Journal of Public Health, 84*, 222–226.

Palloni, A. & Morenoff, J. D. (2001). Interpreting the paradoxical in the Hispanic paradox: demographic and epidemiologic approaches. *Annals of the New York Academy of Sciences, 954*, 14–174.

Patel, V., Cohen, A., Thara, R., & Gureje, O. (2006). Is the outcome of schizophrenia really better in developing countries? *Review Brasil Psiquatry, 28*, 149–152.

Pederson, P. (1999). *Multiculturalism as a fourth force.* Philadelphia: Brunner/Mazel.

Pettigrew, T. F. (1998). Intergroup contact theory. *Annual Review of Psychology, 49*, 65–85.

Ponterotto, J. G., Casas, J. M., Suzuki, L. A., & Alexander, C. A. (2001). *Handbook of Multicultural Counseling* (2nd ed.). Thousand Oaks, CA: Sage.

Poston, C. W. (1990). Biracial identity development model: a needed addition. *Journal of Counseling and Development, 69*, 152–155.

The President's New Freedom Commission on Mental Health (2003). *Achieving the promise: transforming mental health Care in America.* Rockville, MD: Author.

Pumariega, A. J., Glover, S., Holzer, C. E., & Nguyen, H. (1998). Administrative update: utilization of services: II. Utilization of mental health services in a tri-ethnic sample of adolescents. *Community Mental Health Journal, 34*(2), 145–157.

Richman, L. S., Kohn-Wood, L. P., & Williams, D. R. (2007). The role of discrimination and racial identity for mental health service utilization. *Journal of Social and Clinical Psychology, 26*, 960–981.

Rogler, L. H. (1999). Methodological sources of cultural insensitivity in mental health research. *American Psychologist, 54*, 424–433.

Ruiz, A. S. (1990). Ethnic identity: crisis and resolution. *Journal of Multicultural Counseling and Development, 18*, 29–40.

Scheffler, R. M. & Miller, A. B. (1991). Differences in mental health service utilization among ethnic subpopulations. *International Journal of Law and Psychiatry, 14*, 363–376.

Sellers, R. M., Caldwell, C. H., Schmeelk-Cone, K., & Zimmerman, M. A. (2003). The role of racial identity and racial discrimination in the mental health of African American young adults. *Journal of Health and Social Behavior, 44*, 302–317.

Sellers, R. M. & Shelton, J. N. (2003). The role of racial identity in perceived racial discrimination. *Journal of Personality and Social Psychology, 84*, 1079–1092.

Sellers, R. M., Smith, M., Shelton, N. J., Rowley, S. J., & Chavous, T. M. (1997). Multidimensional model of racial identity: a reconceptualization of African American racial identity. *Personality and Social Psychology Review, 2*, 18–39.

Seng, J. S., Kohn-Wood, L. P., & Odera, L. (2005). Explaining racial disparities in diagnosis of posttraumatic stress disorder between African American and White American female Medicaid recipients. *Journal of Obstetric, Gynecological, and Neonatal Nurses, 34,* 521–530.

Simon, G. E., Goldberg, D. P., VonKorff, M., & Ustun, T. B. (2002). Understanding cross-national differences in depression prevalence. *Psychological Medicine, 32,* 585–594.

Simon, G. E., VonKorff, M., Piccinelli, M., Fullerton, C., & Ormel, J. (1999). An international study of the relation between somatic symptoms and depression. *New England Journal of Medicine, 341,* 1329–1335.

Smart, J. & Smart, D. W. (1995). Acculturative stress: the experience of the Hispanic immigrant. *The Counseling Psychologist, 23,* 25–42.

Smedley, B. D., Stith, A. Y., & Nelson, A. R. (2003). *Unequal treatment: confronting racial and ethnic disparities in health care.* Institute of Medicine. Washington, DC: National Academies Press.

Smith, D. P. & Bradshaw, B. S. (2006). Rethinking the Hispanic paradox: death rate and life expectancy for U.S. non-Hispanic White and Hispanic populations. *American Journal of Public Health, 96,* 1686–1692.

Smith, T. B., McCullough, M. E., & Poll, J. (2003). Religiousness and depression: evidence for a main effect and the moderating influence of stressful life events. *Psychological Bulletin, 129*(4), 614–636.

Snowden, L. R. (2001). Barriers to effective mental health services for African Americans. *Mental Health Services Research, 3,* 181–187.

Snowden, L. R. & Thomas, K. (2000). Medicaid and African American outpatient mental health treatment. *Mental Health Services Research, 2,* 115–120.

Somervell, P. D., Leaf, P. J., Weissman, M. M., Blazer, D. G., & Bruce, M. L. (1989). The prevalence of major depression in black and white adults in five USA communities. *American Journal of Epidemiology, 130,* 725–735.

Spencer, M. S., Kohn, L. P., & Woods, J. R. (2002). Labeling vs. early identification: the dilemma of mental health service utilization among low-income African American children. *African American Research Perspectives, 8,* 1–14.

Substance Abuse and Mental Health Services Administration (2006). *Transforming mental health care in America: the Federal Action Agenda: first steps.* Rockville, MD: Author. Retrieved March 31, 2008 from http://www.samhsa.gov/Federalactionagenda/NFC_FMHAA.aspx.

Sue, S. (1998). In search of cultural competence in psychotherapy and counseling. *American Psychologist, 53,* 440–448.

Sue, S., Fujino, D. C., Hu, L.-T., Takeuchi, D. T., & Zane, N. W. S. (1991). Community mental health services for ethnic minority groups: a test of the cultural responsiveness hypothesis. *Journal of Consulting and Clinical Psychology, 59,* 533–540.

Sue, W. W. & Sue, D. (2008). *Counseling the culturally diverse: theory and practice* (5th ed.). Hoboken, NJ: Wiley.

Sussman, L. K., Robins, L. N., & Earls, F. (1987). Treatment-seeking for depression by Black and White Americans. *Social Science and Medicine, 24,* 187–196.

Swerdlow, M. (1992). Chronicity, "nervios," and community care: a case study of Puerto Rican psychiatric patients in New York City. *Culture, Medicine and Psychiatry, 16,* 217–235.

Takeuchi, D., Leaf, P., & Kuo, H. S. (1988). Ethnic differences in the perception of barriers to help-seeking. *Social Psychiatry and Psychiatric Epidemiology, 23,* 273–280.

Tanaka-Matsumi, J. (2001). Abnormal psychology and culture. In D. Matsumoto (Ed.), *The handbook of culture and psychology* (pp. 265–286). New York: Oxford University Press.

Taylor, R. J. C., Levin, J. S., & Joseph, R. (2004). *Religion in the lives of African Americans: social, psychological, and health perspectives.* Thousand Oaks, CA: Sage.

Thomas, K. C. & Snowden, L. R. (2002). Minority response to health insurance coverage for mental health services. *Journal of Mental Health Policy and Economics, 4,* 35–41.

Thompson, V. L. S. & Alexander, H. (2006). Therapists' race and African American clients' reactions to therapy. *Psychotherapy: Theory, Research, Practice, Training, 45,* 99–110.

Uba, L. (1994). *Asian Americans: personality patterns, identity, and mental health.* New York: Guilford.

U.S. Census Bureau (2004). *The face of our population.* Retrieved March 7, 2008 from http://factfinder.census.gov/jsp/saff/SAFFInfo.jsp?_pageId=tp9_race_ethnicity.

U.S. Department of Health and Human Services (1999). *Mental health: A report of the Surgeon General.* Rockville, MD: Author.

U.S.D.H.H.S. (2001). *Mental health: culture, race, and ethnicity — A supplement to mental health: a report of the Surgeon-General.* Rockville, MD: U.S. Department of Health and Human Services, Public Health Service, Office of Surgeon General.

Vega, W. A., Karno, M., Alegria, M., Alvidrez, J., Bernal, G. Escamilla, M., et al. (2007). Research issues for improving treatment of U.S. Hispanics with persistent mental disorders. *Psychiatric Services, 58,* 385–394.

Vega, W. A., Kolody, B., Aguilar-Gaxiola, S., Alderete, E., Catalano, R., & Caraveo-Anduaga, J. (1998). Lifetime prevalence of DSM–III–R psychiatric disorders among urban and rural Mexican Americans in California. *Archives of General Psychiatry, 55,* 771–782.

Vega, W. A. & Lopez, S. R. (2001). Priority issues in Latino mental health services research. *Mental Health Services Research, 3,* 189–200.

Ward, E. C. (2007). Examining differential treatment effects for depression in racial and ethnic minority women: a qualitative systematic review. *Journal of the National Medical Association, 99,* 265–274.

Weisman, A. G. (1997). Understanding cross-cultural prognostic variability for schizophrenia. *Cultural Diversity and Mental Health*, 3, 23–35.

Weisz, J. R., McCarty, C. A., Eastman, K. L., Chiyasit, W., & Suwanlert, S. (1997). Developmental psychopathology and culture: ten lessons from Thailand. In S. S. Luthar, J. A. Burack, D. Cicchetti, & J. R. Weiss (Eds.), *Developmental psychopathology: perspectives on adjustment, risk, and disorder* (pp. 568–592). Cambridge: Cambridge University Press.

Wells, K., Klap, R., Koike, A., & Sherbourne, C. (2001). Ethnic disparities in unmet needs for alcoholism, drug abuse and mental health care. *The American Journal of Psychiatry*, 158, 2027–2032.

Wells, K. B., Sherbourne, C. D., & Miranda, J. (2007). The cumulative effects of quality improvement for depression on outcome disparities over 9 years: results from a randomized, controlled group-level trial. *Medical Care*, 45, 1052–1059.

Whaley, A. L. (2001). Cultural mistrust and mental health services for African Americans: a review and meta-analysis. *Counseling Psychologist*, 29, 513–531.

Williams, D. R., González, H. M., Neighbors, H. W., Nesse, R., Abelson, J. M., Sweetman, J., et al. (2007a). Prevalence and distribution of major depressive disorder in African Americans, Caribbean Blacks, and Non-Hispanic Whites: results from the National Survey of American Life. *Archives of General Psychiatry*, 64, 305–315.

Williams, D. R., Haile, R., Gonzalez, H. M., Neighbors, H., Baser, R., & Jackson, J. S. (2007b). The mental health of Black Caribbean immigrants: results from the National Survey of American Life. *American Journal of Public Health*, 97, 52–59.

Williams, T. (2008). *Black pain: it just looks like we're not hurting*. New York: Simon & Schuster.

World Health Organization (1979). *Schizophrenia: an international follow up study*. New York: Wiley.

World Health Organization, World Mental Health Survey Consortium (2004). Prevalence, severity and unmet need for treatment of mental disorders in the World Health Organization World Mental Health Surveys. *Journal of the American Medical Association*, 291, 2581–2590.

Zhang, A. Y., Snowden, L. R., & Sue, S. (1998). Differences between Asian- and White-Americans help-seeking and utilization patterns in the Los Angeles area. *Journal of Community Psychology*, 26, 317–326.

Clinical Psychology Practice

Radhika Krishnamurthy
Florida Institute of Technology

OUTLINE

Clinical psychology graduate students have a considerable amount to contend with as they proceed toward completing the requirements of their graduate programs and preparing for their careers in the field. While students begin laying the foundations for practice through an array of practicum experiences, the first major step toward practice preparation occurs in the selection of predoctoral internship site. Students who plan well generally consider the type of training site and its available rotations as well as the geographic location, recognizing that this training year often sets the stage for how and where their careers will be launched. The intern has to begin the search for postdoctoral positions within a few months into internship, which requires decisions about whether to apply to a formal postdoctoral training program or pursue job opportunities with attendant negotiations for obtaining the supervision necessary for licensure. The intern or new graduate also needs to decide the state where he or she intends to be licensed, and the new practitioner has to become quickly acquainted with issues such as health-care provider panels, billing codes and methods, licensing, and credentialing. Thus, numerous tasks and decisions lie ahead for the developing professional.

New graduates often enter the career field with insufficient knowledge and guidelines of how to navigate the practice territory, having had their hands full with various other demands during their graduate school years. The National Register's 2005 online survey of 3,835 doctoral students in the United States and Canada found, for example, that more than 50% of respondents had *not* investigated licensure requirements and fewer than 50% were acquainted with prominent credential organizations (Hall, Wexelbaum, & Boucher, 2007). The transition from student to practitioner therefore requires a considerable amount of time and attention devoted to "learning the ropes," even as the graduate contends with settling into life after graduate school, establishing a balance between work and family, and developing his or her professional identity.

In writing this chapter, I recall the various comments from my own students that range from the beginning student's "What kinds of jobs are out there?" and "What do psychologists earn?" to the intern's "I can't believe I have to look for a job already when I'm just settling into internship" and "Is there a 'how-to' guide or 'psychology practice for dummies' book for someone like me?" I am also reminded of their emotional reactions, ranging from eagerness and excitement to unsureness and apprehension. This chapter is intended to address such questions and engender confidence in entering the practice domain. It is certainly not exhaustive in coverage; rather, the goal is to provide an introduction to issues that will be faced by the typical entry-level practitioner.

LICENSURE

An initial task for the new graduate is to embark on the steps needed to secure **licensure**, which involves successfully completing the national and state examination components and securing the requisite postdoctoral supervised experience. Clinical psychology graduate students should ideally become acquainted with the regulations set by the Association of State and Provincial Psychology Boards (ASPPB) while they are still in school. The general requirements for licensing include achieving a doctoral psychology degree from an accredited graduate program or its equivalent, passing the Examination for Professional Practice in Psychology (EPPP) and the examination set by the state in which licensure is sought, and completing 2 years of supervised experience (typically, 1 year of predoctoral internship and 1 year of postdoctoral supervised practice). ASPPB's recommended passing score for the EPPP is a scaled score of 500 (equivalent to a passing raw score of 140) to become licensed to practice independently. Candidates for licensure may avail themselves of practice exams and other preparatory materials available at ASPPB's Web site (http://www.asppb.org/) and should also examine the supervision guidelines provided on that site. The state examination is typically focused on laws, rules, and regulations that govern psychology practice in the particular state and therefore varies in content from state to state.

The candidate for licensure should examine the specific guidelines set by the regulatory body of the relevant state. In the state of Florida, for example, the requirements for licensure set by the Florida Department of Health and implemented by the Florida Board of Psychology include the following: obtaining a PsyD, EdD, or PhD degree in psychology from an accredited program; completing 2 years or 4,000 hours of experience under the supervision of an eligible licensed psychologist; and achieving passing scores on the EPPP (scaled score of 500) and the Florida laws and rules examination administered by the Department of Health (raw score of 32/40 representing 80% success). The examinations can be taken before completing the postdoctoral supervised experience. Prior to the first renewal of the license, the new licensee in Florida is also required to obtain the 2 credit hours of **continuing education** on domestic violence that is required every third biennial license renewal period and 2 hours of continuing education on prevention of medical errors; thereafter, 40 hours of continuing education credit are required within each 2-year period that should include the aforementioned mandated areas of study as well as 3 hours of professional ethics and Florida laws and rules affecting psychology practice. It should be noted that in Florida, as in most states, professional identification of oneself as a "psychologist" is limited to individuals who are licensed per the criteria set by the Florida Department of Health, so that attainment of a doctoral clinical psychology degree alone does not enable one to claim to be a psychologist. Other states have somewhat different criteria for the various components of licensure, license renewal, and professional designation. Links to the licensing boards of all U.S. and Canadian state/province licensing boards are provided on the ASPPB Web site. Once licensure is secured, the new professional can embark on his or her career as an independent practitioner.

THE PRACTICE LANDSCAPE

Clinical psychology practitioners are employed in a broad range of practice settings such as independent practices, private hospitals, Veterans Administration Medical Centers (VAMCs), state psychiatric hospitals, correctional centers, community mental health centers (CMHCs), outpatient clinics, rehabilitation settings, and university counseling centers. A substantial segment of practicing clinical psychologists are self-employed independent practitioners. For example, data from the American Psychological Association's (APA) Center for Psychology Workforce Analysis and Research (CPWAR) survey identified that among the nearly 3,000 respondents who self-identified as clinical psychologists, child clinical psychologists, or clinical neuropsychologists involved in the direct delivery of mental health services, 60% were employed in independent practice settings. Approximately 25% of respondents reported working in organized health-care settings such as general hospitals, VAMCs, and CMHCS, whereas only about 5% were employed in other settings (Kohut, Li, & Wicherski, 2007). Regardless of the type of work setting, all practitioners have to be knowledgeable of several issues related to health-care delivery that are discussed in this section.

Managed Health Care

Unlike previous generations of new professionals, current cohorts of clinical psychology graduates enter into a practice environment in which a **managed care** model is well established and is the dominant structure for delivery and payment for services. Managed health care came into existence in the 1980s largely as a result of the need to control the escalating costs of healthcare. Various reports have indicated that health care costs have risen at a considerably higher rate than would have been predicted from rates of inflation, population growth, or growth in the gross national product. For example, reports indicate cost increases from $50 billion in 1960 to $500 billion in 1986 (Maruish, 1994), and to $1.55 trillion in the early years of the twenty-first century (Garcia-Shelton, 2006). Moreover, treatment costs for mental health and substance abuse disorders have increased at a faster rate than those found for other insured health conditions, attributed partly to a significant increase in utilization of mental health services by a larger segment of the public. An associated goal of the managed care movement was to improve the effectiveness of treatment delivery, based on the recognition that long-term inpatient and outpatient treatments were not necessarily yielding desirable outcomes or proving to be more effective than short-term intermittent interventions.

With a prominent focus on cost containment, the ensuing strategies of the managed care initiative were directed toward (a) risk shifting (through higher **insurance premiums** and **deductibles**, thus transferring some cost responsibility to the patient), (b) risk capitation (through limiting the maximum dollar amount paid for treatment or number of sessions, thus prompting greater efficiency and effectiveness by the treatment provider and greater responsiveness by the patient), and (c) establishment of managed care organizations (MCOs) charged with overseeing both financial and service components of treatment (Maruish, 1994). There are currently several forms of MCOs. The most common ones are (a) health maintenance organizations (HMOs) in which providers contract with the organization to provide all the relevant services for a set fee; (b) preferred provider organizations (PPOs) in which approved providers join a panel of providers who have contracted to deliver services at discounted rates in exchange for receiving a certain volume of clientele; (c) individual practice organizations (IPOs) in

which a group of independent practitioners contract directly with companies or agencies to provide health-care services; and (d) employee assistance programs (EAPs) in which providers contract with companies to serve their employees' health-care needs (O'Donohue & Cucciare, 2005). Psychologists who are independent practitioners typically seek to establish contracts with various MCOs to secure a steady clientele and reliable income. For those who are employed in hospitals or mental health centers, the agency rather than the individual maintains the contract with the MCO. All psychology practitioners, regardless of work setting, are influenced by managed care practices that have left an indelible print on the nature and scope of practice. For example, psychological treatment today essentially consists of brief and intermittent treatment, the therapist serves to activate change rather than dispense a cure, more patients are treated for shorter duration, and community-based support groups or self-help programs are additional alternatives to traditional individual psychotherapy (Cummings, 1995).

The past decade has also witnessed a backlash against the managed care structure, involving strong critiques extended by medical and mental health practitioners across multiple disciplines. These criticisms have centered on two central themes: (a) the

---

HIGHLIGHT BOX 19.1

ESTABLISHING MEDICAL NECESSITY

In a managed care setup, the practitioner is required to address questions concerning the medical necessity of the service in order to receive reimbursement from the MCO. Most private carriers require preauthorization and/or authorization after a specified number of

sessions, depending on the type of service provided (e.g., there are differences for psychological testing and psychotherapy services). Definitions of medical necessity vary somewhat across MCOs but generally converge on the following criteria:

- There is a diagnosed condition that will be the focus of psychological intervention.
- The intervention is necessary to address the health-care needs of the patient.
- The intervention will help alleviate the condition or prevent its deterioration.
- The intervention meets current and generally accepted standards of practice.
- The intervention represents the most appropriate and cost-effective care.
- The intervention is no more intensive and restrictive than necessary.

Specific questions to be answered by the service provider may include the following:

- What are the patient's current symptoms and diagnoses?
- What is the patient's level of functioning?
- What prior treatments did the patient receive for this condition?
- What is the focus of the treatment plan?
- What is the patient's suitability for the proposed intervention?
- What is the expected duration of the intervention?
- What is the expected outcome of the intervention?

restrictions imposed by managed care on service options and the resulting burdens and loss of income experienced by health-care providers, and (b) the adverse impact of managed care on the quality of health care received by patients. Lawsuits by patients and providers abounded. One effect has been the initiation of legislative actions that have curtailed various aspects of behavioral and medical care management (Cummings, 2005). There is also an increasing movement, particularly among independent practitioners offering specialized services, toward returning to fee-for-service structures whenever possible and establishing private service contracts instead of serving on provider panels of MCOs.

Health Insurance Portability and Accountability Act of 1996

An important practice issue that applies to all medical and mental health care providers deals with compliance with the regulations of the Health Insurance Portability and Accountability Act of 1996 (HIPAA; Public Law 104-191). These federal regulations were enacted to increase the efficiency of health-care delivery and ensure the confidentiality and security of individuals' health information. Of particular relevance is the component known as the HIPAA Privacy Rule, which consists of federal standards designed to (a) protect the privacy of patients' medical records and other health-related information, (b) facilitate patients' access to their medical records, and (c) enable patients to exert control over use and disclosure of their personal health information. Compliance with the Privacy Rule was required as of April 14, 2003. The HIPAA Security Rule, which is focused specifically on protecting electronic versions of health information, went into effect on April 21, 2003, with compliance effective as of April 21, 2005 (APA Practice Organization, 2005). More recently, effective May 23, 2007, health-care entities using electronic communications became required to use a single National Provider

Identifier (NPI) for submitting claims to private and public insurance companies (Department of Health and Human Services, 2004).

For the practicing psychologist, the HIPAA regulations translate into several steps that must be taken within his or her agency or practice. Per the Privacy and Security Rules, practitioners and agencies are required to develop specific procedures to safeguard patient privacy. These might include storing patient records in locked file cabinets, safeguarding access to computers that contain patient information, and using password protection to keep electronic files secure. Practitioners/agencies are also required to inform their patients of their privacy rights, and this is typically done through provision of a written "notice of privacy practices" document. The document would inform patients of their rights; report when, how, and in what circumstances their health information may be disclosed to another party; and indicate how and where any complaints of violations could be filed. The policies and procedures of the practice should be saved in written or electronic form and available for inspection. Practitioners may consult the HIPAA Web site (http://www.hipaa.org) for information and updates, and the APA practice organization (http://APApractice.org) provides a link to online guides and tips for HIPAA compliance specifically geared to practicing psychologists.

Although HIPAA regulations seem to be producing the intended improvements in health-care practice, they have also created some complications for the mental health practitioner. For example, HIPAA grants patients the right to examine and receive a copy of their protected health information (PHI) with the exception of the therapist's psychotherapy notes. Thus, they have potential access to intake interview reports, psychological test reports, treatment plans, and so forth, all of which were previously considered the private domain of the mental health practitioner. Patients even have the right to request

amendments to these and other documents. Furthermore, much confusion has ensued around psychological testing practice due to modifications made in the APA's recent revision of its ethical standards (APA, 2002) to accommodate HIPAA rules. For example, although the prior standards (APA, 1992) prohibited the release of raw test data to unqualified individuals, the 2002 standards allow that *test data* may be released to such individuals, including the patient him- or herself, when authorized by the patient (standard 9.04). This has created new worries about test security, test validity, and copyright protection obligations, which the psychologist is enjoined to protect in standard 9.11, because of the difficulty in separating *test data* (inclusive of patient's test responses) from *test materials* (test stimuli that need to be protected). Concerns about harm to the profession, patients, and others have been expressed (Rogers, 2004; Smith & Evans, 2004), although some solutions have also been proposed (see Erard, 2004). Overall, the new professional has to achieve a good understanding of the HIPAA rules and abide by them in his or her work, hopefully with appropriate guidance and oversight by the supervising psychologist during his or her postdoctoral training year. He or she would also benefit from exploring the discussions and debates among his or her fellow professionals to comprehend the various issues that are at play.

Current Procedural Terminology (CPT) Codes

Clinical psychology students and practitioners are well acquainted with the diagnostic codes provided in the *Diagnostic and Statistical Manual of Mental Disorders*, fourth edition, text revision (DSM-IV-TR; American Psychiatric Association, 2000). However, these are not the only numbers they will be dealing with when billing for reimbursement for services by third-party payers. First, the psychologist often has to use International Statistical Classification of

Diseases and Related Health Problems, 9th revision, clinical modification (ICD-9-CM) codes corresponding to the DSM-IV diagnostic codes; a selected listing is provided in Appendix G of the DSM-IV-TR. Furthermore, billing procedures require the use of CPT codes in reporting clinical services when seeking payment from Medicare and private insurance carriers. The CPT code manual published by the American Medical Association is very extensive, listing all the codes utilized by the full spectrum of health-care providers. The psychology practitioner uses a subset of these codes such as those relating to assessment and psychotherapy services. For example, there is a specific five-digit code for psychotherapy services involving the typical 45- to 50-minute outpatient therapy session and another one for its counterpart session in an inpatient hospital, partial hospital, or residential care setting; the numerical codes are different when the service duration is 20–30 minutes and 75–80 minutes. In January 2002, a new set of health and behavior codes was made available to practicing psychologists to bill for assessment and intervention services for patients with diagnosed physical health problems. On January 1, 2006, a revised and expanded set of CPT codes was issued for psychological and neuropsychological testing to better reflect the professional work values associated with testing by a psychologist as separated from testing done using a technician and computer-based testing. Information and guidelines concerning use of these codes are available in links from the APA practice Web site (http://apapractice.org/). It should be noted that there are currently several complications in the use of the newer testing codes, because they are not uniformly understood and implemented by insurance carriers across the country, creating much confusion and hardship for psychologists and necessitating ongoing efforts in clarification and advocacy. For example, a recent scenario has involved inconsistencies across insurance carriers in reimbursing psychologists

for the time and expertise involved in integrating information across tests administered by a technician and generating a professional report, based on confusion about whether combinations of testing codes are permissible. Practicing psychologists need to stay on top of these issues and their resolutions in order to achieve appropriate levels of reimbursement for their professional work.

INDEPENDENT PRACTICE

Establishing Credentials

An independent practitioner needs to take several additional steps beyond getting licensed to practice to order to become visible in the local practice community, establish contacts with referral sources, secure a clientele, and engage in the full range of desired services.

One step would be to secure appointment to the medical staff of local medical and psychiatric facilities, which includes gaining admitting privileges and authorization to attend to patient care when one's outpatient client is hospitalized. Another mechanism is to become listed in the National Register of Health Service Providers in Psychology (see http://www.nationalregister. org/). This becomes a form of self-certification achieved by paying dues and submitting information about one's professional qualifications (Trull, 2005). The register functions as a directory that consumers can search to locate local psychologists. Additionally, it may be used by insurance carriers to verify a psychologist's credentials and therefore potentially offers the practitioner an easier entry into a provider panel.

The practitioner can also pursue specialty **certification** if he or she wants to be recognized as an expert in a particular area, which would also serve to direct specific types of referral to him or her. The most established and widely known specialty certification is that of the American Board of Professional Psychology, Inc. (ABPP;

see http://www.abpp.org/), which offers certification in 13 specialty areas; clinical psychology, clinical neuropsychology, rehabilitation psychology, cognitive and behavioral psychology, couple and family psychology, and child and adolescent psychology are some of the areas of ABPP certification. Currently, ABPP offers an "early entry" mechanism whereby graduate students, interns, and postdoctoral trainees can commence the process so as to achieve diplomate status as a early career professional. Other prominent board certification options include those offered by the American Board of Forensic Psychology (http://www.abfp.com/) and American Board of Assessment Psychology (http://www.assessmentpsychologyboard.org/).

Becoming Acquainted with the Practice Community

A psychologist seeking to establish an independent practice in a given community would want to get a sense of the range of practitioners in that area. Some communities are highly saturated with professionals, each seeking to get a piece of the same practice pie. Others may be less densely populated by service providers or may contain professionals offering more diverse forms of services. New professionals would likely benefit from joining their state psychological association and participating in its annual conferences to start building relationships with their colleagues. Attending meetings of the local chapter is a particularly good way to interact with practice colleagues, discuss common interests, become knowledgeable of local practices and specialties, and become known to others, and it is also a means of obtaining continuing education credits needed for license maintenance.

One of the byproducts of the managed care approach to health-care delivery is that master's-level practitioners and practitioners trained in allied disciplines have become active participants in mental health service delivery. Thus, the psychologist is frequently competing with social workers, mental health counselors, or psychological associates in his or her community, depending on the type of licenses provided in the given state. Indeed, these individuals may have an advantage over doctoral-level psychologists in joining provider panels because they are more cost-effective for the MCO (Trull, 2005). However, psychologists retain several advantages. They have extensive training in psychological testing and assessment, in empirically supported treatment, and in statistical methods and research, which makes them highly qualified to evaluate outcomes. New professionals should emphasize these skills and take advantage of opportunities to demonstrate them, even as they become familiar with the types of services offered by master's-level and allied professionals in the local community.

The new practitioner may determine that joining a group practice would be a good first step into the practice world and one that offers the protection of cost sharing. Joining an established practice of psychologists offers natural opportunities to observe others' practice methods and be mentored in the pragmatics of running a practice. Some practices are composed of professionals from multiple disciplines—psychiatry, social work, and psychology, for example—and offer the opportunity for the psychologist to establish a unique role, for example, of assessing treatment outcomes using standardized testing. Another recent trend has been to join a regional group practice (RGP) that is essentially a large network of providers within a wide geographic area (Cummings, 1995). The RGP's appeal is that it offers a higher level of job and income security and negotiating power with MCOs than an individual practice, and it is therefore a desirable option to consider.

Establishing a Practice Niche

Depending on the nature and composition of the local practice community, an independent practitioner is likely to become most successful when he or she has something distinctive to offer and is able to carve out a unique niche in the professional marketplace, and especially if he or she offers services that meet current service needs. For example, with the expansion of an aging population and associated illnesses such as Alzheimer's disease and other dementias, there is an increased demand for qualified neuropsychologists. Forensic psychology is another area that is experiencing a tremendous growth with psychologists increasingly being called to serve as evaluators and expert witnesses in civil litigation cases, in family court cases involving child custody and related matters, and in criminal cases ranging from evaluation and treatment of sexual offenders to competency evaluations. The foundations of this niche may have been developed in graduate school through an area of concentration or during internship through specialized rotations, and further developed during the supervised postdoctoral training year. Completing a formal postdoctoral specialization is a useful way to establish a specialization and secure a niche in the practice arena and is best achieved with forethought and planning initiated during graduate school or internship. This is because some specialty areas have specific criteria that go beyond the typical licensure-related requirements of supervised postdoctoral experience. For example, the National Academy of Neuropsychology (NAN) has issued a policy statement that specifies completing the equivalent of 2 years of full-time postdoctoral residency to qualify as a clinical neuropsychologist (Hannay et al., 1998), and many postdoctoral training programs have moved in this direction. Although not all current neuropsychology practitioners meet this criterion, it is fast becoming the expectation. Note that the issues of specialization discussed here are not identical to the issues of specialty certification discussed earlier. **Specialization** involves bringing a set of skills to the workplace, developed through training and experience consistent with established criteria or guidelines. This enables the psychologist to pursue and obtain *specialty certification* if he or she chooses, affirmed by the granting of **diplomate** status that enables him or her to be recognized as an expert in that area. Achieving one or both of these milestones facilitates one's ability to occupy a distinctive place in the practice setting and secure a reliable stream of clients.

Alternatively, the practitioner may seek to achieve a new specialization or respecialization, based on new interests developed after entering practice and/or awareness of gaps in mental health services in his or her community. This typically involves undergoing continuing education in the identified area. In fact, the delivery of some types of specialized services *requires* appropriate training and certification in some states. In Florida, for example, three specialty practices—juvenile sexual offender therapy, practice of hypnosis, and practice of sex therapy—require additional coursework and training and warrant maintaining currency in that area.

Overall, the successful practitioner would be aware of, and responsive to, the mental health needs and opportunities in his or her community, creative in diverting a segment of the local mental health clientele into his or her practice, and able to adapt to changing local and national trends in the field. Ultimately, however, being successful depends on building a reputation as a professional who demonstrates high-quality work; who is expedient, efficient, and reliable in his or her work; and who adheres to the highest ethical and professional standards.

Issues in Setting Up a Practice

Clinical psychology professionals who seek to establish an independent practice should have a good understanding of the fact that independent practitioners are proprietors in addition to helpers and have to do some groundwork in terms of developing and applying business

---

HIGHLIGHT BOX 19.2

SEXUAL OFFENDER RISK ASSESSMENT

Over the past couple of decades, sexual offenses against children have become a heightened concern in society, and a variety of legislative actions have been taken at federal, state, and local levels to address them. For example, the Jacob Wetterling Crimes against Children and Sexually Violent Offender Registration Act of 1994 mandated states to implement a sex offender registry. The Megan's Law of 1996 amended the Wetterling Act by requiring states to establish a community notification system. Most recently, the Adam Walsh Child Protection and Safety Act of 2006 created a national sexual offender registration and notification program.

Efforts to register and manage sexual offenders, and concerns about recidivism rates, have created a market for mental health professionals to conduct recidivism risk assessments. Risk assessments, using standardized and empirically evaluated measures as part of a comprehensive evaluation, are used to inform sentencing determinations and civil commitments, provide treatment recommendations, and advise probation and parole officers on the level of supervision they should provide for each individual case. In many states, regular reassessment is required. This has created opportunities for psychologists to gain the qualifications, based on state licensing board regulations and guidelines provided by the Association for the Treatment of Sexual Abusers, to conduct sexual offender risk assessments and work as contracted risk assessment evaluators.

---

skills and acumen. This is an area that may be unknown to them; at the most, their graduate programs may have offered one course in practice management. Broadly speaking, developing a practice involves securing a business license, leasing or purchasing office space and equipment, hiring the necessary office personnel, and developing resources and procedures for advertising and marketing, billing and collections, and record keeping. Careful budgeting and planning are necessary for determining start-up and maintenance costs and for projecting the length of time and volume of work needed to break even and get ahead. The beginning practitioner may need to secure a business loan and would likely need to consult with an accountant and/or tax attorney to get information on tax obligations associated with various self-employment scenarios (e.g., sole proprietorship versus partnership). There are several good resources available for practitioners to consult in developing their practice. For example, Pope and Vasquez (2005) provide detailed resources for setting up, maintaining, and expanding one's practice, and Stout and Grand (2004) also discuss various practice-related issues such as developing and financing the business, setting fee schedules, marketing the practice, generating referrals, and managing risk.

The independent practitioner has to be active in minimizing risk and **liability** associated with his or her professional work. There are two primary mechanisms for risk management. One involves obtaining **malpractice** insurance, which is a necessity rather than a choice. The APA Insurance Trust (APAIT; see http://www.apait.org) provides professional liability coverage for individual and group practice that addresses various issues such as claims of misconduct and personal injury, and numerous other choices are also available through private insurance companies. The practitioner would do well to engage in comparison shopping to find the type of coverage best suited to his or her practice setup. A second major way to reduce liability is to be well versed in laws and regulations, to be appropriately conservative in one's professional and personal actions, and to exercise good judgment.

Although new professionals may relish the autonomy of having an independent practice, especially after experiencing several years of supervision, they may discover that many practitioners establish service contracts with federal and state agencies or departments in order to achieve some degree of income predictability and are therefore subject to the provisions of the contract. Some examples that come to mind include contracts with the Social Security Administration to conduct disability evaluations, contracts with the state's social service agency (Department of Children and Families or its equivalent) to assess and treat child sexual abuse, contracts with the state's juvenile justice system for conducting evaluations and treatment, and contracts with public and private schools for providing psychological testing and psychotherapy. Thus, it would be prudent to devote some time and effort toward selecting and establishing contracts alongside developing the components of one's own practice.

psychologists in community mental health centers, hospitals, and clinics. However, a noteworthy number of graduates are hired into directorial and supervisory positions within the first few years of becoming a licensed professional. Among my own students, early-career positions of recent graduates have included those of assistant director of a counseling center, clinical director of a mental health and addiction treatment facility, president and CEO of a behavioral services organization, director of a hospital's psychology division, and director of neuropsychology services within a medical center, to name a few. Moreover, a substantially larger number of graduates are involved in supervising practicum students and interns. These are anecdotal data, and there are virtually no published survey data on the frequency of administrative and supervisory roles of beginning psychologists. However, colleagues in other graduate programs supply similar anecdotes, and many programs offer some coursework in mental health administration, consultation, and supervision in response to such observations. The overall impression is that clinical psychology professionals are often called upon to serve in positions of responsibility and leadership that go beyond the responsibilities of direct service. Psychologists are also experiencing increased opportunities to serve as consultants to service organizations, courts, and the media and to play important roles in program development and shaping of public policy.

OTHER SETTINGS, ROLES, AND FUNCTIONS

Most clinical psychology students and interns envision that their future employment would involve providing the traditional assessment and psychotherapy services in which they are trained. Indeed, many of those seeking non-academic career paths secure positions as staff

INCOME POTENTIAL

Clinical psychologists' earnings depend on a number of factors such as geographic location (with its associated factors of cost of living and normative billing or salary rates for the locale) and nature of practice. The volume of work undertaken is another influential factor, particularly for independent practitioners; however, agency psychologists may also choose to supplement their salaries with part-time practice or adjunct teaching positions in colleges and universities. Recent data provided by the APA's Center for Psychology Workforce Analysis and Research show the following median salaries by setting for clinical psychology practitioners with under 10 years of experience: $90,000 for VA hospitals, $87,000 for individual private practices, $82,000 for medical/psychological group practices, $75,000 to $77,000 across public and private general and psychiatric hospitals, $76,000 for criminal justice settings, and $62,000 for university counseling centers (CPWAR, APA, 2007). The CPWAR data also show that incomes tend to be slightly higher for administrative positions compared to direct service positions across all settings. These data may serve as guideposts for the new practitioner. It should be also noted that specialty areas such as forensic psychology and neuropsychology offer higher income potential compared to standard areas of mental health practice.

THE FUTURE OF PRACTICE

Psychology practice is very much influenced by changing trends in society and the demands of the marketplace. For example, recent decades have seen an increased medicalization of mental health care, reflected in a shift in focus away from humanism and personal growth to symptom management and short-term restoration. Working within the parameters of managed care has required justifying psychological assessment and treatment services using medical rather than psychological terminology and criteria (Acklin, 1996). This is the context in which psychologists have sought, and obtained, prescription authority in some states and will likely continue to be the framework in which

collaborative work with allied medical professionals will expand.

Several authors have reflected on the changes occurring in our field over the past several decades and predicted that psychology practice will continue to take new forms in the coming years. For example, Cummings (1995) observed that the current era marks the greatest resocialization of psychologists since World War II and that transformations in professional psychology have been a matter of survival rather than choice. In the same vein, Benjamin (2005) noted that whereas psychology dominated the practice of psychotherapy in the 1960s and 1970s, clinical psychologists have needed to reinvent themselves in response to managed care demands, including having to adopt brief intervention practices and changing their focus to areas of practice other than psychotherapy. Trends observed by both authors include a movement toward large-scale group practices, enabling them to increase the range of services and consequently their marketability. Predictions for the future include the expectation that integrated health-care systems involving collaboration between behavioral health care and primary care medicine will evolve, creating new roles for practicing psychologists (Sanchez & Turner, 2003).

Primary Care

The future professional psychologist is increasingly envisioned to be a health psychologist, given the rapid growth of health psychology (Benjamin, 2005; Cummings, 1995). Reports indicate that hospitals constitute the largest area of employment growth for clinical psychologists, and medical school settings and academic health-care centers are other rapidly expanding employment settings (Benjamin, 2005). In fact, there have been several discussions within the field of redefining psychology as a health profession, and there are expanding needs and opportunities for professional psychologists to function as **primary care** providers in the health-care system (Garcia-Shelton, 2006). The recent introduction of the health and behavior CPT codes has made it possible for psychologists to expand their scope of practice by applying their skills to a new group of consumers—patients with medical disorders that are the focus of behavioral medicine interventions — and to bill for primary care provided in nonpsychiatric settings (Garcia-Shelton, 2006; Miyamoto, 2006). Thus, the coming years will likely offer increased options to new professionals, and the possibility of a revised national health-care policy may prompt further adaptations to a changing practice milieu.

For the independent practitioner, moving into the primary care realm means transitioning to working with a health-care team that, collectively, provides comprehensive services. This may include developing collaborative relationships with referring providers (e.g., physicians or nurses) and holding conjoint sessions with them or serving as a consultant to a health-care team. In doing so, the psychologist has to become familiar with the approach taken by other professions in conceptualizing problems, adapt to the faster pace of decision making and service delivery, and restructure his or her products in a manner suited to the consumers of these products (e.g., writing concise and focused psychological reports), essentially adapting to a modified "culture" of service (Haley et al., 1998). Psychologists' roles and functions within a primary care delivery system are expected to be markedly different from their traditional roles in mental health systems in terms of being directed toward health promotion activities. Specifically, their interventions are likely to be focused on issues such as pain management, weight reduction, smoking cessation, coping with chronic disease, and compliance with medical regimens, delivered as complements to the interventions of primary care physicians and allied professionals (Gray, Brody, & Johnson, 2005).

Prescription Authority

The redefinition of psychology as a health-care profession and the management of health care through MCOs created the context in the 1990s in which clinical psychology professionals began to seek authorization to prescribe psychiatric medication. Basically, this reflects an effort to expand the scope of practice and achieve increased parity with physicians and other health-care providers. Advocacy in this area has pointed to the shortages of physicians/psychiatrists particularly in underserved regions, the limited knowledge of mental disorders by primary care physicians who constitute a dominant sector of those who prescribe **psychotropic medications**, and the advantages of integrating psychological and pharmacological treatment through a single treating professional. There have been raging debates about the pros and cons of psychologists acquiring prescribing authority, well documented in numerous articles and commentaries (for a sample, see DeLeon & Wiggins, 1996, and DeNelsky, 1996; for recent summaries, see Gutierrez & Silk, 1998, and Long, 2005). Regardless of this dissension, the profession embarked on a path of advocacy aimed at the passage of legislation to achieve prescription privileges. An early experimental effort toward training psychologists to prescribe medication was conducted through the Department of Defense, involving creation of a 2-year postdoctoral psychopharmacology training program for military psychologists in Bethesda, Maryland. The training included 1 year of intensive didactic training and 1 year of clinical practicum involving treating a specified number of patients under medical supervision (Gutierrez & Silk, 1998). The APA has since developed an outline of a model program that, in essence, requires 300 contact hours of didactic instruction and evaluation by examination as well as supervised treatment of 100 patients (Long, 2005). In 2002, New Mexico became the first state to pass a law allowing psychologists to prescribe psychotropic medication, followed by Louisiana in 2004, and numerous other states have introduced bills with different levels of progress and success.

In the coming years, individual practitioners will make their own decisions about whether they intend to get trained to prescribe psychotropic medications and incorporate it into their professional work. However, regardless of these individual decisions, expansions in prescriptive authority to other states will inevitably affect the practice of clinical psychology. For example, it is quite likely that malpractice insurance premiums will increase across the board for all practitioners, and there will be new expectations (and perhaps requirements by licensing boards) to obtain continuing education in this area, contributing to overall increases in professional costs. It is also quite probable that practice patterns of psychologists will change in the direction of approximating psychiatry practice, although this may arguably happen anyway as a result of the health-care revolution. On the positive side, psychologists may enjoy greater respectability and greater earning power when the public perceives them as analogous to physicians. More significantly, psychologists will have the opportunity to make critical contributions to patients' overall care, a privilege that must not be taken lightly.

Rural Mental Health

An important emerging direction for psychological practice involves addressing the health and mental health service needs of underserved areas. There is now a substantial literature indicating that many regions of the United States, especially rural locations, are experiencing a scarcity of health-care services. This is consequential, given 2000 U.S. census figures showing that approximately 21% of the U.S. population, or about 60 million individuals, live in rural areas (U.S. Census Bureau, 2000). The APA Office of Rural Health's 2000–2001 report indicates that 55% of U.S. counties are characterized by an absence of psychologists, psychiatrists, and social workers (APA, 2001). Moreover, there is a dearth

of inpatient facilities in rural communities (Jameson & Blank, 2007). The APA further reports the following facts: rural regions contain a higher proportion of individuals who are at risk for mental and behavioral health problems; suicide, stress, depression, and anxiety disorders are major rural mental health issues; rural women have more than twice the likelihood of depression as women in urban areas; rural men above the age of 15 have a significantly higher rate of suicide than those in urban areas. Also reported in that fact sheet are the following data: greater than 85% of areas characterized as federally designated mental health professional shortage areas are rural; one-third of counties with populations under 2,500 residents have no health-care professionals to treat mental and behavioral disorders; up to 60–70% of mental and behavioral health services in rural areas are being provided by primary care physicians who lack the training and experience to deal with these issues (APA Government Relations, 2008). Overall, rural America faces considerable difficulty in attracting mental health providers, causing rural residents to travel great distances to receive needed services or to turn to nonprofessional sources (e.g., church, family, and friends) to receive supportive aid (Jameson & Blank, 2007). Thus, practicing psychologists have a great deal to offer to meet the mental health needs of rural America and have opportunities to utilize their training in serving specific disadvantaged groups, such as women and the elderly, in rural locations. Notably, the demand for practitioners in these areas enables the new professional to position himself or herself as a valuable service provider and rapidly develop a sizeable clientele.

New professionals might take advantage of an important resource—the National Health Services Corps (NHSC) loan repayment program, which offers the dual advantages of an entry into rural psychology service/development of a unique specialization and relief from student loan debt. This program was implemented in 1987, and through initiatives undertaken by the APA's Education Directorate in 1994, psychologists came to be included as eligible clinicians for the program (Whiting, 2006). The program pays up to $50,000 of the student loan for 2 years of service in a designated community site; further details may be seen at http://nhsc.bhpr.hrsa.gov/applications/lrp/benefits.htm. This is clearly an excellent opportunity for clinical psychology graduates. My former students who have taken advantage of this resource have had uniformly positive comments about it and have benefited from it.

SUMMARY

Clinical psychologists today have a broad range of practice opportunities across various specialty areas, settings, and locations. Today's new professionals enter a field that is quite different from that experienced by many of their professors and supervisors and may therefore have had relatively little preparation and mentoring for charting the course of their professional careers. This practice landscape presents exciting new prospects as well as potentially daunting challenges. Initial tasks for the clinical psychology practitioner include becoming licensed, considering additional specialization and credentialing, and deciding on the nature and type of practice to undertake (e.g., independent practice, group practice, or agency positions, and urban versus rural service locations), while becoming knowledgeable of regulations and structures governing mental health practice. As their career development progresses, clinical psychologists could avail themselves of emerging options in primary care and rural mental health sectors and redefined roles as integrated health-care professionals with prescription authority.

THOUGHT QUESTIONS

1. As an independent practitioner, what are some steps you can take to ensure a reliable source of income?
2. A severely depressed patient asks to review the intake assessment report in her records. Upon reading the recorded information about her prior suicidal gestures, she becomes angry, denies having reported this information, and demands that you delete it, invoking her rights under the HIPAA Privacy Rule. What action would you take in response to this situation?
3. What are some advantages and disadvantages of working as a primary care provider within a multidisciplinary health-care system?

Glossary

Certification: the affirmation from a professional board of being a specialist or expert, based on meeting advanced criteria of knowledge and competence.

Continuing education: a course of study undertaken after completing the terminal degree, usually as a requirement for maintaining one's license to practice. In psychology, continuing education is typically provided through workshops, seminars, or online courses that are approved by the American Psychological Association.

Current Procedural Terminology (CPT): a set of numerical codes used by practitioners to describe health-care services when billing third-party payers for the services.

Diplomate: a person who has received a diploma reflecting being board certified as a specialist within the profession.

Insurance deductible: the amount required to be paid by the insured party before the health-care plan will begin to reimburse for the insured services.

Insurance premium: the amount paid by the insured party to receive insurance coverage.

Liability: the status of being at risk for legal action based on a claim of professional negligence or harm.

Licensure: receiving a license to engage in professional practice from a professional regulatory board based on meeting the educational, training, and experience criteria of the relevant state and passing the requisite examinations.

Malpractice: the failure to follow generally accepted professional standards, resulting in damage to the patient and subject to professional censure and legal action.

Managed care: a system of health-care delivery aimed at controlling costs.

Primary care: the provision of community-based health care by the professional who is the first point of contact for the patient.

Psychotropic medication: medications used to treat psychiatric disorders, such as antidepressant and antipsychotic agents.

Specialization: a specialty within the broader field (e.g., child psychology within the field of clinical psychology).

References

Acklin, M. W. (1996). Personality assessment and managed care. *Journal of Personality Assessment, 66,* 194–201.

American Psychiatric Association (2000). *Diagnostic and statistical manual of mental disorders* (4th ed., Text Revision). Washington, DC: Author.

American Psychological Association (1992). Ethical standards and code of conduct. *American Psychologist, 47,* 1597–1611.

American Psychological Association (2001). *Caring for the rural community: 2000–2001 report.* Retrieved June 22, 2008 from http://www.apa.org/rural/APAforWeb72.pdf.

American Psychological Association (2002). Ethical standards and code of conduct. *American Psychologist, 57,* 1060–1073.

American Psychological Association Government Relations (2008). *The critical need for psychologists in rural America.* Retrieved June 22, 2008 from http://www.apa.org/ppo/issues/needrural.html.

American Psychological Association Practice Organization (2005). The HIPAA Security Rule primer. Retrieved June 22, 2008 from http://www.apapractice.org/apo/hipaa.html.

Benjamin, L. T., Jr. (2005). A history of clinical psychology as a profession in America (and a glimpse at its future). *Annual Review of Clinical Psychology, 1,* 1–30.

Center for Psychology Workforce Analysis and Research, American Psychological Association (2007). *2007 salaries in psychology: preliminary data. Table 5: Direct human services positions (licensed only), clinical psychology, and Table 9: Administration of human services.* Retrieved June 22, 2008 from http://research.apa.org/07salariestables.html.

Cummings, N. A. (1995). Impact of managed care on employment and training: a primer for survival. *Professional Psychology: Research and Practice, 26,* 10–15.

Cummings, N. A. (2005). Resolving the dilemmas in mental healthcare delivery: access, stigma, fragmentation, conflicting research, politics, and more. In N. A. Cummings, W. T. O'Donohue, & M. A. Cucciare (Eds.), *Universal healthcare: readings for mental health professionals* (pp. 47–74). Reno, NV: Context Press.

DeLeon, P. H. & Wiggins, J. G., Jr. (1996). Prescription privileges for psychologists. *American Psychologist, 3,* 225–229.

DeNelsky, G. Y. (1996). The case against prescription privileges for psychologist. *American Psychologist, 3,* 207–212.

Department of Health and Human Services (2004). HIPAA administrative simplification: standard unique health identifier for health care provides; final rule. *Federal Register, 69*(15), 3434–3469.

Erard, R. E. (2004). Release of test data under the 2002 ethics code and the HIPAA Privacy Rule: a raw deal or just a half-baked idea? *Journal of Personality Assessment, 82,* 23–30.

Garcia-Shelton, L. (2006). Meeting U.S. health care needs: a challenge to psychology. *Professional Psychology: Research and Practice, 37,* 676–682.

Gray, G. V., Brody, D. S., & Johnson, D. (2005). The evolution of behavioral primary care. *Professional Psychology: Research and Practice, 36,* 123–129.

Gutierrez, P. M. & Silk, K. R. (1998). Prescription privileges for psychologists: a review of the psychological literature. *Professional Psychology: Research and Practice, 29,* 213–222.

Haley, W. E., McDaniel, S. H., Bray, J. H., Frank, R. G., Heldring, M., Johnson, S. B., et al. (1998). Psychological practice in primary care settings: practical tips for clinicians. *Professional Psychology: Research and Practice, 29,* 237–244.

Hall, J. E., Wexelbaum, S. F., & Boucher, A. P. (2007). Doctoral student awareness of licensure, credentialing, and professional organizations in psychology: the 2005 National Register international survey. *Training and Education in Professional Psychology, 1*, 38–48.

Hannay, H. J., Bieliauskas, L. A., Crosson, B. A., Hammeke, T. A., Hamsher, K., & Koffler, S. P. (1998). Proceedings of the Houston conference on specialty education and training in clinical neuropsychology. *Archives of Clinical Neuropsychology, 13*, 157–250.

Jameson, J. P. & Blank, M. B. (2007). The role of clinical psychology in rural mental health services: defining problems and developing solutions. *Clinical Psychology: Science and Practice, 14*, 283–298.

Kohut, J., Li, C., & Wicherski, M. (2007, December). *Snapshot of practicing clinical psychologists: extract from the 2007 salaries in psychology survey.* Retrieved June 22, 2008 from http://research.apa.org/07salaryextract.html.

Long, J. E., Jr. (2005). Power to prescribe: the debate over prescription privileges for psychologists and the legal issues implicated. *Law and Psychology Review, 29*, 243–260.

Maruish, M. E. (1994). Introduction. In M. E. Maruish (Ed.), *The use of psychological testing for treatment planning and outcome assessment* (pp. 3–21). Hillsdale, NJ: Lawrence Erlbaum Associates.

Miyamoto, R. E. S. (2006). Billing effectively with the new health and behavior current procedural terminology codes in primary care and specialty clinics. *Journal of Clinical Psychology, 62*, 1221–1229.

O'Donohue, W. & Cucciare, M. A. (2005). Behavioral health economics and policy: an overview. In N. A. Cummings, W. T. O'Donohue, & M. A. Cucciare (Eds.), *Universal healthcare: readings for mental health professionals* (pp. 19–45). Reno, NV: Context Press.

Pope, K. S. & Vasquez, M. J. T. (2005). *How to survive and thrive as a therapist: information, ideas, and resources for psychologists in practice.* Washington, DC: American Psychological Association.

Rogers, R. (2004). APA 2002 ethics, amphibology, and the release of psychological test records: a counterperspective to Erard. *Journal of Personality Assessment, 82*, 31–34.

Sanchez, L. M. & Turner, S. M. (2003). Practicing psychology in the era of managed care: implications for practice and training. *American Psychologist, 58*, 116–129.

Smith, B. L. & Evans, F. B., III. (2004). The end of the world as we know it (and I feel fine): comment on Erard. *Journal of Personality Assessment, 82*, 39–43.

Stout, C. E. & Grand, L. C. (2004). *Getting started in private practice: the complete guide to building your mental health practice.* New York: Wiley.

Trull, T. J. (2005). *Clinical psychology* (7th ed.). Belmont, CA: Thomson Wadsworth.

U.S. Census Bureau (2000). GCT-P1. *Urban/rural and metropolitan/nonmetropolitan population: 2000.* Retrieved June 22, 2008 from http://factfinder.census.gov/servlet/GCTTable?_bm=y&-geo_id=01000US&-_box_head_nbr=GCT-P1&-ds_name=DEC_2000_SF1_U&-redoLog= false&-mt_name=ACS_2005_EST_G00_GCT0101_US37&-format=US-1&-CONTEXT=gct .

Whiting, M. R. (2006). Rural America in need. *Monitor on Psychology, 37*, 64.

Dissemination of Research Findings

Mark B. Powers
University of Amsterdam

Paul Emmelkamp
University of Amsterdam

OUTLINE

Empirically supported treatments (ESTs) are highly effective across multiple mental disorders. They have been rigorously tested and found to be superior to no-treatment controls and other treatments. However, these methods are not often used in clinical practice. Why are these findings not effectively disseminated? Jacqueline Persons stated that **dissemination** is "Behavior Therapy's Next Challenge" (Persons, 1997). However, the challenge of dissemination is not unique to psychology.

In 1847 Ignaz Philipp Semmelweis discovered that hand washing before attending to birthing mothers reduced the incidence of fatal puerperal fever from 20% to only 1% (Wyklicky & Skopec, 1983). However, at the time the prevailing theory of disease etiology was an imbalance of the basic "four humors" (blood, black bile, yellow bile, and phlegm) also known as dyscrasia. As a result, practitioners and the scientific community did not welcome his findings. To make matters worse, he was unable to explain *why* hand washing reduced fatal infections. At the time, he received such criticisms as "Doctors will not want to take the time to wash their hands" and "If practitioners adopt the procedure and the death rate dramatically drops, they will be blamed for the deaths that occurred before the procedure." After Semmelweis left the obstetrics ward, the death rate then rose back to 35% by 1860. Nevertheless, antiseptic procedures were not widely adopted until the twentieth century after his death and the subsequent work of Louis Pasteur and Joseph Lister, among others. This is just one example of how evidence-based medical research is also slow to be adopted in practice (Boissel, 1989; Chalmers, 1974; Ketley & Woods, 1993; Sackett, Richardson, Rosenberg, & Haynes, 1997; Wyklicky & Skopec, 1983).

Similarly, supporters have proposed evidence-based psychotherapy for mental disorders will result in superior outcomes in clinical settings compared to treatment as usual (Wilson, 1995, 1996). Indeed, data suggest superior outcomes in research therapy studies compared to studies of care as usual in clinics (Bickman, Lambert, Andrade, & Penaloza, 2000; Weisz, Weiss, Han, Granger, & Morton, 1995). However, these innovations are often not used in clinical practice.

In this chapter we discuss the dissemination of psychological research findings. We define *dissemination* here as the process of transferring empirically supported treatments into clinical practice. The measurable outcome is the extent to which empirically supported treatments are then actually used in clinical practice. We use the terms *empirically supported* and *evidence-based* interchangeably. First, we discuss why a clinician would use ESTs. Second, we consider several criticisms of ESTs. Third, we review whether the effectiveness of empirically supported treatment is comparable in research facilities and community settings. This determines if results *can* be replicated in clinics. Fourth, we present data on how often empirically supported treatments are actually used in community settings. Finally, we discuss obstacles to dissemination and some potential solutions.

WHY WOULD A CLINICIAN CONSIDER USING AN EST?

Before we discuss whether ESTs are effective and used outside of research facilities, it is important to understand why a clinician should even consider adopting evidence-based methods. The EST movement in the United States was largely influenced by the emergence of evidence-based medicine in the United Kingdom (Chambless & Ollendick, 2001; Sackett et al., 1997). The desire to disseminate ESTs (or evidence-based medicine) to clinical practice was primarily motivated by the assumption that patient outcomes would improve compared to care as usual. Indeed, ESTs have proven more effective than other therapies, placebos, and no-treatment controls for adult and child anxiety disorders (Borkovec & Costello, 1993; Fals-Stewart, Marks, & Schafer, 1993; Hodgson et al., 1972; Lindsay, Crino, & Andrews, 1997; Marks, Hodgson, & Rachman, 1975; Ollendick, 1995). Chambless and Ollendick (2001) summarized the premise that research should be disseminated to practice by stating,

> (a) Patient care can be enhanced by acquisition and use of up-to-date empirical knowledge and (b) it is difficult for clinicians to keep up with newly emerging information pertinent to their practice but (c), if they do not, their knowledge and clinical performance will deteriorate over the years after their training; consequently, (d) clinicians need summaries of evidence provided by expert reviews and instructions on how to access this information during their routine practice. (p. 686)

In summary, ESTs are most attractive for their perceived relative advantage over other available treatment options.

CRITICISM OF THE EST MOVEMENT

Although the EST approach is now increasingly acknowledged in many countries around the world, there are also a number of opponents to this approach. For example, Westen, Morrison, and Thompson-Brenner (2004) have criticized this approach for a variety of reasons. First, the EST movement relies heavily on the results of randomized controlled trials, or RCTs. Second, relatively brief therapies as typically studied in such RCTs may not be suitable if treatment goals include long-term or permanent personality change. Third, it is unrealistic to assume that most patients present with only one isolated problem. Patients in mental health settings often suffer from comorbid disorders. Fourth, psychological problems/disorders may not be effectively treated without dealing with underlying personality pathology. Finally, he questioned the value of RCTs in establishing empirically sound interventions. Correlational analyses are required to supplement RCT findings.

Fonagy, Roth, and Higgitt (2005) have argued that the current categorization in evidence-based psychotherapies does not make a distinction between two radically different groups of treatments: those that have been adequately tested and found ineffective for a specific patient group, and those that have not been tested at all.

> It is important to make this distinction, because the reason that a treatment has not been subjected to empirical scrutiny may have little to do with its likely effectiveness. It may have far more to do with the intellectual culture within which researchers operate, the availability of treatment manuals, and peer or third-party payer perceptions of the value of the treatment. (p. 3)

It is important to keep these criticisms in mind when reading the rest of this chapter. Although many of the ESTs are from cognitive-behavioral origin, it should be stressed that a number of other approaches are also clearly empirically supported including interpersonal psychotherapy (Elkin et al., 1989), mentalization-based treatment (Bateman & Fonagy, 2004), transference focused psychotherapy (Clarkin, Levy, Lenzenweger, & Kernberg, 2007), and panic-focused dynamic psychotherapy (Milrod et al., 2007), to mention just a few.

DO ESTS WORK OUTSIDE OF RESEARCH FACILITIES?

It is now generally acknowledged that results from RCTs are not necessarily generalizable to clinical practice under routine care conditions. Generally, **efficacy** is distinguished from **effectiveness**. Efficacy refers to the effects of treatment under controlled "laboratory" conditions in RCTs. Effectiveness refers to the effects of psychotherapy in clinical practice. Why can we not generalize results from RCTs conducted in academic settings to clinical settings? There are a number of reasons (e.g., Stirman, DeRubeis, Crits-Christoph, & Brody, 2003). First, treatments in research studies follow strict protocols, which is usually not the case in routine clinical practice. Further, patients and therapists in RCTs are not necessarily representative of those in typical clinical practice. In research studies, therapists are extensively trained and intensively supervised throughout the project. Moreover, therapists are often selected who are already highly trained and experienced in the therapy to be delivered. In research studies, patients are selected who are quite homogeneous in terms of complaints. Because statistical power increases as samples become increasingly homogeneous, inclusion and exclusion criteria effectively reduce error variance by removing, as much as possible, individuals with multiple complaints or comorbid disorders. This means that often patients with comorbid conditions are excluded from participation. Further, in research studies patients must undergo an extensive battery of tests and (structured) clinical interviews, not only at baseline but at posttest and follow-up as well. It is not unusual for patients to spend more time undergoing assessments in the context of a research study than in the therapy provided (see Highlight Box 20.1 for an example). Lab-based research is designed to demonstrate that an effect exists at all under tightly controlled conditions. Thus, lab research may be said to be high in internal validity but of questionable external or ecological validity. Field research, however, is stronger in the latter.

Generally, to estimate the effectiveness of treatments shown in RCTs, these interventions are compared with treatments delivered in natural settings. In these studies, ESTs are investigated in real clinical settings rather than academic settings, and their effects are compared with treatments as usual (TAUs) as offered on a routine basis in these settings and/or with results of the ESTs in efficacy studies. A distinguishing characteristic of effectiveness studies is the use of therapists already working in a clinical setting who may have experience in using a variety of techniques and treating a variety of disorders but who may be less experienced in the specific treatment studied. Experiential diversity is also reflected in the patients used in effectiveness trials, because many will be diagnosed with comorbid psychiatric disorders. Finally, in efficacy studies, the emphasis is on a study's internal validity, whereas in effectiveness studies, emphasis is placed on maximizing external validity.

It is encouraging to note there are now positive results from effectiveness trials of

---

HIGHLIGHT BOX 20.1

The MATCH study is presented here as an example. In the largest multicenter psychotherapy trial ($N = 1,726$) ever conducted, three different treatment programs for alcohol abuse and dependence were evaluated using strict research criteria. Patients were followed for up to 3 years after treatment. Patients received either (1) 12 sessions of cognitive-behavioral therapy, (2) 12 sessions of 12-step facilitation therapy, or (3) 4 sessions of motivational enhancement therapy. All three conditions resulted in significant and sustained improvement on a range of alcohol-related outcome variables. All three types of interventions were equally effective. The major results of the MATCH project were summarized in two publications (Project MATCH research group, 1997, 1998). The major value of this mammoth project (which some have compared to the *Titanic*!) is not the finding on matching it was designed for but the fact that a 4-session motivational enhancement therapy was as effective as 12 sessions of CBT or 12-step facilitation therapy. Thus, the MATCH study suggests that 4 sessions of motivational interviewing are just as effective as 12 sessions of the other two therapies for substance abuse. However, in addition to the 4 treatment sessions of motivational interviewing, patients received a substantial number of very lengthy assessment sessions. It is likely that these lengthy assessment sessions were also therapeutic, adding to the efficacy of all three treatments. It is odd to see that the results of this study are often used to implement motivational interviewing in routine care given its cost-effectiveness while totally neglecting the many additional "clinically relevant" hours devoted for research purposes in the original study.

cognitive-behavioral therapy (CBT) for many disorders, including panic disorder (Garcia-Palacios et al., 2002; Stuart, Treat, & Wade, 2000; Wade, Treat, & Stuart, 1998), post-traumatic stress disorder (PTSD) (Foa et al., 2005), obsessive compulsive disorder (Franklin, Abramowitz, Kozak, Levitt, & Foa, 2000), agoraphobia (Bitran, Morissette, Spiegel, & Barlow, 2008; Hahlweg, Fiegenbaum, Frank, Schroeder, & von Witzleben, 2001), social phobia (Gaston, Abbott, Rapee, & Neary, 2006; McEvoy, 2007), depression (Merrill, Tolbert, & Wade, 2003; Minami et al., 2008; Organista, Munoz, & Gonzalez, 1994; Persons, Bostrom, & Bertagnolli, 1999), mixed anxiety and depression (McEvoy & Nathan, 2007), bulimia (Tuschen-Caffier, Pook, & Frank, 2001), chronic fatigue (Scheeres, Wensing, Knoop, & Bleijenberg, 2008), and oppositional-defiant disorder (Taylor, Schmidt, Pepler, & Hodgins, 1998; Tynan, Schuman, & Lampert, 1999). All the studies just cited found that CBT in their clinical settings produced outcomes more or less comparable to benchmark research studies. For example, one study showed that treatment outcome for chronic PTSD patients was similar at a

research facility and a community clinic (Foa et al., 2005). See Figure 20.1.

The largest study to date was reported by Westbrook and Kirk (2005), who studied routine clinical practice in National Health Service psychology clinics in the United Kingdom. In this study, results from several hundred patients with anxiety disorders, depression, and eating disorders were compared with outcome standards in research trials for the same disorders. About half of the sample reliably improved and a third recovered to normal range. Generally, results were comparable to the efficacy benchmark: only in generalized anxiety disorder were the results slightly less than the benchmark of efficacy studies.

Although the studies just cited demonstrate that CBT conducted in routine care conditions can result in comparable improvements found in rigorously controlled efficacy trials, it is questionable whether these results generalize to other treatments. For example, Weersing and Weiss (2002) investigated the usual care provided in community clinic treatment of depressed youth with results of CBT in research trials. Generally, results were substantially less than those typically achieved in research trials.

Overall, findings suggest that ESTs *can* be as effective in practice as they are in carefully controlled research trials. However, further studies are needed to confirm the effectiveness of ESTs in clinical settings.

ARE ESTS USED OUTSIDE OF RESEARCH FACILITIES?

There are several methods to assess how frequently ESTs are used outside of research settings (e.g., private practice, community clinics). First, researchers may survey patients about what kind of therapy they received. Second, researchers can survey practitioners about the

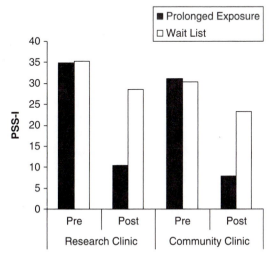

FIGURE 20.1 PTSD Symptom Scale-Interview (PSS-I) data from Foa et al. (2005).

methods they routinely use. Finally, researchers can examine records at provider locations (e.g., Veterans Affairs hospitals) in order to identify the kinds of therapy they are conducting. Next we summarize research using these methods grouped by population, including adult psychopathology in general, anxiety disorders, substance use disorders, eating disorders, and child psychopathology.

Adult Psychopathology

Unfortunately, data suggest most people in the United States with a mental disorder do not receive any treatment (Wang et al., 2005b), and most who do receive help do not get an empirically supported therapy. The National Comorbidity Study suggested that only 20% of people with a 12-month psychiatric disorder received professional treatment within the previous year (Kessler et al., 1994). Similar results were found in the National Comorbidity Study Replication, with 22% of people with a 12-month psychiatric disorder receiving professional treatment within the previous year (Wang et al., 2005b). In addition, less than 20% of children receive necessary interventions (McGee et al., 1990; Tuma, 1989). Another survey of 3,032 adults in the United States showed that 54% of respondents with a mental disorder had received treatment within the previous 12 months (Wang, Berglund, & Kessler, 2000). However, only 14% of these cases received evidence-based treatments. Even if patients seek help, there is most often a delay of 9 to 23 years for anxiety disorders, 6 to 8 years for mood disorders, and 5 to 9 years for substance use disorders (Wang et al., 2005a). For example, patients have panic disorder for an average of 10 years before receiving treatment (Telch, Lucas, Schmidt, Hanna, LaNae, & Lucas, 1993).

What type of treatments are patients receiving? Most patients are managed with pharmacotherapy alone rather than with empirically supported psychological treatments (Olfson,

Marcus, Druss, & Pincus, 2002; Wang et al., 2000). In fact, over a 10-year period, medication prescriptions for mental disorders increased from 45% to 79% while treatment with psychotherapy declined from 71% to 60% (Olfson et al., 2002). This all happened in the context of research finding (a) lower refusal rate, cost, and attrition from psychotherapy versus pharmacotherapy, (b) greater treatment effects favoring psychotherapy, (c) longer-lasting effects of psychotherapy, and (d) fewer side effects with psychotherapy (Fava et al., 1998; Gould, Otto, & Pollack, 1995; Gould, Otto, Pollack, & Yap, 1997; Healy, 2003; Hofmann et al., 1998; Liebowitz et al., 1999; Otto, Pollack, & Maki, 2000; Otto, Tuby, Gould, McLean, & Pollack, 2001).

Anxiety Disorders

Another study used an interesting strategy to survey 500 psychologists about what type of treatments they used to treat anxiety disorders (Freiheit, Vye, Swan, & Cady, 2004). The authors feared that if they asked about using "evidence-based methods," the respondents would simply answer "yes." Therefore, they omitted the term *empirically supported therapy* and instead had each therapist fill out a checklist of the individual strategies they used for each anxiety disorder. For comparison, they separately asked which orientation the therapist identified with most. The results showed that 91% of therapists reported a history of training in CBT. Further, 88% of therapists reported current use of CBT, but only 7% to 38% used exposure therapy regularly. This suggests that dissemination changed verbal behavior of therapists but not their actual use of some of the most important empirically supported methods. By way of contrast, they found that bibliotherapy was used as often or more than exposure-based treatment. Figure 20.2 shows the relative use of exposure, cognitive therapy, and bibliotherapy by anxiety disorder.

Although these data are encouraging regarding the use of cognitive therapy, exposure-based

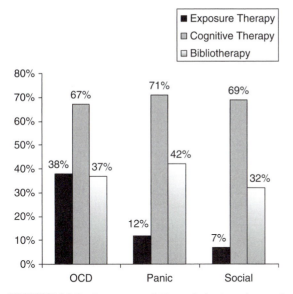

FIGURE 20.2 Percentage of 78 psychologists who used exposure therapy, cognitive therapy, or bibliotherapy to treat OCD, panic disorder, or social anxiety disorder (Freiheit et al., 2004).

treatment was strikingly underutilized. This is particularly alarming given the importance of exposure in effective treatment for anxiety disorders (Barlow, 2002; Emmelkamp, 2004). Why would therapists not use exposure therapy? There is reason to believe that therapists fear symptom worsening or dropouts due to the use of exposure. However, the evidence suggests that exposure therapy shows dropout rates similar to or lower than other methods (Hembree et al., 2003) and reduces symptom worsening (Cahill, Foa, Hembree, Marshall, & Nacash, 2006). For example, the usual dropout rates for clinical services range between 30% and 60% (Baekeland & Lundwall, 1975; Garfield, 1986; Wierzbicki & Pekarik, 1993). This is higher, for example, than the 20% dropout rate seen with prolonged exposure for PTSD (Hembree & Cahill, 2007; Hembree et al., 2003). Another concern may be that using exposure therapy may increase one's liability exposure. However, Richard and Gloster (2006) found no evidence

of legal entanglements for using exposure therapy even though, relative to other techniques, exposure therapy is often perceived as more aversive (Devilly & Huther, 2008). In a Veterans Affairs progress report, less than 20% of the 4,000 PTSD cases examined included exposure, and it was the primary treatment in only 1% (Fontana & Rosenheck, 1993). Similarly, a survey of 217 psychologists from three states showed that only 17% of their patients received any imaginal exposure for PTSD (Becker, Zayfert, & Anderson, 2004). This may be due to the perceived aversiveness of exposure therapy. However, it could also simply reflect the fact that many behavior therapists did not receive training in exposure therapy even if they went through a behaviorally oriented program.

Substance Use Disorders

Behavioral couples therapy is one of the most effective treatments for married or cohabiting substance use disorder patients (Powers, Vedel, & Emmelkamp, 2008). However, a survey of 398 randomly selected community clinics showed that only 27% of programs used any couples-based approach, fewer than 5% used a behaviorally oriented couples therapy, and 0% used the full behavioral couples therapy package (Fals-Stewart & Birchler, 2001). Fals-Stewart, Logsdon, and Birchler (2004) assessed the lasting impact of conducting clinical effectiveness trials of behavioral couples therapy at community outpatient clinics. They revisited (3–5 years after being absent) clinics formerly involved in the delivery of behavioral couples therapy as part of effectiveness trials. To their disappointment they found that four of five programs no longer offered behavioral couples therapy (Fals-Stewart et al., 2004).

Eating Disorders

Patients with eating disorders do not appear to fare any better. CBT is considered the first-line treatment of choice for eating disorders (Fairburn, Agras, & Wilson, 1992; Garner, Vitousek, & Pike, 1997; Marcus, 1997; Wilson, 1996; Wilson, Fairburn, & Agras, 1997). However, a survey of 60 psychologists (who reported at least 5% of their caseload included individuals with eating disorders) showed that only about one-third of the respondents endorsed CBT as their primary approach (Mussell et al., 2000).

Child Psychopathology

As in most other disorders discussed here, CBT is the treatment of choice and highly effective for a variety of child behavior disorders (Casey & Berman, 1985; Kazdin, Bass, Ayers, & Rodgers, 1990; Weisz, Weiss, Alicke, & Klotz, 1987; Weisz et al., 1995). A survey of 467 mental health providers from the Comprehensive Community Mental Health Services for Children and Their Families Program found that 98% of the respondents reported familiarity with CBT. However, only 62% endorsed using cognitive-behavioral methods (Walrath, Sheehan, Holden, Hernandez, & Blau, 2006).

The research reviewed earlier suggests that although ESTs can be used effectively in clinical practice, they are most often not actually used by the majority of providers. Because most ESTs are derived from cognitive-behavioral principles, clinician resistance to their use may reflect a priori theoretical predispositions rather than objections to using empirically supported treatments per se.

OBSTACLES TO DISSEMINATION

What are the obstacles to use of ESTs in clinical practice? Giel and colleagues group factors that mediate EST utilization into three levels: individual, provider, and systemic (Giel, Koeter, & Ormel, 1990). Barriers at any or all of these levels may prevent patients from getting the best treatment available (Collins, Westra, Dozois, & Burns, 2004). Next we discuss factors at each of these levels in turn.

Obstacles at the Level of the Individual

Individual obstacles refer to problems encountered by the client or patient suffering from a disorder. These obstacles include awareness, perceived efficacy of the treatment offered, and their state of readiness for change.

Awareness

Although we do not expect people to diagnose and treat themselves, it is alarming to note how little the public is aware of ESTs. Most patients with mental health problems report being unaware of ESTs. For example, 73% of claustrophobics in one study reported they would have sought treatment earlier if they had known about effective nonpharmacological methods (Öst, Johansson, & Jerremalm, 1982). Further, research indicates that people with mental disorders often assume their symptoms are either biological in origin (Brown et al., 2001; Moeller-Leimkuehler, 2002) or transient and not severe enough to warrant treatment (Mojtabai et al., 2002).

Perceived Efficacy of Treatment

Individuals are more likely to seek effective help if they believe treatment will alleviate their symptoms (Dozois & Westra, 2005; Miller & Rollnick, 2002). Unfortunately, most people suffer from mental disorders for years unaware that effective short-term treatments are available. Even after treatment begins, the patient's belief in the treatment rationale is critical. Indeed, treatment outcome significantly improves when therapists provide an adequate rationale for the selected treatment (Abramowitz, Franklin, Zoellner, & DiBernardo, 2002; Addis & Jacobson, 2000; Devilly & Borkovec, 2000; Oliveau, Agras, Leitenberg, Moore, & Wright, 1969).

Readiness for Change

Even if patients are aware of their diagnosis and treatment options, there is no guarantee that they are ready or willing to undergo the treatment. This state may be referred to as readiness for change within a stages of change model (Prochaska, 1994). The point at which a client is most likely to benefit from therapy is when he or she is in the action-taking stage of this model. Research shows that only about 20% of individuals with mental or physical health problems are in an action-taking stage of change (O'Hare, 1996; Prochaska, 1994). It is also clear that information alone is not sufficient to motivate clients for therapy (Burgoon & Ruffner, 1978; Higbee, 1969).

Obstacles at the Level of the Provider

General Practitioners and Psychiatrists

These obstacles include problems encountered once an individual approaches a healthcare provider (general practitioner, psychiatrist, etc.). Approximately 83% of individuals with anxiety or mood disorders have consulted their general practitioner within the past year (Ohayon, Shapiro, & Kennedy, 2000). Consistent with this finding, general practitioners spend up to one-quarter of their time managing psychiatric conditions (Howard, 1992). However, providers accurately detect only 15% to 40% of these cases (Kessler, Lloyd, Lewis, & Gray, 1999; Kroenke, Spitzer, Williams, Monahan, & Lowe, 2007; Lecrubier, 1998; Ustun & Sartorius, 2002). For example, panic disorder patients see an average of 10 physicians before finally being diagnosed (Sheehan, 1982). Even when detected, most cases are misdiagnosed (Wittchen et al., 2002), remain unreferred for mental health treatment (Stein et al., 2004), or are not managed with evidence-based methods (Stein et al., 2004). Unfortunately, management of such patients is not improved when healthcare providers are given information about

their patients' mental health status (Hoeper, Kessler, Nycz, Burke, & Pierce, 1984).

Mental Health Providers

Misdiagnosis Because ESTs are primarily geared toward specific DSM disorders, reliable and accurate diagnosis is important. One of the most common and reliable instruments for diagnosis is the Structured Clinical Interview for the DSM-IV (First, Spitzer, & Gibbon, 1994). However, for a number of reasons, most clinics do not have the time allotted in the treatment process needed to complete the interview. Also, insurance companies will often not cover treatment without a diagnosis. For these reasons most clinics are forced to make quick diagnostic decisions that may not be as accurate as in research facilities where there are no time constraints (Weisz et al., 2004).

Inadequate Training Even if a correct diagnosis is made, therapists must be trained to deliver ESTs. Greist (2000) concluded there is a discrepancy between the number of patients with mental disorders and the number of therapists trained in evidence-based psychotherapies. Up to 30% of psychology graduate students do not receive any training in empirically supported treatments (Karekla, Lundgren, & Forsyth, 2004). Similarly, approximately 60% of students do not receive supervision in CBT for depression (Crits-Christoph, Frank, Chambless, Brody, & Karp, 1995). Even in graduate programs that emphasize ESTs in their curriculum, a library of treatment manuals or video demonstrations of empirically supported techniques are often missing. In a study of PTSD therapists, only one-third of the respondents reported a history of training in imaginal exposure for PTSD. Further, they identified lack of training as the most common reason for not using exposure therapy (Becker et al., 2004). If therapists are not being trained in ESTs during graduate school, a proposed solution is to train therapists in workshops and at conferences. One study suggested that 77% of therapists using CBT techniques reported training at conferences (Freiheit et al., 2004). Unfortunately, data show that workshops may not always result in changes in clinical practice (Miller & Mount, 2001). Indeed, continuing education does not appear to effectively change practitioner behavior (Davis, Thomson, Oxman, & Haynes, 1992; Vandecreek, Knapp, & Brace, 1990). Rather, therapists who already use CBT may attend the workshops to expand this skill. However, if therapists do not have previous CBT training, the workshop is not likely to change practice. Thus, traditional continuing education workshops may be effective at conveying theoretical perspectives (Amsel, Neria, Marshall, & Eun, 2005) but not for teaching new skills or changing behavior (Davis, Thomson, Oxman, & Haynes, 1995). If workshops are not entirely effective, it is not surprising to find that publication of EST study results does not change therapist behavior either. In this model, researchers assume that practitioners will adopt ESTs once they read about the positive results in a journal article. This model assumes that therapists read the journals where outcome studies are reported. However, only a minority of therapists (35%) read such journals (Beutler, Williams, & Wakefield, 1993). Unfortunately, even education in evidence-based practice does not increase journal reading (McCluskey & Lovarini, 2005). Further, therapists often trust personal experience over scientific findings (Meehl, 1993).

High Turnover Most efforts to directly disseminate ESTs to clinics involve training existing therapists. Unfortunately, the benefits that accrue with training are lost when a therapist leaves a clinic. This is particularly important given the high rates of staff turnover in community clinics (Cahill et al., 2006; Strosahl, 1998). For example, in substance abuse clinics annual therapist turnover rates are approximately 50% (Carise, McLellan, Gifford, & Kleber, 1999). This

suggests that approaching clinics to train therapists in ESTs is a losing battle over time.

Negative Views of Treatment Manuals Another problem has been negative views regarding treatment manuals (Carroll & Nuro, 2002). Treatments were originally manualized to increase the internal validity of RCTs (Luborsky & DeRubeis, 1984; Waltz, Addis, Koerner, & Jacobson, 1993). It was then assumed that once the manualized treatment was validated in research, practitioners in the community would adopt them for routine care (Torrey et al., 2001). However, only 20% of psychologists even report being clear on what a treatment manual is, and only 7% use them regularly (Addis & Krasnow, 2000). Manuals are often criticized for presenting only one theoretical perspective (Goldfried & Wolfe, 1998), neglecting the role of individual therapists (Garfield, 1996, 1998), emphasizing techniques over theory (Silverman, 1996), and focusing on diagnostic criteria rather than case conceptualization (Fensterheim & Raw, 1996). In addition, handing out treatment manuals to clinicians and expecting them to be used can be viewed as a "top-down" process (Cook, Schnurr, & Foa, 2004). In this model, the researcher conceives treatment and the clinician executes (Fensterheim & Raw, 1996). This may result both in resistance from the therapist and in a certain indignation at the implication that a researcher would know more about effective practice than a clinician. In addition, treatment manuals do not appear sufficient to disseminate effective treatments. One study showed the transfer failure rate for a new protocol was 96% when manuals alone were used for training (81% with workshops and 72% with intensive on-site training; Sorensen et al., 1988).

Perceived Efficacy of Treatments Therapists are more likely to adopt an EST if they perceive it as more effective than what they are already doing in their practice. Indeed, positive or negative perceptions of innovations (such as ESTs) account for 49% to 87% of the variance in the extent to which dissemination is successful (Berwick, 2003). However, there is a striking lack of research comparing ESTs to care as usual in effectiveness trials of therapy (Addis, 2002; Weisz et al., 2004). Without this direct comparison, we are left unsure of the relative effects of ESTs and care as usual in any given clinic. If therapists view the new empirically supported therapy as no more effective than what they are already doing, why would they change their practices? Although, at first glance, it may seem obvious that ESTs would outperform care as usual, one study showed there was no difference between an EST and care as usual for substance abuse and treatment on any outcome measures (Morgenstern, Blanchard, Morgan, Labouvie, & Hayaki, 2001). In this case, the EST did not enhance clinical outcome and, therefore, is unlikely to be seen as critical in that clinic setting. This negative finding stresses both the clinical and scientific importance of such comparisons. Although ESTs, by definition, may possess demonstrated efficacy, it is not a given that results will generalize from highly controlled research settings. For example, approximately 20% to 30% of patients do not improve with evidence-based treatments (Chambless, 2002). Further, the effectiveness of ESTs will need to incrementally exceed those of other widely used treatments to a clinically meaningful degree before clinicians would feel compelled to change their practice.

Efficiency, Access, and Transportability of ESTs

Some providers may not use ESTs because of the number of sessions required (i.e., 5–20 sessions). With managed care limitations, longer treatments may be ignored in favor of shorter interventions. In addition, a therapist may practice in an area that does not have access to expert training or other therapists who use

ESTs. These obstacles have led to efforts to develop more efficient and transportable interventions. For example, treatment through the Internet and virtual-reality exposure therapy have proven effective in these areas, which will be discussed later. However, some therapists are still reluctant to adopt the technology. Reasons might include the costs, lack of technical support, and, in a number of cases, also a "technology phobia." Treatment through the Internet has proven effective and could potentially be accessed by patients anywhere. However, to develop the programs requires some interest and knowledge in computer programs, access to a server, and the time to create a Web site.

Obstacles at the Level of the System

Unfortunately, advertising (publishing books, articles, media appearances) may not be sufficient to significantly change how therapists practice. Most often this type of behavior change is a result of external pressure from insurance companies, licensing boards, and consumer demands (Antony, 2005). For this reason, some psychologists suggest the development of treatment guidelines that are enforced by licensing boards or insurance companies. A significant obstacle, however, is lack of consensus as to the content of proposed training guidelines. For example, the Agency for Health Care Policy and Research Depression Guideline Panel suggested psychotherapy only after failure on two antidepressants (AHCPR, 1993). Obviously this set of guidelines is outdated given recent research findings (e.g., Dimidjian et al., 2006; Turner, Matthews, Linardatos, Tell, & Rosenthal, 2008). Another problem in creating practice guidelines is that there are multiple ESTs for each diagnosis. Experts are then charged with the decision to recommend either all the supported therapies or only one. Recommending all the supported therapies is difficult because of the large number involved. For example, Chambless and Ollendick (2001) identified 108 ESTs for adults and 37 for children. On the other hand, if experts attempt to recommend only one supported therapy, they often disagree on which treatment to recommend (Weisz et al., 2004). However, even if more than one EST is recommended, this may not be an insurmountable problem. The critical issue is transparency in communicating the pros and cons of each approach with the clinician always keeping the client's best interests in mind. If the treatments are equally efficacious and effective, and the delivery distinctions between them are relatively trivial, then it may not matter from a consumer perspective which treatment is chosen.

SOLUTIONS FOR DISSEMINATION

Now that we have reviewed some of the common obstacles to dissemination, we turn to some of the solutions that have been proposed. These are also discussed at the levels of the individual, provider, and system. Some solutions are directly from research, whereas others are borrowed from other disciplines, because the study of dissemination is still only beginning.

Solutions at the Level of the Individual

Awareness

To address the lack of awareness of ESTs among the public, one potential solution is to educate consumers of mental health services (Antony, 2005). These efforts may include multiple outlets including popular media (e.g., magazines, television), the Internet, national screening/information days, and self-help books. Unfortunately, the public is primarily exposed to inaccurate and outdated information regarding mental health. One reason may be the hesitancy of researchers to appear in the popular media. There is a notion in the field that too much media exposure detracts from

the credibility of research. Certainly one step in the right direction is for researchers to become more comfortable with these outlets for accurate and state-of-the-art information. For example, Dr. David Tolin (an expert researcher and clinician in anxiety disorders) has participated in several interviews with the *New York Times*, the Associated Press, the *Today Show, Good Morning America*, and the *Oprah Winfrey Show*. Such appearances are often followed by patient calls to specialty research clinics requesting ESTs. Millions of people around the world access the Internet every day. It is no surprise that this medium is a ripe area for dissemination possibilities as well. For example, the American Psychological Association posts consumer-oriented information about ESTs online at http://www.apa.org/divisions/div12/rev_est/index.html. Likewise, the Anxiety Disorders Association of America sponsors national screening days (National Stress Out Week) and posts information regarding anxiety disorders online (http://www.adaa.org/stressOutWeek/default.asp). Self-help resources at bookstores offer another potential outlet to educate and offer treatment for consumers. For example, individuals who read the book *Feeling Good: The New Mood Therapy* have shown significantly reduced symptoms of depression (Burns, 1980; Scogin, Hamblin, & Beutler, 1987; Scogin, Jamison, Floyd, & Chaplin, 1998). In fact, meta-analyses show large effect sizes (0.76–1.19) for self-help approaches (Cuijpers, 1997; Gould & Clum, 1993; Scogin, Bynum, Stephens, & Calhoon, 1990). However, a quick trip to the bookstore (and even to book exhibits and scientific conferences) will demonstrate how difficult it is for an individual to identify self-help books with empirical support from those that are untested.

Perceived Efficacy of the Treatment

In addition to awareness of ESTs, patients are motivated to seek treatment to the extent they believe it will work. Even though individual success stories may not be sufficient scientific evidence for a treatment, they may be one of the most important factors individuals attend to when considering treatment efficacy. Few images are more powerful than watching an actual patient go from start to finish through an effective treatment. In reality, however, the public is bombarded with only selected success stories despite the fact that many treatments, across all treatment-seeking individuals, are no more effective than placebo. In addition, when ESTs are featured in the media, they are often not differentiated from other untested methods. It would be helpful to see a therapist treat a patient with an EST followed by an explanation as to why EST are advised over others. Otherwise, the public will not be cognizant of the differences among diverse treatments with regard to empirical support. It is encouraging to note, however, that CBT is consistently rated by patients as more credible and likely to be effective than medication (Walker, Vincent, Furer, Cox, & Kjernisted, 1999; Zoellner, Feeny, Cochran, & Pruitt, 2003).

Readiness for Change

As mentioned earlier, some individuals may not feel ready or willing to seek help even if a problem is acknowledged. One solution is to conduct motivational interviewing (Miller & Rollnick, 2002). Motivational interviewing is a strategy that emphasizes collaboration, evocation, and autonomy rather than confrontation, education, and authority. The responsibility for change is left with the client rather than the therapist telling them what to do. The "four general principles" of motivational interviewing include expressing empathy, developing discrepancy, rolling with resistance, and supporting self-efficacy. Discrepancy here refers to the difference between the current status of the patient and a desired goal. The therapist helps the patient explore how things are now in their life versus how they would like them to be. These methods have proven effective at reducing treatment resistance in substance use, anxiety, and mood disorders (Miller & Rollnick, 2002; Westra, 2004).

Solutions at the Level of the Provider

General Practitioners and Mental Health Providers

Misdiagnosis There are several potential solutions to increasing diagnostic accuracy. First, clinics may appeal to insurance companies based on evidence to include extra time for assessment. Using this method, many treatment facilities have been granted reimbursement approval for the extra time spent on assessment. Second, researchers could focus on developing shorter (while still accurate) diagnostic instruments and methods. For example, the Child Behavior Checklist (Achenbach, 1991) is a far more practice-friendly instrument than many alternative measures. Third, and related to this, the use of current brief screening instruments could be employed. For example, the Anxiety and Depression Detector is a five-item questionnaire designed to screen for mental disorders in primary care (Means-Christensen, Sherbourne, Roy-Byrne, Craske, & Stein, 2006). This instrument could be routinely administered in primary care settings to increase detection of anxiety and depression. In addition, computerized assessment might be a way of increasing the reliability and accuracy of diagnosis (e.g., Peters & Andrews, 1995). Whether done via computer or the Internet, computerized assessment is something that an individual can do on his or her own time, that is highly cost-effective, and that yields reliable data. Plus, it can be used not just for initial assessment but for process monitoring and outcome assessment. All data can be saved to a database, which would facilitate analyses of the effectiveness of ESTs.

Inadequate Training One positive step to address the lack of training in ESTs has been the inclusion of CBT as a requirement for psychiatry residence programs (Beck, 2000). In addition, continuing education workshops are now regularly offered at national conferences for all disciplines. As stated earlier, however, workshops may not be sufficient to impart new skills. One study suggested that demonstrations by experts (e.g., role plays, video) were more effective than didactic lectures for teaching treatment techniques (Amsel et al., 2005). Therefore, inclusion of demonstrations through role plays or videotaped sessions may be critical to increase the chance therapists will actually use the new treatment strategies (Calhoun, Moras, Pilkonis, & Rehm, 1998). In addition, there is evidence that training in graduate school leads to more positive attitudes and use of CBT and ESTs (Freiheit & Overholser, 1997; Shapiro & Lentz, 1985). Accreditation requirements by the American Psychological Association (APA) are often the most powerful influences in guiding implementation of EST training in graduate schools. Interested students may decide to join the

APA as full members in the future and work to strengthen these requirements. In addition, graduate programs would benefit from maintaining a library of treatment manuals and video demonstrations of techniques.

As the number of ESTs grows, it becomes more and more difficult to train therapists in the myriad protocols. One possibility is to train therapists in empirically supported *strategies* rather than individual treatment packages (Stirman, Crits-Christoph, & DeRubeis, 2004). However, there is currently no evidence that a mixture of empirically supported strategies is more effective than adherence to a manualized intervention (Gonzales, Ringeisen, & Chambers, 2002). In fact, tailoring treatment to each client may be no more effective (Emmelkamp, Bouman, & Blaauw, 1994; Jacobson et al., 1989) or less effective than standardized empirically supported therapy (Schulte, Kunzel, Pepping, & Schulte-Bahrenberg, 1992) (see Highlight Box 20.2 for an example).

HIGHLIGHT BOX 20.2

Many clinicians hold that an individualized approach is better than providing treatment according to a standardized manual. The aim of the study by Emmelkamp, Bouman, and Blaauw (1994) was to investigate whether individualized, tailor-made behavioral treatment based upon a problem analysis of each case led to greater behavioral change and better treatment outcome than a standardized behavioral treatment protocol. Obsessive compulsive patients were randomly assigned to two treatment conditions: (1) customized cognitive-behavioral therapy and (2) standardized exposure *in vivo* therapy. Treatment in both conditions led to significant improvements on obsessive compulsive targets and on the Maudsley Obsessional-

Compulsive Inventory. Improvement generalized to general levels of psychopathology, depressed mood, and social anxiety. Contrary to expectations, however, the individualized treatment was no more effective than the standardized exposure therapy. Thus, contrary to clinical lore, manualized treatment was just as effective as a treatment specifically tailored to the needs of each patient. The results cannot be explained by the fact that patients in the individualized condition also received only exposure and response prevention. Actually, individualized treatment consisted of a variety of techniques in addition to exposure, including social skills training, cognitive therapy, and treatment for bereavement.

Nevertheless, research is currently underway to test an effective unified protocol for emotional disorders (Allen, McHugh, & Barlow, 2008). If this protocol proves effective, it would be much easier to train therapists in one EST rather than hundreds. Another possibility is to encourage therapists to view the entire treatment process as evidence-informed rather than using EST research merely as a guide for treatment selection (Weisz et al., 2004). An evidence-based approach to treatment suggests adopting an hypothesis-testing approach in which clients are assessed, treated, and reassessed with treatment adjusted based upon measured outcomes. Continued monitoring of patient outcomes during the course of therapy permits evidence-based iterative adjustment of treatment.

High Turnover Typical dissemination training at clinics and conference workshops is focused on training individual therapists to implement ESTs. One solution to high rates of staff turnover in clinics is to train "trainers" instead of individual therapists (Cahill et al., 2006). For example, Cahill and coworkers (2006) describe a model where experts first provided an intensive training workshop for interested therapists. Next, a subgroup of workshop members was trained for an additional 2 weeks and became trainers/supervisors. Training supervisors has the advantage of exponentially influencing the number of therapists exposed to an EST and avoids the pitfalls of therapist turnover at clinics provided the supervisors do not leave.

Negative Views of Treatment Manuals As stated earlier, many therapists hold negative views of treatment manuals. One solution is to educate providers on exactly what a treatment manual is and what it is not (Addis & Krasnow, 2000). For example, it may be helpful to let clinicians know that manuals can be used with a degree of flexibility and creativity while still being effective (Kendall, Chu, Gifford, Hayes, & Nauta, 1998). In addition, researchers could conduct a baseline assessment of what empirically supported strategies therapists at a given clinic are already using and then simply add training in the missing features (Chorpita & Nakamura, 2004). Another option is to reconsider the conceptualization of manuals to begin with. We are now at a time when manuals do not have to be delivered in print—they could be delivered as video series over the Web, on CD-ROM, as Web pages, etc. Alternative delivery systems would address a number of issues, including (1) providing modeling of proper therapeutic technique; (2) integrating modeling with text directives; (3) providing online assessment of the degree to which the individual understands concepts (fidelity checking, etc.); (4) providing easy access to check concepts using search functions; and (5) potential the providing for online help to answer questions.

Perceived Efficacy of Treatments Several authors have suggested that effectiveness research should include treatment-as-usual conditions to determine whether the new EST outperforms what therapists are already using (Weisz et al., 2004). For example, researchers could include a baseline assessment of outcomes with standard clinic care before initiating an effectiveness trial. Alternatively, they could include a treatment-as-usual arm in the study. A model example is the collaborative care study by Roy-Byrne et al. (2005). They designed an abbreviated version of CBT for panic disorder (six sessions) and a panic disorder–specific medication prescription algorithm for deployment in primary care settings. The design of this effectiveness trial included collaboration between primary care physicians and mental health specialists, and the treatment was compared to care as usual. The collaborative care intervention was superior to care as usual (Roy-Byrne et al., 2005). Researchers are also starting to develop databases comparing efficacy trials to clinical practice (Southam-Gerow, Weisz, & Kendall, 2003).

Efficiency, Access, and Transportability of ESTs
Efforts are currently underway to make ESTs more efficient. For example, exposure therapy may be enhanced by supplementing treatment with a pharmacological agent known to speed associative learning and extinction, such as D-cycloserine (Hofmann et al., 2006; Kushner et al., 2007; Ressler, Davis, & Rothbaum, 2007; Ressler et al., 2004). In addition, aerobic exercise may be an effective method of interoceptive exposure for panic disorder (Smits et al., in press). A prescription for three 20-minute exercise bouts at 70% maximum heart rate is easier to learn and administer than a complete CBT package. To address complaints that empirically supported protocols developed for research populations do not transport well to practice, therapists and clinics could be included in research from the beginning (Weisz et al., 2004). The current model for treatment development is to first conduct efficacy trials in a controlled environment followed by more open effectiveness trials. Only then is the treatment presented (for the first time) to community therapists. Because of differences in research and community settings, the protocol often needs extensive revision. If practicing clinicians are involved from the beginning, much time may be saved. One example of collaboration between clinicians and researchers is the **Pennsylvania Practice Research Network** (Borkovec, Echemendia, Ragusea, & Ruiz, 2001). In this network, clinical outcomes are evaluated with direct feedback from clinicians who help design the studies. Another example is the development and evaluation of treatments for avoidant personality disorder (Emmelkamp et al., 2006), which was done in close cooperation with clinicians from mental health centers. Rather than first evaluating

these protocols under strict conditions in efficacy studies, the protocols were directly tested with routine cases in mental health centers and treatment was conducted by regular therapists.

Technology-based treatment. The advent of desktop computers ushered in a new era in terms of mental health service delivery. One of the first applications was the use of computers to deliver tests and questionnaires. Results so far show that computer-based assessment can gather information of greater quantity, higher reliability, and potentially higher quality than clinician-administered assessment. Further, there is some evidence that people tend to disclose more information about themselves to computers than in face-to-face contact and that computer-based measures are better predictors of suicidal feelings than clinical interviews (Emmelkamp, 2005; Richard & Gloster, 2006). Nevertheless, many clinicians are still reluctant to use computers for clinical assessment.

More recently, stand-alone computers have been used for psychological treatment. In computer-guided therapy, the computer itself both determines and provides the feedback to the patient. Currently available programs for which effectiveness has been established include Fear Fighter for phobias and panic (Marks et al., 2004), BTSteps for OCD (Greist et al., 2002), Cope (Osgood-Hynes, Greist, & Marks, 1998), the Overcoming Depression Course (Williams, 2001), the Behavioral Self-Control Program for Windows (BSCPWIN) (Hester & Delaney, 1997), and the Drinker's Check-UP (DCU) for problem drinking (Squires & Hester, 2004). Finally, Beating the Blues (BtB) is a self-help treatment program for patients in general practice with anxiety, depression, or mixed anxiety/depression. Generally, results of computer-guided therapy in anxiety-disordered and moderately depressed patients are comparable to those achieved with face-to-face cognitive-behavioral therapies, but computer-guided therapy is more cost-effective (Gega, Marks, & Mataix-Cols, 2004).

Treatment delivered through the Internet. When treatment is delivered by stand-alone computers, no personalized feedback from therapists is possible. The Internet enhances the therapeutic possibilities of computers by offering the possibility to deliver more tailor-made treatment, including therapist feedback, although the field is at the very beginning stages of development. Most current Internet applications deliver self-help interventions in addition to face-to-face contact with a clinician. Patients living in remote areas, physically disabled patients with restricted mobility including severe agoraphobic and obsessive compulsive patients, or patients who are reluctant to seek face-to-face therapy due to anxiety or fear of stigmatization may be reached through the World Wide Web.

Earlier studies using the Internet involve psychoeducation followed by treatment through email. Lange, van de Ven, Schrieken, Bredeweg, and Emmelkamp (1999) described an Internet treatment for post-traumatic stress that did not involve email, which was called Interapy. The entire treatment takes place using a database system implemented on the Internet. Interapy treatment is based on elements from established therapies for post-traumatic stress. Two mechanisms are widely considered to be crucial in overcoming traumatic events: (1) habituation to aversive stimuli, which is achieved by exposure to the traumatic memories and avoided stimuli, and (2) cognitive reappraisal of the traumatic experiences. In Interapy, the treatment consists of structured writing assignments delivered through the Internet without any face-to-face contact. The writing assignments consist of self-confrontation to enable habituation to the traumatic experiences, cognitive reappraisal of the traumatic experiences, and social sharing.

In two randomized controlled studies (Lange, van de Ven, Schrieken, & Emmelkamp, 2001; Lange et al., 2003), the usefulness of Internet-delivered treatment was demonstrated. In the Lange et al. (2003) study, participants from the community with severe post-traumatic stress symptoms displayed clinically meaningful and statistically significantly improvement in symptoms of post-traumatic stress, anxiety, and depression than participants in a waitlist control condition.

Another recently developed Interapy program addresses burnout and work-related stress. It consists of relaxation, time management, cognitive restructuring, and social skills training. This cognitive-behavioral program (CBT) was found to be as effective as face-to-face treatment (De Jong & Emmelkamp, 2000). In an RCT, the Interapy CBT program for work-related stress was found to be more effective than a control condition consisting of psychoeducation only (Lange, van de Ven, Schrieken, & Smit, 2004).

The potential for treatment through the Internet is not limited to post-traumatic stress and work-related stress. Randomized controlled studies (RCTs) have been conducted on teletherapy with other disorders as well. In contrast with Interapy, this form of treatment is less technologically advanced and consists of using the Internet to present self-help material and email correspondence for interacting with participants. Self-help treatments with email support have proven to be effective in individuals with panic disorder, agoraphobia, and depression with community samples. Internet treatment has also been studied as self-help in treatment for headache, insomnia, tinnitus, and obesity (for a review, see Emmelkamp, 2005). Taking the results of these RCTs together, there is now robust evidence that treatment through the Internet is feasible. Further, a series of RCTs has shown that Internet-based treatment may be as effective as conventional face-to-face therapy in various disorders.

Virtual reality therapy. Exposure in vivo is well established as a treatment for anxiety disorders (Emmelkamp, 2004). There is now considerable evidence that exposure can be conducted using virtual reality technology (Powers & Emmelkamp, 2008). Virtual reality (VR) integrates real-time computer graphics, body tracking devices, visual displays, and other sensory inputs to immerse individuals in computer-generated virtual environments. Most VR therapy applications utilize a head-mounted display (HMD) that contains video screens and speakers. The patient focuses his or her attention on computer-generated images that are controlled by the therapist and becomes immersed in the virtual world. VR systems typically permit the therapist to see what the patient is viewing, allow collection of subjective distress data, aggregate data across sessions, and control exposure to clinically meaningful aspects of the virtual environment. VR exposure therapy is conducted like any other form of graded exposure therapy. In general, patients are instructed during treatment to expose themselves to anxiety-provoking virtual simulations in a gradual manner. As habituation occurs and anxiety decreases, patients are encouraged to expose themselves to more stressful virtual scenarios, thereby increasing anxiety (for instance, climb one more virtual floor, take off in a virtual airplane, touch a virtual spider).

VR exposure has several advantages over exposure in vivo. Most obviously, it possesses tremendous logistical advantages in that treatment can be conducted in the therapist's office. Further, VR exposure permits graduated treatment (sequence and intensity of treatment) and creation of highly idiosyncratic exposure paradigms. For example, in the treatment of fear of flying, the advantages of VR exposure over standard exposure therapy are enormous. It is highly cost-effective, components of the flight can be repeated endlessly in the therapist's office, and different flight destinations, different crews, and different weather conditions can be created in seconds. Another advantage is that VR treatment can also be applied to patients who are too anxious to undergo real-life exposure in vivo. Studies demonstrating the feasibility of VR exposure therapy have been published on specific phobias, such as claustrophobia, spider phobia, fear of driving, acrophobia, and fear of flying. Other anxiety disorders that have been treated with VR exposure therapy include PTSD, social phobia, and agoraphobia (Krijn, Emmelkamp, & Olafsson, 2004). Results of a recent meta-analysis show that VR exposure therapy is more effective than control conditions in phobic patients and may even be slightly more effective than the gold standard, exposure in vivo (Powers & Emmelkamp, 2008).

The application of treatment using VR technology is not limited to anxiety disorders. Research into the possibilities of the VR treatment of addictions (by means of virtual cue exposure) has been reported in nicotine addiction and opiate dependence. Other applications have focused on eating disorders, sexual dysfunction, pain control, and palliative rehabilitation with poststroke patients (Emmelkamp, 2005; Riva, 2005).

Implementation of information technology in routine clinical practice. The use of computer-driven assessment and treatment is no longer far-fetched and forms an exciting development for the mental health field. The advantages, especially with regard to Internet-provided assessment and treatment programs, are numerous and include cost-effectiveness, ease and rapidity of getting advice, and reduced stigma. Further, there is evidence that, for some patients, lack of face-to-face contact facilitates the sharing of sensitive information (e.g., suicidal ideation). Some patients prefer to confide in a computer rather than a therapist. Especially in remote areas with few mental health resources, the Internet has the potential to address previously unmet mental health needs for a substantial portion of the population. Further, because the demand for evidence-based therapy exceeds the supply of trained therapists, Internet-based assessment and treatment may help shorten wait lists. Thus computer- and Internet-delivered treatment could be used as a first step in the stepped care of mental disorders, leaving clinicians more time for more severely disordered patients.

Presumably, more and more clinicians will perform Internet-based assessment in the coming years, given its many advantages and few disadvantages. Currently, there are a number of technological limitations that limit the widespread clinical application of VR and, to a lesser extent, Internet-delivered treatment. Apart from these technical impediments, which may be solved by technological developments, there is some reason to expect that technology-based interventions may not be routinely applied in clinical practice in the near future. For example, it took decades for behavior therapy to be accepted as a legitimate form of psychotherapy, despite its evidence-based stance and hundreds of controlled outcome studies (Emmelkamp, 2004).

There is some controversy about the need for face-to-face therapist contact to augment computer-delivered treatment. Although some data suggest that self-treatment utilizing computer technology may be effective in some cases of mild depression, PTSD, and panic disorder, it is questionable whether treatment without any therapist contact is feasible, or even advisable, with more severe cases (e.g., agoraphobic patients and severely depressed patients). For example, it is much easier for an individual to avoid a difficult exposure assignment suggested by an Internet program than a therapist. Further, it is questionable how representative the patients are who apply for treatment through teletherapy. Internet-based programs may only be effective for a subset of well-motivated patients who have an interest in this form of intervention (Tate & Zabinski, 2004), and knowing what personality and situational factors predispose a person to have a positive reaction to the prospects of Internet-delivered treatments would be useful. However, given the widespread use of the Internet, we expect that in the near future Internet-delivered services will be commonplace for many treatment-seeking individuals.

There are a number of reasons that preclude large-scale implementation of VR treatment and Internet-based assessment and therapy. First, resistance to use of computers in the mental health field (see also Bouchard, Côte, & Richard, 2006) comes primarily from clinicians, not from patients. Research has shown that most patients find interacting with a computer acceptable or even preferred. However, therapists often contend that technology may interfere with the development of a therapeutic relationship or dehumanize the patient. For many psychotherapists, the quality of the therapeutic relationship is paramount. When discussing clinical research on VR and psychotherapy delivered through the Internet, hostile reactions by psychotherapists are common, because they feel it has no place in the therapeutic relationship. It may be comforting for therapists to know that the therapeutic relationship does not necessarily suffer as a result of introducing computer-delivered interventions. For example, in the Interapy program reported by Lange et al. (2003), 75% of the patients rated the relationship with their therapist as personal and 88% as pleasant although they never had met the therapist. Similarly, in a direct comparison between face-to-face-therapy and

Internet-delivered therapy, the quality of the therapeutic relationship was rated as higher in the online group (Cook & Doyle, 2002). An issue that deserves more attention, however, involves treatment attrition and early dropout in Internet-delivered treatments. The dropout figure is usually somewhat higher in Internet-delivered treatments than in face-to-face therapy, so there is reason for some concern. Future studies should address this issue, identify predictor variables for dropout, and develop protocols to prevent dropout.

Another obstacle in the more widespread application of technology-based treatments may be related to a technology phobia among psychotherapists (Emmelkamp, 2005). Many psychotherapists are not current with technological innovations and may be anxious about their applications. Some therapists feel threatened by the prospect that computer-delivered therapies will supplant the psychotherapist. Perhaps it is more realistic to expect the further development of specialized centers that will provide specific technology-based interventions rather than to expect computer- and Internet-delivered assessment and therapy to be routinely integrated into clinical care. In fact, several specialized VR treatment centers have already been established in Atlanta, San Diego, and other cities in America.

Surprisingly, ethical concerns with respect to patients' safety and privacy associated with tele-assessment and therapy are rarely discussed. Clearly, teletherapy is not suited for all patients (e.g., patients who dissociate, psychotic and suicidal patients), and adequate measures have to be taken that such patients are not enrolled in teletherapy programs, measures that are already provided in the Interapy programs. Further, the system must allow appropriate actions to be taken in case of emergencies. There is a clear and urgent need for guidelines and formal regulation of assessment through the Internet, teletherapy, and treatment by VR. Other issues that deserve continued attention include those surrounding liability and licensing. As to liability: What if something goes wrong during treatment? Is the therapist, who may be in a different state or country, liable? What kind of care will be available locally to the client? Further, if a therapist is delivering treatment on the Internet across state lines and the therapist is not licensed in the state where the user resides, how do licensing issues apply?

Solutions at the Level of the System

One solution at the system level is greater collaboration between primary care and mental health. Integrating mental health services within primary care can reduce total costs. For example, Von Korff et al. (1998) found that collaborative care of depression reduced the total cost per patient by half. This collaborative environment has proven successful in the treatment of both depression and anxiety (Katon et al., 1995, 1996; Roy-Byrne et al., 2005). An exciting recent development in dissemination research is the emergence of comprehensive models of dissemination. These models draw from several disciplines and offer the potential for testable hypotheses in how best to disseminate innovations. Stirman, Crits-Christoph, and DeRubeis (2004) combined and synthesized three prominent dissemination models. The three models included were Diffusion of Innovations (Rogers, 1995, 2002), Community Organization (Bracht, Kingsbury, & Rissel, 1999), and Social Marketing (Kotler & Zaltman, 1971; Martin, Herie, Turner, & Cunningham, 1998). Stirman et al. (2004) proposed a 5-year dissemination model. The model includes a 1- to 2-year planning phase followed by a 3-year implementation phase (training, implementation, measurement, publication, and maintenance). In Table 20.1 we list their recommendations along with our own. The table is

TABLE 20.1 Synthesis of Dissemination Models (Stirman et al., 2004)

Recommendations for Dissemination	Model
Planning phase	
Conduct focus groups (with researchers and clinicians)	SM, CO, TC
Appoint an advisory board	SM, CO
Secure adequate funding	
Consider and address barriers to dissemination	DI, SM
Conduct a readiness analysis	DI, SM
Match the appropriate innovation to the appropriate agency	DI, SM, CO
Determine the appropriate innovation decision	DI
Training and implementation	
Conduct intensive training (for therapists and future trainers)	SM, TC
Have experts available for ongoing support	SM
Pilot the study to refine the protocol and training	SM
Modify the protocol to accommodate clinical realities	SM, DI
Provide support for administrative structure	DI
Measuring and publicizing success	
Measure clinician and client satisfaction as well as outcome	SM
Include treatment-as-usual comparisons	TC
Publicize findings to other agencies and clinicians	SM, CO
Publicize findings through press releases to the media	TC
Maintenance and follow-up	
Remain available to support continued adoption	DI
Follow up with measures of sustained adoption	SM
Reassess the needs of the agency periodically	CO
Consider developing practice guidelines based on findings	TC

DI, Diffusion of Innovations (Rogers, 1995); CO, Community Organization (Bracht et al., 1999); SM, Social Marketing (Martin et al., 1998); TC, this chapter.

coded by model including DI (Diffusion of Innovations), CO (Community Organization), SM (Social Marketing), and TC (this chapter). See Table 20.1.

Finally, accreditation and professional governing boards may continue to draw attention to the empirical base of psychological methods (e.g., APA, 1996; Barlow, Levitt, & Bufka, 1999).

SUMMARY

In conclusion, empirically supported treatments tested in research facilities are often equipotent when delivered in clinical practice. However, surveys of patients, providers, and medical records show these treatments are not used with great frequency in private and community settings. A review of the literature suggested that obstacles at the individual, provider, and systemic level are to blame. Solutions proposed at the individual/patient level include educating the public through media, Web sites, self-help books, and national screening days. In addition, motivational interviewing was discussed as a method to reduce resistance to seeking help. At the provider level, we discussed (1) increasing accurate detection of mental disorders, (2) training both therapists and other trainers in empirically supported treatments in both graduate school and continuing education (with demonstrations and subsequent supervision), (3) correcting faulty negative beliefs about treatment manuals, (4) involving community therapists earlier in the research-to-practice continuum, and (5) increasing the efficiency and availability of interventions. Finally, at the systemic level we discussed a comprehensive model for dissemination including collaboration between researchers and clinicians and oversight by accreditation and professional governing boards.

THOUGHT QUESTIONS

1. Suppose you are a clinical psychology researcher who just discovered and tested a new empirically supported treatment. This treatment has been replicated in another RCT by another investigator with outstanding results. You now hope patients around the world will benefit from this new treatment. What steps would you take to disseminate your treatment?

2. Imagine that you are a director of a new outpatient psychology clinic. Assume you decide to adopt an evidence-based orientation. What steps would you take to ensure that your clinic used evidence-based methods?

Glossary

Dissemination: the process of transferring research findings into clinical practice.

Effectiveness: how well a treatment works in clinical practice. These studies often include less training in the target treatment and include more heterogeneous patient populations.

Efficacy: how well a treatment works under controlled "laboratory" conditions in randomized controlled trials. The treatments follow strict protocols, the therapists are highly trained in the treatment, and patients with comorbidity are typically not included.

Pennsylvania Practice Research Network: a large group of therapists and researchers in Pennsylvania that was developed in 1994. It was created to increase collaboration between practicing clinicians and researchers and to collect data on the effectiveness of psychological interventions.

References

Abramowitz, J., Franklin, M. E., Zoellner, L. A., & DiBernardo, C. L. (2002). Treatment compliance and outcome in obsessive-compulsive disorder. *Behavior Modification, 26*, 447–463.

Achenbach, T. (1991). *Manual for the Child Behavior Checklist/4-18 and 1991 profile.* Burlington, VT: University of Vermont, Department of Psychiatry.

Addis, M. E. (2002). Methods for disseminating research products and increasing evidence-based practice: promises, obstacles, and future directions. *Clinical Psychology: Science and Practice, 9*(4), 367–378.

Addis, M. E. & Jacobson, N. S. (2000). A closer look at the treatment rationale and homework compliance in cognitive-behavioral therapy for depression. *Cognitive Therapy and Research, 24*(3), 313.

Addis, M. E. & Krasnow, A. (2000). A national survey of practicing psychologists' attitudes toward psychotherapy treatment manuals. *Journal of Consulting and Clinical Psychology, 68*(2), 331–339.

Agency for Health Care Policy and Research (AHCPR) (1993). *Recommendations for treating depression within the primary care setting.* Paper presented at the Agency for Health Care Policy and Research: Depression Guideline Panel, Silver Spring, MD.

Allen, L. B., McHugh, R. K., & Barlow, D. (2008). Emotional disorders: a unified protocol. In D. Barlow (Ed.), *Clinical handbook of psychological disorders: a step-by-step treatment manual* (4th ed., pp. 216–249). New York: Guilford.

American Psychological Association (1996). *Guidelines and principles for accreditation of programs in professional psychology.* Washington, DC: Author.

Amsel, L. V., Neria, Y., Marshall, R. D., & Eun, J. S. (2005). Training therapists to treat the psychological consequences of terrorism: disseminating psychotherapy research and researching psychotherapy dissemination. *Journal of Aggression, Maltreatment and Trauma, 10*(1–2), 633–647.

Antony, M. M. (2005). Five strategies for bridging the gap between research and clinical practice. *Behavior Therapist, 28*, 162–163.

Baekeland, F. & Lundwall, L. (1975). Dropping out of treatment: a critical review. *Psychological Bulletin, 82*(5), 738–783.

Barlow, D. H. (2002). *Anxiety and its disorders* (2nd ed.). New York: Guilford.

Barlow, D. H., Levitt, J. T., & Bufka, L. F. (1999). The dissemi-nation of empirically supported treatment: a view to the future. *Behaviour Research and Therapy*, *37*, S147–162.

Bateman, A. W. & Fonagy, P. (2004). Mentalization-based treatment of BPD. *Journal of Personality Disorders*, *18*(1), 36–51.

Beck, J. S. (2000). *Finally! Cognitive therapy enters psychiatry training!* Bala Cynwyd, PA: Beck Institute for Cognitive Therapy and Research.

Becker, C. B., Zayfert, C., & Anderson, E. (2004). A survey of psychologists' attitudes towards and utilization of exposure therapy for PTSD. *Behaviour Research and Therapy*, *42*(3), 277–292.

Berwick, D. (2003). Disseminating innovations in health care. *JAMA—Journal of the American Medical Association*, *289*, 1969–1975.

Beutler, L. E., Williams, R. E., & Wakefield, P. J. (1993). Obstacles to disseminating applied psychological science. *Applied and Preventive Psychology*, *2*(2), 53–58.

Bickman, L., Lambert, E. W., Andrade, A. R., & Penaloza, R. V. (2000). The Fort Bragg continuum of care for children and adolescents: mental health outcomes over 5 years. *Journal of Consulting and Clinical Psychology*, *68*(4), 710–716.

Bitran, S., Morissette, S. B., Spiegel, D. A., & Barlow, D. H. (2008). A pilot study of sensation-focused intensive treat-ment for panic disorder with moderate to severe agora-phobia: preliminary outcome and benchmarking data. *Behavior Modification*, *32*, 196–214.

Boissel, J.-P. (1989). Impact of randomized clinical trials on medical practices. *Controlled Clinical Trials*, *10*(4, suppl. 1), 120–134.

Borkovec, T. D. & Costello, E. (1993). Efficacy of applied relaxation and cognitive behavioral therapy in the treat-ment of generalized anxiety disorder. *Journal of Consult-ing and Clinical Psychology*, *61*, 611–619.

Borkovec, T. D., Echemendia, R. J., Ragusea, S. A., & Ruiz, M. (2001). The Pennsylvania practice research network and future possibilities for clinically meaningful and scientifi-cally rigorous psychotherapy effectiveness research. *Clin-ical Psychology: Science and Practice*, *8*(2), 155–167.

Bouchard, S., Côte, S., & Richard, D. C. S. (2006). Virtual real-ity applications for exposure. In D. C. S. Richard & D. Lauterbach (Eds.), *Handbook of exposure therapies* (pp. 347–388). San Diego, CA: Academic Press/Elsevier.

Bracht, N., Kingsbury, L., & Rissel, C. (1999). Community organization principles in health promotion: a five-stage model. In N. Bracht (Ed.), *Health promotion at the commu-nity level 2: new Advances*. Thousand Oaks, CA: Sage.

Brown, C., Dunbar-Jacob, J., Palenchar, D. R., Kelleher, K. J., Bruehlman, R. D., Sereika, S., et al. (2001). Primary care patients' personal illness models for depression: a pre-liminary investigation. *Family Practice*, *18*, 314–320.

Burgoon, M., & Ruffner, M. (1978). *Human communication*. New York: Holt, Rinehart, & Winston.

Burns, D. D. (1980). *Feeling good: the new mood therapy*. New York: Wm. Morrow.

Cahill, S. P., Foa, E. B., Hembree, E. A., Marshall, R. D., & Nacash, N. (2006). Dissemination of exposure therapy in the treatment of posttraumatic stress disorder. *Journal of Traumatic Stress*, *19*(5), 597–610.

Calhoun, K. S., Moras, K., Pilkonis, P. A., & Rehm, L. P. (1998). Empirically supported treatments: implications for training. *Journal of Consulting and Clinical Psychology*, *66*, 151–162.

Carise, D., McLellan, A. T., Gifford, L. S., & Kleber, H. D. (1999). Developing a national addiction treatment infor-mation system: an introduction to the Drug Evaluation Network System. *Journal of Substance Abuse Treatment*, *17*, 67–77.

Carroll, K. M. & Nuro, K. F. (2002). One size cannot fit all: a stage model for psychotherapy manual development. *Clinical Psychology: Science and Practice*, *9*(4), 396–406.

Casey, R. J. & Berman, J. S. (1985). The outcome of psychother-apy with children. *Psychological Bulletin*, *98*(2), 388–400.

Chalmers, T. C. (1974). The impact of controlled trials on the practice of medicine. *Mount Sinai Journal of Medicine*, *41*(6), 753–759.

Chambless, D. L. (2002). Beware the Dodo bird: the dangers of overgeneralization. *Clinical Psychology: Science and Practice*, *9*(1), 13–16.

Chambless, D. L. & Ollendick, T. H. (2001). Empirically supported psychological interventions: controversies and evidence. *Annual Review of Psychology*, *52*, 685–716.

Chorpita, B. F. & Nakamura, B. J. (2004). Four considera-tions for dissemination of intervention innovations. *Clinical Psychology: Science and Practice*, *11*(4), 364–367.

Clarkin, J. F., Levy, K. N., Lenzenweger, M. F., & Kernberg, O. F. (2007). Evaluating three treatments for borderline personality disorder: a multiwave study. *American Jour-nal of Psychiatry*, *164*(6), 922–928.

Collins, K. A., Westra, H. A., Dozois, D. J. A., & Burns, D. D. (2004). Gaps in accessing treatment for anxiety and depression: challenges for the delivery of care. *Clinical Psychology Review*, *24*(5), 583–616.

Cook, J. E. & Doyle, C. (2002). Working alliance in online therapy as compared to face-to-face therapy: prelimi-nary results. *Cyber Psychology and Behavior*, *5*, 95–105.

Cook, J. M., Schnurr, P. P., & Foa, E. B. (2004). Bridging the gap between posttraumatic stress disorder research and clinical practice: the example of exposure therapy. *Psy-chotherapy*, *41*(4), 374–387.

Crits-Christoph, P., Frank, E., Chambless, D. L., Brody, C., & Karp, J. F. (1995). Training in empirically validated treatments: what are clinical psychology students

learning? *Professional Psychology: Research and Practice, 26*
(5), 514–522.

Cuijpers, P. (1997). Bibliotherapy in unipolar depression:
a meta-analysis. *Journal of Behavior Therapy and Experimental Psychiatry, 28*(2), 139–147.

Davis, D. A., Thomson, M. A., Oxman, A. D., & Haynes,
R. B. (1992). Evidence for the effectiveness of CME — a
review of 50 randomized controlled trials. *JAMA—
Journal of the American Medical Association, 268*(9), 1111–1117.

Davis, D. A., Thomson, M. A., Oxman, A. D., & Haynes,
R. B. (1995). Changing physician performance: a systematic review of the effect of continuing medical education
strategies. *JAMA—Journal of the American Medical Association, 274*(9), 700–705.

De Jong, G. M. & Emmelkamp, P. M. G. (2000). Implementing a stress-management training: comparative trainer
effectiveness. *Journal of Occupational Health Psychology,
5*, 309–320.

Devilly, G. J. & Borkovec, T. D. (2000). Psychometric properties of the credibility/expectancy questionnaire.
*Journal of Behavior Therapy and Experimental Psychiatry,
31*(2), 73–86.

Devilly, G. J. & Huther, A. (2008). Perceived distress and
endorsement for cognitive- or exposure-based treatments following trauma. *Australian Psychologist, 43*(1),
7–14.

Dimidjian, S., Hollon, S. D., Dobson, K. S., Schmaling, K. B.,
Kohlenberg, R. J., Addis, M. E., et al. (2006). Randomized
trial of behavioral activation, cognitive therapy, and
antidepressant medication in the acute treatment of
adults with major depression. *Journal of Consulting and
Clinical Psychology, 74*, 658–670.

Dozois, D. J. A. & Westra, H. A. (2005). Development of the
Anxiety Change Expectancy Scale (ACES) and validation in college, community, and clinical samples. *Behaviour Research and Therapy, 43*(12), 1655–1672.

Elkin, I., Shea, M. T., Watkins, J. T., Imber, S. D., Sotsky, S. M.
Collins, J. F., et al. (1989). National Institute of Mental
Health Treatment of Depression Collaborative Research
Program: general effectiveness of treatments. *Archives of
General Psychiatry, 46*(11), 971–982; discussion, 983.

Emmelkamp, P. M. G. (2004). Behavior therapy with adults.
In M. Lambert, Bergin, & Garfields (Ed.), *Handbook of
Psychotherapy and Behavior Change* (5th ed., pp.
393–446). New York: Wiley.

Emmelkamp, P. M. G. (2005). Technological innovations in
clinical assessment and psychotherapy. *Psychotherapy
and Psychosomatics, 74*, 336–343.

Emmelkamp, P. M. G., Benner, A., Kuipers, A., Feiertag,
G. A., Koster, H. C., & van Apeldoorn, F. J. (2006). Comparison of brief dynamic and cognitive-behaviour therapies in the treatment of avoidant personality disorder.
British Journal of Psychiatry, 189, 60–64.

Emmelkamp, P. M. G., Bouman, T., & Blaauw, E.
(1994). Individualized versus standardized therapy:
a comparative evaluation with obsessive-compulsive
patients. *Clinical Psychology and Psychotherapy, 1*, 95–100.

Fairburn, C. C., Agras, W. S., & Wilson, G. T. (1992). The
research on the treatment of bulimia nervosa: practical
and theoretical implications. In G. H Anderson & S. H.
Kennedy (Eds.), *The biology of feast and famine: relevance
to eating disorders* (pp. 317–340). San Diego, CA:
Academic Press.

Fals-Stewart, W. & Birchler, G. R. (2001). A national survey
of the use of couples therapy in substance abuse treatment. *Journal of Substance Abuse Treatment, 20*(4),
277–283.

Fals-Stewart, W., Logsdon, T., & Birchler, G. R. (2004). Diffusion of an empirically supported treatment for substance abuse: an organizational autopsy of technology
transfer success and failure. *Clinical Psychology: Science
and Practice, 11*(2), 177–182.

Fals-Stewart, W., Marks, A. P., & Schafer, J. (1993). A comparison of behavioral group therapy and individual
behavior therapy in treating obsessive-compulsive disorder. *Journal of Nervous and Mental Disorders, 181*(3),
189–193.

Fava, G. A., Rafanelli, C., Grandi, S., Conti, S., & Belluardo, P.
(1998). Prevention of recurrent depression with cognitive
behavioral therapy: preliminary findings. *Archives of
General Psychiatry, 55*, 816–820.

Fensterheim, H. & Raw, S. D. (1996). Psychotherapy
research is not psychotherapy practice. *Clinical Psychology: Science and Practice, 3*(2), 168–171.

First, M. B., Spitzer, R. L., & Gibbon, M. (1994). *Structured
clinical interview for DSM–IV Disorders, SCID-I.* New
York: Biometrics Research.

Foa, E. B., Hembree, E. A., Cahill, S. P., Rauch, S. A., Riggs,
D. S., Feeny, N. C., et al. (2005). Randomized trial of prolonged exposure for posttraumatic stress disorder with
and without cognitive restructuring: outcome at academic and community clinics. *Journal of Consulting and
Clinical Psychology, 73*(5), 953–964.

Fonagy, R. A., Roth, A., & Higgitt, A. (2005). Psychodynamic
psychotherapies: evidence-based practice and clinical
wisdom. *Bulletin of the Menninger Clinic, 69*, 1–58.

Fontana, A. & Rosenheck, R. (1993). *The long journey home,
III: the third progress report on the specialized PTSD pro-
grams.* West Haven, CT: Department of Veterans Affairs
Northeast Program Evaluation Center.

Franklin, M. E., Abramowitz, J. S., Kozak, M. J., Levitt,
J. T., & Foa, E. B. (2000). Effectiveness of exposure
and ritual prevention for obsessive-compulsive disorder: randomized compared with nonrandomized samples. *Journal of Consulting and Clinical Psychology, 68*
(4), 594–602.

Freiheit, S. R. & Overholser, J. C. (1997). Training issues in cognitive-behavioral psychotherapy. *Journal of Behavior Therapy and Experimental Psychiatry, 28*(2), 79–86.

Freiheit, S. R., Vye, C., Swan, R., & Cady, M. (2004). Cognitive-behavioral therapy for anxiety: Is dissemination working? *Behavior Therapist, 27*(2), 25–32.

Garcia-Palacios, A., Botella, C., Robert, C., Baños, R., Perpiña, C., Quero, S., et al. (2002). Clinical utility of cognitive-behavioural treatment for panic disorder: Results obtained in different settings: a research centre and a public mental health care unit. *Clinical Psychology and Psychotherapy, 9*(6), 373–383.

Garfield, S. L. (1986). Research on client variables in psychotherapy. In S. L. Garfield & A. E. Bergin (Eds.), *Handbook of psychotherapy and behavior change* (3rd ed., pp. 213–256). New York: Wiley.

Garfield, S. L. (1996). Some problems associated with "validated" forms of psychotherapy. *Clinical Psychology: Science and Practice, 3*(3), 218–229.

Garfield, S. L. (1998). Some comments on empirically supported treatments. *Journal of Consulting and Clinical Psychology, 66*(1), 121–125.

Garner, D. M., Vitousek, K. M., & Pike, K. M. (1997). Cognitive-behavioral therapy for anorexia nervosa. In D. M. Garner & P. E. Garfinkel (Eds.), *Handbook of treatment for eating disorder* (2nd ed., pp. 95–144). New York: Guilford.

Gaston, J. E., Abbott, M. J., Rapee, R. M., & Neary, S. A. (2006). Do empirically supported treatments generalize to private practice? A benchmark study of a cognitive-behavioural group treatment programme for social phobia. *British Journal of Clinical Psychology, 45*, 33–48.

Gega, L., Marks, I., & Mataix-Cols, D. (2004). Computer-aided CBT self help for anxiety and depressive disorders: experience of a London clinic and future directions. *Journal of Clinical Psychology, 60*, 147–157.

Giel, R., Koeter, M. W. J., & Ormel, J. (1990). Detection and referral of primary-care patients with mental health problems: the second and third filter. In D. Goldberg & D. Tantum (Eds.), *The public health impact of mental disorder* (pp. 25–34). Toronto: Hogrefe and Huber.

Goldfried, M. R. & Wolfe, B. E. (1998). Toward a more clinically valid approach to therapy research. *Journal of Consulting and Clinical Psychology, 66*(1), 143–150.

Gonzales, J. J., Ringeisen, H. L., & Chambers, D. A. (2002). The tangled and thorny path of science to practice: tensions in interpreting and applying "evidence." *Clinical Psychology: Science and Practice, 9*(2), 204–209.

Gould, R. A. & Clum, G. A. (1993). A meta-analysis of self-help treatment approaches. *Clinical Psychology Review, 13*(2), 169–186.

Gould, R. A., Otto, M. W., & Pollack, M. H. (1995). A meta-analysis of treatment outcome for panic disorder. *Clinical Psychology Review, 15*(8), 819–844.

Gould, R. A., Otto, M. W., Pollack, M. H., & Yap, L. (1997). Cognitive behavioral and pharmacological treatment of generalized anxiety disorder: a preliminary meta-analysis. *Behavior Therapy, 28*(2), 285–305.

Greist, J. H. (2000). Effective behavioral therapy constrained: dissemination is the issue. In M. Maj, N. Sartorius, A. Okasha, & J. Zohar (Eds.), *Obsessive-compulsive disorder. WPA series: Evidence and experience in psychiatry,* vol. 4. New York: Wiley.

Greist, J. H., Marks, I. M., Baer, L., Kobak, K. A., Wenzel, K. W., Hirsch, M. J., et al. (2002). Behavior therapy for obsessive-compulsive disorder guided by a computer or by a clinician compared with relaxation as a control. *Journal of Clinical Psychiatry, 63*, 138–145.

Hahlweg, K., Fiegenbaum, W., Frank, M., Schroeder, B., & von Witzleben, I. (2001). Short- and long-term effectiveness of an empirically supported treatment for agoraphobia. *Journal of Consulting and Clinical Psychology, 69*(3), 375–382.

Healy, D. (2003). Lines of evidence on the risk of suicide with selective serotonin reuptake inhibitors. *Psychotherapy and Psychosomatics, 72*, 71–79.

Hembree, E. A. & Cahill, S. P. (2007). Obstacles to successful implementation of exposure therapy. In D. C. S. Richard & D. Lauterbach (Eds.), *Handbook of the exposure therapies* (pp. 389–408). Burlington, MA: Academic Press.

Hembree, E. A., Foa, E. B., Dorfan, N. M., Street, G. P., Kowalski, J., & Tu, X. (2003). Do patients drop out prematurely from exposure therapy for PTSD? *Journal of Traumatic Stress, 16*, 555–562.

Hester, R. K. & Delaney, H. D. (1997). Behavioral self-control program for windows: results of a controlled trial. *Journal of Consulting and Clinical Psychology, 65*, 685–693.

Higbee, K. L. (1969). Fifteen years of fear arousal: research on threat appeals: 1953–1968. *Psychological Bulletin, 72*, 426–444.

Hodgson, R., Rachman, S., & Marks, I. M. (1972). The treatment of chronic obsessive-compulsive neurosis: follow-up and further findings. *Behaviour Research and Therapy, 10*, 181–189.

Hoeper, E., Kessler, L., Nycz, G., Burke, J., & Pierce, W. (1984). The usefulness of screening for mental illness. *Lancet, 323*(8367), 33–35.

Hofmann, S. G., Barlow, D. H., Papp, L. A., Detweiler, M. F., Ray, S. E., Shear, M. K., et al. (1998). Pretreatment attrition in a comparative treatment outcome study on panic disorder. *American Journal of Psychiatry, 155*, 43–47.

Hofmann, S. G., Meuret, A. E., Smits, J. A., Simon, N. M., Pollack, M. H., Eisenmenger, K., et al. (2006). Augmentation of exposure therapy with D-cycloserine for social anxiety disorder. *Archives of General Psychiatry, 63*(3), 298–304.

Howard, K. I. (1992). The psychotherapeutic service delivery system. *Psychotherapy Research, 2*, 164–180.

Jacobson, N. S., Schmaling, K. B., Holtzworth-Munroe, A., Katt, J. L., Wood, L. F., et al. (1989). Research-structured vs.

clinically flexible versions of social learning-based marital therapy. *Behaviour Research and Therapy, 27,* 173–180.

Karekla, M., Lundgren, J. D., & Forsyth, J. P. (2004). A survey of graduate training in empirically supported and manualized treatments: a preliminary report. *Cognitive and Behavioral Practice, 11*(2), 230–242.

Katon, W., Robinson, P., Von Korff, M., Lin, E., Bush, T., Ludman, E., et al. (1996). A multifaceted intervention to improve treatment of depression in primary care. *Archives of General Psychiatry, 53,* 924–932.

Katon, W., Von Korff, M., Lin, E., Walker, E., Simon, G. E., Bush, T., et al. (1995). Collaborative management to achieve treatment guidelines: impact on depression in primary care. *JAMA—Journal of the American Medical Association, 273,* 1026–1031.

Kazdin, A. E., Bass, D., Ayers, W. A., & Rodgers, A. (1990). Empirical and clinical focus of child and adolescent psychotherapy research. *Journal of Consulting and Clinical Psychology, 58*(6), 729–740.

Kendall, P. C., Chu, B., Gifford, A., Hayes, C., & Nauta, M. (1998). Breathing life into a manual: flexibility and creativity with manual-based treatments. *Cognitive and Behavioral Practice, 5*(2), 177–198.

Kessler, D., Lloyd, K., Lewis, G., & Gray, D. P. (1999). Cross sectional study of symptom attribution and recognition of depression and anxiety in primary care. *British Medical Journal, 318*(7181), 436–440.

Kessler, R. C., McGonagle, K. A., Zhao, S., Nelson, C. B., Hughes, M., Eshleman, S., et al. (1994). Lifetime and 12-month prevalence of DSM-III-R psychiatric disorders in the United States: results from the National Comorbidity Survey. *Archives of General Psychiatry, 51*(1), 8–19.

Ketley, D. & Woods, K. L. (1993). Impact of clinical trials on clinical practice: example of thrombolysis for acute myocardial infarction. *Lancet, 342*(8876), 891–894.

Kotler, P. & Zaltman, G. (1971). Social marketing: an approach to planned social change. *Journal of Marketing, 35*(3), 3–12.

Krijn, M, Emmelkamp, P. M. G., & Olafsson, R (2004). Virtual reality exposure therapy in anxiety disorders. *Clinical Psychology Review, 24,* 259–281.

Kroenke, K., Spitzer, R. L., Williams, J. B. W., Monahan, P. O., & Lowe, B. (2007). Anxiety disorders in primary care: prevalence, impairment, comorbidity, and detection. *Annals of Internal Medicine, 146*(5), 317–325.

Kushner, M. G., Kim, S. W., Donahue, C., Thuras, P., Adson, D., Kotlyar, M., et al. (2007). D-Cycloserine augmented exposure therapy for obsessive-compulsive disorder. *Biological Psychiatry, 62,* 835–838.

Lange, A., Rietdijk, D., Hudcovicova, M., van de Ven, J. P., Schrieken, B., & Emmelkamp, P. M. (2003). Interapy: a controlled randomized trial of the standardized

treatment of posttraumatic stress through the Internet. *Journal of Consulting and Clinical Psychology, 71*(5), 901–909.

Lange, A., van de Ven, J. P., Schrieken, B., Bredeweg, B., & Emmelkamp, P. M. G. (1999). Internet-mediated, protocol driven treatment of psychological dysfunction. *Journal of Telemedicine and Telecare, 6,* 15–21.

Lange, A., van de Ven, J. P., Schrieken, B., & Emmelkamp, P. M. G. (2001). Interapy: treatment of posttraumatic stress through the Internet: a controlled trial. *Journal of Behavior Therapy and Experimental Psychiatry, 32,* 73–90.

Lange, A., van de Ven, J. P., Schrieken, B., & Smit, M. (2004). Interapy burn-out: prävention und behandlung von burn-out über das Internet. *Verhaltenstherapie, 14,* 190–199.

Lecrubier, Y. (1998). Is depression under-recognized and undertreated? *International Clinical Psychopharmacology, 13,* 3–6.

Liebowitz, M. R., Heimberg, R. G., Schneier, R. R., Hope, D. A., Davies, S., Holt, C. S., et al. (1999). Cognitive-behavioral group therapy versus phenelzine in social phobia: long-term outcome. *Depression and Anxiety, 10,* 89–98.

Lindsay, M., Crino, R., & Andrews, G. (1997). Controlled trial of exposure and response prevention in obsessive-compulsive disorder. *British Journal of Psychiatry, 171,* 135–139.

Luborsky, L. & DeRubeis, R. J. (1984). The use of psychotherapy treatment manuals: a small revolution in psychotherapy research style. *Clinical Psychology Review, 4*(1), 5–14.

Marcus, M. D. (1997). Adapting treatment for patients with binge eating disorder. In D. M. Garner & P. E. Garfinkel (Eds.), *Handbook of treatment for eating disorders* (2nd ed., pp. 484–493). New York: Guilford.

Marks, I. M., Hodgson, R., & Rachman, S. (1975). Treatment of chronic obsessive-compulsive neurosis by in-vivo exposure: a two-year follow-up and issues in treatment. *British Journal of Psychiatry, 127,* 349–364.

Marks, I. M., Kenwright, M., McDonough, M., Whittaker, M., O'Brien, T., & Mataix-Cols, D. (2004). Saving clinicians' time by delegating routine aspects of therapy to a computer: a randomized controlled trial in panic/phobia disorder. *Psychological Medicine, 34,* 9–17.

Martin, G. W., Herie, M. A., Turner, B. J., & Cunningham, J. A. (1998). A social marketing model for disseminating research-based treatments to addictions treatment providers. *Addiction, 93*(11), 1703–1715.

McCluskey, A. & Lovarini, M. (2005). Providing education on evidence-based practice improved knowledge but did not change behaviour: a before and after study. *BMC Medical Education, 5*(1), 40.

McEvoy, P. M. (2007). Effectiveness of cognitive behavioural group therapy for social phobia in a community clinic: a benchmarking study. *Behaviour Research and Therapy*, 45, 3030–3040.

McEvoy, P. M. & Nathan, P. (2007). Cognitive behavioural therapy for diagnostically heterogenous groups in a community mental health clinic: a benchmarking study. *Journal of Consulting and Clinical Psychology*, 75, 344–350.

McGee, R., Feehan, M., Williams, S., Partridge, F., Silva, P. A., & Kelly, J. (1990). DSM-III disorders in a large sample of adolescents. *Journal of the American Academy of Child and Adolescent Psychiatry*, 29(4), 611–619.

Means-Christensen, A. J., Sherbourne, C. D., Roy-Byrne, P. P., Craske, M. G., & Stein, M. B. (2006). Using five questions to screen for five common mental disorders in primary care: diagnostic accuracy of the Anxiety and Depression Detector. *General Hospital Psychiatry*, 28, 108–118.

Meehl, P. E. (1993). Philosophy of science: help or hindrance? *Psychological Reports*, 72, 707–733.

Merrill, K. A., Tolbert, V. E., & Wade, W. W. (2003). Effectiveness of cognitive therapy for depression in a community mental health center: a benchmarking study. *Journal of Consulting and Clinical Psychology*, 71, 404–409.

Miller, W. R. & Mount, K. A. (2001). A small study of training in motivational interviewing: does one workshop change clinician and client behavior? *Behavioural and Cognitive Psychotherapy*, 29, 457–471.

Miller, W. R. & Rollnick, S. (2002). *Motivational interviewing: Preparing people for change* (2nd ed.). New York: Guilford.

Milrod, B., Leon, A. C., Busch, F., Rudden, M., Schwalberg, M., Clarkin, J., et al. (2007). A randomized controlled clinical trial of psychoanalytic psychotherapy for panic disorder. *American Journal of Psychiatry*, 164(2), 265–272.

Minami, T., Wampold, B. E., Serlin, R. C., Hamilton, E. G., & Brown, G. S. (2008). Benchmarking the effectiveness of psychotherapy treatment for adult depression in a managed care environment: a preliminary study. *Journal of Consulting and Clinical Psychology*, 76, 116–124.

Moeller-Leimkuehler, A. M. (2002). Barriers to help-seeking by men: a review of sociocultural and clinical literature with particular reference to depression. *Journal of Affective Disorders*, 71, 1–9.

Mojtabai, R., Olfson, M., & Mechanic, D. (2002). Perceived need and help-seeking in adults with mood, anxiety, or substance use disorder. *Archives of General Psychiatry*, 59, 77–84.

Morgenstern, J., Blanchard, K. A., Morgan, T. J., Labouvie, E., & Hayaki, J. (2001). Testing the effectiveness of cognitive-behavioral treatment for substance abuse in a community setting: within treatment and posttreatment findings. *Journal of Consulting and Clinical Psychology*, 69(6), 1007–1017.

Mussell, M. P., Crosby, R. D., Crow, S. J., Knopke, A. J., Peterson, C. B., Wonderlich, S. A., et al. (2000). Utilization of empirically supported psychotherapy treatments for individuals with eating disorders: a survey of psychologists. *International Journal of Eating Disorders*, 27(2), 230–237.

O'Hare, T. (1996). Readiness for change: variation by intensity and domain of client distress. *Social Work Research*, 20, 13–17.

Ohayon, M. M., Shapiro, C. M., & Kennedy, S. H. (2000). Differentiating DSM–IV anxiety and depressive disorders in the general population: comorbidity and treatment consequences. *Canadian Journal of Psychiatry*, 45(2), 166–172.

Olfson, M., Marcus, S. C., Druss, B., & Pincus, H. A. (2002). National trends in the use of outpatient psychotherapy. *American Journal of Psychiatry*, 159(11), 1914–1920.

Oliveau, D. C., Agras, W. S., Leitenberg, H., Moore, R. C., & Wright, D. E. (1969). Systematic desensitization, therapeutically oriented instructions and selective positive reinforcement. *Behaviour Research and Therapy*, 7(1), 27–33.

Ollendick, T. H. (1995). Cognitive behavioral treatment of panic disorder with agoraphobia in adolescents: a multiple baseline design analysis. *Behavior Therapy*, 26(3), 517–531.

Organista, K. C., Munoz, R. F., & Gonzalez, G. (1994). Cognitive-behavioral therapy for depression in low-income and minority medical outpatients — Description of a program and exploratory analyses. *Cognitive Therapy and Research*, 18(3), 241–259.

Osgood-Hynes, D. J., Greist, J. H., & Marks, I. M. (1998). Self-administered psychotherapy for depression using a telephone-accessed computer system plus booklets: an open US-UK study. *Journal of Clinical Psychiatry*, 59, 358–365.

Öst, L. G., Johansson, J., & Jerremalm, A. (1982). Individual response patterns and the effects of different behavioral methods in the treatment of claustrophobia. *Behaviour Research and Therapy*, 20(5), 445–460.

Otto, M. W., Pollack, M. H., & Maki, K. M. (2000). Empirically supported treatments for panic disorder: costs, benefits, and stepped care. *Journal of Consulting and Clinical Psychology*, 68(4), 556–563.

Otto, M. W., Tuby, K. S., Gould, R. A., McLean, R. Y., & Pollack, M. H. (2001). An effect-size analysis of the relative efficacy and tolerability of serotonin selective reuptake inhibitors for panic disorder. *American Journal of Psychiatry*, 158(12), 1989–1992.

Persons, J. B. (1997). Dissemination of effective methods: behavior therapy's next challenge. *Behavior Therapy*, 28(3), 465–471.

Persons, J. B., Bostrom, A., & Bertagnolli, A. (1999). Results of randomized controlled trials of cognitive therapy for depression generalize to private practice. *Cognitive Therapy and Research*, 23(5), 535–548.

Peters, L. & Andrews, G. (1995). Procedural validity of the computerized version of the Composite International Diagnostic Interview (CIDI-Auto) in the anxiety disorders. *Psychological Medicine*, 25(6), 1269–1280.

Powers, M. B. & Emmelkamp, P. M. (2008). Virtual reality exposure therapy for anxiety disorders: a meta-analysis. *Journal of Anxiety Disorders*, 22, 561–569.

Powers, M. B., Vedel, E., & Emmelkamp, P. M. (2008). Behavioral couples therapy (BCT) for alcohol and dug use disorders: a meta-analysis. *Clinical Psychology Review*, 28, 952–962.

Prochaska, J. O. (1994). Strong and weak principles for progressing from precontemplation to action on the basis of twelve problem behaviors. *Health Psychology*, 13(1), 47–51.

Project MATCH research group (1997). Matching alcoholism treatments to client heterogeneity: Project MATCH posttreatment drinking outcomes. *Journal of Studies on Alcohol*, 58, 7–29.

Project MATCH research group (1998). Matching alcoholism treatments to client heterogeneity: Project MATCH three-year drinking outcomes. *Journal of Studies on Alcohol*, 58, 7–29.

Ressler, K. J., Davis, M., & Rothbaum, B. O. (2007). Pharmacological enhancement of learning in exposure therapy. In D. C. S. Richard & D. L. Lauterbach (Eds.), *Handbook of exposure therapies*. New York: Academic Press/Elsevier.

Ressler, K. J., Rothbaum, B. O., Tannenbaum, L., Anderson, P., Graap, K., Zimand, E., et al. (2004). Cognitive enhancers as adjuncts to psychotherapy: use of D-cycloserine in phobic individuals to facilitate extinction of fear. *Archives of General Psychiatry*, 61(11), 1136–1144.

Richard, D. C. S. & Gloster, A. (2006). Technology integration and behavioral assessment. In M. Hersen (Ed.), *Clinician's handbook of adult behavioral assessment* (pp. 461–495). San Diego, CA: Elsevier Academic Press.

Richard, D. C. S. & Gloster, A. (2006). Exposure therapy has a public relations problem: A dearth of litigation amid a wealth of concern. In D. C. S. Richard & D. Lauterbach (Eds.), *Handbook of the exposure therapies* (pp. 109–126). Burlington, MA: Academic Press.

Riva, G. (2005). Virtual reality in psychotherapy. *CyberPsychology & Behavior*, 8, 220–230.

Rogers, E. (1995). *Diffusion of innovations* (4th ed.). New York: Free Press.

Rogers, E. (2002). Diffusion of preventive innovations. *Addictive Behaviors*, 27(6), 989–993.

Roy-Byrne, P., Craske, M., Stein, M., Sullivan, G., Bystritsky, A., Katon, W., et al. (2005). A randomized effectiveness trial of cognitive-behavioral therapy and medication for primary care panic disorder. *Archives of General Psychiatry*, 62(3), 290–298.

Sackett, D. L., Richardson, W. S., Rosenberg, W., & Haynes, R. B. (1997). *Evidence-based medicine*. New York: Churchill Livingstone.

Scheeres, K., Wensing, M., Knoop, H., & Bleijenberg, G. (2008). Implementing cognitive behavioral therapy for chronic fatigue syndrome in a mental health center: A benchmarking evaluation. *Journal of Consulting and Clinical Psychology*, 76, 163–171.

Schulte, D., Kunzel, R., Pepping, G., & Schulte-Bahrenberg, T. (1992). Tailor-made versus standardized therapy of phobic patients. *Advances in Behaviour Research and Therapy*, 14(2), 67–92.

Scogin, F., Bynum, J., Stephens, G., & Calhoon, S. (1990). Efficacy of self-administered treatment programs: meta-analytic review. *Professional Psychology: Research and Practice*, 21(1), 42–47.

Scogin, F., Hamblin, D., & Beutler, L. (1987). Bibliotherapy for depressed older adults: a self-help alternative. *Gerontologist*, 27(3), 383–387.

Scogin, F., Jamison, C., Floyd, M., & Chaplin, W. F. (1998). Measuring learning in depression treatment: a cognitive bibliotherapy test. *Cognitive Therapy and Research*, 22(5), 475–482.

Shapiro, E. S. & Lentz, F. E. (1985). A survey of school psychologists' use of behavior modification procedures. *Journal of School Psychology*, 23(4), 327–336.

Sheehan, D. (1982). Current concepts in psychiatry: panic attacks and phobias. *New England Journal of Medicine*, 307, 156–158.

Silverman, W. H. (1996). Cookbooks, manuals, and paint-by-numbers: psychotherapy in the 90's. *Psychotherapy*, 33(2), 207–215.

Smits, J. A., Berry, A. C., Rosenfield, D., Powers, M., Behar, E., & Otto, M. W. (in press). Reducing anxiety sensitivity with exercise. *Depression & Anxiety*.

Sorensen, J. L., Hall, S. M., Loeb, P., Allen, T., Glaser, E. M., & Greenberg, P. D. (1988). Dissemination of a job seekers' workshop to drug treatment programs. *Behavior Therapy*, 19, 143–155.

Southam-Gerow, M. A., Weisz, J. R., & Kendall, P. C. (2003). Youth with anxiety disorders in research and service clinics: examining client differences and similarities. *Journal of Clinical Child and Adolescent Psychology*, 32(3), 375–385.

Squires, D. D. & Hester, R. K. (2004). Using technological innovations in clinical practice: the Drinker's Check-up software program. *Journal of Clinical Psychology*, 60, 159–169.

Stein, M. B., Sherbourne, C. D., Craske, M. G., Means-Christensen, A., Bystritsky, A., Katon, W., et al. (2004). Quality of care for primary care patients with anxiety disorders. *American Journal of Psychiatry*, 161(12), 2230–2237.

Stirman, S. W., Crits-Christoph, P., & DeRubeis, R. J. (2004). Achieving successful dissemination of empirically supported psychotherapies: a synthesis of dissemination theory. *Clinical Psychology: Science and Practice*, *11*(4), 343–359.

Stirman, S. W., DeRubeis, R. J., Crits-Christoph, P., & Brody, P. E. (2003). Are samples in randomized controlled trials of psychotherapy representative of community outpatients? A new methodology and initial findings. *Journal of Consulting and Clinical Psychology*, *71*, 963–972.

Strosahl, K. (1998). The dissemination of manual-based psychotherapies in managed care: promises, problems, and prospects. *Clinical Psychology: Science and Practice*, *5*(3), 382–386.

Stuart, G. L., Treat, T. A., & Wade, W. A. (2000). Effectiveness of an empirically based treatment for panic disorder delivered in a service clinic setting: 1-year follow-up. *Journal of Consulting and Clinical Psychology*, *68*, 506–512.

Tate, D. F. & Zabinski, M. F. (2004). Computer and Internet applications for psychological treatment: update for clinicians. *Journal of Clinical Psychology*, *60*, 209–220.

Taylor, T. K., Schmidt, F., Pepler, D., & Hodgins, C. (1998). A comparison of eclectic treatment with Webster-Stratton's Parents and Children Series in a children's mental health center: a randomized controlled trial. *Behavior Therapy*, *29*(2), 221–240.

Telch, M., Lucas, J., Schmidt, N. B., Hanna, H., LaNae Jaimez, T., & Lucas, R. (1993). Group cognitive-behavioral treatment of panic disorder. *Behaviour Research and Therapy*, *31*, 279–287.

Torrey, W. C., Drake, R. E., Dixon, L., Burns, B. J., Flynn, L., Rush, A. J., et al. (2001). Implementing evidence-based practices for persons with severe mental illnesses. *Psychiatric Services*, *52*(1), 45–50.

Tuma, J. M. (1989). Mental health services for children: the state of the art. *American Psychologist*, *44*(2), 188–199.

Turner, E. H., Matthews, A. M., Linardatos, E., Tell, R. A., & Rosenthal, R. (2008). Selective publication of antidepressant trials and its influence on apparent efficacy. *New England Journal of Medicine*, *358*, 252–260.

Tuschen-Caffier, B., Pook, M., & Frank, M. (2001). Evaluation of manual-based cognitive-behavioral therapy for bulimia nervosa in a service setting. *Behaviour Research and Therapy*, *39*(3), 299–308.

Tynan, W. D., Schuman, W., & Lampert, N. (1999). Concurrent parent and child therapy groups for externalizing disorders: from the laboratory to the world of managed care. *Cognitive and Behavioral Practice*, *6*(1), 3–9.

Ustun, T. B. & Sartorius, N. (2002). *Mental illness in general health care: An international study*. London: Wiley.

Vandecreek, L., Knapp, S., & Brace, K. (1990). Mandatory continuing-education for licensed psychologists — its rationale and current implementation. *Professional Psychology — Research and Practice*, *21*(2), 135–140.

Von Korff, M., Katon, W., Bush, T., Lin, E. H., Simon, G. E., Saunders, K., et al. (1998). Treatment costs, cost offset, and cost-effectiveness of collaborative management of depression. *Psychosomatic Medicine*, *60*, 143–149.

Wade, W. A., Treat, T. A., & Stuart, G. L. (1998). Transporting an empirically supported treatment for panic disorder to a service clinic setting: a benchmarking strategy. *Journal of Consulting and Clinical Psychology*, *66*(2), 231–239.

Walker, J., Vincent, N., Furer, P., Cox, B., & Kjernisted, K. (1999). Treatment preference in hypochondriasis. *Journal of Behavior Therapy and Experimental Psychiatry*, *30*, 251–258.

Walrath, C. M., Sheehan, A. K., Holden, E. W., Hernandez, M., & Blau, G. (2006). Evidence-based treatments in the field: A brief report on provider knowledge, implementation, and practice. *Journal of Behavioral Health Services and Research*, *33*(2), 244–253.

Waltz, J., Addis, M. E., Koerner, K., & Jacobson, N. S. (1993). Testing the integrity of a psychotherapy protocol: assessment of adherence and competence. *Journal of Consulting and Clinical Psychology*, *61*(4), 620–630.

Wang, P. S., Berglund, P., & Kessler, R. C. (2000). Recent care of common mental disorders in the United States: prevalence and conformance with evidence-based recommendations. *Journal of General Internal Medicine*, *15*(5), 284–292.

Wang, P. S., Berglund, P., Olfson, M., Pincus, H. A., Wells, K. B., & Kessler, R. C. (2005a). Failure and delay in initial treatment contact after first onset of mental disorders in the National Comorbidity Survey Replication. *Archives of General Psychiatry*, *62*(6), 603–613.

Wang, P. S., Lane, M., Olfson, M., Pincus, H. A., Wells, K. B., & Kessler, R. C. (2005b). Twelve-month use of mental health services in the United States: results from the National Comorbidity Survey Replication. *Archives of General Psychiatry*, *62*(6), 629–640.

Weersing, V. R. & Weiss, W. R. (2002). Community clinic treatment of depressed youth: benchmarking usual care against CBT clinical trials. *Journal of Consulting and Clinical Psychology*, *70*, 299–310.

Weisz, J. R., Chu, B. C., & Polo, A. J. (2004). Treatment dissemination and evidence-based practice: strengthening intervention through clinician-researcher collaboration. *Clinical Psychology: Science and Practice*, *11*(3), 300–307.

Weisz, J. R., Weiss, B., Alicke, M. D., & Klotz, M. L. (1987). Effectiveness of psychotherapy with children and adolescents: a meta-analysis for clinicians. *Journal of Consulting and Clinical Psychology*, *55*(4), 542–549.

Weisz, J. R., Weiss, B., Han, S. S., Granger, D. A., & Morton, T. (1995). Effects of psychotherapy with children and adolescents revisited: a meta-analysis of treatment outcome studies. *Psychological Bulletin, 117*(3), 450–468.

Westbrook, D. & Kirk, J. (2005). The clinical effectiveness of cognitive behaviour therapy: outcome for a large sample of adults treated in routine practice. *Behaviour Research and Therapy, 43*, 1243–1261.

Westen, D., Morrison, K., & Thompson-Brenner, H. (2004). The empirical status of empirically supported psychotherapies: assumptions, findings, and reporting in controlled clinical trials. *Psychological Bulletin, 130*, 631–663.

Westra, H. A. (2004). Managing resistance in cognitive behavioural therapy: application of motivational interviewing in mixed anxiety/depression. *Cognitive and Behavioral Therapy, 33*, 1–16.

Wierzbicki, M. & Pekarik, G. (1993). A meta-analysis of psychotherapy dropout. *Professional Psychology: Research and Practice, 24*, 190–195.

Williams, C. J. (2001). *Overcoming depression: a five areas approach*. London: Arnold.

Wilson, G. T. (1995). Empirically validated treatment as a basis for clinical practice: problems and prospects. In S. Hayes, V. M. Follette, R. M. Dawes, & K. E. Grady (Eds.), *Scientific standards of psychological practice: issues and recommendations*. Reno, NV: Context Press.

Wilson, G. T. (1996). Manual-based treatments: the clinical application of research findings. *Behaviour Research and Therapy, 34*(4), 295–314.

Wilson, G. T., Fairburn, C. C., & Agras, W. S. (1997). Cognitive-behavioral therapy for bulimia nervosa. In D. M. Garner & P. E. Garfinkel (Eds.), *Handbook of treatment for eating disorders* (2nd ed., pp. 67–93). New York: Guilford.

Wittchen, H.-U., Kessler, R. C., Beesdo, K., Krause, P., Höfler, M., & Hoyer, J. (2002). Generalized anxiety and depression in primary care: prevalence, recognition, and management. *Journal of Clinical Psychiatry, 63*(suppl. 8), 24–34.

Wyklicky, H. & Skopec, M. (1983). Ignaz Philipp Semmelweis, the prophet of bacteriology. *Infection Control, 4*(5), 367–370.

Zoellner, L. A., Feeny, N. C., Cochran, B., & Pruitt, L. (2003). Treatment choice for PTSD. *Behaviour Research and Therapy, 41*, 879–886.

CHAPTER

21

The Future of the Profession

Elaine M. Heiby
University of Hawaii at Manoa

Janet D. Latner
University of Hawaii at Manoa

OUTLINE

INTRODUCTION

This is a very exciting time for the future of professional psychology. Many issues have emerged that could lead to vast changes in the discipline. We will discuss six of these issues. The first three issues are controversial within the field. Two are controversial in part because they have been imposed upon the field by the leadership of psychology guild organizations (i.e., prescription privileges and participation in interrogation and torture). The third controversial issue reflects differing values among members of the profession regarding what guidelines should be used in selecting assessment and treatment approaches (i.e., evidence-based practice). Whether these controversial issues become established trends depends upon choices made by individual psychologists, including the readers of this textbook. The remaining three issues are not controversial and represent trends that have emerged from basic psychological science (i.e., giving psychology away, psychopathologizing natural behavior, and acknowledging the role of spirituality in human functioning). These trends are expected to be welcomed by the field and to naturally become part of training and practice.

PRESCRIPTION PRIVILEGES

One of the most significant questions facing the discipline of psychology is whether a transformation into a medical specialty would be a positive change for both science and practice. Clinical psychology is facing the possibility of a radical overhaul by becoming far more medical and far less psychological in nature.

Whether the field medicalizes in the form of expanding the scope of practice to include **prescription privileges** (also referred to as *RxP* or *PPP*) depends upon how many people choose to follow the American Psychological Association's (APA) policy to change state licensing laws (APA, 1996a). The APA policy to expand the practice of psychology by crossing boundaries with the field of invasive physical medicine has proven to be one of the most disputed in the history of the profession.

The prescription privileges issue has been divisive since the proposal was introduced in the mid-1980s (Fowler, 1996). Since then, whether to medicalize the field has continued to spur intensive debate (e.g., Albee, 2002; Barron, 1989; Bush, 2002; Caccavale, 2002; Cantor, 1991; DeLeon, 1990; DeLeon, Dunivin, & Newman, 2002; DeLeon & Wiggins, 1996; DeNelsky, 1996; Fox, 1988; Hayes & Heiby, 1998; Hayes, Walser, & Bach, 2002; Hayes, Walser, &

Follette, 1996; Heiby, 2002a, 2002b; Heiby, DeLeon, & Anderson, 2004; Jansen & Barron, 1988; Kingsbury, 1992; McFall, 2002; Norfleet, 2002; Piotrowski 1989–1990, Winter; Robiner et al., 2002; Sechrest & Coan, 2002; Stuart & Heiby, 2007; Weene, 2002).

What Is Controversial about Prescription Privileges?

There have been numerous reasons provided by proponents to medicalize psychology. The four major reasons for prescription privileges concern an acknowledgment of the popularity of psychoactive drugs, an assertion that the discipline of psychology is evolving to be more medical in nature, a claim that psychologists need less medical training than that required of other prescribing professions, and a prediction that medicalizing the field will not harm psychological science and practice (e.g., DeLeon & Wiggins, 1996). At the same time, each reason has been refuted by those who oppose prescription privileges (e.g., DeNelsky, 1996). A summary of four pro-con arguments is provided in Highlight Box 21.1, Should Psychology Medicalize? One of the most debated issues concerns the nature of medical training for prescription privileges. Some aspects of the context of this training issue are discussed in the following section.

Although the explicit reasons for prescription privileges have been subjected to debate, it has been argued that other contextual factors also have led the APA leadership to seek ways for psychologists to increase their share of the mental health services market. Hayes (1995) argued that the primary reason for seeking this expansion of the scope of practice is financial. He pointed out that capitated systems of health care have led to a revenue loss for clinical psychologists. He also indicated that the income of all prescribing professionals has also declined under managed care so that prescribing by psychologists would not address the cause of

HIGHLIGHT BOX 21.1

SHOULD PSYCHOLOGY MEDICALIZE?

Some of the issues commonly raised by those who introduced the prescription privileges debate are listed here. For each issue, a typical pro and con argument is provided.

Issue 1: Psychoactive Medications Are a Popular Form of Treatment

There is growing evidence that some psychoactive drugs attainable only by prescription can help some people cope with problems in living. Although these drugs are widely used, they usually are prescribed by nonpsychiatric physicians with little training in psychology or biological psychiatry.

PRO: There is a shortage of psychiatrists, particularly in rural areas. Psychologists are in a position to serve consumers without access to a psychiatrist. It is the societal duty of licensed psychologists to prescribe psychoactive drugs. Clinical psychologists would provide more effective services than any physician given their extensive training in basic and clinical psychology. Collaboration with physicians for a medication prescription impedes integrative care and increases expenses by requiring additional appointments.

CON: The evidence does not support a shortage of psychiatrists but does show a geographic maldistribution of all professionals, including psychologists. It is the ethical duty of licensed psychologists to be educated about psychopharmacology. When medication seems indicated, clinical psychologists currently are in the position to provide integrative services by collaboration with physicians and nurses. Collaboration has been shown to be common and deemed effective.

Issue 2: Medicalizing Psychology Is a Natural Process

Practicing medicine is an evolutionary extension of the discipline and profession of psychology.

PRO: The discipline of psychology includes subspecialties that overlap with the biological and life sciences, such as behavioral neuroscience and health psychology. Psychologists commonly collaborate with physicians regarding medication or other invasive procedures with humans and often do research and practice in medical settings. Other health professionals, such as nurses and optometrists, have obtained prescription privileges. Transformation of training and practice is being driven by commonalities with the allied medical professions. Most psychologists support obtaining prescription privileges.

CON: The overlap in subspecialties and collaboration between psychology and other disciplines are inherent to psychological science and practice. Psychology is not outmoded and is not driven to assimilate with medicine. If collaboration were sufficient to evolve an expansion of scope of practice, then psychologists would practice many other professions, such as law and veterinary medicine. Unlike psychology, the training of health professionals who prescribe is already medical in nature, and expansion of scope of practice was supported from within those fields. Surveys do not indicate that a majority of psychologists support prescription privileges.

Issue 3: Medical Training Requirements to Prescribe Are Minimal

The current training required to become a licensed psychologist uniquely prepares one to practice medicine in terms of prescription

---

HIGHLIGHT BOX 21.1   *(continued)*

---

authority. Clinical psychologists already have extensive training in the etiology, diagnosis, and treatment of mental disorders. Appropriate medical training for prescription privileges is far less than that required for other prescribing professions.

PRO: The adequacy of less medical training for psychologists to prescribe psychoactive medication has support. The U.S. Department of Defense's (DoD) demonstration project indicated that postdoctoral training that is similar to that required for nurses to prescribe is adequate for clinical psychologists. Some of the 10 graduates of the project are permitted to prescribe in the military. The APA carefully considered the DoD curriculum and concluded that only half of the amount of training required in the project is needed for clinical psychologists to independently prescribe psychoactive medications to the general population. That APA's training model involving less medical training than the DoD project is adequate is supported by the attainment of prescription privileges for licensed psychologists in the U.S. Territory of Guam and the states of New Mexico and Louisiana.

CON: What constitutes adequate training for clinical psychologists to practice medicine remains an empirical question. The evaluation of the DoD project does not apply to the APA training model, which involves half the amount of training. The APA model has not been implemented in any jurisdiction or evaluated for consumer safety and feasibility. The impact of the regulatory laws in Guam, New Mexico, and Louisiana awaits independent evaluation. Meanwhile, the standards of other prescribing professions and the training in the DoD project provide benchmarks. It is incumbent upon proponents of the APA model to demonstrate that the training protects the consumer and preserves the integrity of psychological science and practice.

Issue 4: Prescription Privileges Will Not Harm Psychology

Medical training for psychologists would not result in resources being allocated away from psychological science, training, and practice.

PRO: The APA medical training model will be inexpensive to implement. The medical training will be additional to what is currently required and will not lead to less training in psychology. Professional schools are well situated to offer the additional training at no cost to the taxpayer because the expenses will be covered by tuition. Psychologists who do prescribe will continue to provide psychological assessment and treatment as much as has been done in the past. Psychologists will often elect to not prescribe medication and will encourage some consumers to stop taking psychoactive medication prescribed by other providers who do not have training in assessment and psychotherapy.

CON: Implementation of medical training at traditional university-based departments of psychology would cost at least an additional $1 million per year. It is likely that these funds will not come from tuition or taxpayer money. Instead, funds will be obtained by replacing psychology faculty with physician faculty and by offering more courses in medicine and fewer in psychology. Psychiatrists abandoned psychotherapy not by choice but by necessity, given the risk and extensive continuing education involved in prescribing. There is no reason to think psychologists will be immune to the same changes. The cross-fertilization between psychological science and practice, which makes the profession distinctive, would quickly vanish.

reduced revenue. Hayes noted that managed health-care systems would readily reimburse empirically supported psychological services because they can be shown to be cost-effective. He concluded psychologists are well positioned to economically survive in a managed care environment if their services are justifiable.

Other contextual factors also have been suggested to help understand why APA is pursuing prescription privileges now even though psychoactive drugs have been available by prescription for over half a century. These other factors include an overreliance on psychotherapy as a way to make a living; an oversupply of doctoral-level clinical psychologists; and the influence of drug companies in broadening the sales of psychotropics (Hayes & Heiby, 1996). Some doctoral programs have focused on training in skills other than psychotherapy, such as program evaluation, integrative care, and supervision. To date, the APA has not attempted to stem the growth of doctoral programs, so the oversupply issue will most likely remain until market factors come into play. Pharmaceutical companies advertising drug use as a way to cope with problems in living remains an influence upon both consumers and providers. However, studies that support the use of psychotherapy alone or in combination with medication for a number of disorders (e.g., Otto, Smits, & Reese, 2005) may counter this influence if psychologists make this option known to the public. Meanwhile, the implications of training for psychologists to prescribe deserve close consideration.

Medical Training Implications

Early proposals for training by advocates of prescription privileges suggested that the training would be brief and comparable to a several-week course taken by a law school graduate preparing for a bar examination (Burns, DeLeon, Chemtob, Welch, & Samuels, 1988). Needless to say, such proposals evoked skepticism. Subsequently, APA organized committees to develop medical curricula. The suggested training approximated that required by allied medical professions with various levels of prescription authority in some states, such as advanced nurse practitioners (e.g., Smyer et al., 1993). APA leadership also prevailed on the U.S. Department of Defense (DoD) to conduct a demonstration project that involved training 10 psychologists in medicine and permitting supervised *prescription authority* at military facilities for patients who had been medically screened. The DoD project required 712 classroom hours and 1 year of full-time supervised practice at a medical hospital, and it permitted psychologists to prescribe only to medically screened adults who were 18 to 65 years old. An evaluation of the DoD project concluded that the graduates were weaker medically than psychiatric physicians, and all 10 graduates argued against proposals for a decreased amount of medical training (American College of Neuropsychopharmacology, 2000).

APA rejected the training recommendations of its committees and the curriculum and practice restrictions required in the DoD demonstration project. Instead, APA issued a reduced medical training model for adoption at either the graduate or postdoctoral level, including prerequisites in the natural and life sciences (APA, 1996b). The APA training model represents an experimental reduction in American standards for medical practice. The medical training in the model is less than half of that required for other prescribing professions, including physician assistants, advanced nurse practitioners, physicians, dentists, and optometrists (Sechrest & Coan, 2002). The APA's prerequisite and graduate or postdoctoral level coursework and practicum included in the medical training model are summarized in Highlight Box 21.2: APA Medical Training Model.

HIGHLIGHT BOX 21.2

APA MEDICAL TRAINING MODEL

The APA policy on medical training for prescription privileges for psychologists is described in a document entitled *Recommended Postdoctoral Training in Psychopharmacology for Prescription Privileges* (APA, 1996b). The Preamble states that the medical training model is designed for both graduate and postdoctoral programs.

Prerequisites for medical training include a planned sequence of didactic coursework (presumably at the undergraduate level) in anatomy, biochemistry, biology, neuroanatomy, physiology, and psychopharmacology, which is equivalent to about 18 semester hours or 288 classroom contact hours. Admission to model training programs involves passing a test of the knowledge covered in the prerequisite courses.

The graduate or postdoctoral medical training consists of about 19 semester hours of didactic coursework, or about 300 classroom contact hours. Courses included are clinical pharmacotherapeutics, neurosciences, pathophysiology, pharmacology, physical and laboratory assessment, physiology, and psychopharmacology.

There is also a practicum requirement, but the description of it in the medical training model is difficult to transform to semester credit or contact hour equivalents. The model specifies that the practicum training be supervised and consist of the trainee being responsible for the medical treatment of at least 100 people seen at both inpatient and outpatient settings.

At least seven programs designed to train psychologists to prescribe are advertised by the APA's Division 55 (American Society for the Advancement of Pharmacotherapy, 2007). Most of the training is offered online, and none of the programs require the prerequisite coursework or an admissions test mentioned in the APA model.

At present, there is no accrediting body for programs that offer training for prescription privileges for psychologists. In addition, there has been no evidence provided by APA that its training model is adequate or that it is being implemented in programs. Therefore, it would be wise for psychology students to consider these factors before embarking on a training program.

Impact on students

If traditional universities elect to add the APA training model (APA, 1996b) to the curriculum, the undergraduate psychology major could be expanded by up to an academic year in order to include typical premedical coursework along with prerequisites (e.g., anatomy, biochemistry, biology, neuroanatomy, physics, and physiology). Graduate or postdoctoral training for licensed clinical psychologists could be extended by 1 to 3 years to include didactic medical training and practicum. However, it has been speculated that most university-based departments of psychology would elect higher standards of training than in the APA model and instead institute requirements that are more similar to those in advanced nurse practitioner and medical schools (Heiby et al., 2004; Robiner et al., 2003).

If the APA medical training model (APA, 1996b) is adopted, the cost of the additional graduate training at a southern state university has been estimated to be at least $155,000 for students, assuming the student lives on $20,000 per year (Wagner, 2002). This estimated cost to the student does not include the additional costs involved in undergraduate premedical training or the higher tuition costs at private universities' graduate programs, including professional schools.

Who Objects to Prescription Privileges?

A consensus to medicalize the training and practice of clinical psychology was not developed before the pursuit of prescription privileges became APA policy. Unlike major past changes to the scope of the profession, such as the regulation of training and independent practice via licensure by state agencies, the pursuit of prescription privileges did not evolve from within the discipline or by members' representatives in the APA Council. Instead, Council rules that would have required a debate among and consultation with constituents were suspended in order for the policy to pass (DeNelsky, 1996).

A **meta-analysis** of opinion surveys (Walters, 2001) indicated that rank-and-file psychologists have been about evenly divided over whether training and practice should expand to include invasive medicine in the form of prescribing psychoactive drugs. Of those who do support this APA policy, only 1 in 20 indicates a desire to undergo the medical training and lifestyle changes required for prescription authority.

In addition to the majority of the rank-and-file psychologists not appearing to be enthusiastic about prescription privileges, various groups of organized psychology have gone on record in opposition (Heiby et al., 2004). The following five organizations publicly expressed objections to prescription privileges before their pursuit became APA policy: (1) the American Association of Applied and Preventive Psychology (AAAPP); (2) the Society for a Science of Clinical Psychology (SSCP); (3) the Council of University Directors of Clinical Programs (CUDCP); (4) the Council of Graduate Departments of Psychology (COGDOP); and (5) the Committee against Medicalizing Psychology

(CAMP). The members of these organizations include scientist-practitioners and those responsible for training psychologists at traditional universities.

Of the five listed organizations, four (i.e., AAAPP, SSCP, CUDCP, and CAMP) explicitly opposed APA policy (APA, 1996a) and encouraged psychologists who wish to prescribe to obtain the authority to do so through already established avenues, such as by obtaining degrees in nursing or medicine. The AAAPP and CAMP also have submitted testimony to state legislatures and governors in opposition of bills enabling prescription privileges. COGDOP'S position was that medical training should not be implemented until all university-based departments of psychology support doing so, which to date has not happened. Clearly, the history of professional psychology did not suggest or endorse prescription aspects until it became APA policy.

Organized opposition to medicalizing psychology obviously was not persuasive to APA leadership, which tried to suppress dissenting opinions. For example, the SSCP's position paper in opposition to APA's prescription privileges policy was removed from its Web site after pressure from the APA, ostensibly because SSCP is one of its divisions (along with being a freestanding organization) and internal dissent is forbidden (Fowles, 2005). However, the SSCP position paper is posted online by the Michigan Society for Psychoanalytic Psychology (2003). More recently, an organization independent of APA has been created to encourage open dialogue: Psychologists Opposed to Prescription Privileges for Psychologists (POPPP, 2007). POPPP also submits testimony to legislatures considering bills that would extend the scope of practice of psychologists to include prescription privileges.

The suppression of opposition to prescription privileges within APA is consistent with how the policy was adopted in the first place, that is, not by APA membership but by APA leadership bypassing their input (DeNelsky, 1996). APA leadership thus chose to take the debate over prescription privileges to the public arena of state legislatures, where psychology presents as a house divided when enabling bills are introduced. Legislators hear testimony from psychologists who support and who oppose prescription privileges. Therefore, it is not surprising that there has been a rocky road in the attempt to transform the profession by legislative fiat.

Progress in Obtaining Prescription Privileges

As of 2007, the U.S. Territory of Guam, the state of New Mexico, and the state of Louisiana have passed laws enabling licensed psychologists to prescribe psychoactive drugs under certain conditions. In each jurisdiction, the requisite training and/or restraints of practice exceed APA policy (APA, 1996a, 1996b).

In 1998, a prescription authority bill was passed in Guam when the legislature overrode the governor's veto. The law requires licensed psychologists to prescribe within a Collaborative Practice Agreement with a physician. No independent prescribing is permitted. Medical training presumably may be completed either before or after licensure. To our knowledge, no psychologist in Guam has obtained prescription authority, although such information is not posted online by the Guam Board of Allied Health Examiners (2007) or the National Register of Health Providers in Psychology (2007).

In 2002, New Mexico's prescription authority law was passed. Whether training takes place at the graduate or postdoctoral level is not specified in the law. New Mexico psychologists with a Conditional Prescription Certificate must work under the supervision of a physician for at least 2 years and then may apply for a Prescription Certificate for independent practice. According to the New Mexico Regulation and Licensing Department, 11 Conditional and three Prescription

Certificates have been issued (New Mexico Board of Psychological Examiners, personal communication, October 23, 2007).

In the 2004 Louisiana prescription authority law, the training must be postdoctoral and involve completion of a regionally accredited program offering a master's degree in clinical psychopharmacology. In addition, 30 medical continuing education credits must be completed annually. Similar to psychologists in Guam, Louisiana psychologists who obtain a Certificate of Prescriptive Authority forgo independent practice and are required to work in consultation with each client's primary physician. The Louisiana State Board of Examiners of Psychologists (2007) lists 45 **medical psychologists**, which is the title used to designate licensed psychologists with the authority to prescribe.

Whether other jurisdictions in the United States will pass enabling legislation is not clear. In response to the APA policy to change licensing laws (APA, 1996a), the state of New York's psychology licensing law was modified to explicitly prohibit prescribing drugs under any circumstances. Enabling bills have been introduced in several other state legislatures over the years but have not become law. Moreover, in 2006, an enabling bill passed by the legislature in Hawaii was vetoed by the governor, who indicated that the proposed medical training did not meet societal standards (Daly, 2007).

Obtaining prescription privileges is clearly an uphill battle with the profession presenting itself without a consensus at state legislatures. Therefore, it is not surprising that legislators have proven hesitant to embark on an experiment regarding a reduction in society's standards for medical training and to impose a transformation of a profession when its members do not fully support the change. Nevertheless, the supporters of prescription privileges remain dedicated to pursuing APA policy (APA, 1996a, 1996b). In 2008, it has been predicted that as many as 16 states will introduce enabling legislation (POPPP, 2007).

Conclusion

It has been more than 30 years since some of the leadership of the APA decided to medicalize psychology in the form of obtaining prescription privileges without the full support of rank-and-file psychologists. For this APA policy to progress, a consensus is needed. Faculty, internship directors, and students in psychology need to be drawn to the medical sciences and understand the significant and multiple risks incurred from the practice of physical medicine (Stuart & Heiby, 2007). The monetary investment in the medical training of psychologists must be deemed desirable to politicians, departments of health, regulatory agencies, consumers, faculty, students, and universities. Psychologists must testify in support of enabling bills at state legislatures and donate to the costs of lobbying. A consensus may be more likely to develop if a neutral party demonstrates that the training required in New Mexico and Louisiana provides consumer safety and does not allocate resources or attention away from psychological science and practice. Such evidence would provide a persuasive argument that social workers and other master's-level mental health providers also should be afforded prescription authority, eliminating any competitive edge for doctoral-level psychologists. Such evidence would also suggest that physician and nursing training are unnecessarily extensive. Given the strong degree to which current psychologists are ambivalent about APA policy (Walters, 2001), perhaps there will be a desire to medicalize psychology among future generations?

PSYCHOLOGISTS' PARTICIPATION IN INTERROGATION AND TORTURE

A major ethical question that is facing psychologists has emerged since the United States entered the second Gulf War in 2003. It became public knowledge in 2004 that American psychologists and physicians were participating in *interrogation* and *torture* techniques with some military prisoners and detainees held in Cuba, in Iraq, and possibly at other locations (Lewis, 2004). Military prisoners and detainees are not being protected by laws relevant to most U.S. civilians, such as evidence of having committed a crime and having the right to an attorney. They also are not being protected by International Human Rights Law and the Geneva Conventions (United Nations, n.d.). At least 200 articles on the ethics of health professionals' roles in interrogation and torture are posted online at http://kspope.com/interrogation/index.php (retrieved January 2, 2008), which speaks to the controversial nature of this type of involvement of psychologists in war.

Interrogation and torture techniques involve using psychological principles that were originally designed to enhance the quality of life by applying them so that they decrease the quality of life. Psychological interventions are used to punish individuals or to elicit information that presumably would support the war effort. These techniques involve creating physical discomfort (e.g., prolonged exposure to extreme cold, loud noises, and bright lights; being hooded; maintaining uncomfortable positions for long periods of time; manhandling; causing sleep deprivation; and near drowning or waterboarding). These techniques also involve inducing psychological discomfort (e.g., exposure to a phobic stimulus; comments designed to create feelings of impotence and humiliation; and induced disorientation to time, person, and place). More information on these techniques and their damaging physical and psychological effects is available from Physicians for Human Rights (2007).

Concerned psychologists and the media quickly questioned the humanity and ethics of health professionals' participation in any aspect of interrogation and torture (e.g., Allhoff, 2006; Annas, 2005; DeClue, 2006). In addition, the

World Medical Association (2003), the American Medical Association (2006), the American Psychiatric Association (2006), and the American Academy of Psychiatry and the Law (2006) explicitly prohibited any involvement whatsoever by physicians in the development or implementation of such techniques.

In sharp contrast to an all-out prohibition of physician involvement in interrogation and torture by medical organizations, the APA created a Task Force and issued a report on Psychological Ethics and National Security (PENS, 2005) to study the issue. The PENS report provides circumstances under which it is ethical for psychologists to participate in interrogation and torture, such as when a psychologist deems participation to be in the nation's interest or to have a humanitarian oversight function. The APA report led to a public outcry with commentaries in the media harshly criticizing psychology for being the only profession endorsing its members deliberately harming prisoners and detainees (e.g., Eban, 2007; Soldz, 2006). Some members of APA also demanded their organization take a zero tolerance position, but these demands were ignored until they reached the level of a public protest at the 2007 APA convention (Zeller, 2007). At that time, the organization Psychologists for an Ethical APA (2007) passed a resolution for the APA to join other health professional organizations by explicitly prohibiting all dehumanizing practices that are deemed not only unethical but in violation of the United Nation's International Human Rights Law and the Geneva Conventions. The APA's Division 19 (Society of Military Psychology) also called for a moratorium on psychologist involvement in interrogation and torture (2007). These groups basically argued that psychologists should do no harm under any circumstance.

In reaction to criticism from its members and the media, the Council of Representatives issued an *APA Resolution against Torture and* *Other Cruel, Inhuman, or Degrading Treatment or Punishment and Its Application to Individuals Defined in the United States Code as Enemy Combatants* (2007). The APA resolution modified its prior blanket endorsement of psychologists' use of interrogation and torture techniques. Instead, the resolution contains qualifiers that seem to permit psychologists to develop these techniques, train others to implement them, monitor their implementation, and evaluate their **effectiveness**.

Psychologists for an Ethical APA (2007) issued a detailed critique of the nonbinding resolution, objecting that it still condones psychologists deliberately harming vulnerable people rather than promoting human welfare. The qualifiers seem to permit psychologists to directly conduct some techniques under some circumstances, but not others. For example, psychologists apparently can conduct these techniques immediately before an interrogation but not during the interrogation. Therefore, psychologists may use torture techniques to prepare a detainee to be interrogated. They also may conduct these techniques as long as they do not inflict "significant" pain or suffering. However, "significant" is not defined and is of course not always immediately obvious. In addition, the resolution speaks to only 19 widely known interrogation and torture techniques and does not address those that are classified.

The APA's resolution was not lauded by other psychologists or the public (e.g., American Civil Liberties Union, 2007; Gill, 2007; Zimbardo, 2007). Psychologists for an Ethical APA (2007) have continued to demand the APA take a clear and comprehensive stance that its objectives are to advance a science and profession that promote human health and welfare, which, in and of itself, forbids interrogation and torture of any kind (Glenn, 2007). Several hundred members of APA have pledged to withhold their dues or resign from the organization because of its explicit endorsement of psychologists' participation in interrogation and torture techniques (http://www.withholdapadues.com/currentpledges.html, retrieved January 3, 2008).

Now that the APA is the only professional association that permits, with some caveats, its members' involvement in interrogation and torture techniques, a job market for psychologists certainly has been secured and future positions created. Psychologists understandably are under high demand by government military agencies and private contractors to do jobs formerly done by physicians who now refuse to do them on ethical grounds. Will psychologists continue to accept these jobs? Will the APA continue to deem involvement in interrogation and torture techniques under certain circumstances as ethical? Will psychology lose its reputation as a discipline and profession dedicated to the promotion of human welfare? Clearly, the reputation of the profession has been harmed in the eyes of the public (Horton, 2007). What direction APA takes regarding involvement in interrogation and torture techniques depends on the moral standards demanded by psychologists themselves. Regardless of the APA's future position on perpetuating torture, clinical psychologists must be prepared to treat the victims of torture, and fortunately this need has been anticipated (Pope & Garcia-Peltoniemi, 1991).

EVIDENCE-BASED PRACTICE

The trend toward comprehensive evidence-based practice in clinical psychology is reflected within several chapters of this book. However, the field's movement toward evidence-based practice has been fraught with controversy and debate (e.g., Norcross, Beutler, & Levant, 2005). Consensus does not yet exist on what constitutes evidence or whether and how evidence should guide care. There is also debate as to what direction the field of clinical

psychology should take in order to advance the evidence base guiding practice.

In 1993, APA's Division 12 (Clinical Psychology) organized a Task Force on the Promotion and Dissemination of Psychological Procedures. Its charge was to develop criteria for judging empirical evaluations of psychological treatments and make recommendations about how to educate psychologists, the public, and mental health service payers about these treatments. It initially identified criteria for evaluating treatments, a short list of treatments that met criteria for being "well-established" or "probably efficacious," and a list of recommendations for disseminating this material. The task force determined several important standards for judging whether treatments had been adequately tested in well-designed and -conducted clinical trials: control/comparison groups, manualized treatments, clearly specified client samples, and independent replication. In addition to randomized controlled trials (RCTs), well-conducted single-case experimental designs using control conditions were also recognized within this framework (Chambless & Hollon, 1998).

These criteria laid out by the task force resulted in the compilation of lists of empirically supported treatments (ESTs). In 1995, 18 treatments were listed as well established and 7 as probably efficacious. In 1998, 16 treatments were listed as well established and 56 treatments as probably efficacious (Chambless et al., 1996, 1998).

What Is Controversial about the EST Movement?

The task force's lists generated an enormous outcry and outrage from the field. Many practitioners expressed concern about whether these lists were final and complete, about the neglect of clinical experience and the prioritization of research findings instead, and about what was viewed as the list's implication that a lack of empirical support for a treatment implied an established lack of **efficacy**. Were widely used treatments not included on the list being blacklisted? And was the list going to guide managed care organizations' decisions about payment for psychological services?

Perhaps the most common criticism leveled at the EST movement concerned the methods of treatment research (Chambless & Ollendick, 2001). Questions were raised as to whether the research methods uniquely privileged cognitive-behavioral therapy and whether they were prohibitive for psychodynamic treatments. Indeed, an examination of 61 of the treatments identified as ESTs demonstrated that 85% of these treatments focus on skill building (rather than insight), 77% involve continuous assessment to monitor client progress, 90% are problem focused, 80% had fewer than 20 sessions, and 85% considered homework essential, while 54% viewed the therapy relationship as a key mechanism of change (O'Donohue, Buchanan, & Fisher, 2000). However, it has been argued that high-quality research methods can be applied to longer-term or more insight-based treatments and that it is the responsibility of the practitioners of such treatments to manualize them and test their efficacy (as has been done with certain long-term treatments, such as dialectical behavior therapy; Linehan, Armstrong, Suarez, Allmon, & Heard, 1991).

Treatments studied in RCTs have also been accused of having limited generalizability to typical clinic patients, where severity and **comorbidity** are thought to be the norm (Westen, Novotny, & Thompson-Brenner, 2004). In contrast, recent studies of actual clinic cases have shown that a large proportion of patients would qualify for at least one RCT from among a series of published trials conducted on 10 common mental disorders (Stirman, DeRubeis, Crits-Christoph, & Brody, 2003). Similarly, a meta-analysis of psychotherapy effectiveness found

robustly effective outcomes for treatments that varied across a wide range of carefully coded measures of clinical representativeness (Shadish, Matt, Navarro, & Phillips, 2000). Indeed, cases may often be excluded from RCTs for not meeting full severity criteria for a given disorder (Crits-Christoph, Wilson, & Hollon, 2005) or for having disorders that have not yet been studied in clinical trials. For example, many clinic cases are given a diagnosis of adjustment disorder (Stirman et al., 2003), which might be used as a catch-all diagnosis by practitioners, yet not a single RCT has examined the efficacy of treatment for this particular disorder.

Critics have charged that RCTs use not only artificially pure patient samples but also arbitrarily limited treatments, such as interpersonal therapy for bulimia nervosa that prohibits discussion of eating behaviors (Persons & Silberschatz, 1998; Westen et al., 2004). The use of treatment manuals has been severely criticized as limiting therapists' creativity, freedom, and ability to individually tailor treatment (Addis, Wade, & Hatgis, 1999). Defenders of manuals, on the other hand, argue that flexibility and individual tailoring are necessary for administering manualized treatment well, as is building rapport with clients in order to facilitate change (Wilson, 1998). In addition, manuals have been recommended for clinical practice outside of research. Defenders explain that treatment manuals can be helpful learning tools in clinical training (Dobson & Shaw, 1988), as well as essential tools to ensure that key ingredients of treatment are not neglected (Wilson, 1998), as may happen in ideographic treatment approaches (e.g., Schulte, Kunzel, Pepping, & Schulte-Bahrenberg, 1992).

In addition to criticism of the methods of RCTs, their results have often been questioned. Proponents of the **"dodo-bird"** hypothesis (a term derived from the story of Alice in Wonderland, in which the dodo-bird pronounces following a race that "Everybody has won, and all must have prizes!") suggest that when the results of many RCTs across different disorders are analyzed together, there is no systematic evidence for differential effects across different treatments. It is argued that where minor differences between treatments do exist, they trend in different directions across different studies, and they can be explained by the researchers' allegiance to their particular favorite treatments (Luborsky et al., 1999, 2002). Other experts contend that for some disorders, such as panic disorder, post-traumatic stress disorder, eating disorders, and others, significantly better outcomes have been shown for ESTs tested against credible alternative treatments (Chambless & Ollendick, 2001). Furthermore, specific treatment procedures have been identified that significantly improve the efficacy of treatment, arguing against the point that *nonspecific* factors account for most of the variance (Lohr, Olatunji, Parker, & DeMaio, 2005).

It has also been argued that most of the differences across treatments can be predicted by the quality of the therapeutic relationship or alliance (Horvath, 2001; Lambert & Barley, 2001) and that the method of treatment adds very little variance to differences in outcomes. In fact, another Task Force on Empirically Supported Therapy Relationships was created by APA's Division 29 (Psychotherapy) to identify important aspects of therapy relationships that have been researched (Norcross, 2001). Therapy alliance is indeed essential and one of the best predictors of treatment outcome. The majority of EST creators regard it as a key mechanism of change (O'Donohue et al., 2000). Because of the nature of the research on therapeutic alliance, many of the findings on the relationship between therapeutic alliance and treatment outcome are correlational. Thus, if there is a causal relationship, the direction is not clear. Further, both alliance and outcome could be the result of another unidentified factor (DeRubeis, Brotman, & Gibbons, 2005). Although such research would be difficult and

unusual, studies that experimentally manipulate the therapist-client relationship would help to determine its causal effect on treatment outcome. Indeed, the success of many self-help interventions, discussed later, may call into question the necessity of having any therapeutic relationship at all in order for change to take place.

Another important criticism of RCTs is that researchers may not be using sufficiently meaningful outcome measures, measures that assess actual improvements in quality of life and functioning across areas that matter most to clients, in addition to symptom improvement (Kazdin, 1999, 2006). More work is needed to validate our outcome measures by assessing their true clinical significance.

Finally, perhaps the most crucial criticism of RCTs and the EST movement is that clinicians are simply not interested in its findings. It has been argued that, rather than treatment outcome, what actually matters most to practicing psychotherapists is the process of change in treatment, the role of the psychologist, and the subjective client experience (Persons & Silberschatz, 1998; Wampold & Bhati, 2004). However, it can also be argued that it is the obligation of the field to disseminate important findings about the efficacy of psychotherapy both to practitioners and to the public. Seven major concerns about evidence-based practice are listed in Highlight Box 21.3. As Barlow (2004) has suggested, if the field of clinical psychology had the budget of pharmaceutical companies, we would surely be launching million-dollar advertising campaigns to promote knowledge about and utilization of the effective psychotherapies that are now available.

Impact of the Movement

Although there is no evidence as yet that any managed care entity has utilized the task force listings to certify or deny payments for psychotherapy, the EST movement has had other

HIGHLIGHT BOX 21.3

CRITIQUES AND DEFENSES OF ESTs

Domain	Critique	Defense
Treatments studied	RCTs necessitate the study of short-term skill-based treatment	Experimental methods can and should be applied to longer treatments
Generalizability	Research isn't generalizable to real clinic cases	Most clinic cases qualify for RCTs
Treatment manuals	Manuals used in RCTs worsen the quality of therapy	Manuals improve treatment adherence and outcome
Dodo-bird hypothesis	There is no evidence for different outcomes across treatments	For certain disorders there is clear evidence of different outcomes
Common factors/alliance	Common factors/therapy alliance explain outcome	Alliance is important in ESTs, but most research on it is correlational
Clinically significant outcomes	RCTs do not measure meaningful change	Measures can and should be validated to reflect key life domains
Lack of broad interest	Practicing clinicians aren't interested in research results	It is our job to get clinicians interested through effective dissemination strategies

far-reaching effects. Consequences of this project have included the publication of numerous books and guidelines for safe and efficacious practice. These included multiple editions of *A Guide to Treatments That Work* (Nathan & Gorman, 2002, 2007) in the United States, which extended from the Division 12 Task Force and broadened in scope to include medical as well as psychological treatments, and *What Works for Whom? A Critical Review of Psychotherapy Research* (Roth & Fonagy, 1996, 2004) in the United Kingdom, based on a report originally commissioned by the National Health Service for use in their strategic policy review of psychotherapy services. APA accreditation now includes a guideline that graduate and internship training programs in clinical psychology must include training in ESTs (http://

www.apa.org/ed/G&P2.pdf, retrieved January 6, 2008); however, the extent and format of this training have not been specified. The Council of University Directors of Clinical Psychology Programs has also encouraged training in ESTs (http://www.am.org/cudcp/Reports/combined%20reports%20on%20competence10-02b3.pdf, retrieved January 6, 2008). Other countries, including Canada and Australia, have created task forces and have placed a similar emphasis on EST (Andrews, 2000).

Extensive guidelines for evidence-based practice have also recently emerged. The U.S. Agency for Health Care Policy and Research (which is part of the Department of Health and Human Services) has compiled extensive clinical practice guidelines (http://www.guideline.gov/, retrieved January 6, 2008), as has the Cochrane collection of research reviews (www.cochrane.org, retrieved January 6, 2008). Similarly, the U.K.'s National Health Service launched the National Institute for Clinical Excellence (NICE) in 2000. This set of guidelines provides especially thorough evidence-based clinical practice guidelines for mental and physical health disorders (www.nice.org.uk, retrieved January 6, 2008). The American Psychiatric Association has also produced a set of practice guidelines for a selection of mental disorders (http://www.psych.org/psych_pract/treatg/pg/prac_guide.cfm, retrieved January 6, 2008).

Despite the amount of research and effort that has gone into the creation of these guidelines, much more work needs to be conducted to successfully implement them (Andrews, 2000). It has been argued that the existence of such guidelines confers a definite responsibility on clinicians: "In effect, these documents set standards of care, which if ignored, leave the clinician both ethically and legally vulnerable" (Sanderson, 2003, p. 293). At the same time, critics of ESTs also make important arguments, as discussed earlier, that the field should not rush to implement practice guidelines based on ESTs, given the problems with generalizability and outcome methods identified in the treatment outcome literature (e.g., Westen et al., 2004).

For ethical and legal reasons, current trends in the fields of both adult and child psychological treatments have recognized the importance of effectiveness research. Research on the feasibility and effectiveness of evidence-based practices in real-world settings is essential in determining their widespread applicability and utility. Emerging literature on the generalizability of treatments to clinical practice settings suggests that they can be taught and practiced effectively, though significant challenges need to be overcome in doing so (Kazdin, 2004; Nathan, Stuart, & Dolan, 2000).

In addition to concerns about the generalizability of ESTs to actual practice settings, critics have also charged that findings on ESTs may not generalize to clients from a range of ethnic groups. As the majority of participants in RCTs have been Caucasian, ESTs have been labeled as culturally sensitive treatments for Caucasians (Hall, 2001). Many culturally sensitive treatments for other ethnic populations still need to be further developed and tested. Ideally, such treatments retain the major ingredients of original treatments but are tailored to also include important considerations for specific minority populations. An emerging literature on such treatments suggests the efficacy of ESTs across cultures, especially among African American and Latino populations in the areas of adult and childhood depression, childhood anxiety, ADHD, and disruptive disorders (Miranda et al., 2005). In applying treatment research both to real-world clinical settings and to the development of culturally sensitive treatments, emerging research suggests that retaining the key active ingredients of ESTs (e.g., exposure, behavioral activation) is crucial for good results across settings and across cultures.

The APA, through a new 2005 Presidential Task Force on Evidence-Based Practice (2006), has published its own definition of evidence-based practice in psychology. Building on a previous definition by the Institute of Medicine, the APA definition takes into account all the different factors that might influence clinical decision making: "Evidence-based practice in psychology (EBPP) is the integration of the best available research with clinical expertise in the context of patient characteristics, culture, and preferences" (p. 273). The APA definition, by refraining from prioritizing research, clinical judgment, or client preferences, appears to be an attempt to please all parties by homogenizing all opinions in the controversy discussed earlier. Indeed, this new task force was made up of many of the outspoken critics and defenders on both sides of the aisle. As a result, it seems likely that most psychologists will find at least some aspects of this definition to be consistent with their existing beliefs and practices. Therefore, it seems likely that it will have little impact on changing or improving the quality of care.

GIVING PSYCHOLOGY AWAY

In 1994, Christensen and Jacobson challenged the field of psychology to "give psychology away." They argued it was likely that

> the psychology that is given away (or at least sold much less expensively) through paraprofessional, self-administered, and mutual-support group treatment may be as effective for some problems as the professional psychology that is sold . . . The current prevalence of psychological disorder [sic] and the available resources to provide treatment suggest that if psychology is not given away, most people in need will not get it, because they cannot afford it. (p. 13)

A major research movement in the field of clinical psychology has developed to demonstrate that self-help is feasible, effective, and comparable to professionally administered treatment. Moreover, newer methods and technologies have sprung up in the past decade to provide even more options for giving psychology away to even greater numbers of consumers.

Benefits of Utilizing and Disseminating Self-help

Self-help may confer several advantages over professionally administered care. A major argument for self-help, as just described (Christensen & Jacobson, 1994), is its affordability and feasibility given the number of people with psychological and behavioral problems and the limited number of professionals available

to treat them. Another potential advantage of self-help is its potential for dissemination. Eliminating or reducing the role of specialist professionals removes a major barrier to the widespread adoption of effective psychological treatments.

In addition, self-help interventions may be viewed by consumers as relatively acceptable. The reasons consumers may prefer self-help include its ease and rapidity of access, lack of stigma and embarrassment, and not wanting a mental health record. Given the recent proliferation of DSM disorders and the tendency to label even common behavioral problems as mental illnesses (discussed later), it is understandable that individuals with circumscribed concerns who may be functioning well in other areas would prefer not to be associated with the mental health system. For similar reasons, self-administered programs have particular promise in the area of prevention (Jorm & Griffiths, 2005; McKendree-Smith, Floyd, & Scogin, 2003). By being made available at earlier stages in the etiology of potential disorders, self-help has the potential to steer individuals toward healthier outcomes rather than developing clinical disorders (Papworth, 2006). The hypothesized psychological advantages of self-help, such as reducing stigma, enhancing self-efficacy, and capitalizing on psychological mindedness, need to be tested in future empirical studies.

Efficacy of Self-help

Several comprehensive reviews have examined the efficacy of self-help interventions (Cavanagh & Shapiro, 2004; Den Boer, Wiersma, & Van Den Bosch, 2004; Jorm & Griffiths, 2005; Kaltenthaler, Parry, & Beverley, 2004; Mains & Scogin, 2003; McKendree-Smith et al., 2003; Papworth, 2006; Rochlen, Zack, & Speyer, 2004). These reviews have generally concluded that for many psychological problems (e.g., depression, anxiety, eating disorders, and others) evidence supports the superiority of self-help treatments to no treatment, waitlist control conditions, or "usual care." The forms of self-help treatments examined have included bibliotherapy, computer- or Internet-based programs, guided self-help, and, to a lesser extent, support groups.

Evidence is more limited concerning whether self-help treatments demonstrate "equivalence" with professionally administered treatments, or even superiority to high-quality, credible control conditions. However, a growing literature of well-designed RCTs in this area is beginning to demonstrate such equivalence (Christensen, Griffiths, & Jorm, 2004; Kenardy et al., 2003; Lidren et al., 1994). An important question in demonstrating the effectiveness of self-help is whether such treatments need to be demonstrated as having as great an impact as professionally administered care. Considering their potential for much more widespread dissemination and lower cost, such treatments might be more cost-effective and have an important population-wide impact even if they proved less efficacious at the individual level than professionally led treatments. However, encouraging research so far suggests that this compromise may not be necessary.

Similar to the guidelines for evidence-based practice compiled by expert reviewers (discussed earlier), certain self-help treatments have been recently reviewed and recommended by expert panels. Specific computerized treatment packages have been recommended by the NICE clinical guidelines (Mayor, 2006). In addition, a review of the most popular self-help books was conducted by a group of clinical psychologists who ranked these books according to ratings of quality (Redding, Herbert, Forman, & Gaudiano, in press). Highly rated books were characterized as (1) being grounded in psychological science, (2) focusing on a limited range of problems, (3) providing clear, specific guidelines for implementing the self-help techniques and monitoring progress, (4) addressing issues related to differential diagnosis, ongoing self-assessment, relapse prevention, and when to seek professional help, and (5) providing realistic expectations about outcome with recommended use. Several best-selling books for anxiety disorders (e.g., *The OCD Workbook*, Hyman & Pedrick, 1999) and mood disorders (e.g., *Feeling Good*, Burns, 1999) were given top ratings (Redding et al., in press).

Applications and Future Directions

Numerous important areas remain for future research to test the acceptability, equivalence, and cost-effectiveness of self-help. With new technologies emerging continually, even computerized and televised interventions may soon give way to newer forms of administration, such as handheld devices with text messaging or instant messaging. Research is needed to create treatment programs that are well suited to the preferences of consumers of all ages and levels of computer literacy. Other creative forms of administration may capitalize on consumers' already existing support networks, such as disseminating self-help manuals through primary care physicians (e.g., Naylor, Antonuccio, Johnson, Spogen, & O'Donohue, 2007) or through parents of children with problems (e.g., Rapee, Abbott, & Lyneham, 2006). Further research is also needed on the use of preventive self-help (e.g., Stice, Burton, Bearman, & Rohde, 2006).

Self-help plays a natural role in stepped-care treatment programs (Bower & Gilbody, 2005). The ethical basis for stepped care emphasizes beginning with the least intrusive treatment possible: "What stepped care does is make explicit the professional and perhaps also the moral applicability of the least restrictive alternative principle to noninstitutional treatment settings" (Davison, 2000, p. 583). For matching consumers to the appropriate initial step of care, it will be important for further research to identify predictors of positive response to self-help (e.g., motivation, self-efficacy, severity). People with more favorable attitudes about self-help were shown to have better attitudes toward reading and stronger self-control orientation and to be more psychologically minded and more satisfied with their lives (Wilson & Cash, 2000).

In addition to stepped-care programs, the process of giving psychology away will be important in the movement toward the integration of psychological care into primary care settings. Psychologists in medical settings often work within a stepped-care framework and must match the individual's treatment needs to the most cost-effective level of treatment (O'Donohue & Cucciare, 2005). The first step often involves minimal care materials such as bibliotherapy or other informational interventions. In a description of the implementation of an integrative care program that effectively administers clinical psychology care into primary care settings, James (2006) has described the brief intervention model used by practitioners. The advantages of integrated service include the treatment of all of the person's health needs at one setting and throughout the life span. Therefore, practitioners provide a form of brief guided self-help for psychological problems: two to three 30-minute sessions in which the psychologist builds on the patient's strengths and offers self-help reading materials, videos, and homework (e.g., reading Burns's *Feeling Good* [1999] and exercising daily), combined with brief cognitive-behavioral therapeutic strategies.

Another unique feature of integrated behavioral health care is that within primary health care settings, it is possible to intervene earlier in the developments of psychopathology. Thus, the patient is less likely to require a full course of professionally led treatment (James, 2006). A recent study by Naylor and colleagues used a **single-case experimental design** to examine the efficacy of using bibliotherapy with depressed patients in a primary care setting (2007). Self-

help books (Burns, 1999) were prescribed by family physicians with little or no mental health training. This study demonstrated that depression decreased following bibliotherapy and that much of this change was maintained at a 3-month follow-up, indicating the feasibility of self-help within integrative care settings.

Relative to the established efficacy of bibliotherapy, there is very little research on self-help groups (Den Boer et al., 2004; Hogan, Linden, & Najarian, 2004). Such research is needed, especially studies comparing group to individual self-help. It is likely that the processes of ongoing group support, public commitments, and role modeling available through groups can improve the effectiveness of treatment (Latner, Stunkard, Wilson, & Jackson, 2006; Latner & Wilson, 2007). The exchange of emotional support, including giving and receiving positive reinforcement, disclosing experiences and empathizing with experiences of others, offering and receiving feedback, and having a supportive network in times of crisis, may be a powerful factor in bolstering confidence and instilling hope (Solomon, 2004).

Studies on self-help also need to routinely include cost-effectiveness analyses, which are often omitted (Barlow, Ellard, Hainsworth, Jones, & Fisher, 2005; Bower, Richards, & Lovell, 2001). And as with any well-designed clinical trials, high standards need to be maintained, with regular adherence/compliance checks conducted; these too are often omitted (Newman, Erickson, Przeworski, & Dzus, 2003). Conflicting research suggests attrition and compliance may be a problem with the self-help approach (Bower et al., 2001; Cuijpers, 1997; Glasgow & Rosen, 1979) and may need to be better prevented in future studies. This is especially crucial given that studies with higher compliance rates have a mean effect size over three times greater than those with the low compliance rates (Gould & Clum, 1993). As discussed earlier in reference to RCTs, research on self-help should utilize outcome measures that reflect clinical significance (e.g., quality of life, subjective well-being, and general functioning) in addition to symptomatic improvement. It is also critical for advocates of self-help to be aware of when psychological problems require professional care so that individuals can receive the level of help they need.

PSYCHOPATHOLOGIZING NATURAL BEHAVIOR

Who will be the consumers of psychological services in the future? Everyone? What types of behaviors will be deemed problems in living that require professional treatment as opposed to natural healthy reactions to challenging life events, such as transient danger and loss? As examples, when is fear an anxiety disorder, and when is sadness a major depressive disorder? What criteria distinguish normal or natural behavior from abnormal or unnatural behavior?

If the number of mental disorders listed in taxonomies published by the American Psychiatric Association is any indicator, most, if not all, people will soon be deemed to be exhibiting psychopathology. Editions of the *Diagnostic and Statistical Manual of Mental Disorders* (DSM) continue to list an escalating number of mental disorders, with only 26 diagnoses from 1940 through 1979 but well over 400 diagnoses since 1980, including the DSM-IV published in 2000 (American Psychiatric Association, 2000). Some current diagnoses in the DSM-IV cover a large sector of people worldwide.

Failure to take into account base rates of a behavior in a population can lead to inflating prevalence of mental disorders. Here are four examples of diagnoses in the DSM-IV (APA, 2000) that can pathologize common behaviors. First, caffeine intoxication is a mental disorder according to the DSM-IV. It has been estimated that in the United States alone, 80% of people regularly consume caffeine in a variety of products (Juliano & Griffiths, 2001). Do people who routinely enjoy these mild stimulants have a mental disorder despite a lack of evidence of distress or dysfunction (DeGrandpre, 2006)? Second, the DSM-IV diagnosis premenstrual dysphoric disorder includes most women during their reproductive years if they experience statistically typical symptoms prior to their menstrual period, such as bloating and breast tenderness (Caplan, 1995). Third, there is the all-encompassing diagnostic category of conditions that are not otherwise specified, so that many life experiences can receive the label of being a mental disorder. Finally, while the DSM-IV ostensibly uses the criteria of distress and dysfunction to define a mental disorder, individuals with some diagnoses, such as schizoid personality disorder, often do not experience either distress or dysfunction.

Mental disorders are included in the DSM based upon committee recommendations to the 25 members on the Council of Representatives of the American Psychiatric Association. The council then votes on whether to deem a cluster of behaviors as abnormal. Votes are highly subject to personal opinions (Caplan, 1995). Moreover, Kirk and Kutchins (1992) argued that these personal opinions are affected more by financial gain than by objective scientific criteria that a syndrome is reliably identifiable and a valid marker of serious problems in living. If the next edition of the DSM continues this trend of adding mental disorders, then the potential market for psychological services is bound to rapidly escalate. Yet what impact will this trend have on people's self-image and self-reliance?

The American Psychiatric Association's taxonomies of mental disorders are not the only factors influencing what behavior is deemed psychopathological. Pharmaceutical companies also seem to "discover" mental disorders fitting their psychoactive drug products (Conrad, 2007). For example, when one drug was found to elicit garrulousness, being introverted or shy was declared in advertisements for this medication to be a "brain disease," even though no biological deficit has been associated with introversion (Lane, 2007). Similarly, feeling sad without considering the context or duration of the dysphoria is regularly touted in advertisements as being an abnormal brain condition that can be cured with a medication (Horowitz & Wakefield, 2007). Therefore, consumers of these advertisements are getting messages that it is not natural to prefer solitary activities or feel grief after a loss.

Whether everyone becomes a potential client for professional psychologists depends on whether psychologists blindly embrace what is deemed psychopathological by the American Psychiatric Association, the APA, and pharmaceutical companies that market psychoactive drugs. Although the monetary incentive to build a customer base is obvious, some psychologists and psychiatrists are troubled about the trend to view what used to be considered normal behavior as being abnormal (e.g., Caplan, 1995; Horowitz, 2002; Horowitz & Wakefield, 2007; Kirk & Kutchins, 1992). It is up to psychologists to decide when to impart information to potential clients that their behavior does not indicate a mental disorder if there is no serious distress or dysfunction. If the only source of distress is a negative self-evaluation based on advertisements from drug companies or knowledge of the current psychiatric taxonomy, then let us hope that future psychologists will take it upon themselves to help normalize some experiences (i.e., differentiate between healthy, natural, adaptive behaviors and exaggerated distortions of healthy functioning). Psychologists are encouraged to be skeptical of diagnoses included in editions of the DSM and to consider evidence of reliability and validity of each diagnosis. Evaluating mental disorders would be far easier if psychologists developed a taxonomy of normal or natural behaviors that can be discriminated from those deemed psychopathological.

SPIRITUALITY IN HUMAN FUNCTIONING

As psychology has become more of an international discipline, both research and practice have become more attentive to the diverse nature of human experiences and how they are categorized within and across cultures. One diversity factor of growing focus is the role of **spirituality** in maintaining a state of well-being (e.g., Bergin, 1991; Brawer, Handal, Fabricatore, Roberts, & Wajda-Johnston, 2002; Brown, 2005; Ellison, 1991; Fabricatore, Handal, & Fenzel, 2000; Hathaway, Scott, & Garver, 2004; Hill & Pargament, 2003; Leshner, 2005; Smith & Richards, 2005). Spiritual factors as used in the professional psychology literature include beliefs, feelings, practices, and phenomenology regarding **incorporeality** and theism. These factors may derive from either organized religion or individual spiritual frameworks and private spiritual practices.

Greater professional attention to spiritual factors is needed. This attention is likely to be welcomed by consumers of psychological services who believe humans have a soul or consciousness that extends beyond the physical body. For example, a Harris Poll (2003) of 2,201 adults in the United States indicated that 90% are monotheistic and more than 80% believe in an eternal soul, miracles, and heaven. A belief in a discarnate creator is often accompanied by other scientifically unverified beliefs, such as psychic and spiritual energy, an unobstructed universe, reincarnation, and impingement from angels or spiritual guides.

By acknowledging that spiritual behaviors and beliefs are common or universal, the practicing psychologist would need to discriminate psychotic and dissociative symptoms from spiritual experiences and, in so doing, may need to obviate standard definitions of psychopathology (O'Connor & Vandenberg, 2005). Assessment devices and treatment approaches may be shown to be more effective if they are tailored to a client's spiritual framework when it is deemed to be relevant to adjustment. It has been suggested that recognition and respect for spiritual diversity are important factors in the provision of culturally sensitive treatment (Hall, 2001). For example, belief in a forgiving creator may prove useful in the cognitive restructuring of attributions that are associated with debilitating guilt. Some clients may desire that spirituality be actively incorporated into treatment. Similarly, some clients may prefer treatment that includes religious teachings and metaphors (Hall, 2001).

Inclusion of spiritual factors in understanding and ameliorating human behavior is not new to psychology. The discipline has its roots in the hypotheses of ancient Greek philosophers who referred to human phenomenology as being the mind or soul that exists in a nonphysical dimension (Hunt, 1993). Up until the mid-twentieth century, some major psychological paradigms included the concept of a human mind or soul that is distinct from the physical body. Examples of psychological theoretical constructs that are attributed to nonmaterial variables include Jung's collective unconscious and Rogers's self-actualization (e.g., Maddi, 1980). The trend of including spiritual factors in psychological theories continued (e.g., Barham & Greene, 1986) but was eschewed by most psychological scientists.

Evidence suggests that spiritual practices can be used as techniques to improve quality of life and reduce distressful symptoms. Emerging literature has indicated that greater spiritual involvement may be associated with reduced morbidity and mortality (Oman & Driskill, 2003). One tool that has been studied for increasing spiritual involvement is mantram repetition, which may improve physical and mental functioning, such as biomarkers of cardiovascular health and self-efficacy (Oman & Driskill, 2003). For example, a mantram repetition intervention group was more effective than an attention control group in improving quality of life and spiritual well-being and reducing anger in HIV-infected adults (Bormann et al., 2006a); those who practiced more had greater improvements. Research in veterans also showed mantram repetition to be helpful in managing stress, negative emotions, insomnia, and unwanted thoughts (Bormann et al., 2006b). Interestingly, repeating a mantram that invokes a holy name, particularly a concept that is consistent with a person's "highest existing or emergent conceptions or aspirations—his or her 'ultimate concerns,'" may be more helpful in improving psychological functioning than a mantram that does not (Oman & Driskill, 2003, p. 11).

Why did mainstream psychology "lose its soul" during the last half of the twentieth century? Possibly because advancements in methodology lent themselves primarily to the study of observable phenomena, and as a result, psychological science burgeoned and evidence-based practice flourished. Why are psychologists rediscovering the soul now? Possibly because the international influences upon the field have led to an acceptance of the study of phenomenological effects of spirituality upon cognitions, emotions, actions, and the physical body that have been central to Eastern studies for millennia (Wallace & Shapiro, 2006). In any case, it is incumbent upon professional psychologists to be "spiritually competent," which is a skill that is not often taught during graduate training (Hage, 2006).

SUMMARY

We have introduced six issues that we believe will shape the future of the profession of clinical psychology. How the profession changes is up to you and your colleagues. We hope you will consider these six issues and become actively involved in them. Otherwise, you may find yourself in a profession that is quite different from what you desire.

Three of the issues described are controversial and invite an active stance. First, the profession will become a medical subspecialty only if a surge of psychologists and graduate students choose to support prescription-privilege scope-of-practice bills at state legislatures across the country and elect to undergo the requisite training. Second, the profession will retain its dubious reputation of being specialists in the perpetuation of interrogation and torture only if one passively accepts APA's current endorsement of these techniques. Third, another movement in the profession that has spawned a great deal of controversy is the trend toward evidence-based practice, which is often defined differently by different parties that vehemently disagree.

It is hoped that the remaining three issues will advise readers of how to adapt to factors that are inherent changes in the profession. First, a great deal of recent research and popular attention has been devoted to the trend toward giving psychology away in the form of self-help treatments. Used individually or within integrated care systems, these programs have the potential to be disseminated more broadly and have an impact on far greater numbers of people than psychology ever has before. Second, whether anyone can experience themselves as adjusted while recognizing that life inherently has positive growth-producing challenges depends in part upon whether psychologists adopt this view themselves in their research and practice or whether we continue to "pathologize the masses." Finally, whether clients can feel free to disclose and utilize spiritual beliefs, feelings, and practices will depend upon whether clinical psychologists accept these experiences as valid.

THOUGHT QUESTIONS

1. Do you think requiring undergraduate majors in psychology to complete an additional 30 semester hours in biological and life sciences would increase or decrease the number of students who declare psychology as their major? Such requirements would include biology, biochemistry, chemistry, anatomy, physiology, and related coursework. What about students who did not have an interest in becoming a clinician? Should they still take the additional courses? Please explain.

2. Would you enter a graduate program in clinical psychology that, along with at least 7 years of study of basic and applied psychology, would include up to an additional 3 years of medical training? Why or why not?

3. The APA medical training model for prescription privileges for psychologists involves far less than half the medical training required for other prescribing professions. Do you think it is appropriate for psychologists to practice medicine with the amount of training proposed in the APA model? Please explain.

4. Psychoactive medications have become popular with the managed care health insurance industry as a "quick fix" to problems in living. Psychiatry has responded to the health insurance industry's reimbursement preferences by abandoning psychotherapy for the most part. Do you think prescribing psychologists would also abandon psychotherapy? Please explain.

5. Should psychologists be involved in interrogation and torture techniques? If yes, under what circumstances? If no, why not?

6. Is it possible to conduct randomized controlled trials to test the efficacy of traditional long-term treatments such as psychodynamic psychotherapy? If so, what are the challenges involved, and how can they be overcome?
7. What do you think primarily accounts for the efficacy of treatment—specific treatment techniques, the therapeutic relationship, or other factors?
8. What do you think are the most important outcome measures that should be assessed in treatment trials? How do symptom-based measures compare to more general measures of functioning, quality of life, and client satisfaction?
9. What are the advantages and disadvantages of stepped-care treatment models? How do the potential benefits to society, such as saved health-care costs, stack up to the possible costs to the individual, such as a delay in effective treatment for some?
10. What possible psychological advantages (or risks) might be conferred by self-reliance in seeking psychological treatment from bibliotherapy or computerized treatments? What possible advantages (or risks) might come from support groups?
11. What criteria can a clinical psychologist use to determine if someone is experiencing a natural life challenge versus a mental disorder? Provide examples of responding to distressful life events that can lead to positive growth versus a maladaptive reaction.
12. How important do you think spirituality is in the psychological treatment of mental disorders? How would your own views of spirituality interact with a client's views? How would you manage a case in which the client's views of spirituality conflicted with your own?
13. What criteria can a clinical psychologist use to differentiate psychopathology from spiritual experiences? Consider what diagnosis, if any, would most likely be given to Moses, Buddha, Jesus, and Mohammed if they underwent a psychological evaluation today.

Glossary

Comorbidity: the presence of one or more disorders in addition to a primary disorder.

Dodo-bird effect: the argument that there is a lack of significant differences among active treatments and that all psychotherapies are equally effective.

Effectiveness: the effects of treatments practiced under real-world conditions, typically across broad populations.

Efficacy: the effects of specific interventions in clinical trials under controlled conditions, typically in clearly defined populations.

EST: an empirically supported treatment.

Incorporeality: the existence of nonphysical forces and beings.

Interrogation: the use of psychological and physical methods to elicit information from or punish an unwilling person who has been detained or imprisoned.

Medicalize: to transform a discipline into a subspecialty of the field of medicine, emphasizing biological causes and treatments rather than psychological ones.

Medical psychologists: licensed psychologists in the state of Louisiana who have the authority to prescribe psychoactive medication.

Meta-analysis: a quantitative analysis of a literature review. The results of individual studies provide the data for additional statistical analyses.

Nonspecific (or common) factors: aspects of psychotherapy beyond specifically identified therapeutic techniques (e.g., therapist warmth or expertise).

PPP: prescription privileges for psychologists. Also referred to as RxP.

Prescription authority: the regulatory authority to prescribe medications. Equivalent to prescriptive authority.

Prescription privileges: see Prescription authority.

RxP: prescription privileges for psychologists. Also referred to as PPP.

Single-case experimental design: a research design in which an experimenter tests the outcome of an intervention in a single participant or small group of participants, who serve as their own control condition.

Spirituality: beliefs, feelings, practices, and experiences related to discarnate entities and an unobstructed universe.

Stepped care: a treatment model where the first treatment recommended is the least restrictive of those available, but still likely to provide significant benefit; nonresponders to first-stage treatments are subsequently moved to a more intensive level of care.

Torture: deliberately harming a detained or imprisoned person using psychological and physical techniques.

References

Addis, M. E., Wade, W. A., & Hatgis, C. (1999). Barriers to dissemination of evidence-based practices: addressing practitioners' concerns about manual-based psychotherapies. *Clinical Psychology Science and Practice, 6,* 430–441.

Albee, G. W. (2002). Just say no to psychotropic drugs. *Journal of Clinical Psychology, 58,* 635–648.

Allhoff, F. (2006). Physician involvement in hostile interrogations. *Cambridge Quarterly of Healthcare Ethics, 15,* 392–402.

American Academy of Psychiatry and the Law (2006). *Psychiatry applauds American Medical Association's new policy against physicians participating in interrogations.* Retrieved September 1, 2007 from http://tinyurl.com/2mc2xo.

American Civil Liberties Union (2007). *ACLU calls on American Psychological Association to ban torture.* Retrieved August 20, 2007 from www.aclu.org/safe-free/torture/31355prs20070817.html.

American College of Neuropsychopharmacology (2000). DoD prescribing psychologists external analysis, monitoring, and evaluation of program and its final report. *American College of Neuropsychopharmacology Bulletin, 6.* Retrieved January 15, 2007 from http://www.acnp.org/Docs/BulletinPdfFiles/vol6no3.pdf.

American Medical Association (2006). *Physician participation in interrogation (Res. 1, I-05), CEJA Report 10-A-06,* Retrieved October 8, 2007 from www.ama-assn.org/ama1/pub/upload/mm/369/ceja_10a06.pdf.

American Psychiatric Association (2000). *Diagnostic and Statistical Manual of Mental Disorders* (4th ed., Text Revision). Washington, DC: Author.

American Psychiatric Association (2006). *Psychiatric participation in interrogation of detainees: position statement.* Retrieved September 15, 2007 from http://www.psych.org/edu/other_res/lib_archives/archives/200601.pdf.

American Psychological Association (1996a). *Model legislation for prescriptive authority.* Washington, DC: Author.

American Psychological Association (1996b). *Recommended postdoctoral training in psychopharmacology for prescription privileges.* Retrieved November 14, 2007 from http://www.apa.org/ed/rx_pmodcurri.pdf.

American Psychological Association Division 19 (Society for Military Psychology) (2007). *Comments on the draft APA Council resolution "Moratorium on psychologist involvement in interrogations at US detention centers for foreign detainees."* Retrieved November 10, 2007 from www.apa.org/ethics/pdfs/div19response.pdf.

American Psychological Association Presidential Task Force on Evidence-Based Practice (2006). Evidence-based practice in psychology. *American Psychologist, 61,* 271–285.

American Psychological Association (2007). *Resolution against torture and other cruel, inhuman, or degrading treatment or punishment and its application to individuals defined in the United States Code as enemy combatants.* Retrieved November 14, 2007 from http://www.ethicalapa.com/Apa_resolution_081907.html.

American Society for the Advancement of Pharmacotherapy (2007). Comparison of programs. Retrieved October 29, 2007 from http://www.division55.org/Comparison_of_Programs.pdf.

Andrews, G. (2000). A focus on empirically supported outcomes: a commentary on search for empirically supported treatments. *Clinical Psychology: Science and Practice, 7,* 264–268.

Annas, G. J. (2005). Unspeakably cruel — torture, medical ethics, and the law. *New England Journal of Medicine, 352,* 2127–2132.

Barham, M. J. & Greene, J. T. (1986). *The silver cord: Lifeline to the unobstructed.* Marina del Rey, CA: DeVorss.

Barlow, D. H. (2004). Psychological treatments. *American Psychologist, 59,* 869–878.

Barlow, J. H., Ellard, D. R., Hainsworth, J. M., Jones, F. R., & Fisher, A. (2005). A review of self-management interventions for panic disorders, phobias and obsessive-compulsive disorders. *Acta Psychiatrica Scandinavia, 111,* 272–285.

Barron, J. (1989). Prescription rights: Pro and con: should psychologists seek the same skills and responsibilities as psychiatrists? *The Psychotherapy Bulletin, 24*(3), 22–24.

Bergin, A. E. (1991). Values and religious issues in psychotherapy and mental health. *American Psychologist, 46,* 394–403.

Bormann, J. E., Gifford, A. L., Shively, M., Smith, T. L., Redwine, L., Kelly, A., et al. (2006a). Effects of spiritual mantram repetition on HIV outcomes: a randomized controlled trial. *Journal of Behavioral Medicine, 29,* 359–376.

Bormann, J. E., Oman, D., Kemppainen, J. K., Becker, S., Gershwin, M., & Kelly, A. (2006b). Mantram repetition for stress management in veterans and employees: a critical incident study. *Journal of Advanced Nursing, 53,* 502–512.

Bower, P., & Gilbody, S. (2005). Stepped care in psychological therapies: Access, effectiveness and efficiency. *British Journal of Psychiatry, 186,* 11–17.

Bower, P., Richards, D., & Lovell, K. (2001). The clinical and cost-effectiveness of self-help treatments for anxiety and depressive disorders in primary care: a systematic review. *British Journal of General Practice, 51,* 838–845.

Brawer, P. A., Handal, P. J., Fabricatore, A. N., Roberts, R., & Wajda-Johnston, V. A. (2002). Training and education in religion/spirituality within APA-accredited clinical psychology programs. *Professional Psychology: Research and Practice, 33,* 203–206.

Brown, K. (2005). Does the psychology of religion exist? *European Psychologist, 10,* 71–73.

Burns, D. D. (1999). *Feeling good: The new mood therapy.* New York: HarperCollins.

Burns, S. M., DeLeon, P. H., Chemtob, C. M., Welch, B. L., & Samuels, R. M. (1988). Psychotropic medication: a new technique for psychology? *Psychotherapy: Research and Practice, 25,* 508–515.

Bush, J. W. (2002). Prescribing privileges: grail for some practitioners, potential calamity for interprofessional collaboration in mental health. *Journal of Clinical Psychology, 58,* 681–696.

Caccavale, J. (2002). Opposition to prescriptive authority: is this a case of the tail wagging the dog? *Journal of Clinical Psychology, 58,* 623–633.

Cantor, D. W. (1991, Fall). The prescription privilege debate: not now, maybe never. *The Independent Practitioner, 11,* 13–14.

Caplan, P. J. (1995). *They say you're crazy: how the world's most powerful psychiatrists decide who's normal.* New York: Addison-Wesley.

Cavanagh, K. & Shapiro, D. A. (2004). Computer treatment for common mental health problems. *Journal of Clinical Psychology, 60,* 239–251.

Chambless, D. L., Baker, M. J., Baucom, D. H., Beutler, L. E., Calhoun, K. S., Crits-Christoph, P., et al. (1998). Update on empirically validated therapies, II. *The Clinical Psychologist, 51,* 3–16.

Chambless, D. L. & Hollon, S. D. (1998). Defining empirically supported therapies. *Journal of Consulting and Clinical Psychology, 66,* 7–18.

Chambless, D. L. & Ollendick, T. H. (2001). Empirically supported psychological interventions: controversies and evidence. *Annual Review of Psychology, 52,* 685–716.

Chambless, D. L., Sanderson, W. C., Shoham, V., Bennett Johnson, S., Pope, K. S., Crits-Christoph, P., et al. (1996). An update on empirically validated therapies. *The Clinical Psychologist, 49,* 5–18.

Christensen, A. & Jacobson, N. S. (1994). Who (or what) can do psychotherapy: the status and challenge of nonprofessional therapies. *Psychological Science, 5,* 8–14.

Christensen, H., Griffiths, K. M., & Jorm, A. F. (2004). Delivering interventions for depression by using the Internet: randomised controlled trial. *British Medical Journal, 328,* 265–269.

Crits-Christoph, P., Wilson, G. T., & Hollon, S. D. (2005). Empirically supported psychotherapies: comment on Westen, Novotny, and Thompson-Brenner (2004). *Psychological Bulletin, 131,* 412–417.

Conrad, P. (2007). *The medicalization of society: on the transformation of human conditions into treatable disorders.* London: Oxford University Press.

Cuijpers, P. (1997). Bibliotherapy in unipolar depression: a meta-analysis. *Journal of Behavior Therapy and Experimental Psychiatry, 28,* 139–147.

Daly, R. (2007). Governor's veto seals fate of Hawaii prescribing bill. *Psychiatric News, 42,* 2–34.

Davison, G. C. (2000). Stepped care: doing more with less? *Journal of Consulting and Clinical Psychology, 68,* 580–585.

DeClue, G. (2006). Review of a question of torture: CIA interrogation, from the Cold War to the War on Terror. *Journal of Psychiatry and Law, 34,* 381–385.

DeGrandpre, R. (2006). *The cult of pharmacology: how America became the world's most troubled drug culture.* Durham, NC: Duke University Press.

DeLeon, P. H. (1990). Psychoactive medications: the debate reaches Hawaii's legislature. *Register Report, 16*(2), 9–10.

DeLeon, P. H., Dunivin, D. L., & Newman, R. (2002). The tide rises. *Clinical Psychology: Science and Practice, 9*, 249–255.

DeLeon, P. H. & Wiggins, J. G. (1996). Prescription privileges for psychologists. *American Psychologist, 51*, 225–229.

Den Boer, P. C. A. M., Wiersma, D., & Van Den Bosch, R. J. (2004). Why is self-help neglected in the treatment of emotional disorders? A meta-analysis. *Psychological Medicine, 34*, 959–971.

DeNelsky, G. Y. (1996). The case against prescription privileges for psychologists. *American Psychologist, 51*, 207–212.

DeRubeis, R. J., Brotman, M. A., & Gibbons, C. J. (2005). A conceptual and methodological analysis of the nonspecifics argument. *Clinical Psychology: Science and Practice, 12*, 174–183.

Dobson, K. S. & Shaw, B. F. (1988). The use of treatment manuals in cognitive therapy: experience and issues. *Journal of Consulting and Clinical Psychology, 56*, 673–680.

Eban, K. (2007). Rorschach and awe. *Vanity Fair*, Retrieved November 16, 2007 from http://www.vanityfair.com/politics/features/2007/07/torture200707?currentPage=1.

Ellison, C. G. (1991). Religious involvement and subjective well being. *Journal of Health and Social Behavior, 32*, 80–99.

Fabricatore, A. N., Handal, P. J., & Fenzel, L. M. (2000). Personal spirituality as a moderator of the relationship between stressors and subjective well-being. *Journal of Psychology and Theology, 28*, 221–228.

Fowler, R. D. (1996, May). A forum for debating prescription privileges. *The APA Monitor, 26*(5), 3.

Fowles, D. (2005). Prescription privileges for psychologists. *Clinical Science, 5*, 6–7. [Electronic version]. Retrieved November 25, 2007 from http://www.bsos.umd.edu/sscp/Fall_2005_Newsletter.pdf.

Fox, R. E. (1988). Prescription privileges: their implications for the practice of psychology. *Psychotherapy, 25*, 501–507.

Gill, R. E. (2007, September–October). Role of psychologists at detention centers approved. *National Psychologist, 16*(5), 1–2.

Glasgow, R. E. & Rosen, G. M. (1979). Self-help behavior therapy manuals: recent developments and clinical usage. *Clinical Behavior Therapy Review, 1*, 1–20.

Glenn, D. (2007, October 12). Resolutions urge Psychology Association to take tougher stand on interrogating prisoners. *Chronicle of Higher Education*. Retrieved October 12, 2007 from http://chronicle.com.

Gould, R. & Clum, G. (1993). A meta-analysis of self-help treatment approaches. *Clinical Psychology Review, 13*, 169–186.

Guam Board of Allied Health Examiners. Retrieved November 19, 2007 from http://dphss.guam.gov/about/licensing.htm.

Guam Prescription Authority Bill (1998). Retrieved November 19, 2007 from http://www.guamlegislature.com/28th_Guam_Legislature/Bills_Introduced_28th/BILL300.htm.

Hage, S. M. (2006). A closer look at the role of spirituality in psychology training programs. *Professional Psychology: Research and Practice, 37*, 303–310.

Hall, G. C. N. (2001). Psychotherapy research with ethnic minorities: empirical, ethical, and conceptual issues. *Journal of Consulting and Clinical Psychology, 69*, 502–510.

Harris Poll (2003). *The religious and other beliefs of Americans 2003*. Retrieved November 24, 2007 from http://www.harrisinteractive.com/harris_poll/index.asp?PID=359.

Hathaway, W. L., Scott, S. Y., & Garver, S. A. (2004). Assessing religious/spiritual functioning: a neglected domain in clinical practice? *Professional Psychology: Research and Practice, 35*, 97–104.

Hayes, S. C. (1995, Spring). Using behavioral science to control guild excesses. *The Clinical Behavior Analyst, 1*, 17.

Hayes, S. C. & Heiby, E. M. (1996). Prescription privileges: does psychology need a fix? *American Psychologist, 51*, 198–206.

Hayes, S. C., Walser, R. D., & Bach, P. (2002). Prescription privileges for psychologists: constituencies and conflicts. *Journal of Clinical Psychology, 58*, 697–708.

Hayes, S. C., Walser, R. D., & Follette, V. M. (1996). Psychology and the temptation of prescription privileges. *Canadian Psychology, 36*, 313–320.

Heiby, E. M. (2002a). Prescription privileges for psychologists: can differing views be reconciled? *Journal of Clinical Psychology, 58*, 589–597.

Heiby, E. M. (2002b). It is time for a moratorium on legislation enabling prescription privileges for psychologists. *Clinical Psychology: Science and Practice, 9*, 256–258.

Heiby, E. M., DeLeon, P. H., & Anderson, T. (2004). A debate on prescription privileges for psychologists. *Professional Psychology: Research and Practice, 35*, 336–344.

Hill, P. C. & Pargament, K. I. (2003). Advances in the conceptualization and measurement of religion and spirituality: implications for physical and mental health research. *American Psychologist, 58*, 64–74.

Hogan, B. E., Linden, W., & Najarian, B. (2004). Social support interventions: do they work? *Clinical Psychology Review, 22*, 381–440.

Horowitz, A. V. (2002). *Creating mental illness*. Chicago: University of Chicago Press.

Horowitz, A. V. & Wakefield, J. C. (2007). *The loss of sadness: how psychiatry transformed normal sorrow into depressive disorder*. London: Oxford University Press.

Horton, S. (2007). *The psychologists and Gitmo*. Retrieved November 19, 2007 from http://www.harpers.org/archive/2007/11/hbc-90001695.

Horvath, A. O. (2001). The alliance. *Psychotherapy, 38*, 365–372.

Hunt, M. (1993). *The story of psychology*. New York: Random House.

Hyman, B. M. & Pedrick, C. (1999). *The OCD Workbook: your guide to breaking free from obsessive compulsive disorders*. Oakland, CA: New Harbinger.

James, L. C. (2006). Integrating clinical psychology into primary care settings. *Journal of Clinical Psychology, 62*, 1207–1212.

Jansen, M. & Barron, J. (1988). Introduction and overview: psychologists' use of physical interventions. *Psychotherapy, 25*, 487–491.

Jorm, A. F. & Griffiths, K. M. (2005). Population promotion of informal self-help strategies for early intervention against depression and anxiety. *Psychological Medicine, 36*, 3–6.

Juliano, L. M. & Griffiths, R. R. (2001). Is caffeine a drug of dependence? *Psychiatric Times, 8*, np. Retrieved November 21, 2007 from http://www.psychiatrictimes.com/p010247.html.

Kaltenthaler, E., Parry, G., & Beverley, C. (2004). Computerized cognitive behavior therapy: a systematic review. *Behavioural and Cognitive Psychotherapy, 32*, 31–55.

Kazdin, A. E. (1999). The meanings and measurement of clinical significance. *Journal of Consulting and Clinical Psychology, 67*, 332–339.

Kazdin, A. E. (2004). Evidence-based treatments: challenges and priorities for practice and research. *Child and Adolescent Psychiatric Clinics of North America, 13*, 923–940.

Kazdin, A. E. (2006). Arbitrary metrics: implications for identifying evidence-based treatments. *American Psychologist, 61*, 42–49.

Kenardy, J. A., Dow, M. G. T., Johnston, D. W., Newman, M. G., Thomson, A., & Taylor, C. B. (2003). A comparison of delivery methods of cognitive–behavioral therapy for panic disorder: an international multicenter trial. *Journal of Consulting and Clinical Psychology, 71*(6), 1068–1075.

Kingsbury, S. J. (1992). Some effects of prescribing privileges. *Professional Psychology: Research and Practice, 23*, 3–5.

Kirk, S. A. & Kutchins, H. (1992). *The selling of DSM: the rhetoric of science in psychiatry*. New York: Walter de Gruyter.

Lambert, M. J. & Barley, D. E. (2001). Research summary on the therapeutic relationship and psychotherapy outcome. *Psychotherapy, 38*, 357–361.

Lane, C. (2007). *Shyness: how normal behavior became a sickness*. New Haven, CT: Yale University Press.

Latner, J. D. Stunkard, A. J., Wilson, G. T., & Jackson, M. L. (2006). The perceived effectiveness of continuing care and group support in the long-term self-help treatment of obesity. *Obesity, 14*, 464–471.

Latner, J. D. & Wilson, G. T. (2007). Continuing care and self-help in the treatment of obesity. In J. D. Latner & G. T. Wilson (Eds.), *Self-help approaches for obesity and eating disorders: research and practice* (pp. 223–240). New York: Guilford.

Leshner, A. I. (2005). Science and religion should not be adversaries. *Psychological Observer, 18* [Electronic version]. Retrieved November 25, 2007 from http://www.psychologicalscience.org/observer/getArticle.cfm?id=1860.

Lewis, N. A. (2004, November 30). Red Cross find detainee abuse in Guantanamo; U.S. rejects accusations; confidential report calls practice tantamount to torture. *New York Times*, Retrieved October 22, 2007 from http://nytimes.com/.

Lidren, D. M., Watkins, P. L., Gould, R. A., Clum, G. A., Asterino, M., & Tulloch, H. L. (1994). A comparison of bibliotherapy and group therapy in the treatment of panic disorder. *Journal of Consulting and Clinical Psychology, 62*, 865–869.

Linehan, M. M., Armstrong, H. E., Suarez, A., Allmon, D., & Heard, H. L. (1991). Cognitive-behavioral treatment of chronically parasuicidal borderline patients. *Archives of General Psychiatry, 48*, 1060–1064.

Lohr, J. M., Olatunji, B. O., Parker, L., & DeMaio, C. (2005). Experimental analysis of specific treatment factors: efficacy and practice implications. *Journal of Clinical Psychology, 61*, 819–834.

Louisiana State Board of Examiners of Psychologists (2007). Retrieved October 22, 2007 from http://www.lsbep.org/index.html.

Luborsky, L., Diguer, L., Seligman, D. A., Rosenthal, R., Krause, E. D., Johnson, S., et al. (1999). The researcher's own therapy allegiances: a "wild card" in comparisons of treatment efficacy. *Clinical Psychology: Science and Practice, 6*, 95–106.

Luborsky, L., Rosenthal, R., Diguer, L., Andrusyna, T. P., Berman, J. S., Levitt, J. T., et al. (2002). The Dodo Bird verdict is alive and well — mostly. *Clinical Psychology: Science and Practice, 9*, 2–12.

Maddi, S. R. (1980). *Personality theories: a comparative analysis*. Homewood, IL: Dorsey.

Mains, J. A. & Scogin, F. R. (2003). The effectiveness of self-administered treatments: a practice-friendly review of the research. *Journal of Clinical Psychology, 59*, 237–246.

Mayor, S. (2006). NICE advocates computerised CBT. *British Medical Journal, 332*, 504.

McFall, R. M. (2002). Training for prescriptions vs. prescriptions for training: where are we now? Where should we be? How do we get there? *Journal of Clinical Psychology, 58*, 659–678.

McKendree-Smith, N. L., Floyd, M., & Scogin, F. R. (2003). Self-administered treatments for depression: a review. *Journal of Clinical Psychology, 59*, 275–288.

Michigan Society for Psychoanalytic Psychology (2003). On prescription privileges for psychologists. Retrieved November 21, 2007 from http://www.mspp.net/SSCPscriptpriv.htm.

Miranda, J., Bernal, G., Lau, A., Kohn, L., Hwang, W.-C., & LaFromboise, T. (2005). State of the science on psychological interventions for ethnic minorities. *Annual Review of Clinical Psychology*, 1, 113–142.

Nathan, P. E. & Gorman, J. M. (Eds.) (2002). *A guide to treatments that work* (2nd ed.). New York: Oxford University Press.

Nathan, P. E. & Gorman, J. M. (Eds.) (2007). *A guide to treatments that work* (3rd ed.). New York: Oxford University Press.

Nathan, P. E., Stuart, S. P., & Dolan, S. L. (2000). Research on psychotherapy efficacy and effectiveness: between Scylla and Charybdis? *Psychological Bulletin*, 126, 964–981.

National Register of Health Providers in Psychology (2007). Retrieved November 19, 2007 from http://www.findapsychologist.org/.

Naylor, E. V., Antonuccio, D. O., Johnson, G., Spogen, D., & O'Donohue, W. (2007). A pilot study investigating behavioral prescriptions for depression. *Journal of Clinical Psychology in Medical Settings*, 14, 152–159.

Newman, M. G., Erickson, T., Przeworski, A., & Dzus, E. (2003). Self-help and minimal-contact therapies for anxiety disorders: is human contact necessary for therapeutic efficacy? *Journal of Clinical Psychology*, 59, 251–274.

New Mexico Prescription Authority Law (2002). Retrieved November 19, 2007 from http://www.rld.state.nm.us/psychology/ruleslaw.html.

New York Psychology Licensing Law. Retrieved October 22, 2007 from http://www.op.nysed.gov/article153.htm#prohibit.

Norcross, J. C. (2001). Purposes, processes, and products of the Task Force on Empirically Supported Therapy Relationships. *Psychotherapy*, 38, 345–356.

Norcross, J. C., Beutler, L. E., & Levant, R. F. (Eds.) (2005). *Evidence-based practices in mental health: debate and dialogue on the fundamental questions*. Washington, DC: American Psychological Association.

Norfleet, M. A. (2002). Responding to society's needs: prescription privileges for psychologists. *Journal of Clinical Psychology*, 58, 599–610.

O'Connor, S. & Vandenberg, B. (2005). Psychosis or faith? Clinicians' assessment of religious beliefs. *Journal of Consulting and Clinical Psychology*, 73, 610–616.

O'Donohue, W., Buchanan, J. A., & Fisher, J. E. (2000). Characteristics of empirically supported treatments. *Journal of Psychotherapy Practice and Research*, 9, 69–74.

O'Donohue, W. & Cucciare, M. A. (2005). Pathways to medical utilization. *Journal of Clinical Psychology in Medical Settings*, 12, 185–197.

Oman, D. & Driskill, J. D. (2003). Holy name repetition as a spiritual exercise and therapeutic technique. *Journal of Psychology and Christianity*, 22, 5–19.

Otto, M. W., Smits, J. A. J., & Reese, H. E. (2005). Combined psychotherapy and pharmacotherapy for mood and anxiety disorders in adults: review and analysis. *Clinical Psychology: Science and Practice*, 12, 72–86.

Papworth, M. (2006). Issues and outcomes associated with adult mental health self-help materials: A "second order" review or "qualitative meta-review." *Journal of Mental Health*, 15, 387–409.

Persons, J. B. & Silberschatz, G. (1998). Are results of randomized controlled trials useful to psychotherapists? *Journal of Consulting and Clinical Psychology*, 66, 126–135.

Physicians for Human Rights (2007). *Leave no marks: enhanced interrogation techniques and the risk of criminality*. Retrieved November 16, 2007 http://physiciansforhumanrights.org/library/report-2007-08-02.html.

Piotrowski, C. (1989–1990, Winter). Prescription privileges: a time for some serious thought. *The Psychotherapy Bulletin*, 16–18.

Pope, K. S. & Garcia-Peltoniemi, R. E. (1991). Responding to victims of torture: clinical issues, professional responsibilities, and useful resources. *Professional Psychology: Research and Practice*, 22, 269–276.

Psychological Ethics and National Security (2005). Retrieved November 16, 2007 from http://www.apa.org/releases/PENSTaskForceReportFinal.pdf.

Psychologists for an Ethical APA (2007). Retrieved November 17, 2007 from http://www.ethicalapa.com/.

Psychologists Opposed to Prescription Privileges for Psychologists (2007). Retrieved January 3, 2008 from http://psychologistsopposedtoprescribingbypsychologists.org/.

Rapee, R. M., Abbott, M. J., & Lyneham, H. J. (2006). Bibliotherapy for children with anxiety disorders using written materials for parents: a randomized controlled trial. *Journal of Consulting and Clinical Psychology*, 74, 436–444.

Redding, R. E., Herbert, J. D., Forman, E. M., Gaudiano, B. A. (in press). Popular self-help books for anxiety, depression, and trauma: how scientifically grounded and useful are they? *Professional Psychology: Research and Practice*.

Robiner, W. N., Bearman, D. L., Berman, M., Grove, W. M., Colón, E., Armstrong, J., et al. (2002). Prescriptive authority for psychologists: a looming health hazard? *Clinical Psychology: Science and Practice*, 9, 231–248.

Robiner, W. N., Bearman, D. L., Berman, M., Grove, W. M., Colón, E., Armstrong, J., et al. (2003). Prescriptive authority for psychologists: despite deficits in education and knowledge? *Journal of Clinical Psychology in Medical Settings*, 10, 211–222.

Rochlen, A. B., Zack, J. S., & Speyer, C. (2004). Online therapy: review of relevant definitions, debates, and current empirical support. *Journal of Clinical Psychology*, 60, 269–283.

Roth, A. & Fonagy, P. (1996). *What works for whom? A critical review of psychotherapy research*. New York: Guilford.

Roth, A. & Fonagy, P. (2004). *What works for whom? A critical review of psychotherapy research* (2nd ed.). New York: Guilford.

Sanderson, W. C. (2003). Why empirically supported psychological treatments are important. *Behavior Modification, 27*, 290–299.

Schulte, D., Kunzel, R., Pepping, G., & Schulte-Bahrenberg, T. (1992). Tailor-made versus standardized therapy of phobic patients. *Advances in Behaviour Research and Therapy, 13*, 67–92.

Sechrest, L. & Coan, J. A. (2002). Preparing psychologists to prescribe. *Journal of Clinical Psychology, 58*, 649–658.

Shadish, W. R., Matt, G. E., Navarro, A. M., & Phillips, G. (2000). The effects of psychological therapies under clinically representative conditions: a meta-analysis. *Psychological Bulletin, 126*, 512–529.

Smith, T. & Richards, P. S. (2005). The integration of spiritual and religious issues in racial-cultural psychology and counseling. In R. T. Carter (Ed.), *Handbook of racial-cultural psychology and counseling*, vol. 4: *theory and research* (pp. 132–159). New York: Wiley.

Smyer, M. A., Balster, R. L., Egli, D., Johnson, D. L., Kilbey, M. M., Leith, N. J., et al. (1993). Summary of the report of the ad hoc task force on psychopharmacology of the American Psychological Association. *Professional Psychology: Research and Practice, 24*, 394–403.

Soldz, S. (2006, August 1). Psychologists, Guantanamo and torture. *Counterpunch.* Retrieved October 6, 2007 from http://www.counterpunch.org/soldz08012006.html.

Solomon, P. (2004). Peer support/peer provided services: underlying processes, benefits, and critical ingredients. *Psychiatric Rehabilitation Journal, 27*, 392–401.

Stice, E., Burton, E., Bearman., S. K., & Rohde, P. (2006). Randomized trial of a brief depression prevention program: an elusive search for a psychosocial placebo control condition. *Behaviour Research and Therapy, 45*, 863–876.

Stirman, S. W., DeRubeis, R. J., Crits-Christoph, P., & Brody, P. E. (2003). Are samples in randomized controlled trials of psychotherapy representative of community outpatients? A new methodology and initial findings. *Journal of Consulting and Clinical Psychology, 71*, 963–972.

Stuart, R. B. & Heiby, E. M. (2007). To prescribe or not prescribe: eleven exploratory questions. *The Scientific Review of Mental Health Practice, 5*, 4–32.

United Nations (n.d.). *International human rights instruments.* Retrieved November 25, 2007 from http://www.unhchr.ch/html/intlinst.htm.

Wagner, M. K. (2002). The high cost of prescription privileges. *Journal of Clinical Psychology, 58*, 677–680.

Wallace, B. A. & Shapiro, S. L. (2006). Mental balance and well-being. *American Psychologist, 61*, 690–701.

Walters, G. D. (2001). A meta-analysis of opinion data on the prescription privilege debate. *Canadian Psychology, 42*, 119–125.

Wampold, B. E. & Bhati, K. S. (2004). Attending to the omissions: a historical examination of evidence-based practice movements. *Professional Psychology: Research and Practice, 35*, 563–570.

Weene, K. A. (2002). The psychologist's role in the collaborative process of psychopharmacology. *Journal of Clinical Psychology, 58*, 817–821.

Westen, D., Novotny, C. M., & Thompson-Brenner, H. (2004). The empirical status of empirically supported psychotherapies: assumptions, findings, and reporting in controlled clinical trials. *Psychological Bulletin, 130*, 631–663.

Wilson, D. M. & Cash, T. F. (2000). Who reads self-help books? Development and validation of the Self-Help Reading Attitudes Survey. *Personality and Individual Differences, 29*, 119–129.

Wilson, G. T. (1998). Manual-based treatment and clinical practice. *Clinical Psychology: Science and Practice, 5*, 363–375.

World Medical Association (2003). *Resolution on the responsibility of physicians in the denunciation of acts of torture or cruel or inhuman or degrading treatment of which they are aware* [adopted by the World Medical Association General Assembly in 2003]. Retrieved June 2, 2007 from http://www.wma.net/e/policy/t1.htm.

Zeller, S. (2007, September 17). Torture issue ties up psychologists association. *Congressional Quarterly Weekly*, p. 2656. Retrieved September 17, 2007 from http://public.cq.com/docs/cqw/weeklyreport110-000002585116.html.

Zimbardo, P. G. (2007). Thoughts on psychologists, ethics, and the use of torture in interrogations: don't ignore varying roles and complexities. *Analyses of Social Issues and Public Policy.* Retrieved August 1, 2007 from http://www.blackwell-synergy.com/toc/asap/0/0.

Index